HUMAN • DEVELOPMENT

ACROSS THE LIFESPAN

Y0-BRB-674

HUMAN · DEVELOPMENT
ACROSS THE LIFESPAN

JOHN DACEY

Boston College

JOHN TRAVERS

Boston College

WCB Wm. C. Brown Publishers

Book Team

Editor *Michael Lange*
Developmental Editor *Carla J. Aspelmeier*
Production Editor *Kay J. Brimeyer*
Designer *Heidi J. Baughman*
Art Editor *Donna Slade*
Photo Editor *Carrie Burger*
Permissions Editor *Karen L. Storlie*
Visuals Processor *Jodi Wagner*

WCB Wm. C. Brown Publishers

President *G. Franklin Lewis*
Vice President, Publisher *George Wm. Bergquist*
Vice President, Publisher *Thomas E. Doran*
Vice President, Operations and Production *Beverly Kolz*
National Sales Manager *Virginia S. Moffat*
Senior Marketing Manager *Kathy Law Laube*
Marketing Manager *George H. Chapin*
Executive Editor *Edgar J. Laube*
Managing Editor, Production *Colleen A. Yonda*
Production Editorial Manager *Julie A. Kennedy*
Production Editorial Manager *Ann Fuerste*
Publishing Services Manager *Karen J. Slaght*
Manager of Visuals and Design *Faye M. Schilling*

Cover illustration by Heidi J. Baughman

The credits section for this book begins on page 647, and is considered an extension of the copyright page.

Copyright © 1991 by Wm. C. Brown Publishers. All rights reserved

Library of Congress Catalog Card Number: 90–81056

ISBN 0–697–07650–4

No part of this publication may be reproduced, stored in a retrieval system, or transmitted, in any form or by any means, electronic, mechanical, photocopying, recording, or otherwise, without the prior written permission of the publisher.

Printed in the United States of America by Wm. C. Brown Publishers, 2460 Kerper Boulevard, Dubuque, IA 52001

10 9 8 7 6 5 4 3 2 1

This book is dedicated with deep affection to the two people who have helped us the most, Linda Schulman and Barbara Travers, our wives.

Brief Contents

❖

Contents

❖

Preface

❖

We realize that you are reading this book for a variety of reasons. You may be required to read it for a particular course in your major program; you may think that studying the human life span will help you in your career choice; or you may have had the luxury of an elective course and decided to pursue a personal interest in human development.

Whatever the reason, you have come to the study of human development at an exciting time. Lifespan courses have permitted authors and instructors to present human development from an integrated perspective. That is, we no longer have to focus on child development to the exclusion of adolescent development and adult development, or on adolescent development to the exclusion of child and adult development.

Childhood, adolescence, and adulthood are part of a person's total life span. Such a perspective permits a unique view into how humans develop. For example, among the several themes in human development you will read about is the notion of "plasticity," which refers to the flexibility of people. That is, can human beings recover fully from a physical trauma or psychological upset experienced early in life, or are they forever scarred by it?

By examining the key aspects of infant or early childhood development, we can obtain deeper insights into adolescent or adult development. How do these early experiences affect later development—or do they? This is an extremely important issue because its answer dictates the extent, or even existence, of intervention programs such as Head Start and drug and alcohol recovery programs.

This is only one example of the benefits to be derived from studying the life span. The value of lifespan studies for those planning to work with others is self-evident. Both personally and professionally, lifespan studies can enrich your relationships with others and provide a solid basis for future work.

Exciting developments in the field itself will hold your attention throughout your reading. For example:

- Studies of infant development in the last decade have completely changed our thinking about infancy. No longer do we think of infants as passive sponges, soaking up what is offered to them. Now we realize that infants are active processors of information who shape their relationships with others as much as they are shaped.

- Investigators studying the childhood years have discovered the critical role of play in physical, cognitive, social, and emotional development. We now realize that children of this age are more sophisticated than we had realized.

- It was long believed that adolescence is a time of "storm and stress." Now we know that the teen years are no more and no less turbulent than other periods of life (although with suicide being a leading cause of death among the youth, it is easy to see why many people see it as a tempestuous time.)

- It wasn't long ago that even experts (e.g., Sigmund Freud) believed that development ends in the middle of the teen years. Now there is convincing evidence that we continue to go through stages of growth of various kinds throughout adulthood.

We have considered it our task to present these topics as issues in a manner calculated to inform, to challenge, and to make our readers as enthusiastic about the study of human development as we are.

Plan of the Book

Any author or instructor in a lifespan course is immediately faced with a fundamental question: what is the best way to present this complex material? There are two possible approaches: topical or chronological. In a topical approach, you study specific topics—physical development, cognitive development, language—as they occur at each stage of life. In a chronological approach, you study the life span as you live it: infancy, early childhood, middle childhood, adolescence, adulthood.

One is not better than the other, so we have decided to incorporate both. The basic framework of this book is chronological but within each of the developmental stages many topics are presented that include the latest theory and research. In this way, we hope that you will adopt a developmental interpretation of the significant and sensitive topics that you will encounter.

To achieve this objective, we have presented the life span in the following developmental epochs:

1. Prenatal beginnings

2. Infancy

3. Early childhood

4. Middle childhood

5. Adolescence

6. Early adulthood

7. Middle adulthood

8. Late adulthood

Special Features

You will find several special features in this book. First, we are well aware that the population of the United States is changing rapidly. Consequently, you will find sections of each chapter devoted to an explanation of pertinent multicultural and multiethnic issues.

Second, as you read each chapter, you will find boxed material about a current issue that invites your active involvement.

Third, at the end of each chapter you are specifically asked to think about the key issues presented in the chapter. These are *not* routine questions. They are intended to take you back into the highlights of the chapter and explore different dimensions of key topics.

Fourth, each chapter opens with a vignette designed to "set the tone" of the chapter and serve as a meaningful introduction to your reading.

Fifth, each chapter contains at least one box entitled "What's Your Opinion?" Here we describe an issue that is as yet unresolved by the experts, and invite you to try and reach your own conclusion.

Sixth, the most important terms in each chapter, the ones you will want to be sure you understand and remember, are presented in boldface type to make them stand out in your reading. They are listed at the end of the chapter and appear in a glossary at the end of the book, accompanied by a brief definition of the term (with the chapter in which each appears noted). Among other things, we think you will find this an aid to studying for exams.

Seventh, although the information in this book is drawn primarily from psychological theory and research, we have also reported on findings from anthropology, sociology, economics, medicine, and the law, where appropriate.

Supplementary Materials

We have worked with the publisher and a group of very talented individuals to put together a quality set of supplementary materials to assist the instructors and students who use this text.

A helpful INSTRUCTOR'S MANUAL has been prepared by Richard Morehouse of Viterbo College. Each chapter of the *Instructor's Manual* includes a chapter overview, learning objectives, key terms page referenced to the text, lecture suggestions, classroom/student activities, and questions for review and discussion.

In addition, a comprehensive TEST ITEM FILE consisting of over 1,000 items has been prepared by Lynne E. Blesz of Cornell College. The Test Item File contains both multiple choice and true/false for each chapter. Each question is referenced to its related learning objective and text page and is classified as factual, conceptual, or applied.

WCB TESTPAK 3.0 is an integrated program designed to print test masters, permit on-line computerized testing, help students review text material through an interactive self-testing, self-scoring quiz program, as well as provide instructors with a gradebook program for classroom management. Test questions can be found in the TEST ITEM FILE, or you may create your own. You may choose to use Testbank A for exam questions and Testbank B in conjunction with the quiz program. Printing the exam yourself requires access to a personal computer—an IBM that uses 5.25- or 3.5-inch diskettes, an Apple IIe or IIc, or a Macintosh. TestPak requires two disk drives and will work with any printer. Diskettes are available through your local WCB sales representative or by phoning Educational Services at 319–588–1451. The package you receive will contain complete instructions for making up an exam.

The WCB Introductory Psychology TRANSPARENCY SET is also available to adopters of this text. This set consists of 139 acetate transparencies designed to aid the instructor in explaining intricate and complex concepts through the use of colorful illustrations, tables, and graphics. These transparencies have been devised to provide comprehensive coverage of all major topic areas covered in developmental psychology.

Acknowledgments

We would like to take this opportunity to thank the individuals who helped in the development of this text.

Three of our graduate students made significant contributions to our research efforts. For their untiring assistance, we thank Tracy Hurd, Martha Moriarty, and Greg Ray.

We are also sincerely thankful to the academic reviewers who have read various drafts of the book and provided helpful suggestions, constructive criticisms, new references, and endless encouragement.

- James A. Blackburn, University of Wisconsin—Milwaukee

- Lynne A. Blesz, Cornell College

- Donald C. Bowers, Community College of Philadelphia

- William J. Dibiase, Delaware County Community College

- Jerry L. Gray, Washburn University

- Don H. Hockenbury, Tulsa Junior College

- Donald E. Houseworth, Lansing Community College

- Nanette P. Manning, Southeastern Community College

- Richard E. Morehouse, Viterbo College

- Linda C. Schwandt, Western Wisconsin Technical College

- Michael F. Shaughnessy, Eastern New Mexico University

- Donald M. Stanley, North Harris County College

- Barry Trunk, Briar Cliff College

- B. D. Whetstone, Birmingham Southern College

Finally, we would like to express our deep appreciation to our secretary, Ann Donaruma, without whose help this large job could never have been completed.

· PART 1 ·

Introduction

· *Chapter 1* ·

Lifespan Psychology: An Introduction

In a fascinating essay, Lewis Thomas, a medical doctor and essayist, comments that we have been "doing science" for about three centuries. This may seem a long time to test the new, scientific approach to human endeavors but to scientists it is only a beginning. Thomas believes that the major discoveries in this century have provided merely a glimpse of our ignorance about nature. His views on psychology and the other social sciences are particularly pertinent for us.

❖ *The social sciences have a long way to catch up, but they may be up to the most important scientific business of all, if and when they finally get down to the right questions. Our behavior toward each other is the strangest, most unpredictable, and most certainly unaccountable of all the phenomena with which we are obliged to live. In all of nature there is nothing so threatening to humanity as humanity itself (Thomas, 1983, p. 23).*

Thomas concludes that we need the brightest and youngest of our most agile minds to grapple with human puzzles.

The great problems remain to be solved: the nature of human consciousness and its development; the mysterious, challenging, and fascinating world of emotions; the manner in which we form relationships with other complicated human beings. These are but a few of the issues that lie before developmental psychologists.

You have embarked on this study at one of the most exciting times in the history of psychology. Read and enjoy.

Lifespan Development

You may not realize it, but you are a statistic in the study of lifespan development. Unknown to you, psychologists, sociologists, statisticians, and demographers, among others, have placed you in a certain age category and have attempted to learn as much as possible about you and those similar to you. Can you guess why?

Psychologists now realize that development, once thought to end at childhood, or possibly adolescence, is a process that continues from conception to death. Today we realize that the changes of adulthood—maturity and aging—are as developmental as those of any other period. By analyzing the various developmental periods—infancy, early childhood, middle childhood, adolescence, and adulthood—researchers are trying to discover the features of each period and to uncover the mechanisms by which we move from one stage to the next.

The Meaning of Life Span

What do we mean by **lifespan psychology** (often referred to as *developmental psychology*)? Perhaps the best way to capture its meaning is to state that *development, as a lifelong process beginning at conception and ending in death, is itself a discipline worthy of study.*

These photos (a–e) show George Bush at various stages of his life span.

(a)   (b)

Table 1.1 Population Projection by Sex and Age: 1900–2000			
Sex and Age	**1990**[a]	**1995**[a]	**2000**[a]
Male			
Under 5	9,827	9,529	9,022
5–17	23,082	24,815	25,458
18–24	13,127	12,072	12,530
25–44	40,624	41,320	40,251
45–64	22,221	25,192	29,468
65 and over	12,637	13,440	13,762
Female			
Under 5	9,371	9,086	8,604
5–17	22,056	23,703	24,305
18–24	12,667	11,630	12,071
25–44	40,753	41,195	39,908
45–64	24,231	27,130	31,418
65 and over	19,061	20,447	21,158

Source: U.S. Bureau of the Census (thousands), 1987.

[a]Numbers represent thousands.

Yet for purposes of research and speculation, we arbitrarily divide the life span into segments, always recalling that each segment is part of a whole. In this book, the life span is divided as follows.

> Prenatal—conception to birth
> Infancy—birth to 2 years
> Early Childhood—2 to 5 years
> Middle Childhood—6 to 11 years
> Adolescence—12 to 18 years
> Early Adulthood—19 to 34 years
> Middle Adulthood—35 to 64 years
> Later Adulthood—65+

Table 1.1 presents the number of males and females in the various age groupings. Find your age group in the table. What do you think this means with regard to consumer spending? family size? future educational policy? future political direction? career opportunities? Do your classmates agree with you?

We could add many more categories here, but the point should be clear. Development does not proceed randomly. It is tightly linked to what psychologists call "context," that is, the society in which an individual develops. This is such an important feature of development that we will return to it frequently throughout this book. To understand development as fully as possible, you must also understand its context.

(c)

(d)

(e)

Why Study Lifespan Development?

There are two major reasons for studying lifespan psychology. As human beings, we are fascinated with ourselves. At first glance this seems to be a remarkably restricted reason. Nevertheless, the more that we know about ourselves, the better will be our relationships with others. Learning about ourselves is important also in order to have a satisfactory and realistic self-concept (Hinde, 1987).

By examining Table 1.1, you can infer that advancing technology, the need for service personnel, and an aging population will create an occupational upheaval. How will these changes affect your career choice? Consider that the following are some of today's fastest growing occupations: retail salespeople, registered nurses, secretaries, general managers, clerks, and physical therapists. On the other hand, among the occupations showing a rapid decline are machine workers, farmers, industrial truck and tractor operators, and stenographers.

Do the figures in Table 1.1 and the occupational trends listed here affect your thinking about the courses you want to take? Do they have any impact on your career choices? If you can identify your strengths and weaknesses, you will be better able to make appropriate education and career choices.

Understanding Yourself

The more education and technical skills you acquire, the greater the range of your opportunities for employment. Consider also the age range of the people with whom you would like to work. For example, if you like working with older individuals, consider looking to the South. With this segment of our population expanding steadily, predictions are that a state such as Florida will provide ample opportunities in service industries.

If you like working with people from a variety of age groups, you may want to consider hotel management, an industry that has grown at an annual rate of 20% each year for the past five years. Perhaps you like helping people of all ages or a particular age. The nursing shortage simply refuses to disappear.

Expectations are that by the year 2000, there will be about 21 million new jobs in the United States. Job availability will be greatest in Los Angeles, Washington, DC, Atlanta, Boston, Phoenix, and Minneapolis-St. Paul. The largest percentage increase will be in Florida cities: Naples, Fort Myers, West Palm Beach, Bradenton, and Orlando.

Learning about yourself and others, understanding the age characteristics of various groups, and projecting yourself—strengths and weaknesses—into future trends are all part of the benefits of studying lifespan psychology (Fischer & Silvern, 1985).

Understanding Others

A sound knowledge of lifespan characteristics also helps us to understand others. We inevitably interact with those of quite different ages. Those relationships can be smoothed by our understanding of what it means to be an infant or teenager. With a growing older population, we also need to be aware of the opportunities and problems of a graying America.

Having a better understanding of people of different ages improves relationships at home, with friends, and at work. As we shall see in chapter 6, relationships consist of a series of interactions. As we react to others, they change accordingly, and these changes in turn affect our behavior. By knowing and understanding people of various ages, we are more inclined to initiate positive interactions (Fischer & Silvern, 1985).

As social conditions change, opportunities for women, minorities, and the handicapped have expanded. The ultimate goal in our society is to remove all obstacles to self-fulfillment, an objective requiring cooperation from all segments of society—government, schools, church, business.

Understanding yourself and acquiring the basic skills needed for a particular occupation can lead to a sense of career satisfaction and self-fulfillment. People who are content in their work tend to look at it creatively and see challenges that keep them constantly interested.

A changing population means changing health needs, especially for the elderly. Technicians, nurses, and doctors require special training for the different challenges that each age group poses. Providing health services during the 1990s will demand a continuing influx of medical personnel.

High technology has become a way of life in modern societies. Advancing in almost any career means acquiring not only basic knowledge but also those technical skills, especially computer-related, that define competence in any field.

As an example of how knowledge of the life span can help, consider the concept of developmental tasks. Developmental tasks were originally proposed by Robert Havighurst to identify critical developmental accomplishments throughout the life span. Our interpretations of the tasks naturally change with time and with new research findings. Havighurst's developmental task concept, however, represents the belief that we continue to develop throughout our lives.

Table 1.2   The Developmental Tasks

Infancy and Early Childhood (0–5)	Middle Childhood (6–12)	Adolescence (13–18)
1. Learning to walk 2. Learning to take solid foods 3. Learning to talk 4. Learning to control the elimination of body wastes 5. Learning sex differences and sexual modesty 6. Acquiring concepts and language to describe social and physical reality 7. Readiness for reading 8. Learning to distinguish right from wrong and developing a conscience	1. Leaning physical skills necessary for ordinary games 2. Building a wholesome attitude toward oneself 3. Learning to get along with age-mates 4. Learning an appropriate sex role 5. Developing fundamental skills in reading, writing, and calculating 6. Developing concepts necessary for everyday living 7. Developing conscience, morality, and a scale of values 8. Achieving personal independence 9. Developing acceptable attitudes toward society	1. Achieving mature relations with both sexes 2. Achieving a masculine or feminine social role 3. Accepting one's physique 4. Achieving emotional independence of adults 5. Preparing for marriage and family life 6. Preparing for an economic career 7. Acquiring values and an ethical system to guide behavior 8. Desiring and achieving socially responsible behavior

From Robert Havighurst, *Developmental Tasks and Education*, 3d ed. Copyright © 1972 David McKay Company, Inc., a division of Random House, New York, NY.

The Developmental Task Concept

Havighurst (1972) defines a **developmental task** as one that arises at a certain period in our lives, the successful achievement of which leads to happiness and success with later tasks, while failure leads to unhappiness, social disapproval, and difficulty with later tasks. Havighurst uses slightly different age groupings, but the basic divisions are quite similar to those used in this book. The initial words of his text *Developmental Tasks and Education* (1972), "Living is learning and growing is learning," are a striking example of his position. To understand the process of human development, one must understand learning; human beings *learn* their way through life.

Sources of Developmental Tasks

Growth and development in a modern technological society require the mastery of a series of tasks. At each level of development, we encounter new social demands and expectations. As we meet these challenges, we acquire new philosophical and psychological resources that, combined with environmental stimulation, constitute a series of developmental tasks that are critical to harmonious development. There are three sources of developmental tasks (Havighurst, 1972):

    1. *Tasks that arise from physical maturation.* For example, learning to walk, talk, and behave acceptably with the opposite sex during adolescence; adjusting to menopause during middle age.

    2. *Tasks that have their source in the pressures of society.* For example, learning to read or learning the role of a responsible citizen.

Table 1.2 *Continued*		
Early Adulthood (19–29)	**Middle Adulthood (30–60)**	**Later Maturity (61+)**
1. Selecting a mate 2. Learning to live with a partner 3. Starting a family 4. Rearing children 5. Managing a home 6. Starting an occupation 7. Assuming civic responsibility	1. Helping teenage children to become happy and responsible adults 2. Achieving adult social and civic responsibility 3. Satisfactory career achievement 4. Developing adult leisure time activities 5. Relating to one's spouse as a person 6. Accepting the physiological changes of middle age 7. Adjusting to aging parents	1. Adjusting to decreasing strength and health 2. Adjusting to retirement and reduced income 3. Adjusting to death of spouse 4. Establishing relations with one's own age group 5. Meeting social and civic obligations 6. Establishing satisfactory living quarters

3. *Tasks that arise from a personal source.* For example, those tasks that emerge from the maturing personality and take the form of personal values and aspirations, such as learning the necessary skills for job success.

The importance of the developmental task concept pervades all developmental levels for two reasons. First, developmental tasks aid in the formulation of more precise and realistic goals for all human beings. Second, as Havighurst states, when the body is ripe, and society requires, and the self is ready to achieve a certain task, the teachable moment has arrived. We can better time what is required in education by identifying the tasks that are suitable for a particular level of development.

Havighurst has identified six major categories: infancy and early childhood (0–5 years), middle childhood (6–12 years), adolescence (13–18 years), early adulthood (19–29 years), middle adulthood (30–60 years), and, rather kindly phrased, later maturity (61+). Table 1.2 presents typical developmental tasks for each period.

An Example of Developmental Tasks

Most of us encounter difficulty with some of the developmental tasks that occur at various ages. How we learn to cope with those difficulties provides excellent clues to our level of adjustment. For example, a friendly but volatile and slightly aggressive girl, Barbara, has two older sisters and an older brother. She is happy at home and close to her parents but she has difficulty with her friends. At 10, 13, and 16 years of age, she is rated (on a scale of 1 through 10) on several developmental tasks.

Getting Along with Age-Mates

Age	Average Rating
10	5.5
13	6.4
16	9.5

How can we explain this improvement? Barbara "learns her way through life." She shifts from aggressive attitudes (perhaps fostered by competition with her brother and sisters) to a feeling of greater self-acceptance. She is discovering who she is and is undoubtedly acquiring a sense of identity and self-worth.

Achieving a Feminine Social Role

Age	Average Rating
10	4.4
13	6.7
16	9.6

The change in ratings here is probably due to the decline in aggression, a quality not usually associated with the feminine role. As Barbara learns that she does not have to fight her way through life, her relations with others improve and she becomes more accepted for herself.

Achieving Emotional Independence

Age	Average Rating
10	4.2
13	5.4
16	8.6

Here we see a different pattern, owing to Barbara's dependence on her parents. Since she lacks satisfactory peer relations, she seeks feelings of security from her parents. Between the ages of 10 and 13, there is not much change in her emotional dependence. Most young people feel emotionally insecure at this time, but Barbara particularly so. She has improved somewhat by the age of 16, but she has yet to achieve the emotional maturity normal for a girl this age.

What can we say about this case? As Barbara encounters the developmental tasks associated with her age, her past learning affects the manner in which she meets each new challenge (Travers, 1982). Thinking that aggressive behavior is necessary, she complicates relationships with her friends. This behavior intensifies her struggle for mastery over other developmental tasks.

An individual's personality is closely related to developmental tasks, since it is the self, reflecting biological and social pressures, that determines any individual's handling of developmental tasks (Harter, 1983). Personality seems to be causally related to performance of tasks. For example, the boy with a healthy, friendly attitude toward girls will obviously be rated more highly on social attitudes.

Finally, emotions, rationality, and self-understanding are more closely related to satisfactory performance of tasks than is intelligence. Our emotional lives are not separated from any endeavors, including the task of achieving intellectual skills.

The developmental-task concept has a long and rich tradition. Its acceptance has been due partly to a recognition of sensitive periods in our lives and partly to the practical nature of Havighurst's tasks. Havighurst has given us all a clear and excellent guide to some of the obstacles that we must overcome at various ages. No inflexible age ranges are given for each task. The age span for each period is quite wide and suggests steady progress toward maturity instead of abrupt steps.

Knowing that a youngster of a certain age (say, 11) is encountering one of the tasks of that period (learning an appropriate sex role) helps adults to understand the child's behavior and to establish an environment that will help the child master the task. Another important task for the middle childhood period is acquiring personal independence. Youngsters will test authority during this phase. If teachers and parents realize that this is a normal, even necessary phase of development, they will react differently than if they see it as a personal challenge (Hetherington & Parke, 1986).

Note Havighurst's developmental tasks for middle adulthood, one of which is a parent's need to help children become happy and responsible adults. Adults occasionally find it hard to "let go" of their children. They want to keep their children with them far beyond any reasonable time. For their own good, as well as that of their children, they must reconcile their wants and needs with those of their children. Once they do, they can enter a happy time in their own lives, especially if the husbands and wives are not only spouses but friends and partners as well.

Havighurst is not alone in placing importance on the developmental task concept (Cole, 1986; Goetting, 1986; Cristante, 1987; Cangemi & Kowalski, 1987). For example, Goetting (1986) has examined the developmental tasks of siblings and identified those that last for a lifetime, such as companionship and emotional support. Other tasks seemed to be related to a particular stage in the life cycle, such as caretaking during childhood and later the care of elderly parents.

We've seen how a knowledge of lifespan development helps us to understand ourselves and others. Now you may be interested in learning about the roots of lifespan studies.

History of Lifespan Studies

Tracing the path along which developmental psychologists have trod leads to interesting, and, in some cases, surprising discoveries. Each developmental epoch—infancy, early childhood, middle childhood, adolescence, and adulthood—has in its turn become a primary focus of research and speculation.

Child Studies

You may be surprised to learn that *children* and *childhood* are relatively new concepts (Aries, 1962). Celebrating a child's birthday, for example, did not begin until the end of the eighteenth century. Robert Sears (1975) has attempted to trace the roots of child development study and concludes that the first stirrings of empathy toward children appeared in the eighteenth century. Concern for mentally ill and delinquent children was followed in the period of the American Civil War by a strong support for the abolition of slavery that signaled solicitude for the welfare of others in general and children in particular.

As professions such as education, medicine, and social work grew and prospered, they slowly became involved with the care, health, and schooling of youth. These more professional commitments to children brought with them organizational support, theories that provided insights into the developmental process, and scientific methods designed to discover the data that would provide solutions to children's problems.

Children were not always prized as they are by most parents today. This photo shows children in a typical 19th century sweatshop, reflecting an attitude in which children, as young as 5 or 6, were valued for their economic work.

BOX 1.1

What's Your Opinion?

Several commentators (Postman, 1982; Winn, 1983) have lamented what they term our society's "loss of childhood." Speaking of children as an endangered species, Postman states:

Everywhere one looks, it may be seen that the behavior, language, attitudes, and desires—even the physical appearance of—adults and children are becoming increasingly indistinguishable. No doubt this is why there exists a growing movement to recast the legal rights of children so that they are more or less the same as adults. The thrust of this movement, which, among other things is opposed to compulsory schooling, resides in the claim that what has been thought to be a preferred status for children is instead only an oppression that keeps them from fully participating in society (1982, p. 5).

Postman argues that there are some things that should be kept from children (e.g., sex) until they can understand its meaning. Once the line between childhood and adulthood is erased—because of the availability of instant information, especially television—childhood ceases to exist.

Nothing is withheld from children. When children and adults view television together, the message is clear: a child is welcomed to the adult world as much because of attention span as developmental readiness. As Postman states, we are in the age of the "disappearance of childhood."

Do you agree with this assessment, or do you believe that today's children are enjoying a typical childhood? What's your opinion?

Great Names in the History of Child Development

You may well recognize some of the famous figures who have been associated with the study of child development over the years. Senn (1975) lists the following as among the major contributors.

- *G. Stanley Hall* is often referred to as the founder of the child development movement in the United States. He became famous for using questionnaires to discover what children are thinking about.

- *Sigmund Freud,* who startled the world with his psychoanalytic theory (see chap. 2), stressed the importance of the early years in a child's life. Belief in their importance remains strong today.

- *John Watson's* views on childrearing were extremely popular in the 1920s and the 1930s, especially his belief that children should be conditioned early in life.

- *Arnold Gesell* pioneered the use of creative methods in child development research, such as using one-way mirrors and motion pictures to record development.

- *Jean Piaget* has dominated our thinking about the cognitive development of children since the 1930s. His views will be presented in detail throughout this book.

These are but a few of the well-known individuals who have contributed much to the child development movement. As Senn states:

❖ *Admittedly, "child development" means different things to different people; to some it has become a slogan, to many a cliché. But the very fact of a large group of supporters of the concept that it is important and something worth working and fighting for in the laboratories, social fields, and political arena is, perhaps, evidence that we are indeed witnessing a movement (1975, p. 88).*

Adolescence

G. Stanley Hall's book, *Adolescence,* published in 1904, signaled the beginning of intense and continuing study of adolescence as a distinct developmental period. Hall's views of adolescence (including seeing it as a period of "storm and stress") greatly influenced those writing about adolescence for the next fifty years. But by the 1950s, a more positive view of adolescence was beginning to emerge (Petersen, 1988). Researchers began to concentrate less on the problems of adolescence and more on the developmental characteristics of the period. A great deal of basic data about adolescents was collected.

Adolescent girls come to their growth spurt earlier than boys, which creates some interesting social situations.

Today, research on this period has increased dramatically. The number of articles and journals devoted to adolescence has grown sharply, and a professional society, The Society for Research on Adolescence, has come into existence. Current research on adolescence emphasizes social development, family relationships, peers, and the wider social environment.

Three topics have recently received considerable attention (Petersen, 1988).

1. *Adolescent adjustment or adolescent turmoil.* Research has seriously questioned the early belief of Hall and others that turmoil is natural for adolescents and is a phenomenon that they outgrow with continued development. For example, Petersen (1988) states that those adolescents demonstrating severe turmoil frequently exhibit later serious problems.

If not all adolescents experience problems, how can we identify those at risk? One marker seems to be gender, which offers the following clues:

▲ Adolescent boys with psychological difficulties usually have a history of childhood problems.

▲ More girls first show signs of psychological problems in adolescence (e.g., greater tendency toward depression).

▲ Anxiety seems to play a key role in the appearance of adolescent difficulties (achievement situations are more likely to arouse anxiety in males, while interpersonal relations are more likely to cause anxiety in females).

2. *Puberty and its effects.* The mechanisms that control pubertal change develop prenatally. For most children, pubertal hormonal levels begin increasing at about 7 years of age, with bodily changes appearing about four or five years later (about a year or two earlier in girls than boys) (Dacey, 1986).

BOX 1.2

Type T Personalities

As a follow-up to the notion of adolescence as a time of turmoil for some teenagers, recent studies have discovered that those adolescents most susceptible to trouble may show clues to this future behavior almost from birth. Known as **Type T personalities** (*T* for *Thrills*), these adolescents seem to have inherited a proneness to taking risks. Taking chances with alcohol and drugs, driving cars at high speeds, fighting, and other impulsive behavior all fit a pattern. As we shall see in the infancy section, we are much more inclined today to accept the notion of inborn temperamental characteristics.

While the biological basis of risk-taking behavior remains unknown, these adolescents share a different physiological profile: heart rate, skin temperature, and sweat glands react more slowly to external stimulation. Frank Farley, a psychologist at the University of Wisconsin, believes that such teenagers seek thrills to satisfy their need for stimulation. Whether Type T personalities take a destructive path depends on home, school, and other environmental contacts.

Farley (1986) estimates that from 10% to 30% of American adolescents have this biological tendency to risk-taking. Among their personality characteristics is an urge for uncertainty, high risk, novelty, variety, complexity, and conflict. This exciting and useful research is just beginning and may eventually shed new light on the causes of adolescent behavior.

Changes in adolescence— physical, social, cognitive—require teenagers to develop different methods of coping. Still searching for identity and susceptible to peer pressure, adolescents can engage in thrill-seeking and dangerous behavior. It is a time when the adults around teenagers need to respond sensitively and treat adolescents as "almost adults."

You probably remember how intensely aware you were of these changes within yourself. Also, the timing of puberty is crucial in relation to others because of the psychological and social processes involved. The well-developed, physically mature girl can only wonder about male classmates still running around in baseball caps and chewing bubble gum.

Here are some of the major findings that have resulted from studies of the relationship between puberty and psychological functioning:

▲ There is little evidence that puberty is linked to psychological problems; its effects may be positive as well as negative.

▲ While puberty may affect psychological variables, its impact is specific— on depression, aggression, or self-concept, for example.

▲ Puberty affects boys and girls differently.

3. *Adolescent-family interactions.* Recent research into adolescent-family relations has focused on the reciprocal effects of the family on the adolescent. (This research focus reflects the current interpretation of development as one of reciprocal interactions—see "Models of Development," this chapter.)

Is there a generational gap between adolescents and their families? As you can see, this question is an extension of the belief that "adolescence is an age of turmoil" for all adolescents. Again, research has shown this belief to be incorrect; parents and their adolescents have more similar attitudes and values than do adolescents and their friends. (Adolescent peer similarities are more common in the adolescent culture, such as dress and music.)

Adolescent-parent conflict, when it exists, results not only from adolescent difficulties but from parental factors, such as divorce, excessive parental control, or a parental midlife crisis. Today's research into

Table 1.3	Numbers of 65+ Population	
Age	**Year**	**No. in Millions**
65–84	1988	15.8
	2020	44.3
85+	1985	2.7
	2020	7.11

Source: U.S. Bureau of the Census, 1987.

Table 1.4	Life Expectancies of 65+ Population	
Group	**1985**	**2020**
Total	74.7 years	78.1 years
Male	71.2	74.2
Female	78.2	82.0
African-American	69.5	75.5
White	75.3	78.5

Source: U.S. Bureau of the Census, 1987.

adolescent-family interactions looks at the family as a system, particularly at the developmental status of the members of this system. If an adolescent does indeed face a problem, are the parents sufficiently mature to adjust (Dacey, 1986)?

In a thoughtful commentary on adolescence as a critical phase in the life span, Petersen states:

❖   *Because there is so much change during adolescence, and these changes require effective coping on the part of the individual, the processes involved are likely to be ones needed to respond to challenges throughout life. If this hypothesis is correct, adolescence will be the first phase of life requiring, and presumably stimulating, mature patterns of functioning that persist throughout life. Conversely, failure to cope effectively with the challenges of adolescence may represent deficiencies in an individual that bode ill for subsequent development (1988, p. 601).*

Adulthood

Adulthood is that time of our lives when we begin a career, form long-lasting relationships, assume personal and civic responsibilities, care for aging parents, and adjust to the aging process. Is it any wonder that this period has attracted the interest of scholars and become a discipline in itself, just as have the periods of childhood and adolescence?

Former president Ronald Reagan in his 70s, Mother Teresa in her 60s, and Jonas Salk in his 70s searching for an AIDS vaccine remind us of the growing number of senior citizens. If we take a more restricted view of population projections and focus on senior citizens, we have the age and numbers categories seen in Table 1.3. By the year 2020, the percentage of the total population 65 years or older will be 17.3%, up from 12% in 1985. The life expectancy figures for the 65+ group is seen in Table 1.4.

Given these figures and the crucial developmental tasks of adulthood, we can understand why these years have attracted so much scholarly attention. As evidence of the continuing interest in adulthood, Birren and associates (1983) note that in reviewing the adult literature over a seven-year period, they found over four hundred pertinent articles. Among the topics most heavily researched was that of intellectual ability: What is the reality and extent of intellectual decline with age? This is an important question when we consider America's aging population, the "graying of America."

As each of these age periods assumed its place in the mainstream of developmental psychology, there was a growing need to integrate findings, to devise some mechanism that would renew focus on the totality of human development. Consequently lifespan development was born, a study committed to the view that development is not confined to any period or periods but rather is a lifelong process, encompassing the time from conception to death.

As in any discipline, there are several controversial issues that lifespan studies must address. These topics engage the time and energy of developmental psychologists and help to give direction to the field.

Issues in Lifespan Psychology

In lifespan psychology, certain basic issues arise that must be addressed because they affect the manner in which we interpret behavior and development. For example, most youngsters begin to utter words, phrases, and sentences beginning at the age of 1. Is this behavior just another link in a continuous progression of developmental steps, or is it distinct from any discernible roots? This problem is commonly referred to as the continuity versus discontinuity issue.

We will now discuss several of these issues, issues that will appear repeatedly throughout the book. In chapter 2 we present the views of the leading developmental theorists, each of whom has taken a position on one or several of these issues.

Normal Versus Exceptional

Do we learn more about development by studying "normal" development or by concentrating on deviations from the typical developmental track (Sameroff, 1986)? You have just read about a growing belief among developmental psychologists that all adolescents are not in turmoil. Do we learn more by studying those teenagers who pass through these years smoothly, or more by focusing on the delinquent or on the adolescent battling drugs?

How one answers these and similar questions leads to different research methods, different publications, different professional organizations, and perhaps—though not always—different interpretations of a particular developmental period (Gloecker & Simpson, 1988).

Inner Versus Outer Control

For those who speculate about the forces that account for development, the issue of control is all important (Hay, 1986). What controls development? Are you inevitably locked into a certain developmental track by influences over which you have no control? Or do you retain the option of choice even in the face of strong compelling forces? For example, if a child has a negative relationship with its mother (let's assume extremes—neglect to the point of deprivation), will that decide the future of later relationships?

Heredity Versus Environment

The "nature-nurture" or "heredity-environment" issue has divided investigators from the days when behavior first began to be studied (Sroufe & Cooper, 1988). What is more important, your genes or your environment? While most developmental psychologists agree that the interaction between the two explains development, there is a tendency to favor one over the other.

While genetic research has proliferated for the past several years, environmental studies have lagged. The difficulty in controlling all the variables that influence development is perhaps the major reason for this difference. (See the research section in this chapter.)

One of the more promising types of environmental research is cross cultural. Recent studies have shown the effect on development of cultural values, educational availability, and childrearing practices.

Continuity Versus Discontinuity

We can summarize the **continuity** versus **discontinuity** issue as follows: do developmental changes appear abruptly, or as the result of a slow but steady progression (Rutter, 1987)? As a rather dramatic illustration, consider the phenomenon known as *attachment* in infancy.

Sometime after 6 months, babies begin to show a decided preference for a particular adult—the infant has attached to that person. During any time of stress—anxiety, illness, appearance of strangers—the child will move to the preferred adult. In regard to continuity or discontinuity, does attachment appear suddenly as completely new and different behavior, or do subtle clues signal its arrival? (For an overview of this topic, see chap. 3.)

Sensitive Periods Versus Equal Potential

Many developmental psychologists believe that there are certain times in the life span when a particular experience has a greater and more lasting impact (Rutter, 1987). These are called **sensitive periods.** For example, the care and attention of a loving adult during the first months of life seems obviously linked to the appearance of attachment.

If such an experience is lacking during these early days, but comes at a later age (say, 5 years), will it produce the same results? Or was the sensitive period missed? Here we have an explosive question that cuts across many of society's activities—social, political, economical.

Let's assume for the sake of argument (and we don't agree with this conclusion) that once a sensitive period is missed, the damage can never be made up. Why, then, should we bother to pour hundreds of millions of dollars into intervention programs (such as Head Start) in the hope of "making up" for lost experiences? Politicians who vote the use of public monies must take a stand on this question; voters either agree or disagree with their decisions.

Most developmental psychologists don't agree that "once missed, never catch up." But they also believe that nobody, child or adult, can withstand severe deprivation, either physical or psychological, indefinitely. We all have our limits (Clarke & Clarke, 1977).

These issues help to identify lifespan psychology as a dynamic discipline, one that has great theoretical and practical implications. But, as fascinating as these issues are, we must never forget the integrated nature of development.

We pride ourselves on being a nation of immigrants, a country that welcomes newcomers with the promise of unrestricted opportunity. To achieve this objective during a time of increasing immigration demands consideration and tolerance for those of different color, nationality, and beliefs.

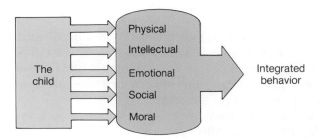

Figure 1.1 The interactive nature of development.

A Biopsychosocial Model of Development

To help us understand the integrated nature of the life span, psychologists have turned to a **biopsychosocial** model of development (Travers, 1982). This term means just what it says: development proceeds by the interaction of biological, psychological, and social forces. Figure 1.1 illustrates the interactive nature of development. It also clearly illustrates the spreading effect of any developmental change on all phases of development. Persons who experience social problems—difficulty with friends, for example—usually will also show problems at home, in school, or at work. It is impossible to confine the problem to one developmental compartment.

If behavior is integrated, it must also be interactive. *Interaction,* however, is a term about which it is easy to be glib. For example, it is true that "development results from the interaction of heredity and environment," but that statement taken alone is almost meaningless. Heredity acts in an incredibly sophisticated, complicated fashion; that is, through gene interaction. Thus genes become the environment for other genes (see chap. 3).

A Systems Analysis

Like heredity, environment acts in ways that we are only beginning to comprehend. Thanks to the work of Uri Bronfenbrenner (1978), we now realize that there are many environments acting on us. For example, there is the **microsystem** (the immediate setting that influences development, such as the family), the **mesosystem** (the relationship among microsystems), the **exosystem** (an environment in which you are not present, but which nevertheless affects you—e.g., your father's job), and the **macrosystem** (society). To illustrate the interactive nature of these forces, consider the youngster whose father has just lost his job (changes in the exosystem), which causes the family to move to another location and results in different friends and schools for the child (changes in the micro- and mesosystems).

Reciprocal Interactions

Heredity and environment produce their results in a complex, interactive manner. But what complicates our analysis even more is that we ourselves are interacting reciprocally with the environment. Remember, at birth we have had nine months of development. So we help to shape the reactions of those around us. Our responses cause parents and siblings to respond in a unique fashion. This process never ceases and is known as **reciprocal interactions** (Brazelton, 1984). We respond to those around us and they change; their responses to us change and we in turn change (Brazelton, 1984).

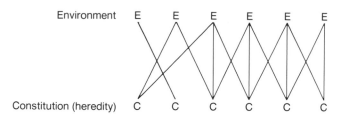

Figure 1.2 Reciprocal interactions.

A Transactional Model

Sameroff (1975) proposes a similar model that incorporates the biopsychosocial notion but is more suited to developmental analysis. He argues against views that attribute development to either heredity or environment. Sameroff summarizes the **transactional model** as follows:

❖　*In order to incorporate these progressive interactions one must move from a static, interactional model to a more dynamic theory of developmental transaction where there is a continual and progressive interplay between the organism and its environment (1975, p. 119).*

The process is similar to that seen in Figure 1.2.

The biopsychosocial and transactional models of development are basically identical. Both emphasize the constant state of reorganization we all experience through development. Both stress the complexity of developmental analysis by recognizing:

1. There is no simple cause-and-effect explanation.

2. All of our internal growth forces are interacting.

3. All relevant external forces are likewise interacting.

4. Internal and external forces are interacting with each other (Travers, 1982).

If you continue to think of development in this manner—that is, employing a biopsychosocial framework—you will appreciate the subtlety and beauty of development, while simultaneously acknowledging the difficulty, but not impossibility, of interpreting developmental data.

Developmental Research

Having identified several key developmental issues and explored a promising model of development, we should now ask: how can we obtain reliable data about these topics?

Today we use many approaches for understanding human behavior. Each has its strengths and weaknesses; none is completely reliable. Most developmental psychologists employ one of three data-collection methods: descriptive studies, manipulative experiments, and naturalistic experiments. In the first type, information is gathered on subjects without manipulating them in any way. In the second two, an experiment is performed before the information is gathered.

BOX 1.3

Multicultural Focus: Culture and Development

We pride ourselves on being a culturally diverse nation that encourages newcomers to share our way of life. Even under the best of conditions, however, immigrants can experience difficulties: language, customs, acceptance, job opportunities. The receiving country also must adapt. Schools, churches, markets, and politics all must change accordingly. We'll explore these ideas in later chapters, but first we'll look at what we know today about immigration.

The United States is now experiencing its third great immigration wave. The federal government began keeping immigration records in 1820, which was the peak of the first significant immigration movement. Most of these immigrants arrived from Great Britain, Ireland, Germany, and Scandinavia, with a smaller number of Chinese entering California (Kellogg, 1988).

The second major wave occurred between 1900 and 1920, mainly immigrants from Italy, Hungary, Poland, and Russia. In 1907, more than 1.3 million immigrants entered the United States; the decade 1900–1910 saw 8.8 million newcomers, representing more than forty countries. It wasn't until the economy collapsed in the late 1920s that immigration slowed.

The third significant wave began in the late 1960s and continues today. If we count the three categories of immigrants—legal immigrants, refugees, and undocumented immigrants—today's migration is the largest in our history. More than two-thirds of this latest migration are Oriental and Hispanic peoples (Kellogg, 1988).

Children from different cultures bring their differences with them. Their different customs may influence the relationships they form. Certainly diet is different. Learning styles vary, which can affect classroom achievement. Frequently fleeing war and poverty, they carry emotional scars. As you can well imagine, all of these conditions have developmental consequences.

They also use one of four time-variable designs: one-time, one-group studies; longitudinal studies; cross-sectional studies; and a combination of the last two, called sequential studies. Each of these types of studies varies in the effect of time on the results. These data-collection methods and time-variable designs will now be described.

Data Collection Techniques

Descriptive Studies

Descriptive studies are quite common. Most are numerically descriptive: for example, how many 12 year olds think the government is doing a good job versus 17 year olds that think so; how much money the average 40-year-old woman has to spend per week; how many pregnant teenage girls were or were not using birth control; how happily or unhappily the average 66-year-old man views his sex life. Some studies ask people their opinions of themselves (called *self-report* studies) or of other people. These may use interviews or questionnaires. Other studies describe people simply by counting the number and types of their behaviors (called *observational studies*). A third type, *case studies,* presents data on an individual or individuals in great detail, in order to make generalizations about a particular age group.

An example of the case study approach is Roll and Miller's (1978) "Adolescent Males' Feelings of Being Understood by Their Fathers as Revealed Through Clinical Interviews." They studied 20 boys who felt they were understood by their fathers and 20 who felt they were not. Although both groups of fathers were equally strict, the first group was seen as fair in their punishment, while the second was not.

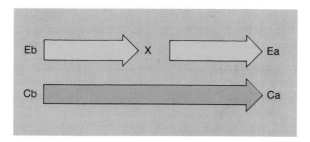

Figure 1.3 The classic experiment.

Descriptive studies have the advantage of generating a great deal of data. But because the sequence of events is not under the observer's control, causes and effects cannot be determined.

Manipulative Experiments

In the quest for the causes of behavior, psychologists have designed many **manipulative experiments.** In these, they attempt to keep all variables (all the factors that can affect a particular outcome) constant except one, which they carefully manipulate. It is called a *treatment.* If there are differences in the results of the experiment, they can be attributed to the variable that was manipulated in the treatment. The experimental subjects must respond to some test selected by the investigator in order to determine the effect of the treatment. Figure 1.3 illustrates this procedure.

E is the experimental group. C is the control group, which receives no special treatment. X stands for the treatment. The lowercase *b* and *a* refer to times before and after the experiment. There is one inescapable conclusion: without the control of all elements, the results remain suspect.

An example is Dacey's study (in progress) in which two similar groups of eighth graders have been randomly selected from all those in two inner-city middle schools. One group is being given the treatment, a series of 16 lessons in self-control, while the other group studies the traditional curriculum. At the end of this experiment, both groups will be observed to see whether there is any decrease in pregnancy, drug use, or dropping out of school. If the experimental group does better in terms of these criteria, we can assume that the 16 lessons in self-control were effective.

Though manipulative experiments often can lead us to discover what causes what in life, there are problems with them. How do you know your results are reliable? Was the treatment similar to normal conditions? Do subjects see themselves as special because you picked them and as a result react atypically? For these reasons, researchers often rely on naturalistic experiments.

Naturalistic Experiments

In **naturalistic experiments,** the researcher acts solely as an observer and does as little as possible to disturb the environment. "Nature" performs the experiment, and the researcher acts as a recorder of the results. (Note: don't confuse these with descriptive studies that are done in a natural setting such as a park—those are not experiments). An example is the study of the effects of the blizzard of 1978 by Nuttall and Nuttall (1979). They compared the reactions of those whose homes were destroyed to those in the same area whose homes suffered only minor damage.

Only with a naturalistic experiment do we have any chance of discovering causes and effects in real-life settings. The main problems with this technique are that it requires great patience and objectivity and it is impossible to meet the strict requirements of a true scientific experiment.

Time-Variable Designs

One-Time, One-Group Studies

As the name implies, **one-time, one-group studies** are those that are carried out only once on one group of subjects. Thus it is impossible to investigate causes and effects, as the *sequence* of events cannot be known.

Longitudinal Studies

The **longitudinal study,** which makes several observations of the same individuals at two or more times in their lives, can answer important questions. Examples are determining the long-term effects of learning on behavior; the stability of habits and intelligence; and the factors involved in memory.

Although much of childhood behavior disappears by adulthood, there has long been a suspicion that some adult traits develop steadily from childhood and remain for life. In his search for such stable characteristics, Benjamin Bloom in his classic work *Stability and Change in Human Characteristics* (1964) notes that the development of some human characteristics appears visible and obvious, while that of others remains obscure. The following are three growth studies in which more than three hundred persons have participated for over thirty years.

1. *The Berkeley Growth Study,* begun in 1928, was designed to study the mental, motor, and physical development of a sample of full-term healthy babies.

2. *The Guidance Study* took youngsters born in 1928 and 1929 and began to study them at 21 months of age. The aim was to study physical, mental, and personality development in a normal group.

3. *The Oakland Growth Study* of 200 fifth and sixth graders was designed to study many interrelations between developmental changes and behavior. The investigators tried to discover whether developmental changes affect a child's potential.

One of the longitudinal growth studies most often quoted is that of the Fels Research Institute (Kagan & Moss, 1962). The subjects were 45 girls and 44 boys, all white, whose personality development was traced from birth through early adulthood. The investigators conducted extensive interviews with both the children and their parents. Among the particular techniques used were the following:

- *Personality tests* given at regular intervals. The child was asked to react to a picture (the Thematic Apperception Test) or to a design such as a Rorschach inkblot. Trained persons analyzed responses for clues to personality, including motives, attitudes, and problems.

- *Observation of the mother* in the home with the child present, and also annual interviews with the mother.

- *Measurement of the intelligence* of both the mother and the father, using the Otis IQ test.

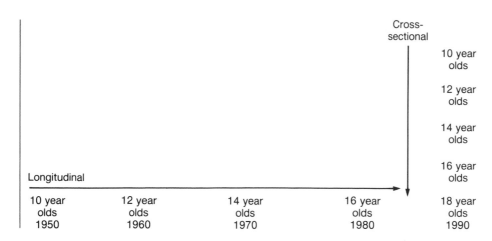

Figure 1.4 *Comparison of the longitudinal and cross-sectional approaches.*

- *Regular observation of the child's behavior* in the home, in school, and at day camp. The child was also interviewed by workers.

Kagan and Moss summarize the obvious advantages of the longitudinal method when they note that it permits the discovery of lasting habits and of the periods in which they appear. A second advantage is the possibility of tracing those adult behaviors that have changed since early childhood.

There are, however, many problems with longitudinal research. It is expensive and often hard to maintain because of changes in the availability of researchers and subjects. Changes in the environment can also distort the results. For example, if you began in 1960 to study changes in the political attitudes of youth from 10 to 20 years of age, you would probably have concluded that adolescents become more and more radical as they grow older. But the war in Vietnam would surely have had much to do with this finding. The results of the same study done between 1970 and 1980 would probably not show this radicalizing trend.

Cross-Sectional Studies

The **cross-sectional study** compares groups of individuals of various ages at the same time, in order to investigate the effects of aging. For example, if you want to know how creative thinking changes or grows during adolescence, you could administer creativity tests to groups of 10, 12, 14, 16, and 18 year olds, and check on the differences of the average scores of the five groups. Jaquish and Ripple (1980) did just this, but their subjects ranged in age from 10 to 84!

As with each of the others, there is a problem with this method. Although the effects of cultural change can be minimized by careful selection, it is possible that the differences you find may be due to differences in *age cohort* rather than to maturation. **Age cohorts** are groups of people born at about the same time. Each cohort has had different experiences throughout its history, and this can affect the results as much as the actual differences in age. Figure 1.4 compares these two approaches.

Table 1.5 Illustration of a Longitudinal/Cross-Sectional Study				
Creativity Test			
Test I March 4, 1970	Test II March 4, 1980	Test III March 4, 1990	
Group A (12 years old)	Group A (14 years old)	Group A (16 years old)	Mean Score Group A
Group B (14 years old)	Group B (16 years old)	Group B (18 years old)	Mean Score Group B
Group C (16 years old)	Group C (18 years old)	Group C (20 years old)	Mean Score Group C
Mean Score 1970	Mean Score 1980	Mean Score 1990	

Table 1.6 Relationships of Data-Collection Techniques and Time-Variable Designs			
	Data-Collection Techniques		
Time-Variable Designs	Descriptive	Manipulated	Naturalistic
One-time, one-group			
Longitudinal			
Cross-sectional			
Sequential			

Sequential (Longitudinal/Cross-Sectional) Studies

When a cross-sectional study is done at several times with the same groups of individuals (such as administering creativity tests to the same five groups of youth, but at three different points in their lives), the problems mentioned before can be alleviated. Table 1.5 illustrates such a **sequential study.** Although this type of research is complicated and expensive, it may be the only type that is capable of answering important questions in the complex and fast-changing times in which we live.

Table 1.6 shows how each of the data-collection methods may be combined with each of the time-variable designs. For each of the cells in this table, a number of actual studies could serve as examples. Can you see where each study mentioned in this section would go?

To conclude this section, Figure 1.5 compares the various research techniques. By *controlled,* we mean the degree to which the investigator can control the relevant variables. By *inclusive,* we mean the degree to which all relevant information is included in the data.

Having explored the history of lifespan studies and examined current issues and research techniques, we turn our attention now to several developmental themes, almost guidelines, that indicate our assumptions about development.

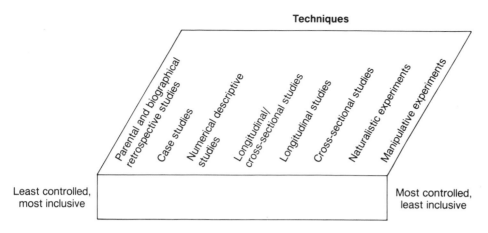

Figure 1.5 A comparison of research techniques.

Themes in Development

The themes that we are about to mention should serve as a guide for understanding human development. As such, they will be a constant presence throughout this book (though discussed only briefly here). They are also the assumptions that we make about how humans develop across the life span.

Human Beings Develop and Change

From the moment of conception until death, human development is a process of change. Each of the periods that we have identified as part of the life span—infancy, early childhood, middle childhood, adolescence, and the stages of adulthood—has its own unique, identifying features.

Infants begin to walk and talk; early childhood youngsters rapidly expand their physical skills; middle childhood youngsters demonstrate an increased symbolic capacity; adolescents struggle to find their own identity; adults mature and help the next generation. Note the categories of development we have identified.

Physical	Moral
Social	Cognitive
Emotional	Linguistic

In each of the age groups that we will discuss, these are the developmental features that we will trace. As you can imagine, any developmental feature can be more significant in one age period than in another. For example, we will discuss language development at length in the early childhood section but refer to it only occasionally in the adolescent and adult sections.

Human Beings Need Relationships

For normal development to occur, humans must establish satisfactory relationships with others. As the noted English scientist Robert Hinde (1979, 1987) has said, "For most of us, relationships with other people are the most important part of our lives." Relationships play a large part in determining what human beings become. The manner in which we form relationships, and the nature of the relationships themselves, can determine happiness and adjustment, or discomfort and frustration at each stage of development.

The reality of reciprocal interactions (discussed earlier in this chapter) testifies to the importance of relationships. We change as the result of our interactions with others, and the change in us produces changes in those with whom we are interacting.

The nature of the relationship will change with development. The interactions of children in early childhood differ from those between teenagers, or between mature men and women.

Human Beings Show Remarkable Plasticity

Human beings show amazing resiliency. Recovery from damage (both physical and psychological) has been a well-documented fact of biological and psychological research (Rutter, 1981). Yet plasticity has its limits, which brings us to a critical question: under what conditions will children and adults recover from damage (Goldman-Rakic, 1983)?

What does **plasticity** mean? It implies flexibility and resiliency; thus plasticity is opposed to continuity. What stand you take on the meaning of these terms has serious implications. Consider, for example, those who believe in continuity: whatever happens to a child in the early years leaves an indelible mark; the damage will be continuous for that child's life.

Adherents of plasticity take exactly the opposite view: since human beings demonstrate tremendous recuperative powers, refusing to offer help to those damaged borders on criminal behavior. The childrearing, educational, economic, and political consequences of either of these positions spread throughout the entire fabric of our society. Although advocates of both views have moderated their ideas somewhat, the lines are clearly drawn and identical evidence has been interpreted differently by the two sides. We will analyze this important topic at greater length in the infancy section.

Human Intelligence Demands Careful Analysis

Psychologists today have become concerned about techniques for measuring human intelligence (Sternberg, 1986). Since a person's intelligence determines in large part successful adjustment to the environment, its developmental consequences are obvious.

Enthusiasm for testing intelligence dimmed when IQ tests failed to resolve several critical issues. These tests also produced conflicting views concerning the relationship between intelligence (or aptitude) and learning performance. For example, advocates of intelligence testing claimed that IQ tests measure a person's innate ability to learn. Results, however, have consistently shown that more education and higher social class are the inevitable partners of rising intelligence test scores.

Also affecting the intelligence testing movement is the nature versus nurture (heredity versus environment) controversy. To what extent do intelligence test scores indicate genetic influences and to what extent environmental forces? The history of psychology is marked by this controversy, with opinion leaning heavily toward the hereditarian view at one time and toward the environmental at another time.

It is an intensely emotional question, and has been accompanied by a distressing tendency to confuse individual differences in ability with group differences. Genetic superiority or inferiority then becomes confused with race or color. If IQ tests can't detect pure potential, the heredity-environment controversy becomes meaningless.

Table 1.7 Age Periods and Chapter Coverage	
Age Periods	**Chapters**
Beginnings	3. The Biological Basis of Development 4. Pregnancy and Birth
Infancy (0–2)	5. The Competent Infant 6. Psychosocial Development in Infancy
Early childhood (2–6)	7. Continuing Competence 8. The Expanding Social World
Middle childhood (7–11)	9. Growth and Cognition 10. The Widening World 11. A Different Path
Adolescence (12–18)	12. Background and Context 13. Rapidly Changing Bodies and Minds 14. The Troubled Adolescent 15. Sexuality and Sex Roles
Early adulthood (19–34)	16. Passages to Maturity 17. Physical and Cognitive Development 18. Psychosocial Development
Middle adulthood (35–64)	19. Physical and Cognitive Development 20. Psychosocial Development
Later adulthood (65+)	21. Physical and Cognitive Development 22. Psychosocial Development 23. Dying and Spirituality

Human Beings Can Become Critical Thinkers

Our previous assumptions lead directly to the idea that humans are critical thinkers. We could probably more accurately entitle this assumption "We *Must* Become Critical Thinkers." Given the shift in our society from an industrial base to an information/technology base, our skills must likewise change (Ennis, 1987).

What is needed is an ability to make clear decisions about choices, choices that will increase in number and complexity as society continues to become more sophisticated (Ennis, 1987). Human beings change. A developing intelligence can solve problems and make decisions if provided with the necessary tools.

Thinking Skills

What are thinking skills? Commonly called *thinking skills* or simply *critical thinking,* they have been praised for both their ultimate value and present utility. (This flush of enthusiasm must not be permitted to turn into a short-lived fad, which occasionally characterizes any science.)

Since an information technology is marked by a swift change in knowledge, sheer factual knowledge will not suffice once we leave school and attempt to become productive citizens. Rather, we need skills and strategies that will enable us to adapt to constant change. As stated in the influential report *Educating Americans for the 21st Century,* schools must return to basics, but not merely the basics of the past. Communication skills and problem-solving skills are the "thinking" tools needed in a technological society.

As you continue your reading throughout the remaining chapters, try to discover clues to a growing ability to adapt to constant change. For those who think critically about the inevitable changes they face, development is greatly enhanced and eased. For those who never fully master this ability, the path is more tortuous.

Finally, as we now realize, lifespan studies focus on successive periods of development. Table 1.7 illustrates how age periods are reflected in this text's coverage.

Transition

In this chapter we have identified the various age groups that constitute the life span and that will be the focus of this book. Lifespan study can help us adjust in a society in which rapid change seems to be inevitable.

By acquiring insights into our own development and recognizing the developmental characteristics of others of differing ages, we can hope to develop more harmonious relationships.

You also, as a result of reading about the strengths and weaknesses of different research methods, should be more analytical and critical of the studies that are presented.

You are urged to search for those developmental themes that were discussed. Can they help you to comprehend more keenly a specific age period?

With these basic ideas firmly in place, we turn to the first age period—infancy. But before we can study infant characteristics, we must understand those forces that help to shape infants: How do our genes act? What effect does the prenatal environment have on the neonate and infant? Are there psychological as well as physical consequences of birth?

Key Ideas

1. As psychologists realized that development does not cease at adolescence but continues into adulthood and old age, lifespan psychology assumed an important place in developmental psychology.

2. The developmental task concept is a good reminder of the critical tasks we face at different ages.

3. Any analysis of lifespan development must address key developmental issues (such as the relative importance of heredity and environment) if it is to present a complete picture of development.

4. To explain the various ages and stages of development, we must use the best data available to enrich our insights and to provide a thoughtful perspective on the life span.

5. Good data demand careful research methods; otherwise we would be constantly suspicious of our conclusions.

6. There are certain themes (such as the significance of different types of change) that act as guidelines for developmental analysis.

Key Terms

Age cohorts
Biopsychosocial
Continuity
Cross-sectional studies
Descriptive studies
Developmental task
Discontinuity
Exosystem
Lifespan psychology
Longitudinal studies
Macrosystem
Manipulative experiments

Mesosystem
Microsystem
Naturalistic experiments
One-time, one-group studies
Plasticity
Reciprocal interactions
Sensitive period
Sequential (longitudinal/cross-sectional) studies
Transactional model
Type T personality

What Do You Think?

1. Believing in the importance of lifespan studies, we urged you to consider its role in your life, especially in helping you better understand yourself and others. Do you think psychological studies can do this? Why?

2. We presented several issues that thread their way through lifespan studies: for example, the role of sensitive periods and a belief in either continuity or discontinuity. Why do you suppose we see these as issues or important developmental features? Discuss each one separately.

3. Even though you're just beginning your reading, would you agree with us that the themes in human development we've mentioned are basic and that understanding them helps us to understand ourselves and others?

Suggested Readings

Havighurst, Robert. (1972). *Developmental tasks and education.* New York: David McKay. Your school library probably has a copy of this little classic. As you read through it, note Havighurst's perceptive explanation of developmental tasks and what they mean for development.

Postman, Neil. (1982). *The disappearance of childhood.* New York: Dell. Amid the growing concern about what's happening to children in our society, this book offers a colorful and thoughtful analysis of the status of childhood. Written by a professor at New York University, it attributes the erosion of childhood to our uncritical acceptance of an electronic world and the disappearing boundaries between adults and children.

Thomas, Lewis. (1983). *Late night thoughts on listening to Mahler's Ninth Symphony.* New York: Viking. A well-known physician's thoughts on life, development, and science.

· *Chapter 2* ·

Theoretical Viewpoints

The Importance of Theories

For many people, the word *theory* means someone's guess about why something happens the way it does. For example, Bob might say, "It's my theory that Joe quit the team because he thinks we don't like him." Used in a textbook, the word *theory* often makes readers think of complicated arguments between experts—"Highbean's theory disagrees with Numbskull's, in that. . . ."

In this book, we use the word differently. We believe that theories are essential in psychology, serving several vital functions. Good theories

- Are helpful tools for organizing a huge body of information. The published studies on human development number in the tens of thousands. The results of these findings would be incomprehensible unless they were organized in some meaningful way. A theory is a shorthand description of this complexity. It forms a framework of "pegs" on which we can hang similar kinds of research findings.

- Help us to focus our search for new understandings. They offer guideposts in our quest for the truth about the complicated human body and its development.

- Do not just describe; they try to explain how findings may be interpreted. They offer building blocks that can help us to understand *which* facts are important, *what* conclusions to draw.

- Draw attention to major disagreements among scholars and scientists. By making these differences clearer, they offer testable ideas that can be confirmed or refuted by research. There can be different interpretations of the same facts. This can be confusing, but it is important that you learn to recognize these differences and draw your own conclusions.

- Provide a preview of much of what is to follow in this book.

We cannot give you the one final answer on how humans develop—no one can do that. We can, however, introduce you to the best current thinking in the study of human development. The three approaches that are briefly described in this chapter serve as overriding themes.

The chapters that follow are organized by age level. As each age is considered, the relevant part of these three approaches will be discussed in greater detail. By the end of the book, we believe you will have a clear understanding of each. This in turn will provide you with the best comprehension of the splendid journey that is known as the human life span.

Critical Issues

Before introducing you to the three approaches and their proponents, let us first remind you of the five major issues to which you were introduced in chapter 1. These questions are central to the study of human development, and thus will arise again and again. The five questions are

- *Normal versus exceptional subjects.* Do we learn more about development by studying "normal" people or by concentrating on deviants?

- *Inner versus outer control.* Are we able to influence our own development (inner control), or is it governed entirely by deterministic forces over which we have no control (outer control)? These forces include genetics, past experience, and current societal influences.

- *Heredity versus environment.* Of these deterministic forces, which is more important to human development, the genes we inherit from our parents, or the specific events in our lives since we were conceived?

- *Continuity versus discontinuity.* Do the changes that happen to us as we grow up occur slowly and imperceptibly, or are they abrupt and discrete?

- *Sensitive periods versus equal potential.* Are there certain times in the life span when a particular experience has a greater and more lasting impact than at any other time, or do all periods have an equal potential for affecting development?

As you will see, each of the theorists we have chosen to highlight in this chapter and in the book takes a position on each of these issues. We will compare and contrast them so that you will be better able to decide where *you* stand on these critical issues.

Three Approaches to Human Development

In terms of the key times of development, three clearly different approaches are taken by our theorists. These positions hold that change in humans involves one of the following:

- *Discrete stages.* Change mainly depends on the person's age. At certain key ages, sharp changes occur that cause mental and personality changes of great importance. These changes are the result of genetic forces. These in turn are influenced by certain factors in the environment. Examples of this approach are Sigmund Freud's **psychoanalytic theory** and Jean Piaget's **cognitive structuralist** theory.

- *Continuous development.* This school of thought is maintained by **behavioral theory** as developed by Ivan Pavlov, John Watson, and B. F. Skinner. They believe that human change depends almost entirely on events in the person's environment. Thus, change for any one individual may be quite abrupt—for example, the death of a parent when one is young is always traumatic—but on the whole, change is slow and imperceptible. Reinforcements and punishments are largely responsible for change.

- *Overlapping stages.* This position lies somewhere between the other two. There are stages of change, as with the discrete view, but they are not as dependent on age and genes. Instead, development results from the presence of stimuli that interact with inherited factors. The stages can be recognized, but they are not nearly as sharp as the discrete view holds.

    Furthermore, each stage involves a specific crisis that must be dealt with if progress to the next stage is to be made. Yet, an individual at the third stage will probably still be working out some aspects of the crisis

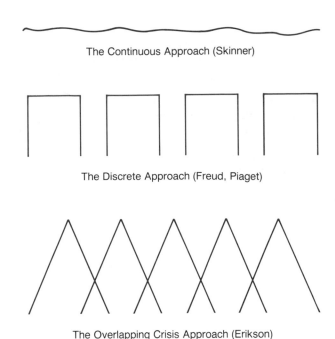

The Continuous Approach (Skinner)

The Discrete Approach (Freud, Piaget)

The Overlapping Crisis Approach (Erikson)

Figure 2.1 *This diagram illustrates the approaches different therapists take toward human development.*

at the second stage, and is already beginning to confront aspects of the crisis at the fourth stage. Thus the stages are said to overlap. A good example of this approach is Erik Erikson's **psychosocial theory.** We hold this theory in very high regard, and will refer to it often in this book. Figure 2.1 graphically depicts the differences in these three concepts.

The Discrete Approach—Psychoanalysis

In more than one hundred years of psychological research, it is impossible to think of anyone who has played a larger role than Sigmund Freud. Even his most severe critics admit that his theory on the development of personality is a milestone in the social sciences. In fact, many people mistakenly think **psychoanalysis,** the name he gave to his theory, is the same as psychology.

Probably because of his experiences as a medical doctor, Freud doubted the reliability of people's testimony about themselves. He also distrusted behavior as a source of the truth. For him, the *unconscious* is the key to understanding the human being. It is here that the most important motives and values reside.

Because many of the ideas in the unconscious are primitive, they are not acceptable to the conscious mind. For example, if a child is furious with her mother, she may not be able to acknowledge it because she is not supposed to hate her mother. Only bad people do that.

Defending the Unconscious Mind

Freud believed that important information in the unconscious is kept from awareness by an array of **defense mechanisms** (Gay, 1988). These are unconscious attempts to prevent awareness of unpleasant or unacceptable ideas. The *psychic censor,*

Dr. Sigmund Freud was a medical doctor before he invented psychiatry.

Table 2.1	Common Defense Mechanisms
1. Repression	Unconsciously forgetting experiences that are unpleasant to remember.
2. Compensation	Attempting to make up for an unconsciously perceived inadequacy by excelling at something else.
3. Sublimation	When unable to fulfill one's drives, making up for it by being creative in some artistic way (e.g., becoming a great violinist).
4. Rationalization	Coming to believe that a condition that was contrary to your desires is actually what you had wanted all along (e.g., sour grapes—"I'm glad I missed the trip; it would have been boring anyway").
5. Identification	Adopting the standards and values of someone you wish you were like.
6. Introjection	Adopting the standards and values of someone with whom you are afraid to disagree.
7. Regression	Reverting to behaviors that were previously successful when current behavior is unsuccessful (e.g., crying about getting a low grade in school with the unconscious hope that the teacher will change the grade).
8. Projection	Ascribing to another person the feelings you actually have about him or her.
9. Reaction formation	Adopting feelings toward another person that are the opposite of your real feelings toward that person.
10. Displacement	When afraid to express your feelings toward one person (e.g., anger at your boss), expressing them to someone less powerful (e.g., you yell at your son).
11. Compartmentalization	Having two mutually incompatible beliefs at the same time (e.g., the politician who sees no problem in belonging to both the local hunting club and the animal protection society).

From J. S. Dacey, *Adolescents Today,* 3d ed. Copyright © 1986 Scott, Foresman and Company, Glenview, IL.

a function of the mind, stands guard over these unconscious thoughts by using defense mechanisms to block awareness. Table 2.1 presents descriptions of some of the most common of these.

It should be noted that sublimation (#3) is a form of compensation (#2), and introjection (#6) is a type of identification (#5). Further, projection (#8) is related to, but significantly different from, reaction formation (#9).

Structures of the Psyche

Freud divided the mind into three structures: the **id,** the **ego,** and the **superego.** These structures appear at different stages of the young child's development. They are empowered by the *libido,* Freud's term for psychic energy. It is similar to the physical energy that fuels bodily functions. He argued that the libido is motivated mainly by sexual and aggressive *instincts.* The characteristics of the three structures are as follows:

1. The *id.* This structure is the only one present at birth. It contains all of our basic instincts, such as our need for food, drink, dry clothes, and nurturance. It is the simplest of the structures, operating only in the pursuit of bodily pleasures. It is not realistic; it can be satisfied merely by imagining that we have gotten what we wanted. It has no clear notion of time or space or any of the other aspects of reality. Think about your dreams; they are a good example of the id in operation.

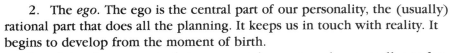

BOX 2.1

What's Your Opinion?

Defense mechanisms function to protect the conscious mind from the truth. They distort the realities that we find too painful to face. Because they mislead us, and because they require spending a lot of energy to maintain that could better be spent elsewhere, many psychologists feel we should try to eliminate them if possible. Others argue that some truths are just too painful to face, and that therefore, at least in the short run, defense mechanisms are useful. They say that most people go through difficult periods (e.g., breaking up with your first love), and that during these periods, defense mechanisms can provide a beneficial buffer for a vulnerable self-image. There will be time enough later to "face the music" of reality. What do you think?

Sigmund Freud suggested that babies react to needful feelings such as hunger in several steps. First, they become aware of the need, then they cry, next they imagine that the need has been met, and they fall back to sleep. Slowly they learn that imagination is no substitute for real satisfaction of a need.

2. The *ego.* The ego is the central part of our personality, the (usually) rational part that does all the planning. It keeps us in touch with reality. It begins to develop from the moment of birth.

Imagining that you get what you want does not work very well, nor for very long. Consider a baby that awakens from a nap and starts to cry. Soon it stops and drifts back into a doze. Before long it awakens again and cries longer this time. If unattended, the dozing periods get shorter and the crying periods longer.

Freud suggested that the awakening baby probably is hungry (or thirsty or wet). At first, it imagines that the problem is solved and is comforted, but this works less and less well as it becomes hungrier. Over time, the baby learns to cry loudly if it wants its mother, and not to stop until she comes. This is the beginning of an ego.

The ego is necessary so that we can learn to live in the real world. The stronger the ego becomes, the more realistic, and usually the more successful, the person is likely to be.

3. The *superego.* Throughout infancy, we gain a clearer and clearer conception of what the world is like. Then, toward the end of the first year, our parents and others begin to teach us what they believe it *should* be like. They instruct us in right and wrong, and expect us to begin to behave according to the principles they espouse. This is the beginning of the superego. Freud disagreed with the religious idea of an inborn conscience. He argued that all morality is learned, as a function of the superego.

Now starts the never-ending battle between the desires of the id and the demands of the superego. The main job of the ego is to strive unceasingly for compromises between these two "bullies."

The Developing Personality

Now we get to the discrete stages. For Freud, development means moving through five instinctive stages of life, each of which he assigns to a specific age range. Each is discrete from the others. Each stage has a major function. Each function is based on a pleasure center, and unless this pleasure center is stimulated appropriately (not too much, not too little), the person becomes **fixated** (stuck at that stage), and is unable to become a fully mature person. The five stages are

---

BOX 2.2

The Psychoanalytic Position

Psychoanalysis takes the following positions on our three major issues:

- The study of deviant persons, those with some type of mental disturbance, is most helpful.
- All change is the result of deterministic forces; that is, people change because of what happens to them, not because of "free will."
- Genetic inheritance and learning (nature and nurture) are involved about equally.
- Development is discrete. It depends on the emergence of sexual pleasure centers and the type of stimulation the person receives at the time each of the various centers is preeminent.
- There are five sensitive periods in life, which end in adolescence.

---

1. The **oral stage** (0 to 1 1/2 years old). The oral cavity (mouth, lips, tongue, gums) is the pleasure center. Its function is to obtain an appropriate amount of sucking, eating, biting, and talking.

2. The **anal stage** (1 1/2 to 3 years old). The anus is the pleasure center. The function here is successful toilet training.

3. The **phallic stage** (3 to 5 years old). The glans of the penis and the clitoris are the pleasure centers in this stage and in the two remaining stages. (That he named this stage the *phallic* stage is one of several reasons Freud is not popular among feminists! [e.g., Horney, 1967]) The major function of this stage is the healthy development of sexual interest. This is achieved through masturbation and unconscious sexual desire for the parent of the opposite sex. Resolution of the conflicts caused by this desire (called the **Oedipal conflict** in males and the **Electra conflict** in females) is the goal.

4. The **latency stage** (5 to 12 years old). During this stage, sexual desire becomes latent. This is especially true for males, through the defense mechanism of introjection (see Table 2.1). They refuse to kiss or hug their mothers, and treat female age-mates with disdain. Because our society is more tolerant of the daughter's attraction to her father, the Electra complex is less resolved and girls' sexual feelings are less repressed during this stage.

5. The **genital stage** (12 years old and older). Now there is a surge of sexual hormones in both genders, which brings about an unconscious recurrence of stage 3. Normally, however, youths have learned that desire for one's parents is taboo, and so they set about establishing relationships (bumblingly at first) with members of the opposite sex who are their own age. Freud believed that if these five stages are not negotiated successfully, homosexuality or an aversion to sexuality itself results. (It should be noted that this concept is not popular among homosexuals, many of whom believe that their sexual orientation goes much deeper than this—see chap. 15.) If fixation occurs at any stage, anxiety results, and defense mechanisms will be used to deal with it.

Jean Piaget was among the first to study normal intellectual development.

The Discrete Approach—Cognitive Structures

While Freud was concerned with the structures of the personality, the Swiss biologist/psychologist Jean Piaget (1896–1980) sought to understand the cognitive structures of the intellect (1953, 1966; Flavell, 1963).

Beginning the Study of Intellectual Development

Piaget is the foremost contributor to the study of intellectual development. Beginning his scholarly career at the age of 11(!), Piaget published numerous papers on birds, shellfish, and other topics of natural history. As a result, the diligent Swiss was offered the curator's position at the Geneva Natural History Museum. He was only 15 at the time and turned it down to finish high school. He received his PhD in biology at the age of 21, and wrote more than fifty books prior to his death.

Piaget began his research on cognitive development in 1920 when he took a position in the Binet Laboratory in Paris. He was given the task of standardizing a French version of an English-language test of reasoning ability, which enabled him to observe how children responded to the questions. He discovered that there were similarities in the wrong answers given by each age group. For example, 5 year olds would give a wrong answer for one reason, whereas older age groups gave the same wrong answer for other reasons. This discovery led Piaget to the idea that children of different age groups have different thinking patterns. Prior to 1920, little research had been done on the nature of intelligence. Most scientists viewed children as miniature adults who used adult thinking methods but used them poorly. The scientists felt that as information was poured into the child, mental maturity gradually developed. Piaget discovered that specific abilities must be acquired before the child's intellect could fully mature; information alone is not enough. Furthermore, he observed that these mental abilities develop in stages, each one preparing the way for the development of the next.

The Role of Intelligence

Piaget's background in biology formed the basis for his view of intelligence. If you have ever seen an episode of "The Undersea World of Jacques Cousteau," you have probably been amazed by the way ocean dwellers adapt themselves to their particular environments. The puffer fish swells to twice its size when threatened by an enemy. The anglerfish uses its dorsal fin as bait to lure smaller fish to its mouth. Nature is filled with examples of superb adaptations of animals to their environments. But nature has not fitted humans to any specific environment. It has equipped us to adapt to most environments through the gift of intelligence. Like the swelling of the puffer fish, human intellect seemed to Piaget to be another example of biological adaptation.

Intelligence matures through the growth of increasingly effective **mental structures.** These structures can best be defined as the blueprints that equip us to affect our environment. They are the tools of adaptation. At birth, all babies simply reflect the environment. When a specific event (a stimulus) occurs, infants react automatically to it. Sucking and crying are examples of these reflexes.

Soon after birth, reflexes are transformed into **schemata.** Schemata are patterns of behavior that infants use to interact with the environment. Figure 2.2 depicts this relationship. Infants develop schemata for looking, for grasping, for placing objects in their mouths. As infants grow older and begin to encounter more elements of their world, schemata are combined and rearranged into more efficient structures. By the time children reach age 7, higher forms of psychological structures are developing. These structures are called **operations.**

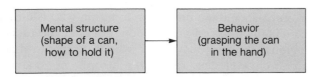

Figure 2.2 Piaget's concept of the schema. Mental structures held in the mind direct and control our behaviors.

According to Piaget, adult thinking is composed of numerous operations that enable the individual to manipulate the environment. Operations are mental, internalized actions. They are similar to programs in a computer. Programs enable the computer to manipulate the data fed into it in various ways. Mental operations do the same. In fact, mental operations are able to take things apart and reassemble them without actually touching the object.

In addition to reflexes, the infant has at birth two basic tendencies or drives that affect intellectual functioning throughout his or her lifetime. They are **organization** and **adaptation,** and they govern the way we use our schemata to adjust to the demands of the environment.

Organization

Our innate tendency to organize causes us to combine our schemata more efficiently. The schemata of the infant are continuously reorganized to produce a coordinated system of higher-order structures. Each time a new schema is acquired, it is integrated into existing schemata. Consider children learning to throw a ball. They may understand the various parts of a good throw, but they will not throw the ball well until they have integrated these parts into a smooth and efficient movement.

Adaptation

The second tendency in all human beings is to adapt to the environment. Adaptation consists of two complementary processes: **assimilation** and **accommodation.** We assimilate when we perceive the environment in a way that fits our existing schemata. That is, we make reality fit our minds. We accommodate when we modify our schemata to meet the demands of the environment. That is, we make our minds fit reality.

We try to assimilate as much as possible because it is easier than accommodation. It is easier to see situations, events, and objects as something we understand and can work with. When asked to describe an unfamiliar object, we say: "It looks like an orange," or "It's hard like a rock." To make these comparisons, we perceive the object in a way that fits what we know. We look for similarities. For example,

mentally to suit the structures in your mind.

You are able to read these words because you altered your perception of them

You may have physically assimilated this idea by turning this book upside down. When we mentally alter what we see, we *recognize* or rethink it and thus assimilate it.

Does ___ . . ___ . ___ . ___ . . 88 ˙ ˙ ˙ 8 ___ ' "? To answer this question written in code, you would have to learn the key. In doing so, you would be acquiring a new schema. This is accommodation. All mental activity uses assimilation and accommodation.

It is necessary to balance these processes. A person who is incapable of assimilation, such as a mentally retarded person, does not have the capacity to take advantage of his previous experiences. A person who is incapable of accommodation is unresponsive to his environment. The rigid schizophrenic is an example.

Stages of Cognitive Development

Mental growth takes place in four discrete stages, each one laying the foundation for the next. They are the **sensorimotor stage** (birth to 2 years old); the **preoperational stage** (2 to 7 years old); the **concrete operational stage** (7 to 11 years old); and the **formal operational stage** (11 years old and up). The change from one stage is quite clear, and regression from later to earlier stages does not happen. Let us look at each stage more closely.

Sensorimotor Stage (Birth to 2 Years Old)

Infants are egocentric at birth: they do not experience the external world as separate from themselves. The existence of objects in the environment of infants is entirely dependent on their sensory perception of them. When an object is removed from their sight or touch, they do not search for it. They act as though it no longer exists. As the sensorimotor stage proceeds, infants develop object permanence, the awareness that objects exist independent of their perception. An example is the child who looks for the rattle he has dropped from his high chair.

Preoperational Stage (2 to 7 Years Old)

Until this stage, children's intellectual tools consist of the ability to use their senses and to interact with the world through movement. When children learn to talk, they acquire the ability to represent objects symbolically in their minds. Consider the statement, "I want a cookie." To make this demand, children must be aware that cookies exist as a class of objects. They must also have acquired the verbal symbol *cookie* and connected feelings of hunger with the symbol for an object that will satisfy it. Now that they have symbols to represent objects in their world, they can manipulate these objects mentally. Now they can think.

Concrete Operational Stage (7 to 11 Years Old)

Children now become concerned with *why* things happen. The intuitive thinking style of the preoperational stage is replaced by elementary logic, as operations begin to develop that enable children to form more complex mental actions on concrete elements of their world.

Logical thinking requires that one have an understanding of the physical properties of the world. Knowing the correct answer to the question "Which is heavier, a pound of feathers or a pound of lead?" depends on understanding the concept of density in relation to measurement. Preoperational children cannot understand that the weight is the same regardless of the density of the objects. The operations necessary for this understanding are developed in the concrete operational stage.

When children acquire these operations, they become able to solve problems logically by the use of elementary deductive reasoning. However, their thinking style still needs refinement. Ask the 9 year old, "How would things be different if we had no thumbs?" and he is likely to respond, "But we *do* have thumbs!" The concrete operational child does not consider possibilities that are not real. The tools of thought are assembled but still need the refinement that takes place in the formal operational stage.

BOX 2.3

Hypothesizing

We presume that all readers of this text are in Piaget's formal operational stage. This means that they already have, or are developing, the ability to make reasonable hypotheses. If you would like to test yourself on this ability, try the following experiment (you may want to do it with several friends/classmates). You will need two sheets of paper 10 × 10 inches in size, both ruled off in one inch squares, with each of the 100 squares numbered consecutively; and three crayons: one yellow, one orange, and one red.

Show the ruled sheets to your friends and ask them to select at random one square on the sheet. Before doing this, however, you should make a hypothesis as to which part or parts of the squared sheet most people will point to. Then you should make a second hypothesis explaining why you think that part or parts will be chosen most often.

You then show one of the ruled sheets to at least fifty people (the more, the better), and ask them to point to one square, any square, at random. Note how many times each of the squares is chosen, and whether the chooser is left- or right-handed. Next, you color the squares on one of the sheets, using your data for right-handers only. Leave those squares with no choices white, and color those with one choice yellow, those with two choices orange, and those with three or more choices red. Do the same thing on the second sheet for the data for left-handers.

Does the data support your hypothesis? If not, can you think of reasons why? Can you think of better ways to go about hypothesizing in general?

Formal Operational Stage (11 Years Old and Up)

In adolescence, one's thinking style takes wing. Formal operations expand thought to the abstract. Reality is represented by symbols that can be manipulated mentally, just as data is represented by electromagnetic code that can be programmed in the computer.

The adolescent is capable of forming conclusions based on hypothetical possibilities. Answering the question, "What would things be like if it rained up?" involves mentally picturing rain rising from the ground. This mental picture is contrasted with reality and various conclusions are produced.

Thinking in the formal stage becomes much more orderly and systematic. Most 8 year olds would be unable to answer the question, "If Jane's hair is darker than Susan's, and Susan's hair is darker than Mary's, whose hair is darkest?" Although an 8 year old is capable of "ranking" the children by darkness of hair, she is unable to manipulate facts concerning imaginary people.

Piaget's ideas, as widely accepted as they have been, have not escaped criticism. For example, some psychologists dispute his belief that cognitive development proceeds through a series of distinct stages, each of which contains important changes in the way that children think. They believe that cognitive development is a gradual process (this will be explained in the next section). It is not all-or-nothing; that is, children are not all preoperational or concrete operational in their thinking (Rest, 1983).

In one of the most famous studies challenging Piaget, Gelman (1969) trained 5 year olds to examine rows of equal-length sticks. Later, when asked to pick rows of equal-length sticks from rows of unequal, they were successful. This seems to show that preschoolers are more competent than Piaget thought. Yet these youngsters may have been "ready" for more complex tasks and just needed the push that Gelman gave them.

In spite of these and similar criticisms, Piaget's ideas remain remarkably popular and his work is a landmark in our studies of cognitive development.

Only when we reach adolescence are we capable of answering questions such as "What would happen if it always rained up?" and "What if we had no thumbs?"

```
╔══════════════════════════════════════════════════════╗
║                     BOX 2.4                          ║
╠══════════════════════════════════════════════════════╣
║            The Cognitive Structural Position         ║
╟──────────────────────────────────────────────────────╢
```

Piaget's **cognitive structuralist theory** takes the following positions on our five major issues:

- The study of normal subjects is usually best, although the study of those below and above average in mental ability is useful.
- All change is the result of genetically inherited schemata and environmental forces. Piaget has little to say about individual control.
- Both genetic structures and learning (nature and nurture) are involved, but the genes probably play the greater role.
- Development is discrete. It depends on the emergence of mental states that are the direct result of the maturation of the brain. Transition between the several age-states is clearly detectable, especially when the person is presented with tasks designed to detect it.
- Sensitive periods play a vital role in development.

The Continuous Approach—Behaviorism

Psychology had its beginnings in Germany in the 1860s. It was concerned with learning how people think, largely by asking them about their perceptions of their experience. This sometimes reached extremes. For example, Edward Tichener of Cornell University requested subjects to swallow raw eggs and then, as they were vomiting (raw eggs will do that to you), he asked them to describe their reactions!

Classical Conditioning—Pavlov and Watson

Soon there were numerous disagreements about the nature of the brain, and researchers found it impossible to resolve them because the data differed from person to person. In fact, for one Russian scientist, they even differed from dog to dog! During the course of his study of digestion in dogs, this scientist, Ivan Pavlov (1849–1936), discovered one of the most important aspects of the brain. This is the ability to form **conditioned reflexes.**

More than fifty years after his death, Pavlov's work (1927, 1928) remains highly influential. His primary observation was that, although at first only the sight of food makes a dog salivate, after a while even the anticipation of food will cause the flow of saliva. He called this *unconditioned response* because it is unlearned. Saliva flowed at the sight of the food dish or the attendant, perhaps even at a sound the attendant usually made during feeding. We can understand how food can cause the flow of saliva, but sights and sounds (the attendant, a bell) do not naturally cause saliva to flow. Somehow Pavlov's dogs "learned" that these sights and sounds signaled the appearance of food.

Pavlov labeled a dog's salivary response to a signal a *conditioned response.* The signal (sights, sounds) he called the *conditioned stimulus.* Pavlov might have considered the search for an explanation of learning to be over, but being an inquiring scientist, he then turned his attention to causing the process on a planned basis.

A hungry dog was harnessed with a ticking metronome present (the conditioned stimulus). After a controlled interval, food (the unconditioned stimulus) was placed in the dog's mouth. After several repetitions, saliva began to flow during the interval when the metronome was ticking, but before any food appeared. Thus Pavlov had established a conditioned reflex, with the metronome acting as the conditioned stimulus.

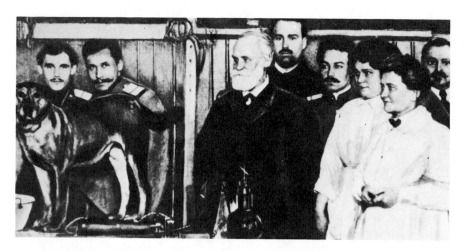

Russian scientist Ivan Pavlov was able to discover many aspects of learning from his experiments on the eating patterns of dogs.

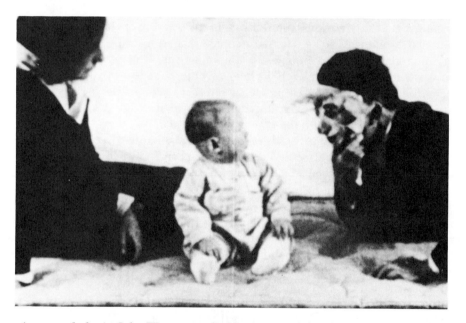

American psychologist John Watson studied how a young boy learned a phobic fear.

Pavlov believed that if he could establish conditioned reflexes through this technique, **extinction** or elimination of reflexes must also be possible. The dog was placed in the usual situation with the metronome ticking and saliva flowing, but the dog was given no food. After several pairings of the ticking metronome and lack of food, saliva no longer flowed when the metronome ticked. Extinction of the conditioned response had occurred.

These two principles, conditioning and extinction, were seen as a possible explanation for why we develop as we do. The American psychologist John Watson (1878–1958) was most impressed with Pavlov's work. He began to explore ways in which Pavlov's laboratory experiments might be occurring in everyday life. His famous findings concerned how a little boy named Albert learned a general fear of furry things.

Through his research, Watson was able to persuade many of his colleagues that the study of perception should be replaced by the study of behavior. He felt much more could be learned this way, and much more objectively. Thus he became the father of the school of psychology known as **behavioral theory.** Many others have followed in his footsteps, but the best known is the Harvard University psychologist B. F. Skinner who died in August, 1990.

Skinner's Theory of Learning

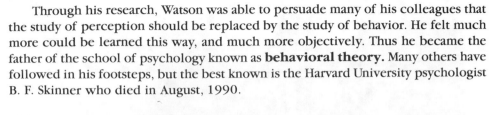

Harvard psychologist B. F. Skinner is known as the father of American behaviorism.

When Skinner (1938, 1948, 1953, 1971, 1983) began to study learning in the late 1920s, he wanted only to satisfy his curiosity about how organisms are changed by their environment. He believed that scientists should start studying simpler organisms and work up to investigating the complexity of humans. Pigeons and rats were chosen for study because their nervous systems are reasonably similar to those of humans. Also, manipulating their lives does not pose the ethical problems that arise with human experimentation. Skinner felt that knowledge gained about these animals would provide clues to the study of humans. If so, this would save the researcher time, effort, and costly mistakes.

Skinner made two basic assumptions about the learning of all organisms, whether an amoeba or a human being. First he assumed that all learning is ultimately determined by forces outside the control of the organism. What we learn and how we learn it is determined completely by genetic inheritance and by the influences of our environment, past and present. He agreed that inside forces such as values and beliefs are involved, but thought that these are formed as the result of the environment. Thus he did away with the concept of **free will.**

He further argued that the study of learning is analogous to a training technique used in engineering schools called the "black box method." In this technique, engineering students are given a black box with two terminals. They vary the voltage, amperage, and wattage of the electricity put in one side, and then meter the results coming out the other side. They are not allowed to know what is inside the black box; it is their job to infer what is in there by watching how the black box responds to the electrical stimuli. Likewise, in the study of learning there is no way for us to know what is going on inside the human head. It is presumptuous to make guesses about the mechanisms of the mind at this time.

Having made these assumptions, Skinner studied the relationship between three variables: stimuli, responses, and the reactions of the environment to responses. His formula for learning is simple. It follows these three steps:

1. *A stimulus occurs in the environment.* For instance, this might be a question from a teacher to a student. Often, it is impossible to tell what the stimulus is.

2. *A response is made in the presence of that stimulus.* An example is a correct or an incorrect answer on the part of the student.

3. *One of three things happens as a reaction to this response.* The response is reinforced; the response is punished; or the response is ignored.

Hence, learning follows this formula:
Stimulus (?) → Response → Reaction of the environment to that response.
Skinner argued that if the response is reinforced, it is more likely to result the next time that stimulus occurs. Thus, if the teacher asks that question again, the student is more likely to give the right answer, because that response was reinforced. If the response is punished, the response is less likely in the future. If the

---

BOX 2.5

Who Can Find the Raisin?

Probably the best way to understand Skinner's view of behaviorism is to apply its principles to teaching someone. For this suggested activity, you need two cups, a raisin, and two squares of paper of different colors big enough to cover the cups.

For 1 to 2 year olds, you must start very simply. Place a raisin in one of the cups and cover that cup with a large square of either color. Cover the empty cup with the large square of the other color. Do this so that the child cannot see what you are doing.

Ask the child to guess which cup the raisin is in by pointing to one of the squares. If the child gets the right one, he or she wins the prize. If not, say, "Too bad. Maybe you'll get it next time. Let's try again."

Now, out of the child's sight, switch the positions of the cups, but cover the cup with the raisin with the same square. Do this until the child regularly guesses correctly. This is called *continuous reinforcement*. Generally speaking, the older the child, the quicker the learning.

Now switch to the two large circles, using the same procedure. Give the child practice with this simple game until you feel it is losing its appeal. For older children, the game can be made more and more complex. Use a greater variety of shape combinations, and use three or even four cups. Finally, try to get the child to verbalize what he or she thinks is the principle behind this activity. Perhaps the child could even invent another way of doing it! As you perform this experiment, you will gain insights into the behaviorist ideas of reinforcement and extinction.

---

response is simply ignored, it also becomes less likely in the future. Each of these three concepts—**reinforcement, punishment,** and no response (which Skinner calls **extinction**)—needs further explanation.

Notice that Skinner did not use the word *reward.* He felt that reward is distinct from reinforcement. A reward is something you give a person because *you* think it will make that person feel good for having made a response. There is a problem with this for Skinner: it assumes that we know what is going on in the mind of another person. We know what is rewarding to us, but we can only guess what is rewarding to someone else. Skinner prefered to define reinforcement as anything that makes a response more likely to happen in the future, without making any reference to how it makes the individual feel inside.

There are two kinds of reinforcement, and the difference between them is important. **Positive reinforcement** refers to any event that, when it occurs after a response, makes that response more likely to happen in the future. **Negative reinforcement** is any event that, when it ceases to occur after a response, makes that response more likely to happen in the future. Notice that both types of reinforcement make a response more likely to happen. Giving your daughter candy for doing the right thing would be positive reinforcement. Ceasing to twist your brother's arm when he gives you back your pen would be negative reinforcement.

To reduce the likelihood of inappropriate responses, Skinner suggested the use of a fourth technique, extinction. Extinction simply means that when an undesirable response occurs, it is disregarded. When a response is unreinforced for a long enough time, it is discontinued.

Skinner's theory is also known as **operant conditioning.** This is because the basis of his theory is that when operants (actions that people or animals take of their own accord) are reinforced, they become conditioned (more likely to be repeated in the future).

BOX 2.6

The Behaviorist Position

Behaviorism takes the following positions on our five major issues:

- Its principles apply to both normal and abnormal development.
- All change is the result of deterministic forces—that is, people change because of what happens to them, not because of ''free will.''
- Both genes and learning (nature and nurture) are involved in development, but learning is by far the most important.
- Development is continuous. It depends on the four forces that control learning: positive and negative reinforcement, punishment, and extinction.
- All times of life have equal potential for change. The environment determines when change will occur.

These concepts of change in human behavior have been enhanced by the ideas of Albert Bandura and his associates. They extend the behaviorist view to specific aspects of social behavior.

Bandura's Theory of Social Learning

Bandura, one of the chief architects of social learning theory, has stressed the potent influence of modeling on personality development. He calls this *observational learning.* In a famous statement on social learning theory, Bandura and Walters (1963) cite evidence to show that learning occurs through observing others, even when the observers do not imitate the model's responses at that time and get no reinforcement. For Bandura, observational learning means that the information we get from observing other people, things, and events influences the way we act.

Social learning theory has particular relevance for development. As Bandura and Walters note, children do not do what adults tell them to do but rather what they see adults do. If Bandura's assumptions are correct, adults can be a potent force in shaping the behavior of children because of what they do.

The importance of models is seen in Bandura's interpretation of what happens as a result of observing others.

> The observer may acquire new responses, including socially appropriate behaviors.
> Observation of models may strengthen or weaken existing responses.
> Observation of a model may cause the reappearance of responses that were apparently forgotten.
> If children witness undesirable behavior that is either rewarded or goes unpunished, undesirable pupil behavior may result. The reverse is also true.

Bandura, Ross, and Ross (1963) studied what effects live models, filmed human aggression, and filmed cartoon aggression would have on preschool children's aggressive behavior. The filmed human adult models displayed aggression toward an inflated doll; in the filmed cartoon aggression a cartoon character displayed the same aggression.

Later, all the children who observed the aggression were more aggressive than youngsters in a control group. Filmed models were as effective as live models in transmitting aggression. The research suggests that powerful, competent models are more readily imitated than models who lack these qualities (Bandura & Walters, 1963).

In summary, the behaviorist position holds that human development does not happen in predictable stages but as the result of stimuli from the environment. Since there are millions of these in a person's lifetime, behaviorists see development as continuous, something that usually happens in small steps every day.

The Overlapping Crises Approach— Psychosocial Crises

Among other important books, Erik Erikson wrote *Childhood and Society* (1963). It is an amazingly perceptive and at times poetically beautiful description of human life. Erikson's view of human development derives from extensive study of people living in an impressive variety of cultures: Germans, East Indians, the Sioux of South Dakota, the Yuroks of California, and wealthy adolescents in the northeastern United States (1959, 1968). His ideas also stem from intensive studies of historical figures such as Martin Luther (1959) and Mahatma Gandhi (1969). He sees human development as the interaction between your genes and the environment in which you live.

According to Erikson, human life progresses through a series of eight stages. Each of these stages is marked by a crisis that needs to be resolved so that the individual can move on. Erikson uses the term *crisis* in a medical sense. It is like an acute period during illness, at the end of which the patient takes a turn for the worse or better. At each life stage, the individual is pressured, by internal needs and the external demands of society, to make a major change in a new direction.

Psychologist Erik Erikson is best known for his theory of psychosocial crises.

The ages at which people go through each of the stages vary somewhat, but the sequence of the stages is fixed. The ages of the first five stages are exactly the same as in Freud's theory (Erikson is an ardent student of his theory). Unlike Freud and Piaget, however, Erikson believes that the stages overlap.

Each of the crises involves a conflict between two opposing characteristics. Erikson suggests that successful resolution of each crisis should favor the first of the two characteristics, although its opposite must also exist to some degree. Table 2.2 gives an overview of his psychosocial theory.

It is necessary to have experienced each crisis before proceeding to the next. Inadequate resolution of the crisis at any stage hinders development at all succeeding stages, unless special help is received. When a person is unable to resolve a crisis at one of the stages, Erikson suggests that "a deep rage is aroused comparable to that of an animal driven into a corner" (1963, p. 68). This is not to say that anyone ever resolves a crisis completely. It is important to note that Erikson's description of the eight stages of life is a picture of the ideal, and that no one ever completes the stages perfectly. However, the better a person does at any one stage, the more progress. Let us look at each stage more closely.

1. *Basic trust versus mistrust (birth to 1 1/2 years old).* In the first stage, which is by far the most important, a sense of basic trust should develop. For Erikson, trust has an unusually broad meaning. To the trusting infant, it is not so much that the world is a safe and happy place, but rather that it is an orderly, *predictable* place. There are causes and effects that one can learn to anticipate. For Erikson, then, trust flourishes with warmth and care, but it might well include knowledge that one will be spanked regularly for disobeying rules.

Stage	Age	Psychosocial Crisis
Table 2.2 Erik Erikson's Psychosocial Theory of Development		
1	Infancy (0 to 1 1/2)	Trust vs. mistrust
2	Early childhood (1 1/2 to 3)	Autonomy vs. shame, doubt
3	Play age (3 to 5)	Initiative vs. guilt
4	School age (5 to 12)	Industry vs. inferiority
5	Adolescence (12 to 18)	Identity and repudiation vs. identity confusion
6	Young adult (18 to 25)	Intimacy and solidarity vs. isolation
7	Adulthood (25 to 65)	Generativity vs. self-absorption
8	Maturity (65+)	Integrity vs. despair

From E. Erikson, *Childhood and Society,* 2d ed. Copyright © 1963 W. W. Norton & Company, Inc., New York, NY.

If the infant is to grow into a person who is trusting and trustworthy, it is essential that a great deal of regularity exist in its early environment. The child needs variation, but this variation should occur in a regular order that the child can learn to anticipate. For example, the soft music of an FM radio can provide regular changes in sound level. So does the movement of the colorful toy birds hanging over a child's crib.

Some children begin life with irregular and inadequate care. Anxiety and insecurity have a negative effect on family and other relationships so important to the development of trust. When a child's world is so unreliable, we can expect mistrust and hostility, which under certain circumstances can develop into antisocial, even criminal, behavior. Of course, not all such people become criminals.

It is also possible to gain basic trust in infancy and then lose it later. Sometimes people who have not suffered an injurious childhood can lose their basic sense of trust because of damaging experiences later in life. Consider this statement of a 14-year-old girl who had had several fights with her mother, and had run away from home. When she was caught, her mother brought charges against her for being a "stubborn child," and she wound up as an inmate in a "school" for delinquent girls:

A Note from Caroline

Locked up. Going on my third day. In a freezing cold room. You sleep in there. Look at four walls. They don't give you nothing but one blanket. The bed is just a rubber mattress and a wooden block for it to go on. A little window with chicken wire. And a pail. And a door and nothing else but four walls. They let you out three times a day for a few minutes and they don't let you speak to nobody. They got nothing in here. You're not even supposed to have a book to read. It's freezing. It's an icebox. One blanket. One! You feel like you want to scream. You feel like you're in a madhouse. There's no need of putting kids in solitary confinement. I see no need of it at all. I wouldn't put a dead dog in this room. I wouldn't. . . . I don't know. You can't really describe this place unless you're here. You've got to live here before you can really tell.

They should send a real good kid here, you know, one that people would believe and have her come to live here for about a week. Or two, three weeks, you know. Then let her report back everything! Tell the people. Just let that person describe this. I know that the State Senate is investigating this place and I hope they tear it down because it needs to be torn down. But I don't think the senate is really going to do anything because it's going to take a lot of people to change this place!

This teenager has not merely lost her faith in the legal system. As a result of this traumatic event, she will no doubt have less trust in all of her fellow humans. Without help, this lack of trust will weaken what she has gained and make future development difficult.

2. *Autonomy versus shame and doubt (1 1/2 to 3 years old).* When children are about 1 1/2 years old, they should move into the second stage, characterized by the crisis of autonomy versus shame and doubt. This is the time when they begin to gain control over their bodies and is the usual age at which toilet training is begun.

Erikson agrees with other psychoanalysts that toilet training has far more important consequences in one's life than control of one's bowels. The sources of generosity and creativity lie in this experience. If children are encouraged to explore their bodies and environment, a level of self-confidence develops. If they are regularly reprimanded for their inability to control excretion, they come to doubt themselves. They become ashamed and afraid to test themselves.

Of course, excretion is not the only target for regulation in this stage. Children of this age usually start learning to be self-governing in all of their behaviors. Although some self-doubt is appropriate, general self-control should be fostered at this stage.

3. *Initiative versus guilt (3 to 5 years old).* The third crisis, initiative versus guilt, begins when children are about 3 years old. Building on the ability to control themselves, children now learn to have some influence over others in the family and to successfully manipulate their surroundings. They should not merely react, they should initiate.

If their parents and others make them feel incompetent, however, they develop a generalized feeling of guilt about themselves. In the autonomy stage they can be made to feel ashamed by others; in this stage, they learn to make themselves feel ashamed.

4. *Industry versus inferiority (5 to 12 years old).* The fourth stage corresponds closely to the child's elementary school years. Now the task is to go beyond imitating ideal models and to learn the elementary technology of the culture. Children expand their horizons beyond the family and begin to explore the neighborhood.

Their play becomes more purposeful, and they seek knowledge in order to complete the tasks that they set for themselves. A sense of accomplishment in making and building should prevail. If it does not, children may develop a lasting sense of inferiority. Here we begin to see clearly the effects of inadequate resolution of earlier crises.

As Erikson puts it, the child may not be able to be industrious because he may "still want his mother more than he wants knowledge." He suggests that the typical American elementary school, staffed almost entirely by women, can make it difficult for children (especially boys) to make the break from home and mother. Under these circumstances, children may learn to view their productivity merely as a way to please their teacher (the mother substitute), and not as something good for its own sake. Children may perform in order to be "good little workers" and "good little helpers" and fail to develop the satisfaction of pleasing themselves with their own industry.

5. *Identity and repudiation versus identity confusion (12 to 18 years old).* The main task of the adolescent is to achieve a state of identity. Erikson, who originated the term **identity crisis,** uses the word in a special way. In addition to thinking of identity as the general picture one has of oneself, Erikson refers to it as a state toward which one strives. If one were in a state of identity, the various aspects of one's self images would be in agreement with each other; they would be identical. Ideally, a person in the state of identity has no internal conflicts whatsoever.

Repudiation of choices is another essential aspect of reaching personal identity. In any choice of identity, the selection we make means that we have repudiated (turned down) all the other possibilities, at least for the present. When youths cannot achieve identity, when *identity confusion* ensues, it is usually because they are unable to make choices. As Biff, the son in Arthur Miller's *Death of a Salesman,* says, "I just can't take hold, Mom, I can't take hold of some kind of life!" Biff sees himself as many different people; he acts one way in one situation and the opposite way in another—a hypocrite. Because he refuses to make choices and shies away from commitments, there is no cohesiveness in his personality. He is aware of this lack, but is unable to do anything about it. (We will have much more to say about his stage in chap. 12.)

6. *Intimacy versus isolation (18 to 25 years old).* In the sixth stage, intimacy with others should develop. Erikson is speaking here of far more than sexual intimacy. He is talking about the essential ability to relate one's deepest hopes and fears to another person, and to accept another person's need for intimacy in turn.

Each of us is entirely alone, in the sense that no one else can ever experience life exactly the way we do. We are imprisoned in our own bodies, and can never be certain that our senses experience the same events in the same way as another person's senses. Only if we become intimate with another are we able to understand and have confidence in ourselves. During this time of life our identity may be fulfilled through the loving validation of the person with whom we have dared to be intimate.

7. *Generativity versus stagnation (25 to 65 years old).* Generativity means the ability to be useful to ourselves and to society. As in the industry stage, the goal here is to be productive and creative. However, productivity in the industry stage is a means of obtaining recognition and material reward. In the generativity stage, one's productivity is aimed at generating a sense of personal fulfillment. Thus, the act of being productive is itself rewarding, regardless of whether recognition or reward results.

According to Erikson, a sense of intimacy with another person of the opposite gender should develop between the ages of 18 and 25. If it does not, a sense of isolation results.

Furthermore, there is a sense of trying to make the world a better place for the young in general, and for one's own children in particular. During the middle of this stage many people become mentors to younger individuals, sharing their knowledge and philosophy of life.

When people fail in generativity, they begin to stagnate, to become bored and self-indulgent, unable to contribute to society's welfare. Such adults often act as if they are their own child.

8. *Integrity versus disgust and despair (65 years old and older).* When people look back over their lives and feel they have made the wrong decisions or, more commonly, that they have too frequently failed to make any decision at all, they see life as lacking integration. They feel despair at the impossibility of "having just one more chance to make things right." They often hide their terror of death by appearing contemptuous of humanity in general, and those of their own religion or race in particular. They feel disgust for themselves.

To the extent that they have been successful in resolving the first seven crises, they achieve a sense of personal integrity. Adults who have a sense of integrity accept their lives as having been well spent. They feel a kinship with people of other cultures and of previous and future generations. They have a sense of having helped to create a more dignified life for humankind. They have gained wisdom.

> ### BOX 2.7
> #### The Psychosocial Position
>
> Erikson's psychosocial theory takes the following positions on our five major issues:
> - Erikson has mainly preferred to study unusual subjects (Luther, Gandhi, pathological adolescents), although he has studied some normal groups, too (e.g., preschool children, Native Americans).
> - Change is the result of a combination of inner and outer forces, but inner forces are emphasized.
> - Genetic inheritance and learning (nature and nurture) are involved about equally.
> - Eight sensitive periods play the central role.
> - Development occurs through dealing with overlapping crises. It depends on the successful resolution of each crisis as it naturally comes up.

Table 2.3   Comparison of Three Developmental Stage Theories

Ages	Psychosexual Stages (Freud)	Psychosocial Stages (Erikson)	Cognitive Stages (Piaget)
0 to 1 1/2	Oral	Basic trust vs. mistrust	Sensorimotor
1 1/2 to 3	Anal	Autonomy vs. doubt, shame	2 years– Preoperational
4 to 5	Phallic	Initiative vs. guilt	
6 to 11	Latency	Industry vs. inferiority	7 years–Concrete operational
12 to 17	Genital	Identity vs. role confusion	11 years– Formal operational
Young adulthood	•	Intimacy vs. isolation	•
Middle adulthood	•	Generativity vs. stagnation	•
Late adulthood	•	Ego integrity vs. despair	•

Note. An asterisk (•) means the theorist suggests no stage for this age group.

Table 2.4   Positions of the Four Theories on Our Five Critical Issues

Critical Issues	Theorists			
	Skinner	Freud	Piaget	Erikson
Normal/exceptional	N/E	E	N	N/E
Inner control/outer control	O	O	O	I/O
Heredity/environment	E	H/E	H/E	H/E
Continuity/discontinuity	C	D	D	C/D
Sensitive periods/equal potential	EP	SP	SP	SP

Table 2.3 presents a summary of the three theories that take a stage view of human development (Reminder: the behaviorists do not take such a view).

Table 2.4 summarizes the positions that each of the four theories takes on each of the critical issues we first described in chapter 1. Please remember that summaries always leave out vital details. The letters in the table stand for the issues—for example, N stands for a preference for studying normal subjects. Thus Skinner's theory is continuous, Freud's and Piaget's are discrete, and Erikson's combines the two.

Transition

This chapter has covered a great deal of important ground. It has introduced you to the framework on which, in many ways, the rest of the book depends. There is a lot to remember, but we will be coming back again and again to these seminal ideas, and this will help you to gain a firm understanding of them. In these first two chapters, you have received an overview of the fascinating study of human development. Now we begin to take a much closer look at each of the major periods of life with the powerful spotlights of theory and research.

Key Ideas

1. Theories are useful tools for organizing information, and for focusing our search for new understandings. They suggest how findings may be explained and draw attention to major disagreements.
2. There are five critical issues we will be looking at in this book: normal versus exceptional subjects; inner versus outer control; heredity versus environment; continuity versus discontinuity; and sensitive periods versus equal potential.
3. There are three approaches to change in human development: that it occurs in discrete stages; that it occurs as continuous development; and that it occurs in overlapping stages.
4. Defense mechanisms play an important role in Freud's theory, as do the id, ego, and superego.
5. Piaget's theory has four stages: sensorimotor, preoperational, concrete operational, and formal operational.
6. In Skinner's theory, there are four major concepts: positive and negative reinforcement, punishment, and extinction.
7. Erikson's stages emphasize eight concepts: trust, autonomy, initiative, industry, identity, intimacy, generativity, and integrity.

Key Terms

Accommodation	Mental structures
Adaptation	Negative reinforcement
Anal stage	Oedipal conflict
Assimilation	Operant conditioning
Behavioral theory	Operations
Cognitive structuralist theory	Oral stage
Concrete operational stage	Organization
Conditioned reflexes	Phallic stage
Defense mechanisms	Positive reinforcement
Ego	Preoperational stage
Electra conflict	Psychoanalysis
Extinction	Psychoanalytic theory
Fixation	Psychosocial theory
Formal operational stage	Punishment
Free will	Reinforcement
Genital stage	Schemata
Id	Sensorimotor stage
Identity crisis	Superego
Latency stage	

What Do You Think?

1. What is your reaction to the statement, "The truth or falseness of a theory has little to do with its usefulness"?
2. Some people say that in his concept of human development Freud emphasizes sexuality too much. What do you think?

3.   Which is better, assimilation or accommodation? If you could do only one, which would it be? Why?

4.   Skinner criticized the other theorists in this chapter for believing they can describe what goes on in the human mind. After all, he said, no one has ever looked inside one. What's your position?

5.   Is it possible for a person to be deeply intimate with another person and still be in a state of identity confusion?

Suggested Readings

Clark, Ronald W. (1980). *Freud: The man and the cause.* New York: Random House. This is one of the most judicious and even-handed books written about the father of psychoanalysis.

Erikson, Erik. (1958). *Young man Luther.* New York: Norton. Martin Luther was the main force behind the Protestant Reformation. In Erikson's penetrating analysis of the causes behind Luther's actions, we have a wonderfully clear example of his ideas about adolescence in general and negative identity in particular.

Skinner, B. F. (1948). *Walden two.* New York: Macmillan. Many students find it hard to see how Skinner's behaviorism would function in everyday life. In this novel, we see how a community based on his principles would operate. In fact, for a while at least, several such communities really existed. This is a good way to understand his theory.

Tyler, Anne. (1986). *The accidental tourist.* New York: Knopf. This story of a man who tries desperately to avoid the bumps of life offers a fine example with which to analyze each of the theories presented in this chapter.

· PART 2 ·

Beginnings

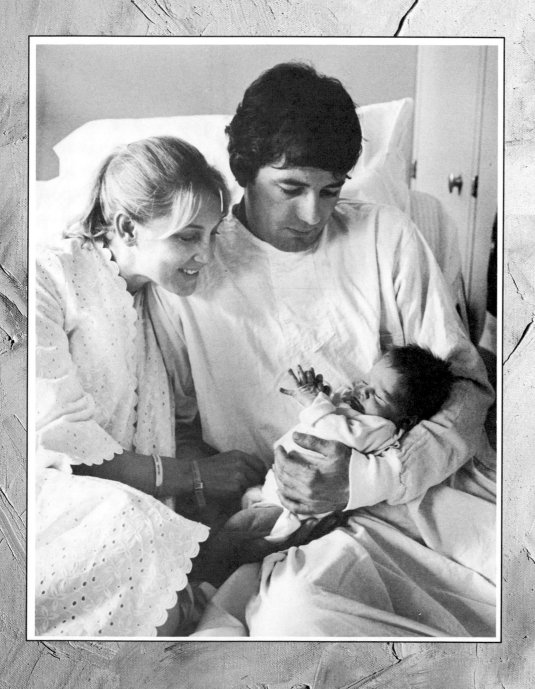

· *Chapter 3* ·

The Biological Basis of Development

In his enjoyable *The Ascent of Man,* Jacob Bronowski states:

❖   *How the message of inheritance is passed from one generation to the next was discovered in 1953, and it is the adventure story of science in the twentieth century. I suppose the moment of drama is the autumn of 1951, when a young man in his twenties, James Watson, arrives in Cambridge and teams up with a man of thirty-five, Francis Crick, to decipher the structure of deoxyribonucleic acid, DNA for short. DNA is a nucleic acid, that is, an acid in the central part of cells, and it had become clear in the preceding ten years that nucleic acids carry the chemical messages of inheritance from generation to generation (1973, p. 390).*

Any journey begins with the first steps, which for students of the life span means that point at which development begins: the merger of sperm with egg and the union of the genetic endowments of mother and father. In this chapter, you will explore a world so tiny that it is almost impossible to imagine. You will read about some of the great biological discoveries of the last century, discoveries that have led scientists to the origins of life itself. As you follow these innovations, you will also come to understand more about development and behavior.

Think for a moment about yourself. You probably think of yourself as a fairly unique individual—and you are right! Thanks to your genetic inheritance, there's no one quite like you in the world. You may or may not be impressed by this fact, but you must have occasionally wondered what made you what you are.

How much of what you are came from your parents and how much came from your contacts with your environment? Remember that heredity and environment are so interrelated that we really can't divide them; they must be considered together. We'll remind you of this at key points in the chapter.

In this chapter we'll try to clarify the process by which heredity and environment immediately begin to interact, in other words, what makes you who you are. You'll read about the fertilization process, during which the sperm and egg unite. Today it's a process filled with the potential for conflict and controversy because of new techniques that enable fertilization to occur outside of a woman's body.

Sometime in your life you probably have said, "Oh, I've inherited that trait." That's the easy answer. How did you inherit that characteristic? Do you remember that DNA you heard about in your science classes? Here you'll learn that the discovery of DNA involved some of the world's greatest biologists in a race to be the first to find the "secret of life."

But traits don't just appear; they're passed on from generation to generation. So following this discussion, we'll trace the manner in which hereditary traits are transmitted. Unfortunately, as we are all aware, occasionally the transmission of traits produces abnormalities, which we will discuss.

Heredity and Environment

With DNA directing development, a child combines the genetic contributions of both parents in a new and original manner from the moment of conception. Remember, however, as you follow development back to its beginnings, none of us is an absolute prisoner of our inheritance. From the moment of fertilization, the environment, in this case the prenatal environment, begins to exercise its influence. We are truly the product of the interaction of heredity and environment (Scarr & Kidd, 1983).

BOX 3.1

The Dragons of Eden

The popular scientist Carl Sagan, writing in his best-selling book *The Dragons of Eden* (1977), has explained how heredity and environment work together about as well as anyone. He believes that as human beings we require tremendous amounts of information to adapt to our world. This information comes from three sources.

1. Most organisms on earth depend on their **genetic** information (which is "prewired"). As humans we are less dependent on genetic information than other species.
2. Even though human behavior is significantly controlled by our genetic inheritance, thanks to our brains we have greater opportunities to create more advanced societies. We also are capable of acquiring what Sagan calls **extragenetic** information. That is, we have an unrivaled capacity for learning, which greatly increases our chances for survival.
3. Finally, we have also shown remarkable ability to create **extrasomatic** sources of information. We store information outside of our bodies, in books and computers, for example.

Sagan's viewpoint is quite optimistic. He believes that we are not just the product of our genes. We can take whatever we were born with and, by means of extragenetic and extrasomatic sources of information, rise to levels that animals are incapable of reaching.

You would enjoy reading *The Dragons of Eden,* not only as a rich source of extrasomatic information but for the pleasure it will give you.

Development = H + E

Heredity and environment. Probably no other phrase has caused as much mischief in interpreting human behavior. Of course behavior results from heredity and environment, but when does the environment begin to exercise its impact? When we use the term *environment,* we mean anything, physical or psychological, that affects the individual (Plomin, 1983).

How much do heredity and environment contribute to different traits? If an infant gives evidence of alertness and competence at birth, why is it impossible to predict future cognitive development?

Many genetic factors are well known. Some genes, such as those for blue eyes, are recessive; others, such as those for brown eyes, are dominant. Children of blue-eyed and brown-eyed parents usually have brown eyes. (The reasons for the various possibilities appear later in the chapter.)

If prenatal conditions are sufficiently adverse, no development will occur, and the ovum or embryo will perish. If development does begin, it is not a question of whether heredity or environment is more important; both contribute (Travers, 1982). But their contribution to a specific trait may differ; that is, both do not contribute equally to each trait. Heredity, for example, exercises primary control over eye color, while the environment contributes significantly to intelligence.

The environment's influence on genetic potential begins at the moment of fertilization—the union of sperm and egg. When you consider the source of a child's potential—the mother's and father's genetic material and the bewildering variety of environmental conditions that children experience—you can better understand why there are seemingly infinite patterns of human behavior.

The strong resemblance of these family members to each other is testimony to the role of heredity in our makeup.

This complicated interaction of heredity and environment also helps to explain the nature and extent of genetic malfunctioning. Most infants are born healthy, but hereditary disease does occur. Estimates are that about 5% of all newborns have some birth defect. For example:

1. Genetic defects cause one-half of all miscarriages.

2. Two-fifths of infant mortality is caused by genetic disease.

3. Four-fifths of the mentally retarded show a genetic defect.

4. Each person carries from five to eight recessive genes for genetic defects.

These figures do not reflect diseases thought to have a genetic link if coupled with certain environmental conditions—cancer, diabetes, and schizophrenia.

First, however, where exactly does development begin?

The Beginnings

The fusion of two specialized cells, the sperm and the egg (or ovum), marks the beginning of development. This fertilized ovum contains all of the genetic material that the organism will ever possess. The zygote (the fertilized ovum) immediately begins to divide, and tissue differentiation commences. During the initial phase of development following fertilization, it is almost impossible to distinguish the male from the female (Travers, 1982).

Any discussion of fertilization today must take into account certain advances in research and technology. Consequently, our discussion will be broken into *two* parts:

1. **Internal,** or natural, **fertilization**

2. **External fertilization** techniques, such as in vitro fertilization (the famous "test-tube" babies).

Table 3.1 contains a glossary of many of the terms in this discussion. Refer to it when you meet an unfamiliar term. Otherwise, the amazing richness of the genetic world can escape you.

In our analysis of genetic material and its impact on our lives, we will examine the manner in which we receive genes from our parents. (Even this fundamental fact today requires further explanation. Genes may come from surprising sources thanks to our technology [Grobstein, 1988]. More about this later.) Our story begins with the male's sperm and the female's egg.

The Sperm

Certain cells are destined to become the sperm and eggs. The chief characteristics of the **sperm** are its tightly packed tip (the *acrosome*), containing 23 chromosomes, a short neck region, and a tail to propel it in its search for the egg. Sperm are so tiny that estimates are that a number of sperm equal to the world's population could fit in a thimble (Travers, 1982).

Males at birth have in their testes those cells that will eventually produce sperm. At puberty, a *meiotic* division occurs that forms the actual sperm. Simultaneously the pituitary gland stimulates the hormonal production that results in the secondary sex characteristics: pubic hair, beard, deep voice.

Table 3.1 A Genetic Glossary

Acrosome: Area at the tip of the sperm.

Allele: Alternate forms of a specific gene; there are genes for blue eyes and brown eyes.

Autosome: Chromosomes other than the sex chromosomes.

Chromosome: Stringlike bodies that carry the genes; they are present in all of the body's cells.

DNA: Deoxyribonucleic acid, the chemical structure of the gene.

Dominance: The tendency of a gene to be expressed in a trait, even when joined with a gene whose expression differs; brown eyes will appear when genes for blue and brown eyes are paired.

Fertilization: The union of sperm and egg to form the fertilized ovum or zygote.

Gametes: The mature sex cells, either sperms or eggs.

Genes: The ultimate hereditary determiners; they are composed of the chemical molecule deoxyribonucleic acid (DNA).

Gene locus: The specific location of a gene on the chromosome.

Genotype: The genetic composition of an individual.

Heterozygous: The gene pairs for a trait differ; a person who is heterozygous for eye color has a gene for brown eyes and one for blue eyes.

Homozygous: The gene pairs for a trait are similar; the eye color genes are the same.

Meiosis: Cell division in which each daughter cell receives one-half of the chromosomes of the parent cell. For humans this maintains the number of chromosomes (46) at fertilization.

Mitosis: Cell division in which each daughter cell receives the same number of chromosomes as the parent cell.

Mutation: A change in the structure of a gene.

Phenotype: The observable expression of a gene.

Recessive: A gene whose trait is not expressed unless paired with another recessive gene; both parents contribute genes for blue eyes.

Sex chromosome: Those chromosomes that determine sex; in humans they are the 23d pair, with an XX combination producing a female, and an XY combination producing a male.

Sex-linkage: Genes on the sex chromosome that produce traits other than sex.

Trisomy: Three chromosomes are present rather than the customary pair; Down's syndrome (mongolism) is caused by three chromosomes at the 21st pairing.

Zygote: The fertilized egg.

The Ovum (Egg)

The **ovum,** or egg, is larger than the sperm, about the size of the period at the end of this sentence (Travers, 1982). When females are born they already have primal eggs. Estimates are that from one to two million eggs have been formed in the ovaries. Since only one mature egg is required each month for about thirty-five years, the number present far exceeds the need.

Many of these primal eggs succumb before puberty. They simply shrivel up and disappear. At puberty the pituitary gland stimulates the hormonal production that produces the female secondary sex characteristics: pubic hair, breasts, wider hips, higher voice.

The Fertilization Process

Although the fertilization process seems similar for males and females, it is far more complicated for females. The interaction between the pituitary and the ovaries occurs in four-week phases—the **menstrual cycle.**

The Menstrual Cycle

The pituitary gland secretes another hormone that stimulates the ripening of eggs, and after two weeks one egg, which has ripened more than the others, is discharged from the ovary's surface. Figure 3.1 illustrates the relationship of the ovum to the ovary, the fallopian tubes, and the uterus.

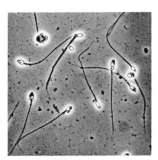

(a)

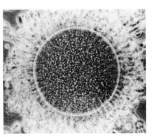

(b)

The sperm (a), in its search for the egg (b), carries the 23 chromosomes from the male.

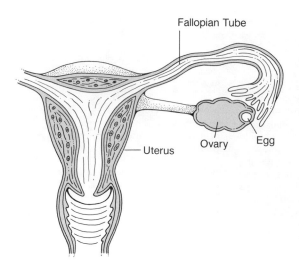

Figure 3.1 *The relationship of ovary, egg, fallopian tube, and uterus.*

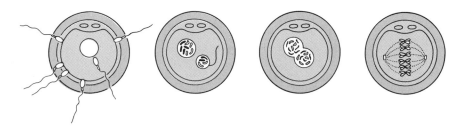

Figure 3.2 *Fertilization of the egg. The sperm, carrying its 23 chromosomes, penetrates the egg, with its 23 chromosomes. The nuclei of sperm and egg fuse, resulting in 46 chromosomes.*

This process, called **ovulation,** triggers a chemical reaction that inhibits the ripening of further eggs. It also prepares the uterine lining for a potential fertilized ovum.

If fertilization does not occur, the prepared uterine lining is shed in menstruation. When the menstrual bleeding ceases, the entire process begins again. During each menstrual cycle many eggs are discarded. As a woman approaches the end of her egg-producing years, these last ova have been present for as many as forty years (Travers, 1982). This may explain why the children of older women are more susceptible to genetic defects. The eggs have been exposed to environmental hazards (such as radiation) too long to escape damage (Singer, 1985).

Ovulation and Implantation

When the egg is discharged from the ovary's surface, it is enveloped by one of the **fallopian tubes.** The diameter of each fallopian tube is about that of a human hair, but it almost unfailingly ensnares the egg and provides a passageway to the uterus. If fertilization occurs, it will take place soon after the egg enters the fallopian tube. Figure 3.2 illustrates the fertilization process.

Fusion of the two cells is quickly followed by the first cell division. As the zygote travels toward **implantation** within the uterus, cell division continues. The cells multiply rapidly and after about seven days reach the uterine wall. The fertilized egg is now called a **blastocyst.** The journey is pictured in Figure 3.3.

BOX 3.2

The Special Case of Twins

Occasionally, and for reasons that still elude us, twins are born. Most twins occur when a woman's ovaries release two ripened eggs (rather than one) and both are fertilized by separate sperm. These twins are called **fraternal,** *nonidentical,* or *dizygotic.* Their genes are no more alike than those of other siblings (i.e., children born of the same parents but at different times).

Less frequently, twins develop from a single fertilized egg that divides shortly after conception. This process leads to *identical,* or **monozygotic,** twins. Their genes are identical, that is, they share the same genotype.

There are estimated to be as many as 50 million pairs of twins around the world, with about 2 million pairs in this country (Powledge, 1983). The frequency of twin births seems to vary according to the ethnic group. For example:

1. In the United States, twins are born once in every 89 white births, and once in every 70 African-American births (Farber, 1981).
2. In Japan, twins occur once in every 155 births.
3. In Nigeria, twins occur once in every 22 births.

As you can well imagine, twins, especially monozygotic or identical twins, have long fascinated psychologists, especially identical twins that have been separated at birth. By comparing these twins from different environments, it is possible to estimate the influence of heredity and environment on behavior.

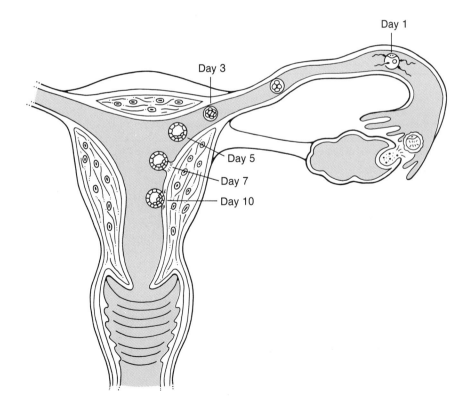

Figure 3.3 From ovulation to implantation.

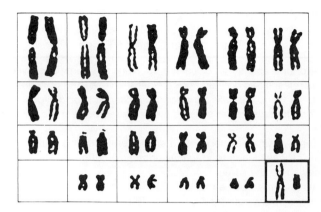

(a)

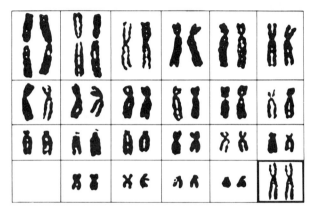

(b)

Figure 3.4 (a) At the top is the chromosome structure of a male, and (b) at the bottom is the chromosome structure of a female. The 23d pair is shown in the bottom right box of each figure; notice that the Y chromosome of the male is smaller. To obtain this chromosomal picture, a cell is removed from the individual's body, usually from the inside of the mouth. The chromosomes are magnified extensively and then photographed.

After the sperm and egg unite, the new cell (the potential individual) possesses 23 pairs of chromosomes, or 46 chromosomes. One member of each pair has been contributed by the father and one by the mother. Figure 3.4 illustrates the chromosomal arrangement of a typical male and female. The fertilized egg at this stage is called the **zygote.**

The 46 chromosomes that the zygote possesses represent the individual's total biological heritage. By a process of division, each cell in the body will have a replica of all 46 chromosomes. The significance of the chromosomes is that they carry the genes, the decisive elements of heredity.

The size of the elements involved is almost bewildering. We have commented on the size of the sperm—so small that it can be seen only microscopically. The head of the sperm, which is about one-twelfth of its total length, contains the 23 chromosomes.

While individuals may change in the course of their lives, their hereditary properties do not change. The zygote, containing all 46 chromosomes, represents the "blueprint" for our physical and mental makeup. Under ordinary circumstances,

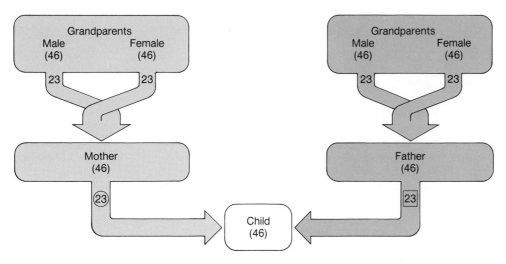

Figure 3.5 The hereditary process.

environmental conditions leave the 46 chromosomes unaltered. (The hesitation expressed by "ordinary circumstances" acknowledges the growing belief that environmental agents such as drugs, viruses, or radiation may cause genetic damage.) Figure 3.5 illustrates the process by which the number of chromosomes remains the same from generation to generation.

Once fertilization occurs, the zygote is not yet free from risk. Let's use a figure easy to work with and assume that 100 eggs are exposed to sperm. The mortality rate from fertilization to birth is estimated as follows.

> Of 100 eggs exposed to sperm:
> 84 are fertilized
> 69 are implanted
> 42 survive one week
> 37 survive seven weeks
> 31 survive to birth

Thus nature's toll results in about a 70% mortality rate.

External Fertilization

Although the fertilization process just described is the normal process for most women, there are exceptions. For some women, infertility, for whatever reason, is an inescapable problem. For those wishing children, external fertilization techniques offer hope.

Today there are hundreds of thousands of childless couples who desperately desire children. They see the new technologies that we are about to discuss as a new hope. These couples represent a growing problem in our society—infertility. Consider these figures:

1. In 1965, 500,000 American couples were childless (about 1.9%). They had no children and failed to conceive after a year of trying.

2. In 1976, the number grew to one million (3.4%).

3. In 1982, the percentage was up to 3.5%.

BOX 3.3

What's Your Opinion?

Closely allied to the new techniques of external fertilization has been the development of sperm banks. The roots of the phenomenon are rather scary since sperm banks grew from a desire to "purify the gene pool"—that is, decide who is to beget of whom, in an attempt to create a superior race. As you recall, it was the Nazi movement that took the principles of *eugenics* (literally means "good birth") to hideous extremes.

Its revival began in 1949 with Hermann Muller's concern over genetic defects and his efforts to further **germinal choice**. Since freezing sperm with liquid nitrogen was a demonstrated success, it now became possible to store frozen sperm indefinitely

for use in vaginal injection. Support came from many sources and led to the founding of the Repository for Germinal Choice.

The repository originally was intended to accept and freeze the sperm of Nobel prize winners, but due to the few who volunteered and their age (most were in their seventies with less vigorous sperm), its acceptance standards were relaxed to include scientists and mathematicians.

The idea remains popular. The largest sperm bank in the world can be found on Madison Avenue in New York City, where there are 35,000 samples of frozen sperm. Do you think this practice should be encouraged or discouraged? What's your opinion?

The major reasons for this increase are thought to be the widespread use of intrauterine devices and the postponement of childbearing by large numbers of women. As a response to childlessness, there are now 153 in vitro fertilization centers around the country and about 100 sperm banks (Guttmacher, 1986).

Although you are probably most familiar with in vitro fertilization, another process, **AID** (*a*rtificial *i*nsemination by *d*onor) is by far the most widely used procedure. Here are some of the techniques now available (Grobstein, 1988):

Artificial insemination
In vitro fertilization (fertilization of egg and sperm occurs in dish)
Embryo transfer (an embryo from one woman's womb is transferred to that of another woman)
Women sell their eggs
Human embryos are frozen for long-term storage
Surrogate motherhood (a woman agrees to be inseminated by the sperm of a man whose wife is infertile and returns the child to the couple after birth)

Consequently, today a child may have as many as five parents:

A sperm donor (father or other male)—1
An egg donor (mother or other female)—1
A surrogate mother—1
The couple who raise the child—2

In Vitro Fertilization

In vitro fertilization is the external fertilization technique with which you are probably most familiar. (At this point we urge you to reexamine Figure 3.1, which details the control system of a woman's menstrual cycle, since the in vitro procedure attempts to imitate both these steps and their timing.) The steps in the procedure are as follows (Grobstein, 1981):

Table 3.2 IVF Success Rates

Problem	Success Rate
Tubal blockage (blocked or damaged fallopian tubes)	15%
Male factor (quantity or quality of sperm is inadequate)	22% (when fertilization is successful—about 60% of time)
Cervical factor (narrow, incompatible with sperm)	14%
Endometriosis (uterine lining found elsewhere)	14%
Unknown causes	17%
DES (mothers of these women took diethystilbestrol)	10%

The woman is usually treated with hormones to stimulate maturation of eggs in the ovary, and she is observed closely to determine the timing of ovulation. (i.e., the time at which the egg leaves the surface of the ovary).

- An incision is made in the abdomen through which a laparoscope (a thin tubular lens through which the physician can see the ovary) is inserted to remove mature eggs.

- The egg is placed in a solution containing blood serum and nutrients.

- Capacitation—a process in which a layer surrounding the sperm is removed so that it may penetrate the egg.

- Sperm are added to the solution; fertilization occurs.

- The fertilized egg is transferred to a fresh supporting solution.

- The fertilized egg is inserted into the uterus.

- The fertilized egg is implanted in the uterine lining.

During this period the woman is being treated to prepare her body to receive the fertilized egg. For example, the lining of the uterus must be spongy or porous enough to hold the zygote. The fertilized egg must be inserted at the time it would normally reach the uterine cavity. What day would that be?

What are the chances of success for couples using this procedure? Table 3.2 presents the rate for various problems. Remember, these are estimates.

A recent interesting development relates to the success rate that in vitro fertilization centers have claimed. Noting that some advertising seemed inflated, the Society for Assisted Reproductive Technology (SART), a division of the American Fertility Society representing most of the IVF centers in this country, reported that it would disclose success rates for its member clinics. This action was in response to congressional criticism of those centers who advertised a success rate of up to 40%. Federal investigations had shown that nationally, a woman has a 9%–10% chance of success from any single treatment attempt.

Many centers resisted the disclosure of results because an apparently low success rate would damage their reputation, resulting in a loss of potential patients. This would be unfair to those centers that honestly report their results but who work with a wide range of patients. That is, some centers work with an older population and make no restrictions about the male's sperm count. Consequently, their success rate is lower than that of centers that accept a more limited group of patients.

As a result of this publicity, demand for IVF has weakened. IVF specialists, however, expect that future improvements in the available techniques will lead to higher success rates and renewed patient confidence.

Chromosomes and Genes

The fertilized egg, the zygote, contains the individual's genetic endowment represented by the 46 chromosomes in its nucleus. Human chromosomes appear in 23 pairs.

Each pair, except the 23d, is remarkably alike. The 23d pair defines the individual's sex: an XX combination indicates a female, while XY indicates a male. The sperm actually determines sex, since it alone can carry a Y chromosome. Thus there are two kinds of sperm: the X chromosome carrier and the Y chromosome carrier.

The Y carrier is smaller than the X, which contains more genetic material. The Y carrier is also lighter and speedier and can reach the egg more quickly. But it is also more vulnerable; if ovulation has not occurred, the X carrier survives longer than the Y carrier.

Consequently, the male, from conception, is the more fragile of the two sexes. Estimates are that 160 are conceived for every 100 females. However, so many males are spontaneously aborted that only 105 males are born for every 100 females. A similar pattern appears in neonatal life and continues throughout development, until women finally outnumber men, reversing the original ratio. Certain conclusions follow:

- Structurally and functionally, females resist disease better than males.

- The male is more subject to hereditary disease and defect.

- Environmental elements expose the male to greater hazards.

- Females are born with and retain a biological superiority over males (Singer, 1985).

The significance of the chromosomes lies in the material they contain—the genes. Each gene is located at a particular spot on the chromosome, called the *gene locus*. The genes, whose chemical structure is **DNA** (deoxyribonucleic acid), account for all inherited characteristics, from hair and eye color to skin shade, even the tendency toward baldness.

Aside from performing their cellular duties, the genes also reproduce themselves. Each gene constructs an exact duplicate of itself, so that when a cell divides, the chromosomes and genes also divide and each cell retains identical genetic material. As the cells divide, however, they do not remain identical. Specialization appears and different kinds of cells are formed at different locations.

The genes, then, are continuously active in directing life's processes according to their prescribed genetic codes. The action of the genes is remarkable not only because of complexity but also because of an elegant simplicity.

For example, the initial goal of the genes is primarily to form the body's basic materials. Although this activity continues throughout our lives, more specialized functions gradually appear and begin to form a circulatory system, a skeletal system, and a nervous system. The process continues until a highly complex human being results (Grobstein, 1988). (Remember the distinction that you read about in the genetic glossary. A **genotype** is a person's genetic composition, while a **phenotype** is the observable expression of a gene.)

BOX 3.4

The Changing Nature of Adoption

For many couples who remain childless in spite of several attempts at external fertilization, adoption is a viable option. The process of adoption has changed radically in the last few years because of a limited number of children and an increase in the number of couples who wish to adopt.

Adoption procedures were formerly *closed*—that is, the biological parents were completely removed from the life of their child once the child was surrendered for adoption. Supposedly, **closed adoption** prevented the natural parents and the adoptive couple from emotional upset. Many biological mothers, however, reported in later interviews that they never recovered from the grieving process.

Today, if a pregnant woman approaches an adoption agency, she gets what she wants. She can insist that her child be raised by a couple with specific characteristics: nationality, religion, income, number in family. She can ask to see her child several times a year, perhaps take the youngster on a vacation, and telephone frequently. The adoption agency will try to meet these demands. This process is called **open adoption**. While many adoptive couples dislike the arrangement, they really have no choice.

Open adoption is a radical departure from the days when a woman who had decided to give up her baby for adoption had to wear a blindfold and earplugs during delivery so she wouldn't see or hear her baby. Today the natural mother may actually select the adoptive couple from several profiles that are given to her. (These profiles contain information about the adoptive couple: food preferences, television, politics, how the couple deals with stress, how they would handle a 2 year old with a temper tantrum.)

Most officials at adoption agencies agree that biological mothers rarely select a couple solely on the basis of income. Religion, life-style, and family stability seem much more important. Face-to-face meetings between the couples are becoming more common and often are decisive in the natural mother's decision.

Although there are problems with open adoption (the adoptive parents frequently resent the continuing presence of the biological mother), most experts agree that a change was needed. Too many adopted children have shown emotional difficulties on learning that they were relinquished, and a large number of biological mothers never recover from relinquishing their babies. Only time can tell how successful this new procedure will be.

Heredity at Work

The original cell, the possessor of 46 chromosomes, begins to divide rapidly after fertilization, until at birth there are billions of cells in the infant. The cells soon begin to specialize: some become muscle, some bone, some skin, some blood, and some nerve cells. These are the somatic or body cells. The process of division by which these cells multiply is called **mitosis** (Figure 3.6). In a mitotic division, the number of chromosomes in each cell remains the same.

A second type of cell is also differentiated: the germ or sex cell that ultimately becomes either sperm or egg. These reproductive cells likewise divide by the process of mitosis until the age of puberty. But then a remarkable phenomenon occurs—another type of division called **meiosis,** or reduction division (Figure 3.7). Each sex cell, instead of receiving 46 chromosomes upon division, now receives 23.

Mitosis is basically a division of cells in which each chromosome is duplicated so that each cell receives a copy of each chromosome of the parent cell. What is doubled in mitotic division is the amount of DNA, the chief component of the genes.

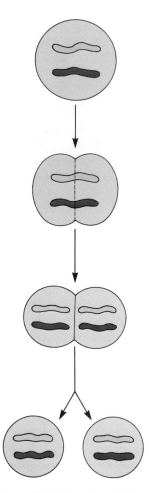

Figure 3.6 A mitotic division is a cell division in which each daughter cell receives the same number of chromosomes as the parent cell—46.

Meiosis, which occurs only in germ cell reproduction, is responsible both for the shuffling of hereditary characteristics received from each parent and for their random appearance in offspring. During the reduction division, the chromosomes separate longitudinally so that 23 go to one cell and 23 to another (Feingold & Pashayan, 1983).

For the male, reduction division begins to occur just before puberty. For the female, the process differs slightly. Since she is required to produce only one mature egg a month, there is no provision for an indefinitely large number of eggs, as there is for sperm.

A woman normally sheds only three to four hundred mature ova in her lifetime, while the normal male in a single ejaculation emits two hundred million to three hundred million sperm. When a female is born, the initial phases of the reduction division have already occurred, and rudimentary eggs are present.

The ovaries at birth contain tiny clusters of all the eggs that will mature in later years. Just before puberty, the final phases of the reduction division occur, and mature eggs are formed. It is as if there is a lengthy waiting period, from birth until about the age of 12 or 13, before the process is finally completed. The 23 chromosomes with their hereditary content are present at birth but must await the passage of time before biological maturity occurs in the female.

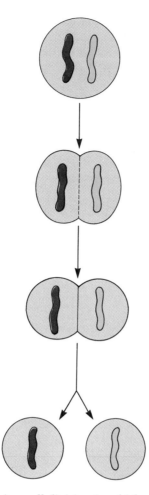

Figure 3.7 *A meiotic division is a cell division in which each daughter cell receives one half of the chromosomes of the parent cell—23.*

Now that we have traced the process by which fertilization occurs and discovered what is passed from parents to child, we still need to know "why I am who I am." This brings us to the discovery of DNA, one of this century's greatest achievements.

DNA: Structure and Function

We know that each chromosome contains thousands of genes, and that each of these thousands of genes has a role in the growth and development of each human being. The chemical key to the life force in humans, animals, and plants is the amazing chemical compound DNA. It constitutes about 40% of the chromosomes and is the molecular basis of the genes. Genes not only perform certain duties within the cell, but join with other genes to reproduce both themselves and the whole chromosome (see Figure 3.8).

Each gene follows the instructions encoded in its DNA. It sends these instructions, as chemical messages, into the surrounding cell. The cell then produces certain substances or performs certain functions according to instructions. These new products then interact with the genes to form new substances. The process continues to build the millions of cells needed for various bodily structures.

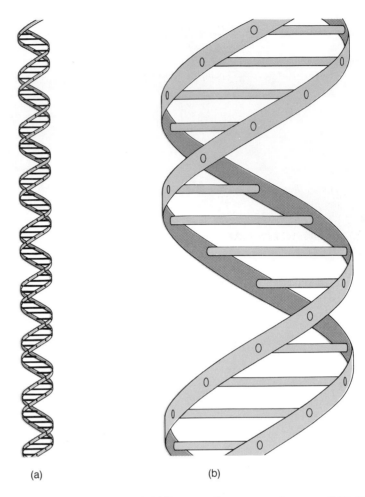

(a)   (b)

Figure 3.8   The DNA double helix. (a) The overall structure that gave DNA its famous name. (b) A closer examination reveals that the sides of the spiral are connected by chemicals similar to the rungs of a ladder.

Examine Figure 3.8 and note how the strands intertwine. The strands, similar to the sides of a ladder, are connected by chemical rings: adenine (A), guanine (G), cytosine (C), and thymine (T). The letters are not randomly connected: A joins with T, G with C. If a code was written as AGCTTGA, it must appear as:

A G C T T G A
T C G A A C T

Thus, one sequence determines the other.

A remarkable feature of DNA is its ability to reproduce itself and ensure that each daughter cell receives identical information. During mitosis the DNA splits as readily as a person unzips a jacket. Each single strand grows a new mate, A to T and G to C, until the double helix model is reproduced in each daughter cell.

The four letter possibilities, A-T, T-A, G-C, C-G, seem to limit genetic variation. But when we consider that each DNA molecule is quite lengthy, involving thousands, perhaps millions of chemical steps (TA, GC, AT, CG, AT, CG, TA), the possible combinations seem limitless. The differences in the DNA patterns account for the individual genetic differences among humans and for differences between species.

BOX 3.5

The DNA Alphabet

If you examine Figure 3.8, you will notice that the various rungs and sides of the DNA ladder resemble small blocks. These are called **nucleotides,** and come in four varieties depending on the AT, GC pairings. Carl Sagan (1977, p. 23) states that although the language of heredity is written in an alphabet of only *four letters,* the final book is very rich. The average DNA molecule consists of about 5 billion pairs of nucleotides.

Sagan attempts to estimate the amount of information that our genes contain. Since there are four different kinds of nucleotides, the number of bits of information in a single chromosome is 20 billion. To what can we compare 20 billion bits of information?

They are the equivalent of about 3 billion letters. Since the average word contains six letters, each chromosome incorporates information equal to about 500 million words. At about three hundred words per typical printed page, this translates into the equivalent of about 2 million pages. The average book consists of about five hundred pages. Thus the information in one human chromosome corresponds to that in four thousand books. As Sagan says, the rungs on the DNA ladder represent a library of information.

Sagan's comment about this human uniqueness is pertinent for lifespan development:

We have made a kind of bargain with nature: our children will be difficult to raise but their capacity for new learning will greatly enhance the chances of survival of the human species (1977, p. 23).

One intriguing question is how the encoded information contained in the DNA is transmitted to the surrounding cell. The process is essentially as follows: RNA (ribonucleic acid) forms within the nucleus of the cell, acts as a messenger for DNA, and moves into the cell body to direct the building of the body's substances.

How Traits Are Transmitted

What color are your eyes? Do your brothers and sisters have the same color eyes? Theirs could be different from yours; the mother and father who produced a brown-eyed child can also have a youngster with blue eyes. For centuries, guesses, myths, and speculation were used to explain the bewildering and mysterious happenings of heredity.

It was not until the end of the nineteenth century that Gregor Mendel offered a scientific explanation. (Note the relatively recent emergence of genetic facts: the transmission of traits by Mendel in the 1860s, the Watson-Crick double-helix model of DNA in 1953, and the number of human chromosomes in 1956.)

Mendel's Work
Mendel, an Austrian monk who studied plants as a hobby, attempted to crossbreed pure strains of pea plants. He used pure sets of plants, that is, peas that were either round or wrinkled, yellow or green, tall or dwarf. He discovered that the first generation of offspring all had the same trait: after crossbreeding round and unwrinkled peas, the offspring were all round. Did the offspring inherit the trait from only one parent?

Mendel quickly eliminated this explanation since the missing trait (wrinkled) reappeared in the second generation. But the trait that was exclusively expressed in the first generation (roundness) was the majority trait in the second generation. That is, the ratio of round peas to wrinkled peas consistently remained at 3 to 1 in the second generation.

Table 3.3   Mendel's Round and Wrinkled Peas

I. First Pairing—R × W

	W	W
R	RW	RW
R	RW	RW

II. Second Pairing—RW × RW

	R	W
R	RR	RW
W	RW	WW

Thus roundness is the **dominant** trait and wrinkled is the **recessive** trait. These two genes, round (R) and wrinkled (W), yield four possible peas: RR, WW, RW, WR. RR and WW are pure strains and breed true; RW and WR contain both the dominant and recessive trait.

A genetic grid based on Mendel's first pairing (round and wrinkled) is shown in Table 3.3. Note how the 3 to 1 ratio appears in the second generation.

What Is Transmitted

The two questions asked most frequently by parents following the birth of a child are, Is it a boy or girl? and Is it healthy? As mentioned earlier, the 23d pair of chromosomes determines the sex of a child: XY = boy; XX = girl. Remember: it is the male who determines the baby's sex since the egg always carries the X chromosome, while the sperm may contain either an X or a Y.

Sperm X + egg X = female
Sperm Y + egg X = male

Hemophilia is an example of sex-linked inheritance, which affected several of the royal families of Europe such as the Romonov's pictured here.

There also occurs what is known as **sex-linked inheritance.** If you recall, the X chromosome is substantially larger than the Y (about three times as large). Therefore the female carries more genes on the 23d chromosome than the male. This difference helps to explain sex-linkage (Feingold & Pashayan, 1983).

Think back now to the difference between dominant and recessive traits. If a dominant and recessive gene appear together, the dominant trait is expressed. There must be two recessive genes for the recessive trait (say, blue eyes) to appear.

But on the 23d set of chromosomes, there is nothing on the Y chromosome to offset the effects of a gene on the X chromosome. As far as is known today, the Y chromosome almost completely lacks genes except for the one that determines maleness—with the possible exception of a condition producing exceptionally hairy ears (Singer, 1985).

Perhaps the most widely known of these sex-linked characteristics is **hemophilia** (the bleeder's disease). The blood of these individuals does not clot properly. Several of the royal families of Europe were particularly prone to this condition.

Another sex-linked trait attributed to the X chromosome is **color blindness.** The X chromosome contains the gene for color vision and, if faulty, there is nothing on the Y chromosome to counterbalance the defect.

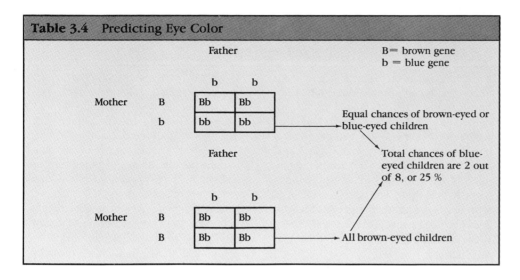

Table 3.4 Predicting Eye Color

| | | Father | | B = brown gene |
| | | | | b = blue gene |

		b	b	
Mother	B	Bb	Bb	→ Equal chances of brown-eyed or blue-eyed children
	b	bb	bb	

Father

Total chances of blue-eyed children are 2 out of 8, or 25 %

		b	b	
Mother	B	Bb	Bb	
	B	Bb	Bb	→ All brown-eyed children

Prospective parents also usually speculate about the color of their child's eyes. What is the genetic explanation for the presence of different eye colors? There is a gene responsible for blue eyes and another responsible for brown eyes. The gene for brown eyes is dominant and the gene for blue eyes is recessive. For example, a child receiving two "brown" genes will have brown eyes; a child receiving two "blue" genes will have blue eyes. Finally, the youngster who receives one of each will have brown eyes, because the gene for brown eyes is dominant.

The basic principle is that genes producing dark eye colors (brown, black) dominate over those producing light eye colors (blue, green, gray). If the mother, for instance, has brown eyes, she may carry only those genes for brown eyes (if her family is mostly brown-eyed) or a brown and a blue (if there are blue-eyed relatives somewhere in the family tree). If the father has blue eyes, he most certainly has two "blue" genes. Let's assume that we don't know anything about the mother's family. Table 3.4 reports the chances of blue-eyed children.

Some Common Abnormalities

Down Syndrome

Down syndrome is caused by a deviation on the 21st pair of chromosomes; the individual may have 47 chromosomes. This defect was discovered in 1866 by a British doctor, Langdon Down, and produces distinctive facial features, small hands, a large tongue, and possible functional difficulties such as mental retardation, heart defects, and an added risk of leukemia.

The appearance of Down syndrome is closely related to the mother's age: chances are about 1 in 750 between the ages of 30 and 35; 1 in 300 between 35 and 39; 1 in 80 between 40 and 45; and after 45 years the incidence jumps to 1 in 40 births. Under age 30, the ratio is only 1 in 1,500 births.

Although the exact cause of Down syndrome remains a mystery, the answer may lie in the female egg production mechanism, which results in eggs remaining in the ovary for forty or fifty years. The longer they are in the ovary, the greater the possibility of damage. There is no treatment for Down syndrome other than good medical supervision and special education. These individuals usually are cheerful,

Down syndrome is caused by a deviation on the 21st pair of chromosomes. These children have distinctive facial features and are usually motorically and mentally retarded.

BOX 3.6
Is It Nature or Is It Nurture?

It may be good for us to pause for a moment in our discussion of the biological basis of development and think about the nature-nurture (or heredity-environment) issue that we mentioned in chapter 1. Earlier in this chapter we spoke of monozygotic twins, those twins who share the same hereditary material. Of particular interest are those monozygotic twins who were separated at birth and lived apart from each other. As you can imagine, differences between these twins would be due to the environment, or their nurture.

An ongoing study at the University of Minnesota (the Minnesota Study of Twins Reared Apart) has collected data on 60 such pairs of twins (Holden, 1987). Among the most interesting findings have been those relating to personality. Personality characteristics such as self-control, impulsiveness, conservatism, and need for achievement were highly similar for both twins, even though they grew up apart.

Among the many findings:

- Emotional reactions that seem long-lasting appear at birth.
- Adopted children whose biological parents are criminal were three times more likely to be arrested as adults.

- A sibling of a schizophrenic has a 12% chance of being afflicted, and an identical twin has a 30%-40% chance; schizophrenia affects about 1% of the population.

Yet we should not jump to conclusions about the genetic influence; genes need an environment for expression and the environment exercises a strong influence. For example, estimates are that 60% of this country's alcohol abusers come from families with no history of alcoholism. Other studies have shown that infants given up for adoption and raised by middle-class families have IQ scores about 20 points higher than peers who remained in the impoverished conditions into which they were born (Scarr, Weinberg, & Levine, 1986).

What can we conclude from these data? Both genes and the environment count. Genes provide a predisposition to certain behaviors and then the environment acts on that initial push, sometimes encouraging it, sometimes changing it. Remember: genes interact with the environment. To understand development and behavior, our guiding principle is heredity plus environment.

perhaps slightly stubborn, with a good sense of mimicry and rhythm. Since the severity of the defect varies, institutionalization of the child is no longer immediately recommended. Some youngsters develop better in the home, especially if the parents believe they can cope successfully.

Other Chromosomal Disorders

Down syndrome results from an extra chromosome. If you recall, the 23d pair of chromosomes are the sex chromosomes, XX for females, XY for males. Estimates are that one in every 1,200 females and one in every 400 males has some disorder in the sex chromosomes.

Occasionally a male will possess an XXY pattern rather than the normal XY. This is called *Klinefelter's syndrome,* and eventually it causes small testicles, reduced body hair, and possible infertility. Another pattern that appears in males is XYY, which may cause larger size and increased aggression. Heated controversy and inconclusive results have surrounded the study of the "super male."

Females occasionally possess an XO pattern (lack of a chromosome) rather than XX. This is called *Turner's syndrome* and is characterized by short stature, poorly developed secondary sex features (such as breast size), and usually sterility.

Jews of Eastern European origin are struck hardest by **Tay-Sachs disease,** which causes death by the age of 4 or 5. At birth the afflicted children appear normal, but development slows by the age of 6 months, and mental and motor deterioration begin. About 1 in every 25 Jews of Eastern European origin carries the defective gene, which is recessive; thus danger arises when two carriers marry. The disease results from a gene failing to produce an enzyme that breaks down fatty materials in the brain and nervous system. The result is that fat accumulates and destroys nerve cells, causing loss of coordination, blindness, and finally death.

Sickle-cell anemia, which mainly afflicts those of African descent, appeared thousands of years ago in equatorial Africa and increased resistance to malaria. Estimates are that 10% of the African-American population in the United States carry the sickle-cell trait. Thus, two carriers who marry have a 1 in 4 chance of producing a child with sickle-cell anemia.

The problem is caused by abnormal hemoglobin. The red blood cells of the afflicted person are distorted and pointed. Because of their shape they encounter difficulty in passing through the blood vessels. They tend to pile up and clump, producing oxygen starvation accompanied by considerable pain. The body then acts to eliminate these cells, and anemia results.

In the population of the United States, **cystic fibrosis** is the most severe genetic disease of childhood, with about 1 in 1,200 children being affected and 1 in 30 being carriers. The disease causes a malfunction of the exocrine glands, the glands that secrete tears, sweat, mucus, and saliva. Breathing is difficult because of the thickness of the mucus. The secreted sweat is extremely salty, often producing heat exhaustion. Cystic fibrosis kills more children than any other genetic disease. Today, if diagnosed early and treated properly, those who are afflicted can lead a fairly lengthy life.

Cystic fibrosis is deadly for several reasons: its causes remain unknown (although recent research has identified a suspect gene) and carriers cannot be detected. It is not until a child manifests the breathing and digestive problems characteristic of the disease that identification is possible. New research, however, offers hope.

Phenylketonuria (PKU) results from the body's failure to break down the amino acid phenylalanine, which then accumulates, affects the nervous system, and causes mental retardation. Most states now require infants to be tested at birth. If PKU is present, the infants are placed on a special diet that has been remarkably successful.

But this success has produced future problems. Women treated successfully as infants may give birth to retarded children because of a toxic uterine environment. Thus at the first signs of pregnancy, these women must return to a special diet. The "cured" phenylketonuric still carries the faulty genes.

Spina bifida (failure of the spinal column to enclose completely) is an example of a genetic defect caused by the interaction of several genes. During the first few weeks following fertilization, the mesoderm sends a chemical signal to the ectoderm that causes the beginnings of the nervous system. The process is as follows:

1. The chemical signal is sent from the mesoderm to the ectoderm.

2. A tube (the neural tube) begins to form, from which the brain and spinal cord develop.

3. Nerve cells are formed within the tube and begin to move to other parts of the developing brain.

4. These neurons now begin to form connections with other neurons.

5. Some of the neurons that don't connect with other neurons die.

If the neural tube does not close, spina bifida results, which can cause mental retardation.

While these are the more common and dramatic genetic diseases, other diseases also have, or are suspected of having, a strong genetic origin: diabetes, epilepsy, heart disorders, cancer, arthritis, and some mental illnesses.

Transition

In this chapter we explored the biological basis of our uniqueness. We were able to see the power and beauty of nature in establishing our genetic endowment as well as the growing influence of technology.

The genes provided by the mother and father unite to produce a new and different human being. Yet this new life still shows many of the characteristics of both parents. We saw how this newness and sameness challenged researchers for decades.

Beginning with the discoveries of Mendel and continuing with those of Watson and Crick, the secrets of hereditary transmission have intrigued scientists to this day. Today's work, building on our knowledge of DNA, provides hope for the future while simultaneously raising legal and ethical questions that have yet to be resolved.

Following fertilization—either by natural or external methods—there begins a 9-month period (at least for most children) that concludes with expulsion into the waiting world. It is this period that occupies us in chapter 4.

Key Ideas

1. Although there have been advances in both genetic and environmental research in recent years, we must remember that development results from the interaction of heredity and environment.

2. With infertility becoming a major problem, several new methods of external fertilization have received considerable attention.

3. The in vitro fertilization technique became possible after detailed information about the menstrual cycle was made available.

4. DNA is now recognized as the source of the genetic codes that are responsible for human development.

5. The Watson-Crick model has been the basis of knowledge about DNA; Mendel's model has been the basis of knowledge about the transmission of traits.

6. Many problems (such as Down syndrome) have been traced to genetic sources.

Key Terms

AID	In vitro fertilization
Blastocyst	Meiosis
Closed adoption	Menstrual cycle
Color blindness	Mitosis
Cystic fibrosis	Monozygotic
DNA	Nucleotides
Dominant	Open adoption
Down syndrome	Ovulation
External fertilization	Ovum
Extragenetic	Phenotype
Extrasomatic	Phenylketonuria
Fallopian tubes	Recessive
Fraternal	Sex-linked inheritance
Genetic	Sickle-cell anemia
Genotype	Sperm
Germinal choice	Spina bifida
Hemophilia	Tay-Sachs disease
Implantation	Zygote
Internal fertilization	

What Do You Think?

1. You may have begun your work in lifespan psychology with the idea that either heredity or environment was all-important. Do you still think that way? Or do you believe that one may be somewhat more important than the other?

2. There have been several controversies lately about surrogate mothers and the children they bear. Do you have any strong feelings about surrogacy? Can you defend it? Regardless of your personal feelings, can you present what you see as the pros and cons of surrogacy?

3. In your reading, you perhaps noticed that the process of in vitro fertilization depended on research findings from studies of the menstrual cycle. Can you explain this, paying particular attention to the administering of hormones and the timing of their administering?

4. James Watson and Francis Crick received a Nobel prize for their discovery of the double-helix structure of DNA. Why is the discovery of DNA so important in our lives? Can you think of anything you have read about in the newspapers or seen on television that derives from this discovery?

5. Given what you know about the role of heredity in development, how would you evaluate the importance of genetic counseling? If you were thinking of having children, and you were concerned about the genetic background of yourself or your partner, would you seek genetic counseling?

Suggested Readings

Sagan, Carl. (1977). *The dragons of Eden.* New York: Random House. Sagan's penetrating and well-written account of genes and their function offers an intriguing entry into the world of heredity. (Available in paperback.)

Watson, James. (1968). *The double helix.* Boston: Atheneum. This personal, colorful look at the discovery of DNA is guaranteed to hold your attention. If you are the least bit intimidated by the thought of reading about your genetic heritage, this book should eliminate your concerns. (Available in paperback.)

· *Chapter 4* ·

Pregnancy and Birth

As you read this book, a myth is being destroyed. In fact, several myths are being destroyed. The notion that babies know nothing at birth and are passive sponges has been totally disproved. We now know that newborns are amazingly competent. After all, they have been flourishing in a highly protected environment for nine months, an environment sometimes humorously called "the prenatal university." Today researchers are asking serious questions about the potential of prenatal life. The basic issue is this: can fetal enrichment (a fancy name for fetal education) produce a better baby?

As evidence of how seriously this topic is taken, books, kits, and videotapes are now available to expectant couples. One company advertises an automated fetal educational communication unit, which consists of a tape player with a speaker belt that can be strapped to the mother's abdomen (Poole, 1987). Cost: $244.95.

Is it fact or fancy to think that prenatal learning is a possibility? While we cannot as yet answer this question with certainty, several clues can help us. First, there is little doubt that the senses (hearing, taste, smell, touch, vision) develop during pregnancy. They do not appear instantly at birth. Taste and smell are present by 20 weeks; touch appears at about 25 weeks; fetuses respond to sound by about 27 or 28 weeks; brain life begins by the seventh month. EEGs (electroencephalograms) taken just before birth show brain waves similar to those of infants.

One of the leading centers of research into fetal life is at the University of North Carolina. Here Anthony DeCasper and his colleagues are attempting to piece together the puzzle of fetal learning. For example, they had infants suck on a nipple attached to a tape recorder. Fast sucking activated a recording of their mothers' voices, while slower sucking produced another woman's voice. The babies showed a preference for their mothers' voices, as indicated by fast sucking.

Taking these results one step further, DeCasper asked a group of pregnant women to read a children's story aloud twice a day for six weeks prior to their expected delivery day. At birth, the infants patterns showed that they preferred the familiar story to one they had never heard (DeCasper & Fifer, 1980). Obviously, there has been some fetal "learning." Results are sufficiently promising to stimulate continued research.

We'll first explore the prenatal world, that nine-month period that provides nourishment and protection and serves as a springboard for birth. Next, we'll turn to those agents that can influence prenatal development. These are both physical and psychological, and can be either positive or negative. We'll then look at birth itself, the completion of a journey that has seen remarkable development.

Finally, for various reasons, some fetuses can't endure this nine-month journey. These early births are called premature. In the past few years, great advances—technological, medical, and psychological—have resulted in more and more of these babies surviving.

Now let's enter the prenatal world.

The Prenatal World

While it may be difficult to imagine, you are the product of one cell, the *zygote,* or fertilized egg. Once the union of sperm and egg took place, it was only a matter of hours (about 24–30) before that one cell began to divide rapidly. The initial phase of this event occurred in a very protected world—the prenatal environment.

The fertilized egg must pass through the fallopian tube to reach the uterus, a journey of about seven days to travel five or six inches. Hormones released by the

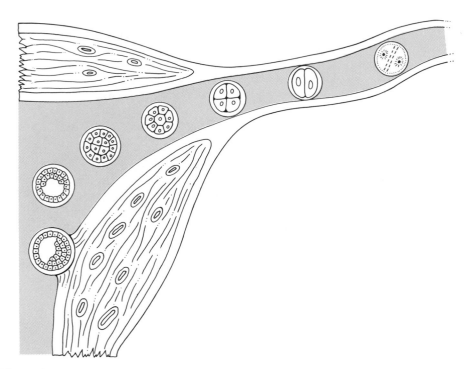

Figure 4.1 *Passage of the zygote into the uterus.*

ovary stimulate the muscles of the fallopian tube wall so that it gently pushes the zygote toward the uterus. During its passage through the fallopian tube, the zygote receives all of its nourishment from the tube. Figure 4.1 illustrates passage into the uterus and implantation.

Recent research (Beaconsfield, Birdwood, & Beaconsfield, 1983) has thrown considerable light on the implantation process. **Implantation** seems to occur in three phases:

- **Apposition,** during which the fertilized egg, now called a blastocyst, comes to rest against the uterine wall.

- **Adhesion,** during which the prepared surface of the uterus and the outer surface of the fertilized egg, now called the **trophoblast,** touch and actually "stick together."

- **Invasion,** during which the trophoblast digs in and begins to bury itself in the uterine lining.

Two events in this process are particularly remarkable:

1. During the invasion phase, the trophoblast penetrates the uterine lining only so far and then stops. The distance varies depending on the species. Why? As of now, we have no answers to this question.

2. Why doesn't the mother reject this invasive tissue? Again, there are no answers to this question.

We can identify three fairly distinct stages of prenatal development: germinal, embryonic, and fetal.

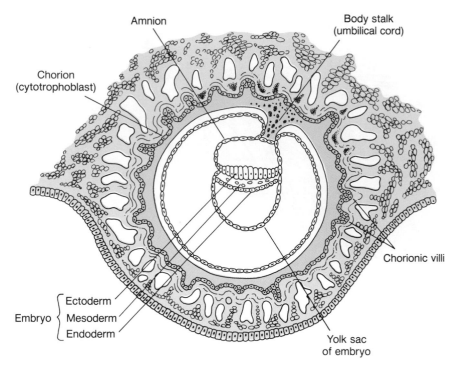

Figure 4.2 During the second week, the blastocyst becomes firmly implanted in the wall of the uterus and the placenta, umbilical cord, and the embryo itself begin to form from its outer layer of cells.

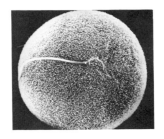

Fertilization through the embryonic period.

(a) The moment of fertilization.

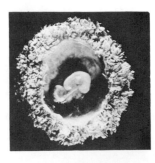

(b) This 4-week-old embryo now has a beating heart, body buds are beginning to emerge, and the eye region is becoming discernible.

The Germinal Period

The **germinal period** extends through the first two weeks. Since the passage through the fallopian tube takes seven days, the zygote is now one week old and called a *blastocyst*. During the second week, the blastocyst becomes firmly implanted in the wall of the uterus. From its outer layer of cells, a primitive **placenta,** an **umbilical cord,** and the **amniotic sac** begin to develop. The inner cell layer develops into the embryo itself. Figure 4.2 illustrates the developmental significance of the blastocyst.

The placenta and the umbilical cord serve a critical function during development. The placenta supplies the embryo with all its needs, carries off all its wastes, and protects it from danger. The placenta has two separate sets of blood vessels, one going to and from the baby through the umbilical cord, the other going to and from the mother through the arteries and veins supplying the placenta.

We can summarize the first two weeks following conception as follows:

Week 1: Movement of the zygote through the fallopian tube to the uterus; continued cell division.
Week 2: Blastocyst adheres to uterine wall; forms placenta, umbilical cord, amniotic sac.

The Embryonic Period

When the second week ends, the germinal period is complete. The **embryonic period,** from the third through the eighth week, sees the development of a recognizable human being. The nervous system develops rapidly, which suggests that the embryo at this time is quite sensitive to any obstructions to its growth.

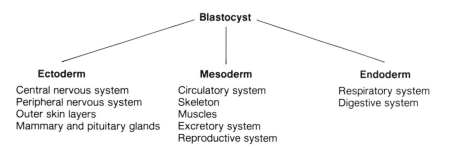

Blastocyst

Ectoderm
Central nervous system
Peripheral nervous system
Outer skin layers
Mammary and pituitary glands

Mesoderm
Circulatory system
Skeleton
Muscles
Excretory system
Reproductive system

Endoderm
Respiratory system
Digestive system

Figure 4.3 *Development from the three layers of the blastocyst.*

Perhaps the most remarkable change in the embryo is cellular differentiation. Three distinct layers are being formed: the **ectoderm,** which will give rise to skin, hair, nails, teeth, and nervous system; the **mesoderm,** which will give rise to muscles, skeleton, and the circulatory and excretory systems; and the **endoderm,** which will give rise to lungs, liver, and pancreas. (See Figure 4.3 for details.)

Usually by the completion of the fourth week, the heart begins to beat—the embryo's first movement. The accompanying photographs show that during the fifth week eyes and ears begin to emerge, bodily buds give clear evidence of becoming arms and legs, and the head area is the largest part of the rapidly growing embryo.

During the sixth and seventh weeks, fingers begin to appear on the hands, the outline of toes is seen, and the beginnings of the spinal cord are visible. While the germinal period saw a rapid increase in number and differentiation of cells, the embryonic period sees the formation of organs **(organogenesis)** (Sadler, 1985).

After eight weeks 95% of the body parts are formed and general body movements are detected. During these weeks embryonic tissue is particularly sensitive to any foreign agents during differentiation, especially beginning at the third or fourth week of the pregnancy.

We can summarize the embryonic period as follows:

> **Weeks 3+:** Rapid development of nervous system.
> **Week 4:** Heart beats.
> **Week 5:** Eyes and ears begin to emerge, bodily buds for arms and legs.
> **Weeks 6 and 7:** Fingers and toes, beginning of spinal cord.
> **Week 8:** About 95% of body parts differentiated—arms, legs, beating heart, nervous system.

The embryonic period can be hazardous for the newly formed organism. Estimates are that about 30% of all embryos are aborted at this time without the mother's knowledge; about 90% of all embryos with chromosomal abnormalities are spontaneously aborted (Travers, 1982).

At the end of this period there is a discernible human being with arms, legs, a beating heart, and a nervous system. It is receiving nourishment and discharging waste through the umbilical cord, which leads to the placenta. The placenta itself never actually joins with the uterus, but exchanges nourishment and waste products through the walls of the blood vessels (Guttmacher & Kaiser, 1986). The future mother begins to experience some of the noticeable effects of pregnancy: the need to urinate more frequently, morning sickness, and increasing fullness of the breasts.

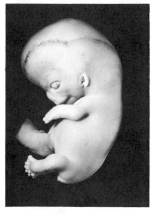

(c) This 45-day-old embryo has visible arms and legs, with the beginnings of toes and fingers. It is possible to detect eyes and ears in the rapidly growing head area.

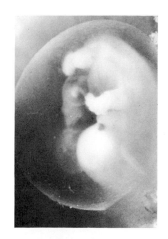

(d) Coming to the end of the embryonic period, this 7-week-old embryo has begun to assume a more human appearance. It is now about 1 inch in length with discernible eyes, ears, nose, mouth, arms, and legs.

Figure 4.4 **The fetus at 4½ months—a time of rapid growth and considerable activity.**

The Fetal Period

The **fetal period** extends from the beginning of the third month to birth. The sex organs appear during the third month and it is possible to determine the baby's sex. Growth is rapid during the fourth month to accommodate an increasing oxygen demand (Nilsson & others, 1987). The fetus produces specialized cells: the red blood cells to transport oxygen and white blood cells to combat disease. The fetus is now active—sucking, turning its head, and pushing with hands and feet—and the mother is acutely aware of the life within her. Figure 4.4 represents the fetus in the fourth month.

The fetus is able to hear sound—the silent world of the fetus is a myth. The fetus hears many environmental sounds: voices, stomach rumblings, and the pulsing of the mother's blood. Macfarlane (1977) reports on research in which investigators inserted small microphones through the cervix into the uterus beside the baby's head. Recordings from these microphones demonstrated considerable uterine noise. Macfarlane describes it as a whooshing noise punctuated by the sound of passing air.

By the end of the fifth month the baby is 10–12 inches long, and weighs about a pound. The fetus sleeps and wakes like the newborn does, even manifesting a favorite sleep position. Rapid growth continues in the sixth month, with the fetus gaining another two inches and one pound, but slows during the seventh month. Viability, the ability to survive if born, is attained.

Preparing For Birth

During the two final fetal months, organ development prepares the fetus for the shock of leaving the sheltered uterine world. The senses are ready to function (some are already functioning), and the brain at birth is 20%–25% of its adult weight.

The fetal period extends from about 8 weeks after conception until birth. The fetus grows rapidly both in height and weight. By the fourth month, the fetus is one-half its birth size, while the fourth to the fifth month is usually the peak growth period. During this time, the mother begins to feel movement. The fetus now swallows, digests, and discharges urine.

Visible sexual differentiation begins, and the nervous system continues to increase in size and complexity. After six months very few new nerve and muscle cells appear. At birth the nervous system must be fully functioning to ensure automatic breathing.

We can summarize these developments as follows.

Third month: sex organs appear
Fourth month: rapid growth, red blood cells, white blood cells; active sucking
Fifth month: fetus hears sound, sleeps, 10–12 inches long, 1 pound
Sixth month: rapid growth, 12–14 inches, 2 pounds
Seventh month: growth slows, viability attained
Eighth and ninth months: preparation for birth, senses ready to function, brain is 25% of adult weight

At the end of the ninth month, the fetus (just before birth) is about 20 inches long and weighs about 7 pounds, 6 ounces.

Table 4.1 Prenatal Development	
Name	**Development**
Zygote	Fertilization (union of sperm and egg)
	Cleavage (about 30 hr)
Blastocyst	Rapid cell division (about four days)
	Implantation (about sixth or seventh day)
Embryo	Begins at third week
	Central nervous system grows rapidly
	Heart begins to beat at about 28 days
	Digestive organs form during the second month
	Muscular system appears during the second month
	Sex differentiation at about seven weeks
	95% of body parts differentiated at the end of the eighth week
Fetus	Organs begin to function from 8–12 weeks
	Rapid growth during fourth month
	Viability at about 27 weeks
	Exercises functioning systems until birth

Most women begin to experience some discomfort as the time of birth approaches. The extra weight, body changes, and sheer effort of movement all contribute to this discomfort. During this period of preparation, the major influence on the growing child is its mother. If the mother is healthy, happy, and reasonably cautious, both she and her child will be the beneficiaries. Table 4.1 summarizes the course of prenatal development.

Development of the Senses

There has been considerable speculation about the role of the senses before birth. The developmental path is as follows (Hetherington & Parke, 1986):

Touch   Touch refers to the reaction to pressure, temperature, and pain, and seems to produce a generalized response. If a stimulus is applied to the fetus, there is a definite reaction. The specialized skin senses are capable of functioning long before birth.

Taste   Taste buds appear as early as the third fetal month and seem to be more widely distributed in fetal life than in adult life. Initially, taste buds appear on the tonsils, palate, and part of the esophagus. In the adult, taste cells are restricted to the tongue. Although the mechanism for taste is present before birth, the presence of the amniotic fluid limits the taste response until after birth.

Smell   Like taste, the neurological basis for smell appears before birth; thus there exists the possibility of response. But since the nasal cavity is filled with amniotic fluid, it is not likely that the sense of smell functions before birth. Premature infants, in the last month, can smell substances when air enters the nasal cavity.

Hearing   As previously noted, most fetuses can hear sound by the fourth month. The auditory mechanism is well developed structurally in later fetal life, but since the middle ear is filled with fluid, the fetus cannot respond to sounds of normal intensity. Strong auditory stimuli, however, produce a response.

BOX 4.1

What's Your Opinion?

As amazing as it may sound, it is now possible to operate on a fetus. Fetal surgery has saved several lives and promises a healthy future for many more. Two types of surgery are most common.

To cure a condition in which the brain regions fill with fluid and expand (called **fetal hydrocephalus**), surgeons now operate within the womb. They must pierce the woman's abdomen and uterine wall and then penetrate the fetal skull. They then insert a tube (*catheter*) into the brain region, draining it until birth.

In a second procedure the surgeon removes the fetus from the womb, operates to correct a blocked urinary tract in the fetus, then returns the fetus to the uterus, adds saline solution (salt water), and sews the uterus. This second technique would not be possible without drugs that prevent labor.

But here again we are faced with the prospect of medical technology outdistancing legal and ethical questions. Think of possible answers to these questions.

- Is the fetus also a patient?
- How can a surgeon weigh the risks to the mother against the potential of saving the fetus?
- If the mother refuses surgery for a treatable fetus, can legal action be taken against her?
- Can a physician who recommends against such surgery, knowing it is available, be charged with malpractice?

Hard questions. Consider the case of a San Diego woman who has been charged with contributing to the death of her infant son because she allegedly abused him as a fetus. The actual charge is of withholding medical treatment before birth; the child was born brain dead due to the mother's use of drugs during the prenatal period. What's your opinion?

Vision   There is general agreement that the absence of adequate retinal stimulation eliminates the possibility of true sight during prenatal life. Macfarlane (1977) states that while muscular development enables the fetus to move its eyes while changing body position, little is known about what or how much the fetus sees. By the end of pregnancy the uterus and the mother's abdominal wall may be stretched so thin that light filters through, exposing the fetus to some light and dark contrast. Visual development begins in the second week following fertilization and continues until after birth. At birth, the eye is sufficiently developed to differentiate light and dark.

This summary of fetal life leads to an inevitable conclusion: given adequate conditions, the fetus at birth is equipped to deal effectively with the transition from its sheltered environment to the extrauterine world.

Influences On Prenatal Development

When we speak of "environmental influences" on children, we usually think of the time beginning at birth. But remember: at birth an infant has already had nine months of prenatal living, with all of its positive and negative features.

Many women today benefit from the latest research and thinking about prenatal care. Diet, exercise, and rest are all carefully programmed to the needs of the individual woman. (Where women, especially pregnant teenagers, lack such treatment, the rates of prenatal loss, stillbirths, and neonatal [just after birth] mortality are substantially higher.)

BOX 4.2

Developmental Risk

Before we discuss the possibility of prenatal problems, the concept of developmental risk will help put this topic in perspective. The term **developmental risk** is used to describe children whose well-being is in jeopardy. Although the term has been widely used for only the past fifteen to twenty years, the problem itself has been a matter of concern since the 1920s (Kopp, 1987).

As you might guess, developmental risks include a range of biological and/or environmental conditions: from the very serious (genetic defects) to the less serious (mild oxygen deprivation at birth). Koop (1987) has summarized the findings of decades of research on biologically based risk:

- The earlier the damage (a toxic drug or maternal infection), the greater is the chance of negative long-term effects.
- Recent research has shown that prenatal risk accounts for the largest percentage of individuals with IQs below 50 and with severe neurological and sensory problems.
- A warm and supportive environment lessens any negative long-term effects.

- Risks that arise just before, during, and after birth show the most serious consequences during infancy and early childhood and gradually recede during the school years.
- With the exception of the most severe risks, the basic behaviors of infants remain unaltered but may be delayed. (For example, certain types of brain damage may remain undetected until school entrance.)
- The developmental outcomes of risk are often associated with the support that a child's environment offers.
- Developmental risk may have negative consequences for all behavior, although it is most frequently associated with lack of intellectual achievement.

As you can well imagine, these findings have important social, financial, and political implications. (You may want to discuss these in class.) They also offer hope for the at-risk child, showing that a sensitive environment can help.

Teratogens

Our major concern is with those substances that exercise their influence in the prenatal environment. Teratogenic agents, which are any agents that cause abnormalities, especially demand our attention. **Teratogens** that can cause birth defects are drugs, chemicals, infections, pollutants, or a mother's physical state, such as diabetes. The study of these agents is called teratology (Kelley-Buchanan, 1988).

To understand the extent of the damage caused by teratogens, consider these statistics.

1. *Two to three percent* of all live births show congenital malformations (serious defects that appear at birth).

2. At the end of the first year following birth, this number *doubles* due to the discovery of malformations not detected at birth.

Before specifying the major teratogens and the damage they can inflict, however, we'll suggest several general principles to help guide your reading. Developmental injury can be traced to two broad causes: *genetic* and *environmental* sources.

The effects of teratogens.

(a) Mothers may pass the AIDS virus to their babies during pregnancy, delivery, and through breast milk. While babies of AIDS-infected mothers may not necessarily receive the virus, those that do are likely to succumb by 5 or 6 years of age.

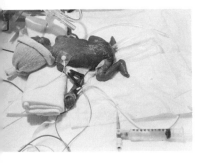

(b) This cocaine addicted baby was born prematurely and suffers from such behavior disturbances as tremulousness, irritability, and muscular rigidity.

Table 4.2   Teratogens, Their Effects and Time of Risk

Agent	**Possible Effects**	**Time of Risk**
Alcohol	Fetal Alcohol Syndrome (FAS), growth retardation, cognitive deficits	Throughout pregnancy
Aspirin	Bleeding problems	Last month, at birth
Cigarettes	Prematurity, lung problems	After 20 weeks
DES	Cancer of female reproductive system	From 3–20 weeks
LSD	Isolated abnormalities	Before conception
Lead	Death, anemia, mental retardation	Throughout pregnancy
Marijuana	Unknown long-term effects, early neurological problems	Throughout pregnancy
Thalidomide	Fetal death, physical and mental abnormalities	The first month
Cocaine	Spontaneous abortion, neurological problems	Throughout pregnancy
AIDS	Growth failure, low birth weight, developmental delay, death from infection	Before conception, throughout pregnancy, during delivery and breast feeding
Rubella	Mental retardation, physical problems, possible death	First three months, may have effects during later months
Syphilis	Death, congenital syphilis, prematurity	From five months on
CMV	Retardation, blindness, deafness	Uncertain, perhaps 4–24 weeks
Herpes simplex	CNS damage, prematurity	Potential risk throughout pregnancy and at birth

Think for a moment how these agents affect a child's life. In some cases, as we shall see, the problem may be sufficiently severe to cause the child to be institutionalized. In others, the defect may strain the relationship between parents and child. Table 4.2 summarizes several of the more common teratogenic agents and the time of greatest potential risk.

Infectious Diseases

Only three viruses have been positively identified as causing malformations.

German Measles (Rubella)   When pregnant women hear the name **German measles** (the technical term is *rubella*), they become worried, and for good reason. German measles is typically a mild childhood disease caused by a virus. Children who become infected develop a slight fever and perhaps swollen glands behind the ears. A rash usually appears at about the second or third day. By the fourth or fifth day all of the symptoms have usually disappeared.

For pregnant women, however, the story is quite different. Women who contract this disease may give birth to a baby with a defect: congenital heart disorder, cataracts, deafness, mental retardation. The risk is especially high if the disease appears early in the pregnancy.

If this happens during the first four weeks of the pregnancy, there is more than a 50% chance that the baby will be born with a major defect. Estimates of the relationship between damage and timing are as follows (Sadler, 1985):

50% chance if the infection occurred during the first four weeks of pregnancy

22% following infection in the 5th to 8th week

7% in the 9th to 12th week

6% in the 13th to 16th week

BOX 4.3

The Special Case of AIDS

AIDS (Acquired Immune Deficiency Syndrome) is caused by a virus that invades the baby's immune system, making it vulnerable to infections and life-threatening illnesses. We know today that the virus can be passed from an infected mother to her baby during pregnancy, during delivery, and occasionally through breast milk (Kelley-Buchanan, 1988). Passing the AIDS virus from mother to child is not inevitable. Estimates are that the virus is transmitted from 30% to 50% of the time. Thus 50% to 70% of these fetuses remain unaffected.

What happens when the virus is transmitted? While data are not yet conclusive, a condition known as AIDS embryopathy may result. This causes growth retardation, small head size, flat nose, widespread and upward slanted eyes, among many other characteristics. Also associated with this disease are higher rates of preterm deliveries, low birth weight, and miscarriage.

These conclusions are still tentative as researchers focus upon this new problem.

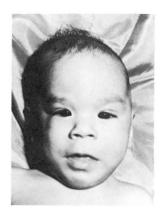

(c) Babies born to women who drank heavily during their pregnancies may manifest distinctive characteristics such as those shown in this photo.

Any woman who has had German measles as a child cannot catch it a second time. She is immune. But it is wise to have a blood test taken to be on the safe side. The American Medical Association recommends that any woman of childbearing age who has not been vaccinated for German measles be immunized. These women should then avoid pregnancy for at least three months.

Cytomegalovirus (CMV) **Cytomegalovirus** can cause damage ranging from mental retardation to blindness, deafness, and even death. One of the major difficulties in combatting this disease is that it remains unrecognized in pregnant women. Consequently, we do not know the difference in outcome between early and late infection.

Herpes Simplex **Herpes simplex** infection usually occurs during birth, and the child develops the symptoms during the first week following the birth. The eyes and nervous system are most susceptible to this disease.

Chemicals/Hormones

The impact of chemicals is difficult to assess, mainly because of the large number of drugs available and used by women before they realize they are pregnant. In a study conducted by the National Institute of Health, researchers discovered that the pregnant women had taken nine hundred different drugs. Only 20% of the women in this study took no drugs at all during their pregnancy (Sadler, 1985).

Thalidomide During the early 1960s, **thalidomide** was popular in West Germany as a sleeping pill and an antinausea measure that produced no adverse reactions in women. In 1962, physicians noticed a sizable increase in children born with either partial or no limbs. Feet and hands were directly attached to the body. Other outcomes were deafness, blindness, and occasionally mental retardation. In tracing the cause of the outbreak, investigators discovered the mothers had taken thalidomide early in their pregnancy.

DES (diethylstilbestrol) In the late 1940s and 1950s, **DES** (a synthetic hormone) was administered to pregnant women supposedly to prevent miscarriage. It was later found that the daughters of the women who had received this treatment were more susceptible to vaginal and cervical cancer. These daughters also experienced more miscarriages when pregnant than would be expected. Recent suspicions have arisen about the sons of DES women: they seem to have more abnormalities of their reproductive systems.

Here are some facts about teratogens that you may find useful to help understand their actions.

1. The extent of the damage caused by teratogens is directly linked to the stage of embryonic development. As we have mentioned repeatedly in these two chapters, timing is critical.

2. Teratogens act in highly specific ways.

3. The effect of a teratogen depends on an individual's genetic makeup. Different individuals will react differently to the same drug.

4. Finally, not all birth defects are caused by teratogens.

As knowledge has spread of the damaging effect of these agents, women have grown more cautious once they realize they are pregnant. We know now that these agents pass across the placenta and affect the growing embryo and fetus. We also know that prenatal growth is more susceptible to damage at certain times (the embryo is especially sensitive). Figure 4.5 illustrates times of greater and lesser vulnerability.

Maternal Nutrition

As you are well aware, the fetus depends on its mother for nourishment. Most women today are keenly aware that a proper diet will help them to give birth to a healthy, happy baby. When you consider the rapidity of prenatal growth (especially from two to seven months), you can understand the importance of a mother's diet, both for her and the child she is carrying.

Most doctors offer the following guide to weight gain for pregnant women:

- If the woman is of normal weight, try to restrict weight gain to 22–28 pounds.

- If the woman is underweight, up to 30 pounds is acceptable.

- If the woman is overweight, the gain should not exceed 16 pounds.

Remember: the baby itself accounts for only one-third or less of the weight gain.

Baker and Henry (1987) recommend that pregnant women should plan to add 300 calories to their regular diets, including calories from the following basic four food groups: (1) milk and dairy products, (2) meat or protein equivalent, (3) fruit and vegetables, and (4) bread and cereal.

The woman's physician will usually recommend supplements such as additional protein, iron, calcium, sodium, fiber, and vitamins. We have previously mentioned the dangers of alcohol use and cigarette smoking. Coffee, tea, and soft drinks should be ingested with caution.

The effects of drugs, disease, and diet, while dramatic, are not the only influences on prenatal development. How a woman feels about her pregnancy is also highly significant.

Maternal Emotions

As Macfarlane (1977, p. 15) says, there are only two ways to have a baby, vaginally or by cesarean section, but each birth is as unique as the woman herself. In a much quoted study, Ferreira (1960) administered an attitude questionnaire to women who were 36 weeks pregnant. He later observed their babies in the hospital nursery and discovered a significant correlation between the mother's emotions during pregnancy and her baby's behavior.

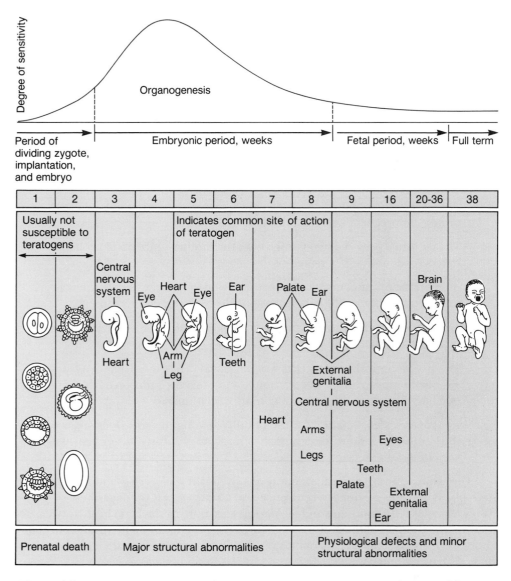

Figure 4.5 *Teratogens and the timing of their effects on prenatal development. The danger of structural defects caused by teratogens is greatest early in embryonic development. This is the period of organogenesis, which lasts for several months. Damage caused by teratogens during this period is represented by the dark-colored bars. Later assaults by teratogens typically occur during the fetal period and, instead of structural damage, are more likely to stunt growth or cause problems of organ function.*

Mothers who were unhappy about their pregnancy and those who feared that they might accidentally harm their babies had "deviant" youngsters who were restless, irritable, or had feeding difficulties or bowel problems. Maurer and Maurer (1988) conclude that the fetus is not perfectly insulated from the mother's stress. Unless the stress that the mother experiences is unusually severe and prolonged, the effects on the fetus are usually of short duration.

There is no direct evidence that a mother's emotions affect prenatal growth. Nevertheless, data continue to accumulate that suggest that a woman under stress releases hormones that may influence prenatal development. While a definite link between maternal emotions and prenatal growth and even later neonatal behavior is still lacking, it is possible to trace a pattern of events. Stress activates the mother's autonomic nervous system to produce hormones, which enter the mother's blood, cross the placenta, and enter the fetal blood stream (Travers, 1982).

Women adjust to pregnancy differently. Since it is a condition that affects the total system, there is an immediate biological difference: some women tire more easily than others and require more sleep and rest. Women differ in their more obvious physical reactions, such as nausea and vomiting: some react better by eating several small servings than two or three large meals. Some women begin their pregnancies with feelings of depression, while others avoid depression completely. How can we explain these differences?

- The events surrounding the pregnancy: career status, money, whether or not the pregnancy was expected or wanted.

- The woman's personal experience with the mother-child bond probably reflects the mother's personality.

- Another major influence on the mother's personality and subsequent attitude toward the child is her relationship with the child's father.

- The mother's acceptance of pregnancy also affects her specific attitudes toward the unborn child.

- The psychological journey that women travel. They usually move from a time of intense self-preoccupation to a gradual recognition of the new person with whom they form a complex relationship.

- The mother's expectation for the child is also significant. Does she see the child as an independent human being who will forge his or her own way, or as an extension of herself?

The woman, as an individual, interprets pregnancy as a crisis and an abnormal state of illness or as a normal occurrence and a state of health. Regardless of pregnancy, everyday life continues and most babies are born normal and healthy because their mothers coped with emotional situations without harming themselves or their child. Perhaps Nilsson and his colleagues (1987) offer the best advice when they suggest that the pregnant woman live her usual life but avoid excesses.

Nevertheless, prenatal problems arise, and today's diagnostic techniques often enable early detection of these difficulties.

Fetal Problems: Diagnosis and Counseling

When a prenatal problem is suspected, both diagnostic procedures and counseling services are available. Among the diagnostic tools now available are the following:

Amniocentesis   **Amniocentesis** is probably the technique you have heard most about. It entails inserting a needle through the mother's abdomen, piercing the amniotic sac, and withdrawing a sample of the amniotic fluid. (Amniocentesis may be done from the 15th week of pregnancy on.) The fluid sample provides information about the child's sex and almost 70 chromosomal abnormalities. For example, spina bifida (see chap. 3) produces a raised level of a protein called *alpha-fetoprotein (AFP),* which may be detected by amniocentesis (Guttmacher & Kaiser, 1986).

In a **fetoscopy,** a tiny instrument called a fetoscope is inserted into the amniotic cavity, making it possible to see the fetus. If the view is clear, defects of hands and legs are visible. (Fetoscopy is usually performed after the 16th week.)

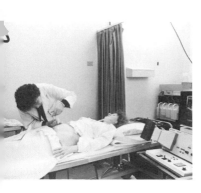

Here a pregnant woman is undergoing amniocentesis. Amniotic fluid is withdrawn and analyzed to determine sex and any chromosomal abnormalities. Amniocentesis may be done from the 15th week onward.

```
┌──────────────────────────────────────────────────────────────────────┐
│                              BOX 4.4                                    │
├──────────────────────────────────────────────────────────────────────┤
│                        Reactions to Pregnancy                           │
├──────────────────────────────────────────────────────────────────────┤
```

In your reading about pregnancy and birth, several viewpoints are apparent.

1. Women can think of these nine months as a natural extension of their femininity and go through this period as gracefully as possible.
2. Women can think of these nine months as an abnormal time in their lives, with the physical and psychological consequences that implies.
3. Woman can think of these nine months as a test of their mental and physical strength, ignoring discomfort and the need for medication.

It seems to us (two males, by the way!) that most women (by that we mean healthy women who have a medical prediction of an uneventful pregnancy) should treat this time as normally as possible, engaging in typical activities as fully and as long as possible. Certain safeguards should be observed, of course, such as avoiding alcohol and cigarettes, and eating nutritional foods.

Many women today, often with the prospective father, participate in prenatal classes that include information and exercise that are designed to help them through the birth. If labor pains become intense, however, women should feel no guilt about requesting medication.

Chorionic Villi Sampling (CVS)   The outer layer of the embryo is almost covered with chorionic villi, fingerlike projections that reach into the uterine lining. A catheter (small tube) is inserted through the vagina to the villi and a small section is suctioned into the tube. **Chorionic villi sampling** is an excellent test to determine the fetus' genetic structure and may be performed beginning at 8 weeks, usually between 8 and 12 weeks.

Ultrasound   **Ultrasound** is a relatively new technique that uses sound waves to produce an image that enables a physician to detect structural abnormalities. Useful pictures can be obtained as early as 7 weeks. Ultrasound is frequently used in conjunction with other techniques such as amniocentesis and fetoscopy (Sadler, 1985).

About 1% of infants suffer from some genetic defect, while another 0.5% suffer from defective chromosomes. As a result, prenatal testing is steadily becoming more common, especially for older women. Testing and counseling are intended to help couples who are concerned about the possibility of inherited problems.

For example, children born with cystic fibrosis or sickle-cell anemia acquire these diseases from parents who are both carriers. Tests are now available to determine if a person is a carrier of a particular genetic disease. If both potential partners are carriers, the chances of children acquiring the disease can be calculated. The counselor would then explain how severe the problem is, what treatment is available, and what the developmental outcomes would be.

Greater access to prenatal testing and genetic counseling raises several ethical and legal issues, such as the following.

- Confidentiality. The issue of confidentiality includes the disclosure of information to third parties and the possibility of unauthorized individuals attaining access to private information stored in data banks.

- Autonomy. One of the major questions about genetic counseling is whether such programs should remain voluntary if there is a known history of family genetic problems. Thus far, opinion is firmly tied to the principle of autonomy: people should have freedom of choice about genetic services.

- Knowledge. Genetic counseling should help people become informed decision-makers about their own well-being. One way of accomplishing this, of course, is to provide as much information as possible. But consider this scenario for a moment: You are a genetic counselor and in the course of obtaining data about a specific problem, you discover that the supposed father is not in fact the biological father. What do you do? There is no easy answer. If you withhold this information, you could cause future problems. If you present it objectively, you could destroy a relationship.

Think about this. Do you have any other suggestions? Prenatal diagnosis and genetic counseling not only identify the existence of genetic defects but raise issues and questions for all involved.

The Birth Process

The odyssey that began approximately nine months earlier reaches its climax at birth. Before this moment arrives, the mother has to make certain decisions. Does she, for example, ask the physician to use an anesthetic, or does she want natural childbirth? Both methods have their advantages and disadvantages.

Natural childbirth provides an unforgettable experience for the mother (and father), but it is hard, painful work that some women prefer to avoid. The use of anesthesia prevents much of the birth pain, but the drug may affect the baby adversely, decreasing alertness and activity for days after birth (Maurer & Maurer, 1988).

Stages in the Birth Process

The mother usually becomes aware of the beginning of labor by one or more of these signs:

1. The passage of blood from the vagina

2. The passage of amniotic fluid from the ruptured amniotic sac through the vagina

3. Uterine contractions and accompanying discomfort

The first two clues are certain signs that labor has begun; other pains (false labor) are occasionally mistaken for signs of true labor.

Three further stages of labor can also be distinguished:

1. *Dilation.* The neck of the uterus (the cervix) dilates to about four inches in diameter. This is the process responsible for labor pains and may last for twelve or thirteen hours, or even longer.

Think of the baby at this stage as enclosed in a plastic cylinder. It is upside down in the mother's abdomen, with the bottom of the cylinder under the mother's rib and the tip buried deep in her pelvis.

The cervix is about one-half inch long and almost closed. Before the next stage, expulsion, occurs, the diameter of the cervix must be stretched to a diameter of four inches. (The comedienne Carol Burnett has said that the only way you can imagine this feeling is if you pulled your upper lip over your head!)

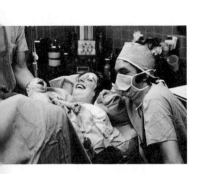

The presence of the father during birth can be a source of physical and psychological support for the mother. Fathers present during birth describe it as an "unforgettable experience."

BOX 4.5

Myths and Facts of Birth

In spite of what you may have heard, no one knows exactly what causes labor to begin or why it begins about 280 days after the first day of the last menstrual period. On the other hand, we do know certain things about birth (Guttmacher & Kaiser, 1986).

- Births are not equally distributed among the days of the week. Deliveries occur much more frequently on Monday through Friday than on weekends. The highest rate is on Tuesdays and the lowest on Sunday.
- Delivery rates seem to peak during August and September, with the lowest rates occurring in December and January.
- When a pregnancy ends spontaneously before the 20th week, a **miscarriage** has occurred. After the 20th week, the spontaneous end of a pregnancy is called a **stillbirth** if the baby is born dead, or a *premature birth* if the baby survives.
- Occasionally a pregnancy occurs outside of the uterus. Called an **ectopic pregnancy,** the fertilized egg attempts to develop outside the uterus, usually in one of the fallopian tubes. This is sometimes referred to as a *tubal pregnancy.* About one in every two hundred pregnancies is ectopic.
- Many women feel "down" a few days after giving birth. This is fairly common and is now thought to be a normal part of pregnancy and birth for some women. Called **postnatal depression,** this condition may be caused by the sudden change in hormones after birth. Also, a woman may have a sense of anticlimax after completing something she has anticipated for so many months. Women also tire easily and feel some tension about care of the baby, especially after a first birth. Postnatal depression usually leaves quickly.

---

2. *The expulsion.* Once the cervix is fully open, the baby passes through the birth canal. This phase typically lasts about 90 minutes for the first child, and about 30 to 45 minutes for subsequent children (although it can last longer). This is the phase when most fathers, if they are present, become exultant. They describe the appearance of the head of the baby (called the crowning) as an unforgettable experience.

With the cervix fully dilated, the fetus no longer meets resistance and the uterine contractions drive it through the birth canal. Uterine pressure at this stage is estimated to be 60 pounds.

It is important to note that the times for expulsion (90 minutes and 30–45 minutes) are averages. If this second stage of labor is prolonged— with no evidence of a problem—surgical intervention remains unnecessary. Occasionally, women spend five or six hours (or more) in a normal first birth.

3. *The afterbirth.* In the **afterbirth** stage, the placenta and other membranes are discharged. It is measured from the birth of the baby to the delivery of the placenta and may last only a few minutes. If the spontaneous delivery of the placenta is delayed, it may be removed manually. Figure 4.6 illustrates the birth process.

For most women, the birth process, as painful as it may be, proceeds normally. Occasionally, however, problems arise.

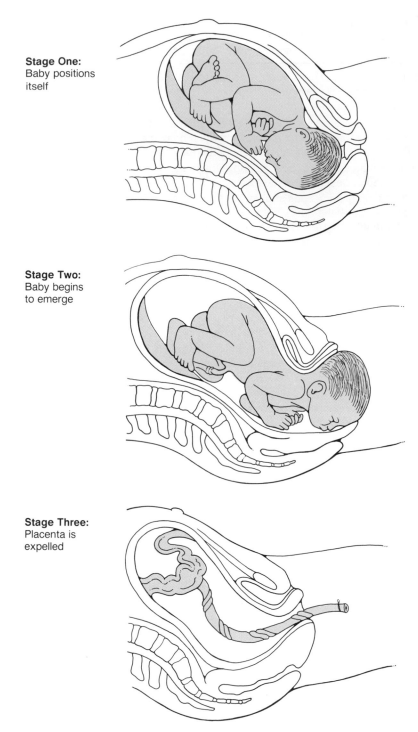

Stage One:
Baby positions
itself

Stage Two:
Baby begins
to emerge

Stage Three:
Placenta is
expelled

Figure 4.6 Stages in the birth process.

Birth Complications

Birth can sometimes be exceptionally difficult, even dangerous. The following are a few of the more common complications.

Breech Birth
About four out of every hundred babies are born feet first, or buttocks first, while one out of a hundred are in a crosswise position (transverse presentation). These are called **breech births.**

Forceps Delivery
Occasionally, for safety, the physician will withdraw the baby with forceps during the first phase of birth. A **forceps delivery** presents some danger of rupturing blood vessels or causing brain damage.

A decision about a forceps delivery depends on two conditions: those involving the fetus and those related to the mother. Is the fetus in such distress that there is a dangerous slowing of the heart rate? Is the baby in the correct position? Has the mother sufficient strength for the final push?

Cesarean Section
If for some reason the child cannot come through the birth canal, surgery is performed to deliver the baby through the abdomen, called **cesarean section.** Although now fairly safe, this operation is considered major surgery and is not recommended unless necessary. About 15% of all live births are cesarean, a figure many consider to be excessive.

Prematurity
About seven out of every hundred births are premature, occurring less than 37 weeks after conception. Fortunately, today it is possible to simulate womb conditions so that the correct temperature and humidity, bacteria control, and easily digestible food can be provided for the child. Still, prematurity presents real dangers, ranging from mental deficiency to death. (We shall shortly discuss this topic in more detail.)

Anoxia (Lack of Oxygen)
If something during the birth process should cut the flow of oxygen to the fetus, there is the possibility of brain damage or death. There is a substantial need for oxygen during birth because pressure on the fetal head can cause some rupturing of the blood vessels in the brain. After the umbilical cord is cut, delay in lung breathing can also produce **anoxia.** Failure here can cause death or brain damage.

Controversy surrounds infants who have experienced anoxia, survived, but show evidence of mental dullness. Does this cause long-term developmental impairment? Sameroff (1975) has reviewed the literature concerning delivery and birth complications and the pertinent studies of anoxia. Investigators assumed that early cerebral oxygen deprivation would cause later intellectual difficulty, so youngsters were studied during infancy, at 3 years of age, and finally at 7 years.

A definite pattern emerged: a few days after birth infants seemed impaired on visual, sensorimotor, and maturational levels. At 3 years, studied with perceptual-motor, cognitive, personality, and neurological tests, they showed lower than normal cognitive functioning and an improved performance on the other items. By 7 years, significant IQ differences had disappeared. Sameroff concludes that anoxia is a poor predictor of later intellectual functioning and that socioeconomic characteristics still remain the best single predictor of future adjustment.

The Rh Factor

Rh factor refers to a possible incompatibility between the blood types of mother and child. If the mother is Rh-negative and the child Rh-positive, miscarriage or even infant death can result. During birth some of the baby's blood inevitably enters the mother's bloodstream. The mother then develops antibodies to destroy fetal red blood cells. This usually happens after the baby is born, so the first baby may escape unharmed. During later pregnancies, however, these antibodies may pass into the fetus' blood and start to destroy the red blood cells of an Rh-positive baby.

Estimates are that about 10% of marriages are between Rh-negative women and Rh-positive men. Today, a protective vaccine has almost eliminated the possibility of Rh incompatibility when Rh-negative women are identified. In a case where the first baby's blood causes the mother to produce antibodies, blood transfusions may be given to the baby while still in the uterus.

Childbirth Strategies

Most babies escape complications and experience little if any birth difficulty. To help the newly born child adjust to a new environment, Leboyer (1975) believes that we must stop "torturing the innocent." Traditionally, newborns encounter a cold, bright world that turns them upside down and slaps them. Leboyer advocates a calmer environment. He suggests extinguishing all lights in the delivery room except a small night light, and making the room silent at the time of birth. Immediately after birth, the child is placed not on a cold metal scale, but on the mother's abdomen, a natural resting place. After several minutes the child is transferred to a basin of warm water. Leboyer claims that this process eases the shock of birth and that babies are almost instantly calm and happy.

Another technique, called **prepared childbirth,** or the Lamaze method after French obstetrician Fernand Lamaze, has become extremely popular with the medical profession. For several sessions women are informed about the physiology of childbirth and instructed in breathing exercises. The technique is intended to relieve fear and pain by relaxation procedures.

A range of birth options is now available to couples. Some, for example, are choosing home births under the guidance of midwives, who are trained delivery specialists. About 50% of all nonhospital deliveries are by midwives. Some hospitals are providing birthing rooms, which have a more relaxed and homelike atmosphere than the typical delivery room. Still, between 95% and 99% of all births occur in hospitals.

The Special Case of Prematurity

The average duration of pregnancy is 280 days. Occasionally, however, some babies are born early; they are premature or preterm, often called "preemies." Formerly these babies had high mortality rates, but with today's sophisticated technology their chances of survival are much greater. Before we discuss the condition of these babies and the reasons for their early appearance, let's establish some pertinent facts.

Facts About Prematures

In 1949 the World Health Organization identified premature infants as those weighing 2,500 grams or less (i.e., about 5 1/2 pounds or less). This figure was problematic, however, since some babies are naturally small but perfectly healthy.

In 1961, the WHO redefined **prematurity** to include those infants with a birth weight of 1,500 grams (about 3 pounds) or less, and who were born before 37 weeks gestation. Thus two criteria were suggested: (1) low birth weight, and (2) immaturity.

Within this definition, two additional classifications are possible (Spreen, Tuppet, Risser, Tuokko, & Edgell, 1983):

1. Infants born before 37 weeks whose weight is appropriate for their age; these are called *preterm AGA*—Appropriate for Gestational Age.

2. Those born before 37 weeks whose weight is low for their age; these are called *preterm SGA*—Small for Gestational Age.

A third classification has recently been proposed—very low birth weight (VLBW), which is defined as below 1,500 grams (about 3 pounds).

Causes of Prematurity

About 5%–8% of all infants in North America and Europe can be classified as premature. Although it is still impossible to predict which women will begin labor prematurely, prematurity has been linked to certain conditions (Avery & Litwack, 1983).

Once a woman has given birth prematurely, the risk of prematurity in the next pregnancy is about 25%. If two pregnancies have ended prematurely, the risk in the third pregnancy rises to 70%. Is this tendency to prematurity inherited? To date, there is no evidence pointing to a genetic connection.

Multiple births—twins or triplets—usually produce babies whose birth weights are lower than that of a single baby. This condition results in prematurity and accounts for about 10% of premature births.

There are signs that *multiple abortions* performed in the second trimester increase the risk of prematurity.

Age has been identified as a correlate of prematurity. If the mother is under 17 and over 35, the risk is substantially increased.

Low socioeconomic status is also a frequent accompaniment. In underdeveloped countries as many as one infant in four is born prematurely. In the United States more premature babies are born to poor than affluent women. The reasons remain a mystery, although frequent pregnancies, maternal malnutrition, and poor (if any) prenatal care may be responsible.

Smoking is a significant factor in any discussion of prematurity. Avery and Litwack (1983) state that, regardless of social class, cigarette smoking is associated with infants of low birth weight. The relationship between prematurity and smoking is found with those who smoke one pack per day. For those women who smoke more than one pack per day, the chances of a baby of low birth weight more than doubles.

Alcohol also increases the likelihood of prematurity. Women who consume alcohol daily during their pregnancy can produce damage in their babies.

Fetal alcohol syndrome (FAS), which came into prominence in 1973, consists of four clusters or clinical features (Vorhees & Mollnow, 1987):

1. Psychological functioning, which may include mild to moderate retardation, irritability, hyperactivity, and possible learning disabilities

2. Growth factors, primarily growth retardation

Tale 4.3 Premature Survival Rates*		
Birth Weight (Grams)	**Percentage Surviving**	
	1977	**1981**
500–600	0	14
601–700	4	14
701–800	23	52
801–900	44	64
901–1000	42	77
1001–1400	87	92
over 1500	99+	99+

*Note: Figures based on survival at two Boston Hospitals.
From Mary Ellen Avery and Georgia Litwack, *Born Early*. Copyright © 1983 Little, Brown and Company, Boston, MA.

3. Physical features such as small head, and possible defects in limbs, joints, face, and heart

4. Structural effects, which may include major malformations

About 60% of American women drink. For those taking 14 drinks per week while pregnant the chance of having an FAS baby rises to 30%.

Other causes of prematurity include maternal infection, cervical problems, high blood pressure, unusual stress, diabetes, and heart disease.

As Avery and Litwack (1983) note, even when all of these causes are enumerated, it still is impossible to explain exactly what happened in any given pregnancy. These authors emphasize that having a baby early is not usually anyone's fault.

A particularly interesting fact about prematures (one that has changed in the past few years) relates to outcome. Early outcome studies indicated that the incidence of major handicaps for prematures ranged from 10% to 40%. (These handicaps include mental retardation, cerebral palsy, serious vision defects.) Recent studies in industrialized nations have shown a reduced rate of problems, from 5% to 15%. We may conclude, then, that preterm birth and low birth weight do not normally place the baby at severe risk.

We can offer nothing but encouragement in this discussion of prematurity. Table 4.3 illustrates the reason for our optimism.

Guidelines for Parents

Although the new technology designed for prematures is marvelous, these babies need to sense parental love. This might seem next to impossible, given the technological nature of the premature nursery.

Here are some guidelines parents of prematures can follow (Harrison, 1983).

*   *Try to understand the baby.* Begin by observing carefully, learning what upsets and soothes. How does the baby respond to different types of stimulation? How long does it take to calm the baby after some upset? What kinds of clues are being given to signal discomfort (changes in skin color, muscular reaction, breathing rate)?

*   *Use as much body contact as possible.* Since these babies came into the world early, they often seem physically insecure (when compared to the normal infant after birth). Touching the baby with the whole hand on back or chest and stomach often relaxes the premature. Massaging both relaxes and shows affection.

- *Talk to the baby.* Studies have repeatedly shown that prematures, while seemingly unresponsive, show better rates of development when exposed to the mother's voice as often as possible.

When the premature infant can be taken from the incubator and given to the parent, a delicate moment has arrived. Some parents find it difficult to react positively to a premature; they feel guilty, occasionally harbor feelings of rejection, and must fight to accept the situation. They are simply overwhelmed. Usually this reaction passes quickly. On the occasion of this initial contact, parents should have been well prepared for holding a baby that is still entangled in wires and tubes.

If you think our discussion is overly optimistic, consider the conclusions of Goldberg and DiVitto (1983). Of the 150,000 premature babies born in the United States each year:

With advances in the treatment of prematures (temperature control, nutrition) the outlook for these babies has greatly improved. Psychological insights into the development of prematures have led to the conclusion that parental support and stimulation are needed during the baby's hospitalization to insure that attachment proceeds as normally as possible.

> Almost all preterms weighing over 3 1/2 pounds survive.
> Of those weighing between 2 1/2 and 3 1/2 pounds, 80%–85% survive.
> Of those weighing between 1 1/2 and 2 1/2 pounds, 50%–60% survive.

Though these children may differ from full-term babies in the early days of their development, most of these differences will eventually disappear. Most prematures will reach developmental levels similar to those of full-term babies. The only difference is that it takes premature babies a little longer to get there.

What can we say about the future development of these infants? Can we predict which youngsters will have later problems? If we eliminate known hazards—genetic defects and congenital malformations—prediction becomes less certain. One conclusion, however, seems inevitable: the younger and smaller the infant, the greater is the risk for later difficulties.

We can best summarize this brief discussion by quoting Avery and Litwack:

❖ *The outlook for normal development has improved for all infants, including those born prematurely. Very small infants continue to have risks for some problems that relate to the reasons for their premature birth, or to the difficulties they may encounter during the precarious days in intensive care. Overall, 90% of them will be normal. The remaining 10% will for the most part represent the infants who are the smallest or most premature. Some will have major disabilities, such as cerebral palsy or blindness. Some will have lesser disabilities such as crossed eyes, wheezing, and perhaps some motor incoordinations. Continuing research into the causes of these problems and means of prevention remains a high priority (1983, pp. 18–19).*

Transition

In this chapter you have seen how a human being begins its journey through the life span. Nature's detailed choreography of prenatal development provides a remarkably complex yet elegantly simple means of ensuring the survival of generations. Once conception occurs, uniting the genetic contribution of both mother and father, the developmental process is underway, sheltered for the first nine months in the protective cocoon of the womb.

For some, the process is interrupted and the uterine stay is shortened. Today these prematures have a heightened chance of survival and of normal physical and psychological development thanks to technological advances.

But what comes next? Once the child—at this point called a neonate—enters the world, what can we expect? Answering this question leads us into the world of infancy, a world of rapid growth, startling changes, and just plain excitement. We begin our explanation of this world in the next part of the book.

Key Ideas

1. Implantation of the zygote (the fertilized egg) occurs in successive stages.
2. The embryonic period is a time of great sensitivity.
3. The fetal period is a time of preparing for birth and life outside the womb.
4. Developmental risk refers to those children who are particularly susceptible to biological or environmental problems.
5. Teratogens are those agents that cause serious abnormalities.
6. Major technological advances have made possible the detection of prenatal problems.
7. Birth, a natural process for most women, occasionally involves complications.
8. Premature babies today show remarkably improved survival rates.
9. Women, as individuals, respond uniquely to their pregnancies, both physically and psychologically.
10. A woman's emotions during pregnancy may affect her baby's behavior at birth.
11. As genetic problems have been identified, genetic counseling has assumed great importance for many couples.

Key Terms

Adhesion
Afterbirth
Amniocentesis
Amniotic sac
Anoxia
Apposition
Breech birth
Cesarean section
Chorionic villi sampling
Cytomegalovirus
DES (diethylstilbestrol)
Developmental risk
Ectoderm
Ectopic pregnancy
Embryonic period
Endoderm
Fetal alcohol syndrome
Fetal hydrocephalus
Fetal period
Fetoscopy

Forceps delivery
German measles
Germinal period
Herpes simplex
Implantation
Invasion
Mesoderm
Miscarriage
Organogenesis
Placenta
Postnatal depression
Prematurity
Prepared childbirth
Rh factor
Stillbirth
Teratogens
Thalidomide
Trophoblast
Ultrasound
Umbilical cord

What Do You Think?

1. There has been considerable discussion recently about the possibility of prenatal learning. Where do you stand on this issue? Be sure to support your opinion with facts from this chapter.

2. You probably have heard how careful women must be when they are pregnant. They are worried about such things as smoking and drinking. Do you think we have become too nervous and timid about these dangers? Why?

3. Turn back to Table 4.2. From your own knowledge (relatives and friends, for example), indicate which of these teratogens you think are most common. Select one and explain why you think it is a common threat and what could be done to help prevent it. (Lead paint is a good example.)

4. There are significant medical and ethical questions surrounding such techniques as fetal surgery. Assume that a physician does not inform a woman that her fetus is a good candidate for fetal surgery. The baby is stillborn. Is the doctor guilty of malpractice or any crime? Can you think of other examples?

Suggested Readings

Avery, Mary Ellen, and Georgia Litwack. (1983). *Born early*. New York: Little, Brown. Vital data, good writing, and a positive outlook make this an excellent introduction to the topic of prematurity.

Guttmacher, Alan, and Irwin Kaiser. (1986). *Pregnancy, birth, and family planning*. New York: Signet. This popular book, available in paperback, has been a best-seller for many years. It carefully presents detailed information about pregnancy and birth.

Olds, Sally. (1983). *The working parents survival guide*. New York: Bantam. A thoughtful, practical, and readable account of the problems and pleasures of working mothers (and fathers).

PART 3

Infancy

· *Chapter 5* ·

The Competent Infant

In these next two chapters you enter the world of infancy. It is a world that has changed dramatically in the last several years. While the newborn was once viewed as "mewling and puking in the nurse's arms" (Shakespeare, *As You Like It*), we are now in danger of treating an infant as "superbaby."

There are those who see a baby as a finely tuned computer, ready to begin such sophisticated activities as reading. If you think we exaggerate, consider this program for infants. In 1983, Glen Doman sponsored a Better Baby Reading Program (marketed through Encyclopedia Britannica). The program is designed to help parents teach their children to read before they reach the age of 3. For your money you would receive:

> *How to Teach Your Baby to Read,* a book by Doman
> A children's storybook
> A set of flash cards with different length words consisting of large red
> letters and smaller black letters

Several years ago Doman had been involved in attempts to raise the developmental levels of brain-damaged children. His work is based on a theory of neurological organization, which he has since applied to teaching one-year-old infants to read. Using Doman's program, infants will supposedly read words on cards and recognize (at 12 months) the differences between similar four- and five-letter words.

Quite different from these ideas was the prevailing view of infancy until the 1960s. Infants were considered passive, little more than absorbent sponges. They came into the world with few if any abilities, unable to see or interact with others.

These two extreme interpretations of infancy provide a sounding board against which you can test the theories and research presented in this chapter. When you are finished with your reading you should be able to take a stand on an important question: just how competent are infants?

To help you understand an infant's world, you'll also examine the methods used to assess the well-being of infants following birth. Then you will be asked to trace various aspects of infant development: physical, motor, perceptual, cognitive, linguistic, and social/emotional.

In this chapter you will also begin to discern the issues and themes discussed in chapter 1. For example, the issue of sensitive periods is particularly important here. Do the events that occur in infancy leave an indelible mark that lasts a lifetime?

Newborn Abilities

In the days immediately following birth until about two weeks to one month, the infant is called a **neonate**. During this period babies immediately begin to use their abilities to adapt to their environment.

Among the most significant of these abilities are the following:

- They display clear signs of *imitative* behavior at 7–10 days. (Try this: stick out your tongue at a neonate of about 10 days—the baby will stick its tongue out at you!)

- Infants can *see* at birth and, if you capture their attention with an appropriate object (such as a small, red rubber ball held about 10 inches from the face), they will track it as you move the ball from side to side. Infants react to color between 2 and 4 months of age, while depth perception appears at about 4 to 5 months.

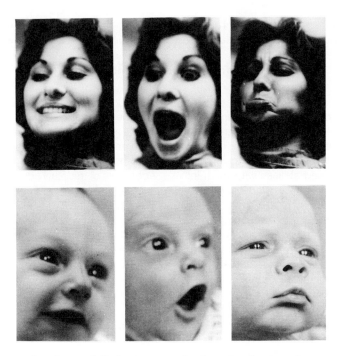

Sample photographs of a model's happy, surprised, and sad expressions, and an infant's corresponding expressions.

- Infants can *hear* at birth (and prenatally) and also can perceive the direction of the sound. In a remarkably perceptive yet simple experiment, Wertheimer (1962) sounded a clicker (similar to those children play with) from different sides of a delivery room only 10 minutes after the infant's birth. The infant not only reacted to the noise but attempted to turn in the direction of the sound.

- Infants are *active seekers* of stimulation. Although their main efforts are devoted to controlling bodily functions, such as breathing and heart rate, they occasionally, for brief moments, pay close attention to the environment. These moments signal their search for stimulation; they indicate an ability to process information.

- Infants manifest a willingness, even a need, *to interact* with other human beings (Hinde, 1987). Compelling evidence suggests that interpersonal relationships have a powerful effect on development. (See Suomi, Harlow & Novak, 1974, for studies of rhesus monkeys and the impact of altered relationships on their development.) What has startled investigators of human relationships is the active role that infants play in controlling their parents' responses, a phenomenon called *reciprocal interactions* (Hinde, 1979).

- Infants, using these abilities, begin their efforts to master the developmental tasks of infancy: learning to take solid foods, learning to talk and walk.

As impressive as these accomplishments are, we must still be rather cautious in overestimating an infant's abilities. Remember: different parts of our brains mature at different rates. The brain fibers for hearing develop early but the brain parts for understanding what is heard develop much later.

BOX 5.1

What's Your Opinion?

Before you continue your reading, try to formulate your idea of how competent a newborn baby is. In one view, infants are neither empty, unresponsive beings nor superbabies designed for instant greatness. Newborn babies bring abilities with them into the world, a cluster of competencies that not only enables them to survive but permits them to engage in a wider range of activities than was previously suspected (Brazelton, 1987). This change in thinking, however, should not create unrealistic expectations. Babies are babies, and to expect them to perform verbal gymnastics, for example, is extremely shortsighted.

Such expectations are not sensible and they may also be emotionally harmful. As we know, babies "tune into" their environments and are quite skillful in detecting the mood of those around them. Adherents of this view advise parents to let babies be babies, using the natural methods that have proven successful: love, attention, and warmth (Brazelton, 1987).

You have just read about attempts to develop superbabies. Which view do you think is most realistic? Which will most help infants to fulfill their potential? What's your opinion?

Physical and Motor Development

As Tanner (1978) has stated, growth is far from being a simple and uniform process of becoming taller or heavier. Growing children experience changes in shape and body composition and in the distribution of tissues. For example, the infant's head at birth is about a quarter of total body length, but in the adult it is about one-seventh. Different tissues (muscles, nerves) also grow at different rates, and total growth represents a complex series of changes. Here are some facts about an infant's physical status you may find interesting (Eichorn, 1979).

- At birth, water accounts for about 75% of an infant's body weight, fat for 11%, and protein for 11%. By comparison, the adult female's weight consists of about 52% water, 31% fat, and 16% muscle, while the male's is 62% water, 14% fat, and 33% muscle.

- An infant's muscles are small and watery; the skeleton is soft and pliable, which is why infants can't support themselves.

- The nervous system, while still immature, is much more advanced.

- Their senses, as we have seen, work quite well.

At birth, of course, the infant must assume those life-sustaining functions that the mother had provided for nine months.

❖ *The major changes are in the respiratory system (the infant begins to breathe in order to oxygenate its own blood) and in the ingestive system (the baby now obtains food through its mouth rather than through the umbilical cord). Most of the other bodily functions have been working previously, though most were supplemented or assisted by the placenta and the mother's body prior to delivery (Lamb & Campos, 1982, p. 38).*

Any analysis of an infant's physical growth must take into consideration the important role that reflexes play.

Table 5.1 Neonatal Reflexes		
Name of Reflex	**How Elicited**	**Description of Response**
Plantar grasp	Pressure applied to bottom of foot	Toes tend to curl
Babinski	Gently stroke sole of foot	Toes spread in an outward and upward manner
Babkin	Press palm of hand while infant lies on back	Mouth opens; eyes close
Rooting	Gently touch cheek of infant with light finger pressure	Head turns toward finger in effort to suck
Sucking	Mouth contacts nipple of breast or bottle	Mouth and tongue used to manipulate (suck) nipple
Moro	Loud noise or sudden dropping of infant	Stretches arms and legs and then hugs self; cries
Grasping	Object or finger is placed in infant's palm	Fingers curl around object
Tonic neck reflex	Place infant flat on back	Infant assumes fencer position: turns head and extends arm and leg in same direction as head
Stepping	Support infant in upright position; soles of feet brush surface	Infant attempts regular progression of steps

Neonatal Reflexes

When a stimulus repeatedly elicits the same response, that behavior is usually called a **reflex.** Popular examples are the eye blink and the knee jerk. All of the activities needed to sustain life's functions are present at birth (breathing, sucking, swallowing, elimination). These reflexes serve a definite purpose: the gag reflex enables infants to spit up mucus; the eye blink protects the eyes from excessive light; an antismothering reflex facilitates breathing. The more important neonatal reflexes are listed in Table 5.1.

Although all infants are born with these reflexes and abilities, not all possess them to the same degree. For example, some neonates demonstrate much weaker reflex action than others, a condition that affects their chances of surviving. Consequently, efforts to develop reliable measures of infant behavior have increased sharply.

Neonatal Assessment Techniques

There are three basic classifications of neonatal tests that assess infant reflexes and behavior.

1. *The Apgar.* In 1953 Virginia Apgar proposed a scale to evaluate a newborn's basic life signs. The **Apgar** is administered one minute after birth, and repeated at three-, five-, and ten-minute intervals. Using five life signs—heart rate, respiratory effort, muscle tone, reflex irritability, skin color—an observer evaluates the infant by a three-point scale. Each of the five dimensions receives a score of 0, 1, or 2. (0 indicates severe problems, while 2 suggests an absence of major difficulties.)

2. *Neurological Assessment.* There are three purposes of the **neurological assessment:**

▲ Identification of any neurological problem.

▲ Constant monitoring of a neurological problem.

▲ Prognosis about some neurological problem.

Table 5.2 Physical Growth—Infancy		
Age (months)	Height (in.)	Weight (lb.)
3	24	13–14
6	26	17–18
9	28	20–22
12	29.5	22–24
18	32	25–26
24	34	27–29

Each of these purposes requires testing the infant's reflexes, which is critical for neurological evaluation and basic for all infant tests (Prechtl, 1977).

3. *Behavioral Assessment.* The Brazelton Neonatal Behavioral Assessment Scale (named after T. Berry Brazelton) has become a significant worldwide tool for infant assessment. While the Brazelton tests the reflexes we have just discussed, its major emphasis is on how the infant interacts with its environment. In other words, it also permits us to examine the infant's behavior. Brazelton believes that the baby's state of consciousness is the single most important element in the examination (1984).

All three of these assessment techniques provide clues about the infant's ability to function on its own. Tests such as these, plus careful observation, have given us much greater insight into infant development. These tests have also helped us to realize that infants are much more competent than we previously suspected.

To summarize, then, we can say that infant growth occurs at a rate unequalled in any other developmental period, with the possible exception of adolescence. If you recall, the average weight at birth is about seven pounds and length is about 20 inches. Table 5.2 illustrates height and weight increases during this period.

Brain Development

The initial stages of the embryonic period saw the appearance of three distinct layers: ectoderm, mesoderm, and endoderm. As we have seen, the ectoderm acts as the basis for the developing nervous system. Estimates are that the baby's brain, at birth, is about a quarter of its adult size. At 6 months it is about 50% of its adult weight, 60% at 1 year, 75% at 2 1/2 years, 90% at 6 years, and 95% at 10 years. The developmental pattern is seen in Figure 5.1.

We know, however, that different parts of the brain develop at different rates. For example, the cerebellum, which controls the fine motor activities, develops more slowly than those brain areas that control the muscles of the upper body. During the first month after birth the cortical areas of the brain show an increasing thickness. Brain development seems to follow a definite schedule. First to show signs of development is the motor area, followed by the sensory region, the auditory area, and then the visual region. Consequently, we should expect motor development to proceed rapidly, which is just what happens.

Motor Development

Motor development proceeds at a steady rate. Since it occurs in a head to feet direction, an infant's ability to control its head signals advancing motor development. The following are several important characteristics of motor control.

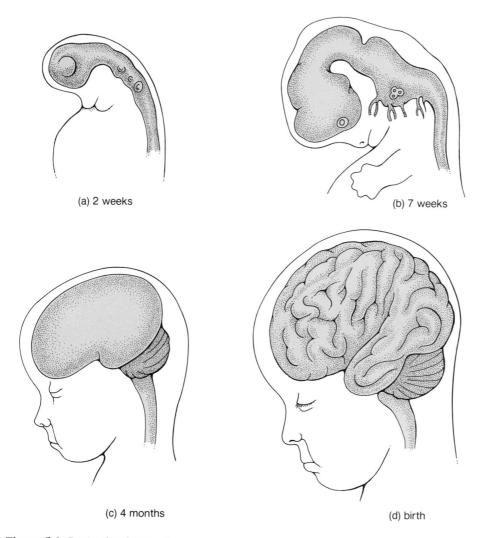

(a) 2 weeks

(b) 7 weeks

(c) 4 months

(d) birth

Figure 5.1 Brain development.

Head Control

The most obvious initial head movements are from side to side, although the one-month-old infant occasionally lifts its head when in a prone position. Four-month-old infants can hold their heads steady while sitting and will lift their head and shoulders to a ninety-degree angle when on their abdomens. By the age of six months, most youngsters can balance their heads quite well.

Locomotion: Crawling and Creeping

Crawling and creeping are two distinct developmental phases. In **crawling,** the infant's abdomen touches the floor and the weight of the head and shoulders rests on the elbows. Locomotion is mainly by arm action. The legs usually drag, although some youngsters push with their legs. Crawling appears in most youngsters after age 7 months.

    Creeping is more advanced than crawling, since movement is on hands and knees and the trunk does not touch the ground. Creeping appears after age 9 months in most youngsters.

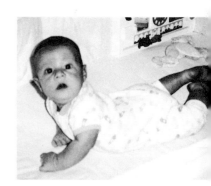

Note the steady development of body control in this picture, especially the head and upper body. Control of the lower body and legs follows by several months.

Most descriptions of crawling and creeping are quite uniform. The progression is from propulsion on the abdomen to quick, accurate movements on hands and knees, but the sequence is endlessly varied. Youngsters adopt a bewildering diversity of positions and movements that can only loosely be grouped together.

Locomotion: Standing and Walking
After about age 7 months, infants when held will support most of their weight on their legs. Coordination of arm and leg movements enables babies to pull themselves up and grope toward control of leg movements. The first steps are a propulsive, lunging forward. Gradually a smooth, speedy, and versatile gait emerges. The world now belongs to the infant.

Once babies begin to walk, their attention darts from one thing to another, thus quickening their perceptual development (our next topic). Tremendous energy and mobility, coupled with a growing curiosity, push infants to search for the boundaries of their world. It is an exciting time for youngsters but a watchful time for parents, since they must draw the line between encouraging curiosity and initiative and protecting the child from personal injury. The task is not easy. It is, however, a problem for all aspects of development: what separates unreasonable restraint from reasonable freedom?

Table 5.3 summarizes milestones in motor development.

Neonatal Problems

Not all infants enter the world unscathed. Occasionally the developmental sequence that we have just discussed does not run smoothly. Among the most prominent of possible problems are the following.

Failure-to-Thrive (FTT)
The weight and height of **failure-to-thrive** infants consistently remain far below normal. They are estimated to be in the bottom 3% of height and weight measures. They account for about 3% of pediatric hospital admissions.

There are two types of FTT: those with organic causes (the problem is usually some gastrointestinal disease and this category accounts for 30% of FTT cases) and those with nonorganic causes (no physical cause for the problem can be found).

Nonorganic FTT is difficult to treat and the problem may originate in family interactions (see chap. 13). The seriousness of this problem is evident from the outlook for FTT infants: almost 50% of them will continue to experience physical, cognitive, and behavioral problems.

Sudden Infant Death Syndrome (SIDS)
Discussion of the survival value of reflexes introduces one of the most perplexing problems facing both parents and researchers, **sudden infant death syndrome** (SIDS). Estimates are that 10,000 infants 2–4 months old die each year from SIDS. There is little warning, although almost all cases were preceded by mild cold symptoms and usually occurred in late winter or early spring.

SIDS rarely occurs before age 1 month or after age 1 year; most victims are between 2 and 4 months old. Deaths peak between November and March. Once again boys are more vulnerable, in this case by a 3-to-2 margin.

Most youngsters somewhere in the seven-to-nine-month period begin to pull themselves up to a standing position. Their legs are now strong enough to support them in a standing position.

Table 5.3	Milestones in Motor Development				
Age	**Head Control**	**Grasping**	**Sitting**	**Crawling-Creeping**	**Standing-Walking**
3 months	Can lift head and chest while prone.	Grasps objects; briefly holds objects; carries objects to mouth.	Sits awkwardly with support.		
6 months	Holds head steady while sitting; balances head.	Develops skillful use of thumb during this period.	Transition from sitting with slight support to brief periods without support.		
9 months	Infant has established head control.	Coordinates hand activities; handedness begins to appear.	Good trunk control; sits alone steadily.	Crawling movements appear (trunk touches floor); begins about 7 months.	
12 months		Handedness pronounced; holds crayon; marks lines.	Can sit from standing position.	Creeping (trunk raised from floor) begins at 9–10 months and continues until steady walking.	Can stand holding onto something; will take steps when held; by 12 months will pull self up.
15 months					Stands alone; begins to walk alone.
18 months					Begins to run.

SIDS is particularly devastating for parents because of the lack of warning. These infants are apparently normal. Parents put them in a crib for a nap or for the night and return later to find them dead. (Hence the common name "crib death.") You can imagine the effect this has on parents, particularly the feelings of guilt: What did I do wrong? Why didn't I look in earlier? Why didn't I see that something was wrong? Today, special centers have been established to counsel grieving parents.

While no definite answers to the SIDS dilemma have yet been found, current research points to a respiratory problem. Control of breathing resides in the brain stem, and autopsies indicate that the infant may not have received sufficient oxygen while in the womb. (This condition is called fetal hypoxia.)

Sleeping Disorder

Most **sleeping disorders** are less serious than FTT or SIDS. Nevertheless, infant sleeping problems negatively affect growth and trouble parents. As Ferber (1985) states:

❖ *The most frequent calls I receive at the Center for Pediatric Sleep Disorders at Children's Hospital in Boston are from a parent or parents whose children are sleeping poorly. When the parent on the phone begins by telling me "I am at the end of my rope" or "We are at our wits' end" I can almost predict what will be said next.*

Children suffering from sleep disorders ordinarily have nothing organically wrong with them. Changing their activities before sleep usually cures the problem.

Ferber goes on to explain that the parent has a child between the ages of 5 months and 4 years who does not sleep readily at night and wakes repeatedly. Parents become tired, frustrated, and often angry. Frequently, the relationship between the parents becomes tense.

Usually a sleep problem has nothing to do with parenting. There is also usually nothing wrong with the child, either physically or mentally. Occasionally problems do exist: a bladder infection, or, with an older child, emotional factors causing night terrors. A sleep problem is not normal and should not be waited out.

Neonates sleep more than they do anything else (usually from 14 to 15 hours per day) and have three sleep patterns: light or restless, periodic, and deep. There is little if any activity during deep sleep (about 25% of sleep). Neonates are mostly light sleepers, with the brain wave patterns associated with dreaming (although infants probably do not dream).

Some internal clock seems to regulate sleep patterns, with most deep sleep spells lasting approximately twenty minutes. At the end of the second week, a consistent and predictable pattern emerges. Neonates sleep in short stretches, about seven or eight per day. The pattern soon reverses itself and infants assume an adult's sleep schedule.

Normal sleep patterns are as follows:

- *During the first month,* infants reduce their seven or eight sleep periods to three or four and combine two of them into one lasting about five hours. (If parents are lucky, this longer period will occur after a late evening feeding.) Infants are thus establishing a night and day routine.

- *During the third month,* sleep patterns are usually regulated. Morning and afternoon naps supplement night stretches ranging from six or seven to as much as ten or eleven hours.

- *At five or six months,* infant sleep patterns change. As part of the night sleep cycles, the infant is usually wide awake at dawn, bursting with excitement, and demanding an audience.

- *By eight months,* naps are shorter and some infants may require only one in the afternoon. A problem that most infants begin to show at this age is a reluctance to go to bed at night. They now begin to sleep most of the night.

- *At twelve months,* napping may be difficult and infants begin to set their schedules; that is, they nap only when tired. There is continued resistance to go to bed at night, but once asleep they usually sleep through the night.

For an idea of normal sleep patterns, see Figure 5.2.

To determine whether a child has a sleeping problem, Ferber (1985) suggests these criteria: (1) the child's sleep patterns cause problems for parents or the infant; (2) obvious problems exist: an inability to sleep or, with older children, sleepwalking and sleep terrors; (3) more subtle symptoms are at work: excessively loud snoring may signal a breathing problem; the child is unable to go back to sleep after waking.

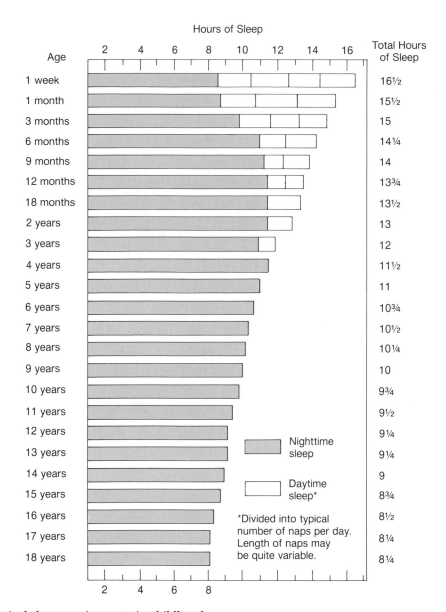

Figure 5.2 *Typical sleep requirements in childhood.*

Respiratory Distress Syndrome (RDS)

The last of the disorders to be discussed is **respiratory distress syndrome** (also called *hyaline membrane disease*). While this problem is most common with prematures, it may strike full-term infants whose lungs are particularly immature.

RDS is caused by the lack of a substance called surfactant, which keeps open the air sacs in the lungs. When surfactant is inadequate, the lung can collapse. Since most babies do not produce sufficient surfactant until the 35th prenatal week, you can see why it is a serious problem for prematures. (Only 10% of a baby's lung tissue is present at full-term birth.)

Full-term newborns whose mothers are diabetic seem especially vulnerable. Babies whose delivery has been particularly difficult also are more susceptible. The good news is that today 90% of these youngsters will survive and, given early detection and treatment, the outlook for them is excellent.

Perceptual Development

From what has been said so far, the current picture of an infant is that of an active, vibrant individual vigorously searching for stimuli. How do infants process these stimuli?

Answering this question moves us into the perceptual world. For babies not only receive stimuli, they interpret them. Before attempting to chart perceptual development, let's explore the meaning of perception in a little more detail.

The Meaning of Perception

Infants acquire information about the world and constantly check the validity of that information. This process defines perception: getting and interpreting information from stimuli. McCall (1979) describes an infant as a "stimulus-detection device" who attends to objects according to the perceptual information they contain.

Seeking information leads to meaning. Objects roll, bounce, squeak—in this way infants learn what objects are and what they do. During infancy, youngsters discover what they can do with objects, which furthers their perceptual development.

Remember: infants are born ready to attend to changes in physical stimulation. Stimuli presented frequently cause a decrease in an infant's attention (*habituation*). If the stimuli are altered, the infant again attends, indicating awareness of the difference. For example, if you show an infant a picture (flower, birds, anything attractive), the child is first fascinated, then becomes bored; the child has habituated. If you now change the picture, you again capture the child's attention.

But infants encounter a wide variety of objects, people, and events, all of which differ on many dimensions: color, size, shape, and so on. They must learn how to react to each.

Brooks and Lewis (1976) studied how infants responded to four different types of strangers, a male and female child, a female adult, and a female midget. In this way, facial configurations and height were varied. The infants reacted to the children by continuous looking and some smiling. They reacted to the midget with considerable puzzlement but no positive response such as smiling or movement toward her. They reacted to the adult by sporadic looking, averting their eyes, frowning, and even crying. Thus the infants used size and facial configuration cues.

We may conclude, then, that perception depends on both learning and maturation. An infant's perceptual system undergoes considerable development following birth, resulting both from greater familiarity with objects and events in the world and from growth.

Visual Perception

Humans are born able to see and quickly exhibit a preference for patterns. Recent research on vision report the following (Aslin, 1987):

- Studies show that **variable accommodation** (focusing on objects at various distances) appears at about age 2 months.

- **Binocular coordination** appears around 4 months. Studies indicate that there may be a critical period for the attainment of stereopsis (three-dimensional vision), since infants born with congenital esotropia (lack of ability to develop three-dimensional vision) have a greater chance of acquiring stereopsis if surgery is performed before the age of 2.

- Infants see *color* sometimes in the 2–4-month period. (A major difficulty in establishing an exact time for color recognition has been in separating color from brightness; it has only recently been overcome.)

- Individual differences in *visual tracking* ability exist at birth.

Visual Preference

Do infants prefer looking at some objects more than others? In an exciting yet simple series of experiments, Robert Fantz provided dramatic documentation of an infant's perceptual ability. Fantz (1961) states that the best indicator of an infant's visual ability is eye activity. Infants who consistently gaze at some forms more than others show perceptual discrimination; that is, there is something in one form that holds their attention.

Using a "looking chamber" in which an infant lies in a crib at the bottom of the chamber and looks at objects placed on the ceiling, Fantz could determine the amount of time that infants fixated on different objects.

He tested 30 infants age 1 week to 15 weeks on four pairs of test patterns: horizontal stripes and a bull's eye, a checkerboard and two sizes of plain squares, a cross and a circle, and two identical triangles. The more complex patterns attracted the infants' attention significantly longer than either the checkerboard and square or the triangle.

The next step involved testing to discover if infants preferred facial patterns. Three flat objects shaped like a head were used. One had regular features painted in black on a pink background; the second had scrambled features; the third had a solid patch of black at one end. The three forms were shown to 49 infants from 4 days old to 6 months old. Infants of all ages looked longest at the real face. The plain pattern received the least attention.

Fantz next tested pattern perception by using 6 objects, all flat discs six inches in diameter: a face, a bull's-eye, newsprint, red disc, yellow disc, and white disc. The face attracted the greatest attention, followed by the newsprint, the bull's-eye, and then the three plain colored discs (none of which received much attention). Infants, then, show definite preferences that are based on as much complexity as they can handle (human faces are remarkably complex).

Visual Adaptation

Studying visual development spurs speculation about how growing visual skill helps infants to adjust to their environment. Gibson and Walk (1960) in their famous "visual cliff" experiment reasoned that infants would use visual stimuli to discriminate both depth and distance.

The visual cliff is a board dividing a large sheet of heavy glass. A checkerboard pattern is attached flush to one half of the bottom of the glass, giving the impression of solidity. The investigators then placed a similar sheet on the floor under the other half, creating a sense of depth—the visual cliff (see Figure 5.3).

Thirty-six infants age 6 to 14 months were tested. After the infant was placed on the center board, the mother called the child from the shallow side and then the cliff side. Twenty-seven of the youngsters moved onto the shallow side toward the mother. When called from the cliff side, only 3 infants ventured over the depth. The experiment suggests that infants discriminate depth when they begin crawling. Thus, infants demonstrate visual ability at birth and quickly show signs of increasing visual skill. Infants at age 3 months also make primitive attempts to organize their visual surroundings and to integrate vision with other infant activities.

To conclude, we can state that by 2–4 months of age infant perception is fairly sophisticated. They perceive figures as organized wholes; they react to the relationship among elements rather than single elements; they perceive color; and complex rather than simple patterns fascinate them.

Cognitive Development

Can infants really think? If they can, what is their thinking like? Do they understand what is happening in the world around them? How do we explain the change in thinking from the newborn to the 2 year old? Answering these questions leads us again to the work of Jean Piaget, whose ideas were initially presented in chapter 2.

Piaget's Sensorimotor Period

Piaget (1967) states that the period from birth to language acquisition is marked by extraordinary mental growth and influences the entire course of development. Several developmental changes occur that reflect what Piaget calls the *decentering process* (not seeing yourself as the center of everything).

Egocentrism describes the initial world of children. Everything centers on them; they see the world only from their point of view. Very young children lack social orientation. They speak at and not to each other, and two children in conversation may be discussing utterly unrelated topics. Egocentric adults know that there are other viewpoints, but they disregard them. The egocentric child simply is unaware of any other viewpoint.

Sensorimotor Achievements

The remarkable changes of this period (about the first two years of life) occur within a sequence of six stages. Most of Piaget's conclusions about these stages were derived from observation of his own three children. (Jacqueline, Lucianne, and Laurent have become as famous in psychological literature as some of Freud's cases or John Watson's Albert.)

Stage 1 During the first stage children do little more than *exercise the reflexes* with which they were born. For example, Piaget (1952) states the sucking reflex is hereditary and functions from birth. Infants will suck anything that touches the

When infants begin to move things to get what they want, they are "coordinating their secondary schemata." This is a clear signal of advancing cognitive development.

Figure 5.3 A child's depth perception is tested on the visual cliff. The apparatus consists of a board laid across a sheet of heavy glass, with a patterned material directly beneath the glass on one side and several feet below it on the other.

lips; then sucking will occur when nothing touches the lips; then they actively search for the nipple. What we see here is the steady development of the coordination of arm, eye, hand, and mouth. Through these activities the baby is building a foundation for forming cognitive structures.

Stage 2   Piaget refers to Stage 2 (from about the first to the fourth month) as the stage of first habits. During Stage 2, **primary circular reactions** appear in which infants repeat some act involving their bodies. For example, they continue to suck when nothing is present. They continue to open and close their hands. There seems to be no external goal, no intent in these actions other than the pleasure of self-exploration. But infants are learning something about that primary object in their world: their own bodies.

Stage 3   **Secondary circular reactions** emerge during the third stage, which extends from about the fourth to the eighth month. During this stage, infants direct their activities toward objects and events outside themselves. Secondary circular reactions thus produce results in the environment, and not, as with the primary circular reactions, on the child's own body.

For example, Piaget's son, Laurent, continued to shake and kick his crib to produce movement and sound. He also discovered that pulling a chain attached to some balls produced an interesting noise, and he kept doing it. In this way, babies learn about the world "out there," and feed this information into their developing cognitive structures.

Stage 4   From about 8 to 12 months of age, infants **coordinate secondary schemes** to form new kinds of behavior. Now more complete acts of intelligence are evident (Piaget & Inhelder, 1969).

The baby first decides on a goal (finding an object that is hidden behind a cushion). The infant attempts to move objects to reach the goal. In Stage 4 part of the goal object must be visible behind the obstacle. Here we see the first signs of intentional behavior.

Stage 5   Tertiary circular reactions appear from 12 to 18 months of age. In the tertiary circular reaction there is again repetition, but it is repetition with variation. The infant is exploring the world's possibilities. Piaget thinks that the infant deliberately attempts to provoke new results instead of merely reproducing activities. Tertiary circular reactions indicate an interest in novelty for its own sake.

A continuing interest in novelty produces the curiosity that motivates continuous growth and change in an infant's cognitive processes. For example, how many times have you seen a baby standing in a crib and dropping everything on the floor? But listen to Piaget: watch how the baby drops things, from different locations and different heights. Does it sound the same when it hits the floor as the rug? Is it as loud dropped from here or higher? Each repetition is actually a chance to learn. Thanks to Piaget, you will be a lot more patient when you see this behavior.

Stage 6   During Stage 6 the sensorimotor period ends and children develop a basic kind of *internal representation*. A good example is the behavior of Piaget's daughter Jacqueline. At age 20 months, she approached a door that she wished to close, but she was carrying some grass in each hand. She put down the grass by the threshold, preparing to close the door. But then she stopped and looked at the grass and the door, realizing that if she closed the door the grass would blow away. She then moved the grass away from the door's movement and then closed it. She had obviously planned and thought carefully about the event before acting. Table 5.4 summarizes the accomplishments of the sensorimotor period.

Progress through the sensorimotor period leads to four major accomplishments:

1. *Object permanence:* children realize that there are permanent objects around them; something out of sight is not gone forever.

2. *A sense of space:* children realize there is a spatial relationship among environmental objects.

3. *Causality:* children realize there is a relationship between actions and their consequences.

4. *Time sequences:* children realize that one thing comes after another.

By the end of the sensorimotor period, children move from purely sensory and motor functioning (hence the name *sensorimotor*) to a more symbolic kind of activity.

Infants and Memory

As infants progress through these first two years, behavior appears that can be attributed only to memory. We have already mentioned how infants show habituation (boredom when viewing the same object).

Kagan and his colleagues (1978) believe that in the last half of the first year, changes in the central nervous system enable infants to recall events and to retain memories longer than they could during the first six months. Thus the growth of memory ability is a significant developmental accomplishment of the last half of the first year of life (Rovee-Collier, 1987).

Olson and Sherman (1983) summarize infant recognition memory as follows. During the first three months, infants show growing ability to retain what they have experienced for a relatively brief time (one to several days). From age 3 to 6 months fairly consistent patterns of memory are present—from 3 to 10 days. From age 6 to

Table 5.4	Outstanding Characteristics of the Sensorimotor Period		
The Six Subdivisions of This Period			
Stage 1.	During the first month the child exercises the native reflexes, for example, the sucking reflex. Here is the origin of mental development, for states of awareness accompany the reflex mechanisms.	Stage 4.	From 8 to 12 months, the child "coordinates secondary schemata." Recall the meaning of schema—behavior plus mental structure. During Stage 4, infants combine several related schemata to achieve some objective. For example, they will remove an obstacle that blocks some desired object.
Stage 2.	Piaget refers to Stage 2 (from 1 to 4 months) as the stage of *primary circular reactions*. Infants repeat some act involving the body, for example, finger sucking. (*Primary* means first, *circular reaction* means repeating the act.)	Stage 5.	From 12 to 18 months, *tertiary circular reactions* appear. Now children repeat acts, but not only for repetition's sake; now they search for novelty. For example, children of this age continually drop things. Piaget interprets such behavior as expressing their uncertainty about what will happen to the object when they release it.
Stage 3.	From 4 to 8 months *secondary circular reactions* appear; that is, the children repeat acts involving objects outside themselves. For example, infants continue to shake or kick the crib.	Stage 6.	At about 18 months or 2 years, a primitive type of representation appears. For example, one of Piaget's daughters wished to open a door but had grass in her hands. She put the grass on the floor and then moved it back from the door's movement so that it would not blow away.

12 months infants show joy when the mother returns; infants also tend to repeat first words, two practical reminders of their improving memory. From 12 to 24 months language usage and reactions to family, friends, and strangers testify to an active, competent memory. You will have noticed in discussing the latter stages of the sensorimotor period how language becomes increasingly important.

Language in Infancy

All children learn their native language at about the same time and in a similar manner. Here is the basic sequence of language acquisition:

> At about age 3 months children use sounds in a similar manner as adults.
> At about age 1 year they begin to use recognizable words.
> At about age 4 years they have acquired the complicated structure of their native tongue.
> In another two or three years they speak and understand sentences that they have never previously used or heard.

The specific sequence of language development appears in Table 5.5.

Table 5.5 The Language Sequence	
Language	**Age**
Crying	From birth
Cooing	5–8 weeks
Babbling	4–5 months
Single words	12 months
Two words	18 months
Phrases	2 years
Short sentences and questions	3 years
Conjunctions and prepositions	4 years

This 3-month-old infant is responding to its mother's face by smiling. In these interactions we see the roots of a child's psychosocial development.

Key Signs of Language Development

Table 5.5 describes the timetable of language acquisition until about age 4. Note that children combine words into sentences and use all categories of vocabulary (conjunctions and prepositions as well as nouns and verbs).

Several things signal difficulty in language acquisition. **Babbling** is a good example. When children babble they make sounds that approximate speech. For example, you may hear an "eee" sound that makes you think that the infant is saying "see." This is to be expected. Deaf children, however, continue to babble past the age when other children begin to use words.

If you have the opportunity, listen to a child's speech when single words begin to appear. You will notice a subtle change before the two-word stage. *Children begin to use one word to convey multiple meanings.* In the initial phase, for example, youngsters say "ball" meaning "give me the ball," "throw the ball," or "watch the ball roll." They have now gone far beyond merely labeling this round object as a ball.

When the *two-word stage* appears (about age 18 months), children initially struggle to convey tense and number. They also experience difficulty with grammatical correctness. Children usually employ word order ("me go") for meaning, only gradually mastering inflections (plurals, tense, possessives) as they begin to form three-word sentences. A youngster's efforts to inject grammatical order into language are a good sign of normal language development.

Sounds to Words

At about age 4 months, children make sounds that approximate speech. These increase in frequency until the children are about a year old, when they begin to use single words. After children commence using words, babbling still appears among the simple words.

We do not yet understand the relationship between babbling and word appearance. Babbling probably appears initially because of biological maturation. (Deaf children babble, which would seem to suggest that babbling does not depend on external reinforcement.)

Late in the babbling period, children use consistent sound patterns to refer to objects and events (Devilliers & Devilliers, 1978). These are called **vocables** and suggest children's discovery that meaning is associated with sound. For example, a lingering *l* sound may mean that someone is at the door. The use of vocables is a possible link between babbling and the first intelligible words.

At about age 1, the first words appear. Often called **holophrastic speech** (one word to communicate many meanings and ideas), it is difficult to analyze. These first words, or **holophrases,** are usually nouns, adjectives, or self-inventive words and often contain multiple meanings. "Ball" may mean not only the ball itself but "throw the ball to me."

Infants "tune into" the speech they hear and immediately begin to discriminate distinctive features. They also seem to be sensitive to the context of the language they hear; that is, they identify the emotional nature of speech. So the origins of language appear immediately after birth in infant gazes and vocal exchanges with those around them.

The precursors of language blend with babbling, which then merges into the first words, and is then continuous with the appearance of two words, phrases, and sentences. Remember: the period of single words is more than a time of merely accumulating more and more words. Although vocabularies increase, there are notable changes in both the kinds of words and the way in which they are used between ages 1 and 2. Counting words is a superficial and perhaps even deceptive method of tracing children's language development.

First Words

Children begin to use multiple words to refer to the things that they previously named with single words. Rather than learning rules of word combination to express new ideas, children learn to use new word forms. Later, combining words in phrases and sentences suggests that children are learning the structure of their language.

At about 2 years of age children's vocabularies expand rapidly and simple two-word sentences appear. They primarily use nouns and verbs (not adverbs, conjunctions, prepositions), and their sentences demonstrate grammatical structure. Although the nouns, adjectives, and verbs of children's sentences differ from those of adults, the same organizational principles are present. These initial multiple word utterances (usually two or three words: "Timmy runs fast") are called **telegraphic speech.** Telegraphic speech contains considerably more meaning than superficially appears in the two or three words.

Word order and inflection (changing word form: e.g., "word"/"words") now become increasingly important. During the first stages of language acquisition, word order is paramount. Children combine words without concern for inflections, and it is word order that provides clues as to their level of syntactic (grammatical) development.

Once two-word sentences are used, inflection soon appears, usually with three-word sentences. The appearance of inflections seems to follow a pattern: first the plural of nouns, then tense and person of verbs, and then possessives.

Vocabulary Growth

Vocabulary constantly expands. The range for each age indicates the growth for that period. Estimating vocabulary is extremely difficult since youngsters know more words than they articulate. Table 5.6 presents the approximate number of words that appear at various ages.

Note how frequently we have said that cognitive development and language development occur in relation to other people. This simple fact points to the critical role that social development plays in an infant's growth.

Table 5.7 illustrates several of the developmental highlights we have thus far discussed.

Now let's turn our attention to the early signs of emotional development.

Table 5.6   The Pattern of Vocabulary Development—Estimates

Age (years)	Number of Words	
	Low	High
1	2–3	4–6
2	50	250
3	400	2,000
4	1,200	6,000
5	1,500	8,000
6	2,500	10,000

Table 5.7   Developmental Characteristics of Infancy

Age (months)	Height (in.)	Weight (lb.)	Language Development	Motor Development	Cognitive (Piaget)
3	24	13–14	Cooing	Supports head in prone position	Primary circular reactions
6	26	17–18	Babbling–single-syllable sounds	Sits erect when supported	Secondary circular reactions
9	28	20–22	Repetition of sounds signals emotions	Stands with support	Coordinates secondary schemata
12	29.5	22–24	Single words— "mama," "dada"	Walks when held by hand	Same
18	32	25–26	3–50 words	Grasps objects accurately, walks steadily	Tertiary circular reactions
24	34	27–29	50–250 words, 2–3 word sentences	Runs and walks up and down stairs	Representation

Early Emotional Development

The study of emotions has had a checkered career in psychology. Interest in emotions and their development has risen to peaks of popularity and plunged to depths of neglect. Today there is once again a resurgence of enthusiasm for its study (Leventhal & Tomarken, 1986).

Smiling

One of the first signs of emotion is a baby's smile, which most parents immediately interpret as a sign of happiness. Two-month-old infants are often described as "smilers." While smiles appear earlier they lack the social significance of the smile that emerges at age 6 weeks. Babies smile instinctively at faces, real or drawn, which probably reflects the human tendency to attend to patterns.

Infants gradually learn that familiar faces usually mean pleasure, and smiling at known faces commences as early as the fifth month. Smiling seems to be a key element in securing positive reinforcement from those around the infant.

Bower (1977) has attempted to move beyond these general observations and notes that smiling has a history. Smiles "for no reason" appear soon after birth and are usually designated "false" smiles because they lack the emotional warmth of the true smile. By age 3 weeks the human female voice elicits a brief, real smile.

BOX 5.2
Language Acquisition: The Theories

Many of the phenomena that we have mentioned so casually are actually amazing accomplishments. For example, imitation does not seem to be the sole explanation of language development, since a child hears so many incorrect utterances. Imitation does not explain the child's seemingly intuitive grasp of syntax, nor the manner by which thoughts are translated into words. How can different surface structures convey an identical meaning?

Attempts to resolve these and similar issues have led to the formulation of four major theories of language development.

1. A *biological,* or *nativist,* explanation focuses on innate language mechanisms that automatically unfold. Language develops similarly under almost any conditions. For example, the language explosion seems to be a cross-cultural phenomenon. Eric Lenneberg (1967) is probably the most famous of the nativists.

2. A *cognitive* explanation views language as part of the youngster's emerging cognitive abilities. Language is a verbal clue to the complexity and level of a child's cognitive structures. Probably the most famous of the cognitive theorists is Piaget (1926).

3. A *psycholinguistic* interpretation attempts to explain how native speakers can understand and produce sentences that were never spoken or written. Children's mastery of their language depends on an intuitive knowledge of the language rules. Noam Chomsky (1957) is probably most widely associated with this theory.

4. A *behavioristic* explanation concentrates on language as a learned skill. Children utter sounds that are reinforced and shaped by the environment, especially parents and teachers, and gradually learn to make distinguishable sounds and to form correct sentences. B. F. Skinner, undoubtedly today's leading behaviorist, proposed a detailed behavioristic theory of language acquisition in one of his early books (1957).

By age 6 weeks the true social smile appears, especially in response to the human face. Bower states that babies smile at a conceptual age of 6 weeks, regardless of chronological age.

Why do infants smile? There are several possible explanations.

• Infants smile at human beings around them.

• Infants smile at any high contrast stimuli, thus eliciting attention from those around them. The infant then links the human face with pleasure.

• Infants smile at discovering a relationship between their behavior and events in the external world.

Several theories of emotional development have been proposed to explain this and other types of emotional development.

Theories of Emotional Development: A Summary
An early theory of emotional development was proposed by Bridges (1930). She believed that neonates demonstrated only the form of emotion: general excitement. As infants grow, specific positive and negative emotions appear: distress at age 3

weeks, anger grows out of distress at age 4 months, disgust from anger at age 5 months, and fear from disgust at about age 6 months. More recently, as researchers have observed specific emotions in the neonate, interest in Bridges' work has faded.

Izard (1978) is probably the theorist most identified with a belief that infants demonstrate specific emotions. Using an infant's facial expressions as the basis for his work, Izard states that emotions emerge as an infant needs them to adapt. He suggests the following pattern of emotional development (Izard & Malatesta, 1987):

- The newborn shows startle, interest, disgust, and distress.

- During the next four months, anger, surprise, and joy appear.

- Fear and shyness emerge during the period from 6 to 12 months.

There are those who disagree with Izard's reliance on facial expression. Sroufe (1979), for example, links emotional and cognitive development. As an infant's cognitive level changes, its ability to express emotion also changes. Sroufe's work has been criticized mainly because it does not explain how cognitive development leads to emotional expression. Table 5.8 summarizes these theories.

First Feelings

As you can tell from this brief excursion into explanations of emotional development, recent interest has yet to be matched by hard evidence. But given the changes in developmental research described in these first five chapters, it can be only a matter of time before the path of emotional development becomes less obscure.

We earlier noted how we view the infant today—as an active partner in development. We also recognize an infant's state with all of its meaning. Finally, we are aware of the number of abilities an infant brings into the world. Using these insights, Greenspan and Greenspan (1985) have begun to probe into the origins of emotions. They believe that the emotional milestones they have identified can lead to parental practices that will help infants to establish more satisfying relationships with others. There are six of these milestones.

1. *Birth to 3 months.* The Greenspans believe that the major features of this period are self-regulation and interest in the world. For normal infants, each of these tasks supports the other.

2. *2–7 months.* The Greenspans refer to this as the infant's time of falling in love. The baby begins to focus on its mother and is delighted by her appearance, voice, and actions.

3. *3–10 months.* During these months an infant attempts to develop intentional communication. It is a time of reciprocal interactions (see chaps. 1 and 6). The mother and infant are responding to each other's signals. When adults (usually the mother) respond to the baby's signals, the infant learns that its actions can cause a response.

4. *9–18 months.* This is a time of dramatic observable achievements: standing, walking, talking. An organized sense of self begins to emerge. For example, at this stage when the mother returns to her infant, the baby may no longer look at her. An infant of this age may walk to the mother, touch her, and perhaps say a word or two. The baby has put together several behaviors in an organized manner.

Table 5.8	Theories of Emotional Development		
Age (months)	**Bridges**	**Izard**	**Sroufe**
0–1	Excitement	Startle, disgust, distress, interest	Stimulus barrier
1–4	Distress, delight	Joy	Turning toward
4–8	Anger, disgust, fear	Anger	Positive affect
8–12	Elation, affection	Fear, shyness	Active participation, attachment
12–18	Jealousy		Practicing
18–24	Joy		Emerging self-concept

BOX 5.3

Multicultural Focus: Cultural Influences on Infancy

It might be wise to pause here and again consider the impact of culture on development. We once more see the truth of the statement that development results from *the interaction of heredity and environment.*

After analyzing recent African studies, Rogoff and Morell (1989) conclude that culture will affect all aspects of development, from physical to cognitive. They illustrate this notion by describing a culture that emphasizes service to the community and manual skills. What Western societies designate as "intelligence" is not as highly valued. Accordingly, social and manual skills are encouraged and rewarded.

Other differences can be found in studies of the interaction between Japanese mothers and their infants. Examining these interactions, a Western observer might be struck by the amount of physical contact between mother and infant. But since this is such commonly accepted behavior in Japan, an observer can't draw too many conclusions about the warmth and quality of the relationship.

Similar studies of infants and their mothers lead to the inescapable conclusion that different cultures value different types of childrearing practices. The outcome of these practices may be quite different from what we would anticipate. Consequently, the research techniques and psychological tests used in one culture may not accurately assess an infant's behavior in another culture. Levine (1977) has summarized this belief nicely when he states that culture, as well as biology, contributes to developmental outcomes. These cultural values are critical for survival in any society, and such values must be clarified to understand the path of development in any society.

5. *18–36 months.* Called the time of creating emotional ideas, this is a period of rapid mental growth. Children can form images of the mother in her absence. They now link these cognitive capacities to the emotional world. They remember their mother reading to them last night—why not tonight? They remember their father wrestling with them last night—why not tonight?

When abilities and behavior are seen in this light, it becomes easier to understand the "terrible twos." Since emotional control is not fully established (remember Piaget's views on egocentrism), difficulties can arise. They are not inevitable. We shall return to this important topic in the next chapter.

BOX 5.4

Toilet-Training: Easy or Difficult?

By the end of the infancy period most parents begin to think about toilet-training for their child. One important fact to remember is that voluntary control of the sphincter muscles (these are the muscles that control elimination) does not occur until about the 18th month. (For some children control is not possible until about 30 months.) Attempting to train children before they are ready can only cause anxiety and stress for the child and frustration for the parents.

As Caplan and Caplan (1983) note, children really can't be trained; they learn when to use the toilet. It is not something parents do *to* a child; rather parents *help* the child without feelings of tension and fear. Certain signs of readiness can alert parents to initiate the process (Caplan & Caplan, 1983).

- As we noted, necessary muscle control does not occur until well into the second year.
- A child must be able to communicate, either by words or gesture, the need to use the bathroom.
- At about 2 years of age, almost all children want to use the toilet: to become more "grown-up" and to rid themselves of the discomfort of wet or soiled diapers.

Parents should try to obtain equipment that the child feels most comfortable with, either a chair that sits on the floor or one that fits over the toilet seat. Brazelton (1981), studying the children in his clinical practice, offers the following estimates for ages of control:

- Most children start training from 24 to 30 months.
- The average age of daytime control was 28.5 months.
- The average age of nighttime control was 33.3 months. (Girls attain nighttime control about two and a half months before boys.)

Most parents expect their children to be toilet trained by the end of infancy. Physiologically most children are ready to learn control; socially it is desirable; psychologically it may be traumatic unless parents are careful. If youngsters are punished for a behavior that they find difficult to master, their perception of the environment is affected, which may produce feelings of insecurity. The common sense of most adults results in a combination of firmness and understanding, thus helping youngsters master a key developmental task. (Travers, 1982, p. 57)

---

6. *30–48 months.* The Greenspans believe that the emotional thinking of these months forms the basis for fantasy, reality, and self-esteem. In other words, children can use their ideas to form a cause-and-effect understanding of their own emotions.

The Greenspans have proposed an outline of emotional milestones that is both theoretically sound and practically helpful. (We have not included their milestones in Table 5.7 because of the overlap of ages.)

When you review this work on emotional development, remember the other phases of development. For example, motor development is involved when a child moves excitedly toward the mother on her return. Language development is involved when infants improve their relationship with their mother by words that are now directed at her.

Cognitive development is probably less obvious but just as significant—the infant remembers. Memory is perhaps a good way to conclude this section. Remember: all development is integrated.

Transition

Your view of an infant now should be of an individual of enormous potential, one whose activity and competence is much greater than originally suspected. It is as if a newborn enters the world with all its systems ready to function and eager for growth.

What happens during these first two years has important implications for future development. Not that setbacks—both physical and psychological—will not occur. They will but they need not cause permanent damage. From your reading in chapter 1, you realize that human infants show remarkable resiliency.

In chapter 2 you read about Erikson's stages of development. In light of what you now know about infant potential, it is easier to accept Erikson's great contribution to our understanding of infants' development of trust.

How do infants first learn that they can trust those around them? The answer lies in the manner in which their initial needs are satisfied. Recognizing infant competence dramatizes their sensitivity to adults. They have the ability to detect and react to parental signals.

We are also now aware that proper need satisfaction entails psychological as well as physical comfort. These first parent-infant interactions furnish the basis for attachment, the knowledge that others can be trusted.

With physical, cognitive, and social development well under way, infants are preparing to leave their "baby" days and enter the exciting world of early childhood.

Key Ideas

1. Today we realize that infants are born with many abilities.
2. We have changed from viewing the infant as a passive organism to one that actively seeks stimuli.
3. Normal reflex activity is critical for a neonate's survival.
4. All aspects of development show remarkable growth.
5. By the end of the period, children show a growing ability to engage in symbolic activity.
6. In the second six months of the first year there is emerging cognitive behavior, especially memory.
7. Beginning with babbling, babies gradually move to the use of words by the end of infancy—about 2 years of age.
8. There is renewed attention to emotional development.

Key Terms

Apgar
Babbling
Binocular coordination
Coordination of secondary schemes
Crawling
Creeping
Egocentrism
Failure-to-thrive
Holophrase
Holophrastic speech
Neonate

Neurological assessment
Primary circular reactions
Reflex
Respiratory distress syndrome
Secondary circular reactions
Sleeping disorders
Sudden infant death syndrome
Telegraphic speech
Tertiary circular reactions
Variable accommodation
Vocables

What Do You Think?

1.   There has been a shift from considering infants as nothing more than passive sponges to seeing them as amazingly competent. This shift carries with it certain responsibilities. We can't be overly optimistic about a baby's abilities. Why? What are some of the more common dangers of this viewpoint?

2.   Testing infants has grown in popularity these past years. One should be cautious however. Remembering what you have read about infants in this chapter, mention several facts you would be careful about.

3.   You have been asked to babysit your sister's 14-month-old baby. When you arrive the mother is upset because she has been picking up things that the baby repeatedly has thrown out of the crib. With your new knowledge, you calm her down by explaining the baby's behavior. What do you tell her?

4.   After reviewing the research on infancy, what do you think about this period as "preparation for the future"? Select one phase of development (e.g., cognitive development) and show how a stimulating environment can help to lay the foundation for future cognitive growth.

Suggested Readings

Greenspan, Stanley, and Nancy Greenspan. (1985). *First feelings*. New York: Viking. Sensitively written by a respected child psychiatrist, this book has become one of the leading statements on emotional development. Detailing the emotional milestones of a child's life, it is a chronicle you would enjoy. It's now available in paperback.

Maurer, Daphne, and Charles Maurer. (1988). *The world of the newborn*. New York: Basic Books. A fascinating explanation of the newborn's experiences—both scientifically sound and enjoyable to read.

Osofsky, Joy (Ed.). (1986). *Handbook of infant development*. New York: Wiley. This book is the "bible" of infancy. If you have any questions about infant behavior, this is the text to use.

Restak, Richard. (1986). *The infant mind*. New York: Doubleday. You will find this popular, well-written account of an infant's world entertaining as well as informative.

· *Chapter 6* ·

Psychosocial Development
in Infancy

Judy Blume's popular book *Otherwise Known as Sheila the Great* provides an excellent example of what this chapter is about: the role of relationships in development. In one scene, Sheila is talking with her best friend Mouse, but she is thinking about the comments that she and her friends have made about one another. She believes that Mouse has said that Sheila is a genius. When Mouse tells her that she (Sheila) has a great idea, Sheila says, "When your brain knows it all it's easy."

❖   *I could tell from Mouse's expression that she was the one who wrote that about me. But I didn't care, because she also wrote that I am an interesting person and I like that idea a lot. . . . And that's what counts. So what if they think I'm bossy sometimes. It's only because I know more than they do. . . . But to be an interesting person! Well, not everyone can be that. That is something special (1972, p. 97)!*

Here we see the true meaning of a relationship. You can judge it only by understanding the meaning of all (or most all) the interactions that make up the relationship.

There is a growing recognition today that relationships with others are the basis of our social development, beginning in those first days after birth. Think for a moment about what you have read about infants, especially their rapid brain and cognitive development. They take in information immediately, and some of this information concerns how they are treated by others, especially their mothers. While they may not grasp the significance of what's going on around them, they can see and hear and understand how they are being treated.

It is what Erikson has called the *time of trust,* which means that children acquire confidence in themselves as well as others. The degree of trust acquired does not depend as much on nutrition and displays of love as it does on the quality of the mother-child relationship. Parents can encourage a sense of trust by responding sensitively to their infant's needs. Physical contact and comfort are crucial for trust to develop. Gradually, as children master motor control, they learn to trust their bodies, thus increasing their psychological sense of security. With the aid of their parents, and their own growing competence, they begin to think of the world as a safe and orderly place.

An infant's relationships begin with its mother and then extend to father, siblings, friends, and so on. We know now that the entire range of a child's relationships contributes to social development. As Michael Lewis states:

❖   *Work in the past decade has broadened our conception of social development from simply looking at the mother as the source of the child's subsequent social development to looking at the child's entire social network (In Trotter, 1987, p. 92).*

Lewis believes that there is considerable evidence to suggest that children form important relationships with others besides their mothers.

Growing knowledge about the emergence of relationships, how they change, and how they affect development has become a key component of developmental research. New findings will create ways to help children master the developmental tasks they face.

Recent research (which we shall discuss) has strikingly demonstrated that everyone in your family is a unique individual, a quite different personality. While growing up, one child might have been exceptionally active while another was shy and quiet. These temperamental differences caused your parents to treat each of you differently.

Table 6.1 Sources of Pupils' Relationships

Parent—Adult	Sibling—Relatives	School	Peers	Others
Mother-father	Brothers	Principal	Male	Day-care personnel
Mother-stepfather	Sisters	Teacher(s)	Female	Friends (family)
Father-stepmother	Stepbrothers	Classmates	Group	Neighbors
Father	Stepsisters	(older, younger)		Religious
Mother	Extended			Medical
Mother-other	(cousins etc.)			Psychological
Father-other	Order of birth			Specialists
Relatives: aunt, uncle, grandparents				(coaches, counselors, music, art teachers etc.)
Foster				
Adopted				
Institutional				

To help us untangle this important network, chapter 6 will first present several basic ideas about relationships (such as the active role that infants play in their own development). We'll then analyze the meaning of relationships: what are they and of what do they consist? Next, we'll examine the source of those first relationships and how they develop and influence later relationships. Finally, we'll explore the research on attachment that has attracted so much attention these past few years. Let's begin by looking at several basic ideas about relationships.

Relationships and Development

Consider for a moment all that a single relationship incorporates:

- Physical aspects of development such as walking, running, and playing with a peer.

- Language aspects, which enable youngsters to share one anothers' lives.

- Cognitive aspects, which allow them to understand one another.

- Emotional aspects, which permit them to make a commitment to another.

- Social aspects, which reflect both socialization and individuation.

All of these features combine as youngsters interact with a remarkable variety of individuals, from those first crucial days with parents, to later interactions with siblings, peers, teachers, and many others. Table 6.1 illustrates the entire range of individuals with whom children interact, from family members to friends.

As you can see from the table, children continue to widen their circle of relationships as they grow. Our concern here, however, is with the origin of relationships in infancy, a concern that has grown out of the changing view of infancy we discussed in chapter 5. How can we link these changes to the current interest in the role of relationships? Let's briefly review several of the developmental concepts we discussed previously.

Infants immediately begin to take in information from their environment and mothers are an important source of this information. From mothers, infants begin to develop a sense of how the world will treat them.

Background of the Relationship Research

One of the major reasons for the interest in relationships is that developmental psychologists became dissatisfied with studying the relationship between mother and child. Greater precision was demanded: what do we know about the content of the interactions between mother and child? Can we study the quality of these interactions? Is it possible to determine the mother's commitment to the relationship?

Another important influence has been the acceptance of a **transactional model of development,** which recognizes the child's active role in its development. Also called *reciprocal interactions,* this model has been described by Brazelton (1984, 1987) and Sameroff (1975). Its meaning is quite simple: I do something to the baby and the baby changes; as a result of the infant's change, I change. The process continues indefinitely.

Finally, the recognition that mothers react differently to different children has introduced the concept of **sensitive responsiveness.** For example, we now know that babies are temperamentally different at birth. While most infants like to be held, some dislike physical contact. How will a mother react to an infant who stiffens and pulls away, especially if previous children liked being held?

This research has contributed to a greater understanding of the role of relationships in development. For example, belief in the reciprocal interactions of relationships as a critical aspect of development has become so widely accepted that a respected commentator can state:

❖   *Over the past decade this emphasis on an interactional model (or transactional, as some may prefer to call it) has swelled to a consensus among leading research workers in human developmental psychology and longitudinal behavioral studies (Thomas, 1981, p. 596).*

Remember: in any adult-child interactions infants also exercise some control over the interactions. We, as adults, respond to infants partly because of the way that they have responded to us. An infant's staring, cooing, smiling, and kicking can all be employed to maintain the interactions. Thus these early interactions establish the nature of the relationship between mother and child, giving it a particular tone or style.

We can usually label relationships, using adjectives such as "warm," "cold," "rejecting," "hostile." But we must be cautious. Any relationship may be marked by apparently contradictory interactions. A mother may have a warm relationship with her child as evidenced by hugging and kissing, but she may also scold when scolding is needed for the child's protection. To understand the relationship, we must understand the interactions.

The Importance of Reciprocal Interactions

Thanks to our changed concept of infants (active not passive), we now recognize the significance of reciprocal interactions in the development of relationships. This new way of looking at infants came about mainly because of the following views.

A Biopsychosocial Model
Developmental psychologists came to believe that a new model, a different way of looking at behavior, was needed to understand infant behavior and development.

This led to what has become known as the **biopsychosocial model.** According to this model, development occurs as the result of an intertwining of biological, psychological, and social forces. For example, an infant who experiences a gastrointestinal problem that produces vomiting has little interest in interacting with others. A biological condition has produced both psychological and social consequences.

Active Processors of Information

A second change came when investigators realized that, from birth, children are active processors of information. They don't only react to stimuli; they see and hear at birth and immediately begin the task of regulating their environment. They fight to control their breathing, and they struggle to balance digestion and elimination.

But brief, calm periods appear after birth when infants take in information from the surrounding world. These fleeting but significant periods are the foundation for the appearance of key developmental milestones during the infancy period. Damon (1983) summarizes this point nicely when he states that infants are born with a natural tendency toward socialization. They are ready to respond to social stimulation. It is not only a matter of responding passively; infants in their own way can initiate social contacts. Many of their actions (such as turning toward their mothers or gesturing in their direction) are forms of communication. Hinde (1987), too, notes that the interchange between infants and their environments is an active one. Those around infants try to attract their attention, but the babies actively select from these adult actions. In other words, infants begin to structure their own relationships according to their individual temperaments.

Sensitive Responsiveness

The use of a biopsychosocial model and a recognition that children are active processors of information prove helpful if parents respond sensitively to their children. Sensitive responsiveness appears to be essential for parenting. It also seems to be more natural for some adults than others. Still, it is a skill that can be acquired and improved upon with knowledge and experience.

Here are several conclusions that can help parents to understand their child's behavior.

- Children are temperamentally different at birth.

- They instantly tune in to their environment.

- They give clues to their personalities.

- A mother's and father's responses to a child's signals must be appropriate for this child.

Transactions or Reciprocal Interactions

As the preceding three views altered our understanding of the active-passive role of children, a different model of development, called *transactional* (Sameroff, 1975), or *reciprocal interactions* (Brazelton & Als, 1979) became widely accepted. The unique temperamental distinctions that infants display at birth cause unique parental reactions. The easy or difficult infant has a decided impact on parents. It doesn't take much effort to visualize how parents respond differently to a crying or cooing infant.

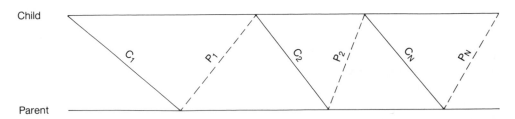

Figure 6.1 *Transactional analysis or reciprocal interactions.*

When parents change their behavior according to their child's behavior, they signal pleasure, rejection, or uncertainty about what their child is doing. Children act on their parents and change the parents; these changes are then reflected in how parents treat their children. The tone of the interactions between children and parents assumes a definite structure that will characterize the relationship for the coming years. Figure 6.1 illustrates the back and forth reaction of parents and their children.

Once developmental psychologists accepted these four views, investigations into bonding, attachment, first relationships, peer relationships, and relationships in special situations (such as with irritable children) could be subjected to more precise and meaningful analysis.

Understanding these views, we can now turn to an analysis of the role of relationships in development. First, however, just what do we mean by relationships?

The Meaning of Relationships

Think for a moment about your friends. What type of relationship do you have with them? with your parents? with a husband or wife? with a child? Now consider this definition of a **relationship.**

❖   *A relationship implies a pattern of intermittent interactions between two people involving interchanges over an extended period of time (Hinde, 1979, p. 14).*

If you have a true relationship with someone, that relationship has *continuity.* That is, you can continue to maintain a relationship with a friend you have not seen for years. An extended series of **interactions,** however, does not necessarily constitute a relationship. The cashier you frequently see at the supermarket, the attendant at the gas station, the receptionist at your dentist's office with whom you exchange pleasantries—none of these become partners in a relationship. If the interactions are nothing more than an exchange of money and a thank you, they cannot be classified as relationships.

As Stern (1977) states, while a relationship is identified by the history of these interactions, it is still more than the sum of these interactions. In a relationship, the interactions are integrated in a manner different from the separate interactions. It isn't just a matter of saying, "Good morning. Isn't it a nice day?" to the cashier. A relationship also involves your perceptions, your mental picture, and your feelings for the other person.

Table 6.2 Categories of Interactions	
Category	**Meaning**
1. Content	a. What the partners do together. b. May distinguish different relationships—mother-child, father-child. c. Enables us to label the relationship.
2. Diversity	a. Indicates the types of interactions making up the relationship. b. The number of things mother and child do together contributes to infant's understanding of others.
3. Quality	a. Not only what partners are doing but also how they are doing it. b. A mother may handle an infant gently or roughly.
4. Relative frequency and patterning of interactions	a. Frequency of interactions but in relation to other types of interactions. b. A pattern of warm interaction may demand hugging and scolding.
5. Reciprocity versus complementarity	a. Doing the same things simultaneously or taking turns. Children's play is an example of reciprocity. b. Interactions are complementary when they are different yet blend together, such as a mother changing or feeding an infant.
6. Intimacy	a. Extent to which partners are prepared to reveal themselves to each other—probably never total. b. Meaningless for infants, but changes quickly with development.
7. Interpersonal perception	a. How the partners see each other. b. Since our sense of self is shaped by reactions of others, the importance of first relationships is clearly evident.
8. Commitment	a. Acceptance of relationship—infant and child have little choice. or b. Decision to work toward continuing a particular relationship.

Infants' Perception of Behavior

Since relationships emerge from the sequence of interactions, mere behavior cannot explain what is happening. What one says or does is significant, but how the partner perceives and judges that behavior is even more important.

These ideas help us to understand the developing relationship between parents and infants. We think today that infants "tune into" their environment from birth. Thus they react to far more than their parents' behavior; the quality of the interactions instantly begins to establish the nature of the relationship.

The Characteristics of a Relationship

Hinde (1979, 1987) argues that eight categories are useful for analyzing relationships: the content of interactions, the diversity of interactions, the qualities of interactions, the relative frequency and patterning of interactions, reciprocity versus complementarity, intimacy, interpersonal perception, and commitment. The meaning of these categories is given in Table 6.2.

The value of Hinde's classification is that we no longer can be satisfied with observing the mother-infant relationship. We can now examine specific features of the relationship (content, quality etc.), study them, conduct research, and determine how, or if, these eight categories are integrated. Hinde's categories are also valuable for discovering just what might be wrong in a relationship. This work promises to help us achieve much deeper insights into the dynamics of relationships.

The Givens in a Relationship

As babies begin to interact with their mothers, a pattern for future relationships is established. The more diverse the interactions that a baby engages in with its mother, the richer the relationship will become.

In the mother-infant relationship (or father-infant), both individuals bring to the relationship physical and biological characteristics ranging from appearance to hereditary endowment. Since we have previously discussed genetic contribution, here we can focus on personal characteristics, such as personal appearance and temperament.

Personal Characteristics

Physical appearance has a powerful effect on a relationship. For good or ill, physical appearance affects the manner in which others react to us. Attractiveness is as important for infants as it is for adults (Langlois & Downs, 1979; Ritter & Langlois, 1988).

You know how appealing the mere sight of a happy baby can be. Their facial expressions and the shape of their features are attractive to most people and help to ensure an infant's survival, given their immaturity and helplessness. The appearance of a sick baby generates concern. We almost instinctively react to their distress. We respond in yet a different manner to an unhappy, crying baby. Tired, frustrated parents may find it difficult to react positively, tending instead to be abrupt and stiff with the baby. Again, an infant's appearance structures our interactions. From what we know of a baby tuning into its environment, we can understand how easily appearance can affect those first relationships.

The first mother-infant interactions quickly establish the style and tone of the relationship (Osofsky, 1976). If the interactions are altered by the infant's physical attractiveness, sensitive responsiveness becomes a matter of prime concern. Given the importance of reciprocal interactions, mothers can initiate a relationship in which an infant quickly realizes that there is something wrong with the quality of the interactions.

Temperament

Temperament is a critical personality trait, especially in the first days and weeks after birth. Carey (1981) states that children's temperaments contribute significantly to their interactions with their environments and immediately begin to structure relationships. Carey defines temperament as the individual's behavioral style in interacting with the environment.

Today's acceptance of the importance of temperament reflects the basic work of Thomas, Chess, and Birch (1970) and Thomas (1981) who believe that in the first half of the twentieth century psychologists overemphasized the role of the environment in development. These authors were struck by the individuality of their own children in the days immediately following birth, differences that could not be attributed to the environment.

To test their hypothesis, Chess and Thomas designed a longitudinal study called the **New York Longitudinal Study.** In 1956 they began collecting data on 141 middle-class children. They observed the behavioral reactions of infants, determined their persistence, and attempted to discover how these behavioral traits interacted with specific elements in the infants' environments. From the resulting data they found nine characteristics that could be reliably scored as high, medium, or low.

1. The level and extent of motor activity.

2. The rhythmicity, or degree of regularity, of functions such as eating, sleeping, and elimination.

3. The response to a new object or person (approach versus withdrawal).

4. Adaptability of behavior to environmental changes.

5. Sensitivity to stimuli.

6. Intensity of responses.

7. General mood or disposition (friendly or unfriendly).

8. Degree of distractibility.

9. Attention span and persistence in an activity.

These ratings provided a behavioral profile of the children, which was apparent by 2 or 3 months of age. Certain characteristics clustered with sufficient frequency for the authors to identify three general types of temperament:

1. **Easy children,** characterized by regularity of bodily functions, low or moderate intensity of reactions, and acceptance of, rather than withdrawal from, new situations (40% of the children).

2. **Difficult children,** characterized by irregularity in bodily functions, intense reaction, and withdrawal from new stimuli (10% of the children).

3. **Slow-to-warm-up children,** characterized by a low intensity of reactions and a somewhat negative mood (15% of the children).

They were able to classify 65% of the infants, leaving the others with a mixture of traits that defied categorization. Knowing what kind of temperament their child has can help parents to adjust their style (way of doing things) to their child's. This can be a distinct advantage in forming positive parent-child relationships. The Thomas and Chess work suggests that infants immediately bring definite temperamental characteristics to the mother-infant relationship, characteristics that will do much to shape those critical initial interactions.

Goodness of Fit
Compatibility between parental and child behavior introduces the concept of **goodness of fit.** A simple way of phrasing this is: How do parents and their children get along together? Thomas and Chess (1977, p. 11) coined the expression *goodness of fit* to signify the match between the properties of the environment, with its expectations and demands, and the child's capacities, characteristics, and style of behaving. Poorness-of-fit is often marked by developmental problems.

Thomas and Chess designed intervention programs to alter the nature of a poorness-of-fit relationship to one more closely approximating goodness of fit. For intervention to be successful, parents need to be reassured that there is nothing wrong with their behavior (if this is the case). With a child of a different temperament, they might have done quite well.

Considering the importance of temperament in any relationship, we will attempt to trace the origin of a child's temperament.

The Origins of Temperament

Carey (1981) states that temperament appears to be largely constitutional. It is observable (at least partially) during the first few days of life, becomes stable at age 3 or 4 months, and constantly interacts with the environment. Studies of twins illustrate the immediate appearance of temperament.

Twin Studies

Matheny (1980) studied twin temperament and discovered differences at each age among the fraternal twins. But in his work with identical twins, he found that they were remarkably alike in temperamental characteristics at all ages.

In another significant twin study, Torgersen (1982) studied the nine categories of temperament identified by Thomas and Chess in a sample of 53 same-sex twins at age 2 and 9 months. The mothers were also asked about similarities and differences between their twins. All temperamental variables for the identical twins at both ages were more similar than those for the fraternal twins, with more marked similarities at age 9 months. Torgersen (1982) next reported a follow-up study of the same twins at 6 years of age. Again using eight of the categories proposed by Thomas and Chess, Torgersen once more found the identical twins to be more alike than the fraternal. Summarizing the data, Torgersen stated (1982) that temperament showed a strong genetic thrust in infancy, and at 6 years of age a genetic influence was still evident in many of the categories.

Goldsmith (1983), analyzing these and similar studies, pointed to strong evidence for genetic effects on sociability, emotionality, and activity. Thus the evidence continues to indicate a strong genetic role in temperament, with all that implies for the mother-infant relationship.

Having considered the nature and givens of relationships, we can now ask, What is the source of the interactions that lead to social relationships? How do an infant's first relationships develop?

First Relationships

Stern has captured the importance of first relationships:

❖   *The infant's first exposure to the human world consists simply of whatever the mother actually does with her face, voice, body, and hands. The ongoing flow of her acts provides for the infant an emerging experience with the stuff of human communication and relatedness. This choreography of maternal behaviors is the raw material from the outside world with which the infant begins to construct knowledge and experience of all things human: the human presence, the human face and voice, their forms and changes that make up expressions, the units and meanings of human behaviors, the relationship between the infant's own behavior and someone else's (1977, p. 9).*

These interactions help infants to form their first relationships and influence how they relate to others. But how do these first relationships actually begin?

As the number of relationships within the family increases, the interactions among family members grow dramatically. Parents, employing the concept of "sensitive responsiveness," engage in reciprocal interactions with their children, thus influencing the path of psychosocial development.

Relationships: Beginnings and Direction

Lisina (1983) has carefully traced the origin and development of the interactions that constitute a relationship by first determining when and if a need for interaction actually exists. She used four criteria:

1. *Attention to an adult,* which would signify that the infant recognizes the adult as the object in some activity; that is, the child does something to the adult.

2. *Emotion displayed toward the adult,* which would indicate that the infant sees the adult not as a mere object, but as someone who brings pleasure or relieves displeasure.

3. *Actions directed at the adult,* which would suggest that the infant is evaluating its role in the relationship—will my overture be accepted?

4. *Reactions to an adult's actions,* which would reflect changes in the adult's behavior brought about by the infant's earlier actions—the infant is beginning to evaluate what has happened.

Motivation and First Relationships

Infants typically react by general states of excitement and distress, which swiftly focus on the mother as infants recognize their mothers as sources of relief and satisfaction. Mothers rapidly discriminate their infants' cries: for hunger, attention, or fright. Thus infants learn to direct their attention to their mothers. Once the pattern is established, infants begin to evaluate the emerging interactions.

Three motives seem to be at work:

1. *Bodily needs*—food, for example—lead to a series of interactions that soon become a need for social interaction. But these basic bodily needs are not the only source of the need for interactions. If you have ever witnessed mother-infant interactions during feeding, you may have been amazed by the infant's intensity in satisfying a basic need. Yet, if you move to a position where the infant can see you, the baby may momentarily stop sucking to attend to the novel sight.

2. *Psychological needs* can cause infants to interrupt one of their most important functions, such as feeding. Consequently, in regard to the origin of relationships, the satisfaction of bodily needs is only the beginning. Children, from birth, seem to seek novelty; they require increasingly challenging stimulation. For infants, adults become the source of information as much as the source of bodily need satisfaction.

3. *Adult response needs.* These first two needs alone are inadequate to explain why, for most of us, relationships with other people are the most important part of our lives (Hinde, 1979). Adults, usually the mothers, satisfy needs, provide stimulation, and initiate communication, thus establishing the basis for future social interactions.

The Developmental Sequence

These three influences at work during the infant's early days—bodily need satisfaction, a search for novelty, and adult responses to their overtures—form a basis for social interaction. In Lisina's scheme (1983), the sequence is as follows:

- During the first three weeks, an adult's appearance has little effect on infants. The only exception, as noted, is during feeding periods.

- From about the beginning of the fourth week, infants begin to direct actions at the adults.

- Emotional reactions also appear at this time, with obvious signs of pleasure at the sight and sound of adults, especially females.

- During the second month, more complex and sensitive reactions emerge, such as smiling and vocalizations directed at the mother, plus animated behavior during interactions.

- By 3 months of age a need for social interactions has formed, which continues to grow and be nourished by adults until the end of the second or beginning of the third year, when a need for peer interactions appears.

Figure 6.2 illustrates the sequence by which the first interactions, combined with developmental changes, gradually lead to specific relationships.

The Significance of the Mother-Infant Interactions

Stern sensitively describes mother-infant interactions:

> ❖ *These are moments that are almost purely social in nature. They often occur at unlikely or unexpected times in the middle of or in the space between other activities. Yet, as I shall try to show, these interpersonal moments are crucial in forming the experiences from which the infant learns how to relate to other people. Here is a detailed example that gives the flavor of the phenomenon and will serve as a reference later on (1977, p. 2).*

Stern then identifies certain characteristics that both mothers and infants bring to the relationship.

The Caregiver's Repertoire

- *Facial expressions.* Facial expressions such as smiling, frowning, showing sympathy, and demonstrating surprise all have social consequences: they are intended to encourage the relationship or, with some mothers and their infants, to avoid interacting.

- *Vocalizations.* Mothers typically exaggerate their speech to their infants and vary its speed. These early speech behaviors seem to function as much for bonding as to convey information.

- *Gaze.* Mothers and infants gaze at each other for relatively long periods, sometimes introducing vocalizations. These behaviors also further the relationship.

- *Face presentations and head movements.* Peek-a-boo and all its variations seem to have both emotional and cognitive consequences: infants enjoy them and learn from them.

Both mother and child bring their own characteristics to the relationship (facial expressions, movements, vocalizations), and, as they do, the interactions between the two become more complex and an attachment slowly develops between the two.

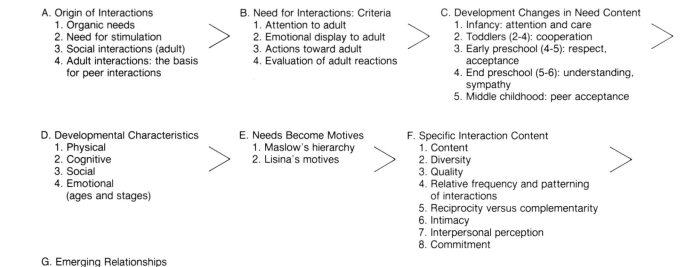

A. Origin of Interactions
1. Organic needs
2. Need for stimulation
3. Social interactions (adult)
4. Adult interactions: the basis for peer interactions

B. Need for Interactions: Criteria
1. Attention to adult
2. Emotional display to adult
3. Actions toward adult
4. Evaluation of adult reactions

C. Development Changes in Need Content
1. Infancy: attention and care
2. Toddlers (2-4): cooperation
3. Early preschool (4-5): respect, acceptance
4. End preschool (5-6): understanding, sympathy
5. Middle childhood: peer acceptance

D. Developmental Characteristics
1. Physical
2. Cognitive
3. Social
4. Emotional (ages and stages)

E. Needs Become Motives
1. Maslow's hierarchy
2. Lisina's motives

F. Specific Interaction Content
1. Content
2. Diversity
3. Quality
4. Relative frequency and patterning of interactions
5. Reciprocity versus complementarity
6. Intimacy
7. Interpersonal perception
8. Commitment

G. Emerging Relationships
1. Ages and stages

Figure 6.2 The origin and development of relationships.

The Infant's Repertoire

- *Facial expressions.* From the time of Darwin, investigators have been impressed by the variety and revealing nature of facial expressions. Conveying a range of emotions from pleasure to displeasure, infants communicate with those around them, firmly establishing a pattern of human relatedness.

- *Gaze.* With steadily improving sight, infants include both people and objects as stimulation. When this occurs the nature of interactions also changes, since infants can now exercise more control over their partner.

As the interactions between mother and child increase and become more complex, an attachment develops between the two. With the preceding ideas in mind, we can turn now to the special topic of attachment.

Attachment

Since the roots of future relationships are formed during the first days of life, we may well ask, How significant is the mother-infant relationship in the minutes and hours after birth? We know that infants who develop a secure **attachment** to their mothers have the willingness and confidence to seek out future relationships. One of the first researchers to recognize the significance of relationships in an infant's life was John Bowlby.

Bowlby's Work

The traditional notion of attachment was developed with great insight by John Bowlby (1969). Bowlby's basic premise is simple: a warm, intimate relationship between mother and infant is essential to mental health since a child's need for its mother's presence is as great as its need for food. A mother's continued absence can

---

BOX 6.1

What's Your Opinion?

We cannot exaggerate the importance of the initial encounters that infants have with the adults around them. In a particularly significant study that was one of the first to focus on the lingering effects of these early interactions, Osofsky (1976) examined the link between neonatal characteristics and early mother-infant relations in 134 mothers and their 2–4-day-old infants. She observed the infants during both a scheduled feeding and a 15-minute stimulation situation during which the mothers presented tasks from the Brazelton Neonatal Assessment Scale to their children. The infants were next evaluated between 2 and 4 days using the full Brazelton scale.

A particularly significant finding was that the overall pattern of interactions indicates *consistent maternal and infant styles that appear soon after birth.* Infants who were highly responsive during the Brazelton assessment were also highly responsive during the stimulation periods. She also found strong correlations between the mother's stimulation and the child's responsiveness: more sensitive mothers have more responsive infants.

Again, note the evidence supporting the importance of the mother-infant interactions. Osofsky concluded that both infant and mother contribute to the style of the relationship. The pattern of interactions forms almost from birth, setting a clearly defined relationship that will undoubtedly shape the course of social development.

Do you agree with Osofsky's conclusions? What's your opinion?

---

generate a sense of loss and feelings of anger. (In his 1969 classic, *Attachment,* Bowlby states quite clearly that an infant's principal attachment figure can be someone other than the natural mother.)

Background of the Theory

Beginning in the 1940s, Bowlby and his colleagues initiated a series of studies in which children age 15–30 months who had good relationships with their mothers experienced separation from them. A predictable sequence of behaviors followed: protest, despair, and detachment.

- *Protest,* the first phase, may begin immediately and persist for about one week. Loud crying, extreme restlessness, and rejection of all adult figures mark an infant's distress.

- *Despair,* the second phase, follows immediately. The infant's behavior suggests a growing hopelessness: monotonous crying, inactivity, and steady withdrawal.

- *Detachment,* the final phase, appears when an infant displays renewed interest in its surroundings, a remote, distant kind of interest. Bowlby describes the behavior of this final phase as apathetic, even if the mother reappears.

From observation of many similar cases, Bowlby defines attachment as follows:

❖   *Attachment behavior is any form of behavior that results in a person attaining or maintaining proximity to some other clearly identified individual who is conceived as better able to cope with the world. It is most obvious when the person is frightened, fatigued, or sick, and is assuaged by comforting and caregiving. At other times the behavior is less in evidence (1982, p. 668).*

Table 6.3	Chronology of Attachment Development	
Age	**Characteristics**	**Behavior**
4 months	Perceptual discrimination; visual tracking of mother	Smiles and vocalizes more with mother than anyone else; begins to manifest distress at separation
9 months	Separation anxiety, stranger anxiety	Cries when mother leaves; clings at appearance of strangers (mother is primary object)
2–3 years	Intensity and frequency of attachment behavior remains constant; increase in perceptual range changes circumstances that elicit attachment	Notices impending departure, signaling a better understanding of surrounding world
3–4 years	Growing confidence; tendency to feel secure in a strange place with subordinate attachment figures (relatives)	Begins to accept mother's temporary absence; plays *with* other children
4–10 years	Less intense attachment behavior but still strong	May hold parent's hand while walking; anything unexpected causes child to turn to parent
Adolescence	Weakening attachment to parents; peers and other adults become important	Becomes attached to groups and group members
Adult	Attachment bond still discernible	In difficulty, adults turn to trusted friends; elderly direct attachment toward younger generation

From John Bowlby, "Attachment and Loss: Retrospect and Prospect" in *American Journal of Orthopsychiatry,* 52:664–678. Reprinted with permission from the American Journal of Orthopsychiatry. Copyright © 1982 by the American Orthopsychiatric Association, Inc.

Bowlby also believes that while attachment is most obvious in infancy and early childhood, it can be observed throughout the life cycle. Table 6.3 presents a chronology of attachment behavior.

Other Explanations of Attachment

Bowlby's is not the only explanation of attachment. As you might expect from your reading of the developmental theories in chapter 2, other theorists have commented on the appearance of attachment.

- *Psychoanalytic theorists,* following Freud, hold that infants become attached to those who provide them oral satisfaction. Thus infants attach to their mothers because mothers usually feed them. Erikson, while accepting the traditional psychoanalytic interpretation of the importance of feeding, also believed that a developing sense of trust between mother and infant contributed to attachment between the two.

- *Behaviorists,* following Skinner, emphasize the importance of reinforcement. For behaviorists, feeding is only one form of reinforcement and not terribly important. Physical contact, comforting, and appropriate types of stimulation (visual, vocal) are equally important. The **total range** of reinforcement provided by parent or caregivers explains attachment.

- *Cognitive theorists,* following Piaget and Kohlberg, believe that attachment is more of an intellectual achievement involving cognitive concepts such as object permanence and a developing sense of competence. While Bowlby's work has provided penetrating insights into attachment behavior, these other theorists have also contributed to our understanding.

Although the interactions between a mother and her child and a father and his child may appear quite different, a child will attach to both mother and father.

BOX 6.2
The Phases of Attachment

Within the chronology of attachment behavior Bowlby has identified four distinct developmental phases:

1. *Orientation and signals without discrimination of figure.* Infants react to people without discriminating them. For most infants, this phase lasts for about the first eight weeks following birth, when they are tracking, grasping, smiling, and babbling.
2. *Orientation and signals directed toward one (or more) discriminated figures.* The identical behaviors observed in Phase One continue, but they are now directed more at the mother. Phase Two lasts until about age 6 months.
3. *Maintenance of proximity to a discriminated figure by means of locomotion as well as signals.* The ability to discriminate others continues to improve, but the effort focuses on the mother. With this sharpened discrimination, friendliness to others diminishes and strangers begin to evoke fear. Phase Three lasts until the third year.
4. *Formation of a goal-connected partnership.* During this phase, children perceive their mothers as independent objects (which parallels their cognitive development) and begin to understand her actions and motives.

Bowlby believes that true attachment does not appear until Phase Three. He also emphasizes the importance of attachment throughout the life span by stating that attachment behavior does not disappear with childhood but persists through life.

Attachment Research

Ainsworth (1973, 1979), who accepts Bowlby's theoretical interpretation of attachment, devised the *strange situation* technique to study attachment experimentally. Ainsworth defines attachment as follows:

> ❖ *The hallmark of attachment is behavior that promotes proximity to or contact with the specific figure or figures to whom the person is attached. Such proximity-and-contact-promoting behaviors are termed attachment behaviors. Included are signaling behavior (crying, smiling, vocalizing), orienting behavior such as looking, locomotions relative to another person (following, approaching), and active physical contact behavior (clambering up, embracing, clinging) (1973, p. 2).*

These behaviors indicate attachment only when they are differentially directed to one or a few persons rather than to others. This is especially noticeable when infants first direct their attention to their mothers, which is the infant's way of initiating and maintaining interaction with its mother. Children also attempt to avoid separation from an attachment figure, particularly if faced with a frightening situation.

To assess the quality of attachment by the *strange situation* technique, Ainsworth had a mother and infant taken to an observation room. Here the child was placed on the floor and allowed to play with toys. A stranger (female) now enters the room and begins to talk to the mother. Observers watch to see how the infant reacts to the stranger and to what extent the child uses the mother as a secure base. The mother now leaves the child alone in the room with the stranger; observers now note how distressed the child becomes. The mother returns and the quality of the child's reaction to the mother's return is assessed. Next, the infant is left completely alone, followed by the stranger's entrance, and then that of the mother.

These behaviors are then used to classify children as follows:

1. *Group A infants (avoidantly attached)*, who rarely cried during separation and avoided their mothers at reunion. The mothers of these babies seemed to dislike or were indifferent to physical contact.

2. *Group B infants (securely attached)*, who were secure and used the mother as a base from which to explore. Separation intensified their attachment behavior; they exhibited considerable distress, ceased their explorations, and at reunion sought contact with their mothers.

3. *Group C infants (ambivalently attached)*, who manifested anxiety before separation and who were intensely distressed by the separation. Yet on reunion they displayed ambivalent behavior toward their mothers; they sought contact but simultaneously seemed to resist it. Examining the nature of these mother-infant interactions, Ainsworth (1979) states that feeling, close bodily contact, and face-to-face interactions seem to be equally important in the child's expectations of the mother's behavior.

A Special Relationship: The Irritable Infant

In a study that integrates many of the topics we have discussed in this chapter, Crockenberg (1981) examined the relationships between mothers and **irritable infants.** Forty-eight 3-month-old infants were assessed on the Neonatal Behavioral Assessment Scale (Brazelton, 1984) and identified as high or low irritable. Low responsive and high responsive mothers were recognized during home observations. Sources of support were elicited in interviews with the mothers. The youngster's degree of attachment was assessed by the "strange situation" procedure.

The results indicated that security of attachment is associated with the mother's social support (from the father, older children, others). For example, anxious attachment was linked to low social support and has its major impact on highly irritable children. Children low in irritability seemed more immune to the benefits of a support system. Aside from the infants' temperaments, the mothers' responsiveness was linked to the amount of support they received, which then affected security of attachment. Insecure attachment could be predicted at age 3 months for those infants whose mothers were unresponsive to their crying and who themselves had little social support.

Several important implications are apparent. First, this study showed how important reciprocal interactions are in a child's life. Irritable infants, especially those from low-support backgrounds, received less responsive mothering. Second, in a time when more children are being raised by single parents, an adequate support system becomes more significant in any consideration of satisfactory social development.

This study, with its far-reaching conclusions for childrearing, also emphasizes that we must accept the partners in a relationship as they are. We are not going to change someone's looks or temperament. All of us—children and adults alike— bring these personal characteristics to any relationship. For example, we have just used irritable infants as an illustration. A mother interacting with an irritable child will experience frustration, perhaps even feelings of hostility, on occasions such as feeding and handling. The mother who feeds, clothes, and talks to her child may well be demonstrating the criteria of adequate mothering. But if the pattern of interactions is examined closely, the mother's resentment about difficult feeding may transfer to the manner in which she treats her child. This may negatively affect the child's perception of the mother as a secure base.

BOX 6.3

Multicultural Focus: Attachment Across Cultures

Mary Ainsworth, who is most closely identified with attachment research, believes that attachment knows no geographic boundaries. After studying infant-mother attachment in Uganda, Ainsworth (1973) reported that of 28 infants she observed, 23 showed signs of attachment. Ainsworth was impressed by the babies' initiative in attempting to establish attachment with their mothers. The babies demonstrated this initiative even when there was no threat of separation or any condition that could cause anxiety. In tracing the developing pattern of attachment behavior, Ainsworth states:

". . . the baby did not first become attached and then show it by proximity-promoting behavior, but rather that these are the patterns of behavior through which attachment grows" (1973, p. 35).

She reports that other studies conducted in Baltimore, Washington, and Scotland indicate that cultural influences may affect the ways in which different attachment-behaviors develop. Nevertheless, although these studies used quite different subjects for their studies, all reported attachment behavior developing in a similar manner.

If you would like to pursue this topic and follow the latest trends in cross-cultural studies of attachment behavior, see *Growing Points of Attachment Theory and Research* (Bretherton & Waters, 1985). This should be available in your school library. You will be particularly interested in the results of recent studies in Germany, Japan, and Israel.

The Klaus and Kennell Studies

Some investigators believe that the initial, intense contacts with the mother have a critical and long-lasting influence on a child's development. Two physicians, Marshall Klaus and John Kennell, both professors of pediatrics at Case Western Reserve University School of Medicine, conducted a series of studies (1976, 1983) concerning the impact of immediate postbirth experiences.

In their initial work, 14 mothers of newborns were given extended contact with their infants. Heat shields (a panel to provide heat) were placed over their beds, and they were given their naked infants for one hour of the first two hours after birth and then for five hours on each of the next three days, for a total of sixteen hours. Fourteen other mothers, matched for age, marital status, and socioeconomic status, received the more standard hospital treatment: they were shown the baby immediately after birth, six or seven hours later they briefly held the baby, and they fed their infants about every four hours.

Kennell controlled the conditions as tightly as possible. The women were randomly assigned to each group, given identical explanations for the study, provided with heat shields (both groups), and had no idea that the mother-infant contacts differed during the three days. The question that Klaus and Kennell pursued was: did the differences in mother-infant contact cause differences in the later mother-child relationship?

The Results

One month after giving birth, all of the mothers returned to the hospital for an interview, a physical examination of the child, and a film of the mother feeding her infant. Klaus and Kennell reported that the extended-contact mothers touched their children more frequently, stood and watched the physical examination more closely, and seemed reluctant to leave their infants with anyone else. Returning at one year after birth for the infant's examination, the extended-contact mothers soothed their

Table 6.4	The Klaus and Kennell Treatment	
	Extended Contact	**Controls**
Number	14	14
At birth	Mothers given child for 1 hour	1. Mother shown the baby
		2. Briefly holds baby 6 hours later
Day 1	Given the baby for 5 hours	Feeding every 4 hours
Day 2	Given the baby for 5 hours	Feeding every 4 hours
Day 3	Given the baby for 5 hours	Feeding every 4 hours
Results	1. Closer attachment	
	2. Greater language involvement	
	3. Higher IQ	
	4. Authors believe results confirm existence of sensitive period for attachment immediately after birth	

From Marshall Klaus and John Kennell, *Bonding.* Copyright © 1983 The C. V. Mosby Company, Inc., St. Louis, MO.

youngsters more when they cried. They also seemed to want to remain closer to their infants than the control mothers.

Two years after birth 5 mothers from each group were randomly selected and interviewed. The extended-contact mothers employed richer language with their children, using more words and asking more questions than the other mothers. When the children were 5 years old, Klaus and Kennell compared 9 of the extended-contact children with 10 of the controls. Children of the extended-contact mothers had significantly higher IQs and higher scores on language tests. (See Table 6.4 for a summary of the results.)

The authors of the study believe that the extra sixteen hours of contact during the first three days of life affected maternal behavior for at least one year after birth (possibly longer) and seemed to have important developmental consequences for the infant. They describe this maternal sensitive period as follows:

❖ *Immediately after the birth the parents enter a unique period during which events may have lasting effects on the family. This period, which lasts a short time, and during which the parents' attachment to their infant blossoms, we have named the maternal sensitive period. . . . During this enigmatic period, complex interactions between mother and infant help to lock them together (1976, pp. 50–51).*

Meaning of the Studies

We should accept the conclusions of Klaus and Kennell with some reservations. Although the authors used careful techniques, one may want to question how different the mothers of the two groups were before birth. Were some mothers more sensitive to their infants' reactions than others? Were the infants temperamentally different at birth, sufficiently so to cause different behavioral responses?

The Klaus and Kennell work has received wide public attention. What concerns both investigators and mothers are the inevitable differences that arise in the mother-infant relationship soon, if not immediately, after birth. For example, some neonates require instant specialized treatment (prematures) and must be separated from the mother. Also, what of the untold mothers who never experienced the intimate relationship described in these studies? Have their youngsters suffered unintended consequences? To their credit, Klaus and Kennell have expressed concern about the impact of their conclusions.

❖ *We faced a real dilemma in deciding how strongly to emphasize the impor-*
tance of parent-infant contact in the first hours and extended visiting for the
rest of the hospital stay, based on the available evidence. Obviously in spite of
a lack of early contact experienced by parents in the past 20 to 30 years, almost
all these parents became bonded to their babies. The human being is highly
adaptable, and there are many fail-safe routes to attachment. Sadly, some par-
ents who missed the bonding experience have thought that all was lost for their
future relationship.

This was, and is, completely incorrect, but it was so upsetting that we have
tried to speak more moderately about our convictions concerning the long-
term significance of this early bonding experience (1983, p. 50).

The authors' insistence on caution in interpreting their results is laudatory but should
not diminish efforts to understand both the nature of relationships and their influence on development.

In an exhaustive review of the literature on bonding, Goldberg (1983) concludes that most of the evidence does not support the existence of a sensitive period
for parent-infant bonding because few careful studies have been done on the actual
beginnings of maternal behaviors. A British study conducted by Packer and Rosenblatt (1979) found that the amount of mother-infant interactions in the delivery
room was quite low: about 500 of the mothers did not touch their infants in the
first 20 minutes; 180 did not even look at their newborn. (The investigators note
the conditions were not ideal; the infant was presented to the mother at the con-
venience of the staff.) This and similar studies cast doubt on the belief that delivery
room contacts are characterized by euphoria. As Goldberg (1983) concludes, we
do not know much more about initial parent-infant contacts and their effects on
later behavior than we knew in the 1970s. But research continues.

Fathers and Attachment

Although we have concentrated on the mother in our discussion of attachment, the
father's role in the process has attracted growing interest. As fathers become more
involved in childcare (by the 1990s about 90% of mothers will work full- or part-
time), questions have arisen about an infant's attachment to both mother and father.

Research has focused on demonstrating the differences between mothers' and
fathers' behavior (nurturant versus playful), the similarity between parental behaviors (both exhibit considerable sensitivity), and the amount of involvement in the
infant's care. Do infants react differently to each parent? The evidence suggests that
while the mother usually remains the primary attachment figure, both mother and
father have the potential to induce attachment.

Can Fathers Bond With Their Children?

Continued findings attest to the ability of fathers to bond with their infants. For
example, during the birth process fathers are frequently present during labor and
delivery, which usually lessens the mother's feeling of distress and may facilitate
father-infant bonding. (The evidence is mixed on this conclusion; see Rutter, 1979.)
Fathers and mothers display quite similar behaviors when interacting with their
newborns, both exhibiting sensitivity to newborn cues. (This finding seems to be
consistent across socioeconomic classes.)

In an ongoing study at Boston's Children's Hospital, Yogman (1982) discovered
that as early as 6 weeks of age infants interact differently with their parents than
they do with strangers. In the study, adults (mothers and fathers) entered from behind
curtains and were told to play with the infant without toys and without taking the

infant from the seat. One camera focused on either the mother or father, the other on the infant. Seven minutes of interaction were recorded—two minutes each with the mother, father, and a stranger, separated by 30-second intervals. By 3 months of age, Yogman reported, infants "successfully interacted with both mothers and fathers with a similar, mutually regulated reciprocal pattern as evidenced by transitions between affective levels that occurred simultaneously for infant and parent" (1982, p. 138).

By 7 or 8 months of age when attachment behavior (as defined by Bowlby and Ainsworth) normally appears, infants are attached to both mothers and fathers and prefer either parent to a stranger. The evidence indicates, then, that fathers possess the potential for establishing a close and meaningful relationship with their infants immediately from birth.

In spite of fathers' increased involvement, most fathers still spend a limited amount of time with their infants and only occasionally are they involved with physical care. As has been well documented, fathers spend more time playing with their children. Fathers tend to be more tactile and physical while mothers are more verbal, which suggests that infants receive qualitatively different stimulation from their fathers (Parke, 1981).

Clarke-Stewart (1978) observed 14 fathers interacting with their infants at 15, 20, and 30 months of age. Mothers and children were also observed with fathers both present and absent. No differences in attachment behavior to the mother or father were noted. Considerable similarity in parental interactions with the children (smiling, vocalizing) was evident, but the children were more responsive to the father's play. Clarke-Stewart attributes this difference not to the fathers themselves but to the type of paternal play. That is, fathers seemed to enjoy the play, praised the children more, and engaged in more physical play.

Current Research Into Attachment

Does deprivation in one generation lead to problems in the next? Recent research points to the reality of **intergenerational continuity,** that is, the connection between childhood experiences and adult parenting behavior. For example, studies have shown that children raised in unhappy or disrupted homes are more prone to unhappy marriages and divorce. A similar pattern has been found among parents who batter their children: these parents suffered seriously disturbed childhoods marked by neglect, rejection, or violence (Rutter, 1981).

Intergenerational Continuity

In an attempt to discover if parental behaviors reach across generations, Ricks (1985) has examined the evidence from two perspectives: the impact of separation or disruption, and parental reports of their childhood attachments. Ricks is concerned with the time involved in these studies. Memory, for example, poses an obstacle since our recall of the past may well be affected by our current thinking, our present mood, and by our present status. As Ricks asks: Do childhood memories accurately reflect childhood experiences (1985, p. 214)?

With these cautions, Ricks then examined the separation and disruption studies. Two findings emerged:

1. Separation from parents in the family of origin (i.e., the parents' original family) was related to problems in parenting.

2. Separation in the family of origin seemed to be associated with marriage problems and with depression in the mother.

The interactions between a father and his child tend to be more physical than those between a mother and her child. The qualitatively different types of stimulation a child receives from each parent would seem to suggest implications for the staffing of daycare centers and preschool facilities.

A key factor in intergenerational effects was disruption (parents remain together but fight and are basically unhappy). Mothers from disrupted families of origin did not manifest the warm relationships with their children that mothers from nondisrupted families manifested. Preschool children of mothers from disrupted families had poorer language skills than youngsters whose mothers had not come from disrupted families. The early attachment relationship was adversely affected by disruption, divorce, or long-term separation in the mother's family of origin.

In the second phase of her study, Ricks turned to the recollections that mothers had of their own relations with their parents. She consistently found significant relations between a mother's recollection of her childhood attachments and her present ability to serve as a secure base for her child. In the development of social relationships, those first bonds, the initial relationships, have a critical function that may carry across generations.

Transition

The role of relationships in development has finally achieved a prominent place in our attempts to understand a child's growth. From the initial contacts with the mother to the ever-expanding network of siblings and peers at all ages, relationships exert a powerful and continuing influence on the direction of development.

We are slowly acquiring data about the function of relationships. For example, we have seen how important and persistent are the first interactions with parents. They set a tone for future relationships and set the direction for social development. Recent research has led to significant findings about the quality of relationships.

In this chapter, you were asked to become familiar with the beginnings of relationships. As you continue your reading and move into the early childhood period, the function of relationships will appear with children's play and their first experiences with school. With middle childhood and adolescence, the effect of peer relationships becomes even more significant. For now, however, we turn our attention to early childhood.

Key Ideas

1. The theme of this chapter has been that relationships with other people are the most important part of our lives.

2. From birth, children begin to establish a network of relationships that influences their development.

3. The notion of infants as active partners in interactions with those around them has helped us to understand the role of relationships in development.

4. One way to understand relationships is to analyze them by categories (such as Robert Hinde has done).

5. There are some features of a relationship (such as personality and temperament) that immediately affect interactions.

6. We know now that an infant's first relationships have an important function in social development.

7. Attachments, those first critical relationships, have been shown to be an important part of a child's life.

8. Research shows that fathers can form close bonds with their children.

9. The Klaus and Kennell studies have had a controversial impact on attachment research.

Key Terms

Attachment
Biopsychosocial model
Difficult children
Easy children
Goodness of fit
Interactions
Intergenerational continuity
Irritable infants

New York Longitudinal Study
Relationship
Sensitive responsiveness
Slow-to-warm-up children
Temperament
Total range
Transactional model of
  development

What Do You Think?

1. Probably the basic issue for you to grasp is the extent of an infant's abilities: physical, social, and psychological. Do you think that infants are as we have described them in these two chapters, or do you think that we have over- or underestimated their competencies?

2. Depending on your answer to the above question, explain how you interpret an infant's participation in developing relationships? That is, given an infant's ability to smile, coo, and make physical responses, how much control do you believe they exercise in their interactions with adults?

3. Think about the role of appearance and temperament in developing relationships. A well-known psychologist once said that some children are so difficult to love that parents may have to fake it. How do you react to this statement? Do you think an infant could detect such parental behavior?

4. Once the Klaus and Kennell studies received wide coverage (which they did in the press and television), many mothers experienced feelings of guilt because their children had not received such treatment immediately after birth. They were afraid that their children would be at a disadvantage. What would you tell them? How would you attempt to relieve their feelings of guilt?

Suggested Readings

Bowlby, John. (1969). *Attachment*. New York: Basic Books. Here is Bowlby's classic statement about attachment. It is very readable and is a reference you should be familiar with.

Manchester, William. (1983). *The last lion: Winston Spencer Churchill, 1874–1932*. A particularly revealing look at Churchill's difficult boyhood and his desperate attempt to please indifferent parents.

Maurer, Daphne, and Charles Maurer. (1989). *The world of the newborn*. New York: Basic Books. This book contains readable summaries of many of the crucial developmental milestones of infancy that we have discussed.

Stern, Daniel. (1977). *First relationships*. Cambridge, MA: Harvard University Press. This is a sensitive and thoughtful summary of those critical first relationships. Stern is rapidly becoming a leading commentator on the beginnings of social development.

PART 4

Early Childhood

· *Chapter 7* ·

Early Childhood: Continuing Competence

The time of infancy is now behind us. By two years, typical children walk, talk, and are eager explorers of their environment. Early childhood children gradually acquire greater mastery over their body. The clumsy actions of infancy are replaced by more coordinated, skillful movements. With walking and talking, new directions in development become more obvious. Children's personalities take on definite shadings.

Their interactions with those around them begin to take shape, setting the stage for the kind of relationships they will form in the future. They will now begin the process of widening their circle of relationships. Children from age 2 to 6 will make new friends and, in our society today, almost inevitably experience preschool teachers. Some youngsters of this age will also be faced with a new sibling(s), which can be a time of great frustration if not handled carefully.

While these changes fascinate us—and deservedly so—we cannot overlook the more subtle internal changes that are occurring simultaneously. Perhaps no one has traced and analyzed these changes with greater sensitivity than Selma Fraiberg (1959). Her little classic, *The Magic Years,* offers an insightful journey through the early years. She gracefully echoes the need not to be blinded by the obvious changes that are taking place:

❖   *Parental wisdom and understanding in the conduct of feeding, toilet-training, sex education, and discipline serve the child's mental health by promoting love and confidence in parents and by strengthening the need to regulate body needs and impulses. But the most ideal early training does not eliminate all anxiety or remove the hazards that exist everywhere in the child's world and in the very process of development itself (1959, p. 4).*

As Fraiberg notes, there is no way that children can be raised without encountering tension and danger. Developmentally, what is important is the manner in which children handle anxiety. Before youngsters develop the inner resources for managing tension, they depend on their parents to remove the source of the danger.

Fraiberg points out that the parents' willingness to help with their children's anxieties will help youngsters cope with future tensions. Gradually children devise their own personal and unique way of dealing with life's problems. These methods of coping emerge during the early childhood years, and discerning parents can help their children achieve healthy, adaptive reactions. Do you recall the discussion of sensitivity in chapter 6? Here is an example of it at work. While we are still uncertain how it functions, we know that some parents are quite sensitive to the cues their children offer. Again, while the surface changes of early childhood are fascinating, be aware of these other, more subtle transformations.

To help you understand the rapid changes that occur during these years, we'll first trace the important physical changes of the period, especially the significance of brain development. We'll then analyze cognitive development, turning to Piaget for an explanation of how these changes occur, and examine a child's growing representational ability. Finally, these years see the "language explosion" with all that it implies for development, so we'll conclude by discussing this critical phase of development.

Characteristics of the Period

Early childhood, extending from age 2 to 6, is a time of rapid change: height increases about 10–12 inches, weight by about 15 pounds; language grows at a phenomenal rate; cognitive changes appear in both thought and language; personality

Early childhood youngsters find the world a fascinating place. Giving these children the freedom to explore and learn, coupled with sensible restrictions, encourages the development of mastery.

BOX 7.1

What's Your Opinion?

In regard to the changes that occur during these years, you can better understand the potential for conflict between adult rules and children's impulses if you consider how a child's world has dramatically widened. A room or house no longer contains these youngsters. They are mobile and wish (rightly so) to push beyond previous limits. They can walk; soon they are running. They also show expanding intellectual interests, which will culminate in reading and school entry by the end of the period. It is precisely here that children meet the demands of an adult world. They probably begin to hear "no" for the first time. They want to run out into the streets and their parents stop them. They reach for that colorful dish on the table and someone says "don't."

During the early childhood years, peers play an increasing role in social development; parents are no longer the sole source of companionship. As children play together, they express their opinion of each other in a way that provides instant feedback to their personalities. As we know today, a major influence on the development of self is the reaction of others, and these formative years steadily shape the developing self-concept.

Given these youngsters' increased abilities, and their awareness of them, what do you think would constitute one of the major causes of child-adult conflict? What's your opinion?

Table 7.1   Some Developmental Characteristics of Early Childhood

Age (years)	Height (in.)	Weight (lb)	Language Development	Motor Development
2½	36	30	Identifies object by use; vocabulary of 450 words	Can walk on tiptoes; can jump with both feet off floor
3	38	32	Answers questions, brief sentences; may recite television commercials; vocabulary of 900 words	Can stand on one foot; jumps from bottom of stairs; rides tricycle
3½	39	34	Begins to build sentences; confined to concrete objects; vocabulary of 1,220 words	Continues to improve 3-year skills; begins to play with others
4	41	36	Names and counts several objects; uses conjunctions; understands prepositions; vocabulary of 1,540 words	Walks downstairs, one foot to step; skips on one foot; throws ball overhand
4½	42	38	Mean length of utterance (morphemes) 4.5 words; vocabulary of 1,870 words	Hops on one foot; dramatic play; copies squares
5	43	41	Begins to show language mastery; uses words apart from specific situation; vocabulary of 2,100 words	Skips, alternating feet; walks straight line; stands for longer periods on one foot
5½	45	45	Asks meanings of words; begins to use more complex sentences of 5 or 6 words; vocabulary of 2,300 words	Draws recognizable person; continues to develop throwing skill
6	46	48	Good grasp of sense of sentences; uses more complex sentences; vocabulary of 2,600 words	Jumps easily; throws ball overhead very well; stands on each foot alternately

and social development enter a new distinct phase; feelings of mastery and independence may conflict with parents and teachers. It is Erikson's time of **autonomy** and **initiative** and Piaget's **preoperational period.** Also, during these years children continue their mastery of Havighurst's *developmental tasks*: toilet training, getting ready to read, the continuing emergence of abstract thinking, the skillful use of language, and the growing ability to distinguish right from wrong.

Youngsters of this age, wanting to do things their way, often clash with the dictates of parents and teachers. Adults often are torn. They want to provide freedom and opportunities, but still must balance the youngster's need to explore and to achieve mastery of self and world against the dangers to a child's safety. The early childhood years require time and adult patience as youngsters explore, test their world, continue to build their sense of trust in adults, and extend trust to others (Anselmo, 1987). They constantly absorb new ideas, widening and deepening their cognitive world and expanding their memory. Proper materials and space are critical, since children's movement through space provides the necessary information about self and world that fuels increasing cognitive demands.

We may casually observe these youngsters and comment on their incessant play. But by examining them psychologically, we can see the interplay of movement, activity, and cognitive curiosity that produces constant improvement in competence. Table 7.1 summarizes many characteristics of early childhood youngsters.

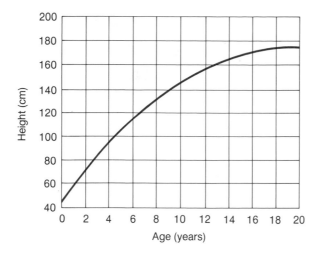

Figure 7.1 The human growth curve.

Physical and Motor Development

As you can see from Table 7.1, growth in childhood proceeds at a less frantic pace than in infancy. For example, if you double a boy's height at age 2, you will have an approximation of his adult height. But it takes another 14 to 15 years to reach that height. Children during this period grow about another 12 inches and continue to gain weight at the rate of about five pounds a year. Body proportions are also changing, with the legs growing faster than the rest of the body. By about age 6, the legs make up almost 45% of body length. The beginning of this period usually sees the completion of baby teeth, and at the end of the period children begin to lose them. Boys and girls show about the same rate of growth during these years.

Characteristics of Physical Development

Look at Figure 7.1, the human growth curve. (Note that 10 centimeters equal 4 inches.) This curve strikingly illustrates the regularity of physical growth. With the exception of the two spurts at infancy and adolescence, growth is highly predictable for almost all boys and girls, given satisfactory conditions.

The Sequence of Early Childhood Growth
We are concerned here with physical growth and development. Optimum growth requires proper nutrition, temperature, and rest to stimulate the genetic elements and growth hormones. Tanner (1978) notes that the growth process is self-stabilizing. It is governed by the control system of the genes and fueled by energy absorbed from the environment. If malnutrition or illness deflects children from the normal growth path, but a corrective force (adequate diet or termination of illness) intervenes, the normal course of development will accelerate until the children "catch up"; thereupon growth slows. These children are often called **developmentally delayed.**

Different cells, tissues, and organs grow at different rates. (Some tissues never lose the ability to grow, such as hair, skin, and nails.) In humans, for example, body length at birth is about four times the length of the face at birth, so the head is relatively large. But the head grows more slowly than the trunk or limbs, so that at age 25 body length is about eight times that of face length.

Children of this age begin to demonstrate greater control of both gross and fine muscles. Note in this picture how the child is grasping the flag, a clear sign of perceptual and motor development.

In an interesting interpretation of the first five years of life, Knobloch and Pasamanick (1974) state that healthy development depends on the integration of five kinds of behavior:

1. *Adaptive,* including perception, sensorimotor reactions, and eye-hand coordination.

2. *Gross motor behavior,* including head balance, sitting, standing, creeping, and walking.

3. *Fine motor behavior,* including the use of hands and fingers in grasping and manipulating an object.

4. *Language behavior,* including facial expression, gestures, words, phrases, sentences, and comprehension.

5. *Personal-social behavior,* including feeding ability, toilet training, self-dependency, and cooperation.

Using and extending the rich and varied work of Arnold Gesell, Yale's famous child psychologist, Knobloch and Pasamanick believe that the key ages of early childhood are 24, 36, 48, and 60 months. By key ages, the authors mean those stages of development during which children seem to integrate their behavior. These ages can be used to determine if a child's behavior is on a normal developmental schedule. Thus children combine different abilities to produce more organized behavior. Table 7.2 illustrates the developmental accomplishments of these five kinds of behavior.

Knobloch and Pasamanick (1974) summarize these early childhood periods as follows:

Table 7.2   Early Childhood Development: Selective Behaviors

Levels of Maturity	Adaptive	Gross Motor	Fine Motor	Language	Personal-Social
24 months	Builds towers, draws circles	Runs well, kicks ball	Can turn pages	Uses phrases, understands directions	Pulls on clothes, plays with toys
36 months	Copies circle, can build bridge of 3 cubes	Stands on one foot, jumps off step	Holds crayon like adult	Uses sentences, answers simple questions	Uses spoon, puts on shoes
48 months	Copies cross, builds with 5 cubes	Skips on one foot, broad jumps	Traces within lines	Uses conjunctions, understands prepositions	Washes and dries face, plays cooperatively
60 months	Counts 10 objects, copies triangle	Skips on alternate feet		Asks "Why?"	Dresses without assistance, asks meaning of words

Source: Data from Hilda Knobloch and Benjamin Pasamanick, *Gesell and Amatruda's Developmental Diagnosis.*
Copyright © 1974 Harper and Row Publishers, Inc., New York, NY.

- In the second year, walking and running develop, children achieve bowel and bladder control, begin to speak, and acquire some sense of self-identity.

- Between the second and third year, children use language as a vehicle for thought.

- In the fourth year, questioning becomes a way of life, and abstract thinking is apparent. Children should be relatively independent in personal life and home routine.

- In the fifth year, motor control has matured, language is fairly articulate, and social adjustment is apparent.

Continuing Brain Development

During these early childhood years, the brain continues to grow, exercising its powerful control of behavior. These years see children showing a decided preference for using one hand or foot over the other. This preference, called "handedness," starts to appear toward the end of infancy and becomes well-established by the age of 5 or 6.

Lateralization

Which hand do you use for writing? If you were to kick a football, would you use the leg on the same side of your body as the hand you use for writing? Pick up a pencil or ruler and assume it is a telescope. Which eye do you use? Are you using the same side of the body that you used for writing and kicking? Your answers to these questions should give you some idea of the meaning of cerebral **lateralization.**

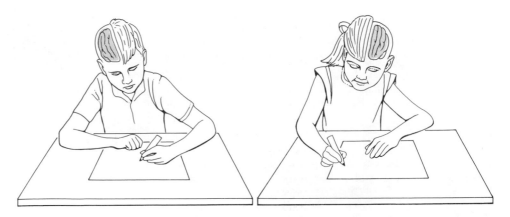

Figure 7.2 Lateralization of handedness.

We tend to think of the brain as a single unit, but actually it consists of two halves: the **cerebral hemispheres.** The two halves are connected by a bundle of nerve fibers (the corpus callosum). The left hemisphere controls the right side of the body, while the right hemisphere controls the left side of the body. Although the hemispheres seem to be almost identical, your answers to the preceding questions reveal important differences between the two. These differences are clues to your brain's organization. If you are right-handed, for example, your left cerebral hemisphere is lateralized for handedness and also for control of your speech—you are "left lateralized." Figure 7.2 illustrates the process.

Much of our knowledge of cerebral lateralization has resulted from studies of brain-damaged patients. Patients with left hemisphere damage, for example, typically have speech difficulties; while damage to the right hemisphere frequently causes perceptual and attentional disorders (Rourke & others, 1983). Because as humans we rely so heavily on language, the left hemisphere came to be thought of as the dominant or "major" hemisphere. Today, however, much importance has been placed on the right hemisphere's control of visual and spatial activities.

Developmental Shifts

As interesting as these data are, we are concerned mainly with the developmental and educational implications. Data clearly suggest differences between the hemispheres at all ages and between both sexes. Rourke and colleagues (1983) report an *age-related shift* in scanning letters from LFA (left-field advantage) to RFA (right-field advantage). The shift occurred from approximately age 6–7 to age 11–12.

They give the example of presenting both a 7 year old and 14 year old with a simple sentence. They believe that these children probably generate different strategies to process the sentence. They also doubt that this processing occurs in the same brain structures. The authors speculate that the younger child is likely to respond to the visual configuration of the sentence, thus signaling visual-spatial predominance. The older reader, however, probably responds, almost automatically, with analytic awareness. You can see the importance of this finding. Teachers can present material more effectively if they are aware of the different processing strategies.

Are there other implications for development and education to be drawn from the lateralization literature? Answering this question requires two significant considerations:

This child is using his right hand to dig, signaling that his left cerebral hemisphere is lateralized for handedness and control of speech.

1. *Are there sex differences related to lateralization?* Without reviewing the enormous literature addressed to this question, we can safely state that sex differences exist in certain abilities. Differences in verbal and spatial skills are especially obvious. Females seem to be decidedly superior in anything relating to language, while males excel in spatial tasks. But these differences tell us nothing about why they exist. They may result from either biological or cultural factors, or both.

Our interest, however, focuses on one question: should teachers use different instructional practices for girls and boys? While research results should be taken into consideration, they should not be the basis for curriculum construction or different instructional techniques. For one thing, males and females are much more alike in brain functioning than they are different. Some women have greater spatial ability than men, and some men have greater language skills than women. Second, we are a nation that cultivates individual differences, and unique talents should be fostered.

2. *To what extent, then, should education recognize these differences?* Since lateralization studies have become known, criticism has been directed at the schools for "teaching to the left hemisphere." Reading, writing, and mathematics all favor logical, sequential processing—left hemisphere functions. Should we teach to the right hemisphere?

Although the temptation to teach to either hemisphere is great, research to date does not clearly show how much either hemisphere is involved in the activities of the other—for example, how much one interferes with the other (Spreen & others, 1984). Perhaps we can best conclude by stating that we should be aware of hemispheric involvement in any particular activity, but also be aware that human activity, especially learning, entails the commitment of both hemispheres. (These findings take on greater significance today since most early childhood youngsters will have some involvement with education, as we shall see in chap. 3.)

Physical Development: An Overview

In an excellent overview of physical development, Tanner (1978) discusses how the interaction of heredity and environment produces the rate and kinds of physical growth. Among the chief contributing forces are the following:

- *Hereditary elements.* Hereditary elements are of immense importance to the regulation of growth. The genetic growth plan is given at conception and functions throughout the entire growth period.

- *Nutrition.* Malnutrition delays growth and, if persistent, can cause lasting damage. Children in Stuttgart, Germany, were studied each year from 1911 to 1953. From 1920 to 1940 there was a uniform increase in average height and weight, but in the later years of each war (first and second world wars) average height declined as food was curtailed. These children recovered, but there remain questions about the effects of chronic malnutrition. For example, does chronic malnutrition produce permanent brain damage in the fetus and the 1- or 2-year-old child?

- *Disease.* Short-term illnesses cause no permanent retardation of the growth rate, although they may cause some disturbance if the child's diet is consistently inadequate. Major disease usually causes a slowing of growth, followed by a catch-up period if circumstances become more favorable.

- *Psychological disturbances.* Stress can slow development and occasionally lead to deprivation dwarfism. Small children under uncompromising strain such as divorce seem to "turn off" their growth hormone and become almost dwarfed.

- *Socioeconomic status.* Children from different social classes differ in average body size at all ages. Tanner gives the example of differences in height between British children of the professional class and those of laborers. Children of the professional class are from one inch taller at age 3 to two inches taller at adolescence. There is a consistent pattern in all such studies, indicating that children in more favorable circumstances are larger than those growing up under less favorable economic conditions. The difference seems to stem from nutrition, sleep, exercise, and recreation.

- *Accelerated trends.* There has been a tendency during the past hundred years for children to become progressively larger at all ages. This is especially true in Europe and America.

Growing Motor Skills

When early childhood children reach the age of 6, no one—parents or teachers—are surprised by what they can do physically. Think back to the infancy period and recall how often we referred to what they *couldn't* do. Stand, walk, run. We tend to take the accomplishments of the 6 year old for granted, but a great deal of neuromuscular development had to occur before these motor skills became so effortless.

We are concerned here with two types of motor skills: gross (using the large muscles) and fine (using the small muscles of the hands and fingers). The well-known chronicler of children's development, Arnold Gesell (1940), has stated that

Table 7.3	The Emergence of Motor Skills	
Age	**Gross Skills**	**Fine Skills**
2	Runs, climbs stairs, jumps from object (both feet)	Throws ball, kicks ball, turns page, begins to scribble
3	Hops, climbs stairs with alternating feet, jumps from bottom step	Copies circle, opposes thumb to finger, scribbling continues to improve
4	Runs well, skillful jumping, begins to skip, pedals tricycle	Holds pencil, copies square, walks balance beam
5	Hops about 50 feet, balances on one foot, can catch large ball, good skipping	Colors within lines, forms letters, dresses and undresses self with help, eats more neatly
6	Carries bundles, begins to ride bicycle, jumps rope, chins self, can catch a tennis ball	Ties shoes, uses scissors, uses knife and fork, washes self with help

thanks to perceptual and motor development, 3- and 4-year-old children can hold crayons, copy triangles, button their clothes, and unlace their shoes. Table 7.3 summarizes the development of motor skills.

Cratty (1979) discusses several motor skills as follows:

- *Running.* The 18-month-old child has a hurried walk. The true run appears between ages 2 and 3. By the age of 5 or 6, youngsters run rapidly (about 11.5 feet per second), employing considerable arm action.

- *Jumping.* At about age 18 months, youngsters step off a low object with one foot, hesitating slightly before placing it on the ground. At age 2, youngsters use what Cratty calls "the two-feet takeoff." Soon they begin to jump over low barriers, and by age 5 they are skillful jumpers (they can broad jump three feet and hurdle one-foot objects).

- *Hopping, skipping, galloping.* Hopping may be on one foot in place, using alternate feet, or hopping for distance. Sometime after age 3 or 4 youngsters can hop from one to three steps on their preferred foot, and by age 5 they can extend hopping to about ten steps. Girls acquire this skill slightly earlier and more successfully than boys. Skillful skipping and galloping appears between the ages of 6 and 7 (Cratty, 1979).

- *Balancing.* Balancing, a measure of nervous system integrity, appears quite early. Three year olds can walk a reasonably straight line. Five year olds can maintain control while standing on one foot with their arms folded. Girls are slightly superior on this task.

The physical picture of the early childhood youngster is one of energy and growing motor skill. Adequate rest and nutrition are critical, and parents should establish a routine to avoid problems. For example, to reconcile a rambunctious child with the necessity of sleep, parents should minimize stimulation through a consistent, easily recognized program: washing, tooth brushing, storytelling, and gentle but firm pressure to sleep. Careful and thoughtful adult care should prevent undue difficulties.

The early childhood years are a time when children show a great love for drawing. Not only are their drawings a sign of motor development, but they also indicate levels of cognitive development and can be emotionally revealing.

The Special Case of Drawing

Children love to draw. No one has to teach them. In a finely tuned sequence, children move from random scribbles to skillful creations. When something is as natural and fascinating for children as drawing, we can only wonder why the vast majority of youngsters lose this desire and skill.

Drawing flourishes during the early childhood years. Brittain (1979) divides early drawings into two levels: **random scribbling** and **controlled scribbling.** Random scribbling lasts until about age 3. Children use dots and lines with simple arm movements. They gradually begin to use their wrists, which permits them to draw curves and loops. They grip the crayon as tightly as possible, usually with the whole hand. Controlled scribbling lasts until age 4. Now children carefully watch what they are doing, whereas before they looked away. They have better control of the crayon and hold it now like an adult.

By age 4 or 5, children begin to paint and hold the brush with thumb and fingers. They hold the paper in place with the free hand. They give names to their drawings and begin to show representation (using one thing for another—see the cognitive section of the chapter).

The well-known psychologist Howard Gardner (1980) has written sensitively about children's drawing and raised several important questions. Noting how drawings develop—from the scribbles of the 2 year old to the 3 year old's interest in design to the 4 and 5 year old drawing representations—Gardner comments on the liveliness and enthusiasm of their work.

And then suddenly it stops! The end of the early childhood period sees the end of creative expression, except for a select few. Why? We simply don't know. Our ignorance breeds other questions: Do all children possess artistic talent or only the gifted few? Are children's drawings truly creative or are they copies? How much depends on teaching?

Children's drawings are not only good clues to their motor coordination but, as we'll see, provide insights into their cognitive and emotional lives (Gardner, 1980).

Cognitive Development

Physical development during early childhood, while observable and exciting, is not the only significant change occurring. Early childhood youngsters expand their mental horizons by their increasing use of ideas and by rapid growth in language. This growing cognitive ability is a fact; explaining it is much more difficult. To help us understand what is happening and how it happens, we turn once more to Piaget.

Piaget's Preoperational Period

Piaget and Inhelder (1969) state that as the sensorimotor period concludes, representation (the ability to represent something by a "signifier" such as language) appears. This period extends roughly from the age of 2 to 7. The child now acquires the ability for inner, symbolic manipulations of reality. Piaget and Inhelder describe the emergence of the symbolic function as the appearance of behavior that indicates representation. They list five of these preoperational behavior patterns.

- **Deferred imitation,** which continues after the disappearance of the model to be imitated.

- **Symbolic play,** or the game of pretending.

- **Drawing,** which rarely appears before age 2½.

- **The mental image,** which is a form of internal imitation.

- **Verbal evocation** of an event not occurring at that particular time. A child may point to the door through which the father left and say "dada gone."

Imitation
For Piaget, imitation is mainly accommodation (see chap. 2), as children attempt to change in order to conform to the environment. When the sensorimotor period ends, children are sufficiently sophisticated for the phenomenon of deferred imitation to appear. Piaget gives the example of a child who visited his home one day and while there had a temper tantrum. His daughter Jacqueline, about 18 months old, watched, absolutely fascinated. Later, after the child had gone, Jacqueline had her own tantrum. Piaget interprets this to mean that Jacqueline had a mental image of the event.

Play
Piaget argues eloquently for recognizing the importance of play in a youngster's life. Obliged to adapt themselves to social and physical worlds that they only slightly

These children, playing doctor and patients, are furthering all aspects of their development. They are discovering what objects in their environment are supposed to do, they are learning about the give and take of human relationships, and they are channeling their emotional energies into acceptable outlets.

understand and appreciate, children must make intellectual adaptations that leave personality needs unmet. For their mental health, they must have some outlet, some technique that permits them to assimilate reality to self, and not vice versa. Children find this mechanism in play, using the tools characteristic of symbolic play.

Drawing

We have previously discussed drawing as a sign of physical growth. Piaget examines children's drawings for their cognitive significance. Piaget considers drawing as midway between symbolic play and the mental image. In drawing a person, for example, children go through some stages that demonstrate the increasing use of symbols.

1. Initially they make a head with arms and legs, but usually no body. The importance of the drawing seems to be merely the act of doing it.

2. Next is a period of intellectual realism where, even if a profile is drawn, it will nevertheless have two eyes.

3. This is followed by what is called visual realism, in which a profile has only one eye and a pattern appears. Trees, houses, and people are all in correct proportion. Visual realism appears at about age 8 or 9.

Mental Images

Mental images appear late in this period because of their dependence on internalized imitation. Piaget's studies of the development of mental images between the ages of 4 and 5 show that there are two categories of mental images. There are **reproductive images,** which are restricted to those sights previously perceived. There are also **anticipatory images,** which include movements and transformation. At the preoperational level, children are limited to reproductive images.

A good illustration of the difference between the two is the previous example of matching tokens. Piaget gave 5- and 6-year-old children red tokens and asked them to put down the same number of blue tokens. At this age children will put one blue token opposite each red one. But if we change the arrangement and spread out the row of red tokens, the children are baffled because they now think there are more red tokens than blue. Thus they can reproduce but not anticipate, which reflects the nature of their cognitive structures and level of cognitive functioning.

Language

Finally, language appears during this period after children have experienced a phase of spontaneous vocalization, usually between the age of 6 and 10 months; a phase of imitation of sounds at about age 1; and one-word sentences at the end of the sensorimotor period. Piaget and Inhelder (1969) note that from the end of the second year the sequence is that of two-word sentences, short complete sentences, and finally the gradual acquisition of grammatical structures.

In his early writings (1929) Piaget described three fascinating developmental characteristics of preoperational thought.

1. **Realism,** which means that children slowly distinguish and accept a real world. They now have identified both an external and internal world.

2. **Animism,** which means that children consider a large number of objects alive and conscious that adults consider inert. For example, a child sees a necklace wound up and then released; when asked why it is moving, the child replies that the necklace "wants to unwind."

Children overcome these cognitive limitations as they recognize their own personalities; that is, they refuse to accept personality in things. Piaget also believes that, as with egocentrism, comparison with the thoughts of others—social intercourse—slowly conquers animism. He identifies four stages of animism:

▲ almost everything is alive and conscious

▲ only those things that move are alive

▲ only those things that manifest spontaneous movements are alive

▲ consciousness is limited to the animal world

3. **Artificialism,** which consists in attributing human creation to everything. For example, when asked how the moon began, some of Piaget's subjects replied, "because we began to be alive." As egocentrism decreases, youngsters become more objective, and they steadily assimilate objective reality to their cognitive structures.

Thus they proceed from a purely human or divine explanation to an explanation that is half natural, half artificial: the moon comes from the clouds but the clouds come from people's houses. Finally, at about age 9 they realize that human activity has nothing to do with the origin of the moon.

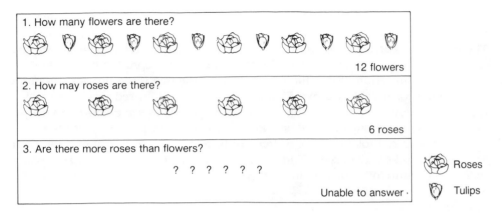

Figure 7.3 Lack of genuine classification.

Limitations of Preoperational Thought

Although we see the steady development of thought during this period, there are still limitations to preoperational thought. As the name *preoperational* implies, this period comes before advanced symbolic operations develop. Piaget has stated constantly that knowledge is not just a mental image of an object or event.

To know an object is to act on it, to modify it, to transform it, and to join objects in a class. The action is also reversible. If two is added to two, the result is four; but if two is taken away from four, the original two returns. The preoperational child lacks the ability to perform such operations on concepts and objects.

There are several reasons for the restricted nature of preoperational thought.

Egocentrism   In the period of preoperational thought, children cannot assume the role of another person or recognize that other viewpoints exist, a state called **egocentrism.** This differs from sensorimotor egocentrism, which is primarily the inability to distinguish oneself from the world. For example, preoperational children make little effort to ensure that listeners understand them. Thus they neither justify their reasoning nor see any contradictions in their logic.

Centration   A striking feature of preoperational thought is the centering of attention on one aspect of an object and the neglecting of any other features—called **centration.** Consequently, reasoning is often distorted. Preoperational youngsters are unable to decenter, to notice features that would give balance to their reasoning.

A good example of this is the process of classification. When youngsters from age 3 to 12 are asked "What things are alike?" their answers proceed through three stages. First, the youngest children group figurally, that is, by similarities, differences, and by forming a figure in space with the parts. Second, children of about age 5 or 6 group objects nonfigurally. They form the elements into groups with no particular spatial form. At this stage, the classification seems rational, but Piaget and Inhelder (1969) provide a fascinating example of the limitations of classification at this age. If in a group of 12 flowers, there are 6 roses, these youngsters can differentiate between the other flowers and the roses. But when asked if there are more flowers or more roses, they are unable to reply because they cannot distinguish the whole from the part (see Figure 7.3). This understanding does not appear until the third phase of classification, about the age of 8.

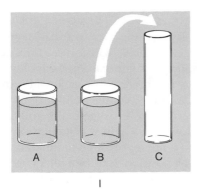 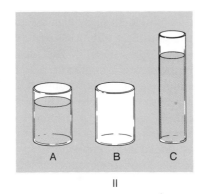

Figure 7.4 Piaget used the beaker task to determine whether children had conservation of liquid. In I, two identical beakers (a and b) are presented to the child; then the experimenter pours the liquid from B into beaker C, which is taller and thinner than A and B. The child is asked if beakers B and C have the same amount of liquid. The preoperational child says no, responding that the taller, thinner beaker (c) has more.

States and Transformations Youngsters concentrate on a particular state or succession of states of an object and ignore the transformation by which one state is changed into another. Their lack of conservation is a good example of the static nature of preoperational thought.

Conservation means understanding that an object retains certain properties, no matter how its form changes. The most popular illustration is to show a 5 year old two glasses, each half filled with water. The child agrees that each glass contains an equal amount. But if you then pour the water from one of the glasses into a taller, thinner glass, the youngster now says that there is more liquid in the new glass (see Figure 7.4). Youngsters consider only the appearance of the liquid and ignore what happened. They also do not perceive the reversibility of the transformation. In their minds they do not pour the water back into the first glass.

Irreversibility A truly cognitive act is reversible if it can utilize stages of reasoning to solve a problem and then proceed in reverse, tracing its steps back to the original question or premise. The preoperational child's thought is **irreversible** and entangles the child in a series of contradictions in logic.

In the water-level problem, for example, the child believes that the taller, thinner glass contains more water. Youngsters cannot mentally reverse the task (imagine pouring the contents back into the original glass). At the conclusion of the pre-operational period, children slowly decenter and learn reversibility as a way of mental life.

The Neo-Piagetians

There are those, usually referred to as neo-Piagetians, who have suggested revisions to Piaget's work. From your reading so far, you realize that Piaget believed in the stage theory of development. That is, development is seen as a sequence of distinct stages, each of which entails important changes in the way a child thinks, feels, and behaves (Scarr & others, 1986). Rest (1983), however, has argued that the acquisition of cognitive structures is gradual rather than abrupt and is not a matter of all-or-nothing (a child is completely in the preoperational or concrete operational stage). A child's level of cognitive development seems to depend more on the nature of the task than on a rigid classification system.

In a careful analysis of Piaget's ideas, Gelman and Baillargeon (1983) state that while the notion of cognitive structures is logical, the idea of broad stages of development is questionable. The idea of distinct stages, with no overlap, seems to lack supporting empirical evidence. For example, if you ask a preschooler if a bouquet composed of six roses and four tulips has more roses or flowers, the child invariably answers more roses. But does that mean the younger child has irreversible structures, while those of the older children are reversible? Is the younger child strictly preoperational and the older operational? In a typical Piagetian experiment, a doll is placed at different positions around a model of three mountains and children are asked how the mountains look at each position. Children under age 6 report their own view and not the doll's. Yet Gelman and Baillargeon (1983) state that when cards with different pictures on each side are shown to 3-year-old children, they correctly report what they saw and what the tester would see.

Can preschoolers be trained to acquire a concrete operational task? In a classic experiment, Gelman (1969) worked with 5 year olds who had failed to conserve number, length, and liquid amount. She trained the children to focus on the relevant relations (teaching them to attend to rows of sticks of equal length, for example). Following this training, when the children were asked to select rows of equal length sticks, they chose correctly. They were later able to transfer this ability to Piagetian conservation tasks.

While this study shows that preschoolers are probably more competent than their failure on concrete operational tasks suggests, we may wonder if these 5 year olds were already on the verge of concrete operations and the training Gelman offered "pushed" them into concrete operational thought.

❖   *There is hesitation in abandoning the stage concept. At one point, many psychologists (including Flavell) were ready to abandon the stage approach for a more gradual, continuous model of cognitive development. Now they are reconsidering. In the beginning or middle of a stage, children may be erratic in their thinking. They may perform better on some tasks (conservation of liquid) than on others (conservation of number). . . . The idea of stages is useful in identifying these major mental reorganizations (Scarr & others, 1986, p. 355).*

Piaget's theory, however, is not the only explanation of cognitive development. A more current theory, called information-processing theory, also helps to explain how children gradually acquire the ability to let one thing represent another. When youngsters represent, they enter a new phase of development.

Another View: Information-Processing Theory

Information processing is the study of how children (and adults) perceive, comprehend, and retain information. As children mature, they steadily devise more sophisticated strategies for extracting information from their world. How many times have you said to yourself, "I wonder what he's thinking?" Or "how could she have arrived at that answer?" You have grappled with the representations in another person's mind. Here, we will discuss how a youngster begins to represent.

The Meaning of Representation
Before tracing the developmental sequence, however, you should have an idea (!) of just what **representation** means. The manner in which you record or express information is a representation of that information (Glass, Holyoak, & Santa, 1987).

BOX 7.2

Children and Their Humor

"Why did daddy tiptoe past the medicine cabinet?"

"Because he didn't want to wake the sleeping pills."

Jokes such as these have spurred Paul McGhee (1979) to analyze children's humor and trace its developmental path. Noting that little is known about how children develop humor, McGhee turned to cognitive development as a possible explanation. While humor also has psychodynamic and social features, McGhee believes that its cognitive properties offer the best basis for unraveling its secrets.

McGhee begins by noting that the basis of most children's humor is incongruity, which is the realization that the relationship between different things just isn't "right." Using this as a basis, he traces four stages of incongruous humor. He treats stages as does Piaget: the sequence of stages remains the same, but the ages at which children pass through them varies.

Stage One: Incongruous Actions Toward Objects. Stage One usually occurs sometime during the second year when children play with objects. They are able to form internal images of the object and thus start to "make-believe." For example, one of Piaget's children picked up a leaf, put it to her ear, and talked to it as if it were a telephone, laughing all the time. One of the main characteristics of Stage One humor is the child's physical activity directed at the object.

Stage Two: Incongruous Labeling of Objects and Events. Stage Two humor is more verbal, which seems to be its most important difference from Stage One. McGhee (1979) notes that the absence of action toward objects is quite noticeable. Piaget's 22-month-old daughter put a shell on the table and said, "sitting." She then put another shell on top of the first, looked at them and said, "sitting on pot." She then began to laugh. They delight in calling a dog a cat, a foot a hand, and then start laughing.

Stage Three: Conceptual Incongruity. Around age 3, most children begin to play with ideas, which reflects their growing cognitive ability. For example, Stage Three children will laugh when they see a drawing of a cat with two heads.

Stage Four: Multiple Meanings. Once children begin to play with the ambiguity of words, their humor approaches the adult level.

- "Hey, did you take a bath?"
- "No. Why, is one missing?"

Children at the Stage Four level (usually around age 7) understand the different meaning of "take" in both instances. Stage Three children could not understand the following.

- "Order! Order! Order in the court."
- "Ham and cheese on rye, your honor."

Stage Four youngsters appreciate its ambiguity.

You can see how cognitive development is linked to humor. As egocentrism wanes, concrete operations appear, enabling children to appreciate more complex meanings in their humor.

The word *car* is a representation since it represents an object. The idea conveyed can also be represented by different words: auto, automobile. In each example, however, the information represented remains the same.

How Do We Represent?

Knowing how children represent information raises important issues for their learning (to be discussed in chap. 8). We appear to employ two types of codes for representing information: **mental imagery** (also called *analog representation*) and **verbal processing** (also called *analytical representation*).

BOX 7.3

How We Code

In a simple, and what has become classic, experiment in cognitive psychology, Conrad (1964) had college students like you memorize lists of six written letters (such as TAVRBK). The students read the letters silently; the letters were removed; the subjects were asked to repeat the letters in order. They would make mistakes and substitute a letter for one they had seen. It was the type of letter substituted that intrigued Conrad.

If the students recalled the letters visually (that is, using the same code in which the letters were originally presented), you would expect them to use a substitute letter that looked like the original letter—C for O. But the students substituted letters that sounded like the original—V for C. Conrad concluded that the students had recoded the letters, substituting a speech code for a visual code. (Incidentally, this is an excellent example of information processing.)

These results are particularly interesting for us because they raise questions about how early childhood children react to instruction.

1. Will they recode visual letters into a speech code?
2. Do individual differences explain their preferences for particular sensory modes? That is, do some children learn better by listening than by reading?
3. Is it possible to identify the mode that a child prefers?

While the answers to these questions remain elusive, some clues are being furnished. For example, Conrad found that with deaf subjects who cannot speak, letter substitutions were visual rather than auditory: they tended to substitute C for O and not V for C.

Consequently, we can conclude that the chances are high that not all children use the same code to represent information in memory. These and similar studies emphasize that parents and teachers must be clear with these children, appealing to as many senses as possible.

Stop for a moment and think about the last time you went to the beach. Were there waves? Was the beach crowded? What color was the water? Answering these questions takes you into the world of mental imagery, a world that has long intrigued philosophers and psychologists. You undoubtedly formed a "picture in your mind" to answer each of the questions. Your mental image represented the waves, the people at the beach, the color of the water (Kosslyn, 1980).

If you think about your answers, you will sooner or later question the accuracy of your image—just how precise is it? Was the water exactly that blue-green color you recall? Today's psychologists are concerned with the reliability of what we report about our images.

Discussing the importance of mental images in our lives, Kosslyn states:

❖ *To get an intuitive feeling for the topic of this book, try to answer the following questions. What shape are a German Shepherd's ears? Is a tennis ball larger than a pear? Does a bee have a dark head? Is a Christmas tree darker green than a frozen pea? Most people report that they mentally picture the named objects in the course of trying to answer these questions. For example, a typical respondent will tell me that he or she pictured the dog's head and "looked at" the ears in order to assess their shape (1980, p. 1).*

Verbal processing, unlike mental imagery, does not resemble what it represents. Language remains the best example of verbal processing: in no way does *car* resemble an actual automobile.

The distinction between mental imagery and verbal processing is important when you consider that although most of us use both codes, we typically prefer one over the other and so do early childhood youngsters. If you can determine which code a child prefers, then you should try to match that code to achieve the best results in learning.

For example, when they memorize, some children begin to use a method called *rehearsal* (repeating something over and over). Others use a technique called *method of loci* (imagining that they put the things to be memorized in different rooms in their house). Children will learn by themselves to use any one (or several) of these techniques (ask your classmates what they do to memorize), but these techniques also can be taught.

In tracing the early childhood youngster's growing memory abilities, we find that, with age, children develop better strategies for remembering. They also learn, although gradually, to use the strategies appropriately and consistently. Preschoolers begin to use rehearsal and acquire the basic idea of planning and helping themselves to remember in various ways, though not in the systematic manner of older children (Gardner, 1982).

As you can tell from our discussion of Piaget's interpretation of the preoperational period and information-processing theory, early childhood children have marched firmly into a symbolic world. A major part of that world, one that has much to do with adaptation, is language.

Language Development

Youngsters soon acquire their native language, a task of such scope and intricacy that its secrets have eluded investigators for centuries. During the early childhood period language ability "explodes." Children proceed from hesitant beginnings to almost complete mastery by the end of the period (about seven years.)

All children learn their native language. At similar ages they manifest similar patterns of speech development, whether they live in a ghetto or in some wealthy suburb. Moskowitz (1979) states that within a short span of time and with almost no direct instruction, children completely analyze their language. Although subtle refinements are made between ages 5 and 10, most youngsters have completed the greater part of the process of language acquisition by the age of 4 or 5.

Language as Rule Learning

By the age of 4 or 5, children will also have discovered several basic rules:

- There are rules for recombining sounds into words.

- Individual words have specific meaning.

- There are rules for recombining words into meaningful sentences.

- There are rules for participating in a dialogue.

What children have acquired naturally, language specialists translate into more technical statements, such as the following:

- The rules of **phonology** describe how to put sounds together to form words.

- The rules of **syntax** describe how to put words together to form sentences.

The attention that adults (especially parents) give children encourages positive interactions and leads to satisfactory and fulfilling relationships. Adult attention will also further language development and enhance a child's self-concept.

- The rules of **semantics** describe how to interpret the meaning of words.

- The rules of **pragmatics** describe how to take part in a conversation.

As we trace the path of language development in the early childhood years, you should remember a basic distinction that children quite clearly demonstrate. At about one year (the infancy period) children show an ability for receptive language ("show me your nose"—they receive and understand these words). Now, in early childhood, they produce language themselves, **expressive language.** How do children acquire these language milestones?

The Pattern of Language Development

All children learn their native tongue, and at similar ages they manifest similar patterns of language development. The basic sequence of language organization is as follows (Travers, 1982):

- At about 3 months children use intonations similar to those of adults.

- At about 1 year they begin to use recognizable words.

- At about 4 years they have acquired the complicated structure of their native tongue.

- In about two or three more years they speak and understand sentences that they have never previously used or heard.

Around age 10 months, children begin to use actual words and can usually follow simple directions. At about one year, or perhaps slightly older, they seem to grasp that words "mean" things, like people or objects. Sometime between the ages

Table 7.4 The Language Sequence	
Language	**Age**
Crying	From birth
Cooing	5–6 weeks
Babbling	4–5 months
Single words	12 months
Two words	18 months
Phrases	2 years
Short sentences and questions	3 years
Conjunctions and prepositions	4 years

of 12 and 18 months children begin to use single words as sentences *(holophrases)*; by age 2 they utter two-word sentences; and usually by age 4 they produce sentences of several words.

As children grow, it is difficult to specify how extensive their vocabulary is. Do we mean spoken words only? Or do we include words that children may not use but clearly understand? Whatever criteria we use, girls seem to surpass boys by about one year of development until the age of 8.

It is an amazing accomplishment. For example, the vocabulary of every language is categorized; that is, some words are nouns, some are verbs, still others are adjectives, prepositions, or conjunctions. If English had only 1,000 nouns and 1,000 verbs, we could form one million sentences ($1,000 \times 1,000$). But nouns can be used as objects as well as subjects. Therefore the number of possible three-word sentences increases to one billion ($1,000 \times 1,000 \times 1,000$).

One billion sentences is the result of a starkly impoverished vocabulary. The number of sentences that could be generated from English, with its thousands of nouns and verbs, plus adjectives, adverbs, prepositions, and conjunctions, staggers the imagination. Estimates are that it would take trillions of years to say all possible English sentences of 20 words. In this context, the ability of children to acquire their language is an astounding achievement. Although most youngsters experience problems with some tasks during this period—difficulty with reading or mathematics—they acquire their language easily and in just a few years. The specific sequence of this accomplishment is seen in Table 7.4. These ages and accomplishments are a good guide to normal language development. Remember, don't confuse youngsters who demonstrate a serious language problem (such as lack of comprehension) with those who experience temporary setbacks.

Speech Irregularities

When speech emerges, certain irregularities appear that are quite normal and to be expected. For example, *overextensions* mark children's beginning words. Assume that a child has learned the name of the house pet—"doggy." Think what that label means: an animal with a head, tail, body, and four legs. Now consider what other animals "fit" this label: cats, horses, donkeys, and cows. Consequently, children may briefly apply "doggy" to all four-legged creatures, but they quickly eliminate overextensions as they learn about their world.

Overregularities are a similar fleeting phenomenon. As youngsters begin to use two- and three-word sentences, they struggle to convey more precise meanings by mastering the grammatical rules of their language. For example, many English verbs add *ed* to indicate past tense.

> I want to play ball.
> I wanted to play ball.

BOX 7.4

The Case of Genie

The startling case of Genie illustrates the durability of language but also demonstrates its vulnerability. Discovered in the upstairs room of a suburban Los Angeles home, Genie was 13 1/2 years old and weighed only 60 pounds when found. She could not stand or chew solid food, nor was she toilet trained (Curtis, 1977).

From the age of 20 months she had been confined to a small, shaded room where she had been kept in a crib or tied to a chair. Any noises that she made were greeted with a beating. Few, if any, words were exchanged with her parents, nor was there any radio or television set in the home. She was usually fed baby food. Genie also had a congenital hip problem that caused her father to think that she was severely retarded. She had emotional difficulties but had normal hearing and vision. Her language comprehension and usage were almost nonexistent.

After treatment in the Children's Hospital of Los Angeles, Genie was placed in a foster home where she acquired language, more from exposure than any formal training. Estimates are that she has acquired as much language in eight years as the normal child acquires in three. She continues to have articulation problems and difficulty with word order.

While Genie has made remarkable language progress, difficulties persist. For example, she does not appear to have mastered the rules of language (her grammar is unpredictable), she continues to use the stereotypic speech of the language-disabled child, and she seems to understand more language than she can produce. Thus the case of Genie suggests that while language is difficult to retard, sufficiently severe conditions can affect progress in language.

Other verbs change their form much more radically.

> Did Daddy come home?
> Daddy came home.

Most children, even after they have mastered the correct form of such verbs as *come, see, run,* still add *ed* to the original form. That is, youngsters who know that the past tense of *come* is *came* will still say:

> Daddy comed home.

Again, this persists only briefly and is another example of the close link between language and thought. We know that from birth children respond to patterns. They look longer at the human face than they will at diagrams because the human face is more complex. (Remember the Fantz study?) Once they have learned a pattern such as adding *ed* to signify past tense, they have considerable difficulty in changing the pattern.

The path of language development is similar for all children. A particular culture has little to do with language emergence, but it has everything to do with the shape that any language assumes. Children will not speak before a certain time—this is a biological given and nothing will change it. But once language appears, it is difficult to retard its progress. Usually only some traumatic event such as brain damage (which we have discussed) or dramatically deprived environmental conditions will hinder development.

Finally, Anselmo (1987) notes that as children come to the end of the early childhood period, several language milestones have been achieved:

- They become skillful in building words, adding suffixes such as *er*, and *ist* to form nouns. The person who performs experiments is an experiment*er*.

- They begin to be comfortable with passive sentences ("the glass was broken by the wind").

- By the end of the period, children can pronounce almost all English speech sounds accurately.

- As we have noted, this is the time of the "language explosion," and vocabulary has grown rapidly.

- Children of this age are aware of grammatical correctness.

Transition

Thus far in our discussion of the early childhood years we have seen that rate of growth slows somewhat but still continues at a steady pace. Physical and motor skills become more refined. Cognitive development during these years leads to a world of representation in which children are expected to acquire and manipulate symbols. Language gradually becomes a powerful tool in adapting to the environment.

There are, however, other aspects of development that affect the direction a child's development takes. Early childhood youngsters seem to "come into their own." The emerging personality of infancy takes on definite dimensions in these years. Children must learn to adjust to family members—perhaps a new brother or sister. Many children of this age experience the shock of parental separation and divorce, with its consequences to development. For many, the idea of family takes on new meaning. These are among the important topics to which we turn in the next chapter.

Key Ideas

1. Early childhood youngsters need a sensitive, and sensible, combination of freedom and restraint.
2. Good physical health during this period requires proper exercise, diet, and rest.
3. Continued brain development is reflected in a child's growing lateralization.
4. Children of this period demonstrate increasing motor skill development.
5. Early childhood youngsters can now represent information and use these representations to guide their behavior.
6. It is the time of Piaget's preoperational period, marked by such characteristics as deferred imitation, symbolic play, drawing, mental imagery, and language fluency.
7. A child's developing sense of humor seems to be tied to cognitive development.
8. During this period, children acquire the fundamentals of their language and begin to enlarge their vocabulary at a rapid rate.

Key Terms

Animism
Anticipatory image
Artificialism
Autonomy
Centration
Cerebral hemispheres
Conservation
Controlled scribbling
Deferred imitation
Developmentally delayed
Drawing
Egocentrism
Expressive language
Information processing
Initiative
Irreversibility

Lateralization
Mental imagery
Overregularities
Phonology
Pragmatics
Preoperational period
Random scribbling
Realism
Representation
Reproductive image
Semantics
Symbolic play
Syntax
Verbal evocation
Verbal processing

What Do You Think?

1.   The data presented in this chapter show that early childhood youngsters continue their rapid growth, although at a less rapid rate than during infancy. Imagine yourself a parent of a child of this age (boy or girl). How much would you encourage them to participate in organized, directed physical activities (swimming, dancing, soccer etc.)? Be sure to give specific reasons for your answer.

2.   As you read Paul McGhee's account of the development of children's humor, could you explain his stages by comparing them to Piaget's work? Do you think this is a logical way to proceed? Why?

3.   When you compared the tragic case of Genie to the enormous language growth of most children, what came to your mind? Did it change your opinion about how language develops? In what way? What do you think this case implies for the existence of a sensitive period for language development?

Suggested Readings

Fraiberg, Selma. (1959). *The Magic Years.* New York: Scribners. We mentioned this little classic at the beginning of the chapter. You'll gain valuable insights into the early childhood years from these pages. It's available in paperback in many bookstores.

Moskowitz, Breyne. (1979). The acquisition of language. *Scientific American,* 92–108. If you're like most readers encountering the basics of language development for the first time, you could use a good summary of the process. This article, which you can get in your library and copy, is clear, thorough, and well written.

Trelease, Jim. (1985). *The Read-Aloud Handbook.* New York: Penguin. An excellent source of ideas for capturing children's attention through books. It includes a fine age-related annotated bibliography.

· *Chapter 8* ·

Early Childhood: The Expanding Social World

The early childhood years see the blossoming of youngsters into distinct personalities. Although temperamental differences are apparent at birth, they now flourish until even the casual observer notices a child's "personality." Early childhood youngsters begin a period in which they must reconcile their individuality with the restrictions of the world around them.

The psychologist William Damon (1983) has described this period as one of socialization versus individuation. By **socialization,** Damon means the need to establish and maintain relations with others and to regulate behavior according to society's demands. **Individuation** refers to the fullest development of one's self. These two functions seem to pull in opposite directions. Society has certain regulations that its members must follow if chaos is to be avoided. Yet these rules must not be so rigid that the individual members who constitute the society cannot develop their potential to the fullest.

Any society, ours included, demands resolution of the tension between the two. Each needs the other. In chapter 7, individuation was stressed, the emergence of individual physical and cognitive abilities. In this chapter, the expression of those talents within a societal context is explored and the possible sources of tension are traced.

But as we examine the great socializing agents of society—family, school, peers, televison—a clear warning sign flashes. Is society driving early childhood youngsters too harshly? Are expectations too great? Do we expect our children to grow up too quickly? The popular child psychologist David Elkind thinks so:

❖   *What is happening in the United States today is truly astonishing. In a society that prides itself on its preference for facts over hearsay, on its openness to research, and on its respect for 'expert' opinion, parents, educators, administrators, and legislators are ignoring the facts, the research, and the expert opinion about how young children learn and how best to teach them (1987, p. 3).*

What concerns Elkind is the academic pressure that parents and educators are placing on their children. Calling this the "**miseducation** of youth," Elkind believes that these parents are in search of superkids. He believes that such parental behavior reflects parental ego more than parental need and has little to do with a child's needs.

In a thoughtful essay on children in our society today, Neil Postman (1982) argues that childhood has actually disappeared. Citing highly paid 12-year-old models, toddlers in designer jeans, and the growing absence of children's games, Postman laments the disappearance of childhood. In a highly technological society with instant and open communication, nothing is withheld from youngsters. Calling television the "total disclosure medium," Postman believes that the lines separating adulthood from childhood are being erased. This loss of a distinct childhood results in a loss of shame. Everything is revealed to children; there are no secrets.

To come to grips with these issues, in this chapter we'll examine the modern family, tracing the stages through which it proceeds, the impact of parenting on children, the effect of divorce on development, and the growing importance of daycare in our society. We'll next explore how these early experiences affect a child's learning by examining the various types of learning. The discussion of learning will lead us to a review of early childhood education—its pros and cons. Throughout these years a child's sense of personal identity is gradually emerging. Its inherent temperamental characteristics are tempered by the reactions of family members, teachers, and peers. Finally, we'll comment on the significance of play to children of this age. Our initial task, though, is to examine that great socializing agent—the family.

Television, one of the major socializing agents in a child's life, can have both prosocial and antisocial consequences. As a given in the lives of most children, parents should carefully monitor what their children watch.

The Family in Development

While this section could have been written for any chapter in a book on the life span, it is particularly pertinent here since the family is still recognized as the great socializing agent. We have previously mentioned (chap. 1) the relatively recent appearance of childhood. Our focus here will be on several current phenomena that have a powerful effect on early childhood.

But before we begin our analysis, we should remember that any family is dynamic, not static. Families change, and as they do, they exercise different effects on a child's development. For example, children who remain in an intact family, or who experience the death of a parent, or who go through a parental divorce all undergo unique experiences that must affect development. But we need not be so dramatic. Families sustain normal change in the course of the lives of their members.

As society changes, the manner in which families respond also changes. Children cannot escape the results—positive or negative—of these twists and turns of family living. We also know that one of the most important characteristics of any family is the way that parents treat their children.

Parenting Behavior

In a careful analysis of the relationship between parental behavior and children's competence, Baumrind (1967, 1971, 1986) discovered three kinds of parental behavior: authoritarian, authoritative, permissive. Here is what she means by each of the types.

Authoritarian Parents
Authoritarian parents are demanding, and for them instant obedience is the most desirable child trait. When there is any conflict between these parents and their

---

BOX 8.1
Family Changes

Any analysis of family life contains two major themes. First is the nature of the family itself. In the late twentieth century, the identification of alternative forms of family living has sharply altered our view of the traditional family. Yet as we have seen throughout our discussion, different family styles have always existed. Population projections and estimates of family styles present a fairly consistent pattern: change will continue, but it will be a modification of current styles. For example, the number of single mothers will increase, but as governmental support also increases, there will undoubtedly be more and better day-care services, increased after-school programs for the older children, and perhaps greater flexibility in the work schedules of working parents.

The second major theme is the developmental consequences of these changes.

Here we find much less certainty, since it is simply too soon to make definite statements. While it is relatively easy to state that there should be no attachment difficulties for youngsters who are placed in daycare centers as early as 3 months of age, this assumption is based on the quality of the original, and continuing, interaction between the mother and child (Brazelton, 1987).

As we noted, however, the nature of that mother-child interaction may be quite different for family-reared and daycare children. What will be the lasting effects of the lack of a male model in families headed by women? There may be few, if any, but it is too soon to tell. Society changes, families adapt (perhaps more rapidly than before), and our clear task is to monitor the developmental consequences of these changes.

Table 8.1　Patterns of Childrearing Behavior

	Authoritarian High	Authoritarian Low	Authoritative High	Authoritative Low	Permissive High	Permissive Low
Control	•		•			•
Clarity of communication		•	•		•	
Maturity demands	•		•			•
Nurturance		•	•		•	

children (Why can't I go to the party?), no consideration is given to the child's view, no attempt is made to explain why the youngster can't go to the party, and often the child is punished for even asking.

Authoritative Parents
Authoritative parents respond to their children's needs and wishes. Believing in parental control, they attempt to explain the reasons for it to their children. Authoritative parents expect mature behavior and will enforce rules, but they encourage their children's independence and search for potential (see Table 8.1). They try to have their youngsters understand that both parents and children have rights. In the resolution of socialization versus individuation, authoritative parents try to maintain a happy balance between the two.

Permissive Parents
Baumrind believes that **permissive parents** take a tolerant, accepting view of their children's behavior, including both aggressive and sexual urges. They rarely use

Table 8.2	Parental Behaviors and Children's Characteristics		
	Parental Behaviors		
	Authoritarian	Authoritative	Permissive
Children's characteristics	Withdrawn Lack of enthusiasm Shy (girls) Hostile (boys) Low need achievement Low competence	Self-assertive Independent Friendly Cooperative High need achievement High competence	Impulsive Low self-reliance Low self-control Low maturity Aggressive Lack of responsibility

punishment, or make demands of their children. Children make almost all of their own decisions. Distinguishing indulgence from indifference in these parents can be difficult.

Beginning with the belief that parents' behaviors are concerned with control, clarity of communication, maturity demands (you can do better than that), and nurturance (love, warmth), Baumrind attempted to link parental characteristics (such as authoritarian, etc.) and qualities in their children (such as outgoing, hostile, etc.). Table 8.1 summarizes these interactions.

Examining Table 8.1, note that authoritative parents are high on control (they have definite standards for their children), high on clarity of communication (the children clearly understand what is expected of them), high in maturity demands (they want their children to behave in a way appropriate for their age), and high in nurturance (there is a warm, loving relationship between parents and children). Thus, according to Baumrind's work, authoritative parents are most desirable.

What do these behaviors mean for children's characteristics? While no hard answers can as yet be given, Table 8.2 illustrates several characteristics associated with each of the parental styles. Since these characteristics may be quite general and may change as research focuses on this topic, we can be quite certain of one conclusion: regardless of style, parental behavior leaves its mark, often indelibly.

Children of Divorce

Divorce, an increasingly important aspect of family life, affects children in many ways. Not only is their physical way of life changed (perhaps a new home, or reduced standard of living), but their psychological lives are touched (Hetherington, Cox, & Cox, 1985). Before examining these effects, let's look first at the divorce phenomenon.

Facts About Divorce
Nearly half of today's marriages will end in divorce. Estimates are that 50% of our children will live with a single parent before the age of 18. Table 8.3 summarizes many of these changes.

Effects on Children
As mentioned earlier, any discussion of the effects of divorce (or any traumatic event) must begin with the child's level of cognitive development. Remember that early childhood youngsters are at Piaget's preoperational level. Their ability to engage in abstract thinking is still limited and they lack that vital aspect of cognition—the ability to reverse their thinking. This colors their reaction to their parents' divorce.

As social conditions change—mothers working, single-parent families—fathers have become more involved in childcare. Children thus see their parents in roles different from the more stereotypical views of the past.

Table 8.3 Children Living With One Parent	
Status of Parent	**Number**
Mothers	
Divorced	5,325,000
Absent spouse	3,288,000
Widowed	821,000
Never married	3,985,000
Fathers	
Divorced	814,000
Absent spouse	432,000
Widowed	95,000
Never married	310,000

Source: Data from Bureau of the Census, 1987.

Other conditions affect children's reactions to their parents' divorce (Wallerstein & Blakeslee, 1989):

- The bitterness of conflict before the divorce

- The child's reaction to the loss of the parent who leaves

- Any change in the relationship between the child and the departed parent

- The effect the divorce has on the parent who retains custody of the children

- Any change in behavior toward the children on the part of the parent who retains custody

Commonly reported reactions of early childhood youngsters to divorce are shock and depression. They fear that their parent (s) no longer love them and are actually abandoning them. These reactions fit the pattern of preoperational thinking. Their cognitive egocentrism prevents them from seeing the problem from their parents' perspective. They cannot realize that their mother or father loves them just as much even though they are leaving. Thus the divorce centers on them.

Second Chances
Wallerstein and Blakeslee (1989) report findings similar to those of Hetherington and others. Beginning in 1971, Wallerstein studied 60 families that had experienced divorce. She worked with 131 children who were between the ages of 2 1/2 and 18 at the time their parents separated. Her analysis of the 34 youngsters who were in preschool at the time of parental breakup reveals important information about early childhood youngsters.

When the parents separated, their children were seriously upset. Acute separation anxiety appeared. Eighteen months later about half of the group was still quite troubled, with boys showing the most severe problems. Five years later the children's adjustment seemed to be tied to the quality of life in the postdivorce or remarried family. About one-third of the group showed signs of depression. Ten years later the children claimed little memory of the circumstances surrounding the divorce. Wallerstein, however, in analyzing their replies to questions, found a high degree of repression in their conversations. Wallerstein also discovered a phenomenon she called **reconciliation fantasies.** Although the divorce had occurred

Children develop within a complex network of family relationships. What they are exposed to during these years can have long-lasting consequences.

BOX 8.2

Children of Single Parents

Studying the long-term effects of divorce on children, Hetherington and colleagues (1985) conclude that divorce has more adverse, long-term effects on boys. Remarriage of a mother who has custody of the children, however, is associated with an *increase* in girls' behavior problems and a slight *decrease* in boys' problems.

The transition period in the first year following the divorce is stressful: economically, socially, and emotionally. Conditions then seem to improve and children in a stable, smoothly functioning home are better adjusted than children in a nuclear family riddled with conflict. Nevertheless, school achievement may suffer and impulsivity increases. Hetherington and Parke make an interesting comment about the relationship between divorced mothers and their children:

Divorced mothers may have given their children a hard time, but divorced mothers got rough treatment from their children, particularly their sons. In comparison with divorced fathers and parents in nuclear families, the divorced mother found that in the first year following divorce her children didn't obey, affiliate, or attend to her. They nagged and whined, made more dependency demands, and were more likely to ignore her. The aggression of boys with divorced mothers peaked at one year following divorce, then dropped significantly, but at six years after divorce was still higher than that of boys in nuclear families. (1986, p. 524)

---

10 years earlier, many of the children stated poignantly that they wished their parents could get together again. Wallerstein concluded that early childhood youngsters who live through the divorce of their parents are less burdened in the future than those who are older at the time of the divorce.

Does Divorce Cause Childhood Problems?

We have one final comment about the difficulties children have after divorce. In a carefully designed study, Block and colleagues (1986) have raised questions about problems that children have after parental divorce. Beginning with data indicating that some youngsters do and others do not have problems, the authors state that one fault of the divorce studies is that they are almost all retrospective (that is, they "look back"). Consequently, they are at the mercy of faulty memories and perhaps an adolescent's or adult's unwillingness to speak of painful experiences.

The authors were able to design a prospective study (looking ahead) of children's personalities before the divorce. They found that 3-year-old boys whose parents eventually divorced already were showing problems, especially self-control. When they were 7 years old, they were still showing the same behavior. Three-year-old girls whose parents would divorce seemed competent, skillful, and competitive. But by age 4 their behavior had changed: they didn't get along with others, were overly emotional, and tended to withdraw. By age 7, these behaviors were still evident, but the girls also showed continuing cognitive competence.

The authors' findings point to several important conclusions:

- Researchers cannot focus on the divorce itself as the cause of children's later problems.

- Some youngsters show these same problems years prior to the divorce.

- Events *preceding* the divorce, especially the stress and conflict involved, may be responsible for problems that appear after the divorce.

- Girls may not be as immune to marital turmoil as we thought. They may simply display their feelings in a manner "appropriate" for girls: anxious, withdrawn, extremely well-behaved.

Hetherington's excellent earlier study (1972) of father absence supports this last conclusion. Girls whose fathers died or who left because of divorce showed little disruption of appropriate sex-role behavior but had later problems in adolescence in relating to males. Daughters of divorced women sought more attention from boys, actively seeking contact with them. Daughters of widows avoided boys and preferred female friends and activities.

Daycare

Almost two-thirds of women with children under age 14, and more than one-half of mothers with children under one, are in the labor force. In fact, the single largest category of working mothers are those with children under age 3 (Zigler & Stevenson, 1987).

What happens to children while mothers are at work? Obviously someone must be taking care of these youngsters, and it is precisely here that questions are raised about **daycare.** How competent are the individuals who offer these services? Is the daycare center healthy and stimulating? Is it safe? What are the long-term developmental consequences of daycare placement? In light of recent exposures of the sexual abuse of children in some centers, America's parents are demanding answers to these questions.

Facts About Daycare

Reliable facts about daycare are hard to come by, chiefly because of the lack of any national policy that would provide hard data. There are about 35,000–40,000 "places" providing daycare services (principal income is from offering childcare). "Places" is perhaps the best way to describe them because of the wide variety of circumstances available. For example, one mother may charge another mother several dollars to take care of her child. A relative may care for several family children. Churches, businesses, and charities may run large operations (Zigler & Gordon, 1982). Some may be sponsored by local or state government as an aid to the less affluent. Others are run on a pay-as-you-go basis. Almost everyone agrees that the best centers are staffed by teachers who specialize in daycare services (about 25% of daycare personnel).

If we now sort out what is known about types of daycare centers, we can group them as follows (Clarke-Stewart, 1982). (Remember: most states now have minimal standards for daycare operation.)

- *Private daycare centers run for profit* have no eligibility requirements and will accept almost anyone who can pay the fee. Typically staffed by two or three people (usually not professionally trained), they may operate in a converted store or shop. They probably are minimally equipped with toys and educational activities and usually offer no social or health services.

Daycare has become an important phenomenon in our society as more and more mothers join the work force. Research indicates that developmental outcomes are closely linked to the quality of daycare.

Among the variety of daycare settings, home daycare centers are quite numerous. Often run by a family member or neighbor, they are smaller and more informal than large centers.

- *Commercial centers* are also private and run for profit. They may be part of a national or regional chain with uniform offerings and facilities. They usually are well equipped with good food and activities. The centers are a business, much as a MacDonald's or Burger King. KinderCare, for example, runs about 900 centers.

- *Community church centers* are often (but not always) run for children of the poor. The quality of personal care (attention, affection) is usually good but they often have minimal facilities and activities.

- *Company centers* are often offered as fringe benefits for employees. They are usually run in good facilities with a well-trained staff and a wide range of services.

- *Public service centers* are government sponsored, well run, and have high quality throughout. Unfortunately, there are few of these available and they are designed to serve low-income children.

- *Research centers* are usually affiliated with some university and represent what the latest research says a daycare center should be. Most studies of daycare have been conducted in these centers. But since the centers are of the highest quality, the results of such studies do not give a true picture of daycare throughout the country.

- *Other centers* include the family-run centers mentioned earlier and co-operative centers where parents rotate responsibility for childcare under professional guidance. In another fairly popular form of care, a neighborhood mother, usually a former nurse or teacher, takes care of two or three children, thus avoiding state requirements concerning number of children, facilities, or insurance.

A National Concern

As you can see, the country is moving into a different era with regard to daycare. Working mothers are now in the majority, and their numbers promise to increase. Given these events, regulation of daycare has taken on new urgency. Legislative

---

BOX 8.3

Desirable Qualities of Daycare Centers

For those parents who wish guidelines to identify important features in a daycare setting, here are several specific suggestions based on Clarke-Stewart's (1982) recommendations.

Health and Safety
No smoking around children
Clean floors
Covered floors
A clean and neat eating area
Children are kept clean
One adult always present
Dangerous materials (drugs etc.) locked up
Electrical outlets covered
First-aid supplies available
Everything in good repair
Heavy furniture secured
Good recordkeeping

Physical Space
Each child has individual space for belongings
Adequate resting space
Good storage space
Good window space
Well-controlled ventilation
Clean, accessible toilet
Easy access to play area
Play area well maintained
Physical space not overcrowded
Physical space can encompass materials and activities

Adults
- Enough adults to meet desired ratio (see Table 8.4)
- Adults work well with children
- Adults have had daycare training
- Staff concerned with all children
- Both males and females employed
- No physical punishment
- Well-organized programs

Table 8.4 Suggested Ratio of Staff to Children			
	Age	**Maximum Group Size**	**Staff-Child Ratio**
For centers	0–2	6	1:3
	2–3	12	1:4
	3–6	16	1:8
For homes	0–2	10	1:5
	2–6	12	1:6

battles over standards for daycare centers have been constant, but the best the federal government has been able to do is to propose general standards. Among the most important of these is the suggested ratio of staff to children.

Despite the minimal salaries of daycare workers, costs are high because daycare is labor intensive. Staff-child ratios usually average from 1:8 to 1:10, much too high considering children's needs and safety. But a new attitude is developing, one with political consequences. National surveys have consistently shown that more than one-half of the voters think there should be a national policy regarding daycare.

Developmental Outcomes
Regardless of what you may have heard or read, there are no definite conclusions concerning the long-term developmental consequences of daycare. One reason is

that careful follow-up of children from daycare is not yet available (Zigler & Stevenson, 1987).

Such studies are only beginning to appear. For example, Belsky and Rovine (1988) reported on the results of two longitudinal studies of infants and their families. They found that when infants were 12–13 months old and had twenty or more hours of nonmaternal care per week, some of the infants were insecurely attached. These same infants were more likely to be aggressive and tended to withdraw. Yet this report also contains puzzling data. Over one-half of the infants who had the twenty hours of nonmaternal care were securely attached. These data reveal the uncertainty of our present knowledge and reinforce our conclusion that we must be careful about either positive or negative statements about daycare.

Another obstacle has been the use of university sponsored research centers to study children. These centers are usually lavishly equipped and overstaffed. They simply do not reflect the national norm. Despite this, some conclusions have been drawn.

- Youngsters from deprived environments show cognitive gains; those from middle- and upper-class homes show no gain or loss.

- Daycare youngsters seem more mature socially.

These are shaky findings and may very well be reversed by additional research.

Given the changing conditions in which many children grow up, it is not surprising that their experiences affect what and how they learn. Consequently, we shall next turn our attention to education in early childhood.

Early Childhood Education

The number of children in early childhood education programs has increased steadily in the last four decades. Project Head Start, for example, was started in 1965 to aid low-income children. While research has shown mixed results for improving children's achievement, other benefits have been claimed.

Lazar and Darlington (1982) studied the long-term results of 12 Head Start programs and reported significant effects on school competence, families, and attitudes about self and school. Among the techniques employed by the various programs were constant communications with parents, training of mothers in the use of educational activities in the home, and periodic home visits. Pooling the data from these studies, Lazar and Darlington (1982) discovered the following:

1. Children who attended these programs were less likely to be retained in grade and more likely to meet their schools' requirements.

2. They attained higher IQ scores than their controls.

3. The children demonstrated higher self-concepts and were proud of their school accomplishment.

4. Mothers of program graduates were more satisfied with their child's school performance than control mothers; they also had higher occupational aspirations for their children than control mothers.

These results were obtained several years after the children had left the program and suggest the benefits of positive parental involvement in school affairs.

There are preschool programs for the middle class and advantaged as well as for low-income children. Some of these schools offer only play as the chance to learn how to get along with others. Others, such as the Montessori schools, are much more structured.

Regardless of the kind of school, several features distinguish preschools: low teacher-child ratio, specially trained teachers, availability of resources, and recognition of children's individual differences. These programs are all child centered; that is, they are designed to emphasize the individual child and to provide the child with enriching, enjoyable experiences.

Miseducation

A different perspective is offered by Elkind (1987), some of whose ideas were presented in the chapter opening. Believing that educating preschoolers too often reflects the parents' needs, Elkind is concerned that many programs are excessively formal and involve inappropriate expectations. Individual differences are sacrificed to some form of attainment, ranging from swimming to reading. Thus pressure can become excessive and the joy and pleasure of these years are lost.

Elkind believes that placement in pressure programs comes from the needs of several classes of parents.

> *Gourmet parents.* They have everything and they want their children to have the same experiences.
> *College-degree parents.* They believe education is the answer to everything, so they want their children to be intellectual "superkids."
> *Gold-medal parents.* These parents want their children to be Olympic-class "in something."
> *Prodigy parents.* They made it on their own and think their children can do likewise if they get a fast start in life.

These are only a few of Elkind's classes of parents, but they illustrate his concern that today's preschoolers are placed in educational pressure cookers because of their parents' needs.

Within these changing conditions of society and family, the early childhood youngster must learn to adjust and survive. It is the give and take between pressure and freedom that helps to shape a definite personality.

The Self Emerges

"You are who you are." This oft-repeated statement summarizes what personality means. Psychologists define personality as the "dynamic organization of those psychophysical systems that define a person's behavior and thought." Our concern is with how children acquire this sense of self.

In chapter 6 we mentioned the growing belief that humans come into this world with inborn temperamental differences. These differences, then, are the foundation upon which children build their unique personalities. Children form their personalities by using their *genetic endowment* that defines their potential: physical and intellectual. (Whether the environment helps or hinders the fulfillment of potential is a story for chap. 9.) They also learn about themselves from those around them. The reactions of others contribute greatly to what children think of themselves (Damon, 1983).

The Development of Self

To understand development, you must always remember it is an integrated process (Harter, 1983). All aspects—physical, cognitive, social, and emotional—

BOX 8.4

Multicultural Focus: Self and Others

As we have seen in this chapter, one of the accomplishments of the early childhood years is a sense of self. This understanding of self comes partially through interacting with others. When children interact with those from other cultures, their self-identity broadens to accept those with different customs, languages, and ideas.

In commenting upon the growing understanding of others, Ramsey states:

While knowledge of unfamiliar people and lifestyles may reduce children's fears and avoidance of differences, their motivation for reaching beyond cultural, racial, and class barriers largely rests on their self-confidence, their ability to empathize with others' experiences and feelings, and their anticipation of pleasure and satisfaction to be derived from expanding their social relationship (1987, p. 112).

Helping youngsters to achieve this objective are the social goals of multicultural education, which include (Ramsey, 1987):

- Positive cultural, racial, and class identities
- High self-esteem
- Awareness of other emotional, cognitive, and physical states

- The ability and willingness to interact with diverse others
- A sense of social responsibility
- An active concern for the welfare of others

Those working with preschool youngsters have a unique opportunity to further a positive multicultural perspective during these years of enthusiasm and rapid learning. As an example, Yao (1988) offers several suggestions for working with Asian immigrant parents. She begins by urging adults to take the time to familiarize themselves with the social, cultural, and personality traits that make these children and their parents unique. Adults should ask themselves questions such as:

- Do I have any prejudices toward this group?
- What stereotypes do I associate with Asian-Americans? (e.g., they're all superior in math and science)
- What do I know about their culture?
- Will there be any conflict between my values and theirs?

These and similar questions can act as guidelines to help us adapt to those of different cultures and also help children adapt to different ways. We can do no less.

contribute to smooth growth. Nowhere is this more evident than in the analysis of self-development.

- If a youngster has normal physical growth, a sense of mastery develops, increasing self-confidence.

- If cognitive development progresses satisfactorily, children acquire vital knowledge that helps them to adjust to their world, increasing self-confidence.

- If relations with others are mostly pleasant, children learn about others and themselves, increasing self-confidence.

Children distinguish themselves from others at about age 18 months, perhaps even a little earlier. In their famous experiment, Lewis and Brooks-Gunn (1979) put rouge on the noses of children. At age 15 to 18 months, youngsters, when placed before a mirror, touched the rouge on their noses, indicating that they knew who they were. They recognized themselves.

Think of what you have learned about cognitive development: children are becoming less egocentric; they are distinguishing themselves from the world. Emotionally, they have begun the process of separating from their mothers, recognizing

The infant shown here touching his nose and mouth against the mirror reveals the development of a sense of self, which most infants accomplish by about eighteen months of age.

that mothers are also individuals. Language is flourishing and others are speaking to them. The convergence of developmental paths helps to further the sense of self. Their growing cognitive ability helps children to represent things, to separate from mothers and the world in general. This leads to acceptance—through cognition, language, and developing relations—of an independent world "out there."

Gender Identity

❖ *Sex identity at first glance appears to be a simple matter of boy/girl. It is in fact, a most complicated phenomenon. Adult sex identity results from a mixture of genetic, hormonal, cultural, and psychological forces in proportions that are largely unknown. The scientific complexity of sex identity is matched by the emotional reaction it evokes. Sex identity is usually the first question that pops into everyone's mind whenever a new human being enters the world (Kilpatrick, 1976, pp. 61–62).*

Kilpatrick, who has written so sensitively about sexual development, emphasizes that gender identity results from a complicated mix of culture and biology. To clarify the meaning of sex identity, we should distinguish sex identity, sex stereotypes, and sex role.

- **Sex identity** is a conviction that one belongs to the sex of birth.

- **Sex stereotypes** reflect beliefs about the characteristics associated with male or female.

- **Sex role** refers to culturally acceptable sexual behavior.

Sex Identity and Biology

Whatever your ideas on sex identity and sex, we start with an unavoidable premise: parts of the sexual agenda are biologically programmed. As Elkin and Handel state:

❖ *If any phenomenon in the human world can be considered an incontrovertible fact, it would be this: a human being can either beget a child or bear a child. No human being can do both. This difference in body functioning between males and females is universal; it occurs in all human societies, and there is not a single known exception (1989, p. 211).*

John Money (1980), working in a Johns Hopkins clinic devoted to the study of congenital abnormalities of the sex organs, believes that sexual differentiation occurs through a series of stages. He has proposed a series of four stages that account for biological sex. (Note: this says nothing about sex role.)

Chromosomal Sex   The biological sexual program is initially carried by either the X or Y sex chromosome. This is called **chromosomal sex.** If you recall from chapter 3, the male can carry either the X or Y to join with the mother's egg, which carries only the X sex chromosome. When a sperm with an X chromosome fertilizes the egg, a female is conceived (XX). If the sperm carries a Y chromosome, a male is conceived (XY).

Gonadal Sex   Chromosomal sex alone does not determine sex. The XX or XY combination passes on the sexual program to the undifferentiated gonads (Money & Ehrhardt, 1972). This is called **gonadal sex.** If the program is XY, the gonads will then differentiate into testes. This, as you recall, occurs during the 6th or 7th week after fertilization. If the program is XX, the gonads differentiate into the ovaries, starting at about the 12th week. So during the first six weeks, the dividing, fertilized egg is essentially sexless.

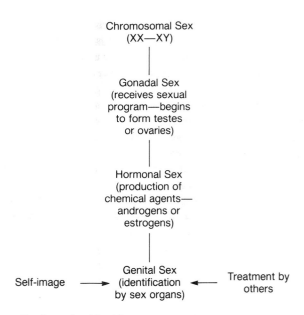

Figure 8.1 The path of gender identity.

Hormonal Sex   Once the testes or ovaries are differentiated, they begin to produce chemical agents called sex hormones. This is called **hormonal sex.** Both testes and ovaries secrete the same sex hormones but in different quantities. Males produce more of the sex hormones called androgens, while females produce more estrogens (the female sex hormone). If no sex hormones were produced, the developing fetus would always be female.

You may have read that aggression seems to be the one personality trait that distinguishes males and females. The male sex hormones, the androgens (especially testosterone) seem to produce a rougher, more aggressive type of behavior. Money (1980) also believes that these prenatal sex hormones may affect brain organization. Though evidence is yet limited, the androgens and estrogens may influence the rapidly developing brain.

Note what has happened so far. The sexual program, originally determined by the chromosomes, has produced a sexual program that dictates body differences between the male and female and also probably a nervous system differentiation.

Genital Sex   A baby's sex is determined not only by chromosomes and hormones but by its external sex organs. This is called **genital,** or morphological, **sex.** Even if males can't produce sperm that are able to fertilize an egg, they are still called male because of their sex organs. The same holds true for women who can't bear children (Elkin & Handel, 1989). Figure 8.1 illustrates these stages.

As you can well imagine, it is genital or morphological sex that determines how society will treat the newly born baby. We shall turn now to sex and socialization.

How Children Learn About Gender

It doesn't take the early childhood youngster long to discover what behavior "fits" men and which "fits" women. If you think about the competencies that we have traced thus far (especially cognitive) and combine these with the acquisition of a sex identity by age 2 or 3, you can understand children's rapid grasp of appropriate sexual behavior. Lott (1989) reports that by preschool age, most children are well aware of their own gender, which parent they are most like, and the gender of family members and peers.

For an idea of how soon children begin to make decisions based on sex, consider Lott's (1989) report on the result of a study that required children ages 2 to 7 to assign various occupations to either a male or female doll. As early as 2 years of age, they assigned male occupations to male dolls. For example, 67% of 2 and 3 year olds chose the male doll for doctors.

Occupational stereotyping seems to be similar for boys and girls and increases with age. These sex stereotypes are not confined to 2 and 6 year olds. When today's college students were asked to list words that describe male and female, here are some of their choices.

Male	**Female**
Aggressive	Kind
Forceful	Gentle
Confident	Understanding
Strong	People-oriented
Career-oriented	Thoughtful
Independent	Emotional
Dynamic	Nurturing

Where do these ideas come from? As we have seen, boys and girls are exposed to the socialization practices of those around them from birth. Among the most influential of these agents are parents, siblings, peers, and media. (The stereotypic treatment of males and females on television has been well documented and will be discussed at length in chap. 10.)

Parents

Evidence clearly suggests that parents treat boy and girl babies differently from birth (Berk, 1989). Adults tend to engage in rougher play with boys, give them stereotypical toys (cars and trucks), and speak differently to them. By the end of the second year, parents respond favorably to what they consider appropriate sexual behavior (i.e., stereotypical) and negatively to cross-sex play (boys engaging in typical girl's play and vice versa). For example, Fagot (1985) observed toddlers and their parents at home. Both mothers and fathers differentially reinforced their children's behavior. That is, they reinforced girls for playing with dolls and boys for playing with blocks, girls for helping their mothers around the house and boys for running and jumping.

Lips (1988) believes that parents are unaware of the extent to which they engage in this type of **reinforcement.** In a famous study (Will, Self, & Datan, 1976) 11 mothers were observed interacting with a 6-month-old infant. Five of the mothers played with the infant who was dressed in blue pants and called "Adam." Six mothers later played with the same infant wearing a pink dress and called "Beth." The mothers offered a doll to "Beth" and a toy train to "Adam." They also smiled more at Beth and held her more closely. The baby was actually a boy. Interviewed later, all the mothers said that boys and girls were alike at this age and *should be treated identically.*

Perhaps no one has summarized the importance of this differential treatment of sons and daughters better than Block (1983). Noting the reality of this parental behavior, Block states that males and females grow up in quite different learning environments, which has important psychological implications for development.

Siblings

What can we say about the influence of brothers and sisters on gender development? Of one thing we can be certain: a youngster with brothers and sisters has unique

Children often find opposite-sex toys extremely attractive. Many parents encourage the use of such toys to help their children avoid the development of stereotypical sexual attitudes.

experiences in the home. Brothers and sisters differ markedly in personality, intelligence, and psychopathology in spite of shared genetic roots. So circumstances within the family dictate that a variety of experiences will help to shape a child's idea of what is appropriate sex-typed behavior.

About 80% of children have siblings, and considering the amount of time they spend with each other, these relationships exercise considerable influence on developmental outcomes (Dunn, 1983). An older brother showing a younger brother how to hold a bat; a younger sister watching her older sister play with dolls; quarrelling among siblings—each of these examples illustrates the impact that sibling relationships have on gender development.

Banks and Kahn (1982) state that the sibling relationship helps to shape a child's identity and also provides reassuring feelings of constancy. But it isn't quite that simple. In a classic study of the influence of siblings on sex typing, Brim (1958) found that children with same-sex siblings had more "sex-appropriate" behavior than those with opposite-sex siblings. In another study, Stoneman, Brody, and MacKinnon (1986) discovered that girls with older brothers shared more masculine activities and boys with older sisters were more interested in feminine activities.

Yet other studies (e.g., Tauber, 1979) showed just the opposite. Children with same-sex siblings enjoyed playing with opposite-sex toys. What should you conclude from these conflicting results?

- The quality of relationships among the siblings (positive or negative) may be responsible. If an older brother tends to bully a younger brother, the younger may turn elsewhere.

- Parents may react differently to brothers/sisters. (We have spoken at length about this possibility in chap. 6.)

- Much more research is needed on this topic.

Siblings play a major role in development. For those children with brothers and/or sisters, older siblings can act as models, help younger brothers and/or sisters in times of difficulty, and help smooth relations with adults.

Peers

When early childhood youngsters start to make friends and play, these activities foster and maintain sex-typed play. Studies show that by the age of 3, children reinforce each other for sex-typed play (Langlois & Downs, 1980). When they engage in "sex-inappropriate" play (boys with dolls, girls with a football), their peers immediately criticize them and tend to isolate them.

Here, again, we see the influence of imitation and reinforcement. During these years, youngsters of the same sex tend to play together, a custom called **sex cleavage** and one that is encouraged by parents and teachers. If you think back on your own experiences, you'll probably remember your friends at this age being either all male or female. You can understand, then, how imitation, reinforcement, and cognitive development come together to intensify what a boy thinks is masculine and a girl thinks is feminine (Dunn, 1983).

Gender Constancy

By now you have probably, and correctly, concluded that gender indentification results from a complex mixture of biology and learning. This interplay produces what is called *gender constancy.* Three steps seem to be involved.

- **Gender identity,** which as we have noted appears anywhere from age 1 1/2 to 3.

- **Gender stability,** which appears from age 3 to 4 and means that youngsters realize that gender normally stays the same throughout life.

- **Gender constancy,** which means that children understand the meaning of gender; even if a woman dresses in a man's suit, shoes, and hat, she remains a woman. Most children acquire gender constancy by age 7 (about the same time they begin to master Piagetian conservation tasks).

At this point, you may be wondering what developmental processes explain gender development. As usual, there are several explanations.

Theories of Gender Development

As Huston notes (1983), two major theories have generated most of the research in gender development during the past ten years: **social learning** theory and **cognitive-development** theory. Since these were treated at length in chapter 2, we will concentrate on their value as explanations of gender development.

Social learning theorists believe that parents, as the distributors of reinforcement, reinforce appropriate sex-role behaviors. By their choice of toys, by urging "boy" or "girl" behavior, and by reinforcing this behavior, parents encourage their children to engage in sex-appropriate behavior. If the parents have a good relationship with their children, they also become models and their children tend to imitate them, acquiring additional sex-typed behavior. Thus children are reinforced or punished for different kinds of behavior. They also learn sex-typed behavior from male and female models who display different kinds of behavior.

A second explanation, quite popular today, is cognitive-development theory, which derives from Kohlberg's speculations about gender development (1966). We know from Piaget's work that children engage in symbolic thinking by about the age of 2. Using this ability, children acquire their gender identity. Then, Kohlberg believes, they begin the process of acquiring sex-appropriate behavior.

A newer, and different, cognitive explanation is called *gender schema* theory. A schema is a mental blueprint for organizing information. You develop a schema

---

BOX 8.5

What's Your Opinion?

What can we say about differences between boys and girls? Do these differences exist? Yes, but our thinking about the reasons for these differences has changed. We no longer say with certainty that biology alone is the cause.

Mathematics is a good example. The myth that "Boys are just better at math and science" is slowly crumbling. As ideas about sex roles have changed, so also have parents' expectations for their daughters. Numerous studies have recently shown that the gap between males and females on math scores has steadily declined (see Berk, 1989). Nevertheless, there are documented differences, including the following. (Note: we are not speculating about the cause of these differences.)

- *Physical size and strength.* Although almost all girls mature more rapidly than boys, by adolescence boys have surpassed girls in size and strength.
- *Language.* Girls do better on verbal tasks almost immediately, a superiority that is retained. Boys also exhibit more language problems than girls.

- *Spatial skill.* Boys display superiority on spatial tasks, a superiority that continues throughout schooling.
- *Mathematical ability.* We have previously commented on boys' better performance.
- *Achievement motivation.* Differences here seem to be linked to task and situation. Boys do better in stereotypical "masculine" tasks (math, science), girls on "feminine" tasks (art, music). In direct competition between males and females, beginning around adolescence, girls' need for achievement seems to drop.
- *Aggression.* Boys appear to be innately more aggressive than girls, a difference that appears early and is remarkably consistent.

Of all the differences mentioned, only aggression seems to have biological roots, and even that will be shaped by the child's environment: family, friends, school. Do you agree? What's your opinion?

---

for gender. This schema helps you to combine your gender identity with sex-typed behavior and an appropriate sex role. You develop an integrated schema or picture of what gender is and should be.

We can perhaps conclude that each of these theories contributes to our understanding of gender development.

The Importance of Play

Children play constantly during these early childhood years, and they play for various reasons. The primary reasons are the following.

Cognitive Development

Play aids cognitive development. Through play, children learn about the objects in their world, what these objects do (balls roll and bounce), what they are made of (toy cars have wheels), and how they work. To use Piaget's terms, children "operate" on these objects through play, and also learn behavioral skills that will be of future use to them. As Bruner and associates state:

❖ *This would suggest, then, that play has the effect of providing practice not so much of survival-relevant instructive behavior but, rather, of making possible the playful practice of subroutines of behavior later to be combined in more useful problem solving (1978, p. 150).*

Social Development

Play helps social development during this period because the involvement of others demands a give-and-take that teaches early childhood youngsters the basics of forming relationships. Social skills demand the same building processes as cognitive skills. Why are some 5 and 6 year olds more popular with their classmates than others? Watching closely you can discover the reasons: decreasing egocentrism, recognition of the rights of others, and a willingness to share. These social skills do not simply appear; they are learned, and much of the learning comes through play (Anselmo, 1987).

Emotional Release

Play provides an emotional release for youngsters. There are not the right or wrong, life and death feelings that accompany interactions with adults. Children can be creative without worrying about failure. They can also work out emotional tensions through play.

Caplan and Caplan (1984) state that play is a powerful developmental instrument for several reasons:

- Play aids learning because children have the freedom to explore and enjoy.

- Play is investigative because children, lacking knowledge, must search for and discover what works and what doesn't.

- Play is voluntary, with no fixed directions.

- Play can provide an imaginary, escape world, which children sometimes need.

- Play helps to build interpersonal relationships.

Aside from these more formal characteristics, Elkind's ideas seem particularly pertinent.

❖ *But children need to be given an opportunity for pure play as well as work. At all levels of development, whether at home or at school, children need the opportunity to play for play's sake. Whether play is the symbolic play of young children, the games with rules and collections of the school-age child, or the more complicated intellectual games of adolescence, children should be given the time and encouragement to engage in them (1981, p. 97).*

The Meaning of Play

"Play" can mean many things: a child experimenting with a new toy, the attempts to master a game, acting out fantasies, or imagining new and different characters and situations. As Gardner (1982) notes, play does not include satisfying biological needs (eating, drinking) or problem-solving behavior (trying to complete a task imposed by someone else).

There are two major categories of play:

1. *Exploratory play* in which children use something as a starting point for novel behavior. For example, children with crayons and paper may begin to draw circles (which they have previously done) and then change the pattern, perhaps forming an ellipse. The behavior is not directed to a goal.

2. *Rule-governed play,* in which children draw circles, then squares, then diamonds; that is, children follow some type of cultural rules.

These two categories help to separate children's tasks into either play or problem solving. When children try out their own ideas rather than focus on a problem or substitute cultural rules for an implied task, then children are playing (Gardner, 1982).

Play cuts across all aspects of development. But how can we be sure that what we see is actually play? In their exhaustive survey, Rubin and associates (1983) have identified several dispositional features of play:

- Play is not forced on children; they do it because they like it.

- They're not concerned with outcome; they enjoy the act of playing.

- There is an "as if" quality to play; reality is suspended and children get great enjoyment from pretending.

- There are no rules to be followed, which distinguishes play from games.

- When children play they are active; they are not daydreaming.

The Development of Play

Does play change over time? Are there age-related features of play that we can identify? It is difficult, if not impossible, to link a specific kind of play to a specific age. But it is possible to link kinds of play with the characteristics of a particular level (early childhood, middle childhood).

Until the age of 18 months to 2 years, children's play is essentially sensorimotor. That is, there is a great deal of repetition involving the body—for example, doing the same things with a toy. Gardner (1983, p. 250) states that at age 2 a great divide is passed since children can engage their world symbolically: letting one thing represent another, adopt different types of roles, and indulge in fantasy and pretend activities. Children may pretend to drink from play cups, or feed a doll with a spoon, or use a clothespin as a doll (Sutton-Smith, 1986).

Play also becomes more social; interactions with other children become more important in play. Gardner (1982) estimates that as much as 25% of a 6 year old's play is **pretend play,** while interactive pretend play increases to about 20%. With the beginning of the school years, play becomes more social and rule dominated. Games with rules become important, which reflects children's ability to use abstract thinking in playing games. A strike in baseball, for example, is a ball thrown over the plate, one that a batter swings at and misses, or a "foul ball." School-age children, with their increased symbolic ability, understand these rules and apply them in their games.

Pretend play characterizes the early childhood years and is a sign of a child's increasing symbolic ability. They practice behavior, learn about roles, and often relieve emotional tension through these activities.

Pretend play, however, seems most characteristic of the early childhood youngster. Children of Piaget's preoperational period show an increasing ability to represent. They are better able to engage in abstract thinking, to let one thing represent another. They can pretend. Rubin, Fein, and Vandenberg (1983) believe that pretend play becomes more social with age and seems to entail a three-stage sequence.

1. Pretend play becomes increasingly dramatic until the early elementary school years.

2. Pretend play becomes more social with age.

3. Pretend play gradually declines and is replaced by games—with rules—during middle childhood.

Pretend play begins with simple actions such as pretending to be eating or asleep. But as symbolic ability increases during the early childhood years, the nature of pretending changes. Youngsters will use toy telephones to talk. Later, they will pick up a banana and pretend to talk on the telephone. Pretend play steadily becomes more elaborate. Youngsters will serve tea to a group of dolls or feed soldiers; they also begin to enact the role of others.

❖   *From a child's play we can gain understanding of how he sees and construes the world—what he would like it to be, what his concerns and problems are. Through his play he expresses what he would be hard pressed to put into words. A child does not play spontaneously only to while away the time, although he and the adults observing him may think he does. Even when he engages in play partly to fill empty moments, what he chooses to play at is motivated by inner processes, desires, problems, anxieties (Bettelheim, 1987, p. 35).*

Table 8.5 Play and Development			
Piaget (1962)	**Parten (1932)**	**Erikson (1950)**	**Howes (1980)**
Practice play: repetitive and sensorimotor	Solitary play: plays alone Onlooker play: observes others	Autocosmic: plays with body	Parallel play: plays beside, not with, others
Symbolic play: use of pretend in childhood	Parallel play: plays beside, not with (3 to 4 years old)	Microcosmic: plays with small toys and objects	Mutual regard: same as parallel but with awareness
Games with rules: use of operations in middle childhood	Associative play: plays with others but play is random, not coordinated	Macrocosmic: plays with others	Social play: smiles, talks with others while playing
	Cooperative play: organized activity, middle childhood		Complementary play: reciprocal (rolling ball back and forth)
			Complementary play 2: reciprocal, social (same as above but with greater social interaction)

Table 8.5 presents the view of several leading theorists concerning the development of play.

Transition

At the beginning of the early childhood years, most children meet other youngsters. By the end of the period, almost all children enter formal schooling. Their symbolic ability enriches all of their activities, although there are still limitations. Given their boundless energy and enthusiasm, they require consistent and reasonable discipline. Yet they should be permitted to do as many things for themselves as possible to help them gain mastery over themselves and their surroundings.

By the end of the early childhood period, children have learned much about their world and are prepared to enter the more complex, competitive, yet exciting world of middle childhood.

Key Ideas

1. The outcome of children's social development depends on the way they resolve the socialization-individuation issue.

2. To understand the influence of the family on development, you must consider the family as a dynamic, changing unit.

3. Parents usually have definite views on bringing up their children, which translates into patterns of childrearing behavior.

4. Recent studies of divorce suggest that it has a longer-lasting impact than was previously realized.

5. Given the large number of divorces in modern societies, more attention must be devoted to the effect of divorce on children of different ages.

6. With many mothers returning to the workforce, the need for daycare has grown rapidly.

7. Many different types of daycare exist, all of which should provide a safe, happy, and healthy environment for children.

8. The early childhood period is a unique time for learning, and adults should be familiar with the various types of learning so that they can be used most effectively.

9.   Although youngsters of this age can learn easily and rapidly, they should not be pushed. Childhood is childhood and parents should plan for their children's enjoyment as well as learning.

10.   Play is a natural expression of an early childhood youngster's natural exuberance and is a marvelous medium for the development of self.

Key Terms

Authoritarian parents
Authoritative parents
Chromosomal sex
Cognitive-development
Daycare
Gender constancy
Gender identity
Gender stability
Genital sex
Gonadal sex
Hormonal sex
Individuation

Miseducation
Permissive parents
Pretend play
Reconciliation fantasies
Reinforcement
Sex cleavage
Sex identity
Sex role
Sex stereotypes
Socialization
Social learning

What Do You Think?

1.   With today's accepted changes in the sex roles of males and females, do you think that a boy or girl growing up in these times could become confused about gender identity? Does your answer also apply to sex roles? Why?

2.   Think back on your days as a child. Can you put your parents' behavior in any of Baumrind's categories? Do you think it affected your behavior? Explain your answer by linking your parents' behavior to some of your personal characteristics.

3.   In this chapter you read about the "sleeper" effect of divorce (effects show up quite a bit later). Do you agree with these findings? Can you explain them by the child's age at the time of the divorce? (Consider all aspects of a child's development at that age.)

4.   You probably have read about child abuse in some daycare centers. Do you think there should be stricter supervision? Why? By whom?

Suggested Readings

Ambrose, Stephen. (1983). *Eisenhower* (Vol. I). New York: Simon & Schuster. Includes the boyhood days of the man who would become soldier, general, and president. A revealing account of the family and community forces that helped to shape his destiny.

Brazelton, T. Berry. (1981). *On becoming a family.* New York: Delacorte. An engrossing account of the development of family relationships by one of America's most renowned pediatricians.

Clarke-Stewart, Alison. (1982). *Daycare.* Cambridge, MA.: Harvard University Press. Well written and easy to read, this overview of daycare will give you a wide-ranging perspective on the problems and promise of daycare. (Available in paperback.)

Elkind, David. (1987). *Miseducation: Preschoolers at risk.* New York: Knopf. Typical Elkind—current, perceptive, and a pleasure to read. Using physical and psychological evidence, Elkind builds a strong case against the tendency of some parents to "push" their children. (Available in paperback.)

Wallerstein, Judith, and Susan Blakeslee. (1989). *Second chances.* New York: Simon & Schuster. This book is must reading for anyone interested in the effect of divorce on children. It summarizes Wallerstein's ten-year follow-up of the children of divorced parents, and furnishes insights into the entire spectrum of divorce in our society today.

PART 5

Middle Childhood

· *Chapter 9* ·

Middle Childhood: Growth and Cognition

This chapter, which analyzes the physical, cognitive, and moral milestones of middle childhood, will often take on the appearance of a mystery. Much is happening to 6–12-year-old youngsters that eludes initial detection. The cognitive complexities and moral reasoning that characterize these years place a youngster in that no man's land between childhood and adolescence.

To help you discover clues to important developmental achievements, this chapter will begin by tracing physical and motor development during the middle childhood years. We'll then turn again to Piaget and analyze his concrete operational period, that time of cognitive development when youngsters begin to engage in truly abstract thinking. Here we'll pause and examine the world of intelligence testing, which has caused so much controversy. But today's children are expected to do much more with their intelligence than just sit and listen and memorize: they're expected to develop thinking skills and to solve problems. We'll explore both of these worlds (cognitive and problem solving) and then trace the moral and language development of middle childhood youngsters.

As observers of this phase of lifespan development, we cannot allow ourselves to be deceived by an apparent lull in development. Too much is going on. Deep-seated developmental currents are changing the very process by which children reason and make their moral decisions.

In tracing the developmental path of children during these years, significant signposts can be found in fiction. Can anyone describe the cognitive ability of a middle childhood youngster better than Mark Twain? Do you recall the memorable scene where Tom is desperately trying to avoid whitewashing Aunt Polly's fence? One of his friends, Ben Rogers, passes by, imitating the "Big Missouri" riverboat. When Ben sympathizes with him, Tom looks at him and says, "What do you call work?"

His friend asks, "Why ain't *that* work?" Tom neatly dodges the question and asks, "Does a boy get a chance to whitewash a fence every day?" By this time Ben is jumping up and down in his eagerness to paint. When this happens,

By this time Ben is jumping up and down in his eagerness to paint. When this happens,

❖   *Tom gave up the brush with reluctance in face but alacrity in his heart. And while that late steamer Big Missouri worked and sweated in the sun, the retired artist sat on a barrel in the shade close by, dangled his legs, munched his apple, and planned the slaughter of more innocents.*

What else can we do but acknowledge a sophisticated and subtle mind at work?

Do you remember Huck Finn meeting the Duke and the Dauphin? Not believing their stories about lost titles, Huck makes a decision.

❖   *It didn't take me long to make up my mind that these liars warn't no kings nor dukes at all, but just lowdown humbugs and frauds. But I never said nothing, never let on; kept it to myself; it's the best way; then you don't have no quarrels and don't get into no trouble.*

As we'll see a little later, such thinking reflects a certain level of moral reasoning. Children of these years use their previous experiences with rewards and punishments and their growing cognitive ability to reach moral decisions.

Think about what you read in this chapter; probe into what lies behind a child's behavior. It will help you to understand the developmental achievements that prepare a youngster to move from these last years of childhood to the different demands of adolescence.

BOX 9.1

The Developmental Tasks of Middle Childhood

Before journeying through the middle childhood years, a review of the developmental tasks of this period can help to provide a deeper insight into your reading. (See Table 1.2 for a listing of these tasks.) According to Havighurst (1972), this period is characterized by three great outward pushes.

1. Children begin to move from parental control to that of the peer group.
2. There is a physical thrust into the world of games and work.
3. There is a mental thrust into the world of concepts, problems, and communication.

From these three great growth thrusts emerge the developmental tasks of middle childhood. For example, children of this age are faced with challenging cognitive tasks in school. Here is one of Havighurst's developmental tasks of middle childhood.

Developing Fundamental Skills in Reading, Writing, and Calculating.

- Nature of the task: To perform these tasks well enough to meet the demands of society.
- Biological basis: The maturation of the nervous system. For example, most youngsters before the age of 6 have inadequately coordinated eye muscles, and their gaze may wander down the page instead of making an accurate return sweep to the beginning of the next line.
- Psychological basis: By the age of 12 or 13 most children have acquired the basic linguistic skills sufficient for them to succeed at a normal level of development.
- Cultural basis: The minimum level of ability that society requires is undoubtedly higher now than a century ago. Socioeconomic status now depends on a high development of intellectual skills.
- Educational implications: The importance of biological maturation for the mastery of these skills indicates that children should not encounter certain of these tasks until they are ready for them.

If youngsters master the developmental tasks of middle childhood, they will usually experience success with later tasks. Failure leads to unhappiness, disapproval by society, and difficulty with later tasks. As we develop, we face increasing demands, but we also acquire new physical and psychological resources.

Physical Development

In contrast to the rapid increase in height and weight during the first years of life, physical development proceeds at a slowed pace during middle childhood (Elkind 1971). As you can see from Table 9.1, most children gain about two inches in height per year. The same pattern applies to weight gains. By 6 years of age, most children are about seven times their birth weight.

Middle childhood youngsters show steady growth, usually good health, and an increasing sense of competence. Physical growth is relatively slow until the end of the period when girls' development may spurt. As we have cautioned constantly, variables such as genetic influence, health, and nutrition can cause wide fluctuations in the growth of these children. Two youngsters may show considerable physical variation and yet both be perfectly normal. Table 9.1 illustrates several of the physical features of middle childhood development.

Changes in height and weight are not the only noticeable physical differences. Body proportion changes also. Head size comes more in line with body size. An adult's head size is estimated to be about one-seventh of total body size; the preschooler's is about one-fourth. This difference gradually decreases during the middle

---

BOX 9.2

What's Your Opinion?

Desiring social acceptance, middle childhood youngsters strike out in many directions in their endeavor to achieve status. There are many paths: the school paper, dancing, band, and sports. During these years many youngsters, both boys and girls, coordinate their physical abilities and show definite signs of athletic skill. Little league baseball, youth hockey, soccer, Pop Warner football—all become showcases for their athletic talent (Bloom, 1985).

If parents, coaches, and youngsters maintain their perspective, sports can be a healthy vehicle for helping children to mature. But adults who encourage a win-at-any-cost attitude do little to help a 10 year old maintain perspective (Elkind, 1987). Parents, realizing that they have a skilled athlete in the family, and facing formidable college tuition costs, frequently push their children too hard and too fast. And now that the availability of federal monies is linked to equitable athletic opportunities for girls, girls are beginning to feel the same pressures from parents that boys have long experienced.

Sports are an *excellent outlet* for youngsters—but in their proper proportion. What happens to personal values if a youngster becomes totally immersed in sports at a time when schooling becomes ever more abstract? The need to read well soars; science becomes an integral part of the curriculum; and mathematics becomes more formidable. The stories of athletes who drop out of college in their senior year, or high school graduates who cannot read and are barely able to write are a grim reminder of a national literacy problem.

Competition in sports is keen, as it is in the classroom, which raises certain issues.

- Competition, as well as cooperation, is a fact of life—in home, in school, in work. Races should be run and scores should be kept.

- Excessive motivation produces negative results. This applies equally as well to competition, which should be a sharp stimulant to motivation. Consider the athlete who, under enormous pressure from some unthinking coach, hides a potentially crippling injury to help the team to win.

- Intense competition with others turns youngsters against one another, and, if prolonged, leads to an undesirable concentration on self—I must win, regardless. Too often under these conditions the end justifies the means, and such behavior becomes routine.

- Competition probably is inescapable, and competition with self should be used as a way of learning to cope with life. What's your opinion?

---

childhood years. Also, the loss of baby teeth and the emergence of permanent teeth change the shape of the lower jaw. By the end of the period, the middle childhood youngster's body is more in proportion and more like an adult's.

Changes in arms, legs, and trunk size also occur. The trunk becomes thinner and longer, and the chest becomes broader and flatter. Arms and legs begin to stretch but as yet show little sign of muscle development. You may have heard children of this age described as "all arms and legs." Hands and feet grow more slowly than arms and legs, which helps to explain some of the awkwardness that we see during these years. These children are tremendously active physically and gradually display a steady improvement in motor coordination (Tanner, 1978).

The middle childhood years are a time when children's abilities demonstrate considerable competence; their continuing mastery of their bodies and their environment lead to emerging skills that are readily observable.

Table 9.1   Physical Development in Middle Childhood

Age (years)	Height (in.)		Weight (lb)		Motor Development
	Girl	Boy	Girl	Boy	
7	48	49	52	53	Child has good balance; can hop and jump accurately
8	51	51	60	62	Boys and girls show equal grip strength; great interest in physical games
9	52	53	70	70	Psychomotor skills such as throwing, jumping, running show marked improvement
10	54	55	74	79	Boys become accurate in throwing and catching a small ball; running continues to improve
11	57	57	85	85	Boys can throw a ball about 95 feet; girls can run about 17.5 feet per second
12	60	59	95	95	Boys can run about 18.5 feet per second; dodge ball popular with girls

Motor Skills

Healthy, active children of this age—both boys and girls—demonstrate considerable motor skill. Cratty (1979) summarizes motor development during these years:

- Skill increases with maturity until, by the end of the period, some youngsters are highly skilled and much in demand for various sports.

- Boys are stronger than girls.

- Girls may be more graceful and accurate.

- Sex differences—especially strength—become more obvious toward the end of the period.

- Balance matures by the end of the period.

Cognitive Development

During the middle childhood years, children's cognitive abilities become remarkably complex and sophisticated. These youngsters now begin formal education, and their cognitive abilities should enable them to meet the more demanding tasks set by the school.

We shall continue our practice of examining cognitive development by beginning with Piaget and his explanation of these years—the concrete operational period.

Piaget and Concrete Operations

Recall the early childhood years and the preoperational period. Piaget believed that preschoolers' thinking is still restricted. *Egocentrism* and *irreversibility* still characterize preoperational children (Gelman & Baillargeon, 1983).

During the period of concrete operations, children overcome these limitations. They gradually employ logical thought processes with concrete materials—that is, with objects, people, or events that they can see and touch. They also concentrate on more than one aspect of a situation, which is called **decentering.** They acquire conservation and can now reverse their thinking. Think of the water jar problem (see chap. 2). Now they can mentally pour the water back.

❖ *About the age of seven, a fundamental turning point is noted in a child's development. He becomes capable of a certain logic; he becomes capable of coordinating operations in the sense of reversibility, in the sense of the total system of which I will soon give one or two examples. This period coincides with the beginning of elementary schooling. Here again I believe that the psychological factor is the decisive one. If this level of the concrete operations came earlier, elementary schooling would begin earlier (Piaget, 1973, p. 20).*

Middle childhood youngsters are at Piaget's stage of concrete operations. Now they demonstrate increasing mental competence such as classifying.

Several notable accomplishments mark the period of concrete operations:

1. **Conservation** appears. In Piaget's famous water jar problem, children observe two identical jars filled to the same height. While they watch, the contents of one container are poured into another, taller and thinner jar so that the liquid reaches a higher level. Seven-year-old children typically state that the contents are still equal. They conserve the idea of

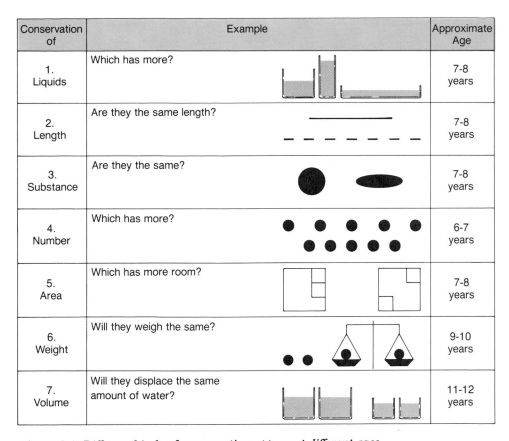

Conservation of	Example	Approximate Age
1. Liquids	Which has more?	7-8 years
2. Length	Are they the same length?	7-8 years
3. Substance	Are they the same?	7-8 years
4. Number	Which has more?	6-7 years
5. Area	Which has more room?	7-8 years
6. Weight	Will they weigh the same?	9-10 years
7. Volume	Will they displace the same amount of water?	11-12 years

Figure 9.1 Different kinds of conservation appear at different ages.

equal amounts of water by decentering, focusing on not only one part of the problem but both. They can now reverse their thinking; they can mentally pour the water back into the original container.

2. **Seriation** means that concrete operational children can arrange objects by increasing or decreasing size.

3. **Classification** enables children to group objects with some similarities within a larger category. Brown wooden beads and white wooden beads are all beads.

Features of Concrete Operational Thinking

Children at the level of concrete operations can solve the water-level problem, but the problem or the situation must involve concrete objects. That's the reason for calling the period *concrete operational.* In the water-level problem, for example, children no longer concentrate solely on the height of the water in the glass; they also consider the width of the glass. But as Piaget notes, concrete operational children nevertheless demonstrate a true logic, since they now can reverse operations.

Concrete operational children gradually master conservation—that is, they understand that something may remain the same even if surface features change.

Figure 9.1 illustrates the different types of conservation that appear at different ages. For example, if preoperational children are given sticks of different lengths, they cannot arrange them from smallest to largest. Or if presented with three sticks,

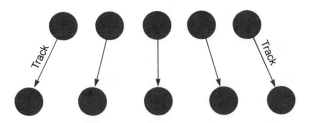

Figure 9.2 Encouraging acquisition of number concept.

A, B, and C, they can tell you that A is longer than B and C, and that B is longer than C. But if we now remove A, they can tell you that B is longer than C, but not that A is longer than C. They must see A and C together. The child at the level of concrete operations has no difficulty with this problem.

But limitations remain. Piaget (1973) gives the example of three young girls with different colored hair. The question is: Who has the darkest hair of the three? Edith's hair is lighter than Suzanne's but darker than Lili's. Who has the darkest hair? Piaget believes that propositional reasoning is required to realize that it is Suzanne and not Lili. Youngsters do not achieve such reasoning until about 12 years of age.

Concrete operational children can also classify—that is, they can group different things that have something in common. For example, wooden objects may include both a table and a chair. In a classic experiment illustrating mastery of classification, Piaget showed a girl about twenty brown wooden beads and two or three white wooden beads. He then asked her to separate the brown from the white beads. Children at both the preoperational and concrete levels can do this. But then he asked her, ''Are there more brown beads or wooden beads?'' The preoperational child answered brown, while an older child answered correctly.

Another interesting feature of this period is the child's acquisition of the number concept, or **numeration.** This is not the same as the ability to count. If five red tokens are more spread out than five blue ones, preoperational children, although able to count, still think there are more red than blue tokens. Piaget then constructed an ingenious device that enables a child to trace the blue to the red. The preoperational child can actually move the blue token to the corresponding red, but still thinks there are more red tokens! It is during the concrete operational period that children understand oneness—that one boy, one girl, one apple, and one orange are all one of something (see Figure 9.2).

Of course, Piaget's way of analyzing cognitive development is not the only way. Another technique attempts to measure the different types of tasks that children of different ages can master. This is called the psychometric view of intelligence.

The Psychometric View of Intelligence

Psychologists have followed many routes in their quest to discover the secrets of the human mind. One of these paths led to a belief that intelligence can be measured. Intelligence, that fascinating yet enigmatic something, promised to discriminate the able from the less able.

At the beginning of this century, there was an influx of immigrants to American shores. Some device was needed to classify individuals for education, for work, and ultimately for military service. This helps to explain why the mental testing movement was readily, almost eagerly, accepted. Here at last was a tool, so went the claim, that cut to the heart of a person's innate capacity. The circumstances that led to the development and acceptance of intelligence tests illustrate the methods that investigators adopted to assess native ability.

Binet and Mental Tests

The story of Alfred Binet and his search for the meaning and measurement of intelligence is famous in the history of psychology. Much of his early work on the intellectual and emotional lives of children resulted from studies of his daughters. But in 1904, Binet was asked by the Parisian Minister of Public Instruction to formulate a technique for identifying the children most likely to fail in school. The problem was difficult, since it meant finding some means of separating the normal from the truly retarded, of determining the lazy but bright who were simply poor achievers, and of eliminating the halo effect (assigning an unwarranted high rating to youngsters because they are neat or attractive).

The items in Binet's early test reflected these concerns. When an item seemed to differentiate between normal and subnormal, he retained it; if no discrimination appeared, he rejected it. (Binet defined normality as the ability to do the things that others of the same age usually do.) Fortunately for the children of Paris and for all of us, Binet was devoted to his task. The fruits of his and his coworkers' endeavors was the publication in 1905 of the Metrical Scale of Intelligence, which evolved into the several versions of the famous **Stanford-Binet Intelligence Test** (Binet & Simon, 1905).

The Wechsler Intelligence Scales

David Wechsler, a clinical psychologist at New York's Bellevue Hospital, was dissatisfied with previous attempts to measure adult intelligence. In his hospital work, Wechsler needed some reliable means to identify level of intelligence in his examination of criminals, neurotics, and psychotics.

There are three forms of the Wechsler test, designed to measure the intelligence of human beings through the life span, beginning at the age of 4. These are

1. **WAIS,** the Wechsler Adult Intelligence Scale, which is a revised form of his first test, originally published in 1939.

2. **WISC-R,** the Wechsler Intelligence Scale for Children—Revised, which first appeared in 1949 and assesses the intelligence of children from age 5 to 15.

3. **WPPSI-R,** the Wechsler Preschool and Primary Scale of Intelligence—Revised, which is designed to measure the intelligence of children from 4 to 6 1/2 years of age.

Wechsler states (1958) that other important aspects of intelligence include motivation and persistence at a task. For example, individuals with precisely the same score on the same intelligence test may adapt quite differently. One youngster with an IQ of 75 may require institutional care, while another child also with an IQ of 75 may function adequately at home. (For an excellent discussion of the nature of intelligence and its many implications, see Sternberg, 1982.)

Other psychologists, not entirely happy with either Piaget's views or the psychometric approach, have devised new ways of explaining children's cognitive abilities.

As youngsters enter the middle childhood years, school offers a series of increasingly abstract tasks. With their growing symbolic abilities (conservation, reversibility, etc.) they should be able to master the challenges posed by a diverse curriculum.

New Ways of Looking at Intelligence

IQ tests, as we have seen, failed to resolve the main issue: how much of intelligence is inherited and how much is learned? For example, advocates of intelligence testing claimed that these instruments measured a person's innate potential for learning. This claim implied that IQ test scores were unaffected by either education or social class. Results, however, have consistently shown that more education and higher social class are the inevitable partners of higher intelligence test scores.

To avoid this pitfall, several recent theories have been proposed. Three of these concern us here.

Sternberg's Triarchic Model of Intelligence

Robert Sternberg (1986) has designed a **triarchic model** of intelligence to answer three questions.

- What is the relationship of intelligence to our internal world? What are the inner processes and strategies that we use?

- What is the relationship of intelligence to our external lives? How does the environment affect intelligence?

- What is the relationship of intelligence to our experiences? How does what we do help to shape our intelligence?

To answer these questions, Sternberg (1986) devised the following three-fold model of intelligence.

1. The Components of Intelligence Sternberg has identified three types of information-processing components: **metacomponents,** which help us to plan, monitor, and evaluate our problem-solving strategies; **performance components,** which help us to execute the instructions of the metacomponents; and **knowledge-acquisition components,** which help us to learn how to solve problems in the first place (Sternberg, 1988). These three components are highly interactive and generally act together.

For example, consider writing a term paper. The metacomponents help you to decide on the topic, plan the paper, monitor the actual writing, and evaluate the final product. The performance components help you in the actual writing of the paper. You use the knowledge-acquisition components to do your research. Figure 9.3 illustrates the manner in which the components work together.

2. Experience and Intelligence Sternberg's second aspect of intelligence includes our experiences, which improve our ability to deal with novel tasks and to use pertinent information to solve problems.

3. The Context of Intelligence The third aspect of intelligence in Sternberg's model refers to our ability to adapt to our culture. It wouldn't make much sense to move a nomadic people to New York City and then test their intelligence on the Wechsler. The major thrust of contextual intelligence is **adaptation.** Adaptation, for Sternberg, has three meanings:

- Adaptation to existing environments, so that you adjust to current circumstances

- Shaping existing environments, which implies changing the present environment to meet your needs

- Selecting new environments

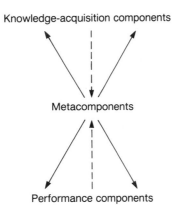

Figure 9.3 *The relationship among the components of intelligence.*

If you apply these descriptions to yourself and others you know, you probably can identify which aspect of intelligence predominates in each person. For example, if you excel in analytical thinking, you probably do quite well on traditional IQ tests.

While Sternberg does not apply his theory directly to children, you can see how his work relates to the developing cognitive competence of the middle childhood youngster. To take one example, with their growing symbolic activity, children can think about their thinking—that is, they are employing metacomponents. Sternberg (1986) has also compiled a list of reasons why we too often fail, which has important implications for children of this age.

Noting that all of us, children and adults, let self-imposed obstacles frustrate us, Sternberg states that what is important is not the level of our intelligence but what we achieve with it. Sternberg has identified the most common obstacles:

- *Lack of motivation.* If children aren't motivated, it really doesn't matter how much talent they have. In a typical classroom situation, for example, the range of intelligence may be fairly narrow and differences in motivation spell success or failure.

- *Using the wrong abilities.* Although children acquire greater cognitive ability, they frequently don't use it or else fail to recognize exactly what is needed. For example, faced with a math test, they may fail to review solutions to word problems (knowledge-acquisition components) and instead depend on their previous experiences.

- *Inability to complete tasks.* Regardless of how skilled children may be in their use of Sternberg's components, if they are unable to sustain their efforts—for whatever reason—they are in danger of failure. The worry here is that this tendency may become a way of life, ensuring difficulty, frustration, and failure.

- *Fear of failure.* Some youngsters may develop a fear of failure early in life. This can prevent them from ever fulfilling their intellectual potential.

These are among the obstacles that adults should be aware of, so they can help middle childhood youngsters develop to the fullest.

Gardner and Multiple Intelligences

Howard Gardner (1983, 1985) has forged a tight link between thinking and intelligence with his theory of *multiple intelligences.* An especially intriguing aspect is that an individual who is capable of penetrating mathematical insights may be quite baffled by the most obvious musical clues. Gardner attempts to explain this apparent inconsistency by identifying seven equal intelligences.

1. Linguistic Intelligence The first of Gardner's intelligences is language—**linguistic intelligence.** For example, we can trace the effects of damage to the language area of the brain; we can identify the core operations of any language (phonology, syntax, semantics, and pragmatics); and language development in humans has been well documented and supported by empirical investigations. Gardner considers language a preeminent example of human intelligence.

As we will soon see, during these years children change their use of language to a more flexible, figurative form. Gardner comments on this by noting that middle childhood youngsters love to expand on their accomplishments. They use appealing figures of speech: "I think I'll get lost," meaning that they're about ready to leave.

2. Musical Intelligence One has only to consider the talent and career of Yehudi Menuhin to realize that there is something special about musical ability. At 3 years of age, Menuhin became fascinated by music and by 10 he was performing on the international stage. The early appearance of musical ability suggests some kind of biological preparedness—**a musical intelligence.** The right hemisphere of the brain seems particularly important for music, and musical notation clearly indicates a basic symbol system. Although not considered intelligence in most theories, musical skill satisfies Gardner's criteria and so demands inclusion.

In regard to the middle childhood years, Gardner notes that most children (except for those who are musically talented) cease musical development after school begins. For the talented, up to the age of 8 or 9, talent alone suffices for continued progress. Around 9 years of age, serious skill-building commences, with sustained practice until adolescence, when these children must decide how much of their lives they want to commit to music. In general, society accepts musical illiteracy.

3. Logical-Mathematical Intelligence Unlike linguistic and musical intelligences, **logical-mathematical intelligence,** Gardner believes, evolves from our contact with the world of objects. In using objects, taking them apart, and putting them together again, children gain their fundamental knowledge about "how the world works." By this process, logical-mathematical intelligence quickly divorces itself from the world of concrete objects. Children begin to think abstractly.

Gardner then uses Piaget's ideas to trace the evolution of thinking. The development of logical-mathematical thinking, as explored by Piaget, is used as an example of the scientific thinking so characteristic of logical-mathematical intelligence. You may want to review Piaget's ideas concerning the unfolding of intelligence to better understand Gardner's views.

4. Spatial Intelligence Brain research has clearly linked spatial ability to the right side of the brain. Here Gardner relies heavily on Piaget, noting that these years see an important change in children's thinking, especially with the appearance of conservation and reversibility. Middle childhood youngsters can now visualize how objects seem to someone else. During these years, children can manipulate objects using their **spatial intelligence,** but this ability is still restricted to concrete situations and events.

Relationships with peers, abstract activities, and developing physical skills all occupy middle childhood youngsters. The success that children achieve in these activities contribute significantly to an emerging sense of competence.

5. Bodily-Kinesthetic Intelligence As Gardner notes, describing the body as a form of intelligence may at first puzzle you, given that we normally divide the mind and reasoning from our physical nature. This divorce between mind and body is often accompanied by the belief that our bodily activities are somehow less special.

Gardner urges that we think of mental ability as a means of carrying out bodily actions. Thus thinking becomes a way of refining motor behavior. Our brain's control of our bodily functions has been well documented. Also, the developmental unfolding of bodily movements has been thoroughly recorded. Gardner states that our control of bodily motions and the ability to handle objects skillfully are defining features of an ''intelligence''—**bodily-kinesthetic intelligence.**

We have commented that middle childhood witnesses the emergence of bodily skills, to the point where they can dominate some children's lives. Gardner poses an age-old question to which we still have no definite answer: Does increasing mental ability affect the performance of a bodily skill?

6. and 7. Interpersonal and Intrapersonal Intelligence Gardner refers to **interpersonal** and **intrapersonal** intelligences as the *personal intelligences.* Interpersonal intelligence builds on an ability to recognize what is distinctive in others, while intrapersonal intelligence enables us to understand our own feelings. Autistic children are good examples of a deficit in this intelligence. Often competent in a certain skill, they may be utterly incapable of ever referring to themselves.

The middle childhood years see greater social sensitivity, a keener awareness of others' motivation, and a sense of one's own competencies. Children begin to develop friendships and devote considerable time and energy to securing a definite place in a circle of friends. This effort can only increase their sensitivity to interpersonal relations. At the same time, they become more aware of themselves, furthering the development of their intrapersonal intelligences. If children of this age do not succeed in establishing harmonious relationships, they may develop feelings of inadequacy and isolation. This fuels a fear of failure that can produce diminished expectations.

Perkins and Thinking Frames

Long concerned with the improvement of thinking skills, Perkins (1987) also urges that we avoid too narrow a view of intelligence. He believes that the key question is: What psychological factors contribute to a broader, more qualitative model of intelligence? Modern psychologists, he says, have adopted one of three concepts of intelligence.

- *A power theory of intelligence,* which is solely dependent on the neurological efficiency of the brain, a genetic interpretation.

- *A tactical theory of intelligence,* which holds that those who think better do so because they have more tactics for how to use their minds.

- *A content theory of intelligence,* which views intelligence as a rich knowledge base. Mastery of factual material is at the heart of thinking and problem solving.

No one of these views contains all the answers about intelligence. A combination of all three seems more promising (Perkins, 1987).

$$Intelligence = Power + Tactics + Content$$

Perkins (1987) argues that tactical intelligence consists of a bag of tricks, and proposes the term *thinking frames* to describe the tricks that make up tactical intelligence.

Thinking frames are representations intended to guide the process of thought. He defines them as a guide to organizing and supporting thought processes (Perkins, 1987). How can children acquire these frames? Perkins believes that we learn thinking frames by a three-stage process.

- *Acquisition,* or mastering the basics of a frame by direct instruction, invention, or unconsciously soaking up frames.

- *Internalization,* or making the process automatic. Internalization comes about through practice on simple examples until it becomes fluent and spontaneous.

- *Transfer,* or using the frame in a wide variety of contexts.

While it is too soon to know if any or all of these theories help us to understand intelligence better, they broaden our perspective by forcing us to look at intelligence in a different way. More significantly, they have the potential to influence how we work with children, particularly of this age. Rather than accepting an all-or-none view, it now seems more possible to enrich children's intelligence by specific measures.

Perkins (1987) addresses this issue when he comments on "making sense of making minds," which seems particularly applicable to the cognitive world of the middle childhood youngster. He shapes his ideas around three questions.

1. **What constitutes better thinking?** Believing that better thinking can best be visualized in his equation of Intelligence = Power + Tactics + Content, Perkins states that tactics and content can be vastly improved. You can see how youngsters of these years can be guided through the steps that lead to the rapid acquisition of thinking frames.

2. **By what process can children learn to think better?** Perkins argues that children can improve their thinking by focusing on the tactics they use. Since power won't change and the acquisition of a rich knowledge base requires considerable time, the quickest route to improvement lies in the sharpening of tactics. Youngsters of this age, with their interest, enthusiasm, and capacity for rapid learning, are naturals to improve tactics.

3. **How can we judge if thinking is improving?** Perkins believes that two principles should direct our efforts with children: (1) use varied and effective frames that offer practical guidance; (2) learn these frames to the point of overlearning.

In regard to improving children's thinking, we can conclude our summary of Perkins' work by noting that events shape minds by art or accident. As Perkins states, our aim must be for more art and less accident.

Our analysis of cognitive development, however, should not be restricted to a purely theoretical look at intelligence or cognition. We are also aware of the complexity of a middle childhood youngster's thinking. What do they do with their intelligence? Can we help them to do better?

Thinking and Problem Solving

Advanced societies demand citizens who can do more with their intelligence than just survive. Rapid change requires the ability to cope. Yet 25% of the 14–18-year-old group no longer are in school. We can only question how many young people are adapting. Concern about these and similar statistics has prompted renewed interest in two topics that have been with us for years: critical thinking and problem solving.

Thinking Skills

Young people—actually all of us—need the skills and strategies that enable us to be productive members of our society. The famous American educator John Dewey was worried about this years ago. In his classic work *How We Think* (1933), Dewey remarked that reflective thinking begins with doubt or uncertainty that causes us to search for the materials that will remove the perplexity. Dewey believed that we go through states of thinking, such as the following:

- We make suggestions as we look for possible solutions.

- We search for the cause of the uncertainty and attempt to be precise about what is blocking us.

- We formulate hypotheses, which we use to guide our search.

- We mentally test these hypotheses.

- We physically test the hypothesis that seems best suited to resolve our difficulty.

Critical Thinking
Dewey, of course, was referring to critical thinking. Critical thinking depends on skills that children can learn, such as improving their memory and attending to the

important part of any problem. Knowledge is also vital, since the more information you have about something the easier it is to understand and solve the problem.

Several attempts have been made to identify the particular skills young people need. Benjamin Bloom's enduring *Taxonomy of Educational Objectives, Handbook 1: Cognitive Domain* (1956) is one example. The thinking skills of the taxonomy are knowledge, comprehension, application, analysis, synthesis, and evaluation.

Robert Ennis (1987), noting that critical thinking skills reflect logical thinking, argues that young people should acquire a thinking disposition. A thinking disposition entails answering four questions:

1. Are you clear about what is going on? Focus on the question; define what is needed; get more information.

2. Do you have a good basis for any judgment you make? Be sure your response is credible; use pertinent data for your decision.

3. Are your inferences logical? Again, get the information. Proceed systematically.

4. Have you discussed the problem with anyone else? Talk to others. Use new ideas.

Parents and teachers can encourage a middle childhood youngster's cognitive potential to think critically. By appealing to their enthusiasms and abilities, adults can encourage these youngsters to begin using "a thinking disposition."

Decision Making and Reasoning

Do you consider yourself logical? How good are you at making decisions? Do you pride yourself on your accurate thinking? While we all want to think that we are models of logical thinking, facts seem to tell us otherwise.

Does Decision-Making Skill Improve With Age?

Addressing the question of whether decision-making skill improves with age, Krouse (1986) studied 90 children, 30 each from grades one, three, and six (48 boys, 42 girls). Employing the Concept Assessment Kit (which measures conservation) and a variety of Tversky-Kahneman tasks, Krouse sought to determine if any relationship existed between children's decision-making behavior (as determined by Tversky-Kahneman tasks) and certain variables: educational level, level of cognitive development, sex of child.

Krouse found that educational level made a difference. Third and sixth graders demonstrated the same variations in decision making as adults, a particularly interesting finding in the light of cognitive theory. Recalling our discussion of attention, perception, representation, classification, and memory, we could conclude, not surprisingly, that children's processing capacities are fairly restricted during the early years. To what do young children attend? Are they capable of discriminating loss of money from loss of object, or is it just something lost?

Younger pupils (preschoolers to grade two) could not judge their mental capabilities as accurately as the older pupils, an ability that gradually and consistently improves during the elementary school years. Whatever the reason, a developmental shift seems to occur around the third grade: children's decision-making skills come to resemble an adult's.

BOX 9.3

How Would You Answer These Questions?

1. Imagine that you were lucky enough to obtain two tickets to the great Broadway musical *Phantom of the Opera* for $100. As you walk down the street to the theater, you discover that you have lost the tickets. You can't remember the seat numbers. Would you go to the ticket window and buy another pair of tickets for $100?

2. Imagine that you are on the way to the theater to buy tickets for the Broadway play *Phantom of the Opera*. They will cost you $100. As you approach the ticket window you discover that you have lost $100. Would you still pay $100 for the tickets?

These questions, originally posed by Tversky and Kahneman (1981) elicit some interesting answers. How did you answer them? Among their subjects, 46% answered yes to question 1, while 88% answered yes to question 2. Note that many more people said they would buy new tickets if they had lost the money rather than the tickets. Yet the two situations are almost identical—in each instance you would have lost $100.

How can we explain the difference in the responses? Tversky and Kahneman believe that the way a problem is framed helps to explain our response. As they state:

The frame that a decision-maker adopts is controlled partly by the formulation of the problem and partly by the norms, habits, and personal characteristics of the decision-maker (1981, p. 453).

The point here is that our decisions are influenced by the way questions and problems are structured and by our personal characteristics, such as motivation, persistence, and the like. We can help children reach better decisions by teaching them the skills and strategies discussed in this chapter.

Problem-Solving Skills

Middle childhood youngsters use their newly developed cognitive accomplishments to solve the problems they face in their daily lives. Some children are better than others at this, but all children can improve their problem-solving skills. To give you an idea of what we're talking about, see how good you are at solving the problem in box 9.4.

Good Problem Solvers

Obviously, some people are better at problem solving than others due to intelligence, experience, or education. But anyone's ability to solve problems can be improved—even children's. Some children and adults don't do well with problems because they're afraid of them. "I'm just not smart enough"; "I never could do these." Here is a good example. Group the following numbers in such a way that when you add them, the total is 1,000.

88888888

Unintimidated elementary school children get the answer almost immediately. Some of you won't even bother trying; others will make a halfhearted effort; still others will attack it enthusiastically. What is important is how you think about a problem. Step back and decide what you have to do; decide on the simplest way to get the answer.

BOX 9.4

Try This Problem

Do you think you're a good problem solver? Before you answer, try to solve the following problem.

Two motorcyclists are 100 miles apart. At exactly the same moment they begin to drive toward each other for a meeting. Just as they leave, a bird flies past the first cyclist in the direction of the second cyclist. When it reaches the second cyclist it turns around and flies back to the first. The bird continues flying in this manner until the cyclists meet. The cyclists both traveled at the rate of 50 miles per hour while the bird maintained a constant speed of 75 miles per hour. How many miles will the bird have flown when the cyclists meet?

Many readers, examining this problem, will immediately begin to calculate distance, miles per hour, and constancy of speed. Actually this is not a mathematical problem; it is a word problem. Carefully look at it again. Both riders will travel for one hour before they meet; the bird flies at 75 miles per hour; therefore the bird will have flown 75 miles. No formulas, no calculations, just a close examination of what is given.

In the 8s problem, think of the only number of groups that would give you 0 in the units column when you add them—five. Try working with five groups and you will eventually discover that $888 + 88 + 8 + 8 + 8$ gives you 1,000.

People who are good problem solvers have several distinct characteristics that are seen in middle childhood youngsters (Hayes, 1981).

- *Positive attitude.* Good problem solvers face problems with confidence, sure that their problems can be solved by careful, persistent analysis.

- *Concern for accuracy.* Good problem solvers seize on the data that are present in the problem. Simply by encouraging children to read more carefully—to reread—and to look for the details that are given, they can grasp the problem more accurately, thus improving their problem-solving skills.

- *Break the problem into parts.* Good problem solvers divide a problem into parts, study each part, and then put the parts back together again.

- *Avoid guessing.* Good problem solvers refuse to guess; they consistently search for the facts.

What can be done to help children improve their problem-solving skills? Here are several helpful suggestions (Hayes, 1981; Bransford & Stein, 1984; Lewis & Greene, 1982).

Determine just what the problem is.
Understand the nature of the problem.
Plan your solution carefully.
Evaluate both your plan and the solution.

Many of life's daily problems facing children are vague, ill-defined. If children lack problem-solving strategies, their task is next to impossible. This is one of the major reasons there is growing pressure for schools to teach problem-solving skills, either as a separate course or as a part of a course's content.

BOX 9.5

The Role of Memory

One of the most powerful strategies in solving problems is the efficient use of memory. All memory strategies, however, are not equally effective. The appropriateness of the strategy depends on the level of material involved. Try this memory problem.

The following list contains 25 words. Take 90 seconds to study these words. When time runs out, write as many of the words as you can without looking at the list.

paper	fruit	street	wheel
white	step	juice	time
spoke	shoe	car	note
ball	word	judge	run
banana	touch	hammer	table
dark	page	bush	official
walk			

How did you do? Or more importantly from our perspective, how did you do it? Were these among the strategies you used?

1. *Rehearse each word* until you have memorized it: tire, tire, tire.
2. *Rehearse several words*: ball, apple, referee; ball, apple, referee.
3. *Organize the words by category.* Note that several words are related to cars; others could be grouped as fruit; still others could be categorized as relating to books.
4. *Construct a story* to relate as many of the words as possible.
5. *Form images of words* or groups of words.

You may have tried one or a combination of these strategies, but note that you were not told to memorize them in any particular manner.

If you had received specific instructions, each of these strategies would not have been equally effective. When we are asked to remember a particular telephone number, the tendency is to rehearse it for as long as we need to recall it. But if you had been directed to memorize them in a certain order (the way that they were presented), grouping them by categories would not have been efficient. Thinking of a story to link them in the correct order would have been much more efficient.

These new ways of examining intelligence and the renewed interest in critical thinking and problem solving seem particularly pertinent to middle childhood youngsters. With their developing cognitive sophistication, they are equal to the challenge posed by new ideas and deserve the opportunity to sharpen their mental skills.

As middle childhood youngsters think better, reason more maturely, and evaluate their actions, moral development becomes a matter of increasing importance.

Moral Development

As youngsters slowly mature, the beginnings of moral development emerge as a consequence of learning: children are rewarded for what their parents believe is right and punished for wrongdoing. With cognitive growth, the time of moral reasoning appears. Control of behavior gradually begins its shift from external sources to more internal self-control.

Piaget's Explanation

Youngsters realize that the opinions and feelings of others matter—what I do might hurt someone else. By the end of the period, children clearly include intention in their thinking. For the 6 year old, stealing is bad because I might get punished; for the 11 or 12 year old, stealing may be bad because it takes away from someone else. During these years, children move from judging acts solely by the amount of punishment to judging acts based on intention and motivation.

As might be expected, Piaget has examined the moral development of children and attempted to explain it from his cognitive perspective. Piaget formulated his ideas on moral development from observing children playing a game of marbles. Watching the children, talking to them, and applying his cognitive theory to their actions, he identified the following stages of moral development—how children actually conform to rules.

- In the first stage, children simply played with the marbles, making no attempt to conform to rules. Piaget (1932) referred to this as the *stage of motor rules.*

- In the second stage, at about ages 3 to 6, children seem to imitate the rule behavior of adults, but they still play by themselves and for themselves. Piaget calls this the *egocentric stage.*

- Between ages 7 and 8, children attempt to play by the rules, even though rules are only vaguely understood. This is Piaget's *stage of incipient cooperation.*

- Finally, between the ages of 11 and 12, which Piaget calls the *stage of codification of rules,* children play strictly by the rules.

After youngsters reach the fourth stage, they realize that rules emerge from the shared agreement of those who play the game, and that rules can be changed by mutual agreement. They gradually understand that intent becomes an important part of right and wrong, and their decreasing egocentrism permits them to see how others view their behavior. Peers help here because in the mutual give-and-take of peer relations, children are not forced to accept an adult view. This is referred to as the *morality of cooperation.*

Kohlberg's Theory

Among the more notable efforts to explain a child's moral development has been that of Lawrence Kohlberg (1975, 1981). Using Piaget's ideas about cognitive development as a basis, Kohlberg's moral stages emerge from a child's active thinking about moral issues and decisions. Kohlberg has formulated a sophisticated scheme of moral development extending from about 4 years of age through adulthood.

Middle childhood youngsters are at Kohlberg's **preconventional level of morality** for most of the period. Only as they approach ages 10 to 12 do they begin to edge into the **conventional level of morality,** where acts are right because that's the way it's supposed to be (determined by adult authority). The **postconventional level of morality** comes at age 13 and over.

Kohlberg's scheme traces moral development through six stages by successive transformations of cognitive structures (see Table 9.2).

Table 9.2 Kohlberg's Stages of Moral Development
Level I. Preconventional (about 4 to 10 years).
During these years children respond mainly to cultural control to avoid punishment and attain satisfaction. There are two stages:
Stage 1. Punishment and obedience. Children obey rules and orders to avoid punishment; there is no concern about moral rectitude.
Stage 2. Naive instrumental behaviorism. Children obey rules but only for pure self-interest; they are vaguely aware of fairness to others but only for their own satisfaction. Kohlberg introduces the notion of reciprocity here: "You scratch my back, I'll scratch yours."
Level II. Conventional (about 10 to 13 years).
During these years children desire approval, both from individuals and society. They not only conform, but actively support society's standards. There are two stages:
Stage 3. Children seek the approval of others, the "good boy-good girl" mentality. They begin to judge behavior by intention: "She meant to do well."
Stage 4. Law-and-order mentality. Children are concerned with authority and maintaining the social order. Correct behavior is "doing one's duty."
Level III. Postconventional (13 years and over).
If true morality (an internal moral code) is to develop, it appears during these years. The individual does not appeal to other people for moral decisions; they are made by an "enlightened conscience." There are two stages:
Stage 5. An individual makes moral decisions legalistically or contractually; that is, the best values are those supported by law because they have been accepted by the whole society. If there is conflict between human need and the law, individuals should work to change the law.
Stage 6. An informed conscience defines what is right. People act, not from fear, approval, or law, but from their own internalized standards of right or wrong.

Source: Based on L. Kohlberg, "A Cognitive-Developmental Analysis of Children's Sex-Role Concepts and Attitudes" in E. Maccoby (ed.), *The Development of Sex Differences.* Copyright © 1966 Stanford University Press, Stanford, CA.

According to Kohlberg, moral judgment requires us to weigh the claims of others against self-interest. Thus youngsters must overcome their egocentrism before they can legitimately make moral judgments. Also, anyone's level of moral development may not be the same as their moral behavior. To put it simply, people may know what is right but do things they know are wrong.

Lickona (1983) has suggested a variation of the moral dilemma for assessing a child's level of moral reasoning. It also forces youngsters to test the limits of their reasoning.

Assume that you are working with an 8-year-old child. You pose this dilemma to the child: "What would you do if you found a wallet with $10 in it and you needed the money for a ticket to a skating party? But the wallet also has the owner's name and address in it." Question the child about returning the wallet: "You found it, so would that be stealing?" "Why should you return it?" "What if you don't get a reward?" Don't accept the answer of stealing. Ask, "Why is it stealing?" If the child says, "I might get into trouble," you have identified a Stage 1 child.

As Lickona notes, if you vary your questions, you will discover the range of the child's moral reasoning. Knowing the upper limits gives you a yardstick for measuring the child's behavior against moral level and helps you to motivate the child to act at the appropriate level.

Not all students of moral development agree with Kohlberg. Strenuous objections have been made to Kohlberg's male interpretation of moral development, especially by Carol Gilligan.

BOX 9.6

The Moral Dilemma

To discover the structures of moral reasoning and the stages of moral development, Kohlberg (1975) has employed a modified clinical technique called the **moral dilemma,** in which a conflict leads subjects to justify the morality of their choices. In one of the best known a husband needs a miracle drug to save his dying wife. The druggist is selling the remedy at an outrageous price, which the woman's husband cannot afford. He collects about half the money and asks the druggist to sell it to him more cheaply or allow him to pay the rest later. The druggist refuses. What should the man do: steal the drug or permit his wife to die rather than break the law? By posing these conflicts, Kohlberg forces us to project our own views.

In A Different Voice

Gilligan (1977, 1982) has questioned how accurate Kohlberg's theory is in relation to women. Gilligan believes the qualities associated with the mature adult (autonomous thinking, clear decision making, and responsible action) are qualities that have traditionally been associated with masculinity rather than femininity. (Kohlberg, for example, places most women at the third stage of his hierarchy because of their desire for approval, their need to be thought nice.) The characteristics that define the good woman (gentleness, tact, concern for the feelings of others, display of feelings) all contribute to their lower scores for moral development.

Noting that women's moral decisions are based on an ethics of caring rather than a morality of justice, Gilligan argues for a different sequence for the moral development of women. For boys and men, separation from mothers is essential for the development of masculinity; while for girls, femininity is defined by attachment to mothers. Consequently, women define themselves through a context of human relationships and judge themselves by their ability to care (Gilligan, 1982).

She notes that a woman's development is masked by a special interpretation of human relationships. A shift in imagery occurs. For example, while cognitive and moral theory clearly trace an 11-year-old boy's thinking, that same theory "casts scant light on that of the girl" (Gilligan, 1982, p. 25). When the 11-year-old boy, Jake, is confronted with the dilemma of the overpriced drug, he has no hesitation— "steal it." The response of the girl, Amy, is quite different. The husband should not steal the drug; rather he should seek other, legal ways of obtaining it. Consequently, Gilligan believes that a new interpretation of a woman's moral development is needed, one that is based on the imagery of a female's thinking.

As a result of her studies, Gilligan has formulated a developmental sequence based on the ethic of care. According to Gilligan, when the outline of women's morality is sketched, the results differ from Kohlberg's speculations about men. Gilligan has described a morality of responsibility based on a concept of harmony and nonviolence and a recognition of the need for compassion and care for self and others (Brabeck, 1983). Gilligan does not argue for the superiority of either the male or female sequence but urges that we recognize the difference between the two. By recognizing two different modes, we can accept a more complex account of human experience.

Whether boy or girl, middle childhood youngsters, through their rapid cognitive development, are aware of right and wrong. How do we know this? They write answers to questions; they talk to us. Language development is another clue to their growing maturity.

BOX 9.7

Multicultural Focus: Language, Thought, and Immigrants

As we conclude our discussion of intelligence and thinking, we should pause and consider some of the characteristics of newly arrived immigrants, characteristics that could lead to labeling. We must remember that children entering the United States come into a culture in which almost all citizens speak only English. Consequently, language is an immediate barrier.

Educators have also come to realize that most immigrant students have difficulty with standardized tests for the following reasons:

- Language
- Difficulty in learning a new language if teachers can't use a student's native language for instruction
- English instruction may be too brief
- Any cultural bias in the tests (e.g., asking a math question using an American sport such as baseball)

As First (1988) has stated, if you're going to test immigrant students, at least teach them the things about which you're testing them.

Students who are learning a second language, adjusting to a new culture, or recovering from emotional trauma may need more than nine months to complete the learning associated with a given grade level (p. 208).

These are common concerns, but from the perspective of our work in this chapter, you can see the potential danger of labeling. Yet immigrants don't always have great difficulty. We are well aware that many Asian-American pupils have a high level of achievement. Nevertheless, immigrant children sound different; they may have difficulty in school; their marks may be low; they may do poorly on standardized tests. Conclusion: they're dumb.

From your reading in this chapter, you now realize that many of these youngsters face a formidable task and that any judgment about their abilities should be suspended. Ask yourself and others a simple question: if you went to another country where you did not know the language and were unfamiliar with the customs, how would you do? Good luck!

Language Development

In middle childhood we find children immersed in a verbal world. Language growth is so rapid that it is no longer possible to match age with language achievements. Table 9.3 presents several language accomplishments of middle childhood with other middle childhood characteristics.

Note the steady progression in motor skills: from the initial grasping of a pencil and printing to the writing of lengthy essays by the age of 10 or 11. Greater visual discrimination is apparent in the accurate description of events and the elimination of letter reversals. The growth in cognitive ability is seen in the detection of cause and effect, and the appeal of science and mystery stories.

Using Language

By the age of 7, almost all children have learned a great deal about their language. They appear to be quite sophisticated in their knowledge, but as Menyuk (1982) notes, considerable development is still to come. During the middle childhood years, children improve their use of language and expand their structural knowledge. By the end of the period, they are similar to adults in their language usage.

Table 9.3	Some Typical Language Accomplishments
Age (years)	**Language Accomplishment**
6	Vocabulary of about 3,000 words
	Understands use and meaning of complex sentences
	Uses language as a tool
	Possesses some reading ability
7	Motor control improves; able to use pencil
	Can usually print several sentences
	Begins to tell time
	Losing tendency to reverse letters (*b, d*)
8	Motor control improving; movements more graceful
	Able to write as well as print
	Understands that words may have more than one meaning (e.g., *ball*)
	Uses total sentence to determine meaning
9	Can describe objects in detail
	Little difficulty in telling time
	Writes well
	Uses sentence content to determine word meaning
10	Describes situations by cause and effect
	Can write fairly lengthy essays
	Likes mystery and science stories
	Masters dictionary skills
	Good sense of grammar

There are three types of change in language usage during these years (Menyuk, 1982).

- *Children begin to use language for their own purposes,* to help them remember and plan their actions. They move from talking aloud when doing something to inner speech. From about age 7 on, children use language to help them recall things. This applies not only to individual items (such as lists) but also the relations between objects or actions (psychologists call this **encoding**).

- *Language during these years becomes less literal.* We saw the beginnings of this change in chapter 7, when we discussed children's humor. Now they use language figuratively. On going to bed, an 11 year old may say, "Time to hit the sack." Children display this type of language by a process called **metalinguistics awareness,** which means their capacity to think about and talk about their language. You can see how this is impossible until children acquire the cognitive abilities that we just discussed.

- *Children are able to communicate with others more effectively.* They understand relationships; they can also express them accurately, using appropriate language. In a sense, more effective communication is the product of the interaction of many developmental forces: physical growth as seen in the brain's development; cognitive development as seen in the ability to use symbols and to store them; and language development as seen in vocabulary development and usage. Language has now become an effective tool in adapting to the environment.

In regard to changes in structural knowledge, most children, especially by the end of the period, begin to use more complexly derived words. Remember when we spoke of the acquisition of morphological rules? Adding *er* to *old* changes its meaning. Children begin to change word stems, which can produce syntactic changes as well.

I really like history.

I really like historical books.

They now understand the rules that allow them to form and use such changes.

The same process applies to compound words. What does your instructor write on? Usually it's a blackboard. Middle childhood youngsters realize a blackboard in this meaning is not a black piece of wood. The awareness of relations helps them to learn that the same relationship can be expressed in different ways.

Liz slapped Janie.

Janie was slapped by Liz.

As Menyuk (1982) states, much of children's language development during these years results from their awareness of language categories and the relationships among them.

During middle childhood the relationship of language development (in the sense of mastering a native tongue) to reading becomes crucial. Between the ages of 6 and 10, children must interpret written words wherever they turn: from signs on buses and streets as they go to school, to schooling that is massively verbal.

When you consider a middle childhood youngster's competence—especially cognitive and linguistic—you conclude that they should be able to read effectively. The topics that engage reading researchers reflect the abilities of these children.

The Importance of Reading

Among the topics that engage researchers are decoding, vocabulary, and reading comprehension. **Decoding,** a controversial and elusive topic, refers to the technique by which we recognize words. There are reading theorists who argue that children should focus on the whole word, and there are those who believe that individual letters must be taught—the phonics method. Research today indicates that early phonics instruction produces the most satisfactory results. Do middle childhood youngsters possess this ability? Absolutely.

Vocabulary, or word meaning, refers to teaching the meaning of a word, not how to pronounce it. Pause for a moment and consider the ramifications of this statement. Knowledge of vocabulary is highly correlated with intelligence, which is highly correlated with reading performance and school success. Is it any wonder, then, that the acquisition of vocabulary is high on any list of reading priorities?

Reading comprehension, which is the ultimate objective in any type of reading instruction, means that a reader not only recognizes words but understands the concepts that words represent. Children of this age should have the capacity to understand the meaning of appropriate words. Wolf and Dickinson furnish a good example.

❖ *Imagine if you will, a small group of children ranging in age from three to ten, huddled around a piece of paper with* die Katze *written in bold letters upon it. The youngest child squeals. A picture! A slightly older four-year-old child shouts, Book! A first grader quickly tries to pronounce it, then says slowly with a puzzled expression, It isn't a picture or a book. It's funny letters. I think it's funny words. The oldest child smiles knowingly and with the slightest disdain says, It's a word all right, but it isn't in English. I'm pretty sure it means cat, but in Italian, maybe French, too (1985, p. 227).*

The 10 year old knows this word is different. To reach this understanding, Chall (1983) believes, children pass through a series of stages:

- In the prereading stage, children up to 6 years of age learn letter and number discrimination and basics of reading.

- In Stage 1 (grades 1.5–2.5), the major emphasis is on decoding as it applies to single words and simple stories.

- In Stage 2 (grades 2.5–4), reading becomes much more fluent and understanding what is read becomes increasingly important.

- In Stage 3 (grades 4–8), reading should be automatic and effort should be put into the comprehension of more complex material.

- Chall's Stages 4 and 5 apply to adolescents and adults.

The goal of reading instruction during these years should be to enable children to control their own reading by directing attention where it is needed.

You can understand why reading is so important to children of this age. As they move through the school curriculum, their work becomes increasingly verbal: they read about the history of their country, the story of science, the symbols of mathematics, or any subject you can mention. A youngster who has a reading problem is a youngster in trouble. To the extent that reading problems increase, we all suffer.

Transition

From our discussion so far, we know several things about middle childhood youngsters. But are they capable of meeting the problems they face? Yes and no. They can assimilate and accommodate the material they encounter, but only at their level. For example, elementary school youngsters up to the age of 10 or 11 are still limited by the quality of their thinking. They are capable of representational thought but only with the concrete, the tangible. They find it difficult to comprehend fully any abstract subtleties in reading, social studies, or any subject.

According to Erikson, the middle childhood period should provide a sense of industry; otherwise youngsters develop feelings of inferiority. With all of the developmental accomplishments of the previous six or seven years, youngsters want to use their abilities, which means that they inevitably experience failure as well as success, especially in their school work. The balance between these two outcomes decisively affects a child's self-esteem.

Physically active, cognitively capable, and socially receptive, much is expected of these children, especially in school. Their widening social horizons, with increasingly influential peer input, introduce joy and excitement but also stress and anxiety. We turn to these concerns in the next chapter.

Key Ideas

1. The typical middle childhood youngster experiences slow, steady growth, and these years are usually a time of robust health.

2. The middle childhood years see the emergence of well-coordinated motor skills, with some children showing unusual ability.

3. Growing cognitive sophistication is a major accomplishment of this period, with symbolic functioning becoming common practice.

4. These years are the period of Piaget's concrete operations, during which children demonstrate their capacity to deal abstractly with their world.

5. As we have seen, Piaget's view is not the only way to interpret children's intelligence.

6. New ways of looking at intelligence offer a better understanding of children's thinking and better methods for improving learning and teaching techniques.

7. With their growing cognitive competence, middle childhood youngsters exhibit an ability to use advanced thinking skills to solve problems.

8. In today's society, children acquire a wide range of experiences that, coupled with their new cognitive skills, should enable them to improve problem-solving skills, to expand their memories, and to move comfortably in a conceptual world.

9. Youngsters' growing cognitive competence also changes the way that they think about moral issues—from the fear of getting caught to concern about hurting someone else.

10. Language becomes increasingly significant in a middle childhood youngster's life—both for communication and as a means of academic success.

Key Terms

Adaptation
Bodily-kinesthetic intelligence
Classification
Competition
Conservation
Content theory of intelligence
Conventional level of morality
Decentering
Decoding
Encoding
Interpersonal intelligence
Intrapersonal intelligence
Knowledge-acquisition components
Linguistic intelligence
Logical-mathematical intelligence
Metacomponents
Metalinguistic awareness
Moral dilemma

Musical intelligence
Numeration
Performance components
Postconventional level of morality
Power theory of intelligence
Preconventional level of morality
Reading comprehension
Seriation
Spatial intelligence
Stanford-Binet Intelligence Test
Tactical theory of intelligence
Thinking frames
Triarchic model
Vocabulary
WAIS
WISC-R
WPPSI-R

What Do You Think?

1.   Imagine an 11-year-old boy—let's call him Tom—who lives in the suburbs of a large northeastern city. He shows signs of becoming a great baseball player (a pitcher). His father realizes that his son could eventually win a college scholarship and go on to become a professional if he continues to develop. He decides that Tom should not play pickup games with his friends because he might hurt himself. He also decides that the family should move to the South so Tom can play ball all year. Neither his wife nor Tom's sister wants to move. As a family friend, you have been asked for advice. What would you suggest?

2.   You are a fourth-grade teacher and you turn to Janice and say, "Janice, Barbara is taller than Janie, who is taller than Liz. Who's the tallest of all?" Janice just looks at you. You sigh and think, "Where's Piaget when I need him?" How would you explain Janice's behavior?

3.   Billy (9 years old) cuts through the parking lot of a supermarket on the way home from school. In the bike rack by the wall he sees a beautiful racing bike that he really wants. It seems to be unlocked and no one is around. With Kohlberg's work as a guide, what do you think is going through Billy's mind?

Suggested Readings

Gardner, Howard. (1983). *Frames of mind.* New York: Basic Books. Gardner's book, which is available in paperback, is an excellent example of the new perspective on studying intelligence. Recognizing that we all seem to demonstrate different abilities, Gardner makes an appealing case for the existence of several intelligences.

Lickona, Thomas. (1983). *Raising good children.* New York: Bantam. This little paperback, based on Kohlberg's work, is one of the clearest and most practical guides to the development of children's moral reasoning.

Young, Jeffrey. (1988). *Steve Jobs: The journey is the reward.* New York: Lynx. A penetrating account of the restless, inquiring mind of the middle childhood years that eventually led to the founding of Apple Computer.

· *Chapter 10* ·

Middle Childhood:
The Widening World

In *Henry and Beezus,* one of Beverly Cleary's popular novels about that great star of middle childhood, Henry Huggins, she has Henry in a desperate search for a new bicycle. As Henry explores many avenues to obtain enough money, he is constantly frustrated. But in his actions, he displays both the growing cognitive competence of the middle childhood years and the expanding network of relationships in which these youngsters move.

Thinking he had failed in all of his efforts, Henry's mother offers to buy him a used bike, which is all she can afford. Henry's answer is a study of a positive mother-child relationship.

❖   *"Gee, thanks a lot, Mom, but I guess not. If I can't have a brand new bike without a single thing wrong with it, I guess I can get along without one." Somehow, Henry found he felt more cheerful.*

Later Henry wins the door prize at the grand opening of a new market: $50 worth of coupons at a beauty salon! Henry's shrewd mind goes to work and he immediately begins to sell the coupons, getting more than enough money to buy his bike.

Think of the world that awaits children of Henry's years. With their ability to think logically and creatively and their skill in anything physical, the world must seem theirs for the taking—as it should. These are the years that Erikson has identified as the time of industry versus inferiority.

Consider the developmental accomplishments that we described in chapter 9. Children's skills—physical, motor, cognitive, linguistic—are beginning to flourish. Now they want an opportunity to demonstrate their prowess and to win recognition from others. But if their efforts meet only failure, the result can be feelings of inferiority. Their experiences with their families, friends, and in school should provide the opportunities for the further development of competence.

With these personal changes come expanding social contacts—perhaps the addition of brothers and sisters, new friends, new adult figures, and school with its challenges and achievements. All of these new contacts—siblings, friends, and teachers—become important influences on a child's development.

One type of positive social contact that a youngster of this age can make is in forming relationships with the elderly. Children 10 or 11 years old visit nursing homes where they find "writing partners," elderly citizens with varied cultural backgrounds and rich personal experiences. The partners write stories and poems that the children use in their language classes. These interpersonal relationships give the children insights into a group they rarely encounter (with the possible exception of grandparents). Such experiences help children to develop those prosocial behaviors so needed in our society: caring, sharing, a sense of responsibility, and a sensitivity to the needs of others. The children also help the elderly. With the enthusiasm and energy of these years, they bring interest and excitement to many whose lives are limited. Here we have an excellent example of what middle childhood youngsters can accomplish and give to others as they begin to move into a wider social context.

In order to trace the impact that these different individuals have on development, it is perhaps wise to begin with those closest to home—siblings. We'll then turn our attention to peer influence. Following that, we'll examine those two great socializing agents: school and television. But we know that children are growing up in difficult times, so we should also consider how stress affects development.

Siblings and Development

❖ *Children grow up within a network of relationships—with parents, grand-parents, friends, and for 80% of children in the United States and Britain, sib-lings. How does this experience of being a sibling affect their development (Dunn, 1983, p. 787)?*

With these words, one of the leading students of **sibling** relationships, Judy Dunn, emphasizes the importance of brothers and sisters in a child's development. Of one thing we can be very sure: growing up with brothers and sisters is quite different than growing up without them. Brothers and sisters, because of their behavior toward one another, create a different family environment. During their early years, for example, siblings probably spend more time with each other than they do with their parents. An older sibling may spend considerable time taking care of younger brothers and sisters. These relationships last a lifetime, longer in most cases than those between husband and wife or parent and child (Dunn, 1988).

When you examine sibling relationships from this perspective, you can see how they affect development. In the early years, young brothers and sisters can provide security for babies who may feel frightened by strangers or anything different. (The attachment literature we discussed in chap. 5 shows that siblings definitely can attach to each other.) Older siblings are also models for younger children to imitate. They can become sounding boards for their younger brothers and sisters—that is, the younger siblings can try out something before approaching a parent. Older siblings often ease the way for the younger by trying to explain to parents that what happened wasn't all that bad. In this way, bonds are formed that usually last a lifetime (Hinde, 1987).

The Developing Sibling Bond

In their attempt to explain the sibling bond, Banks and Kahn (1982) begin with parents' conflicting guidelines for their children's relationships.

- Be close, but remain distinct individuals.

- Be loving, but beware of sex.

- Be cooperative, but retain your independence.

- Be admiring, but don't let your brothers and sisters take advantage of you.

- Be competitive, but don't dominate.

- Be aggressive, but not ruthless.

- Be tolerant, but hold on to your own point of view.

These authors believe that several cultural changes have combined to strengthen sibling relationships. Family size, for example, continues to shrink. In the common two-child family, the relationship tends to become intense, with each sibling exercising a strong influence on the other.

Longer life spans mean that brothers and sisters spend a longer period of their lives together than ever before, as long as seventy or eighty years! When parents have died, their own children have left, and spouses die, siblings tend to tighten the bond and offer each other needed support.

Older siblings can help their younger brothers and sisters and ease many of the normal upsets in development. By being models, offering advice, and interceding with adults, bonds are formed that survive distance and time.

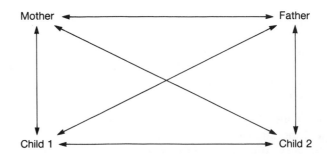

Figure 10.1 Increasing relationships with a second child.

Geographic mobility means unavoidable separation. Friendships are broken; schools and teachers change; adjustments to new situations must be made. For many children, the one anchor to be found is a brother or sister.

Divorce and remarriage typically bring unhappiness and hurt. Relationships change, which causes most children to experience emotions ranging from relief to fear. We have previously commented on the developmental effects of divorce, but pause for a moment and consider how relationships can multiply when divorced parents remarry (Banks & Kahn, 1982; Schibuk, 1989).

In what has become a classic analysis, J. P. Scott (1968) has illustrated how family relationships become more complex with each birth. With the addition of one child, the number of relationships increases to three. With the addition of a second child, the number of relationships increases to six, double the original figure. The first child adds two relationships; the second child adds three; the third child adds four. Figure 10.1 shows the increase in relationships with a second child. If a third child adds four new relationships to the family, the total increases to ten.

> Third child—4
> Second child—3
> First child—2
> Mother-father—1
> _____
> 10 relationships

For younger children, then, the social environment becomes increasingly complex.

How Siblings Help Each Other

As you might conclude from what we've said about siblings, conditions may exist that link siblings in a lifelong relationship. After all, why not? Think of the functions that siblings perform for one another, functions that contribute to the cementing of the bond. Among them are the following (Banks & Kahn, 1982).

1. *Identification and differentiation.* Calling identification the glue of the sibling relationship, Banks and Kahn state that the process by which one youngster learns from a sibling's experiences is a powerful phenomenon. Observing, imitating, and tentative trials, on the younger sibling's own terms (i.e., without parental pressure), can become an effective means of acquiring competence. Accepting some of an older sibling's behaviors and rejecting others leads to differentiation, an important and necessary step in developing a healthy self-concept.

2. *Mutual regulation.* Siblings can act as nonthreatening sounding boards for each other. New behaviors, new roles, and new ideas can be

Siblings perform many functions for each other. Not only do they directly help each other but also by observing older sibling's behaviors they decide what to accept and what to reject, thus contributing to their own sense of identity.

tested on siblings, and the reactions, whether positive or negative, lack the doomsday quality of many parental judgments. The emotional atmosphere is less charged. These simple experiments can give children confidence or prevent them from embarrassing incidents.

3. *Direct services.* Cooperative siblings can ease many a burden. From the exchange of clothes as teenagers, to the borrowing of money before a paycheck, to support in life's crises, siblings provide valuable services for each other.

4. *Dealing with parents.* Sibling subsystems are the basis for the formation of powerful coalitions often called the *sibling underworld.* Older siblings can warn their younger brothers and sisters about parental moods and prohibitions, thus averting problems. Older siblings frequently provide an educational service to parents by informing them of events outside the home.

But we also know that sibling relationships can be negative. *Rivalry,* whatever the cause, may characterize any bond. An older sibling can contribute to those feelings of inferiority that Erikson so elegantly describes as contributing to the crises of this period. Imagine the difficulty of a first-born sibling forced to share parental attention, especially if the spacing between the children is close (less than two years). If the firstborns must also care for younger children, they can become increasingly frustrated.

But the causes for rivalry are not one-sided. Younger children may see only the apparent privileges that are extended to the oldest: a sharing in parental power, authority, and more trivial matters such as a later bedtime or greater use of the television set. Yet the bond remains.

How Siblings Affect Development

In an early and careful investigation, Koch (1960) found that school-age children have unique attitudes toward their siblings. For example:

- Some said they played frequently with their brothers and sisters; others rarely did.

- About one-third of the children said they fought constantly; another one-third said they seldom quarreled.

- Some said they liked playing with a sibling; others much preferred a friend.

When Koch specifically asked the youngsters if they would be happier without their siblings, she received definite answers. One-third replied they would be happier without the sibling. (Could you make her disappear? She's too bossy.) The majority, however, said they preferred keeping the sibling (although they phrased their answer in less than glowing terms: "I'll keep him. He's bad but not that bad.").

Their replies reflected many of the functions provided by siblings—help, money, support. Those who preferred life without a sibling commented on conflicts, bossiness, and abuse. ("He makes me cry." "She's so mean.") The emotional quality of the relationship was apparent in both the positive and negative responses, much more so than when referring to anyone else. Commenting on these findings, Dunn states:

❖ *The children talked about affection, comforting, and helping, but also about antagonism and quarreling. And it is striking that these different qualities of the relationship were not closely linked. Children who described their relationship with a brother or sister as very warm, close and affectionate, for instance, were not necessarily those children who experienced little conflict with the sibling or who expressed little rivalry with each other. And the children who fought a great deal with their siblings were not necessarily the children who reported much jealousy about the parents (1985, p. 51).*

What specific developmental implications can we draw from our discussion?

- As with our previous analysis (see chap. 5), the early *affective* quality of the relationship persists through the years. The content of the interactions between siblings will obviously change throughout the years, but its affective quality remains consistent.

- Younger siblings tend to *imitate* older brothers or sisters. Which children imitated gives insight into the relationship. Second-borns imitate most frequently, especially if the firstborn had been affectionate. Same-sex pairs imitate each other more frequently than mixed-sex pairs (Dunn, 1983).

A question that has long divided psychologists is the role, if any, that birth order plays in sibling relationships and development.

During middle childhood, peer relationships become increasingly important for social development. Children are attracted to those who share their interests, who play well with them, and who help them to learn about themselves.

Birth Order

Fascinated by the belief that **birth order** can predict a child's intelligence and personality, psychologists have made repeated attempts to identify precise effects of birth order. In an early study, Schachter (1959) examined the relationship between anxiety and affiliation (being with others), suspecting that there could be differences between firstborn and later-born children. What he discovered confirmed his suspicions: anxiety is related to the needs of firstborn, and only children want to be with other people more so than later-born children.

Birth Order and Personality Characteristics

In another, widely publicized work, Toman (1976) argued that children's position in the birth order influences the appearance, or lack of, certain personality characteristics. Only children, for example, are supposed to develop certain traits because of intense parental concern: conscientious, methodical, concerned with achievement, comfortable with older people, and avoiding conflict.

Middle children, given the difficulty of defining middle, are thought to feel neglected, have many friends outside the family, leave home early, and carry feelings of insecurity for years, if not a lifetime. There is an old saying about middle children: they seldom forgive and never forget.

Birth Order and Intelligence

There have also been attempts to determine if any relationship exists between birth order and intelligence. Research does not give us any clear evidence. Perhaps the best known effort to analyze this relationship has been done by Robert Zajonc.

Beginning in the 1970s, Zajonc and Marcus (1975) attempted to discover any underlying cause between birth order and intelligence. In their search, they developed the **confluence model,** which attempts to assess the effects of the environment on intellectual performance. The confluence model rests on the premise that the intellectual growth of each family member depends on the intellectual level of all the other family members. Any family's intellectual environment becomes the average of the absolute intellectual levels of its members (Zajonc & Marcus, 1975). When family size changes, the intellectual average changes; as children develop, the intellectual average changes.

For example, arbitrarily setting the intellectual levels of the parents at 30 units each, the newborn child's level is zero. The average score of the intellectual environment for the firstborn is calculated as follows:

$$\frac{30 + 30 + 0}{3} = 20$$

Now assume a second birth when the firstborn's intellectual level is four.

$$\frac{30 + 30 + 4 + 0}{4} = 16$$

But a careful examination of the model reveals that increasing birth order need not be associated with decreasing intellectual performance if there is sufficient spacing between the children. If the second child is not born until the firstborn reaches an intellectual level of 24, the average intellectual environment then becomes:

$$\frac{30 + 30 + 24 + 0}{4} = 21$$

This is superior to the environment that the firstborn initially experienced. Conversely, if one of the parents is lost, the family's intellectual level declines.

There are problems with this explanation. For example, as you can see, unreasonable periods of child spacing are necessary to produce brighter children born later in the birth order. Continued interest in this issue has produced new research that raises serious doubts about any real effects of birth order. Analyzing data on 150,000 individuals, Blake (1989) notes that family background seems to account for birth order effects. Family size, for example, seems to be a much better predictor of achievement than birth order. Researchers such as Blake now believe that Zajonc's model reflects family background, such as the number of siblings and the spacing between them.

Even a child's personality seems immune to the impact of birth order. Blake (1989) states that the effects of birth order on personality once thought to exist probably are the results of the particular subjects who were available for analysis. Only children, for example, formerly believed to be self-centered, selfish, and spoiled are now seen (as the result of more careful analysis) to be similar to children raised with siblings.

Many of these studies were of children born after World War II, a time of large families. Consequently, any study of high achievement would show more eldest children because small families were underrepresented in any group of firstborns. We can perhaps best summarize recent findings by noting that a child's position in the family means little apart from such factors as family size, family norms, and cultural norms.

What can we conclude from this discussion of the influence of brothers and sisters on development? First we can agree with the initial premise of this section:

children who have brothers and/or sisters grow up in a different environment from those who don't. Second, a child's position in the birth order probably has few significant developmental consequences, in spite of past beliefs.

Middle childhood youngsters will bring to their interactions with those outside of the family the characteristics that they formed within the family circle. With this in mind, let's turn now to the impact of peers on development.

The Influence of Peers

Peer: One of Equal Standing

We typically use the word **peers** to refer to youngsters who are similar in age, usually within 12 months of each other. But as Hartup (1983) notes, equal in age does not mean equal in everything—intelligence, physical ability, or social skills. Also, research shows that many of a child's interactions are with those who are more than 12 months older.

With these cautions, we turn now to the influence of peers during middle childhood. (Here you may want to return briefly to chap. 5 and the analysis of relationships. We'll assume that you understand the basics of a relationship at this point.)

When we turn to same-sex—and mixed-sex—interactions, we can summarize the obvious findings quickly. Children of all ages associate more frequently with members of their own sex. Why? Adults encourage such relationships. Children of the same sex also share more mutual interests, and sex-role stereotypes operate powerfully to reinforce same-sex relationships.

Children's Friendships

In his engaging book *Children's Friendships,* Rubin (1980) states that the word *friend* reflects the common functions of peer relationships for people of all ages. It refers to nonfamilial relationships that are likely to foster a feeling of belonging and a sense of security. How youngsters think about friends, of course, changes with age.

Middle childhood youngsters, with the abilities that we have traced, can reach logical conclusions about their friends. Children of this age search for friends who are psychologically compatible with them. For example, does Jimmy share my interests? Does he want to do the same things I do? Children begin to realize, especially toward the end of the period, that friends must adapt to each other's needs.

Rubin (1980) believes that friends provide certain resources that adults can't provide. For example:

- *Friends offer opportunities for learning skills.* They teach children how to communicate with one another, which gradually leads to the ability to recognize the other person's needs and interests. (We'll discuss this shortly with Selman's work.) Friendship also means that a child has to learn how to cooperate and how to deal with conflict.

- *Friends give children the chance to compare themselves to others.* "I can run faster than you" is not just a competitive statement. It's also a means of evaluating oneself by comparison with others.

- *Friends give youngsters the chance to feel that they belong to a group.* By age 10 or 11, groups have become important, and, as we saw earlier in our discussion of gender, sex cleavage is the rule. Here children find a social organization that includes not just individual friendships but

School is an important milestone for all aspects of development. Children must learn to respond appropriately to authority outside of the family and to get along with peers. It is an important part of psychosocial as well as cognitive development.

roles, collective participation, and group support for activities. You can see, then, how being included in a group can further development, and how feelings of isolation and self-doubt can come from being excluded. Friendships are one means of traveling the normal path of social development.

Peers in Middle Childhood

Think of the world these children are now encountering. Physical and cognitive abilities enable them to move steadily, although slowly, toward others such as neighborhood friends. Upon entering school, they increase their contacts and begin to realize that other children have ideas that may differ from their own. Cognitive development helps them to accept these differences. For Piaget, one of the major obstacles to more mature thinking is egocentrism, that tendency to relate everything to me. With its decline during middle childhood, children gradually see that other points of view exist. This in itself is an important developmental phenomenon, one that has been carefully explored by Robert Selman (1980).

Perspective Taking
In his efforts to clarify emerging interpersonal relationships, Selman has developed a theory of **social perspective-taking** levels that spring from a social cognitive developmental framework. Selman (1980) states that you can't separate children's views on how to relate to others from their personal theories about the traits of others. Thus, children construct their own version of what it means to be a self or other.

Table 10.1 Selman's Theory of Interpersonal Understanding

Level 0 3–6 years

Undifferentiated and Egocentric
Concept of Persons: undifferentiated—does not separate physical and psychological characteristics of persons.
Concept of Relations: egocentric—no accurate notion of relations.

Friendship

Friendship depends on physical closeness and functional similarity; admires strength and quickness

Level I 5–9 years

Differentiated and Subjective
Concept of Persons: differentiates physical and psychological characteristics—intentional acts recognized.
Concept of Relations: seen as one-way.

Friendship

Someone does what child wants or child does what other wants—implies recognition of an inner self.

Level II 7–12 years

2d Person and Reciprocal
Concept of Persons: can look at self objectively and realize that others can too.
Concept of Relations: reciprocal in that children realize that others do what they do (i.e., I know that she knows that I know)—sees people this way but not relationships (i.e., not mutual)

Friendship

Interactions become desirable in themselves—a "meeting of the minds"—but only for specific interests. Still sees interactions as helping self.

Level III 10–15 years

3d Person and Mutuality
Concept of Persons: 3d person—self and others as subjects and objects. Can have mixed thoughts and feelings about something (love and hate).
Concept of Relations: 3d person view of self, others, and system. Looks on interpersonal interactions as including self, others, and the relationship.

Friendship

Goal is mutual interest and sharing.

Level IV 12+ years

In-depth and Societal-Symbolic
Concept of Persons: individual seen as complicated, many things going on inside.
Concept of Relations: interactions and relationships become complicated because they may reflect deeper levels of communication.

Friendship

Realizes that complex needs can be met by different relationships. Relationships are seen as open and flexible—helps in own self-identity.

As a result of careful investigations of children's interactions with others, and guided by such theorists as Piaget, Flavell, Mead, and Kohlberg, Selman has identified several levels of social perspective-taking. Table 10.1 presents a summary of thinking at each level and how it affects a child's perception of friends. Note that in the middle childhood years a youngster gradually realizes that those out there are different and have ideas of their own. By the end of middle childhood, a youngster's views of a relationship include self, someone else, and the kind of relationship between them.

We have mentioned cognitive development, diminished egocentrism, and a striving for competence as factors in getting along with others. Youngsters of this age are also better able to communicate with one another and to use reinforcements from their peers to shape their own behavior (Boivin & Begin, 1989). Because of their cognitive, language, and perspective-taking skills, they cooperate better with one another than younger children and aggression decreases somewhat. The desire to conform becomes important, especially at the end of the period.

Given the increase in friends during the school years, we can question the role of schooling itself. How does it influence the development of middle childhood youngsters?

Schools and Middle Childhood

❖ *For almost a dozen years during a formative period of their development children spend almost as much of their waking life at school as at home. Altogether this works out at some 15,000 hours (from the age of five until school leaving) during which schools and teachers may have an impact on the development of the children in their care. Do a child's experiences at school have any effect; does it matter which school he goes to; and which are the features of school that matter (Rutter, 1979, p. 1)?*

Answering his own questions, Michael Rutter emphasizes that schools do indeed matter. Examining 12 London schools over a period of years, Rutter found that there were several characteristics that marked the effective school.

- A mixture of children rather than a homogeneous group showed better results.

- The ample use of rewards, praise, and appreciation were associated with better pupil outcome. (Pupil outcome refers to achievement, behavior, attendance, and delinquency rates.)

- A pleasant and comfortable school environment (good care of the building, good working conditions, responsiveness to pupils' needs) was also linked to better outcomes.

- Encouraging pupils to share responsibility in running the school helped to improve achievement, attendance, and behavior.

- Pupils showed greater academic and behavior gains in those schools that stressed academic matters.

- Pupil behavior was best in those schools whose teachers were positive models: they were on time, knew their subjects, and were willing to see pupils at any time. Pupil behavior was worse in those schools whose teachers relied on physical punishment.

Research today clearly shows that differences between schools are strongly associated with characteristics of the schools and produce powerful effects on pupils. How can we interpret these findings? Schooling affects behavior, and perhaps one of the greatest influences on middle childhood youngsters (outside of the family) is the teacher (see box 10.1).

Schools and Social Development

Schools are different social contexts at preschool, elementary, and secondary levels. They are organized differently, children perceive them differently, and different aspects of social behavior appear to meet pupils' changing needs (Minuchin & Shapiro, 1983). Preschool experiences are more protective and caring than educational. The children interact with one or two teachers, perhaps an equal number of aides, and several peers.

During the middle childhood years, the elementary school classroom becomes more of a true social unit, with more intense interactions between teacher and pupil

BOX 10.1

The Influence of Outstanding Teachers

Several outstanding public figures have testified to the impact schools and teachers have on children's development (Lynn, 1985).

- Ralph Nader (consumer advocate) commented on the fifth-grade teacher who stressed the value of time: she was driving home that to waste time is to lose it forever. "I never forgot that advice."
- Elizabeth Dole (U.S. Secretary of Labor) recalled that her concept of service was inspired by teachers who took the concept of leadership seriously.
- Sally Ride (first woman astronaut) was motivated to continue her interest in science by an outstanding high school chemistry teacher.
- Steve Jobs (co-founder of Apple Computers) remembers his fourth-grade teacher saying that somewhere in a classroom, sitting at a desk just like yours, is someone who is going to change the world.
- Hugh Downs (TV newscaster) remembers those teachers who didn't patronize or talk down. He believes that we must have people telling young people that they can do it—"that's what I built on."

Both research and testimonials illustrate the influence that schools exercise on development. Your common sense has probably brought you to the same conclusion. How can any event as intense and prolonged as schooling not leave its imprint on a child's growth?

and among peers (Travers, 1982). Teachers, as authority figures, establish the climate of the classroom and the kinds of relationships permitted. Peer group relationships stress friendship, belonginess, and status (Adalbjarnardottir & Selman, 1989).

Two different types of interactions can be identified, both of which will shape the direction of a middle childhood youngster's growth. First is the relationship with the teacher: usually intense, goal-directed, and subject to evaluation. Second is the relationship with peers, which will open up a new world. When you examine these relationships objectively, the school's role in development for children of these years seems critical.

Think now of the many aspects of development that we have mentioned: the inborn temperamental disposition of children, the pattern of childrearing behavior parents adopt, the relationships within the family. All of these determine how a child reacts to what happens in a classroom. Does it match the child's needs?

- During the kindergarten and elementary school years pupils are being socialized. They are learning to respond to teachers and get along with their peers—and taught the basic skills. Discipline is typically not a major concern since youngsters of this age usually react well to authority and seek teacher praise and rewards. Adjustment to the school as a major socializing agent and mastery of the fundamentals are the two chief tasks of these years (Hetherington & Parke, 1986).

- Pupils in the middle elementary school grades know a school's routine and have worked out their relationships with their peers. They must concentrate on curricular tasks in a clearly defined classroom atmosphere (Minuchin & Shapiro, 1983).

The first day of school is stressful for youngsters. For most children, however, this upset to their psychological equilibrium passes and they adapt quickly.

- The upper elementary years are a time when peer pressure mounts and most youngsters are concerned with pleasing friends. Teachers are authority figures and more challenging to students. Classroom control becomes more of an issue. Children should have mastered the basics and to an extent can function independently. Classroom procedures and rules should be distinct, understandable, and fair (Wittrock, 1986).

Thus, with growing maturity, middle childhood youngsters face greater demands and higher expectations. From our brief discussion, you can see how the schools should contribute to the youngster's sense of competence, which Erikson identifies as the psychosocial strength of these years. Competence is not confined to academics but extends into the physical and social worlds, helping middle childhood youngsters develop a needed self-confidence.

If the challenges to these youngsters are great, so are the opportunities. One opportunity for social growth comes with the charge to American schools to educate all the children of all the people (Rutter & Garmezy, 1983).

Our Multicultural Schools

In our pluralistic society, children will meet pupils from many different cultures. We know that cultural differences in the classroom can affect both achievement and adjustment. Consequently, an important goal for our schools is to prepare children to enter the larger society and develop positive relationships with those from different cultures. The focus of multicultural education is on helping youngsters develop positive gender, racial, cultural, and class identities and to accept others from different cultures (Ramsey, 1987).

Integrating Our Pupils

Attempting to avoid misunderstandings that could affect relationships among children, our schools have emphasized several means of integrating youngsters from different backgrounds (Ramsey, 1987).

Student Learning Style   Good examples of student learning style can be found in the literature on various cultural groups. For example, studies of Hispanic students have shown that these students tend to be influenced more than other students by personal relationships and praise or disapproval from authority figures. Pueblo Indian children from the American Southwest show higher achievement when instruction utilizes their primary learning patterns (those that occur outside the classroom). These pupils respond well when instruction incorporates the concerns and needs of the community in a global manner. That is, they learn more effectively when a subject, such as mathematics, is taught in a more applied manner—for example, as it is related to specific community needs.

Recognition of Dialect Differences   If dialects hinder academic progress, how should the schools attempt to remedy the problem? Should they use standard (proper) English with these students and risk alienating them or causing them to reject their cultural heritage? Or should English be taught as a foreign language? What of students who speak Black English? Should they be taught using Black English until they master standard English?

Unfortunately, research offers no clear guidance. Students do not seem to gain academically if initially taught in their own dialect. Also, many parents believe that their children should be taught in standard English so that they can master the language skills for future success. Perhaps the best advice here is to adapt to the community's wishes as much as possible. The key to a school's success in teaching these pupils is to establish and maintain close contact with parents.

Bilingual Education School involvement with bilingual programs has increased substantially since 1968 when Congress passed the **Bilingual Education Act.** In 1974, the United States Supreme Court ruled that schools must make provision for students who find instruction incomprehensible because they do not understand English.

Legislation and court orders, however well intentioned, are inadequate vehicles in themselves. For example, estimates are that at least 50,000 Vietnamese and Cambodian school-age children arrived on these shores during the influx of 1975. Unless cultural differences were recognized, the schools, and children and parents, experienced considerable problems (e.g., children were accustomed to writing their surnames first; married women retained their given names).

We may conclude that multicultural education, while desirable, has certain risks accompanying its implementation. Separatism can become divisive if difference is overemphasized.

As our schools attempt to remain a strong force in a child's development, middle childhood children are increasingly drawn to that strong competitor of school—television.

Television and Development

Do you have a television set in your home? Don't you laugh at what appears to be a ridiculous question? You probably have at least one, more likely two or three. When you consider that American homes have at least one set and realize the colorful appeal of TV, you can better understand why television has become the school's great competition (Pinon, Huston, & Wright, 1989).

In the Surgeon General's report on television viewing, *Television and Behavior: Ten Years of Scientific Progress and Implications for the Eighties* (1982), one of the questions asked was, who watches television? The answer was simple: almost everyone. Elementary school children watch at least four hours each day.

The beginning of school attendance slows the time spent watching, but at about age 8 the rate increases dramatically. Are there developmental effects from all of this viewing?

Children's Viewing Habits
The 1982 Surgeon General's report reflects the pattern of development discussed thus far. Babies are briefly attracted by the color and sound; 2 and 3 year olds watch longer and with some understanding; elementary school children watch for long periods; and the teen years see a lessening in viewing time. These viewing habits are fairly well established. Specifically, the report presented several findings related to development.

Television and Cognitive Development

The moment we concede that children learn from watching television, certain questions arise:

> How active are children in the process?
> To what do they attend?
> How much do they understand?
> How much do they remember?

Answering these questions gives us insight into how TV watching and cognitive development are associated. For example, when you studied Piaget's work, especially

---

BOX 10.2

Take a Guess

For an idea of the role that television plays in our society, try to answer these questions, which have been drawn from several national surveys.

1. What percentage of American homes have a TV set?
2. How long (on the average) is the set on per day?
3. By age 85, how many years of television has the average viewer seen?
4. How many hours of TV does the average viewer watch per week?
5. By age 18, a student has watched how many hours of TV?
6. By age 15, how many killings has a child seen on television?
7. Can television influence a child's behavior?

If you had any doubts about the extent of television viewing, these figures should dispel them.

3. 9 years
2. 6 hours
1. 99%
7. yes
5. 15,000
4. 28 hours
6. 13,000 killings

---

his views on operations, you saw how Piaget insisted that children were active participants in their cognitive development. They actively construct their cognitive world.

The same is true of their TV watching. They bring a unique set of cognitive structures to the TV set, structures that reflect their level of cognitive development. Remember what we said about middle childhood youngsters: attention span lengthens, memory improves, and comprehension increases. Children don't drop these abilities when they watch TV; they apply them to what they are seeing (Liebert, Sprafkin, & Davidson, 1988). Specifically we know that:

- *Children remember what is said,* even when they are not looking at the screen. Auditory attention is also at work (voices, sound changes, laughing, and applause).

- *The amount of time spent looking at the set is directly related to age.* By age 4 children will attend to TV about 55% of the time, even when there are many other distractions in the room.

- *Specific features of programs attract children:* women, movement, and camera angles; they look away during stills and animal shots.

- *Children quickly learn to relate sound to sight:* chase music means a chase scene. (Note the ideal combination of auditory and visual effects that produces powerful attractions.)

- *Comprehension* depends on age and experience.

This last finding requires additional comment. To understand television, children need three accomplishments:

1. They must know something about story form—how stories are constructed and understood.

2. World knowledge or general knowledge about situations and events are needed to grasp television's content.

3. Knowledge of television's forms and conventions helps viewers to understand what is happening on the screen. Music, visual techniques, and camera angles all convey information (Liebert & others, 1986).

Consideration of these three requirements helps to put children's viewing in perspective: they simply lack the maturity and experience to grasp fully much of what they are watching. For example, they have the perceptual skills to see and recognize a car moving away. But now the camera may cut to another scene (the sky, a police officer, or corner of a house). The significance of the cut introduces another theme, embedded in the story, that completely eludes them.

We can conclude, then, that much of what children see on television is not just content. They also learn TV's codes: sound effects, camera techniques, and program organization. Some researchers believe that changes in children's behavior following the viewing of televised violence come from their responding to fast action, loud music, and camera tricks. Children understand television programs according to their level of development, and their level of development is affected by their television viewing.

Television and Violence

If we were to summarize the Surgeon General's report (1982), we would say:

**BE CAREFUL OF WHAT CHILDREN WATCH;
TELEVISION MAY BE HARMFUL TO THEIR HEALTH.**

After decades of research, we can safely conclude that televised violence causes aggressive behavior in the children who observe it (Parke & Slaby, 1983). Are children exposed to much television violence? Think of what we've said so far.

- Almost every American home has at least one television set.

- Children watch for many hours each day.

- Much of television's programming contains violence as a common feature. Estimates are that over 70% of all prime time dramatic shows contain violent scenes.

- Most children watch television with few, if any, parental restrictions. (Our concern here is with middle childhood youngsters who tend to watch adult shows.)

- Boys prefer to watch TV violence more than girls.

- Younger children (up to about the third or fourth grade) are less likely to associate violence with motivation and consequences.

Grouping these facts has caused Parke and Slaby (1983) to reach two conclusions:

1. Televised violence *increases* children's level of aggression.

2. Televised violence *increases* children's passive acceptance of the use of aggression by others.

Can the American public force television producers to decrease the level of violence in their programming, a level that slowly but steadily seems to be increasing? For many reasons, ranging from the appeal of violence to issues of free speech, this is a difficult question to answer. But all responsible adults can take one step with far-reaching consequences: be alert to what children are watching because television affects development.

```
┌─────────────────────────────────────────────────────────────────────┐
│                              BOX 10.3                                 │
├─────────────────────────────────────────────────────────────────────┤
```

What's Your Opinion?

We have repeatedly noted how different theorists (especially the major theorists discussed in chap. 2) can interpret the same data differently. Television violence is a good example. Two theories have been widely used in attempts to understand television's impact on children: cognitive and behaviorist.

Cognitive theorists, reflecting Piaget's views, believe that children understand what they see according to their level of cognitive development. The cognitive structures that children form can be altered by what they see on television. Children attend to what they see; they learn from what they see; and they remember what they see. They can also apply these new ideas in new settings. Since we have discussed cognitive theory in detail, let's turn to the behaviorists.

Behaviorists, especially in the social learning theory of Bandura (1986), offer a different interpretation. Bandura believes that considerable evidence exists to show

that learning can occur by observing others, *even when the observer doesn't reproduce the model's responses.* Referring to this as **observational learning,** Bandura states that the information we obtain from observing other things, events, and people influences the way we act.

On what does Bandura base his conclusions? With his colleagues (Bandura, Ross, & Ross, 1963), Bandura conducted a now famous experiment. Preschool children observed a model displaying aggression toward an inflated doll under three conditions: in one situation the children saw a film of a human model being aggressive toward the doll. In the next, children witnessed filmed cartoon aggression. Finally, live models exhibited the identical aggressive behavior. The results: later all children exhibited more aggression than youngsters in a control group!

Which theory do you think offers the best explanation? What's your opinion?

Television and Prosocial Behavior

The Surgeon General's report also refers to television's potential for encouraging **prosocial behavior** in children. Prosocial behavior includes such things as friendliness, self-control, and being helpful (Mussen & Eisenberg-Berg, 1982).

Testing this potential, Sprafkin and associates (1975) selected two episodes from the "Lassie" series. One of these episodes had the lead child character risk his life to save a puppy. The other episode had no such dramatic incident. An episode from the "Brady Bunch" show was also used. The researchers created a situation in which children would have to make a choice between alerting adults that an animal needed help or continuing to work on a task that could win them a prize. If they pushed a help button, they lost time on their task (a game). They had to make a choice, then, between sacrifice or self-interest.

The children who had seen the prosocial "Lassie" episode were more willing to help than those who watched either of the other two programs. They pressed the help button for 93 seconds compared with 52 and 38 seconds for those who had watched the other programs. The Surgeon General's report concludes:

❖   *The clear and simple message derived from the research on prosocial behavior is that children learn from watching television and what they learn depends on what they watch. The programs they see on television change their behavior. If they look at violent or aggressive programs, they tend to become*

BOX 10.4
Should Television Be Used as a Prosocial Agent?

Your initial response to the title question is probably a firm yes. Would everyone agree with you? We're not so sure.

In 1975, the United Methodist Church provided money for producing 30-second television spots intended to help children become more cooperative. Psychologists and experienced television personnel combined to make as professional a presentation as possible. The format was identical to that of regular commercials.

Children, ages 4 to 10, watched while sitting on a comfortable sofa, in a relaxed, den-like setting with natural distractions such as toys and books. They were later tested for comprehension of the program and were observed playing.

In the best-known spot, "The Swing," a boy and a girl, about 10 years old, both run to a swing. They argue and struggle over it, each claiming the first ride. They scowl and look menacingly at each other. Suddenly one of them steps back and suggests that the other go first. They are then shown taking turns, happily swinging through the air. The announcer's voice concludes that "this is how you (children) should behave" (Liebert & others, 1982).

Tens of millions of children all over the world saw "The Swing." After seeing the film, children's cooperation increased and all seemed well. Then a reaction set in amid charges of psychological behavior control. Who has a right to impose values on children? Should all children be taught cooperation? Don't some youngsters need to be aggressive to survive? Isn't this brainwashing children? Are we infringing on that fundamental right we all cherish in our society—the right to freedom?

Would you still answer the title question in the same way? Are you sure?

more aggressive and disobedient. But if they look at prosocial programs, they will more likely become more generous, friendly and self-controlled. Television can have beneficial effects; it is a potential force for good (1982, p. 51).

A new brother or sister, budding friendships, school challenges, televised violence, inevitable upset at home—put them all together and they spell *stress*.

Stress in Childhood

Do you recall the title of this chapter, "Middle Childhood—The Widening World"? As youngsters of this age spend more of their time away from home, new contacts and new tasks can upset them. There is no escape; we all have faced them. Were we scarred for life by these encounters? Probably not.

In her excellent and practical analysis of childhood stress, Brenner (1984) describes a spectrum of stressors:

Ordinary	**Moderate**	**Severe**
Jealousy of sibling	One-parent home	Separation from parent (divorce, death, illness)
Typical school anxiety	Multiple parents (biological mother, stepmother, biological father, stepfather)	Abuse Parental alcoholism

But first, let's link what is known about childhood stress to development. We begin by admitting that there is no definition of **stress** with which everyone agrees. Let's use this definition.

> Stress is anything that upsets our equilibrium—
> both psychological and physiological.

Types of Stress

Different kinds of stress can cause similar reactions. Think of a time when your parents were really angry with you or when you were faced with a severe challenge (perhaps speaking before a large group for the first time; or just after you had been given some bad news). Some children react in the same way to all of these events, either with high anxiety, fear, avoidance, weakness, or vomiting.

Different kinds of stress also can cause different reactions of varying intensity. If we group these ideas, we can begin by stating that (Honig, 1986):

- Stress can come from internal sources, usually illness.

- Stress can come from external sources, such as family, school, or peers.

- Stress can be chronic, such as the child who is trapped for years with an alcoholic or abusive parent or with an insensitive teacher.

Table 10.2, based on Brenner (1984), summarizes specific childhood stressors.

Individual Reactions of Children

When each of us is faced with stress, we react differently. To begin with, not all of us would agree on what stress is. For example, some are probably terrified of flying, while others see it as a pleasant, relaxing adventure. While there are many reasons for these different responses, we can isolate several important individual differences.

Sex   As we have repeatedly seen, boys are more vulnerable than girls. This includes their reaction to stress. Select any event that is likely to induce stress and boys are more susceptible: death, divorce, new sibling, hospital admission.

Age   Children of different ages respond differently to stress. There is good evidence that infants are relatively immune to the stress of hospital admission; the age of greatest risk is from age 6 months to 4 years. Children above the age of 4 can rationalize that hospitalization, for example, does not mean abandonment by parents. Middle childhood youngsters are less vulnerable to stress caused by a new sibling, while younger children show a great deal of clinging.

The grief reactions of young children are shorter and milder than those of older youngsters. Cognitive level probably explains the difference; younger children can't understand the concept of death itself (Rutter, 1988). Long-term effects may be greater if family breakup causes change in socioeconomic status, and if moving is involved.

Temperament   Recall that we are all born with unique temperaments, differences that affect the way we interact with the environment. Consequently, children's temperament influences the intensity of their reactions after a stressful event—for example, parental separation.

These are but a few of the many factors that help to explain different reactions to stress. But what can we say about their developmental effects?

Children need emotional support from those in their environment. Even under the most difficult circumstances (divorce, death of a parent, hospitalization), the presence of a "significant other" can help a child to cope, to deal with stress in an appropriate manner for the child's developmental level.

Table 10.2 Specific Childhood Stressors	
Type	**Example**
Two-parent families	Changes associated with normal growth: new siblings, sibling disputes, moving, school, working parents
One-parent families	Multiple adults, lack of sex-role model, mother vs. father, financial difficulties
Multi-parent families	New relationships, living in two households
Death, adoption	Parental death, sibling death, possible institutional placement, relationships with different adults
Temporary separation	Hospitalization, health care, military service
Divorce	Troubled days before the divorce, separation, the divorce itself
Abuse	Parental, sibling, institutional; sexual, physical, emotional
Neglect	Physical (food, clothes), emotional (no response to children's needs for attention and affection)
Alcoholism	Secrecy, responsibility for alcoholic parent, suppress own feelings

Developmental Effects of Stress

If we attempt to link development and vulnerability to stress, we reach certain conclusions. For example, Maccoby (1988) notes that we cannot be upset by events whose power to harm us we do not understand. We can't be humiliated by failure to handle problems whose solutions are someone else's responsibility. Maccoby compares why some events are stressful and others are not and formulates several hypotheses.

- *Age changes alone don't explain vulnerability.* While the events that cause stress change with age, we all experience periods of stabilization and destabilization. In other words, we may be more vulnerable to change at certain times (e.g., we may react emotionally to bad news if we have been quite sick).

- *Environmental structure can lessen vulnerability.* Youngsters can handle stress better if all other parts of their lives are stable. For example, entering school is stressful for almost all children. If home conditions are warm and supportive, it helps to ease what can be a difficult transition. On the other hand, if parents have separated during these days, children can find school entrance quite painful.

- *Although middle childhood youngsters face more stressful situations than younger children, they have learned better ways to cope.* Also, as they move away from sole dependence on parents as attachment figures, peers begin to form a strong supportive network, especially toward the end of middle childhood.

- *Recognizing adults as authority figures* gives children a sense of security, which acts as a buffer against stress.

- *With their growing cognitive ability,* children of this age begin to develop coping skills that help them to combat stress. Think of our discussion of this growing cognitive capacity: the ability to think abstractly, solve problems, reach decisions, and to plan ahead. All of these abilities help to combat stress.

These are no guarantees of successful coping, for obvious reasons: the intensity of the stress, the immaturity of the children, and the amount of support they receive. Yet we also know that there is a small number of children who seem oblivious to stress, at least for a time.

The Invulnerable Child

The mother of three children was beset by mental problems. She refused to eat at home because she was sure someone was poisoning her. Her 12-year-old daughter developed the same fear. Her 10-year-old daughter would eat at home only if the father ate with her.

Her 7-year-old son thought they were all crazy and always ate at home. The son went on to perform brilliantly in school and later in college and has now taken the first steps on what looks like a successful career. The older daughter is now diagnosed schizophrenic, while the younger girl seems to have adjusted after a troubled youth. Why? How?

Answering these questions takes us into uncharted territory. We simply don't know much about invulnerability. But what is known points to one of the human characteristics discussed in chapter 1: *resiliency,* or *plasticity.* This is the ability to recover from either physiological or psychological trauma and return to a normal developmental path.

Who are these **invulnerable children** who grow up in the most chaotic and adverse conditions, yet manage to thrive? They seem to possess some inner quality that protects them from their environment and enables them to reach out to an adult who can offer critical support (Garmezy, 1987).

The ratio seems to be about 1 in 10; that is, for every 10 children who succumb to adverse conditions, 1 develops normally. In each case studied, an adult was there to offer the emotional support needed: a teacher, aunt, uncle, grandparent (Garmezy, 1987). Invulnerable children seem to possess a winning personality. (Remember the discussion of inborn temperamental differences in chap. 6.) They also seem to have a special interest or talent. For example, some of these youngsters were excellent swimmers, dancers, and artists; others had a special knack for working with animals; some showed talent with numbers quite early. Whatever their interest, it served to absorb them and helped to shelter them from their environment.

Such characteristics—a genuinely warm, fairly easy-going personality, an absorbing interest, and the ability to seek out a sympathetic adult—helped these children to distance themselves emotionally from a drugged, alcoholic, or abusive parent (sometimes a parent with all of these problems). Recent studies have shown that children who are emotionally close to a disturbed parent frequently develop problems.

Michael Rutter (1987) a leading researcher in the study of invulnerable children, has attempted to sort out some of the characteristics that help to explain either invulnerability or vulnerability. Among them are the following.

- *Sex.* As with any other problem we discuss, boys are more vulnerable than girls. Whether or not psychological vulnerability is innate is difficult to determine. Boys tend to be exposed to psychological stress more than girls, and typically display disruptive behavior.

- *Temperament.* Children with negative personality features are more frequently the target of a disturbed parent. Parents with a problem do not take it out equally on all children.

- *Parent-child relationship.* While not much is known about this characteristic, a good relationship with one parent acts as a buffer for the child.

- *Positive school experience.* The experience could be either academic or nonacademic. The pleasure associated with success seems to help raise a youngster's sense of self-esteem.

- *Early parental loss.* The results of losing a parent, especially a mother, do not become evident until later in life. Even then its effects are not apparent unless combined with another threatening event.

For those working with youngsters who may be exposed to severe adverse conditions, Rutter suggests:

- Try to reduce the risk impact by teaching children methods of stress reduction and by helping them to gain success and pleasure in other activities.

- Try to reduce any negative chain reaction by providing emotional support.

Table 10.3   Children's Patterns of Coping

Avoiding Stress	Facing Stress
Denial: children act as though the stress does not exist; may use fantasy (imaginary friends to talk to)	*Altruism:* by helping others, children ease their own pain
Regression: children act younger than their years, show greater dependency	*Humor:* children joke about their problems
Withdrawal: children remove themselves, either physically or mentally; they may run away, or attempt to fade into the background	*Suppression:* they push their troubles from their minds; they may play unconcernedly for a while
Impulsive Acting Out: children speak and act impulsively to avoid thinking about reality; by making others angry they attract attention, thus temporarily easing pain	*Anticipation:* these children plan how to meet stress; they tend to protect themselves and accept what can't be avoided

- Help these children to acquire a greater sense of self-esteem by offering a secure relationship and an opportunity for successful achievements.

How Children Cope

Before we begin to discuss coping in childhood, we should remember that for most children psychosocial stress is the villain. That is, a child's hospital admission or a mother's temporary absence is really not the issue here. In most cases of psychosocial stress, the tension is persistent and unrelenting. The child with an alcoholic father or abusive mother has little chance of escaping. Table 10.3 illustrates children's ways of coping with stress.

Yet some children seem invulnerable, as we noted earlier. Remember, however, that invulnerability does not imply that these are super-children who can resist all stress.

❖   *There is no single set of qualities or circumstances that characterizes all such resilient children. But psychologists are finding that they stand apart from their more vulnerable siblings almost from birth. They seem to be endowed with innate characteristics that insulate them from the turmoil and pain of their families and allow them to reach out to some adult—a grandparent, teacher, or family friend—who can lend crucial emotional support (Goleman, 1987, p. 82).*

Continuing deprivation or problems will eventually scar them, but they are better able to function in settings that disable other children. The characteristics of these children are summarized in Table 10.4 (based on work by Farber & Egeland, 1987).

We can best summarize all that we know about coping skills and child development in this list of guidelines for adults.

- To encourage coping skills in children, demonstrate them yourself, especially self-control.
- Encourage children to develop self-esteem.
- Be sympathetic to their feelings and learn to recognize when a child is under stress.
- Urge children to adopt a positive attitude, which then helps them to search for solutions.
- Talk to them; get them to examine their problems openly so that they can obtain any available support.

Table 10.4 Characteristics of Invulnerable Children	
Age	**Characteristics**
At birth	Alert, attentive
1 year	Securely attached infant
2 years	Independent, slow to anger, tolerates frustration well
3–4 years	Cheerful, enthusiastic, works well with others
Childhood	Seems to be able to remove self from trouble, recovers rapidly from disturbance, confident, seems to have a good relationship with at least one adult
Adolescence	Assumes responsibilities, does well in school, may have part-time job, socially popular, is not impulsive

Transition

This chapter followed middle childhood youngsters as they moved away from a sheltered home environment and into a world of new friends, new challenges, and new problems. Whether the task is adjusting to a new sibling, relating to peers and teachers, or coping with difficulties, youngsters of this age enter a different world.

But the timing of their entrance into this novel environment is intended to match their ability to adapt successfully, to master those skills that will prepare them for the next great developmental epoch, adolescence. From Tom Sawyer's subtlety to children learning to cope with stress, middle childhood youngsters require skills that will enable them to deal with their widening social world.

Inevitably, though, they face times of turmoil, which can come from internal or external sources. For some youngsters, these periods of stress are brief interludes; for others, there is no relief for years. Children cope uniquely, using temperamental qualities and coping skills as best they can.

For some, however, the path is always different; the developmental trajectory seems off target. They are the subjects of our next chapter.

Key Ideas

1. Having brothers and sisters creates a different developmental environment for children.

2. While psychologists recognize the influence of siblings, there is still little evidence of specific effects.

3. Each birth in a family introduces a new, complex set of relationships.

4. Children with brothers and sisters also feel the effects of birth order, a phenomenon that intrigues and puzzles psychologists.

5. We are still not certain of the effect of birth order on personality and intelligence.

6. In the middle childhood years, peers emerge as a powerful force in a child's social development.

7. Studies of children's friendships have traced the gradual widening of the circle of friends, including both individual friendships and group membership.

8. School, with its demands and opportunities, should be a critical stimulus to all aspects of development.

9. Television has been widely accepted and recognized as an influential force in development, and so deserves our study as a powerful socializing agent.

10. Today's children are exposed to almost unlimited environmental stimuli and so have become more vulnerable to stress.

Key Terms

Bilingual Education Act

Birth order

Confluence model

Invulnerable children

Observational learning

Peer

Prosocial behavior

Sibling

Social perspective-taking

Stress

What Do You Think?

1.   Recall your relationship with your brothers and sisters. How would you evaluate the experience, positive or negative? Why? Does your answer reflect some of the topics mentioned in this chapter? If you are an only child, do you think you missed out on something? Why?

2.   Where were you in the birth order? From your assessment of your personality characteristics, do you think you match Toman's list of characteristics for your birth position?

3.   It is generally accepted that friendships and groups become more important during the middle childhood years. With your knowledge of the developmental features of these years, do you think children of this age are ready for group membership?

4.   For individuals to experience stress, they must understand the forces that are pressing on them. Do you think middle childhood youngsters are capable of such an interpretation of the events surrounding them?

Suggested Readings

Liebert, Robert, Joyce Sprafkin, and Emily Davidson. (1988). *The early window.* 3d ed. New York: Pergamon. This paperback is one of the best single sources on the impact of television on our society today. Once you read this, you'll understand why TV is considered a major socializing force in a child's life.

Parmet, Herbert. (1980). *Jack: The struggles of John F. Kennedy.* New York: Dial. An insightful glimpse of those childhood years when the give-and-take of family interactions was colored by a constant sense of "great expectations."

Rubin, Zick. (1980). *Children's friendships.* Cambridge, MA: Harvard University Press. This widely quoted little book is a storehouse of insights into the role that friends play in a child's social development. (It is part of the *Developing Child* series, a collection of paperbacks you would find quite interesting and helpful.)

Ward, Geoffrey. (1989). *A first-class temperament: The emergence of Franklin Roosevelt.* New York: Harper & Row. To the end of her days, Eleanor Roosevelt felt that no one loved her for herself. In this intriguing account of the young Roosevelts, Ward traces the effect of an alcoholic father and an indifferent mother on the emotional life of a young girl.

· *Chapter 11* ·

A Different Path: Children
Who Are Exceptional

Up to this point we have described the typical course of development for most children. Some youngsters, however, follow a different path. Consequently, this chapter is devoted to an analysis of those children who are exceptional to some degree. We'll focus on children with physical and health impairments, those who are intellectually different, those who experience communication difficulties, behavior disorders, and emotional problems, and those who are learning disabled.

As you read this chapter, remember that a child's early difficulties do not necessarily mean a lifetime of continuous problems. This depends on the nature, severity, and timing of the difficulty. Think back to chapter 1 and recall our discussion of sensitive periods and continuity when we emphasized the human ability to "bounce back." It is a comforting thought.

As an example of a youth who got off to a rocky start, consider Winston Churchill. Beginning school at 7 years of age, Churchill immediately set his own agenda: refusing to learn anything he wasn't interested in, rebellious, troublesome—in a constant battle with authority. At the bottom of his class, Churchill maintained this pattern through his years at Harrow, the famous British prep school. As one of his biographers, William Manchester, writes:

❖ *Churchillian stubbornness, which would become the bane of Britain's enemies, was the despair of his teachers. He refused to learn unless it suited him. He was placed in what today would be called a remedial reading class, where slow boys were taught English. He stared out the window. Math, Greek, and French were beneath his contempt (1983, p. 157).*

These words describe one of the world's greatest leaders, a statesman who led the English people through the darkest days of the second world war and ultimately triumphed. Yet, by today's standards, he probably would be termed a child "with a behavior disorder." So we should reserve judgment until we have all the facts about any developmental difficulty.

Before we continue, you may wish to review several of the major accomplishments of youngsters as they proceed through the normal stages of development. These milestones, which appear in Table 11.1, will help you to compare typical growth with the developmental difficulties described in this chapter.

Different Paths—Different Development

Not all children follow the developmental sequence that we have sketched in the previous chapters. Some find themselves on a different path. Problems ranging from a genetic defect to disease to an accident can cause twists and turns in development. Consider these cases.

A 9-year-old girl was referred by her family doctor for neuropsychological testing. She had been having school problems with writing and arithmetic. Her motor abilities seemed quite limited. She also had difficulty relating to other children (Rourke and others, 1983). She was friendly but easily distracted during the testing, requiring constant guidance and encouragement. Her IQ was 88, but she did poorly on the performance section of the test (WISC, see chap. 9). The examiners suspected that her visual-perceptual and verbal-spatial abilities were impaired.

Continued testing supported these initial findings. She seemed to have particular trouble when she had to use her left hand, suggesting difficulty in the functioning of the right cerebral hemisphere. This would also explain the quality of her social relationships. She could not understand nonverbal communication such as facial expressions, gestures, and body postures. After intensive perceptual motor training and exercises to improve visual-spatial organization, the girl showed considerable improvement and was ready to return to regular schooling.

Or take the case of the famous Koluchova twins in Czechoslovakia (Clarke & Clarke, 1976). Their mother died shortly after birth and they were placed in a children's home for 11 months. The father then remarried and the boys came to this new household. They had two older sisters and the stepmother had two children.

The next five years can only be described as a nightmare for the twins. The stepmother, for some reason, despised them. She forbade the other children to talk to them; they were almost totally isolated and kept in a small closet. Occasionally they were locked in the cellar for long periods of time. They lacked adequate food, exercise, and fresh air. They were beaten often.

When the father finally had to take one of the boys to a doctor, the physician alerted authorities and the boys were taken from the family. The children were hospitalized, where physical and psychological tests were given. They showed fear of toys, other children, and television. It was impossible to measure their intelligence and their language was impaired.

The children were next placed in a children's home and eventually taken by a foster family headed by two unmarried, middle-aged sisters. Simultaneously they were sent to a school for the mentally retarded where they steadily showed improvement. They were later placed in a normal school where they were older than their classmates but equal to the educational tasks. At the most recent assessment the twins showed normal intelligence and were developing well socially.

Finally, consider Eric, 3 years old. His parents were mildly surprised when, on kissing him soon after birth, they detected a salty taste. The weren't bothered by this until they noticed that his growth seemed slow and he was wracked by a chronic cough. As you may have guessed, Eric was showing some of the classic symptoms of cystic fibrosis. Caused by a genetic defect, cystic fibrosis is the most severe genetic disease of childhood, affecting about one in 1,200 youngsters. Cystic fibrosis kills more children than any other genetic disease (Travers, 1982).

In reading about each of these cases, you can understand how difficult it is to classify many children's problems. In the first case, the results of a brain dysfunction could easily have been attributed to a lack of intelligence, poor attention, developmental delay, or to being a troublemaker. In the second case, the twins might have been judged mentally retarded, rather than the victims of horrible family conditions. Finally, Eric's parents could easily have thought he was suffering from repeated flu infections.

Trying to identify the chief cause of exceptionality requires patience, careful observation, and good methods of evaluation. In the remainder of the chapter, think constantly about how the problem being discussed could affect other aspects of development. Before beginning, however, read these symptoms and see if you can identify the individual described (Webb and others 1981).

- Cocaine abuse

- Compulsive, narcissistic

- Gunshot wound

- Psychosocial stress (result: personal and financial loss)

- Adapts well; functions well

Table 11.1 Milestones in Development and Learning

Age (years)	Physical	Cognitive	Social	Emotional	Language
Infancy (0–2)	1. Can hear and see at birth 2. Rapid growth in height and weight 3. Rapid neurological development 4. Motor development proceeds steadily (crawling, standing, walking)	1. Seek stimulation 2. An egocentric view of the world begins to decrease 3. Demonstrates considerable memory ability 4. Begins to process information	1. Need for interaction 2. Smiling appears 3. Reciprocal interactions begin immediately 4. Attachment develops	1. Beginnings of emotions discernible in first months 2. Infant passes through emotional milestones	1. Proceed from cooing and babbling to words and sentences 2. Word order and inflection appear 3. Vocabulary begins to increase rapidly
Preschool (2–6)	1. Extremely active 2. Mastery of gross motor behavior 3. Refinement of fine motor behavior	1. Perceptual discrimination becomes sharper 2. Attention more focused 3. Noticeable improvement in memory 4. Easily motivated	1. Attachment 2. Beginning of interpersonal relationships a. parents b. siblings c. peers d. teachers 3. Play highly significant	1. Still becomes angry at frustration 2. Prone to emotional outbursts 3. Emotional control slowly appearing 4. Aware of gender 5. Fantasies conform more to reality 6. May begin to suppress emotionally unpleasant memories	1. From first speech sounds (cooing, babbling) to use of sentences with conjunctions and prepositions 2. Acquires basic framework of native language
Middle childhood (7–11)	1. Mastery of motor skills 2. Considerable physical and motor skills	1. Attention becomes selective 2. Begins to devise memory strategies 3. Begins to evaluate behavior 4. Problem-solving behavior shows marked improvement	1. Organized activities more frequent 2. Member of same-sex group 3. Peer influence growing 4. Usually have "best" friend	1. Pride in competence 2. Confident 3. Growing sensitivity 4. Volatile 5. Striving, competitive 6. Growing sexual awareness	1. Rapid growth of vocabulary 2. Uses and understands complex sentences 3. Can use sentence content to determine word meaning 4. Good sense of grammar 5. Can write fairly lengthy essays

Note: he shows remarkable persistence and always gets his man; relaxes playing the violin. **WHO IS THIS MAN?**
Answer: Sherlock Holmes

This brief vignette illustrates the difficulty of diagnosis. It would be easy to say that our subject suffers from drug abuse, or a physical problem, or stress. When we identify all of the symptoms, we can more accurately suggest programs of intervention and predict the future. Keep this in mind as we follow children on their different paths in this chapter.

A Classification Scheme

Over the years many classifications for identifying children's problems have been proposed, but none have been thoroughly satisfactory. The latest effort, **DSM III-R** (Diagnostic and Statistical Manual III—Revised) has had wide acceptance and we will use applicable sections from it as a basis for our work.

Developmental Domains		
Piaget	Erikson	Kohlberg
Sensorimotor 1. Use of reflexes 2. Primary circular reactions 3. Secondary circular reactions 4. Coordination of secondary schemata 5. Tertiary circular reactions 6. Representation	1. Development of trust	1. Begins to learn wrong from right
Preoperational 1. Deferred imitation 2. Symbolic play 3. Mental imagery 4. Drawing 5. Language	1. Growing competence and autonomy 2. Initiative and purpose	1. Beginning of preconventional moral reasoning
Concrete Operational 1. Conservation 2. Seriation 3. Classification 4. Number 5. Reversibility	Industry and competence	1. Continued development of preconventional moral reasoning 2. Conventional moral reasoning

Table 11.1 *Continued*

We will discuss seven categories of exceptionality in this chapter.

- *Physical and health impairment*. Here we discuss such topics as sight, hearing, and orthopedic problems.

- *Intellectual differences*. The focus here will be on slow learners and the gifted.

- *Communication disorders*. This category includes children who have difficulty acquiring language as well as difficulties such as stuttering.

- *Behavioral problems*. Conduct disorders and hyperactivity are the major issues.

- *Emotional problems*. Included are problems ranging from anxiety to schizophrenia.

BOX 11.1

Children at Risk

Children at risk—what does it mean? Those children who give early signs of physical or psychological difficulties, unless helped by appropriate intervention, may continue to experience problems, perhaps with increasing intensity, throughout the life span. In response to a growing national concern about these children, many leaders (medical, educational, psychological, business) have recognized the importance of the preschool years in any intervention planning.

Although the significance of these years is readily acknowledged, we also know that only 18% of children eligible for Head Start are actually enrolled. Recognizing this, the United States Congress has taken steps to expand funding for preschool programs. For example, to battle the problems that arise from social disadvantage, certain key needs have been identified.

- Good prenatal care for the mother
- Good medical care for babies of low birth weight
- Developmental information for mothers
- Access to reliable early childhood education
- Access to jobs and housing

The medical community's concern with these years can be seen in the hospital programs that have sprung up across the country. At Boston's City Hospital, for example, a child development project attempts to identify potential learning disabilities in children who are being treated at the hospital. Realizing that medical personnel often see these children before anyone else, a team of early childhood developmental specialists and pediatricians have treated over a thousand youngsters and identified about 25% of them as having some form of learning disability.

Suffering from such problems as lead poisoning, prematurity, low birth weight, poor maternal care, stress, and neglect, these children, without help, frequently become the school dropouts of the future. With early diagnosis, however, they can be referred to appropriate services.

In a similar manner, educators are addressing such problems more aggressively. There is a growing recognition that teachers need

- A better understanding of poverty and its effects
- A thorough grounding in multicultural issues
- Insight into the role that these factors can play in curriculum and instruction

With this multidisciplinary approach, efforts at helping children at risk have a much greater chance of succeeding.

- *Learning disabilities.* Discussion will center on children who are achieving less than they should.

- *Abused children.* These youngsters deserve special attention due to their upbringing.

Perhaps you disagree with the topics that we have included in each of our groups. For example, you may think that giftedness should be treated separately. Gifted children, however, are exceptional. At least we have a common classification scheme to which to refer.

That these children require separate analysis is further reflected in federal legislation. Public Law 94–142, The Education for All Handicapped Children Act, requires communities to provide an appropriate education for children with special needs. This law is expressly designed to accommodate such youngsters by requiring that they be placed in the least restrictive environment in which they can achieve success.

Called **mainstreaming,** this legislation was passed in 1975 and imposed a mandate on every school in the country. ''Least restrictive'' means that pupils are to be removed from the regular classroom and home and family as *infrequently as possible.*

❖   *That is, his or her life should be as normal as possible and the intervention should be consistent with individual needs and not interfere with individual freedom any more than is absolutely necessary. For example, children should not be placed in a special class if they can be served adequately by a resource teacher and they should not be placed in an institution if a special class will serve their needs just as well (Hallahan & Kauffman, 1988, p. 8).*

The Dangers of Labeling Children

As you undoubtedly discerned from our groupings of children's difficulties, some youngsters are handicapped, while others are talented. In either case, the children have some characteristic—physical, mental, behavioral, social—that requires special attention in order for them to achieve to their potential. It is important to remember that *a youngster may be handicapped in one situation but not another.* A child in a wheelchair may be an outstanding scholar; a physical handicap does not imply cognitive difficulties. As Gloecker and Simpson (1988) note, those students who are exceptional do not possess different traits; they demonstrate differences in the quantity of these traits.

While labels may be necessary for identifying and helping pupils and making available appropriate services, any rigid classification system can cause problems. These pitfalls range from indiscriminate exclusion from a regular classroom to the danger that the label becomes self-fulfilling. Sensitive to these problems, today's parents and educators emphasize the skills possessed by an exceptional child and attempt to improve any inadequate skills.

Physical and Health Impairment

We'll begin our discussion with those children who suffer from physical difficulties, such as visual and hearing problems.

Visual Impairments

Children with a **visual impairment** are those who have any reduction in vision. The National Society for the Prevention of Blindness recommends that children be referred for an eye examination if, on the Snellen Chart, they are unable to read the following lines:

3 year olds	20/50 or less
4 year olds through third grade	20/40 or less
Fourth grade and above	20/30 or less

(20/50 means that this youngster can see at 20 feet what the ordinary child can see at 50 feet. Normal vision is 20/20.) We still lack an accurate account of visually impaired children since data collection varies from state to state. The most widely used figure suggests that 1 in every 1,000 children is either visually impaired or blind.

The best way to summarize the developmental characteristics of visually impaired children is to remember that they are like other children in many more ways than they are different (Haring & McCormick, 1986).

Visual impairment can be a major cause of academic problems. Careful testing is needed to prevent visual problems affecting all aspects of a child's life.

Hearing Impairments

Children with a **hearing impairment** are those who suffer a hearing loss that ranges in severity from mild to profound. Estimates are that about 8% or over 17 million Americans experience some form of hearing difficulty. Within this group, approximately 100,000 preschool youngsters, 600,000 elementary and junior high pupils, and almost a million high school and college students have some degree of hearing loss.

Once the problem is detected and corrected, the outlook for these children is good. Of course, the earlier the detection, the better. Pupils with a mild hearing loss (and even some with a more severe loss) often adapt sufficiently to go several years in school without being identified. They compensate in such ways that teachers miss the problem. But these pupils suffer because they cannot work to full potential and frequently become frustrated and anxious (Berdine & Blackhurst, 1985).

Physical problems, such as visual and hearing problems, are not the only potential hazard facing children. Intellectual difficulties, deriving from many sources, also appear.

Intellectual Differences

As you might expect, children reflect the entire range of intellectual ability, from severely retarded to gifted. Both extremes of this intellectual continuum have attracted considerable attention. In chapter 9 you read about classifying intelligence. Most people have an IQ of about 100 on the Binet test. Let's move in opposite directions from this so-called average and examine the characteristics of both slow and gifted children.

Slow Learners

Any discussion of slow learners takes us into the world of **mental retardation.** Who are these individuals? A widely accepted definition has been proposed by the American Association on Mental Deficiency.

❖   *Mental retardation refers to significantly subaverage general intellectual functioning resulting in or associated with concurrent impairments in adaptive behavior and manifested during the development period (Grossman, 1983, p. 11).*

In this definition, *subaverage* refers to an IQ of approximately 70 or below. Estimates are that about 2%–3% of the population is below average. By *adaptive,* Grossman means the extent to which an individual meets the standards of personal independence and social responsibility expected for age and culture group. Table 11.2 presents the AAMD classification scheme. The meaning of the categories is as follows.

* *Mild:* Development slow. Children capable of being educated ("educable") within limits. Adults, with training, can work in competitive employment. Able to live independent lives.

* *Moderate:* Slow in their development, but able to learn to care for themselves. Children capable of being trained ("trainable"). Adults need to work and live in sheltered environment.

* *Severe:* Motor development, speech, and language are retarded. Not completely dependent. Often, but not always, physically handicapped.

BOX 11.2

Someone Who Is Making It

Today Billy is 11 years old, physically strong, and delivers newspapers. Usually pleasant, Billy is perfectly capable of knowing which houses on his route are to receive papers. It is only on the day when payment is due that you notice Billy's difficulty. If you are a new customer, his father or older brother comes to the door with Billy and helps with the change. If you are known and trusted, you tell Billy what change to give you.

Billy is a good example of a mentally retarded youngster who is functioning satisfactorily. Experiencing immediate difficulty in school, he has been in a special class for several years and has managed to acquire basic skills. The newspaper distributor feels strongly about him and has given him an opportunity that many other youngsters never receive.

Billy enjoys a unique situation where he has proven himself a valuable asset and shows the wisdom of attempts to bring these children as close as possible to normal lives. If they receive similar social support, many youngsters such as Billy will blend into society, leading lives that are not dramatically different from the rest of us. Note that Billy fits the behavioral classification of mildly mentally retarded in Table 11.2.

Table 11.2 Classification of Retardation		
Mild	52–67 (Binet)	55–69 (WISC—R)
Moderate	36–51	40–54
Severe	20–35	
Profound	Below 20	

From American Association on Mental Deficiency. Copyright American Association on Mental Deficiency, Washington, DC.

- *Profound:* Need constant care or supervision for survival. Gross impairment in physical coordination and sensory development. Often physically handicapped.

Kessler (1988) reinforces the comments that we made at the chapter's opening when she notes that any person (child or adult) may meet the criteria of mental retardation at one time in life and not another. Thus it is possible for both IQ and adaptive functioning to change.

If you should have a slow learner in the family or occasionally meet them in your neighborhood or in circumstances such as Billy's, remember that these youths

Have the same basic needs as the nonretarded
Demonstrate considerable individual differences
Are a changing population because of society's evolving perception and
    treatment

At the other end of the intellectual continuum are gifted children.

The Gifted/Talented

❖ *Jimmie is six years and eight months as of this writing and this year he has shown a deep interest in paleontology, meteorology (he has his own weather station), and electronics. He builds his own radio and transmitter sets with little assistance. He has forged ahead with his inventions, too. . . . This year, when he heard about the airplane disasters at Idlewild and La Guardia airfields, he felt quite dismayed and decided to do something about it. Using a*

Many children who are exceptional, such as the mildly mentally retarded, with support, can acquire social skills that enable them to function in an appropriate setting.

> *cardboard shoe box, two strips of paper and two magnets, he invented a device which the pilot could use in the cockpit of his plane which would tell him when it is off course on approaching. Needless to say, Thomas Edison is his idol (Goertzel & Goertzel, 1962, p. 289).*

The abilities of this boy, taken from the Goertzels' enduring description of a gifted youngster, nicely define what we mean by gifted. But, though immensely talented, these children frequently grow up in environments (including schools) that don't understand them and often display hostility toward them.

Defining Gifted

Even defining the **gifted and talented** has caused considerable controversy. Initially, an IQ of 120 or 140 (or some number) was used to identify the gifted. But these measures were too restrictive. Youngsters who have exceptional talent in painting or music or who seem unusually creative are also gifted. As a result, The Gifted and Talented Children's Education Act of 1978 defined these children as follows:

❖   *The term gifted and talented children means children, and, whenever applicable, youth who are identified at the preschool, elementary, or secondary level as possessing demonstrated or potential abilities that have evidence of high performance capabilities in areas such as intellectual, creative, specific academic or leadership ability, or in the performing and visual arts, and who by reason thereof, require services or activities not ordinarily provided by the school.*

Who Are the Gifted and Talented?

Estimates are that about 5% of school-age children fit this definition. If these children are so talented, why do they require special attention? For every Einstein who

Thomas Edison's creative genius was not immediately recognized. As with many of the gifted, their talents may go unrecognized or arouse hostility in those around them.

Gifted children may approach tasks quite differently than typical children. Einstein, for example, was thought to be almost incapable of learning because of his delayed language and unique methods of problem solving.

One of history's great figures, Churchill had an inauspicious beginning. School failures and personality clashes with instructors disguised the genius that was to appear later.

is identified and flourishes, there are probably dozens of others whose gifts are obscured. Thomas Edison's mother withdrew him from first grade because he was having so much trouble; Gregor Mendel, the founder of scientific genetics, failed his teacher's test four times; Isaac Newton was considered a poor student in grammar school; Winston Churchill had a terrible academic record; Charles Darwin left medical school.

One major difficulty with the way that our society deals with gifted children is that interest in them comes and goes. Initially, interest in gifted children was aroused when the results of IQ tests showed that some children were outstanding. Later, when the Soviets launched their Sputnik satellite, there was concern in the United States for providing opportunities for the gifted that could offer us a chance to catch up (Bloom, 1985; Fox & Washington, 1985).

Today, with our national concern for unusual students of all types, interest in the gifted has increased dramatically. Government reports insist that the gifted are a minority who need special attention. They are indeed a minority, characterized by their special ability, who come from all levels of society, all races, and all national origins, and who include both sexes equally. They are the Einsteins, the Edisons, the Lands.

The Gifted—A Neglected Group

The gifted have been neglected for several reasons. Among them are the following.

- *Failure to be identified.* In a recent survey, the U.S. Office of Education reports that 60% of schools reported no gifted students. Teachers and administrators simply fail to recognize them.

- *Hostility of school personnel.* Hostility has traditionally been a problem for the gifted. Resentment that they are smarter than teachers, dislike for an intellectual elite, and antagonism toward their obvious boredom or even disruptive behavior have all produced a hostile atmosphere for the gifted.

- *Lack of attention.* The inconsistent interest in these children that we described causes a lack of attention to their needs. Estimates are that only 3%–4% of the nation's gifted have access to special programs.

- *Lack of trained teachers.* There are remarkably few university programs to train teachers of these children.

Working from different assumptions about the gifted and talented, Benjamin Bloom and his colleagues (1985) reached several interesting conclusions about this group. Defining talent as an unusually high level of demonstrated ability, achievement, or skill in some special field of study or interest, they investigated the development of talent in several fields: psychomotor (including athletic), aesthetic (including musical and artistic), and cognitive.

Selecting Olympic swimmers and world class tennis players, concert pianists and sculptors, and finally research mathematicians and research neurologists, Bloom and his team subjected the participants to intensive interviewing. They also interviewed the parents and teachers of these individuals, with the subjects' permission. From these interviews, the following general conclusions were made:

- Young children usually view latent ability as play and recreation, followed by a long period of learning and hard work, eventually focusing on one particular learning activity (math, science).

- The home environment structured the work ethic and encouraged a youngster's determination to do the best at all times.

- Parents strongly encouraged children in a specialized endeavor in which they showed talent.

- No one made it alone; families and teachers or coaches were crucial at different times in the development of a youngster's talent.

- Clear evidence of achievement and progress was necessary for a youngster to continue learning even more difficult skills.

Bloom concludes that for talent to develop, several qualities must be present, such as a strong interest and emotional commitment to a particular talent field, a desire to reach a high level of attainment, and finally a willingness to expend great amounts of time and effort to reach high levels of achievement in the field of talent.

Remember, however, that these children are similar to other boys and girls in their interests and feelings. Every effort should be made to have them socialize with other youngsters. Terman, for example, found that the gifted have the same interest in games and sports. Also, remember that the intellectually gifted student is not necessarily physically gifted; nor is the artistically talented necessarily mathematically superior.

From the gifted, we turn to those children who may have difficulty with communication. The consequences of this problem range from difficulty in relating to others to underachievement in school.

BOX 11.3

What's Your Opinion?

About nine-tenths of the money spent in the United States on special education goes to the remedial teaching of children whose intellectual abilities are below average. In the Soviet Union, the ratio is just about the opposite.

Some people argue that the United States needs to try to bring as many of its people as possible up to a minimum level of cognitive ability, because living in a democracy demands it. The Soviet Union, being a totalitarian state, doesn't have to worry about "the best education possible for all the children of all the people." Besides, gifted children don't need as much support because they'll learn it anyway.

Others claim that the Soviet Union has done quite well with its policy, having moved from an illiterate state in 1917 to a position of world power. The United States today is fighting a fierce battle for her economic life and cannot afford to neglect a valuable resource: her gifted children.

Do you think we've neglected the gifted? Should we change our policy? What's your opinion?

Communication Disorders

Some children have language problems that are unrelated to sensory handicaps or cognitive difficulty. They are delayed in demonstrating language or have difficulty in expressing themselves.

Children With Language Problems

Those children with language problems fall into one of two categories. **Speech disorders** refer to difficulties children have with how they speak. **Language disorders** refer to the difficulty some children have in learning their native language—its content, form, and usage—and possibly to delayed language development.

What can we say about these children? In a widely used analysis of language development and language disorder, Bloom and Lahey (1979) suggest that the expression **communication disorders** be used to identify those language behaviors that differ from what is expected, given a child's chronological age.

Content, Form, and Use

Bloom and Lahey urge that we think of language behavior as the interactions among content, form, and use. *Content* refers to the ideas that children have about the world and that they have coded in their language. *Form* means the sounds and words of a child's native language along with the rules for combining them. *Use* refers to the context and functions of language. Language disorders, then, are any upsets or deviations in these three categories or in the interactions among the three categories, such as seen in the following.

Here are examples of disorders in each of the categories.

- *Content.* These children can express their ideas, but the ideas seem more appropriate for a child two or three years younger.

- *Form.* Some children have ideas about the world that they are simply unable to express in their language. For example, you may find a 6- or 7-year-old child who points to herself and says "milk." She communicates the idea that she wants milk but can't string the words together to convey the idea.

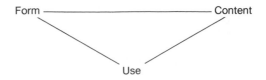

Language as the interaction among content, form, and use.

- *Use*. Children who have usage problems usually have ideas and words to express them but still have difficulty communicating. They may ramble or talk about something out of context. Sometimes these children withdraw and don't want to speak at all.

You can see how the Bloom and Lahey view of communication disorders emphasizes what children can and cannot do with their language. Being aware of the type of disruption of children's language (in content, form, and use) allows one to plan an effective remedial program.

Think for a moment about communication problems and you'll realize their seriousness. Children who have trouble communicating with others are susceptible to a wide range of disorders. They can quickly acquire learning difficulties; they miss out on much that is going on around them. Perhaps most important, their relationships with others suffer.

Other youngsters, unable to converse normally with these children, will gradually ignore them, or even make them the source of their jokes, which can be one cause of behavior disorders. As you can see, identification and attempts to ease the problem should commence as soon as possible (Bos & Vaughn, 1988).

Behavior Disorders

Parents, teachers, and adults in general agree that fighting, temper tantrums, defiance, destructiveness, and other similar behaviors are among the most disturbing problems that children display. You can probably guess why. Examine Table 11.3 and note how these **behavior disorders** can reach out and disturb others.

Before we analyze the behavior of these children, note that children with emotional problems are not included here. There are several good reasons for this distinction (Rutter & Garmezy, 1983). For example, while boys and girls display emotional problems in equal numbers, *behavior problems are much more common in boys*. Behavior problems are closely linked with reading difficulties, but emotional disorders are not. Behavior problems also seem to be tied to family troubles, while this isn't as apparent in emotional difficulties. For these reasons we will discuss emotional disorders separately.

The Development of Behavior Disorders

Fighting, screaming, hitting, temper tantrums, rebellion, stealing—these are behaviors that make life miserable for some children and those around them. A particular concern is that this antisocial behavior is associated with the later appearance of delinquency and crime (Hallahan & Kauffman, 1988).

We know that temper tantrums seem to peak at the end of the second year and then gradually diminish, giving way to periods of sulking and pouting. During the fourth and fifth years, disagreements with playmates become a major cause of outbursts. For an idea of how this problem originates, consider these recent findings:

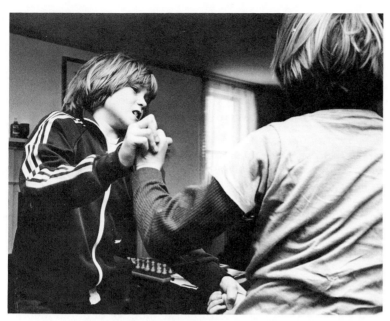

Some children are prone to acting out behaviors such as fighting, screaming, and kicking that cause problems for them and those around them. These children may need help in acquiring and maintaining self-control.

Table 11.3 Selected Behavior Disorders			
Aggression	**Antisocial Behavior**	**Noncompliance**	**Personal Characteristics**
Fights with peers	Lies	Ignores directions	Impatient
Attacks others	Steals	Resents discipline	Impulsive
Shouts at parents	Sets fires	Stays out late	Easily upset
Extremely competitive	Vandalizes	Lacks respect for adults	Excitable
Constantly quarrels with peers			

- Harsh punishment of children increases the likelihood of aggressive behavior. So also does the example of violence, whether at home, on the streets, or on television.

- Extremely impulsive and aggressive people have low levels of a brain chemical (serotonin) that inhibits aggression.

- Highly aggressive males have high levels of testosterone (see chap. 4).

Reporting on an ongoing longitudinal study at the University of Illinois, Pines (1985) stated that children who pushed, shoved, and started fights at age 8 turned into more aggressive adults. These children had parents who punished them much more harshly than the less aggressive children. Pines also noted that aggressive children as adults were more aggressive with their children than their own parents had been with them. A vicious cycle continued.

Study after study confirms these findings. Fischer and associates (1984) studied 541 children, 9–15 years of age, and found that both internalizing (shy, withdrawn) and externalizing (conduct disorders) behaviors persisted. Children who were identified as either type when they were ages 2 to 6 showed similar behavior in junior high school. There were no differences between the sexes.

Similar findings were reported by Rutter and Garmezy, who stated that conduct problems show little change between ages 6 and 18.

❖   *In summary, many forms of socially disapproved behavior tend to be at a peak during the preschool years, diminishing markedly during the early years of schooling. However, this early phase of negativism associated with a tendency to pull toys apart, write on walls, and take other people's belongings may not have the same meaning as the conduct disorders seen in older children. The latter show little change in overall prevalence between 8 and 18 years of age, although delinquents reach a peak in adolescence. However, there is a marked and real drop in antisocial behavior over the early years of adult life (1983, p. 819).*

What can we say about the continuity of these problems for individual children? Studies have shown that difficulty with parents and temper tantrums in kindergarten are associated with aggression and hostility in school. For children identified at age 3 as having behavior problems, 62% still showed disorders at age 8. These disorders were seen especially in males.

Conduct disorders are more common in boys than girls at all ages. While there are many possible explanations for this sex difference, undoubtedly the basic reason is the male's increased vulnerability to biological and psychosocial factors from conception on. (See chap. 3.)

These are not only persistent problems, especially for boys, but are quite stable across the years. For example, aggression and antisocial behavior not only persist throughout the childhood years but also predict similar behavior in adulthood (though with less frequency). *We can conclude, then, that antisocial adults were almost always antisocial children, while antisocial children have a one in four chance of becoming antisocial adults* (Kessler, 1988).

Remember: these children, for whatever reason, lack self-control and need an appropriate external structure that offers a reasonable balance between freedom and restraint. But what of those children whose activity is so unusual that they require special treatment?

Attention-Deficit/Hyperactivity

As we have seen, one of the characteristics of children with behavior disorders is their activity. There is another type of child whose degree of activity alone is his or her main behavioral characteristic. These youngsters, the hyperactive, are never still, can't remain seated, and are constantly on the move. As Rutter (1975) has noted, the key features that differentiate such activity are its severity, its early onset, its persistence, and its association with disorders of attention and concentration.

Hyperactivity usually appears at about age 3 or 4. Parents begin to notice that their children have a short attention span and are easily distracted. The problem seems to lie in an **attention-deficit** whose underlying cause may be a brain problem; only occasionally can hyperactivity be traced to temperament. These youngsters typically experience educational difficulties and developmental delays.

You can see how hyperactivity affects relationships with other children, often leading to aggression and fighting. While the problem may be neurological in origin,

Table 11.4   Criteria for Attention-Deficit/Hyperactivity

A

(Eight of the following must be present for six months.)

 1. Constant fidgeting
 2. Can't remain seated
 3. Easily distracted
 4. Can't wait for turn
 5. Interrupts
 6. Difficulty in completing tasks
 7. Can't sustain attention

 8. Jumps from one incomplete task to another
 9. Difficulty in playing quietly
10. Talks too much
11. Breaks in on others
12. Doesn't listen
13. Loses things frequently
14. Heedless physical activity that can be dangerous

B

These difficulties appear before the age of 7.

C

Not a developmental disorder.
(This condition may be mild, moderate, or severe, depending on the number and intensity of the symptoms.)

environmental conditions such as parental care or classroom treatment affect the kind and intensity of the behavior problem. The outlook for these youngsters is not good.

The Meaning of Hyperactivity

For many years investigators have attempted to distinguish hyperactivity from the usual activity associated with a behavior problem. One of the most accepted classification schemes appears in DSM-III—R, previously mentioned. Table 11.4 presents the criteria needed for a diagnosis of hyperactivity. Note that eight of the fourteen criteria must be present if hyperactivity is to be diagnosed.

To summarize, these children are marked by poor problem solving, poor self-control, attention problems, and impulsiveness. These characteristics may well persist into adult life.

Treatment Procedures

Hyperactive children are often treated with a stimulant called *Ritalin.* Why use a stimulant on children who are already excessively active? Stimulants succeed with hyperactive children because, until adolescence, they have the reverse effect: they help children to concentrate and maintain attention for a longer time.

Ritalin treatment has become controversial because of its possible side effects, such as increased irritability and mood swings. Its long-term positive effects have also been questioned. The bizarre behavior of several children on Ritalin has received widespread publicity, heightening the controversy. Most successful treatments have combined drugs with a program of behavior modification. Remember, however, that stimulants are effective with 70%–80% of children, which leaves a large percentage either unaffected or made worse.

Finally, Rutter (1983) has noted that hyperactivity has been diagnosed fifty times more often in North America than in Britain. It seems unlikely that such a vast difference reflects real differences in the two populations. Differences in the populations may indeed exist, but there must also be differences in making the clinical diagnoses.

BOX 11.4
Hyperactives: The Future

In a follow-up study of hyperactive children, Weiss (1983) and her colleagues studied 76 hyperactive children and matched them with 45 control subjects on age, sex, socioeconomic class, and IQ. They were originally identified at 6 to 12 years of age. The children had been identified as restless with poor concentration, in trouble at home and school, but none were psychotic, epileptic, or had cerebral palsy. All the children lived at home and had IQs of about 85 on the Wechsler. Among the results were the following.

- Fewer of the hyperactives were still living with their parents. They also had significantly more geographic moves than the controls, and had far more car accidents. Their educational history showed that they had completed less schooling and failed more subjects than the controls. They also had more court referrals.
- More hyperactives were diagnosed as having personality trait disorders and noted their childhood as unhappy.
- Poorer social skills, lower self-esteem, more impulsiveness, and greater restlessness distinguished the two groups in the follow-up study.

The results suggest that hyperactivity remains a persistent problem and that early intervention programs need to focus on methods of impulse control. As for that minority of hyperactive youngsters who go on to lives of delinquency and crime, we urgently need means of predicting this outcome.

Emotional Disorders

You should read this section with one warning in mind: *discussion of a child's emotional problems does not imply psychiatric disorders.* All children will experience passing difficulties that differ somewhat from typical development. For example, a youngster may experience temporary fear of darkness; another may show signs of anxiety after the family has moved. Such behavior does not differ significantly from that of other youngsters either in severity or abnormality. Most children will go through the same type of stage. Most importantly, it does not persist.

At the other end of the emotional spectrum are serious problems such as autism and schizophrenia, but these affect only a small number of children. Most children who have gone through emotional difficulties recover; the outlook for emotional disorders is good.

Let's begin our discussion with a cluster of problems that used to be called neurosis but now have been separated into fears, phobias, and anxiety.

Fears, Phobias, Anxieties

Fears, phobias, and anxieties can occur at any age, but are most common during early childhood and at puberty. For example, fear of dogs and cats is usually seen at age 2 or 3, fear of the dark appears during the fourth year, and an array of social and sexual fears occur during adolescence.

Jersild and Holmes, in their classic study (1935), studied 25 boys and 25 girls ranging in age from 5 to 12 years. Only 19 of these children denied that they had ever experienced fear. Fear of the mysterious, giants, corpses, and witches were most common, followed by fear of animals, strangers, and being alone. Next were fears of bodily injury, and nightmares. The fears of the 5 and 6 year olds differed from the older youngsters. The frequency of fears rose sharply during early childhood and at age 11. Figure 11.1 illustrates the pattern.

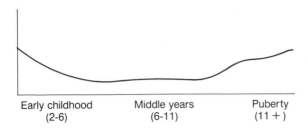

Early childhood (2-6)	Middle years (6-11)	Puberty (11 +)

Figure 11.1   The appearance of fears.

Fear, which usually arises from a child's personal experience, can spread (by conditioning) to other objects, persons, or events in the child's environment. Understanding and emotional support are the best means of helping a child eliminate such fears.

Fear may focus on one object, person, or situation, or it may generalize widely. Childhood fears usually arise from some personal experience or from observation. A youngster who has been bitten by a dog may be terrified by the sight of any dog. Children who are insecure in their relations with parents may be fearful in most situations. Children who have watched parents or siblings exhibit fear in a specific situation (crowded elevators, flying) may develop similar fears.

Interesting developmental patterns appear as children age and their experiences widen (Rutter & Garmezy, 1983). Among the age trends are the following.

- *During infancy* most fears are normal: fear of noise, falling, strange objects, and strange persons. These peak before age 2 and then rapidly decline.

- *During early childhood,* fear of animals peaks at about age 3, fear of the dark between ages 4 and 5, and fear of imaginary creatures slightly after age 5.

- *During early or middle childhood,* fears of such things as snakes and storms appear and show an inconsistent pattern that may last throughout life.

- *During late childhood,* infrequent fears and phobias, such as the forerunner to agoraphobia, may arise and persist throughout life.

Anxiety lacks the specific focus of fear. Chess and Hassibi (1978) define anxiety as an unpleasant sensation that is usually experienced as feelings of apprehension and general irritability accompanied by restlessness, fatigue, headaches, a funny feeling in the stomach, and a heaviness in the chest.

When fears and anxieties become so overwhelming that they dominate a child's feelings and behavior for lengthy periods, the term *phobic reaction* is used (Chess & Hassibi, 1978). Harre and Lamb (1983) define a **phobia** as an unrealistic and disproportionate fear of an object or situation. Children who develop such a fear of animals that they refuse to leave the house, older children who develop a morbid fear of dying, and the special case of refusing to attend school are all examples of phobias.

School phobia is a particularly interesting example of this disorder. It usually appears at one of two times. The first occasion may be at the time of school entrance. Children fear new situations and are reluctant to separate from the mother. These youngsters develop symptoms before departing for school that are instantly relieved when they are allowed to stay at home. With older children who have not previously demonstrated this phobia, the phobia is typically linked to an examination, fear of a teacher, or difficulty with peers.

The symptoms of school phobia are early morning stomach problems, headaches, and nausea. They may cry and cling to the mother, begging to stay home. Most authorities recommend a quick return to school. For younger children the outlook is good, but the prognosis for older youngsters is less optimistic.

Depression

❖   *Less common—but frequent enough to constitute a major psychiatric concern—is the sorrow that does not abate with the passage of time, that seems exaggerated in relation to the supposed precipitating event, or inappropriate, or unrelated to any discernible cause, or replacing a more congruous emotion. This sorrow slows down, interrupts, or disrupts one's actions; it speaks a sense of anguish which may become difficult to contain; at times it tends to expand relentlessly into a psyche which seems endless in its capacity to experience mental pain; often it recurs even after appearing to be healed. This emotional state is generally called depression (Arieti & Bemporad, 1978, p. 3).*

You can feel only sympathy for *anyone* in such a state. It is more troubling to think of children experiencing such feelings. In fact, for many years, some psychologists doubted that children could be depressed. But as Rutter and Garmezy (1983) noted, studies have repeatedly shown that

- Feelings of misery and unhappiness are common in children

- Feelings of misery and unhappiness are equally common for boys and girls

- Depression seems to be a part of other irrational disorders in children

- The overwhelming depression seen in adults is rare among children

Depression can be linked to environmental conditions and is distinguished by the severity of the behavior. Depression is characterized by a depressed mood, difficulty in thinking, fatigue, lack of enthusiasm, and numerous other complaints. Childhood depression may take one of several forms (Haring & McCormick, 1986):

- A chronic (lasting) depressive reaction of childhood, which characterizes children who have experienced separation from loved ones or who have an emotionally disturbed mother.

- Acute depressive reaction, which marks a child's response to a great personal loss.

- Marked depressive reaction, which is distinguished by serious behavior problems.

Finally, any discussion of childhood depression should contain one warning: most low spots in a child's mood are not signs of depression.

Autism

Autism is a severe and rare disorder that appears before 30 months of age. It was first described by Leo Kanner (1944). The autistic child shows the following characteristics:

1. Withdrawal from contact with other people

2. Severe language problems

Autistic children manifest distinctive, and destructive, behaviors that require special treatment. Living in a world of their own, these children have particular difficulty with language.

3. Obsessive preservation of the status quo (insists on sameness, exhibits repetitive behavior)

4. Skill in fine motor movements

5. Inability to deal with people

Autism strikes about 5 in 10,000 children and causes destructive behavior. During infancy these children often resist bodily contact; if you pick them up, they stiffen and attempt to pull away (even weeks after birth). Parents worry about deafness because the child simply doesn't respond to them. Repetitious body movements appear. During the second year, the lack of responsiveness becomes more apparent. They rarely turn toward the person who is speaking to them. They also avoid eye contact. Their delayed speech becomes noticeable.

Erickson (1982) states that many clinicians believe that autistic characteristics are most pronounced by age 3 or 4. Eye contact and speech development are almost completely absent. Some of these youngsters show rapid motor development and almost all of them seem to enjoy music.

Finally, while there have been decades of controversy concerning the intelligence of autistic children, evidence now points to a basic cognitive deficit (Rutter & Garmezy, 1983). This deficit involves impaired language, sequencing, abstraction, and coding functions. While the IQs of autistic children range from severely retarded to superior, three-quarters of these children show some type of intellectual difficulty.

Autism appears more frequently in boys, and most of these youngsters require special education. The prognosis is poor. Autistic children who possess normal intelligence may complete basic school and possibly secure employment; they rarely marry.

Childhood Schizophrenia

Childhood schizophrenia is a severe disorder characterized by a combination of extreme isolation, noncommunicative use of speech, repetitive body movements, self-injurious behavior, abnormal responses to light or sound, problems in eating and sleeping, abnormal fears or lack of fears, and delusional behavior. Many of these characteristics apply to infantile autism, but the age of onset differs: *autism appears before 30 months, while childhood schizophrenia appears mainly from age 4 to 7*. Current research points to neurological difficulties, genetic elements, or both as chief causes, although environmental agents have not been discounted.

If we turn once again to the DSM-III—R classification, the criteria for childhood schizophrenia include:

- Gross and sustained difficulty in social relationships (unusual emotional reactions, inappropriate clinging, asocial behavior)

- At least three of the following:
  Sudden anxiety
  Lack of appropriate fear, unexplained rage
  Resistance to change
  Strange motor movements (peculiar hand or finger movements, walking on toes)
  Abnormal speech
  Hyper- or hyposensitivity to stimuli
  Self-mutilation

- Appears after 30 months and before 12 years

- Absence of delusions and hallucinations

As you can imagine when you consider their lack of contact with reality and the disturbances in emotion, movement, language, cognition, and personal relations, the prognosis for these children is poor.

The Learning Disabled

Learning disability is a general term that refers to multiple disorders leading to difficulties in listening, speaking, reading, writing, reasoning, or mathematical abilities. The belief today is that learning disabilities are due to a central nervous system problem. A learning disability may occur along with other handicapping conditions (**sensory impairment, mental retardation, social and emotional disturbance**) or environmental influences (cultural differences, insufficient/inappropriate instruction, psychogenic factors). But it is **not** the direct result of those conditions or influences.

Morsink (1983) has suggested the following criteria:

- *Discrepance*. There is a difference between what these students should be able to do and what they are actually doing.

- *Deficit*. There is some task others can do that an LD child can't do (such as listen, read, or do arithmetic).

- *Focus*. The child's problem is centered on one or more of the basic psychological processes involved in using or understanding language.

- *Exclusions.* These problems are not the direct result of poor vision or hearing, disadvantage, or retardation, but these students still aren't learning.

Learning disabled children usually have a normal IQ, are having difficulty in one or more school subjects, do not seem to be suffering from any basic behavioral-emotional disorders, and family conditions do not seem to be a cause (though they may help or hinder). The problem is widespread. The U. S. Department of Education estimates that *almost 5% of all school-age children were receiving learning disabilities services in the public schools.*

Here are the most frequently found characteristics of learning disabled children (Hallahan & Kauffman, 1988):

> Hyperactivity
> Perceptual motor impairments
> Emotional instability
> General coordination problems
> Attention disorders
> Impulsiveness
> Memory and thinking problems
> Specific academic difficulty (reading, arithmetic, writing, spelling)
> Neurological difficulties

Note: Not all learning disabled children have all of these symptoms. Any one child may have only a few, but enough to cause problems.

Abused Children

Most people consider the United States to be a nation of child lovers. It always comes as a shock, then, to discuss child abuse. Before we discuss this topic, we should agree on what is meant by the term. For our purposes, **child abuse** includes physical injury, physical neglect, sexual abuse, and, occasionally, some instance of forced drug use.

As Kempe and Kempe (1978) stated, child abuse was not discussed in the last century, although evidence of it was everywhere. Sensitivity to children's needs plus a willingness to admit that abuse existed brought the issue to public attention in the past quarter-century. It still remains an elusive subject that defies precise definition because of the many forms of abuse. While physical and sexual abuses that leave evidence are easy to detect and describe (if they are reported), other forms of abuse that emotionally wound youngsters are perhaps never detected.

Professionals believe that abusive behavior involves direct harm (physical, sexual, deliberate malnutrition), intent to harm (which is difficult if not impossible to detect), and intent to harm even if injury does not result. In 1974, Congress passed Public Law 93–247, Federal Child Abuse Prevention and Treatment Act. This act defines child abuse as follows:

❖ *The physical or mental injury, sexual abuse, negligent treatment, or maltreatment of a child under the age of 18 by a person who is responsible for the child's welfare under circumstances which indicate that the child's health or welfare is harmed or threatened thereby, as determined in accordance with regulations prescribed by the Secretary.*

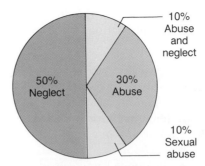

Figure 11.2 Estimates of types of abuse.
Source: Data from the U.S. Department of Health and Human Services, 1984.

Another problem is determining incidence. Figures show tremendous variability. The actual data are only for reported cases and undoubtedly represent only the tip of the iceberg. The true extent of the problem may be staggering. Estimates are that almost 4% of all children between the ages of 3 and 17 are at risk for abuse each year, with an estimated mortality rate of 5% to 27%. This estimate is undoubtedly low. Figure 11.2 illustrates the various types of abuse and estimated incidences of each.

The Nature of the Problem

Although child abuse is an age-old problem, not until recently did it become widely publicized. In the 1920s Dr. John Caffey, studying bone fractures and other physical injuries, suggested that parents might have caused the injuries. The skepticism that greeted his conclusions prevented him from officially reporting his findings until the late 1940s. In 1961, C. Henry Kempe and his associates startled the annual meeting of the American Academy of Pediatrics by their dramatic description of the battered child syndrome.

You may well ask, What kind of person could ever hurt a child? While the parental characteristics leading to child abuse are not rigidly defined, several appear with surprising frequency. Here are some of those:

- The parents themselves were abused as children.

- They often are loners.

- They refuse to recognize the seriousness of the child's conditions.

- They resist diagnostic studies.

- They believe in harsh punishment.

- They have unreasonable expectations for the child. (Children should never cry or drop things.)

- They lack control and are often immature and dependent.

- They feel personally incompetent.

The most consistent feature of the histories of abusive families is the repetition, from one generation to the next, of a pattern of abuse, neglect, and parental loss or deprivation. In each generation we find, in one form or another, a distortion of the relationship between parents and children that deprives children of the consistent love and care that would enable them to develop fully.

Table 11.5 Indicators of Abuse and Neglect

Neglect	Abuse— Physical	Abuse— Behavioral	Abuse— Sexual Physical	Abuse— Sexual Behavioral
Lack of supervision	Bruises, welts (especially facial)	Overly passive Developmental lag	Difficulty in walking, sitting	Unwilling to change for gym
Lack of adequate clothing	Burns	Extremely aggressive[a]	Bloody clothing	Withdrawn
Lack of medical/ dental care	Cuts	Extremely dependent[a]	Bleeding Disease	Unusual sexual knowledge for age
Absence from school	Fractures			Poor peer relations
Poor hygiene	Head injuries (including missing teeth)			Reports assault
	Internal injuries			

[a]These two opposite sets of behaviors both act to satisfy a parent's need for fulfillment.

Summarizing, there are four categories of parental abuse:

1. The parents have a background of abuse and neglect.

2. Parents perceive the child as disappointing or unlovable.

3. Stress and crisis are usually associated with abusive behavior.

4. No lifeline exists; that is, there is no communication with helpful sources in times of crisis.

But what of the children themselves? Some observers believe that certain types of children are more prone to be abused than others. Remember: children shape their parents as much as parents shape their children. If a child's acts or looks irritate a parent predisposed to violence, the results of the parent-child interaction may be preordained (which doesn't mean that the child is at fault).

Children growing up in a hostile environment feel that to survive they must totally submit to their parents' wishes. They often exhibit continual staring, and a passive acceptance of whatever happens. It is only later in a permissive setting that the pent-up fury explodes. They slowly develop complete distrust of others, which often translates into school problems.

What to Look For

Today we know of certain signals that alert us to the possibility of an abused child. Table 11.5 summarizes many of these. A child's family also may offer clues to either actual or potential abuse. For example, many abusive parents lacked emotional support as children. These unmet needs may carry over into their relations with their own children. They lack the skills to provide for their own emotional needs and lack the ability to cope with the anger and rage they may feel as a result. Their lack of self-esteem leads to feelings of being unloved, unappreciated, and unwanted. What could be easier than to take out these frustrations on a close, helpless target— a child?

When you consider all the factors that may trigger abuse—parents, children themselves, poor family relations, socioeconomic conditions, lack of support—it becomes clear that understanding the problem requires considerable and careful research.

The Special Case of Sexual Abuse

Sexual abuse refers to any sexual activity between a child and an adult whether by consent or force. It includes fondling, penetration, oral-genital contact, intercourse, and the use of children in pornography (Kelly, 1986).

Estimates are that between 50,000 and 500,000 children are sexually abused each year. Most of the victims are female, but the number of male victims is on the rise.

Kelly believes that children feel that they have lost control and are helpless when sexually abused by an adult. All of their lives they have been taught to obey adults, so they feel forced to comply. This is particularly troublesome since most abusers are known to the family: a relative, friend, or some authority known to the children.

What are the developmental effects of this violation and betrayal of a child by an adult? Browne and Finkelhor (1986), summarizing several major studies, report both short-term and long-term effects of sexual abuse. Different ages seem to suffer different types of effects. For example, the highest rate of problems was found in the 7–13-year-old group. Forty percent of the abused children of this age showed serious disturbances; 17% of the 4–6-year-old group manifested some disturbance. About 50% of the 7–13-year-old group showed greatly elevated levels of anger and hostility compared to 15% of the 4–6 year olds. An increase in anxiety, fear, and distress was common to all age groups.

Are there long-term effects for adults who were sexually abused as children? Among the effects are the following:

- Depression (probably the most common finding)

- Above normal levels of tension

- A negative self-concept

- Sexual problems

Sexual abuse is a problem that every reader will find repugnant. Yet we can offer some positive conclusions. We are now better able to identify these children and provide help. Treatment techniques offer hope for the future. As the problem becomes more widely publicized, parents, teachers, and concerned adults are becoming increasingly sensitive to its possible occurrence.

Transition

And so our journey through childhood is finished. We have seen how normal development—physical, cognitive, and socioemotional—prepares a youngster for the continuing challenges of adolescence and adulthood. Children's *physical* growth permits them to cope with the inevitable needs of daily living: walking, running, strength demands, motor coordination. Their *cognitive* growth prepares them for the abstract demands that await—in school, in work, and in existing in a technological society. Their *psychosocial* growth supports them in the inevitable tense and anxious situations that life presents. But we also know that some youngsters experience a troubled journey. There are deviations—some serious and long lasting, others less so.

No matter the path, our discussion has identified several elements that all children need in order to fulfill whatever potential they possess.

Proper diet
Proper care
Stimulating environment
Parental love and support

With these in place, children have a better than even chance of maximum individual development. Now, on to adolescence.

Key Ideas

1. Although most children follow the developmental path that we have traced, some will encounter developmental difficulties.

2. Classifying the problems that children can experience is confusing, so most psychologists today turn to the DSM-III-R as a guide.

3. For some children, physical and health impairments create early developmental challenges.

4. Among children—and adults—there is a wide range of intellectual differences, extending from slow learners to gifted youngsters.

5. Communication disorders refer to those language and speech problems that can, if unchecked, hinder children's interactions with their environment.

6. A particularly troublesome problem are those behavioral disorders that affect others and that have a tendency to persist if left unchecked.

7. Children are subject to emotional problems ranging from fears and anxieties to more serious disorders such as autism and schizophrenia.

8. Some children are not functioning at the level that their tested abilities suggest they should; these are the learning disabled.

9. Finally, some children find themselves in homes or situations in which they are abused physically, emotionally, or sexually.

Key Terms

Anxiety
Attention-deficit
Autism
Behavior disorders
Child abuse
Childhood schizophrenia
Children at risk
Communication disorders
Depression
DSM-III-R
Fear

Gifted and talented
Hearing impairment
Hyperactivity
Language disorders
Learning disability
Mainstreaming
Mental retardation
Phobia
Sexual abuse
Speech disorders
Visual impairment

What Do You Think?

1.   Some teachers are nervous about mainstreaming. While they sincerely want all their pupils to achieve as much as possible, they worry about the impact of exceptional students in their classes. Will these students take too much of the teacher's time? Are teachers equipped to deal effectively with these students? How will the other students react to them? Recalling the categories of exceptionality we discussed in this chapter and the different ages of pupils, how would you answer these questions?

2.   Think back to the case of Billy, the newsboy, whom we identified as a slow learner. You probably know similar youngsters. We stated that such children will blend into the range of abilities we see every day and manage to function outside of an institution. Do you agree with this? Why? Discuss the circumstances that would permit this to happen.

3.   Have you ever known, or known of, a gifted child? How would you describe that child? Different? The same as others but quicker, better able to find solutions? How did the school treat any signs of giftedness? Do you think they should be treated differently in school? What would you suggest? Discuss the pros and cons of your answers with the class.

Suggested Readings

Bloom, Benjamin. (1985). *Developing talent in young people*. New York: McGraw-Hill. Bloom's discussion of how to foster talent in our youth is at once theoretically sound and practically attractive.

Crawford, Christina. (1979). *Mommie dearest*. New York: Morrow. A chilling account of child abuse that remained hidden for years.

Kempe, Ruth, and Henry Kempe. (1978). *Child abuse*. Cambridge, MA: Harvard University Press. This little paperback, part of the Harvard Developing Child series, is one of the best overviews of child abuse that you could read. Don't be put off by the date; it's as current today as when it was published.

Thompson, Charlotte. (1986). *Raising a handicapped child*. New York: Morrow. A sympathetic, readable account of the journey from first diagnosis to ultimate success for physically handicapped children.

· PART 6 ·

Adolescence

· *Chapter 12* ·

Adolescence: Background and Context

"Who are you?" said the caterpillar. Alice replied, rather shyly, "I—I hardly know, Sir, just at present—at least I know who I was when I got up this morning, but I must have changed several times since then."
Lewis Carroll, Alice in Wonderland, *1865*

Is adolescence a period of abrupt change, or is that only a stereotype? Is it a soul-wrenching time, or no more difficult than any other period of life? Has it always been recognized as a special part of development, or is its recognition something new? This brings us to the main question of Part 6 of this book: What is adolescence?

How Should We Define Adolescence?

When Does It Start?

At what point did your adolescence begin? Many answers have been offered:

Is interest in the opposite sex the best sign that a young person has reached puberty? What other indicators could you name?

- When you began to menstruate, or when you had your first ejaculation.

- When the level of adult hormones rose sharply in your bloodstream.

- When you first thought about dating.

- When your pubic hair began to grow.

- When you became 11 years old (if a girl); when you became 12 years old (if a boy).

- When you developed an interest in the opposite sex.

- When you (if a girl) developed breasts.

- When you passed the initiation rites set up by society: for example, confirmation in the Catholic Church; bar mitzvah and bas mitzvah in the Jewish faith.

- When you became unexpectedly moody.

- When you became 13.

- When you formed exclusive social cliques.

- When you thought about being independent of your parents.

- When you worried about the way your body looked.

- When you entered seventh grade.

- When you could determine the rightness of an action, independent of your own selfish needs.

- When your friends' opinions influenced you more than what your parents thought.

- When you began to wonder who you really were.

Although there is at least a grain of truth in each of these statements, they don't help us much in defining adolescence. For example, although most would agree that menstruation is an important event in the lives of women, it really isn't a good criterion for determining the start of adolescence. The first menstruation (called *menarche*) can occur at any time from 8 to 16 years of age. We would not say that

---

BOX 12.1

An Average Day in the Life of an American Teen

Today (and every other day this year):

7,742 teenagers have become sexually active.

623 teenagers have gotten syphilis or gonorrhea.

2,740 teenagers have gotten pregnant (at a cost to taxpayers of over 2 billion dollars).

1,293 teenagers have given birth to a child.

1,105 teenagers have had an abortion.

369 teenagers have miscarried.

1,375 teenagers have dropped out of school before graduation.

3,288 have run away from home.

1,629 teenagers are locked up in adult jails.

6 teenagers have died of suicide.

? teenagers are being beaten or psychologically or sexually abused.

? teenagers have parents who are or soon will be divorced.

Source: Data from the Children's Defense Fund, 1989.

the menstruating 8 year old is an adolescent, but we would certainly say the non-menstruating 16 year old is one.

Probably the most reliable indication is a sharp increase in the production of the four hormones that most affect sexuality: progesterone and estrogen in females, testosterone and androgen in males. But determining this change would require taking blood samples on a regular basis, starting when youths are 9 years old. Not a very practical approach, is it?

Clearly, identifying the age or event at which adolescence begins is not a simple matter. We will need to look at it much more closely, from the standpoints of biology, psychology, sociology, and several other sciences, and we will do so in other chapters in this book.

❖ *These are the best years of your life! You'd better enjoy them now, because before you know it, you'll be weighed down with adult responsibilities!*

Can you remember your parents saying this, or something like it? At some time during their teen years, most people are advised not to waste their youth. It used to be a common belief that adolescence is a carefree period, a stage of life when people "sow their wild oats" before settling down to the more rigorous demands of adult maturity.

This view is not so common any more. In fact, some observers believe that it has become the *worst* time of life. Is adolescence an unusually difficult period of life? Are the changes that accompany it more abrupt and disruptive than those of earlier and later stages? Those who think so support their view with statistics such as those in Box 12.1.

Obviously, adolescence is a *very* bad time for *some* people. But does that mean that adolescents in general are becoming more of an affliction to themselves and to society? Do *average* adolescents have a harder time of it than their predecessors? For an answer, let us use the perspective of history. What follows is a brief summary of the ways adolescence was viewed in earlier times.

Prior to the twentieth century, it appears that children moved directly from childhood into adulthood with no period of adolescence in between.

Ancient Times

It appears that teenagers were no more popular with early writers than they are with many people today. Take, for example, this rather cranky statement written in the eighth century B.C. by the Greek poet Hesiod:

❖   *I see no hope for the future of our people if they are dependent on the frivolous youth of today, for certainly all youth are reckless beyond words. When I was a boy, we were taught to be discreet and respectful of elders, but the present youth are exceedingly wise and impatient of restraint.*

The famous Greek philosopher and reknowned teacher of the young, Socrates, was no great fan either. He wrote this in the fifth century B.C.:

❖   *Our youth now love luxury. They have bad manners, contempt for authority; they show disrespect for their elders and love chatter in place of exercise. They no longer rise when others enter the room. They contradict their parents, chatter before company, gobble up their food and tyrannize their teachers.*

Socrates' notable student, Plato, had a more positive outlook. In his view of the life span, childhood is the time of life when the spirit (meaning life values) develops, and so children should study sports and music. In the teen years, the reason starts to mature, and so youth should switch to the study of science and mathematics. For Plato's student, Aristotle, the teens are the years in which we develop our ability to choose, to become self-determining. This passage is not an easy one, however, and he felt it caused youth to be impatient and unstable.

The Middle Ages

During the Middle Ages, the concept of human development became unrelentingly negative. Now children came to be seen as "miniature adults." Children rarely appear in paintings from those times, but when they do, they are always dressed in cut-down versions of their parents' clothes. It was generally agreed that the way to help them become mature adults was through strict, harsh discipline, so that they could overcome the natural evils of the childish personality.

The word *teen* meaning a person from 11 to 19 years old, is an inflected form of *ten,* used as a suffix (e.g., *four-teen*). In Middle English, however, there was a word *teen* that meant "injury; misery, affliction; grief." The obsolete *teen* and the suffix *-teen* are not related etymologically. But coincidentally, *teen* is an accurate description of how youth was looked at in the period from the Romans to the Renaissance in Western culture.

The "Age of Enlightenment"

The beginning of the "Age of Enlightenment" (from the 1600s to the early 1900s) saw no major change from the previous period in terms of the view of adolescence. For example, Hesiod's and Socrates's observations were echoed by an old shepherd in Shakespeare's *The Winter's Tale* (1609).

❖   *I would there were no age between ten and three-and-twenty, or that youth would sleep out the rest; for there is nothing in the between but getting wenches with child, wronging the ancientry, stealing, fighting.*

This position held sway until the 1700s, when Jean Jacques Rousseau argued forcibly through his book *Emile* (1762) that children and youth need to be free of adult rules so they can experience the world naturally. He compared childhood to the lives of the American Indians, whom he referred to as "noble savages." He believed that both groups are basically good, and that Indians grow into kind and insightful adults because they are not corrupted by civilization.

In early America, this view did not gain much support. Life at that time was not easy, and everyone was expected to work hard, including children. Most youths worked on farms, but as the population grew, more and more went into apprenticeships in the cities. By the nineteenth century, however, a dual pattern began to emerge. By the 1840s, the country was clearly splitting into a large lower and middle class.

The children of the poor continued in the old apprenticeship mold, but middle class youth began to stay in school longer and longer. The technical demands of the Industrial Revolution called for more extensive education. The reform movement by the "muckrakers" at the turn of the twentieth century, which brought about stricter labor and compulsory education laws, created a more equitable situation between the two social classes. Only in the early 1900s did adolescence, as we know it today, begin.

The Twentieth Century

Now began the age of *empiricism*. Early in our century, those who were interested in understanding youth ceased speculating about the nature of adolescence and began to make careful observations of them. This is what empiricism means.

It should be noted that psychology itself began only in the late nineteenth century. It took as its first task learning how the brain perceives the environment around us, but soon turned to understanding human development. The new science quickly accepted the challenge of explaining the transition from childhood to adulthood. In this task, it was greatly influenced by the writings of G. Stanley Hall and a number of other social scientists who followed him.

G. S. Hall and the Theory of Recapitulation

G. Stanley Hall (1844–1924) is known as the father of adolescent psychology. Building upon Charles Darwin's theory of evolution, Hall constructed a psychological theory of teenage development, published in two volumes and entitled *Adolescence* (1904).

Hall posited four periods of development of equal duration, which he felt correspond to the four lengthy stages of development of our species: infancy/animal, childhood/anthropoid (humanlike apes), youth/half-barbarian, and adolescence/civilized.

- *Infancy: birth–4 years.* In this stage children recapitulate the animal stage in which mental development is quite primitive. Sensory development is the most important aspect of this period, together with the development of sensorimotor skills.

- *Childhood: 4–8 years.* Hunting and fishing, using toy weapons, and exploring caves and other hiding places are common activities of childhood. Language and social interaction begin to develop rapidly, as they did during the nomadic period of the human race.

- *Youth: 8–12 years.* This period corresponds to the more settled life of the agricultural world of several thousand years ago. This is the time when children are willing to practice and to discipline themselves; this is when routine training and drills are the most appropriate—especially for language and mathematics.

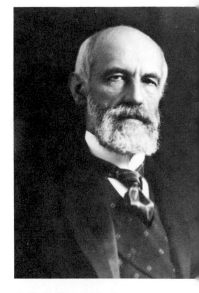

G. S. Hall was the first American to publish research on the teen years, with his book Adolescence *(1904).*

BOX 12.2

The Table of Contents of *Adolescence* (1904)

Although Hall's *Adolescence* seems laughable today because of some of the subjects covered (note in particular the titles of chaps. 5, 6, 13, 17, and 18), it provides a wonderful view of the state of psychology at the turn of the century.

Volume I

Chapter

1 Growth in Height and Weight
2 Growth in Parts and Organs During Adolescence
3 Growth of Motor Power and Function
4 Diseases of Body and Mind
5 Juvenile Faults, Immoralities, and Crimes
6 Sexual Development: Its Dangers and Hygiene in Boys
7 Periodicity
8 Adolescence in Literature, Biography, and History

Volume II

Chapter

9 Changes in the Sense and Voice
10 Evolution and the Feelings and Instincts Characteristic of Normal Adolescence
11 Adolescent Love
12 Adolescent Feelings toward Nature and a New Education in Science
13 Savage Public Initiations, Classical Ideals and Customs, and Church Confirmations
14 The Adolescent Psychology of Conversion
15 Social Instincts and Institutions
16 Intellectual Development and Education
17 Adolescent Girls and their Education
18 Ethnic Psychology and Pedagogy, or Adolescent Races and their Treatment

---

- *Adolescence: 12–25 years.* **Storm and stress** typify human history for the past 2,000 years, as well as this developmental period. Adolescence is a new birth, for now the higher and more completely human traits are born.

Hall believed that each person's development passes through the same four stages as the human species. He thought that all development is determined by physiological (i.e., genetic) factors. Development occurs in an unchangeable, universal pattern, and the effects of the environment are minimal. For example, Hall argued that some socially unacceptable behavior in children, such as fighting and stealing, is inevitable. He urged parents to be lenient and permissive, assuring them that children must have this catharsis, and that when they reached the later developmental stages, these behaviors would simply drop out of existence.

Hall made a major point of the "contradicting tendencies" of adolescence—the experience of violent mood swings—which he felt tended to make youth more human. Some of the turbulent variations he noted are

- energy and enthusiasm versus indifference and boredom

- gaiety and laughter versus gloom and melancholy

- vanity and boastfulness versus humiliation and bashfulness

- sensitivity versus callousness

- tenderness versus cruelty

Hall felt that the development of most human beings stopped short of this fourth stage, in which appreciation of music and art are achieved. Most people seemed fixated at the third stage, in the dull routine of work. A social reformer, Hall believed that adolescence is the only period in which we have any hope of improving our species. He felt that placing teenagers in enriched environments would improve their genes, which their children would then inherit. Hence we could become a race of superanthropoids.

Most psychologists today argue that **recapitulation theory** is an interesting but quite inaccurate picture of human social development. They believe Hall tried to force reality to fit an outmoded conception of evolutionary development. His theory is considered wrong for several reasons. While it may have described children of the early 1900s with some accuracy, it does not coincide with our knowledge of them today. It most particularly does not present a true picture of adolescence. Although the majority of youth in his time may not have had much appreciation for civilized culture, this was clearly due not to genetic imperfections but to such factors as having been forced to leave school to work on the farm. In addition, Hall's belief in the genetic transmission of acquired (improved) characteristics is scientifically false. Since Hall looked only at American culture, and since most individuals in the culture did develop similarly, he mistakenly thought that genes were responsible for this similarity. Later studies of other cultures have shown wide differences in developmental patterns.

Although Hall is to be admired for his efforts to bring objectivity to adolescent psychology through the use of empiricism, it has been suggested that he had several personal agendas. He was a strong preacher against what he viewed to be teenage immorality, and was especially concerned that educators try to stamp out the "plague of masturbation," which he considered to be running rampant among male youth. Here is a little speech that he recommended high school teachers and clergy give to their youthful charges:

❖   *If a boy in an unguarded moment tries to entice you to masturbatic experiments, he insults you. Strike him at once and beat him as long as you can stand, etc. Forgive him in your mind, but never speak to him again. If he is the best fighter and beats you, take it as in a good cause. If a man scoundrel suggests indecent things, slug him with a stick or a stone or anything else at hand. Give him a scar that all may see; and if you are arrested, tell the judge all, and he will approve your act, even if it is not lawful. If a villain shows you a filthy book or picture, snatch it; and give it to the first policeman you meet, and help him to find the wretch. If a vile woman invites you, and perhaps tells a plausible story of her downfall, you cannot strike her; but think of a glittering, poisonous snake. She is a degenerate and probably diseased, and even a touch may poison you and your children (1904 p. 136).*

To conclude this brief excursion into the historical point of view, let us say that distrust of adolescence has not died in the second half of this century. As noted adolescent sociologist Edgar Friedenberg remarked in 1959:

❖   *A great many young people are in very serious trouble throughout the technically developed world, and especially the Western world. Their trouble, moreover, follows certain familiar common patterns; they get into much the same kind of difficulty in very different societies (p. 6).*

We cannot accept these historical views with confidence, however, because each of them suffers from the same critical flaw: they are primarily reflections of subjective opinion, not of scientifically objective measurement. This is not to say that subjective experience has no place in our considerations. For example, another

---

BOX 12.3

What's Your Opinion?

Hall is hardly the only adolescent psychologist who can be accused of bias in his thinking. In a fascinating study, Enright and colleagues (1987) looked at 89 articles published during two economic depressions and two world wars to see if these events had an influence on research. The results were striking:

In times of economic depression theories of adolescence emerge that portray teenagers as immature, psychologically unstable, and in need of prolonged participation in the educational system. During wartime, the psychological competence of youth is emphasized and the duration of education is recommended to be more retracted than in depression. (p. 541)

Is it likely that youth were viewed as immature during depressions in order to keep them from competing with adults for scarce jobs, and that their maturity is seen as greater during wartime because they are needed to perform such adult tasks as soldiering and factory work? If so, is this bias conscious or unconscious? What do you think?

As you read the other theories in this chapter, see if you can spot what you believe to be biases in them.

---

reasonable way to determine whether adolescence is an especially troubled period is through the **retrospective accounts** of those who have lived through it. They are called "retrospective" because they involve a backward look at the period by a wide variety of individuals. What follows are some vignettes from the lives of living adults who were asked to "tell us of an incident from your adolescence which you believe most typifies it." As you read them, see if they clarify for you the meaning of adolescence.

Memorable Incidents From Several Adolescences

Betty, age 22: I remember getting caught by my mother with one of my girl friends in the closet. We were 11. Well, we were exploring each other's bodies—juvenile adolescent masturbating, I guess you'd call it. My mother just freaked out. She screamed, "What are you doing?" It was embarrassing. We denied everything, and her whole reaction to the thing finally was to give me a pamphlet put out by the Tampax Company on "Your Growing Years." She wouldn't talk about it, though. She didn't punish me—I don't think she even told my father about it. I guess this must be just our secret.

Clare, age 25: The summer of eighth grade my friend Judi and I were working on painting and redoing the CYO room in my parish. It was a very big deal because we were associating with high school people on almost equal terms. I liked this boy, Ross, who was a sophomore. He was a wrestler during school and worked outdoors during the summer, so he had a tanned, muscular body. I was 14, and he appealed to me enormously. One day the other people who were working on the place left and we were alone. He asked me to massage his back, so I did that. I loved the feel of his body. He kissed me, and we ended up lying on a couch all afternoon. He taught me to French kiss and to neck and make "hickies" in an almost formal, teacher-to-student manner. I loved it. I went home with a hicky on my neck, made sure all my friends knew about it and who put it there, and it was fun going through all the effort it took to hide it from my mother.

BOX 12.4

What Were You Like?

Following are some questions about your personality that you might enjoy answering. Pretend you are in the eighth grade. Let your mind drift back to that time, and imagine yourself sitting in your favorite classroom. Look around the room and see who is sitting there. Try to answer these questions as you would have then.

A. Are the following statements true or false?

1.	Most of the other kids in the class are stronger than I am.	T	F
2.	I am about as intelligent as anybody in this classroom.	T	F
3.	I am certainly not one of the teacher's favorite students.	T	F
4.	Most people would say I am above average in athletic ability.	T	F
5.	I am probably one of the more attractive students in this class.	T	F
6.	I am one of the shortest of the kids here.	T	F
7.	I would say that I am more mature than most of my friends.	T	F
8.	I am more popular than most of my classmates.	T	F
9.	I am very moody and I seem to get upset easily.	T	F
10.	I am unhappy with several of my physical traits.	T	F

B. Fill in the blanks in the following sentences:

1. The thing I would like to change most about my life is _____

   _____

2. My best friend is (give a brief description) _____

   _____

3. My deepest secret is _____

4. My fondest memory is _____

5. The thing of which I am most ashamed is _____

C. Rank the following characteristics in the order in which they are true of you. Put a 1 in front of the characteristic that best describes you; put a 2 in front of your second most typical trait; and so on.

_____ Good student		_____ Handsome/pretty
_____ Sports enthusiast		_____ Kind and generous
_____ Boy/girl crazy		_____ A loyal friend
_____ Shy		_____ Well mannered
_____ Humorous		_____ Reliable

   There are several things that can be done with this list to enhance your understanding and empathy for adolescents. You and your other classmates might want to compare answers. Go around the room and have each person read their answers to some of the questions, one at a time. You may wish to analyze the answers for clues about the definition we are seeking. On the other hand, you might share your answers with a small group of your most trusted friends, or even with your parents and siblings.

Eddie, age 19: I was 14 when I first did a crime. Me and a friend were going to bust into this house, because he saw where the lady hid the back door key, but then he chickened out. I went in at two in the morning, and I was hardly even scared. I went into the bedroom and I remember I was excited to hear the people breathing. I grabbed all the stuff on the dresser and knocked over the lamp. The man jumped out of bed and grabbed me—he was strong as hell. I thought I had it, but then I bit him hard on the arm and he let go. I beat it fast. I still held on to the jewelry, but when I took it to a guy the next day, he said it was all cheap junk. I still don't know if it was or not. I been in some trouble since then, but never again for busting into houses!

When we examine some of the major themes of adolescence in these episodes—sex, guilt, loyalty, parental conflict, friendship, confused values—and the
emotional intensity with which they are experienced, we can begin to define adolescence. But many more factors must be considered before we can honestly say we
have an acceptable definition. For an understanding of the most important of these
factors, we turn to several experts on adolescence.

Theories of Adolescence: Anna Freud

A trained psychoanalyst like her father, Anna Freud (1895–1983) believed that his
definition of adolescence was too sketchy. She suggested (1968) that her father had
been too involved with his discovery that sexuality begins not at puberty but in early
infancy. As a result, he overemphasized the importance of that earlier stage in the
total developmental picture. Anna Freud spent the major part of her professional
life trying to extend and modify psychoanalytic theory as applied to adolescence.

Anna Freud saw the major problem of adolescence as being the restoration of
the delicate balance between the ego and the id, which is established during latency
and disrupted by puberty. Latency, she felt, is the time when children adopt the
moral values and principles of the people with whom they identify. Childhood fears
are replaced with internalized feelings of guilt that are learned during this period.
The id is controlled during latency by the strength of the superego. At puberty,
however, the force of the id becomes much greater and the delicate balance is destroyed.

The problems brought about by this internal conflict cause the adolescent to
regress to earlier stages of development. A renewed Oedipal conflict (see chap. 2)
brings about fears that are entirely unconscious and often produce intense anxiety.
Therefore, the unconscious defenses of the ego tend to multiply rapidly, especially
the typical ones of repression, denial, and compensation. The problem, of course,
is that the use of these defense mechanisms causes new stresses within the individual and tends to further increase the level of anxiety.

Anna Freud described two additional adolescent defense mechanisms:

- *Asceticism,* in which, as a defense against the sexual, "sinful" drives of
  youth, the teenager frequently becomes extremely religious and devoted to God

- *Intellectualization,* in which the adolescent defends against emotionality of all kinds by becoming extremely intellectual and logical about
  life

*Sociologist Robert
Havighurst suggested a
series of developmental
tasks for each stage of life.*

Theories of Adolescence: Robert Havighurst

By the 1950s and 1960s, several new theories developed as a reaction to the earlier
viewpoints. Robert Havighurst (b. 1900), a sociologist at the University of Chicago,
became a major spokesperson (also see chap 1). He suggested that there are specific
developmental tasks at each stage of life, which lie midway between the needs
of the individual and the ends of society. He defined these tasks as skills, knowledge,
functions, and attitudes that are needed by an individual in order to succeed in life.

As with Freudian theory, the inability to negotiate successfully any particular stage interferes with success at all succeeding stages.

For the adolescent period, Havighurst (1951) describes nine developmental tasks:

- Accepting one's physique and accepting a masculine or feminine role.

- Forming new relations with age-mates of both sexes.

- Achieving emotional independence of parents and other adults.

- Achieving assurance of economic independence.

- Selecting and preparing for an occupation.

- Developing intellectual skills and concepts necessary for civic competence.

- Desiring and achieving socially responsible behavior.

- Preparing for marriage and family life.

- Building conscious values in harmony with an adequate scientific world-picture.

Although written 40 years ago, Havighurst's list holds up rather well today. Research has lent considerable support to Havighurst's theory, and educators and therapists have found his ideas useful.

Theories of Adolescence: Erik Erikson

According to Erik Erikson (b. 1902), the main task of the adolescent is to achieve a **state of identity.** Erikson (1958, 1959, 1963, 1968, 1969), who originated the term **identity crisis,** uses the term in a special way. In addition to thinking of identity as the general picture one has of oneself, Erikson refers to it as *a state toward which one strives.* If you were in a state of identity, the various aspects of your self-images would be in agreement with each other; they would be identical.

Repudiation of choices is another essential aspect of reaching personal identity. In any choice of identity, the selection we make means that we have repudiated (given up) all the other possibilities, at least for the present. All of us know people who seem unable to do this. They cannot keep a job, they have no loyalty to their friends, they are unable to be faithful to a spouse. For them, "the grass is always greener on the other side of the fence." Thus they must keep all their options open and must not repudiate any choices, lest one of them should turn out to have been "the right one."

Erikson suggests that identity confusion is far more likely in a democratic society because there are so many choices. In a totalitarian society, youths are usually given an identity, which they are forced to accept. The Hitler Youth Corps of Nazi Germany in the 1930s is an example of a national effort backed by intense propaganda to get all the adolescents in the country to identify with the same set of values and attitudes. In democratic societies, where more emphasis is placed on individual decision making, choices abound; some children may feel threatened by this over-abundance of options. Nevertheless, a variety of choices is essential to the formation of a well-integrated identity.

Further, it is normal for identity confusion to cause an increase in self-doubt during early adolescence (Seginer & Flum, 1987; Shirk, 1987). Shirk states that such doubts should decrease during the middle teen years, "as social norms for self-evaluation are acquired through role-taking development" (p. 59). He studied self-doubt in 10, 13, and 16 year olds, and found significant decreases with advancing age.

You may recall that in chapter 2 we described Erikson's complete theory as "an amazingly perceptive and at times poetically beautiful description of human life." He probably has done more research and writing on this fifth stage of identity formation than on all the others combined. We believe that most psychologists would call him the foremost theorist on adolescence today. This does not mean, however, that all agree with his view that adolescence is a time of identity crisis.

The Search for Identity

Goethals and Klos (1976) argue that if an identity crisis exists at all, it comes only at the end of adolescence:

❖ *It is our opinion that college students do not typically have a firm sense of identity and typically have not undergone an identity crisis. College students seem to be in the process of identity seeking, and experience identity crisis toward the end of senior year and in their early post-college experience. A male or female's disillusionment with their job experience or graduate study, a female's disappointment at being at home with small children, is often the jolt that makes them ask what their education was for, and why they are not as delighted with their lives as they had been led to believe they would be (p. 129).*

University of Michigan researchers (Bachman, O'Malley, & Johnston, 1978) have studied changes in the attitudes and goals of 2,000 male adolescents. They conclude that contrary to the view "of adolescence as a period of great turbulence and stress, we found a good deal of consistency along dimensions of attitudes, aspirations, and self-concept." Few of their subjects gave any evidence of having experienced an identity crisis.

Erikson, who himself had an extensive and rather difficult identity crisis in his youth, supposed that "My friends will insist that I needed to name this crisis in everybody else in order to really come to terms with it" (1975, p. 26). Born Erik Homberger, he seems to have rejected his past. It was difficult. His Danish mother remarried a German Jew, and he found himself rejected both by Jewish and Christian children. His identity crisis was resolved by the creation of a brand-new person with a new name, religion, and occupation. Some biographers (e.g., Berman, 1975; Roazen, 1976) have suggested that the surname he chose, *Erikson,* means he is the "son of himself." His theory of human development is no doubt colored by these experiences. At the same time, the intensity and degree of his identity crisis have made him extremely sensitive to the problems that all adolescents go through.

Perhaps the best conclusion we can reach, based on the available evidence, is that while the teen years are definitely a time of *concern* over one's identity, major decisions about it may be postponed by many until they reach early adulthood. This is probably truer today than ever, because of the phenomenon that Erikson calls the **moratorium of youth,** which seems to be lasting longer and longer.

The Moratorium of Youth

Erikson sees adolescence as a period of moratorium—a "time out" period during which the adolescent experiments with a variety of identities, without having to assume the responsibility for the consequences of any particular one. We allow adolescents this moratorium so that they can try out a number of ways of being, the better to come to their own particular identity. The moratorium period does not exist in preindustrial societies. Some have suggested that only Western industrial societies can afford the luxury of a moratorium. Others say that only because the values in Western industrial societies are so conflicted do adolescents *need* a moratorium.

Erikson stated that indecision is an essential part of the moratorium. Tolerance of it leads to a positive identity. Some youth, however, cannot stand the ambiguity of indecision. This leads to **premature foreclosure.** The adolescent who makes his choices too early usually comes to regret them. He or she is especially vulnerable to identity confusion in later life.

Erikson suggested that religious initiation ceremonies such as Catholic confirmation and Jewish bar and bas mitzvah can limit the young, forcing them into a narrow, negative identity. This can happen if the ceremony dogmatically spells out the specific behaviors expected by adults. On the other hand, such ceremonies can suggest to youths that the adult community now has more confidence in their ability to make decisions. The effect depends on the explanation of the goals of the ceremony.

Although some youths tend to be overly idealistic, Erikson believes that idealism is essential for a strong identity. In young people's search for a person or an idea to be true to, they are building a commitment to an ideology that will help them unify their personal values. They need ideals in order to avoid the disintegration of personality that is the basis of most forms of mental illness.

Negative Identity

While most adolescents do not go through changes as great as Erikson did in his youth, many do take on what he calls a **negative identity.** People with negative identities adopt one pattern of behavior because they are rebelling against demands that they do the opposite. An example is the boy who joins a gang of shoplifters, not because he wants to steal, but because he doubts his masculinity and seeks to prove that he is not a coward through the dangerous act of theft. Another example is the sexually permissive girl who is punishing her mother for trying to keep unreasonably strict control over her. Sex is not her goal; proving that she is no longer her mother's baby is.

In his psychohistorical biography of German religious leader Martin Luther (1483–1546), called *Young Man Luther* (1958), Erikson paints a somber picture of negative identity. Luther's greatness as a leader, says Erikson, was partly built on the enormous anger and unresolved conflict he experienced in his late teens. Luther's decision to become a monk and enter the monastery was the assumption of a negative identity. The choice expressed his rejection of fifteenth-century society rather than his devotion to Catholicism. Luther indulged in further contrariness by trying to be a better monk than anyone else. Luther's strong internal conflict is illustrated by the story of his falling into a faint while performing in the choir. As he fell to the ground, he is said to have cried out, "It isn't me!" Many other incidents also indicate that he couldn't accept being who he was.

Members of the Hitler Youth Corps were victims of "premature foreclosure," in which their identity was designed for them without their having any choice. They were taught exactly what to wear, how to act, what to think. Some actually turned their parents in to the secret police for what they believed to be violations of Hitler's creed.

Erikson suggests that the young Martin Luther was an excellent example of his concept of negative identity. Because of what happened in his youth, he spent his adulthood rebelling against what he had been taught. Here Frau Cotta, the woman who cared for him when he was 11 (in 1494) introduces the shy boy to her family.

BOX 12.5
The Erikson Psychosocial Stage Inventory

The Erikson Psychosocial Stage Inventory (EPSI) was developed as a research tool to examine adolescents' resolutions of conflicts associated with Erikson's first six stages in psychological development. We remind you that these stages are concerned with basic trust, autonomy, initiative, industry, identity, and intimacy.

Because Erikson regarded adolescence as central to his theory of human development, an investigation of how the adolescent forms an identity is of value. EPSI was tested in a study of 622 adolescents and has 12 items for each of Erikson's stages (Rosenthal, Gurney, & Moore, 1981). On the basis of their extensive research, the authors concluded that the EPSI is a useful measure for studying early adolescence and for "mapping changes as a function of life events" (p. 525). This means that the test can be used to find out the relationships between a person's stage of development and his or her age, IQ, personality traits, and many other characteristics. Here are some sample items, which the respondent is asked to check true or false:

Item Number	Subscale
	Trust
36.	Things and people usually turn out well for me.
	Autonomy
13.	I know when to please myself and when to please others.
	Initiative
34.	I'm an energetic person who does lots of things.
	Industry
60.	I stick with things until they are finished.
	Identity
10.	I've got a clear idea of what I want to be.
	Intimacy
59.	I have a close physical and emotional relationship with another person.

From Rosenberg, et al., *The Journal of Youth and Adolescence,* 10(6): 525–37. Copyright © 1981 Plenum Publishing Corporation, New York, N.Y.

Erikson believes that Luther had an extended identity crisis. His monkhood was used as the time and place for working out a positive identity. As his identity evolved, Luther devoted himself without reluctance to God and turned all his fury against the Pope, fomenting the Protestant religious upheaval. Like Erikson, Luther's identity crisis was not resolved until he reached 30.

Identity Status

Erikson's ideas on adolescence have generated considerable research on identity formation. The leader in this field is James Marcia, who has made a major contribution to our understanding through his research on **identity status.** He and his colleagues have published numerous studies on this topic (Marcia, 1966, 1967, 1968, 1980, 1983; Cote & Levine, 1988; Craig-Bray, Adams, & Dobson, 1988; Dellas & Jernigan, 1987; Kroger & Haslett, 1988; Raphael, Feinberg, & Bachor, 1987; Rogow, Marcia, & Slugowski, 1983; Rowe & Marcia, 1980; Schiedel & Marcia, 1985; Slugoski, Marcia, & Koopman, 1984).

Marcia believes that there are two essential factors in the attainment of a mature identity. First, the person must undergo several *crises* in choosing among life's alternatives, such as the crisis of deciding whether to hold to or give up one's religious beliefs. Second, the person must come to a *commitment,* an investment of

Table 12.1	Summary of Marcia's Four Identity Statuses			
	Identity Status			
	Confusion	Foreclosure	Moratorium	Achievement
Crisis	Absent	Absent	Present	Present
Commitment	Absent	Present	Absent	Present
Period of adolescence in which status often occurs	Early	Middle	Middle	Late

self, in his or her choices. Since a person may or may not have gone through the crisis of choice and may or may not have made a commitment to choices, there are four possible combinations, or statuses, for that person to be in.

Status 1. **Identity confusion:** no crisis has been experienced and no commitments have been made.

Status 2. **Identity foreclosure:** no crisis has been experienced, but commitments have been made, usually forced on the person by the parent.

Status 3. **Identity moratorium:** considerable crisis is being experienced, but no commitments are yet made.

Status 4. **Identity achievement:** numerous crises have been experienced and resolved, and relatively permanent commitments have been made.

Table 12.1 summarizes these definitions.

Erikson's eight stages (in addition to the six mentioned earlier, there are the stages of generativity and integrity) follow each other in a more or less unchangeable sequence. Research indicates that Marcia's identity statuses have a tendency toward an orderly progression, but not so clearly as Erikson's stages. For example, Meilman (1979) studied males at the ages of 12, 15, 18, 21, and 24. They were rated on attitudes toward occupation, religion, politics, and, for the older subjects, sexual matters. For each of these areas, the older the group, the fewer the individuals in the confusion status and the more in the achieved status.

In fact, most of Meilman's results fit Marcia's theory well. For instance, the number of teens in the achievement category increased progressively through age 24. The largest percentages of those in the identity confusion category were age 12, 68%; and age 15, 64%; at age 18, 48% were still seen to be in this category. The foreclosure category was also greater in the younger age brackets: age 12, 32%; age 15, 32%; and age 18, 24%. None of the 12 year olds were found to be in the achievement category, and only 4% of the 15 year olds were. The moratorium category also increased in each of the age brackets.

Carol Gilligan (1982) and others have focused on possible gender differences in identity formation. They have concluded that women are less concerned than men with achieving an independent identity status. Women are more likely to define themselves in terms of their relationships and responsibilities to others. Society gives women the predominant role in transmitting social values from one generation to the next. This role requires a stable identity, and therefore a stable identity appears to be more important to women than it is to men. The result is that women may tend to foreclose on an identity defined by others around them rather than compete to form a more independent identity.

BOX 12.6

Identity Rating

Try placing people you know into one of Marcia'a four statuses. Choose 10 friends and write their names in the spaces below. Put the number of the identity status you choose for each person after his or her name. Do the rating quickly, without thinking about it too much—this tends to make the rating more accurate.

Name	Status
1. _____	_____
2. _____	_____
3. _____	_____
4. _____	_____
5. _____	_____
6. _____	_____
7. _____	_____
8. _____	_____
9. _____	_____
10. _____	_____

Notice how many of your ratings fall into each category. Were most of them in the fourth category, identity achievement? If so, was this because most of the friends you chose for this activity have an achieved identity, or perhaps because you unconsciously chose them on that basis? Have most adults achieved identity? Have you? Once achieved, is identity a permanent possession?

Grotevant and associates (1982) have expanded Marcia's research into the interpersonal realm, including friendships, dating, and sex roles. They feel that before forming intimate relationships, adolescents explore and commit themselves to interpersonal relationships as part of their identity formation.

In summary, it may be said that the adolescent's personality is undergoing many changes, but they are probably no more traumatic than at any other stage of life. The major concern is to begin to form an adult identity, which means choosing certain values and repudiating others. There is the danger of staying in the moratorium period too long, and of forming a negative identity. It is considered necessary to work one's way from identity confusion through the moratorium to an achieved identity, while avoiding foreclosure. In the next half of this chapter, we will be dealing with the two foundations of the identity process: relationships with family and peers.

The Changing American Family and Its Role in Adolescent Life

❖   *It is, after all, the simplest things we remember: A neighborhood softball game, walking in the woods at twilight with Dad, rocking on the porch swing with Grandma.*

   Now, no one has time to organize a ballgame. Our woods have turned to malls. Grandma lives three states away. How will our children have the same kind of warm memories we do?

   B. F. Meltz, Saving the Magic Moments, *1988*

Table 12.2. The Family's Changing Role	
Former Family Roles	**Societal Elements That Perform Them Now**
Economic-productive	Factory, office, and store
Educational	Schools
Religious	Church or synagogue
Recreational	Commercial institutions
Medical	Doctor's office and hospital
Affectional	Family

Of all the changes in American society in recent years, those affecting the family have probably been the most extensive (also see chap. 7). Curiously, researchers have spent little of their time studying adolescent-parent relations—until recently. Steinberg (1987) offers an explanation for the change:

❖ *The reasons for the rekindled interest in adolescents' relations with mothers and fathers are many, but among them surely is the increased public attention that family issues in general (e.g., divorce, stepfamilies, maternal employment, family violence) have received during the past five years (p. 192).*

Let us begin with a look at the family's changing role in modern society.

The Loss of Functions

In 1840 the American family fulfilled six major functions (Sebald, 1977). Table 12.2 lists those functions and suggests which elements of society now perform them. Today the first five functions—economic-productive, educational, religious, recreational, medical—have been taken over by professionals. It appears that the family has been left to provide but one single function—affection for its members. In the nineteenth century, parents and children needed each other more than now, for the following three major reasons (Coleman, 1961).

Vocational Instruction
For both males and females, the parent of the same sex taught them their adult jobs. Most men were farmers and most women housewives. Parents knew all the secrets of work, secrets passed on from generation to generation. Today, nearly 100% of men work at jobs different from their fathers, and an increasing percentage of women are not primarily housewives, as their mothers were.

Economic Value
Adolescents were a vital economic asset on the farm; without children, the farm couple had to hire others to help them. Work was a source of pride to the children. It was immediately and abundantly clear that they were important to the family. Today, instead of being an economic asset, most children are an economic burden on the family's resources.

Social Stability
When families almost never moved from their hometowns, parents were a crucial source of information about how to live in the town, knowing all the intricacies of small-town social relationships. One depended on one's parents to know what to

do. Today, when the average American moves every five years, the adults are as much strangers in a new place as the children. In fact, with Dad, and now frequently Mom, driving out of the neighborhood to work, the children may well know the neighborhood better than their parents do.

The constant migration to new places in which the elders are as much strangers as the young, and the development of new forms of technology in which the elders are not expert, has caused a change of huge importance. It has resulted in a culture in which the young pattern their behavior on that of their peers rather than on older models. Margaret Mead (1970) coined a term for this, calling it a **cofigurative culture.**

The Increase in Age-Related Activities Among Older Adolescents

The change from family to peer group influence during middle adolescence is accelerating these days. This is mainly caused by the specialization of the entertainment industry and the media. Both participatory entertainment, such as sports, and spectator entertainment, such as television, are more and more aimed at specific age groups. Therefore, everyone, teenagers included, tend to watch or participate in recreational activities only with members of their own age group.

Television has been especially powerful in this changeover. When teenagers reach the age of 18, they typically will have watched twice as many hours of television as they will have spent in the classroom. These activities isolate teenagers more and more from adults (who spend less time watching television) and force them to rely on friends for security and values orientation.

Bronfenbrenner (1977) found that as teenagers depend more on their friends, they are more likely to view their parents as lacking in affection and not very firm in discipline. They also show greater pessimism about the future, rank lower in responsibility and leadership, and are more likely to engage in antisocial behavior. Even when such detrimental tendencies are not present, life changes that the child and parents usually are undergoing can make life especially difficult.

The Effects of Divorce

A smoothly functioning family can provide support and nurturance to an adolescent during times of stress. But when the family is itself in a state of disarray, such as during a divorce, not only is the support weakened but the family often becomes a source of stress.

Divorce has become commonplace in American society. Even with slight decreases in the divorce rate in recent years, there are still over one million divorces every year, which is roughly half the number of marriages performed during the same time (U.S. Bureau of Census, 1986). Divorce tends to occur most in families with a newborn, and second most in families with an adolescent present. It is estimated that as many as one-third to one-half of the adolescent population is affected by divorce (Jurich, Schumm, & Bollman, 1987).

What, then, are the effects of divorce on the development of the adolescent? Unfortunately, conclusions are often based as much on speculation as research findings, due to problems in the research. Divorcing parents often refuse to let themselves or their children participate in such studies, which makes random samples difficult to obtain (Santrock, 1987).

Bronfenbrenner suggests that teenagers today depend more on their friends and less on their families for their values than in earlier times. Possibly because of this, they seem to have less positive feelings toward their parents.

Nevertheless, it is clear that the divorcing family does contribute additional stress to a developing adolescent. One obvious effect is economic. The increased living expenses that result from the need to pay for two domiciles (usually paid by the father) most often leads to a significant decrease in the standard of living for the children. Most adolescents, particularly young adolescents, are extremely status conscious, and status is often obtained with the things money can buy (clothes, stereos, cars, etc.). Young adolescents may well resent being unable to keep up with their peers in this regard. Older adolescents are better equipped to cope with this type of additional stress, both psychologically and financially, since they can enter the workforce themselves.

Another obvious effect of a divorce is the absence of one parent. Often, custodial rights are given to one parent (usually the mother), and so the children are likely to lose an important source of support (usually that of the father). What support the noncustodial parent provides is sometimes jeopardized by the degree of acrimony between the divorced parents. One or both of the parents may attempt to "turn" the adolescent against the other parent. This sometimes results in disturbing, negative tales about a mother or father, forcing adolescents to cope with adult realities while they are still young.

Some single parents find life without their spouse quite difficult, others find they like it. Regardless of the effect on the parents, the children in a divorce virtually always suffer.

Such distractions also can disrupt the disciplinary process during adolescence. Under any circumstances, administering consistent and effective discipline during this time often requires the wisdom of King Solomon. A difficult job for two parents becomes the primary responsibility of one. Preoccupied parents, perhaps feeling guilty over subjecting the child to a divorce, find it difficult to provide the consistent discipline that the child was used to previously.

Because it is the father who typically leaves a family during divorce, there are often more negative effects for males than for females (Hetherington, 1973). During the teenage years, the father often assumes primary responsibility for disciplining the male adolescents in the family. An abrupt change in disciplinary patterns can lead some adolescents to exhibit more antisocial and delinquent behavior.

Despite the negative aspects we've outlined, you should keep in mind that not all aspects of a divorce impact negatively on adolescents. Divorce is often a better alternative than keeping a stressful, unhappy family intact. In fact, the few studies that have compared adolescents from the two groups have shown that teenagers from divorced families do better in general than adolescents from intact but feuding families (Hetherington, 1973). Obviously the ability of the two parents to resolve their divorce as amicably as possible is an important factor in lessening the burden on the children. And although too many new or inappropriate responsibilities may inhibit ego formation, some added responsibilities may increase self-esteem and independence in the long run. It is also the case that many of the negative consequences of the single-parent family are often relieved by a remarriage.

The Effects of Gender

A spate of new studies have investigated the part that gender plays in family life. Three generalizations may be drawn from this research (Steinberg, 1987):

1. Boys and girls do not differ markedly in the way they relate to their families in general (Hauser, Houlihan, & Powers, 1987; Hill & Holmbeck, 1987; Montemayor & Brownlee, 1987). An important exception is that for healthy development, females need to become more independent from the family, whereas males do better when they maintain close ties (Cooper & Grotevant, 1987; Hakim-Larson & Hobart, 1987; Hill & Holmbeck, 1987; Steinberg & Silverberg, 1986).

2.   Mothers and fathers relate to their families quite differently. Fathers are more likely to be helpful in family discussion than mothers (Hauser & others, 1987); fathers spend most of their time with their adolescent children playing, while mothers spend about half of their time with them in household matters (Montemayor & Brownlee, 1987); and mothers are more likely to be involved in conflicts (Silverberg & Steinberg, 1987).

3.   Mother-daughter relationships are the most intense, positively and negatively, and father-daughter relationships are the most bland (Silverberg & Steinberg, 1987; Youniss & Smollar, 1985).

Creativity and the Family

As was discussed in chapter 8, most family researchers have agreed that there are three styles of parenting (Baumrind, 1983).

1.   **Authoritarian parenting style:** The parents strive for complete control over their children's behavior by establishing complex sets of rules. They enforce the rules through the use of rewards and, more often, strong discipline.

2.   **Permissive parenting style:** The parents have little or no control, and refrain from disciplinary measures.

3.   **Authoritative parenting style:** In this, the most common style, parents are sometimes authoritarian and sometimes permissive, depending to some extent on the mood they are in. They believe that both parents and children have rights, but that parental authority must predominate. They maintain their superiority in as nurturing a way as they can.

Authoritarian parents insist on strict adherence to the rules they set. The authoritarian parent is unlikely to cultivate her child's creativity.

In an extensive study of 56 families in which at least one of the adolescents was highly creative (Dacey, 1989), a picture of a fourth style clearly emerged. The parents in these families were found to be devotedly interested in their children's behavior, but they seldom made rules to govern it. Instead, by modeling and family discussions, they espouse a well-defined set of values, and expect their children to make personal decisions based on these values.

After the children make decisions and take actions, the parents let the children know how they feel about what was done. Even when they disapprove, they rarely punish. Most of the teens in the study said that their parents' disappointment in them was motivation enough to change their behavior. All of the parents agreed that if their child were about to do something really wrong, they would stop her or him, but that this virtually never happens. We call this the **creative parenting style.** Only some of the parents in the study are themselves creative, but all appear committed to this approach.

In addition to fostering values formation, creative parenting also means cultivating certain personality and intellectual traits that help children to make sound, insightful decisions. Among the traits are tolerance of ambiguity, risk-taking, delay of gratification, androgyny, problem-solving skills, and balanced use of brain hemispheres.

The success of creative parenting is based on a well-established principle: people get better at what they practice. These parents provide their children with ample opportunities to practice decision-making skills, self-control, and, most vital of all, creative thinking. They serve as caring coaches as their children learn how to live.

It should be obvious that your interactions with your family make a big difference in how your personality develops. Now let's turn to a consideration of the second aspect of social interaction, the peer group.

Interactions With Peers

❖   *[Adolescents spend] only 4.8 percent of their time with their parents and 2 percent with adults who are not their parents—for a total of only 7 percent of waking hours spent with adults (Nightingale & Wolverton, 1988, p. 8)!*

In the decade following World War I, a spirit of liberality and experimentation prevailed. Many of the young "flappers" of the 1920s had unconventional and even rebellious attitudes toward adulthood, but no one suggested that they had a culture all their own. It was not until the 1950s that social scientists began to suspect that young people were creating significant new subcultures. Among the earliest and most antagonistic to the cultural mainstream were the beatniks and the Hell's Angels.

Adolescent Subcultures

During the 1960s there was a debate among social scientists over whether adolescents were forming their own distinctive subcultures. Many felt that the high visibility of the more defiant youth was exaggerating the differences between teenagers and adults (Douvan & Adelson, 1966; Hill & Aldous, 1969). Even in the 1970s some authors argued that the youth culture exists more in theory than in fact (Bandura, 1972; Davis, 1971; Larson, 1972; Schwartz & Baden, 1973; Stein, Soskin, & Korchin, 1974; Thomas, 1971). Stein and associates (1974) found that most teenagers have a strong sense of trust in adults over 30 years old, especially caretaking adults. Larson (1972) found that children and teens complied more often with the desires of parents than with the desires of peers. This was true at least among the 4th-, 9th-, and 12th-graders he studied.

Nevertheless, there were some (Coleman, 1961; Green, 1968; Williams, 1960) who began to argue for the existence of a separate teenage subculture during the 1960s. By the 1970s, the majority of researchers shared this view (Coleman, 1974; Manaster, 1977; Rogers, 1977; Sebald, 1977). Today, most agree not only that an adolescent subculture exists but that adolescents are differentiating themselves from adults more thoroughly than ever.

The Origins of Subcultures

How do subcultures get started? Why are there so many of them? Three major theories have attempted to explain the origin of subcultures: the psychogenic, the culture transmission, and the behavioristic theories (Sebald, 1977).

The Psychogenic Model
A subculture, any subculture, arises when a large number of people have a similar problem of adjustment, which causes them to get together to deal with the problem and help each other resolve it. Modern teenagers receive a much less practical and more abstract introduction to life than formerly. They see the world as complex and ambiguous. They often feel it is unclear how they fit in and what they ought to be doing. Many try to escape from ambiguity into a world that they create with other teenagers. In the past, this way of creating an identity was used almost solely by

delinquent youngsters who were unable to find a respected place in society. Today, escape or avoidance of reality is becoming a much more common reaction to personal difficulty. This is known as the **psychogenic model** because it assumes that today's teens are psychologically disturbed by the world they are living in. Not mentally ill, but disturbed.

The Culture Transmission Model

According to the **culture transmission model,** a new subculture arises as an imitation of the subculture of the previous generation. This takes place through a learning process by which younger teenagers model themselves after those in their twenties. Magazines, movies, and television programs aimed at teenagers have been effective mechanisms for perpetuating the so-called teenage subculture. Thus, though new forms of behavior may *seem* to evolve, in actuality most are only new versions of the solutions older people found for their problems when they were teenagers. Not surprisingly, this model argues that teenagers today are really not all that different from those of previous decades.

The Behavioristic Model

The **behavioristic model** sees subcultures starting out as a result of a series of trial-and-error behaviors, which are reinforced if they work. It is like the psychogenic model in that a new group is formed by people with similar problems. It differs in that the psychogenic model views teen behavior as innovative, whereas the behavioristic model sees peer group members behaving the way they do because they have no other choice.

According to behaviorism (see chap. 2), teenagers experience adults as "aversive stimuli"; that is, it is painful to interact with adults because in clashes over values, adults almost always win. In an attempt to escape from aversive stimuli, adolescents try out different behaviors with each other. They receive both positive reinforcement (their interactions with their peers make them feel better about themselves) and negative reinforcement (the pain they experience in interacting with adults stops when they stop interacting with the adult world).

Another factor in the perpetuation of youth subculture is **inconsistent conditioning.** For example, teenagers are expected to act responsibly in their spending, but on the other hand, they have to get parental permission for all but the smallest purchases, because they are not legally responsible for their debts. An example of inconsistent conditioning, one that no longer exists in the United States, is when teenagers are asked to fight and possibly die for their country, but are not allowed to vote and help influence their country's policies.

Which of these models best explains the origins of the youth subculture? What would you say? Can you think of a fourth explanation?

Elements of the Adolescent Subculture

Whether it has a similar or different origin from other subcultures, the teenage subculture clearly has a number of common elements, including the following.

Propinquity

An obvious but often overlooked factor in the adolescent subculture is that the members of a group live near one another and know one another prior to joining the group. Gold and Douvan (1969) have suggested that physical closeness is the single most important factor in the makeup of teenage groups.

Unique Values and Norms

All group members try to overcome limitations that they feel they would have if they did not belong to the group (Block & Langman, 1974). Whatever the underlying reason for the group—race, age, politics, ethnic background—its members see a clear advantage in joining with others of similar values. In the teen years, adult domination creates a major motivation for attaching oneself to one's age-mates. In their study of peer attachments, Armsden and Greenberg (1987) found that teens who are devoted members of their group "reported greater satisfaction with themselves, a higher likelihood of seeking social support, and less symptomatic response to stressful life events" (p. 427).

Gender Differences

There are some important gender differences in peer group values (Smart & Smart, 1973). Girls seek satisfaction of a wider variety of emotional needs in their friendships than boys, but tend to seek just a few close friends. Girls value loyalty, trustworthiness, and emotional support most of all. Boys, on the other hand, seek friendships that help them assert their independence and resist adult control.

Peer Group Identity

The youth subculture tends to force its members into a deeper involvement with one another. Because teenagers spend so little time with, and derive so little influence from, those older and younger than themselves, they have only one another to look to as models. Today, those under 17 make up a much larger percentage of the population than formerly, and they continue their education for a much longer period. As a result, they spend much more time with other youths and much less time with adults.

Regardless of the orientation of the group, the youth culture tends to force its members into a deeper involvement with each other.

A proposal by Newman and Newman (1976) recognizes the growing importance of this tendency. They suggest that we divide Erikson's identity stage into two stages: early adolescence (ages 13 through 17), called the *group identity versus alienation stage,* and later adolescence (ages 18 through 22), called the *individual identity versus role diffusion stage.* This division recognizes that it is also necessary that one identify with a group or groups in order to achieve a well-resolved personal identity.

Although we agree with their two-stage concept, we disagree with the ages they suggest. On the basis of our view of the research, early adolescence starts at about 11 for females and about a year later for males (this difference will be explained in the next chapter). Middle adolescence starts at about 14, and late adolescence occurs at about 17, leading into early adulthood at 19. We have chosen 19 because this is the age at which youth have usually been out of high school and into jobs or college for one year. We think this year represents a major turning point in the development of most individuals in the Western hemisphere.

Transition

Being an adolescent is no easy task these days. It probably never was, but now there are so many choices, and there is a great temptation to try and take them all! It is unclear whether adolescent peer group relationships are all that different from earlier times, but the family in the United States appears to be undergoing major alterations. What is clear is that with every passing year, the peer group plays a greater and greater role in the adolescent's life, while the role of the family continues to decline.

As Nightingale and Wolverton put it in their report to the Carnegie Council on Adolescent Development (1988),

❖   *Adolescents have no prepared place in society that is appreciated or approved; nonetheless they must tackle two major tasks, usually on their own: identity formation, and development of self-worth and self-efficacy. The social environment of adolescents today makes both tasks very hard. . . . We must change the view that many people hold of all youth as troubled and harmful to the rest of society (pp. 1, 16).*

In this chapter, we have given an overview of the personality and social development of early and middle adolescents. This is only half of the picture, though. Of at least equal importance are the critical factors of physical and mental development, which we report on in the next chapter.

Key Ideas

1.   There are several ways to define adolescence. These include social, psychological, physical, economic, and legal definitions.

2.   The nature of the passage from childhood to adulthood has been a topic of concern since earliest times.

3.   G. Stanley Hall, the first adolescent psychologist, argued that there are four stages in human development: infancy, childhood, youth, and adolescence. He felt that development ends at the beginning of adulthood.

4.   Robert Havighurst suggested nine developmental tasks that all adolescents should complete.

5.   Erik Erikson's psychosocial theory of development calls the adolescent stage ''a crisis in identity formation'' and ''repudiation versus identity confusion.''

6.   Two important aspects of Erikson's adolescent theory are ''negative identity'' and ''the moratorium of youth.''

7.   James Marcia has defined four identity statuses: confusion, foreclosure, moratorium, and achievement.

8.   The modern American family is seen as having lost five of its original six functions.

9.   Changes in age-related activities, puberty, divorce rate, parenting styles, and sibling and race relations have had powerful effects on the family.

10.   The establishment of adolescent subcultures in recent decades has meant that adolescents are more isolated than ever from other age groups.

Key Terms

Authoritarian parenting style
Authoritative parenting style
Behavioristic model
Cofigurative culture
Creative parenting style
Culture transmission model
Developmental tasks
Identity achievement
Identity confusion
Identity crisis
Identity foreclosure
Identity moratorium

Identity status
Inconsistent conditioning
Moratorium of youth
Negative identity
Permissive parenting style
Premature foreclosure
Psychogenic model
Recapitulation theory
Repudiation
Retrospective accounts
State of identity
Storm and stress

What Do You Think?

1. Do you believe you have had an "identity crisis"? If so, what makes you think so?

2. Which explanation in this chapter best explains the origins of the youth subculture? What is your own explanation?

3. What would you say are the characteristics of an adolescent? Try to state your list in terms of actual behavior.

4. In what ways do you think adolescence may have changed over the centuries?

5. Do you know anyone who, you feel, has a negative identity? What is this person like?

6. In what ways is your nuclear family different from your mother's or your father's?

Suggested Readings

Auel, Jean. (1981). *Clan of the cave bear*. New York: Bantam. Auel's wonderful imagination and excellent knowledge of anthropology make this book on the beginnings of the human family a winner. In fast-paced fiction, she describes the relationships between two types of primitive peoples—those who communicate by voice and those who do so with their hands!

Erikson, Erik. (1958). *Young man Luther*. New York: Norton. Erikson picked Martin Luther as a subject because, in Erikson's view, he was a famous case of negative identity. This book also closely examines the Protestant Reformation and so may appeal to you if you are interested in the beginnings of the Protestant religions.

Goldman, William. (1962). *Lord of the flies*. New York: Coward-McGann. This tale of a group of teenage boys whose plane crashes on a Pacific island, killing the adults, is must reading. You watch the subgroups develop and proceed to the shocking ending.

McCullers, Carson. [1946] (1985). *The member of the wedding*. New York: Bantam. Twelve-year-old Frankie yearns desperately to join her brother and his bride on their honeymoon. She learns a great deal about the transition from childhood to maturity from the devoted housekeeper.

Moravia, Alberto. (1958). *Two women*. New York: Farrar, Straus & Giroux. This moving, compassionate tale describes the relationship between a peasant mother and her daughter in war-torn Italy. It involves the struggles of the mother to deal with her adolescent daughter's needs under these extremely trying circumstances.

Wright, Richard. (1945). *Black boy*. New York: Harper & Row. This is a moving autobiography of the novelist's adolescence in the deep South. Its insights are entirely relevant to today's world.

Chapter 13 ·

Adolescence: Rapidly Changing Bodies and Minds

Puberty

Gretchen, my friend, got her period. I'm so jealous, God. I hate myself for being so jealous, but I am. I wish you'd help me just a little. Nancy's sure she's going to get it soon, too. And if I'm last, I don't know what I'll do. Oh, please, God. I just want to be normal.
        Judy Blume, Are You There, God? It's Me, Margaret, *1970*

Since humans began writing about the experience of living, they have speculated about **puberty.** However, the scientific study of puberty started only at the turn of this century when, because of child labor laws, teenagers were increasingly kept from working so they could continue in school. Teachers and psychologists became more interested in the way children developed—much more so than were the factory owners who had governed the lives of so many teenagers in the nineteenth century.

Early Studies

❖   *The girls are clearly beginning to look like young ladies, while the boys with whom they have thus far played on scarcely equal terms now seem hopelessly stranded in childhood. This year or more of manifest physical superiority of the girl, with its attendant development of womanly attitudes and interests, accounts in part for the tendency of many boys in the early teens to be averse to the society of girls. They accuse them of being soft and foolish, and they suspect the girls' whispering and titterings of being laden with unfavorable comments regarding themselves (King, 1914, p. 13).*

This quaint and somewhat condescending description of the differences between males and females is typical of many of the adolescent theorists of the early twentieth century (e.g., Boas, 1911; Bourne, 1913; Burnham, 1911; King, 1914). Understandably, these writers had far less data available than we do today, and their opinions were largely subjective. For example, King (1914) stated that for girls puberty peaks at 12, and for boys at 13. Using data gathered in Boston in 1913, he found that there were fewer deaths per thousand among 12-year-old girls and 13-year-old boys than for any other female and male age group, respectively. Because relatively few died at these ages, King argued, this must be when their "vital force" was highest, and thus was an indication of the onset of puberty. This is an interesting but wrong hypothesis. For one thing, the age at which the death rate is lowest changes from year to year and from place to place. Biological factors such as the timing of puberty are now known to be less variable than death rate.

King (1914) also suggested that the major cause of **delayed puberty** was "excessive social interests, parties, clubs, etc., with their attendant interference with regular habits of rest and sleep" (p. 25). He further stated that the *second* major cause of delayed puberty was "an excess of physical work." It is unlikely that the work itself caused the delay, but rather that poor children, who were most likely

BOX 13.1

What's Your Opinion?

At one residential center for delinquent adolescent males, female college seniors were invited to a meeting to explain sexuality. At first the questions were taken from cards the boys had prepared, but soon there was a more open exchange of ideas. One boy asked exactly where various organs are located, and one of the young women demonstrated by pointing to her body.

When another asked what a Tampax looked like, a real one was passed from hand to hand. (The boys were quite puzzled until the young women realized that they had forgotten to remove the paper wrapper!) The session was so successful that several more were held.

Unfortunately, new techniques and materials in sex education are not being given much of a chance these days. Sex education courses are actually on the wane. Hence, the sex information "underground" is still functioning. In this process, 14 year olds teach 12 year olds how sex works:

- "Babies come out of their mother's breasts—the nipples open up to let them out."
- "You get a girl pregnant if you put your tongue in her mouth while kissing."
- "The two weeks after a girl's period is her 'safe' time."
- "If you masturbate too much, hair will grow on your palms, and eventually you'll go crazy."
- "Most girls really don't like sex, but they can't help getting excited if you rub the back of their neck."
- "If you don't have at least one orgasm per month, your penis will shrivel up."

Many psychologists feel that young teenagers tend to repress sexual learning because it embarrasses them. Therefore, they argue that there is a great need for sex education programs, and that such programs should start early in the child's studies, perhaps as early as in kindergarten. Others argue that sex education in the schools inevitably involves teaching a set of values, and there is no one set of values with which the general public can agree. Furthermore, they say, most teachers lack the knowledge, and many lack the ability, to teach a sexual curriculum well. What do you think?

to work excessively, were also likely to be poorly fed. It is well known today that malnutrition, whether from poverty or from an eating disorder, will delay puberty.

The Human Reproductive System

Much more is known today about many aspects of puberty. We know more about the organs of our reproductive system and how these organs function together. And we are learning how to present this knowledge to adolescents effectively.

How well do you know your own reproductive system? Take the test in Box 13.2, then read the following sections on the female and the male sexual systems.

	BOX 13.2

How Well Do You Know Your Reproductive System?

Most of us seem to think we understand the workings of sex and reproduction well enough, yet when asked to define the various parts of our sexual system, we don't do very well. How high would you rate your knowledge?

If you would like to learn how much you really know (and this knowledge is important, if only because the adolescents you deal with may ask you questions about it), take this test. Put an M after each male sex organ, an F after each female sex organ, or M/F if it is both. The correct answers may be found by examining Figures 13.1 and 13.2.

	M, F, M/F		M, F, M/F
Bartholin's glands	___	Mons pubis (mons veneris)	___
Cervix	___	Ova	___
Clitoris	___	Ovary	___
Cowper's glands	___	Pituitary gland	___
Epididymis	___	Prostate	___
Fallopian tubes	___	Scrotum	___
Fimbriae	___	Testes	___
Foreskin	___	Ureter	___
Glans penis	___	Urethra	___
Hymen	___	Uterus	___
Labia majora	___	Vas deferens	___
Labia minora	___	Vulva	___

This test has been given to groups of college sophomores and graduate students. The possible score is 24. The sophomores, whose mean age is 18, averaged 19 on the test. The graduate students, whose mean age is 27, averaged 13! Why do you suppose the older students did worse?

The Female Sexual System

The parts of the female sexual system are defined here and are illustrated in Figure 13.1.

Bartholin's glands   A pair of glands located on either side of the vagina. These glands provide some of the fluid that acts as a lubricant during intercourse.

Cervix   The opening to the uterus located at the inner end of the vagina.

Clitoris   Comparable to the male penis. Both organs are extremely similar in the first few months after conception, becoming differentiated only as sexual determination takes place. The clitoris is the source of maximum sexual stimulation and becomes erect through sexual excitement. It is above the vaginal opening, between the labia minora.

Fallopian tubes   Conduct the ova from the ovary to the uterus. A fertilized egg that becomes lodged in the fallopian tubes, called a fallopian pregnancy, cannot develop normally and if not surgically removed will cause the tube to rupture.

Fimbriae   Hairlike structures located at the opening of the oviduct that help move the ovum down the fallopian tube to the uterus.

Hymen   A flap of tissue that usually covers most of the vaginal canal in virgins.

Labia majora   The two larger outer lips of the vaginal opening.

Labia minora   The two smaller inner lips of the vaginal opening.

Mons pubis or mons veneris   The outer area just above the vagina, which becomes larger during adolescence and on which the first pubic hair appears.

Ova   The female reproductive cells stored in the ovaries. These eggs are fertilized by the male sperm. Girls are born with more than a million follicles, each of which holds an ovum. At puberty, only 10,000 remain, but they are more than sufficient for a woman's reproductive life. Since usually only one egg ripens each month from the midteens to the late forties, a woman releases fewer than 500 ova during her lifetime.

Ovaries   Glands that release one ovum each month. They also produce the hormones estrogen and progesterone, which play an important part in the menstrual cycle and pregnancy.

Pituitary gland   The "master" gland located in the lower part of the brain. It controls sexual maturation and monthly menstruation.

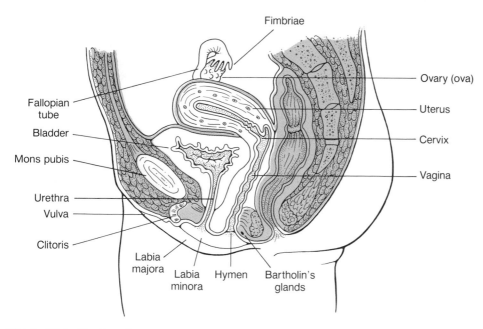

Figure 13.1 *The female reproductive system.*

Ureter A tube connecting the kidneys with the bladder.

Urethra A canal leading from the bladder to the external opening through which urine is excreted.

Uterus The hollow organ (also called the womb) in which the fertilized egg must implant itself for a viable pregnancy to occur. The egg attaches itself to the lining of the uterus from which the unborn baby draws nourishment as it matures during the nine months prior to birth.

Vulva The external genital organs of the female.

The Male Sexual System

The parts of the male sexual system are defined here and are illustrated in Figure 13.2.

Cowper's glands Located next to the prostate glands. Their job is to secrete a fluid that changes the chemical balance in the urethra from an acidic to an alkaline base. This fluid proceeds up through the urethra in the penis where it is ejaculated during sexual excitement just before the sperm-laden semen. About a quarter of the time, sperm also may be found in this solution, sometimes called *preseminal fluid*. Therefore, even if the male withdraws his penis before he ejaculates, it is possible for him to deposit some sperm in the vagina, which may cause pregnancy.

Epididymis A small organ attached to each testis. It is a storage place for newly produced sperm.

Foreskin A flap of loose skin that surrounds the glans penis at birth, often removed by a surgery called *circumcision*.

Glans penis The tip or head of the penis.

Pituitary gland The "master" gland controlling sexual characteristics. In the male it controls the production of sperm, the release of testosterone (and thus the appearance of secondary sexual characteristics such as the growth of hair and voice change), and sexual excitement.

Prostate glands Produce a milky alkaline substance known as semen. In the prostate the sperm are mixed with the semen to give them greater mobility.

Scrotum The sac of skin located just below the penis, in which the testes and epididymis are located.

Testes The two oval sex glands suspended in the scrotum that produce sperm. Sperm are the gene cells that fertilize the ova. They are equipped with a tail-like structure that enables them to move about by a swimming motion. After being ejaculated from the penis into the vagina, they attempt to swim through the cervix into the uterus and into the fallopian tubes where fertilization takes place. If one penetrates an egg, conception occurs. Although the testes regularly produce millions of sperm, the odds against any particular sperm penetrating an egg are enormous. The testes also produce testosterone, the male hormone that affects other aspects of sexual development.

Ureter A tube connecting each of the kidneys with the bladder.

Urethra A canal that connects the bladder with the opening of the penis. It is also the path taken by the preseminal fluid and sperm during ejaculation.

Vas deferens A pair of tubes that lead from the epididymis up to the prostate. They carry the sperm when the male is sexually aroused and about to ejaculate.

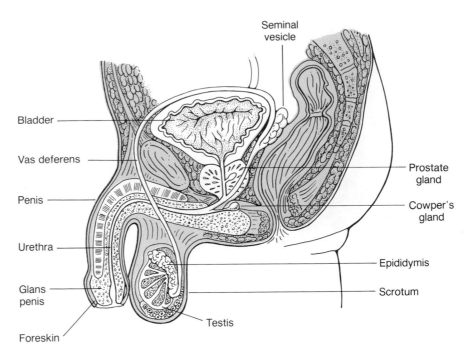

Figure 13.2   The male reproductive system.

When Does Puberty Start?

Is there any one physiological event that marks the beginning of adolescence? The sequence of bodily changes in puberty is surprisingly constant. This holds true whether puberty starts early or late and regardless of the culture in which the child is reared. Table 13.1 lists the sequences of physiological change.

Which of these physical events in the life of the adolescent might we choose as the actual beginning of puberty? Change in hormonal balance is first, but its beginning is difficult to pinpoint. Skeletal growth, genital growth, pubic hair, breast development, voice change, growth spurt—all are inconvenient to measure. Menarche has been suggested as the major turning point for girls, but many women do not recall menarche as a particularly significant event. Sometimes the first ejaculation is suggested as the beginning of adolescent puberty for males, but this too is often a little remembered (and possibly repressed) event.

Despite the fact that puberty is primarily thought of as a physical change in a child, the psychological impact can be significant. This is especially true with menstruation. Even in these "enlightened" times far too many girls experience menarche without being properly prepared. As a result, an event in a young girl's life that should be remembered as the exciting, positive beginning of the transition to adulthood is instead viewed as a negative, sometimes frightening, experience. Research suggests that better preparation for first menstruation results in more positive attitudes about it (Koff, Rierdan, & Sheingold, 1980).

Given our understanding of the physiology of adolescents and differences in individual psychology and culture, we would have to conclude that *there is no*

Table 13.1   The Sequence of Physiological Change in Males and Females

Females
- Change in **hormonal balance.**
- The beginning of rapid **skeletal growth.**
- The beginning of breast development.
- Straight, pigmented pubic hair.
- **Maximum growth spurt** (when growth is at its fastest rate).
- The appearance of hair on the forearms and underarms.

Males
- Change in hormonal balance.
- The beginning of skeletal growth.
- The enlargement of the genitals.
- The appearance of straight, pigmented pubic hair.
- Early voice changes (voice "cracks").
- First ejaculations (wet dreams, nocturnal emissions).
- The appearance of kinky, pigmented pubic hair.
- Maximum growth spurt.
- The appearance of downy facial hair.
- The appearance of hair on the chest and underarms.
- Late voice change (the voice deepens).
- Coarse, pigmented facial hair.

Note: For more on these physiological changes, see Muuss (1982).

single event marking the onset of puberty but rather a complex set of events, whose effects may be sudden or gradual.

The Effects of Timing on Puberty

In a general sense, the onset of puberty affects all adolescents in the same way. However, the *age* at which these changes begin has some very specific effects on the adolescent's life. (The photo in figure 13.3, taken in 1912, illustrates how 14-year-old adolescents can differ greatly in their stage of physiological development—and did so even many years ago!)

In this section, eight adolescents, four males and four females, are compared in order to illustrate the differences that often occur among children even though they are all in the **normal range of development.** Each adolescent is 14 years old. The first female and male are early maturers, the second are average maturers, and the third are late maturers. They all fall within the typical range of all adolescents. The fourth female and male represent average adolescents of one hundred years ago.

The Early-Maturing Female: Ann

At 5 feet, 5 inches and 130 pounds, Ann is considerably bigger than her age-mates. Her growth accelerated when she was 8 years old, and by the time she was 10 1/2, her maximum growth spurt crested. She is still growing taller but at a slower rate. Her *motor development* (coordination and strength) had its greatest rate of increase two years ago. She is stronger than her age-mates, but her strength and coordination have reached their maximum.

Figure 13.3 *Comparison of male and female growth (King, 1914).*

BOX 13.3

Sleeping Beauty: A Tale of Menstruation?

Once upon a time Sleeping Beauty was born, and her parents, the King and Queen, invited fairies to her christening. These good fairies endowed her with beauty, grace, health, and other fine qualities. Unexpectedly, a jealous, evil fairy came to the christening. She uttered a dreadful curse: Sleeping Beauty would prick her finger on the distaff of a spinning wheel and bleed to death. One of the good fairies was able to change this threat of death into one hundred years' sleep. The King tried to prevent the curse from taking effect; he removed all the distaffs from the kingdom. While her parents were away, the 15-year-old Sleeping Beauty discovered a locked chamber. She walked into the room and saw an old woman who was spinning. Sleeping Beauty was fascinated by the spinning wheel, touched it, and pricked her finger on the distaff. She fell into a deep sleep for one hundred years until she was awakened by the kiss of her lover, Prince Charming.

The famous child psychologist Bruno Bettelheim (1976) believes that fairy tales such as "Sleeping Beauty" instruct us about the emotional turmoils of childhood and adolescence. In the Sleeping Beauty story, all of the parents' attempts to prevent their child's sexual awakening fail, because such aspects of sexuality as menstruation are inevitable. Bettelheim believes that the dreadful "curse" that causes bleeding is symbolic of menstruation, and turns out to be a blessing in disguise for Sleeping Beauty. During her hundred years of inward-turning contemplation, Sleeping Beauty was struggling to attain the physical and emotional maturity she needs to be ready for love and marriage. After this long withdrawal into a deathlike sleep, she is awakened by Prince Charming. Can you think of other fairy tales that are symbolic stories of adolescence?

She started menstruating three years ago, at age 11, and her breasts are already in the secondary (adult) stage. Her pubic and underarm hair are also at an adult stage.

Ann is confused about the way her body looks. She feels conspicuous and vulnerable because she stands out in a crowd of her friends. Her greater interest in boys, and their response, often causes conflicts with other girls. They envy the interest the boys show in her more mature figure. She often has negative feelings about herself because she is "different."

Other girls tend to avoid her now because her early **maturation** makes her older than them. In later adolescence, she may experience some difficulties; she may find herself in situations (such as with drugs, sex, or drinking) for which she is not yet ready. It also will not always be easy to find a boy tall enough to dance with.

In summary, we can say that while Ann is experiencing difficulties with her early maturity, she will begin to feel better about herself as she approaches 16.

The Average-Maturing Female: Beth

Although Beth is also 14, she is different in almost every way from Ann. She represents the typical adolescent today in the sense of being average in her measurements and physical change. It is clear that there is no "average" adolescent from the standpoint of personality and behavior.

Beth is 5 feet, 3 inches tall and weighs 120 pounds. She reached her maximum growth spurt two years ago and is also starting to slow down. She is presently at the peak of her motor development.

Her breasts are at the primary breast stage; she is beginning to need a bra, or thinks she does. She started menstruating two years ago. She has adult pubic hair, and her underarm hair is beginning to appear.

Girls who reach puberty late are usually unhappy about it, but not as unhappy as boys who are late. Boys who reach physical maturity early are usually quite happy about it, and more happy than are girls who are early.

Sleeping Beauty: Metaphor for menstruation?

She feels reasonably happy about her body, and most but not all of her relationships with her peers are reasonably satisfying. Although she does have some occasional emotional problems, they are not related to her physical development as much as are Ann's.

The Late-Maturing Female: Cathy

Cathy is at the lower end of the normal range of physical development for a 14-year-old girl. She is only 4 feet, 8 inches tall, weighs 100 pounds, and is just beginning her growth spurt. She is not too happy about this, as she feels that the other girls have advantages in relationships with boys.

Cathy's breasts are at the bud stage; her nipples and encircling areolae are beginning to protrude, but she is otherwise flat-chested. She has just begun menstruation. Pubic hair growth has started, but as yet no hair has appeared under her arms.

Other girls tend to feel sorry for her, but they also look down on her. She is more dependent and childlike than the others. She feels a growing dislike for her body, and she is becoming more and more introverted and self-rejecting because of it. At this stage her immaturity is not a great disability; at least she is more mature than some of the boys her age. As she reaches later adolescence, her underdeveloped figure may be a more serious source of unhappiness for her if she accepts conventional standards of sexual desirability.

The Average Adolescent Female of One Hundred Years Ago: Dorothy

Although records of adolescent physical development of one hundred years ago are less than adequate, we can be fairly certain about some of the data. Dorothy, who was typical for her time, was physically much like Cathy is now. At 4 feet, 7 inches, she was one inch shorter, and at 85 pounds, she weighed 15 pounds less than Cathy.

At age 14, Dorothy would still have had four years to go before her peak of motor development, and she would not have started to menstruate for another year. In all the other physical ways she looked a great deal like Cathy. The major difference between the two girls is that while Cathy is unhappy about her body's appearance, Dorothy, who was typical, felt reasonably good about hers.

The Early-Maturing Male: Al

Al finds that at 5 feet, 8 inches tall, he towers over his 14-year-old friends. He reached his maximum growth spurt approximately two years ago and weighs 150 pounds. He is now about two years before the peak of his motor development. His coordination and strength are rapidly increasing, but contrary to the popular myth he is not growing clumsier.

As adolescents reach their peak of motor development, they usually handle their bodies better, although adults expect them to have numerous accidents. It is true that when one's arms grow an inch longer in less than a year, one's hand-eye coordination suffers somewhat. However, the idea of the gangling, inept adolescent is more myth than fact.

Al's sexual development is also well ahead of that of his age-mates. He already has adult pubic hair, and hair has started to grow on his chest and underarms. He began having nocturnal emissions almost two years ago, and since then the size of his genitals has increased almost 100%.

Because our society tends to judge male maturity on the basis of physique and stature, Al's larger size has advantages for him. He is pleased with his looks, although once in a while it bothers him when someone treats him as though he were 17 or 18 years old. Nevertheless, he uses the advantages of his early maturity whenever possible.

His friends tend to look up to him and to consider him a leader. Because size and coordination often lead to athletic superiority, and because success in school sports has long meant popularity, he has the most positive self-concept of all the adolescents described here, including the females. He has a good psychological adjustment, although he is sometimes vain, and is the most confident and responsible of this group. He engages in more social activities than the others, which also occasionally gets him into trouble, because he is not psychologically ready for some of the social activities in which he is permitted to participate.

The Average-Maturing Male: Bob

Interestingly, Bob is exactly the same height as his "average" female counterpart, Beth, at 5 feet, 3 inches tall. At 130 pounds, he outweighs her by 10 pounds. He is currently in the midst of his maximum growth spurt and is four years away from reaching the peak of his coordination and strength.

His sexual development began about a year ago with the start of nocturnal emissions, and he is just now starting to grow pubic hair. As yet he has no hair on his chest or under his arms. However, his genitals have reached 80% of their adult size.

Bob gets along well with his age-mates. He is reasonably happy with the way his body has developed so far, although there are some activities that he wishes he could excel in. Most of the attributes that he aspires to are already possessed by Al, whom he envies. This causes few problems, as Bob still has every reason to hope his body will develop into his ideal physical image.

The Late-Maturing Male: Chuck

Chuck is also similar in stature to his counterpart, Cathy. They are both 4 feet, 8 inches tall, although at 90 pounds, Chuck is 10 pounds lighter than Cathy. He is a year and a half away from his maximum growth spurt and must wait six years before his motor development will peak.

Chuck's sexual development is also lagging behind those of the other two boys. His genitals are 50% larger than they were two years ago, but as yet he has no pubic, chest, or underarm hair. He has not yet experienced nocturnal emissions, although these are about to begin.

He is the least happy with his body of the adolescents described here. His voice has not yet changed, he is not as strong and coordinated as the other boys, and he is much smaller than they. They tend to treat him as a scapegoat and often ridicule him. He chooses to interact with boys who are younger than himself and is attracted to activities in which mental rather than physical prowess is important, such as chess and band. He avoids girls, almost all of whom are more physically mature than he. This lack of heterosexual experience may later affect his self-concept.

Chuck lacks confidence in himself and tends to be dependent on others. He was of almost average size in grammar school and now feels he has lost prestige. He frequently does things to gain the attention of others, but these actions seldom bring him the acclaim he craves. Probably as a result, he is more irritable and restless than the others and engages in more types of compensating behaviors.

The Average Adolescent Male of One Hundred Years Ago: Dan

At 4 feet, 7 inches, Dan was shorter than Chuck by one inch, and weighed the same, 90 pounds. He trailed Chuck in sexual development by two years, and, at age 14, his genitals had increased only 20% in size.

However, the major difference between Chuck and Dan lies in self-satisfaction. While Chuck is extremely unhappy about the way he is developing, Dan was as happy as Bob is now because he was quite average for that time. Although we cannot know what his relationship with peers was like or how he viewed himself, we can guess that these were quite similar to Bob's.

The preceding descriptions illustrate the great variability in adolescent growth and in adolescent responses to growth. It should be kept in mind, however, that self-image and peer relationships are not entirely determined by physique. "Average-sized" adolescents do not always lead a charmed life, and many late and early maturers are quite comfortable with themselves. Adolescents who have clarified their values and set their own standards are not likely to be overly affected by pubertal changes or the peer approval or disapproval brought about by them.

The small size of Dorothy and Dan, who were average teenagers one hundred years ago, is part of the phenomenon called the **secular trend.** In recent centuries, adolescents have been entering puberty sooner and growing taller and heavier. An example is the onset of menstruation, called **menarche,** which occurs about two and a half years earlier than it did a century ago in the United States (14.75 years old in 1877, 12.25 today).

What if the secular trend goes on forever? "Imagine a toddler displaying all the features of puberty—a three-year-old girl with fully developed breasts, or a boy just slightly older with a deep male voice. That is what we will see by the year 2250 if the age at which puberty arrives keeps decreasing at its current pace" (Santrock, 1989, p. 84).

Almost certainly, this won't happen. For one thing, it appears that the trend is relatively recent. Several writers in early times refer to menarche as occurring in the late teen years. If we were to project the trend back for 1,000 years, women would have started menstruating in their thirties and forties, but most of them did not even live that long. It is likely that the trend is a special case that pertains only to the period from the 1700s to today, and is the result of improvements in nutrition, medicine, and health care in general.

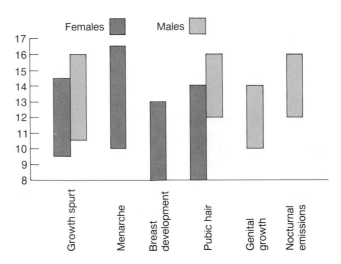

Figure 13.4   Normal age ranges of puberty.

According to Wyshak and Frisch (1982), this change in the onset of menarche since one hundred years ago ranges from three years earlier in Scandinavian countries to about one year in France. Surveying 218 reports, these authors learned that menarche is delayed by malnutrition and by strenuous physical activity. For example, the age of menarche is relatively late in poor girls in the poorer developing countries and among dancers and athletes in affluent countries: it occurs in these cases at about 15 years (Frisch, 1978). This delay is almost certainly due to the lesser amount of fat in the bodies of these girls—menstruation does not occur unless a certain level of fat cells is maintained. This is also the cause of **amenorrhea** (the suppression of menstruation) in anorexics and bulimics (see chap. 15).

Figure 13.4 details the age ranges considered normal for development. Adolescents who experience these changes earlier or later may have no medical problem, but it is probably a good idea to consult a doctor. If a glandular imbalance exists, the doctor can usually remedy the problem with little difficulty.

Inappropriate Physical Growth and Its Effects

Inappropriate physical development, while rare, will be described briefly here. The two major types are **gynecomastia,** excessive male breast growth (some breast growth in the male is not unusual in male teens), and **virilism,** the development of several masculine traits in the girl, including **hirsutism** (facial and chest hair) and voice deepening. Gynecomastia often results from excessive use of marijuana. Both conditions can usually be reversed with hormone therapy (Money & Ehrhardt, 1972).

Another problem that occasionally occurs is **psychosocial dwarfism,** in which puberty is so delayed that the teenager looks like a child. This condition is the result of an extremely negative environment. In one case, a boy had been severely beaten by his mother and by his six brothers and sisters, who were themselves beaten if they refused to participate. He was found naked in a closet, the door of which had been nailed shut. His doctor described his situation:

❖   *In the manner typical for victims of the battered child syndrome, this partic-*
    ular sixteen-year-old boy fits the formula of being forced to suffer punishment
    by way of atonement for his parents' own shortcomings and transgressions.
    In particular, the stepmother may have been pathologically destroying in him,
    by proxy, an image of what she could not tolerate in herself, namely, her own
    illegitimacy (Money & Wolff, 1974, p. 128).

Removal to a positive environment usually helps the child recover some, but seldom all, of the lost growth and development. The earlier this is done, the greater the recovery.

In summary, we may say that the vast majority of human bodies proceed toward maturity in the same way, but that in the last few centuries the timing of the process has changed radically.

Intellectual Development

I was about twelve when I discovered that you could create a whole new world just in your head! I don't know why I hadn't thought about it before, but the idea excited me terrifically. I started lying in bed on Saturday mornings till 11 or 12 o'clock, making up "my secret world." I went to fabulous places. I met friends who really liked me and treated me great. And of course I fell in love with this guy like you wouldn't believe!

Susan Klein, a eighth-grade student

Adolescence is a complex process of growth and change. Because biological and social changes are the focus of attention, changes in the young adolescent's ability to think often go unnoticed. Yet it is during early and middle adolescence that thinking ability reaches the fourth and last level—the level of abstract thought (see chap. 2). To understand how abstract thought develops, we have to know more about the intellect itself.

Variables in Intellectual Development—Piaget

According to Jean Piaget's theory (as we hope you remember from chap. 2), the ability to think develops in four stages:

- The sensorimotor stage (birth to 2 years), in which the child learns from its autonomic interactions with the world.

- The preoperational stage (2 to 7 years), in which behaviors such as picking up a can are gradually internalized so that they can be manipulated in the mind.

- The concrete operational stage (7 to 11 years), in which actions can be manipulated mentally, but only with things. For example, a child of 8 is able to anticipate what is going to happen if a can is thrown across the room without actually having to do so.

- The formal operational stage (11 years +), in which groups of concrete operations are combined to become formal operations. For example, the adolescent comes to understand democracy by combining concepts such as putting a ballot in a box and hearing that the Senate voted to give money for the homeless.

The ability to understand that the rules of games can be fairly changed is an aspect of the formal operation stage. Even though these young men are unlikely to change the rules of their chess game, they are now at the intellectual level at which they recognize this is a possibility.

We are like other animals, especially the primates, in many ways. They, too, can make plans, can cooperate in groups, and may well have simple language systems. But it is the ability to perform formal operations that truly separates us. Piaget's conception of the formal operation is a remarkable contribution to psychology.

It was also Piaget who first noted the strong tendency of early adolescents toward democratic values because of this new thinking capacity. This is the age that youth first become committed to the idea that participants in a group may change the rules of a game, but once agreed on, all must follow the new rules. This tendency, he believes, is universal; all teenagers throughout the world develop this value.

Having considered Piaget's ideas about adolescent cognition in some detail earlier in this book, let us turn now to a review of the findings of those researchers who have been diligently following him.

Variables in Intellectual Development—Flavell

Psychologist John Flavell (1977), on the basis of his own studies and his review of the literature, has suggested that there are seven aspects of the transition from childhood to adolescent and adult thinking. These seven aspects are considered in the following sections, from the standpoint of an imaginary adolescent situation.

We would like you to imagine the following scenario. Your local television station has decided to sponsor a new program called "Young Women Today." It has already hired a 29-year-old woman to host the show, a person who has had considerable experience in the talk-show format.

In addition, they want to hire a 17-year-old high school girl as an assistant hostess. This has been announced at the local high school. Because the employers are sure that many female students will apply for this job, they have designed a simple application form. With it, they hope to identify the better candidates whom they will then interview. On this application form, the applicants are to describe two characteristics that would make them an especially good choice for the job. Here are Flavell's seven aspects of the childhood-adolescent cognitive transition, analyzed from the standpoint of this scenario:

The Real versus the Possible

For Piaget (1966), probably the most important cognitive change from childhood to adolescence has to do with the growing ability of the adolescent to imagine possible and even impossible situations—the aspect Flavell calls **the real versus the possible.** Elementary school children tend to approach problems by examining the data firsthand and attempting to make guesses about the solution to the problem on the basis of the first piece of information they look at. As Flavell (1977) suggests, the child has "an earthbound, concrete, practical-minded sort of problem approach, one that persistently fixates on the perceptible reality there in front of him" (p. 103). The preliminary approach is a series of guesses as to what information can mean.

This is no longer the case for 17-year-old Ellen, who would very much like to get the television show job. As it happens, she is the daughter of an unemployed actor. She wonders whether she should mention this. She thinks that it may help her, both because her father has been in show business and because her family could use the money. On the other hand, she suspects that the television people might think that if her father has been unsuccessful in show business, she may be, too. Whereas a 9-year-old child might put this fact down on the application, hoping that it will make some difference, Ellen tries to think of all the possible ramifications of this piece of information before deciding whether to use it.

Ellen is obviously a formal operational thinker. For her, as Flavell (1977) would describe it, "reality is seen as that particular portion of the much wider world of possibility which happens to exist and hold true in a given problem situation" (p. 103).

Empirico-Inductive versus Hypothetico-Deductive Methods

A further major difference between concrete and formal operational thinkers is in their *method* of problem solving. Younger children use an **empirico-inductive** approach; that is, they are likely to look at available facts and try to induce some generalization from them. Adolescents, on the other hand, are likely to use **hypothetico-deductive** reasoning to hypothesize about the situation and then deduce from it what the facts *should be* if the hypothesis is true. Adolescents tend to look at what might be, in two senses: they attempt to discover several possibilities in a situation before starting to investigate it empirically. Then they try to imagine the possible outcomes of each possibility.

Whereas the younger child might be satisfied with simply putting down two possible characteristics on the application, Ellen is likely to think of what the ramifications are for each of a number of possible characteristics. For example, she might hypothesize that if the station has a reputation for being concerned with poor people, they will be sympathetic with the fact that her father is out of work and needs a job. On the other hand, if the station has a reputation for fierce competition, it might look negatively on this information, thinking that perhaps her whole family are "losers."

Intra-propositional versus Inter-propositional Thinking

Elementary school-age children, especially older ones, may well be able to think of a number of possible outcomes that would result from a single choice. It is only in later adolescence, however, that they are able to think of the ramifications of *combinations* of propositions.

In Ellen's case, for example, she may decide that her father's unemployment could hurt her, but she may balance this by stating that she herself has maintained a paper route successfully for the past four years. **Inter-propositional thinking** can become infinitely more complex than **intra-propositional thinking.** Logicians (students of logical thinking) have discovered many aspects of the interrelationships that can occur between sets of propositions. These complexities usually become part of the repertoire of thinkers as they develop into adulthood.

An important aspect of this complexity is the ability to think logically about statements that may have no relationship to reality whatsoever. As Flavell (1977) states, "formal operational thinkers understand that logical arguments have a disembodied, passionless life of their own" (p. 106). Most persons find thinking about abstract concepts—for example, the laws of trigonometry—more difficult than thinking about the construction of a table, but the laws of logic in each case do not differ. During adolescence and adulthood, the person becomes aware of this.

Combinations and Permutations

Because concrete operational thinkers look at propositions only one way at a time, they are often unable to imagine all of the possible **combinations** or **permutations** of a set of data. During adolescence, the thinker becomes able to realize that systematically generating combinations (A with B, A with C, B with C etc.) can aid in thoroughly examining the possible solutions of a problem.

It is entirely likely that Ellen would sit down and draw up a list of all her good characteristics before even starting to decide which of these would be best to put on her application. To improve her creativity, she might write all of these characteristics on separate sheets of paper, put them in a hat, and draw them out in pairs to see if she comes across a pair that she thinks will be unusually appealing. Without such a technique, she might never have thought of that particular pair.

Inversion and Compensation

Suppose you have before you two containers with an equal amount of water in each, hanging evenly from each side of a balance scale. Obviously, if a cup of water is added to the container on the right, it will sink to a level lower than the container on the left. If you were asked to make the containers even again, you would probably recognize that it could be done in one of two ways: withdraw a cup of water from the container on the right (**inversion**), or add a cup of water to the container on the left (**compensation**).

Concrete operational thinkers are likely to think of one or the other of these solutions, but not both. They usually will not recognize that there is more than one possible way to solve the problem. Having solved it one way, they no longer pay attention to the task. Because formal operational thinkers are able to imagine both inversion and compensation as being useful in solving a problem, they have a better chance of coming up with other fruitful solutions.

Ellen would be using compensation if she mentioned her newspaper job to balance her father's unemployment. She might be using inversion if she simply left out the fact that her father is unemployed.

Information-Processing Strategies

Older thinkers are not only more likely to have a large array of problem-solving strategies, but are more likely to attempt to devise a plan to use this array. Such a plan is an **information-processing strategy.**

Flavell (1977) points to the game of "Twenty Questions" as an example of this difference. In this game, the problem solver is allowed twenty questions of the yes-or-no type to solve a problem. For example, if the problem is to guess what person the questioner is thinking of, an excellent question would be, "Is the person alive?" This eliminates a tremendous number of possibilities. Other questions such as "Is the person a woman?" or "Is the person an adult?" are examples of this effective problem-solving strategy. Concrete-operational problem solvers are more likely to name twenty particular individuals and thus (unless they are lucky) lose the game.

Ellen has the problem of attempting to discover what major criteria the television people have in mind in selecting their talk show host. She might go to several individuals in the community who know about those criteria. Furthermore, she might use a good strategy in asking questions of those informed persons. At any rate, to the extent that she has reached the formal operations stage, she is much more likely to do so.

Consolidation and Solidification

The changes from childhood to adulthood mentioned so far have been qualitative. There are also two quantitative aspects of this transition. The mental gains that are being made are slowly consolidated—show **consolidation.** Not only are the improved problem-solving techniques learned, but they are employed in a wider variety of situations and with greater skill. Furthermore, these gains seem to be solidified—show **solidification.** That is, the thinker is more certain and confident in the use of the newly gained mental skills and is more likely to use them in new situations.

If Ellen were 12 years old instead of 17, she may have tried some of the same tactics but she might very well have given up quickly and just put down any two traits that seemed acceptable to her. It is her greater experience with these thinking styles that gives her the motivation to persevere at the task. Table 13.2 offers an overview of Flavell's variables.

Adolescent Egocentrism

Parents often feel frustrated at the seemingly irrational attitudes and behaviors of their adolescent children. One explanation is the re-emergence of a pattern of thought that marked early childhood, egocentrism. **Adolescent egocentrism**

Table 13.2   Overview of Flavell's Variables in Intellectual Development

Concrete Operational Thinking		Formal Operational Thinking
1. The real	vs.	1. The possible
2. Empirico-inductive method	vs.	2. Hypothetico-deductive method
3. Intrapropositional thinking	vs.	3. Interpropositional thinking
4. Unable to see combinations and permutations	vs.	4. Able to see combinations and permutations
5. Can use inversion *or* compensation	vs.	5. Can use inversion *and* compensation
6. Poor information-processing strategies (weak plan)	vs.	6. Good information-processing strategies (clear plan)
7. Mental gains not consolidated and solidified	vs.	7. Mental gains consolidated and solidified

From John Flavell, *Cognitive Development.* Englewood Cliffs, NJ: Prentice-Hall, Inc.

(Elkind, 1978) refers to the tendency to exaggerate the importance, uniqueness, and severity of social and emotional experiences. Their love is greater than anything their parents have experienced. Their suffering is more painful and unjust than anyone else's. Their friendships are most sacred. Their clothes are the worst or the best. Developmentally speaking, adolescent egocentrism seems to peak around the age of 13 (Elkind & Bowen, 1979), followed by a gradual and sometimes painful decline.

Elkind sees two components to this egocentrism. First, teenagers tend to create an *imaginary audience*. They are on center stage, and the rest of the world is constantly scrutinizing their behavior and physical appearance. This accounts for some of the apparently irrational mood swings in adolescence. The mirror may produce an elated, confident teenager ready to make his appearance. Then one pimple on the nose can be cause for staying inside the house for days. In fact, school phobia can become acute during early adolescence because of concerns over appearance.

The second component of egocentrism is the *personal fable*. This refers to adolescents' tendency to think of themselves in heroic or mythical terms. The result is that they exaggerate their own abilities and their invincibility. This type of mythic creation on the part of an adolescent can sometimes lead to increased risk-taking, such as drug use, dangerous driving, and disregard for the possible consequences of sexual behavior. Many teenagers simply can't imagine an unhappy ending to their own special story.

Critical Thinking

Divergent thinking is an important aspect of critical thinking.

Although we discussed critical thinking at some length in chapter 9, we should make a number of points about its role in adolescence. Guilford's distinction between convergent and divergent thinking (1975) will be helpful here, because critical thinking is made up of these two abilities.

Convergent thinking is used when we want to solve a problem by *converging* on the correct answer. For example, if we were to ask you to answer the question, "How much is 286 times 469," you probably could not produce it immediately. However, if you used a pencil and paper or a calculator, you would almost certainly arrive at the same answer as most others trying to solve the problem. There is only one correct answer. Critical thinking is like this. As Moore and Parker (1986) put it, it is "the correct evaluation of claims and arguments."

Divergent thinking, on the other hand, is just the opposite. This is the type of thinking used when the problem to be solved has many possible answers. For example, what are all the things that would be different if it were to rain up instead of down?

Other divergent questions are "What would happen if we had no thumbs," and "What should we do to prevent ice buildup from snapping telephone lines." Divergent thinking can be right or wrong, too, but there is considerably greater leeway for personal opinion than with convergent thinking. Not all divergent thinking is creative, but it is more likely to produce a creative concept. To be a good critical thinker, it is not enough to analyze statements accurately. Often you will need to think divergently to understand the possibilities and the implications of those statements, too.

Because adolescents are entering the formal operations stage of intellectual development, they become vastly more capable of critical thinking than younger children. As they move through the teen years, they grow in their ability to make effective decisions. This involves five types of newly acquired abilities (Moore, McGann, & McGann, 1985):

Phase 1. Recognizing and defining the problem.
Phase 2. Gathering information.
Phase 3. Forming tentative conclusions.
Phase 4. Testing tentative conclusions.
Phase 5. Evaluation and decision making.

In the next section, we will make a distinction between critical and creative thinking, but it is important that we not make too great a distinction, especially at this age level. Paul (1987) describes this concern well:

❖ *Just as it is misleading to talk of developing a student's capacity to think critically without facing the problem of cultivating the student's rational passions—the necessary driving force behind the rational use of all critical thinking skills—so too it is misleading to talk of developing a student's ability to think critically as something separate from the student's ability to think creatively. . . . The imagination and its creative powers are continually called forth (p. 143).*

Creative Thinking

❖ *This is the story about a very curious cat named Kat. One day Kat was wandering in the woods where he came upon a big house made of fish. Without thinking, he ate much of that house. The next morning when he woke up he had grown considerably larger. Even as he walked down the street he was getting bigger. Finally he got bigger than any building ever made. He walked up to the Empire State Building in New York City and accidentally crushed it. The people had to think of a way to stop him, so they made this great iron box which made the cat curious. He finally got inside it, but it was too heavy to get him out of again. There he lived for the rest of his life. But he was still curious until his death, which was 6,820,000 years later. They buried him in the state of Rhode Island, and I mean the whole state.*
Ralph Titus, a seventh-grade student

The restless imagination, the daring exaggeration, the disdain for triteness that this story demonstrates—all are signs that its young author has great creative potential. With the right kind of encouragement, with the considerable knowledge we now have about how to foster creativity, this boy could develop his talents to his own and society's great benefit.

Creative thinking appears to have many elements—divergent thinking, fluency, flexibility, originality, remote associations. We will look more closely at these elements when we get to adult creativity later in this book, but one element that seems to be of special importance in adolescence is the use of metaphor.

The Use of Metaphor

A metaphor is a word or phrase that comes by comparison or analogy to stand for another word or phrase. Common sense suggests a relationship between efficient metaphor use and creativity. Using a metaphor in speech involves calling attention to a similarity between two seemingly dissimilar things. This suggests a process similar to divergent thinking, and there is a growing body of research support for this relationship (Jaquish, Block, & Block, 1984; Kogan, 1973, 1983; Wallach & Kogan, 1965).

Kogan (1983) believes that the **use of metaphor** can explain the difference between ordinary divergent thinking and high quality divergent thinking. A creative person must be able not only to think of many different things from many different categories, but to compare them in unique, qualitatively different ways. Although metaphors are typically first used by older children and adolescents, research has extended to looking at the symbolic play of very young children and how it relates to creativity (see Kogan, 1983, for a good review). The early imaginative play of children is now being viewed as a precursor of later metaphor use and creativity.

Howard Gardner and his associates at Harvard University have studied the role of metaphor. Gardner's seminal *Art, Mind, and Brain: A Cognitive Approach to Creativity* (1982) offers many insights into the process. Gardner has based his research on the theories of three eminent structuralists: Jean Piaget, Noam Chomsky, and Claude Levi-Strauss. He states that "These thinkers share a belief that the mind operates according to specifiable rules—often unconscious ones—and that these can be ferreted out and made explicit by the systematic examination of human language, action, and problem solving" (p. 4).

Gardner's main efforts have focused on the relationship between children's art and children's understanding of metaphor, both in normal and brain-damaged children. He describes talking to a group of youngsters at a Seder (the meal many Jews eat to commemorate the flight of the Hebrews from Egypt). He told them how, after a plague, Pharaoh's "heart was turned to stone." The children interpreted the metaphor variously, but only the older ones could understand the link between the physical universe (hard rocks) and psychological traits (stubborn lack of feeling). Younger children are more apt to apply magical interpretations (God or a witch did it). Gardner believes that the development of the understanding of metaphoric language is as sequential as the stages proposed by Piaget and Erikson, and is closely related to the types of development treated in those theories.

Examining children's metaphors such as a bald man having a "barefoot head" and an elephant being seen as a "gasmask," Gardner and Winner (1982) found clear changes with age in the level of sophistication. Interestingly, there appear to be two opposing features:

- When you ask children to explain figures of speech, they steadily get better at it as they get older. There is a definite increase in this ability as the child attains the formal operations stage.

Studying the stories of the Bible is an excellent way to learn about metaphors.

BOX 13.4

Tommy

Tommy was an unkempt child, whose physical health was poor due to frequent bouts with viral infection. His teachers reported that the quality of his schoolwork was generally poor, and he had considerable difficulty with spelling and rote learning. He cared little for reading or writing and had a consistently negative attitude toward school in general. He frequently interrupted classes by "asking foolish questions," being rude to the teachers, and playing practical jokes on others.

He set fire to a portion of his home, and when asked why, his reply was, "because I wanted to see what the flames would do." The boy was given a beating by his father, in full view of the neighborhood. He attempted to hatch chicken eggs by sitting on them, and when this didn't work, he encouraged his playmates to swallow some raw. Neighbors frequently noted explosions coming from the basement of the boy's home, where his mother permitted him to play with chemical substances.

The boy's father had little regard for his son's intelligence, and stated that strong disciplinary intervention and obedience training were the best methods for dealing with Tommy. Nevertheless, his mother, a former school teacher, insisted that he be allowed to stay at home and receive the rest of his education from her. Ultimately, she had her way.

When asked their diagnosis of 11-year-old Tommy, many psychology students label him emotionally disturbed, and recommend he be taken from his parents and institutionalized for his own good. Actually, he eventually turned out pretty well—Tommy's full name is Thomas Alva Edison!

- However, very young children seem to be the best at making up their own metaphors. Furthermore, their own metaphors tend to be of two types (Gardner & Winner, 1982):

❖ *the different patterns of making metaphors may reflect fundamentally different ways of processing information. Children who make their metaphors on visual resemblances may approach experience largely in terms of the physical qualities of objects. On the other hand, children who base their metaphors on action sequences may view the world in terms of the way events unfold over time. We believe that the difference may continue into adulthood, underlying diverse styles in the creation and appreciation of artistic form (p. 164).*

It is exciting to think that this discovery by Gardner and Winner may explain why some people become scientists and others writers. If this is so, it certainly is an important key to fostering such talent. Of course, this is not to say that they have the answers to such questions as why children develop one of the two forms of "metaphorizing" (or neither), but their work appears to be a giant step in the right direction.

These researchers believe that the spontaneous production of metaphors declines somewhat during the school years. This is probably because the child, having mastered a basic vocabulary, has less need to "stretch the resources of language to express new meanings" (1982, p. 165). In addition, there is greater pressure from teachers and parents to get the right answers, so children take fewer risks in their language. Gardner and Winner (1982) point to the *Shakespeare Parallel Text Series,* which offers a translation of the bard's plays into everyday English ("Stand and unfold yourself" becomes "Stand still and tell me who you are") as a step in the wrong direction. "If, as we have shown, students of this age have the potential to deal with complex metaphors, there is no necessity to rewrite Shakespeare" (p. 167).

Creativity, Giftedness, and the IQ

As Feldman (1979) has pointed out, there have been many studies of "giftedness," but only a few of exceptionally creative, highly productive youth. He believes that this unfortunate situation is mainly the fault of "the foremost figure in the study of the gifted," Lewis M. Terman. Terman (1925) was well known for his research on 1,000 California children whose IQs in the early 1920s were 135 or higher. Terman believed these children to be the "geniuses" of the future, a label he kept for them as he studied their development over the decades. His was a powerful investigation, and has been followed by scholars and popular writers alike.

Child prodigies are distinguished by the passion with which they pursue their interests. Here we see the young Wolfgang Amadeus Mozart performing for a group of admiring adults. He was not merely precocious—able to perform at levels typical of older children; he was prodigious—able, at a young age to write music that is still performed by professional musicians.

Precisely because of the notoriety of this research, Feldman argues, we have come to accept a *numerical* definition of genius (an IQ above 135), and a somewhat low one at that. Feldman notes that the *Encyclopedia Britannica* now differentiates two basic definitions of genius: the numerical one fostered by Terman; and the concept first described by Sir Francis Galton (1870, 1879): "creative ability of an exceptionally high order as demonstrated by actual achievement."

Feldman (1979) says that genius, as defined by IQ, really only refers to **precociousness**—doing what others are able to do, but at a younger age. **Prodigiousness** (as in child prodigy), on the other hand, refers to someone who is *qualitatively* higher in ability from the rest of us. This is different from simply being able to do things sooner. Further, prodigiousness calls for a rare matching of high talent and an environment that is ready and open to creativity. If such youthful prodigies as Mozart in music or Bobby Fischer in chess had been born two thousand years earlier, they may well have grown up to be much more ordinary. In fact, if Einstein had been born *fifty* years earlier, he might have done nothing special—particularly since he did not even speak well until he was five!

So if prodigies are more than just quicker at learning, what is it that truly distinguishes them? On the basis of his intensive study of three prodigies, Feldman states that

❖ *Perhaps the most striking quality in the children in our study as well as other cases is the passion with which excellence is pursued. Commitment and tenacity and joy in achievement are perhaps the best signs that a coincidence has occurred among child, field, and moment in evolutionary time. No event is more likely to predict that a truly remarkable, creative contribution will eventually occur (1979, p. 351).*

In summary, critical and creative thinking are similar in that they both employ convergent and divergent production. The main difference between them is that critical thinking aims at the correct assessment of *existing* ideas, whereas creativity is more aimed at the invention and discovery of *new* ideas. While each requires a certain amount of intelligence, creativity also depends on such traits as metaphorical thinking and an independent personality.

BOX 13.5

Guidelines for Improving Your Own Creativity

Here are some suggestions (Dacey,1989) that should help you become a more creative problem solver:

- Avoid the "filtering out" process that blocks problems from awareness. Become more sensitive to problems by looking for them.
- Never accept the first solution you think of. Generate a number of possible solutions; then select the best from among them.
- Beware of your own defensiveness concerning the problem. When you feel threatened by a problem, you are less likely to think of creative solutions to it.
- Get feedback on your solutions from others who are less personally involved.
- Try to think of what solutions someone else might think of for your problem.
- Mentally test out opposites to your solutions. When a group of engineers tried to think of ways to dispose of smashed auto glass, someone suggested trying to *find uses* for it instead. Fiberglass was the result!
- Give your ideas a chance to incubate. Successful problem solvers report that they frequently put a problem away for a while, and later on the solution comes to them full blown. It is clear that they have been thinking about the problem on a subconscious level, which is often superior to a conscious, logical approach.
- Diagram your thinking. Sometimes ideas seem to fork, like the branches on a tree, with one idea producing two more, each of which produces two more, and so on. Diagramming will let you follow each possible branch to its completion.
- Be self-confident. Many ideas die because the person who conceived them thought they might be silly. Studies show that females have been especially vulnerable here.
- Think about the general aspects of a problem before getting to its specifics.
- Restate the problem several different ways.
- Become an "idea jotter." A notebook of ideas can prove surprisingly useful.
- Divide a problem, then solve its various parts.
- Really good ideas frequently require some personal risk on the part of the problem solver. In this we are like the turtle, which can never move forward until it sticks its neck out.

Transition

We wish that all children could go through the sometimes turbulent period of puberty and reach the other side with a normal, healthy body. We wish they could negotiate adolescence so successfully that they become energetic, creative, lifelong learners.

Unfortunately, we know that this is not the case. Drug abuse, deep depression or other mental illness, delinquency—these are a major part of the lives of too many of our youth today. If we are to have a complete view of this developmental stage, we must also investigate this negative side of life. That is what we will do in chapter 14.

Key Ideas

1. The speculations of early theorists, who lacked adequate data, led to a number of wrong conclusions.
2. There is no single event marking the onset of puberty but rather a complex set of events, whose effects may be sudden or gradual.
3. Jean Piaget describes the early-middle adolescent periods as the formal operational stage, in which groups of concrete operations are combined to become formal operations.
4. John Flavell suggests there are seven aspects of this fourth Piagetian stage: the real versus the possible; empirico-inductive methods versus hypothetico-deductive methods;

intra-propositional versus inter-propositional thinking; combinations and permutations; inversion and compensation; information-processing strategy; and consolidations and solidification.

    5. Critical thinking, the "correct assessment and interpretation of statements," may be said to be composed of convergent and divergent thinking.

    6. The use of metaphor is an important aspect of the creative process, especially during the teen years.

    7. Creativity, giftedness, and intelligence are three different traits, although they are related.

Key Terms

Adolescent egocentrism	Maturation
Amenorrhea	Maximum growth spurt
Combinations	Menarche
Compensation	Normal range of development
Consolidation	Permutations
Delayed puberty	Precociousness
Empirico-inductive method	Prodigiousness
Gynecomastia	Psychosocial dwarfism
Hirsutism	Puberty
Hormonal balance	Real versus the possible
Hypothetico-deductive method	Secular trend
Information-processing strategy	Skeletal growth
Inter-propositional thinking	Solidification
Intra-propositional thinking	Use of metaphor
Inversion	Virilism

What Do You Think?

    1. Should children be taught about their body functions in school? Should this teaching include sexuality? If so, at what grade should it start?

    2. What was the beginning of puberty for you? Why do you think so?

    3. Do you think fairy tales are really symbolic descriptions of real-life events? Can you suggest some?

    4. In reading about the progress the mind makes during adolescence, could you remember these changes happening to you? Describe some of your memories of those times.

    5. Studies show that most people believe they are below average in creativity, which cannot be true, of course. By definition, half of all people are above average. Where do you fit as compared to all of your acquaintances on this trait? Why?

    6. Do you believe you can "disinhibit" (free up) your creative abilities? How should you start? Why don't you?

Suggested Readings

Blume, Judy. (1970). *Are you there, God? It's me, Margaret*. New York: Bradbury. Although written for teens, this book has a wealth of insights into pubertal change, at least for females. Our women friends tell us that Blume really understands.

Erikson, Erik. (1969). *Gandhi's truth*. New York: Norton. This is one of the best examples of "psychohistory," which is the biography of a person as seen from the two disciplines of psychology and history. Mahatma Gandhi's quest to free India from British domination makes for good reading. The stories about the forces that influenced his youthful thinking are particularly instructive.

Potok, Chaim. (1967). *The chosen*. New York: Fawcett. This is the story of a boy whose father is a rabbi in the strict Hassidic (Jewish) religion. It chronicles the struggle he has over his desire to be a good student and still be "normal."

· *Chapter 14* ·

The Troubled Adolescent

In my dream I saw the world
in a frame of imitation gold.
I heard fear pounding in my ears
And in the white light I could see only black.
Blinded by the sound of darkness
I saw invisible fingers
And heard nonexistent sounds.
I was a nonexistent person
In a nonexistent world.
God help me
As I stab myself with a
Rubber knife.
By a 16-year-old girl living in an adolescent residential center

Although the transition from childhood to adulthood can be difficult, the majority of adolescents are able to negotiate it successfully. Add the problems of substance abuse, mental disturbance, and/or crime, however, and a great deal of unhappiness always results. As the poem above suggests, some teens suffer from two or even all three of these problems. In fact, sad to say, having one of the problems increases the chance that you will suffer from the other two. Therefore, no study of American adolescence is complete without taking a hard look at these distressing areas.

How widespread are these difficulties? The teenagers themselves can probably best answer this question. In a recent and highly scientific poll of 13–17 year olds (Roper, 1987), they were asked how often certain behaviors occurred "a lot" and "sometimes" among their fellow students. Figure 14.1 presents the results.

The overall numbers are not a cause for rejoicing. Females and those in middle adolescence see the problems as more widespread than their counterparts. Whites are tied or ahead of African-Americans in all categories but crime and pregnancy. Surprisingly, upper and upper middle-class youths are tied or ahead of the other two groups in all areas but crime and pregnancy (and this difference may be due to their greater access to lawyers and doctors). No region of the country has a monopoly on the problems, but public schools are ahead of private schools in every category. Of course this latter finding is probably more tied to socioeconomic background than to the type of schooling.

Let us turn now to a review of the research in each of the three general problem areas: substance abuse, mental disturbance, and delinquent behavior.

Substance Abuse

Prevalence of Use

It is difficult to say with precision how widespread substance abuse is. Studies differ, from year to year, region to region, and disappointingly, from one another even when year and region are the same. One of the most recent intensive studies of high school seniors (Johnston, O'Malley, & Bachman, 1987) found a decrease in marijuana, an increase in cocaine and crack cocaine, and a leveling off in alcohol (which could not get a lot higher than it is).

The Roper study mentioned above also looked at how many teens have used a variety of drugs, and how recently they used them. These data are presented in Figure 14.2. Unlike Figure 14.1, which reports what teens think their *fellow students* are doing, Figure 14.2 summarizes what they say *they themselves* are doing.

The newest drug to hit the adolescent subculture is MDMA (also known as Adam or Ecstacy). It produces a smoother, longer euphoria than cocaine and is one of the

There has been considerable change in the choices drug users are making in recent years. For example, crack cocaine has become much more popular than hallucinogens such as LSD. Unfortunately, the newer drugs are much more likely to be lethal.

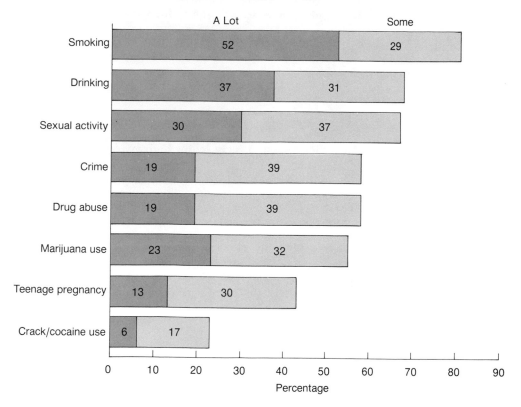

Figure 14.1 *What goes on among fellow students? (Asked of teenagers only)*

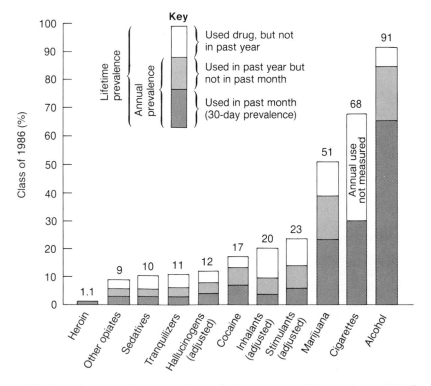

Figure 14.2 *Prevalence and recency of use of eleven types of drugs, class of 1986.*

Table 14.1   Frequently Seen Stages in Adolescent Substance Use

A. Experimental Use (late grade school or early junior high years)

Intake

1. Occasional beer drinking, pot smoking, or use of inhalants (glue sniffing, sniffing aerosols, etc.). Usually done weekends or during the summer, mostly with friends.
2. Easy to get high (low tolerance).
3. Thrill of acting grown up and defying parents is part of the high.

What the World Sees

Often unplanned, using beer sneaked from home, model glue, etc.

Little use of "harder" drugs at this stage.

B. More Regular Use (late junior high and early senior high years)

Intake

4. Tolerance increases with increased use. More parties involving kegs, pot, possibly pills or hash. Acceptance of the idea that "everyone does it" and wanting to be in on it. Disdain of "local pot" or 3.2 beer. Staying out later, even all night.
5. Use of wine or liquor *may* increase, but beer remains the most popular drink. Willing to suffer hangovers.
6. Consumption increases and pride in being able to "handle it" increases.
7. Use on week nights begins, and school skipping may increase.
8. Blackouts may begin, and talk with friends about "What did I do last night?"
9. Solitary use begins—even smoking at home (risk-taking increases). Concentration on fooling parents or teachers when high.
10. Preoccupation with use begins. The next high is carefully planned and anticipated. Source of supply is a matter of worry.
11. Use during the day starts. Smoking before school to "make it through the morning." Use of "dust" may increase, or experiments with acid, speed, or barbs may continue.

What the World Sees

More money involved, false IDs used. Alcohol or pot bought and shared with friends.

Parents aware of use. May start a long series of "groundings" for late hours. Lying to parents about the extent of use and use of money for drugs.

School activities are dropped, especially sports. Grades will drop. Truancy increases. Friends not using drugs are dropped. Weekend-long parties may start.

From *Adolescent Chemical Use Chart.* © Dennis D. Nelson. Published by CompCare Publishers, Minneapolis, MN. Used by permission.

so-called designer drugs (Buffum, 1988; Buffum & Moser, 1986). Its use is definitely on the rise, in part because a number of psychiatrists have said that it can cure psychological ills.

As you can see, drug use among teens is a serious problem in this country. But people who use drugs do not become abusers overnight. What is the usual sequence of events leading to the problem?

Stages of Substance Abuse

As a result of his study of high school students, Nelson (1980) has suggested that certain stages represent the sequence that usually occurs in the use of illegal drugs (see Table 14.1). This stage theory does not imply that all students go through all the stages, but almost all follow the same sequence up to some point. It should be noted that in this theory, as in most studies, hallucinogens include PCP, LSD, psilocybin, mescaline, peyote, and chemical hallucinogens (DMT, DOM, PMA, and MDA). Sedatives include tranquilizers, barbiturates, and methaqualone (Young, 1987).

As you can see from reading Table 14.1, the road to addiction is usually quite predictable. The steps that lead to the last stage are many and may not proceed in just this order, but if no one intervenes, they lead inexorably to disaster. The change

Table 14.1 *Continued*

C. Daily Preoccupation

Intake

12. Use of harder drugs increases (speed, acid, barbs, dust).
13. Number of times high during the week increases. Amount of money spent for drugs increases (concealing savings withdrawals from parents).
14. "Social use" decreases— getting loaded rather than just high. Being high becomes normal.
15. Buying more and using more—all activities seem to include drug use and/or alcohol.
16. Possible theft to get money to ensure a supply. There may be a contact with "bigger" dealers.
17. Solitary use increases. User will isolate self from drug-using friends.
18. Lying about or hiding the drug supply. Stash may become concealed from friends.

What the World Sees

Possible dealing or fronting for others.

Possible court trouble for minor consumption or possession. May be arrested for driving while intoxicated. Probation may result.

May try to cut down or quit to convince self that there is no problem with drugs.
Most straight friends are dropped.

Money owed for drugs may increase. More truancy and fights with parents about drug use.

D. Dependency

Intake

19. Getting high during school or at work. Difficult to face the day without drugs. Drugs are used to escape self.
20. Possible use of injectable drugs. Friends are "burnouts" (and may take pride in the label).
21. Can't tell what normal behavior is any more—normal means being stoned nearly constantly.
22. Physical condition worsens. Loss of weight, more frequent illnesses, memory suffers. Flashbacks may increase. Thoughts of suicide may increase.

What the World Sees

Guilt feelings increase. Questioning own use but unable to control urge.

Low self-image and self-hate. Casual sexual involvement. Continued denial of problem. School dropped. Dealing may increase along with police involvement. Parents may "give up."

Paranoia increases. Cost of habit increases, with most of money going to habit.

Loss of control over use.

is often so gradual that the abuser fails to realize it is happening. And of course most abusers use an array of defense mechanisms to justify their behavior. One rationalization is that drugs enhance their sexual performance.

Drugs and Sex

A number of researchers have looked at the relationship between the use of drugs and sexual functioning (Buffum, 1988; Buffum & Moser, 1986; Higgins & Stitzer, 1986; Solow & Solow, 1986; Zabin, Hardy, Smith, & Hirsch, 1986). The purpose of these studies was to evaluate the claims of many youths that drugs make them more sexually capable and increase their enjoyment of the sex act. It is alleged that drugs stimulate sexual activity through releasing inhibitions and through direct stimulation of desire.

There has been remarkable accord in the findings. Only amphetamines actually enhance sexual performance, and they do so only for a limited time. Marijuana may stimulate sexual desire under some circumstances because it disinhibits the fears some people have of sexuality. Alcohol also has a disinhibitory effect in small doses, but in moderate and heavy doses it decreases the ability to function. Barbiturates and psychedelics, the other two drugs investigated in these studies, appear to have no effect on sex whatever.

Some youth erroneously believe that the use of drugs or alcohol will heighten their sexual performance and enjoyment.

The studies all conclude that response is mainly dependent on the psychological makeup of the individuals involved and on the setting. Those experienced in the use of drugs with sex say that even when there is a good result, it is only transitory.

Another interesting finding of several of the studies was that those who use drugs regularly are more sexually active than those who do not. Goode (1972) discovered that drug users are not only sexually more active, but they start their sexual activity at an earlier age and with a more diverse selection of partners. Again, the studies seem to agree that the major reason that drugs are helpful in the sex act is because the drug users *think* they are going to be. It may also be that high risk-takers are more likely to indulge in both sex and drugs.

Of particular concern is the finding that those most likely to combine drug use (including alcohol) with sex are also those who are most likely to engage in unprotected sex (Buffum, 1988). They are also most likely to engage in activities that involve the highest risk of getting AIDS.

Table 14.2 offers some essential information on the most used controlled substances.

Ethnic Group and Abuse

Although there is not a great deal known about the comparative abuse of substances by ethnic groups, one study looked at the number of arrests for drug use per 10,000 members of an ethnic group, with seven groups being considered (Asian-American Drug Abuse Program, 1978). It was found that African-American, Mexican-American, and Native American arrests outnumbered white arrests by three to two. Arrests for Japanese- and Chinese-Americans were negligible. Of course, these data may reflect biases of the legal system rather than actual use.

One of the most interesting factors in substance abuse has to do with whether or not a teen's family has arrived in this country in the previous generation or two, as has been the case with so many Asian-Americans. Tessler (1980) suggested a series of interrelationships between these variables, as presented in Table 14.3. This table shows that conflicts between traditional cultural patterns, immigration factors, and the mores of American society often bring about an increase in the use of drugs, particularly alcohol. This is especially so for adolescents, who are in the most vulnerable age group. The table is not meant to represent what always happens, but a high percentage of the time this is what occurs.

Estrada and colleagues (1982) reported on the use of alcohol by a group of 107 Hispanic seventh- and eighth-grade junior high school students (age 13 to 16) in Los Angeles. Subjects responded to a self-administered questionnaire concerning personal issues, social characteristics, and family composition. Also studied were alcohol consumption, school performance, and a number of other behaviors. Findings suggest that the strongest link is between the use of alcohol and marijuana.

Dembo (1981) questioned whether the degree of drug involvement of 1,101 African-American and Puerto Rican seventh graders resulted from their home composition, relationships with parents, attitudes toward school, machismo values, and/or identification with drug-involved peers. Data were obtained via questionnaires and surveys. Results showed that peer-oriented attitudes and behaviors probably provide the most likely prediction of drug use for these minority youth.

Table 14.2 Controlled Substances: Uses and Effects

Drugs	Usual Methods of Administration	Possible Effects	Effects of Overdose	Withdrawal Syndrome
Narcotics				
Opium	Oral, smoked	Euphoria, drowsiness, respiratory depression, constricted pupils, nausea	Slow and shallow breathing, clammy skin, convulsions, coma, possible death	Watery Eyes, runny nose, yawning, loss of appetite, irritability, tremors, panic, chills and sweating, cramps, nausea
Morphine	Oral, injected, smoked			
Codeine	Oral, injected			
Heroin	Injected, sniffed, smoked			
Hydromorphone	Oral, injected			
Meperidine (pethidine)	Oral, injected			
Methadone	Oral, injected			
Other narcotics	Oral, injected			
Depressants				
Chloral Hydrate	Oral	Slurred speech, disorientation, drunken behavior without odor of alcohol	Shallow respiration, cold and clammy skin, dilated pupils, weak and rapid pulse, coma, possible death	Anxiety, insomnia, tremors, delirium, convulsions, possible death
Barbiturates	Oral, injected			
Glutethimide	Oral, injected			
Methaqualone	Oral, injected			
Benzodiazepines	Oral, injected			
Other depressants	Oral, injected			
Stimulants				
Cocaine	Sniffed, injected, smoked	Increased alertness, excitation, euphoria, increased pulse rate and blood pressure, insomnia, loss of appetite	Agitation, increase in body temperature, hallucinations, convulsions, possible death	Apathy, long periods of sleep, irritability, depression, disorientation
Amphetamines	Oral, injected			
Phenmetrazine	Oral, injected			
Methylphenidate	Oral, injected			
Other stimulants	Oral			
Hallucinogens				
LSD	Oral	Illusions and hallucinations, poor perception of time and distance	Longer, more intense "trip" episodes, psychosis, possible death	Withdrawal syndrome not reported
Mescaline and peyote	Oral, injected			
Amphetamine variants	Oral, injected			
Phencyclidine	Smoked, oral,			
Phencyclidine analogs	Injected			
Other hallucinogens	Oral, injected, smoked, sniffed			
Cannabis				
Marijuana	Smoked, oral	Euphoria, relaxed inhibitions, increased appetite, disoriented behavior	Fatigue, paranoia, possible psychosis	Insomnia, hyperactivity, and decreased appetite occasionally reported
Tetrahydrocannabinol				
Hashish				
Hashish oil				

Source: Drug Enforcement Administration, *Drug Enforcement Fall 1982*. Washington, DC: U.S. Department of Justice.

Table 14.3.   Asian-American Cultural Clashes

Traditional Cultural Patterns	vs. Immigration Factors	vs. American Society
Close-knit family with strong father.	Father has to hold down more than one job to support family and is unable to provide the strong influence tradition demands.	More democratic approach to family structure. Mothers work. Increase of single-parent families.
High parental expectations.	Language difficulties; inability to make friends; difference in educational systems.	More tolerance of children who are not high achievers.
Shame associated with having a problem.	Immigration brings many adjustment problems.	More openness regarding problems, and more willingness to seek professional help when necessary.
Pride in one's worth and value to oneself, the family, and the community.	Inability to communicate, obtain a job, achieve a level of academic excellence.	Prejudice, stereotyping, both old and new; exotic, humble, inscrutable, studious, gang member or participant in Tong Wars.
Women are supposed to stay home and raise the children.	Women may have to enter job market to help support family.	Acceptable for women to enter job market and lead a more independent life-style.
Drinking is perceived in many cases as being an acceptable part of family and community life. Alcohol a part of ritual and festivals.	Increased drinking because of pressure may not be considered a problem.	Drinking not perceived as being culturally important.

From *Drugs, Kids and Schools: Practical Strategies for Educators and Other Concerned Adults* by Diane Jane Tessler. Copyright © 1980 by Diane Jane Tessler. Reprinted by permission of Scott, Foresman and Company.

BOX 14.1

Do You Have a Drinking Problem?

The following questions may help you to decide whether you have a drinking problem:

- Do you drink to escape from the pressures of college life?
- Do you sometimes skip classes because of hangovers?
- Do you drink more than your friends?
- Do you drink to escape from reality, boredom, or loneliness?
- Do your friends or loved ones express concern about your drinking?
- Do you drink and get drunk even when intending to stay sober?
- Do you drink when you are alone?
- Do you drink frequently to a state of intoxication?
- Have you had two or more "blackouts" (can't remember some or all of what happened while you were drinking) in the past year?
- Have you gotten into trouble with the police and/or college officials as a result of your behavior while drinking?

If you must answer *yes* to any of these questions, you may have a problem with alcohol, and perhaps you should seek advice from trained personnel. If you must answer *yes* to more than two of the questions, especially those on the second half of the list, you definitely have reason for concern, and should seek help.

Source: Adapted from Chebator, 1984.

BOX 14.2

Talking to Teenagers about Drinking

The U.S. Department of Transportation (1976) has made a number of suggestions for talking to teenagers about their drinking behavior:

- Honestly explore your own drinking behavior before you talk with teenagers.
- Be honest in expressing your feelings and in stating your own values and preferences. Encourage the same from them.
- Be calm, firm, and consistent.
- Remember that you're sharing ideas and information about drinking.
- Don't put teenagers on the witness stand or demand a confession.
- Recognize that adolescents are not always able to control the situation they find themselves in.
- Tell teenagers you want to hear what they have to say and to learn what they know about drinking and driving.
- Be a good listener, even when you may not agree.
- Keep to the point. No matter where the discussion leads, and no matter what kind of reaction you may get or may feel, keep forcefully in mind that this discussion concerns only the problem of drinking.

Crime and Abuse

Although it is commonly thought that drug users, especially those who use hard drugs, are regularly involved in criminal activities, reliable data on this aspect of drug use is surprisingly limited. FBI statistics (Federal Bureau of Investigation, 1989) indicate that the drug most associated with crime is alcohol. In 40% of assaults and 35% of rapes, those convicted had been "under the influence."

Research into the relationship between substance abuse and crime (and other undesirable behaviors) was carried out by Santana (1979). This study looked at 19 types of undesirable behavior, and compared their occurrence among drug abusers to their occurrence among nonusers. The disturbing finding of this study was that, in every case but one, the users were much more likely to commit undesirable behaviors than nonusers. Even in the single exception, for arson, the behavior was evenly divided. This does not prove that drug use causes crime, but does indicate a strong relationship between the two.

Substance Use and Personal Relationships

There has long been a debate as to whether adolescent drug usage is related more to family circumstances than to interaction with peers (Detting & Beauvais, 1987). Most studies have indicated that the typical drug user has problems with his or her parents. Tudor and colleagues (1980) found that drug users had conflicts with their parents in the following areas:

- They wanted to be allowed to make their own decisions without having any advice from their parents.

- They did not believe that they should be limited to only those friends their parents endorsed.

- They were less likely to desire affection from their mothers and fathers, nor did they feel close to them.

- They did not desire to imitate their parents.

Anti-drug media campaigns have encouraged drug addicts to seek help through drug rehabilitation programs. A number of these programs, such as the Straight Program, have a high success rate in rehabilitating these addicts.

One other series of studies (Huba, Wingard, & Bentler, 1979, 1980a, 1980b, 1980c) found that although relationships with parents do affect substance abuse in early adolescence, as students get to high school the parental effect drops off:

❖ *The finding that by the ninth grade boys and girls have drug use patterns that are related more to perceived patterns in the peer culture than to perceived patterns in the adult culture suggests that adult models become* relatively *less important (1980b p. 464).*

Combating Substance Abuse

The first step toward reducing the effects of drugs and alcohol on our youth is improving our ability to determine, in the early stages, who is at risk. There is good news on this front. A recent study (Christiansen, Roehling, Smith, & Goldman, 1989) found that a number of measures administered in the seventh and eighth grade were significant predictors of drinking behavior one year later. These measures included a questionnaire on attitudes toward drinking and such demographic variables as parental ethnic background, religious affiliation, parents' occupations, and parental drinking attitudes.

The effectiveness of treating those identified as having a problem is another story. It is estimated that as many as 15% of all American teens need treatment for compulsive drug/alcohol use (Falco, 1988). Unfortunately, there is very little research on treatment programs, and those that do exist, such as the Washington-based Straight Program, are expensive and hard to gain admittance to. There is even less known about educational and prevention programs designed to reduce the *demand* for drugs, which drug abuse experts now believe to be the best approach to this problem. It is even more difficult to reach those youth who have left school and are at even higher risk for substance abuse. In many of our larger cities, nearly half of all teens fall into this category.

Falco (1988) suggests that

❖ *The Anti-Drug Act of 1986 provides an opportunity to develop a comprehensive national strategy which addresses both supply control and demand reduction efforts. A key part of such a strategy will be to plan effective use of substantial new prevention and treatment research funds (p. v).*

She recommends that a major part of these funds be spent researching the mechanisms underlying adolescent risk-taking behavior, and the impact of social policy on abuse.

No prevention program is likely to be effective if the climate in the school is conducive to drug abuse. Tessler (1980) argues that to find out what the climate is in any particular school, it is necessary to administer a survey such as the one in Box 14.3. The survey is easy to administer to students, teachers, and administrators alike. It takes only a few minutes to complete. Tessler claims that

❖ *the results will help everyone get in touch with some of the silent agents responsible for a poor school environment which would make the success of any effective drug education impossible (p. 114).*

You may wish to answer the questions in the box in regard to your high school. That would be a good way to remind yourself of the factors that can lead to serious substance abuse. You may also want to send a copy to the high school's principal.

BOX 14.3

School Climate Survey

Does your school

1. Have racial or ethnic problems?   Yes _____   No _____
2. Have a high truancy rate?   Yes _____   No _____
3. Have cases of vandalism? Violence? Serious fights? Gangs? Drug problem?
   Yes _____   No _____
4. Have many cases of student arrests?   Yes _____   No _____
   (If you don't know the answer to all the above, local law enforcement agencies
   may be able to give you some information.)
5. Plan events that encourage school unity?   Yes _____   No _____
6. Have good recreational and extracurricular activities that are well supported by
   the student body and staff?   Yes _____   No _____
7. Provide good counseling and health services?   Yes _____   No _____
8. Give everyone the opportunity to respect their own heritage and those of
   others?   Yes _____   No _____
9. Involve parents in important school decisions and events?   Yes _____   No _____
10. Seek a constructive bond with the community: through urban or neighborhood
    improvement projects, with law enforcement, with the handicapped, with the
    elderly, and so on?   Yes _____   No _____
11. Use community agencies or the expertise of residents to help with school
    programs?   Yes _____   No _____
12. Direct students and parents to community resources that will improve their
    lives?   Yes _____   No _____
13. Provide students with real leadership opportunities (not simply token positions)?
    Yes _____   No _____
14. Have an "emotional climate" in which students, faculty, and administrators feel
    free to express their thoughts and feelings?   Yes _____   No _____
15. Encourage students to be creative and curious?   Yes _____   No _____
16. Help students explore and appreciate their own special talents?
    Yes _____   No _____
17. Allow students to clarify values?   Yes _____   No _____
18. Help students to deal effectively with inner and outer conflicts?
    Yes _____   No _____
19. Provide problem-solving and decision-making experiences for students?
    Yes _____   No _____
20. Help students develop goals for the future?   Yes _____   No _____

From *Drugs, Kids and Schools: Practical Strategies for Educators and Other Concerned Adults* by Diane Jane Tessler. Copyright © 1980 by Diane Jane Tessler. Reprinted by permission of Scott, Foresman and Company.

Questions 1 to 4 relate to situations that can cause antisocial or antiauthority behavior. School and police records can also reveal whether this kind of problem exists in the school. Questions 5 to 9 concern school services and special programs. Responses here can indicate a lack of school unity.

Responses to questions 10 to 12 reveal how members of the school community feel the school fits into the life of the larger community it serves. They also indicate whether or not neighborhood resources are used for the benefit of those attending the school. Questions 13 and 14 deal with whether or not the three main segments of the school community—students, faculty, and administrators—are able to communicate effectively with each other. Responses to questions 15 to 20 will indicate whether or not there are opportunities for students to develop self-respect and self-awareness. One should tabulate both the total responses and the three subtotals for the three segments of the school population. If these data indicate a problem in one of the six areas—antisocial responses, services and programs, community relations, communications, affective areas, and general responses—then committees should be established to improve the situation in the problem area. Tessler says that her experience with this approach shows that such changes can go a long way in making the abuse of substances less desirable to students.

It must be admitted that much of the information we have on abuse is not totally reliable, because of the situations in which drug use must be studied. In the next area that we will consider, the problems of mental disturbance, there is better data because it is usually studied in the controlled setting of the hospital.

Mental Disturbance

A number of psychologists and psychoanalysts (most notably Freud) have suggested that it is normal in adolescence to have distressing, turbulent, unpredictable thoughts that in an adult would be considered pathological. Here is an example of this view:

❖   *The fluidity of the adolescent's self-image, his changing aims and aspirations, sex drives, unstable powers of repression, and his struggle to adapt his childhood standards of right and wrong to the needs of maturity, bring into focus every conflict, past and present, that he has failed to solve. Protective covering of the personality is stripped off, and the deeper emotional currents are laid bare (Ackerman, 1958, pp. 227–228).*

This disruptive state is partly characteristic of the identity stages of confusion and moratorium (see chap. 12). Identity confusion is sometimes typified by withdrawal from reality (Erikson, 1958, 1968). There can be occasional distortions in time perspective. Mental disturbance also often makes intimacy with another person impossible. These characteristics are also seen in the moratorium stage, but they tend to be of much shorter duration.

How common and how serious are these problems? The picture is not clear. Summarizing decades of research, Kimmel and Weiner (1985) conclude that true **psychopathology** (mental illness) is relatively rare during adolescence. It is impossible to determine the frequency of mental illness, however, because of current disagreements over its definition. Weiner (1970) cites numerous studies, most notably Masterson's, which give us considerable reason to believe that "adolescent turmoil," while common, does not really constitute psychopathology.

Studies *do* indicate that when adolescents become seriously disturbed and do not receive appropriate treatment quickly, the chances of them "growing out" of their problems are dim (Walker & Greene, 1987; Wilson, 1987). Weiner (1970) warns that

❖   *An indiscriminate application of "adolescent turmoil" and "he'll-grow-out-of-it" notions to symptomatic adolescents runs the grave risk of discouraging the attention that may be necessary to avert serious psychological disturbance (p. 66).*

It is not clear that a greater number of adolescents are experiencing mental illness, but the number of them being *admitted* for psychiatric care is skyrocketing. From 1980 to 1984, for example, admissions of teens to psychiatric hospitals increased 480%—from 10,764 to 48,375 nationally (Select Committee on Children,

The number of adolescents being admitted for psychiatric care has been skyrocketing in recent years.

Table 14.4	Juvenile Psychiatric Admissions in the Minneapolis/St. Paul Area		
Year	**Number**	**Rate per 1,000**	**Patient days**
1976	1,123	91	46,718
1977	1,062	88	53,730
1978	1,268	107	60,660
1979	1,623	142	68,949
1980	1,775	158	74,201
1981	1,745	159	72,381
1982	1,813	165	71,267
1983	2,031	184	76,899
1984	3,047	299	83,015

Youth, and Families, 1985). Table 14.4 shows the amazing change from 1976 to 1984 in the Minneapolis/St. Paul area. These data may reflect a more positive societal attitude toward receiving help with emotional problems.

Types of Mental Disorders

The question of what kinds of mental illness make up this increase has not received much attention recently. The study by Rosen and colleagues (1965), though dated, examined a very large number of cases. It gives us an idea of the types of mental disorders that adolescents suffer, and there is no reason to assume that these data have changed greatly. Approximately 4% of the illnesses of both males and females were accounted for by acute and chronic brain disorders (a malfunction of some part of the brain), 10% by mental retardation, and 6.5% by schizophrenia (a serious distortion of reality).

In Britain, Rutter (1980) reviewed surveys and found that about 15% of 15 year olds were afflicted by psychiatric disorders, although as many as 6% more went undetected. In a more recent study, Horwitz and White (1987) studied differences between male and female adolescents. They found that 11% of the males suffered from neurotic disorders, such as anxiety, depression, and obsessive-compulsive reaction, compared to 18% of the females.

Although the overall picture is less than clear, we have a great deal of data on specific adolescent mental disturbances. Chief among them are eating disorders and depression and suicide.

Anorexia Nervosa

Anorexia nervosa is a syndrome of self-starvation that mainly affects adolescent and young adult females, who account for 95% of the cases (Larson & Johnson, 1981; Mintz & Betz, 1988). It is characterized by an "intense fear of becoming obese, disturbance of body image, significant weight loss, refusal to maintain a minimal normal body weight, and amenorrhea. The disturbance cannot be accounted for by a known physical disorder" (American Psychiatric Association, 1985).

Health professionals have seen an alarming rise in the incidence of this disorder in the last fifteen to twenty years among young women (Bruch, 1981; Rosen, Gross, & Vara, 1987). Whether there is an actual increase of anorexia nervosa or whether it is now being more readily recognized has yet to be determined.

Anorexia nervosa has become an increasingly frequent problem among adolescent females.

The specific criteria for anorexia nervosa are

- Onset prior to age 25.

- Weight loss of at least 25% of original body weight.

- Distorted, implacable attitudes toward eating, food, or weight that override hunger, admonitions, reassurance, and threats, including:

     Denial of illness, with a failure to recognize nutritional needs.

     Apparent enjoyment in losing weight, with overt manifestations that food refusal is a pleasurable indulgence.

     A desired body image of extreme thinness, with evidence that it is rewarding to the person to achieve and maintain this state.

     Unusual hoarding and handling of food.

- No known medical illness that could account for the anorexia and weight loss.

- No other known psychiatric disorder, particularly primary affective disorders, schizophrenia, or obsessive, compulsive, or phobic (fearful) neuroses. (Even though it may appear phobic and obsessional, food refusal alone is not sufficient to qualify as an obsessive, compulsive, or phobic disorder.)

- At least two of the following manifestations: amenorrhea (loss of menses); lanugo (soft downy hair covering body); bradycardia (heart rate of less than 60); periods of overactivity; episodes of bulimia; vomiting (may be self-induced).

Bulimia Nervosa

Bulimia nervosa is a disorder related to anorexia nervosa and sometimes combined with it. It is characterized by

❖ *. . . episodic binge-eating accompanied by an awareness that the eating pattern is abnormal, fear of not being able to stop eating voluntarily, and depressed mood and self-deprecating thoughts following the eating binges. The bulimic episodes are not due to Anorexia Nervosa or any known physical disorder (American Psychiatric Association, 1985).*

Bulimia has been observed in women above or below weight, as well as in those who are normal (Lowenkopf, 1982).

The specific criteria of bulimia are

     Repeated episodes of binge-eating.
     Awareness that one's eating pattern is abnormal.
     Fear of not being able to stop eating.
     Depressed mood and self-deprecation after binges.

Anorectics and bulimics share emotional and behavioral traits, despite their clinical differences. The most characteristic symptoms specific to these disorders are the preoccupation with food and the persistent determination to be slim, rather than the behaviors that result from that choice (Bruch, 1981).

A number of new approaches to treatment and therapy are currently being researched (Scott, 1988). Although success rates are not high, the situation in either disorder is usually so complex and potentially hazardous that only qualified personnel should attempt to treat victims.

Depression[1]

The term *depression* can have many different meanings and manifestations. Originally a word for a pathological symptom, it has found its way into common usage by the general public, and its meaning has been greatly broadened.

Depression is not a specific syndrome or illness in itself. It is considered to be a basic affective state that, like anxiety, can be of long or short duration, of low or high intensity, and can occur in a wide variety of conditions at any stage of development. In certain circumstances, such as in reaction to a death in the family, it is a normal and appropriate affective response.

Depression becomes pathological when it occurs in inappropriate circumstances, is of too long duration, or is of such great intensity as to be out of proportion to the cause. Depression is harmful to a person's development when it interferes with the capacity to work, to relate to others, or to maintain the healthy functioning of essential physical needs for sleep and nutrition. Serious depressive conditions can upset a person's functioning in all of these areas and more.

Symptoms of Depression

The symptoms of depression may be classified in one of four areas (Beck, 1967):

- *Emotional manifestations:* dejected mood, negative self-attitudes, reduced experience of satisfaction, decreased involvement with people or activities, crying spells, and loss of sense of humor.

- *Cognitive manifestations:* low self-esteem, negative expectations for the future, self-punitive attitudes, indecisiveness, and distorted body image.

- *Motivational manifestations:* loss of motivation to perform tasks, escapist and withdrawal wishes, suicidal thoughts, and increased dependency.

- *Physical manifestations:* appetite loss, sleep disturbance, decreased sexual interest, and increased fatigability.

Not all depressed individuals will show all of these symptoms, of course, but they are likely to exhibit one or more symptoms from these four categories.

There is some evidence that African-Americans may be more vulnerable to depression than white Americans. Freeman (1982) examined emotional distress, as assessed by the Hopkins Symptom Checklist, among 607 urban African-American high school students 15 to 18 years of age. Subjects reported high distress primarily about feelings of disadvantage, volatile anger, interpersonal sensitivity, and loneliness. Females were significantly more likely than males to suffer emotional distress, although several of the leading distress items were experienced equally by both groups.

Causes of Depression

Adolescents develop depression for a variety of reasons:

- *Capacity for denial.* Young persons appear able to deny the reality of painful conditions or affects with greater effectiveness than adults.

- *Tendency to act out feelings.* The impulsiveness of adolescence makes it more likely that feelings will find expression in actions.

---

[1]The authors wish to acknowledge the contribution of Dr. David Curran to this section.

The desire to avoid dependence and helplessness. Most adolescents want to feel independent, strong, and able to control their problems. They do not want to feel dependent on adults or at the mercy of events or feelings.

The causes of depression, both normal and pathological, can usually be generalized under the heading of *loss* (Cantwell & Carlson, 1983; Carlson, 1983; Crumley, 1982; Curran, 1984; Petzel & Cline, 1978; Seiden & Freitas, 1980; Shaffer & Fisher, 1981; Tishler & McHenry, 1983; Weiner, 1970). Seriously depressed individuals have usually experienced a series of losses, which may include losses of loved ones through death or relocation.

Depressed adolescents will often recount a history of parental separation, death, or divorce; a series of moves; death or loss of pets; moving away from trusted friends; or express the feeling that childhood was a far better state than adolescence. There ensues a feeling of hopelessness or despair at not being able to regain the lost objects or status. The anger born of this frustration is often turned against the self with harmful results.

Depression is manifested with increasing frequency during mid- and late adolescence. Females are three times more likely to be affected by depression than males. This is probably because girls, when they are unhappy, tend to be intrapunitive, that is, take some action that is harmful to themselves. Boys tend to be extrapunitive and hurt others. Both tendencies clearly seem to result from the sex roles society has assigned to us.

Masked Depression

Toolan (1975) states that "especially in the adolescent we seldom see a clear picture of depression" (p. 407). He refers to this situation as "masked" depression. It is a distinctive quality of adolescent depression that the symptoms listed on page 367 are often not seen or are in some way obscured (Tishler & McHenry, 1983). It is especially true with boys, who "have a need to hide their true feelings, and particularly the softer, tender, weak sentiments" (Tishler & McHenry, 1983, p. 732).

Depressive Equivalents

Adolescents are predisposed, then, toward alternative forms of dealing with depression. These different symptoms for the same disorder are called *depressive equivalents.* They serve the purpose of allowing adolescents to discharge and seek relief for their feelings, and at the same time avoid a recognition of their problems and feelings. Activity of this type distracts teenagers from thinking of their problems and facing the unpleasant image they hold of themselves and their lives.

Examples of depressive equivalents are:

- *Concentration difficulty.* Often difficulty in concentrating is the earliest, most frequently cited, and only symptom present and the only one of which adolescents are aware. There is a defensive quality to these problems in concentrating. As the mind seeks to avoid awareness of painfully sad thoughts and feelings, it may skip actively from thought to thought, unable to stay still for fear of it being caught by the waiting depressive alternative. The effect on school performance can be devastating.

- *Running away.* Depressed teenagers sometimes run away from the family home, foster home, or other residential setting as a means of actively

Young teens run away from home for a variety of reasons. Sometimes teenagers run away in order to deal with their overwhelming feelings of depression. A recent study found that 160,000 teens are locked out of their homes by their parents and many wind up living on the streets.

dealing with overwhelming feelings that often originate in family relations. Running away provides a temporary release of tension and gives the feeling that one is in control.

- *Sexual acting out.* The urgent necessity to ward off underlying feelings of being unloved and unwanted may push the adolescent toward promiscuous sexual behavior. Close physical contact with another person provides relief. Females are especially vulnerable.

- *Boredom and restlessness.* Depressed adolescents often manifest their condition by swinging between states of short-lived but unbounded enthusiasm and periods of intolerable boredom, listlessness, and generalized indifference. It is to avoid coming any closer to an awareness of depressive effects that the cycle of excited activity and restlessness is again renewed. "I'm bored" is often an unconscious code phrase for "I'm depressed."

- *Aggressive behavior and delinquency.* Depressed adolescents, especially boys, sometimes carry out angry and destructive behavior, such as vandalism, in place of the depressive feelings. These actions may be designed to counteract the poor self-image and feelings of helplessness by artificially inflating the youth's self-image as a strong, fearless, and clever person.

Masked depression and its depressive equivalents are dangerously unhealthy because they obscure the nature and extent of the individual's distress from the teenager and from significant adults. In some cases these behaviors are very self-destructive and jeopardize normal adolescent development in favor of temporary but ineffectual relief.

The Crisis of Death

Although not a true mental disturbance, the death of a loved one almost always causes teens great disturbance. Teenagers seldom have to deal with their own mortality or the deaths of relatives or friends. How do they become aware of death? The development of children's understanding of death closely parallels other aspects of their cognitive development (Nagy, 1982) as described by Piaget (see chap. 2). Until about 2 years of age (the sensorimotor stage), children lack an understanding of death; they become anxious at the absence of a parent or sibling, but this is a temporary state. As children reach the preoperational stage, from 2 to 7 years, they begin to form a concept of death, but they think of it as quite reversible, as a gradual sleeplike state from which the person will probably soon return. Their sense of loss is similar to the feeling that attaches to the loss of a favorite toy, which can be replaced later by another. Toward the end of this stage, death becomes personified, so that it seems to be an invisible being lurking about. For some children, death becomes frightening at this time.

During the years 7 through 11 (the concrete operational stage), death becomes much more of a reality. Children learn that it is not reversible, and become anxious when thinking of the loss of parents or other loved ones. However, they still cannot think of death in terms of themselves. It is only during adolescence (the formal operations stage) that children realize they are mortal and will die someday. Now they have a sense of their own future and a clearer sense of the time dimension itself. As they begin to plan their lives, the inevitability of death becomes real and they develop a new anxiety about death.

❖   *Many adolescents have a clear feeling of the passing of this life stage with the expectation of a specific ending. This sense of the anticipated end of adolescence might be an important parallel to the concept of the finality of death. . . . I would add that ruminations over suicide and forms of actively promoted death encounters would serve to provide the adolescent with a sense of greater temporal definition in his life (Hankoff, 1975, p. 76).*

Adolescents who have a clear sense of their own values, and who have been helped by their parents to form a set of values, are more likely to have a realistic and less fearful attitude toward death. This is not to say that parents can simply give their adolescents an appropriate attitude toward death. Those adolescents in James Marcia's stages of identity diffusion and foreclosure (see chap. 12) are the most likely to have difficulty with the concept of death because of their unwillingness to confront reality.

Kastenbaum (1959) found that youth who are highly religious and who believe in life after death are more likely to show an active interest in the topic and are more likely to conduct their daily lives on the basis of their expectations for the future. They are more apt to have confronted the formal aspects of death.

This is supported by a more recent study by Gray (1987). He administered the *Beck Depression Inventory* to 50 12 to 19 year olds who had had a parent die not less than six months and not more than five years prior to testing. Gray found that those who had achieved a healthy adaptation had had "high levels of informal social support postloss, good relations with the surviving parent prior to loss, a balanced personality style, and presence of religious beliefs" (p. 511).

In her popular book *On Death and Dying,* Elisabeth Kübler-Ross (1969) points out that in "old country" and "primitive" cultures, children have contact with death from an early age. In technological societies, children are shielded from death because it is considered too upsetting. She suggests that when:

❖ *children are allowed to stay at home where a fatality has stricken, and are included in the talk, discussions, and fears, [it] gives them the feeling that they are not alone in the grief and gives them the comfort of shared responsibility and shared mourning. It prepares them gradually and helps them to view death as part of life, an experience which may help them grow and mature. (p. 6)*

Kübler-Ross has concluded from her studies that most persons who know that their death is imminent pass through a sequence of five stages in their attempts to deal with it: denial and isolation, anger, bargaining, depression, and acceptance. Her description of these stages can be useful to those helping an adolescent cope with the dying of a loved one.

Hankoff (1975) has suggested that the absence of initiation rites in technological societies is responsible for the deep fear of death common among adolescents (for more on this, see chap. 17). Initiation rites offer youth a meaningful encounter with this most important aspect of life, death:

❖ *In brief, [initiations into] these mysteries involve sexuality, the spirit world, and death. The mystery of death is brought to the initiand through a ritualized performance in which he is symbolically made to die and be born. This initiatory ritual thus is a template for the important human spiritual experience of self-renewal. In traditional cultures the initiatory ritual tangibly and powerfully provides the youth with knowledge of the spiritual world, the mysteries and privileges of adult status, and emotional participation in death and rebirth experiences (p. 379).*

Suicide

Suicide and attempted suicide among contemporary adolescents is cause for great concern. The extent to which it occurs will be discussed in the last chapter. In this chapter we discuss the psychological aspects of it.

The Meaning of Suicide Attempts Among Teenagers

Only a small percentage of teenagers who make suicide attempts actually die. This is not true of older age groups. With advancing age, suicide attempts increasingly result in death. The relative infrequency of suicidal deaths in teenagers raises questions about the actual meaning and intent of these apparently self-destructive acts.

Several studies have explored the lethal intent in adolescent suicide attempts. Bancroft (1979) reported that among a general population of those admitted to a hospital emergency room because of self-poisoning, 42% stated that they had no intention of dying. Persons in Bancroft's study were considered to have the lowest level of suicidal intent, compared to the 21–35 and the 36-and-over age groups, as learned from the self-reports of subjects. Curran (1984, 1987) asked teenagers who attempted suicide if they thought that adolescents who attempt suicide intend to die. Only 16% named "wish to die" as the primary motive.

Self-poisoning (usually through drug overdose) is by far the most common mode of attempting suicide among female and younger adolescents in general. Self-poisoning, however, is rarely of high lethality. McIntire (1980) reported that only 12% of cases intended to cause death.

It is safe to say that most teenage injuries to self are not attempts to end life. What then is the actual meaning of and reasons for such dramatic acts? What are the hoped-for effects of the suicidal act of low lethality?

Considerable research points to the highly communicative quality of this type of suicidal behavior, particularly in younger and female populations. Further, teenage suicide attempts appear to occur within an interpersonal context (Hawton, 1982a;

Self-poisoning is the most common method of suicide attempts among females and young adolescents.

Topal & Reznikoff, 1984; Wenz, 1979; White, 1974). Often the hope of the suicidal adolescent is to regain a lost love or influence the lover to feel more positively. Bancroft (1979) found that 45% of the 16–20-year-old suicide attempters studied were "seeking help" by means of their suicide attempt, while 35% sought to "influence someone."

The finding that teenage suicide attempts are usually of low lethality in no way diminishes the seriousness of the action. The adolescent who attempts suicide is a needy person whose act should be treated with the utmost seriousness. This is also true for those who "only talk about committing suicide." Their remarks should always be referred to qualified personnel.

Adolescent suicide and attempted suicide can derive from a variety of conditions. However, certain common factors have been found. In every case, suicidal behavior occurs as the culmination of multiple, longstanding, significant problems, both within the person and between that person and the environment. The problems involve three major areas: personality problems, family problems, and societal problems.

Personality Problems as Causes of Suicide

Historically speaking, adolescent suicidal behavior has been viewed as behavior of an impulsive nature, often indulged in by relatively normal teenagers (Crumley, 1982; Jacobziner, 1965). It has become increasingly clear, however, that teenage suicide attempters are significantly troubled individuals whose emotional problems are impressive, if not easily labeled. Labeling has proved difficult because of the myriad ways in which teenagers manifest their symptoms and hide or obscure their real feelings to the adult world. Hudgens (1975) stated that "considered by itself, the fact that a teenager has attempted suicide or made a serious suicidal communication tells little about him except that he probably has a psychiatric disorder" (p. 150). The primary personality problems are the following:

Depression   The feature most often seen in the literature on adolescent suicide is depression. Therapists and other mental health workers have become better at spotting it in its various "masked" forms (Tishler & McKenry, 1983). Further research has suggested that the mental health state of the adolescent suicide attempter and committer is now more disturbed than in previous years. Psychosis, however, is seen in only about 2% of the adolescent suicidal population and is especially rare in female adolescents (McIntire, 1980; Schowalter, 1978).

Overreliance on Limited Support   Adolescents who attempt suicide tend to overinvest themselves in very few, but very intense, interpersonal relationships. They appear to have a limited capacity to support themselves emotionally or to cope with their lives by means of internal strength alone. Rather, they rely heavily on the support of others, usually peers (Topol & Resnikoff, 1984; Walch, 1976).

Their peer relationships are supercharged but often painfully shortlived. They often overwhelm their friends with their neediness, which leads those friends to distance themselves. Suicidal teenagers often go through a series of failed relationships of this type without the internal strength to support themselves.

Communications Skills   Suicidal adolescents tend to express troubled feelings through behavior rather than internal or interpersonal dialogue. They are usually not in counseling at the time of their attempt and usually have never been in counseling (Weiner, 1970). In many instances, the suicide attempt itself is an attempt at communicating to specific individuals or the human environment at large the desperation and loneliness they feel. Adolescents who are aware and tolerant enough of their unhappiness to talk about it are at far less risk of suicide than those who have no other expressive medium available to them.

Reality Testing Adolescents who attempt suicide often lack an adequate capacity to accurately assess their condition in the world. It is difficult for them to put things in perspective. Troubles in one area of their lives are generalized to other areas. This inability to evaluate their world objectively may be a transitory condition in response to a stressful event, or it may be a more chronic condition. This manner of thinking allows them to be overwhelmed by events that may seem trivial to an outsider. It causes them to feel more hopeless about their future and at the mercy of events in the present.

Hypersensitivity All adolescents occasionally overreact to situations, but the **hypersensitive youth** will have an extreme reaction to situations that would only mildly disturb most people. The disruptions caused by seemingly trivial events may come together in a suicide attempt.

Suggestibility Sabbath (1969) has described the "expendable child," who believes that his parent or parents wish him dead. This parental wish may be conscious or unconscious, spoken or unspoken, true or untrue. But to the extent that children are suggestible, they are likely to comply with this perceived wish. The role of the parents in the suicide attempts of highly suggestible children is clear. Lorand and Schneer (1961) have studied parents whose sadistic behavior conveys to children that they are unwanted. Glaser (1965, 1978) has studied the emotionally detached parent, who is unwilling or unable to demonstrate love. Such parents may care deeply for their children, but suggestible adolescents tend to take their apparent detachment as a wish for their death. Teicher and Jacobs (1966) found that 88% of adolescent suicide attempts occur in the home, quite frequently with one or both parents right in the next room, an indication that parental behavior is a factor.

Magical Thinking Many adolescents have an unrealistic view of death's finality and use suicide as a means to radically transform the world and solve problems or to join a loved one who has already died. We call this **magical thinking.** These feelings are often aided and abetted by the glorification of suicide that sometimes occurs in the media (Garner, 1975).

Religious Fanaticism Some adolescents, whose faith in the omnipotence and omniscience of God is particularly strong, and who are doubtful about whether they are good enough to continue living, decide to attempt suicide and leave the outcome to God. Just as in medieval times when disagreements were settled by jousting matches, extremely religious youths expect God to intervene and save them from death by their own hand if He judges them worthy of life.

Lack of Control Over the Environment Corder and colleagues (1974) cite the inability to change one's environment as a frequent cause of attempted suicide. This concept was first studied by Rotter (1971), and a review of the studies of personal control has appeared elsewhere (Dacey, 1976). People tend to fall into one of two categories in terms of their sense of control over their lives. "Internals" see control as self-derived; they have a sense that they can influence what happens to them by their own actions. "Externals" see control as imposed by outside factors; thus, they see life as a matter of chance or luck. Some externals really do not have much control; others only imagine they do not. In either case, external individuals are far more likely to commit suicide than internals.

Family Problems as Causes of Suicide
Considerable research has been devoted in recent years to the constitution, dynamics, and histories of the families of suicidal adolescents (Angle, 1983; Crumley, 1982; Hawton, 1982a, 1982b, 1982c; McKenry, Tishler, & Kelley, 1982). It has

been shown that the families of suicidal adolescents experience significantly more dysfunction, disorganization, mobility, and loss than the families of normal teens.

Parental Losses   Parental losses tend to occur at an earlier age for the suicidal adolescent than for comparison groups of disturbed, nonsuicidal adolescents. A high incidence of parental deprivation, both physical and emotional, has often been reported (Wade, 1987; White, 1974). Physical abuse in the home has been cited by Green (1978) as a relatively more common element. Jacobs (1971) stressed that suicidal teens often feel they are a burden to their families and that the family would be better off without them. In many cases this perception was covertly or overtly reinforced by home life.

Parent-Child Role Reversals   Parents and children sometimes exchange traditional role behaviors—called **parent-child role reversals.**

❖   *In the parent-child interaction, the child adopts some parent-type behavior (for example, care-taking, supporting, nurturing, advising), and the parent acts more as a child would be expected to act (for example, seeking support, acting helpless, or unable to cope) (Kreider & Motto, 1974, p. 365).*

Role reversal occurs frequently in a home where there is one parent or one child. It tends to produce anxiety, pain, frustration, and hostility in adolescents. They are not ready to handle such a burden of adult behavior and may blame themselves for their inability. They may seek to alter the family environment, or to escape it, or may collapse under the pressure. They sometimes see suicide as the only way out of the double bind of having to act as both child and adult.

The Appearance of Not Being Needed   When we feel that no one needs us, we tend to become lonely and self-centered:

❖   *Suicide is not so much the outcome of "pressure," but pressure without social support. Suicide does not automatically mean that a person has not been loved or cared for. It probably does mean that he was not needed by others in an immediate, tangible fashion. 'Needed' should be understood in the sense we imply when we say we need the first-string member of an athletic team, the paper delivery boy, the only secretary in a small office, or the only wage earner in a family. The person needed must be obviously relied upon by others, and his absence should create a disruptive and foreseeable gap. In this light, it is understandable that one of the highest suicide rates is that of middle-aged bachelors and one of the lowest is that of married women with children. . . . It is nice to know we are loved, but essential to know we are needed (Wynne, 1978, p. 311).*

Children who feel they have to take care of their parents have a higher than average incidence of suicide attempts.

Communications   Finally, serious impairment of communication between father and daughter is increasingly being noted and treated as a factor in the dynamics of the female adolescent suicide (Angle, 1983; Hawton, 1982a, 1982b, 1982c; McKenry & others, 1982; White, 1974).

Societal Problems as Causes of Suicide

Problems with Peers   Peer problems are considered a critical factor in the development of adolescent suicidal behavior (Celotta, Jacobs, & Keys, 1987; Jacobs, 1971; Rohn, 1977; Teicher, 1973; Tishler, 1981; Walch, 1976; Wenz, 1979). This is especially true for disturbed, suicidal adolescents whose family life has often been inadequate. They tend to feel that they have little else in the world to support them, and with the departed friend or lover goes their sense of worth, esteem, and belonging (Hawton, 1982c; Weiner, 1970; White, 1974).

Imitation "Epidemics" of teenage suicides and suicide attempts in single localities recently have caused researchers and laypersons alike to wonder about the contagiousness of adolescent suicidal behavior. The National Center for Disease Control in Atlanta, Georgia, is mounting a major effort to study this. Some excellent research does suggest that well-publicized suicides bring out latent suicidal tendencies in adults and significantly increase the rate of suicide in the geographic area covered by the publicity (Ashton & Donnan, 1981; Bollen & Phillips, 1982; Phillips, 1979). It is reasonable to assume that adolescents are at least as readily influenced as adults.

Curran (1984) has demonstrated that teenagers are quite familiar with suicide as a behavioral alternative to coping with life's problems. He reported that 87% of the female high school students questioned knew someone who had attempted or committed suicide. In 55% of the cases, it was a person known well by the teenager—a friend, close relative, or family member. Among the males questioned, 57% knew someone who had attempted suicide; 29% knew the attempter well.

Other Societal Factors Individuals behave within the context of the society in which they live and are influenced by the pressures and changes within that society. It would seem that our society is becoming more suicidogenic for our adolescents. Some of the factors that promote dangerous stresses have been studied by McAnarney (1979). She found that the high suicide rates in the United States appear to be related to the following societal factors:

- *Family status.* Family status refers to the strength of family ties. In societies where family ties are strong, fewer suicides occur. American adolescents who are experiencing the current changing status of the family may suffer in their achievement of identity. Also, when families are not close, parents may not be able to recognize early warning signs and help their teenagers before suicide becomes an alternative.

- *Religion.* Studies have indicated that in societies where the majority of the people belong to a formal religious organization, suicide attempts are low.

- *Transition and mobility.* Groups in transition tend to have higher suicide rates than stable ones. For example, many American teenagers experience disorganized urban environments or frequent moves when one or both parents are transferred at work.

- *Achievement orientation.* Cultures such as the United States in which achievement is a major priority have higher suicide rates. Japan and Sweden are other achievement-oriented societies that exhibit high suicide rates.

- *Aggression.* Sometimes suicide is defined as aggression turned inward. In cultures where the expression of aggressive feelings is discouraged or suppressed, suicides are more prevalent. This may help to explain the higher rate of suicide attempts among females.

Blumenthal and Kupfer (1988) have made an effort to incorporate all of these factors into "a new approach to early detection and intervention for the prevention of youth suicide" (p. 1). Their proposal is certainly the most comprehensive to date; research on its effectiveness will be worth careful scrutiny.

BOX 14.4
Warning Signs of Potential Suicide Attempt

1. Change in school grades	6. Talking about killing oneself
2. Withdrawal or moodiness	7. Talking about "not being" or not
3. Accident proneness	having any future
4. Change in eating or sleeping	8. Giving away prized possessions
habits	
5. Other significant changes in usual	
behavior	

Delinquent Behavior

You have probably been a juvenile delinquent. Juvenile delinquency is defined as "any illegal act by a minor." Does this apply to you? Well, it does to your authors, each of whom can remember committing some petty crime in his youth. Studies indicate that between 90% and 100% of high school students admit to having committed some illegal act, such as dime store theft, using a fake ID, or drinking alcohol while under age (Manaster, 1989). For most teens, delinquency is no problem. Less than 20% of all crime in the United States is committed by teens (Federal Bureau of Investigation, 1989). Nevertheless, the problem is serious enough for us to review here.

Although juvenile delinquency has usually been differentiated from adult crime only in terms of age (usually 18), in this chapter, adolescent delinquent behavior is distinguished according to three groups: **nonaggressive status offenders,** that is, persons who commit crimes that are mainly harmful to themselves (runaways, prostitutes); the **juvenile delinquent** acting alone, who usually commits theft or destruction to property; and the **aggressive gang,** which engages in a variety of illegal group activities.

The Nonaggressive Offender

Persons labeled *nonaggressive offenders* are lawbreakers, technically, but they usually do not do physical harm to another person's body or property. Females constitute the majority of teenagers in this category, although the number of males is growing. About 25% of juvenile court cases are of this type (Haskell & Yablonsky, 1982).

The Runaway
According to the U.S. Department of Commerce (1988), the number of children leaving home without permission of their parents has been increasing in recent years. They estimate that 1 out of 10 12–17 year olds has run away from home at least once. Why do children run away from home? Clashes with family members and the commission of petty crimes are major causes. Almost 70% of the runaways interviewed have low achievement and little, if any, involvement with school. Runaways give as reasons the unfairness of laws that make it necessary to get parental permission for such actions as seeing a doctor of their choice or obtaining a job.

Although the problem of the runaway has been almost totally disregarded until recently, a number of services to runaways and their parents have been instituted in the last five years. Among these experiments are

---

BOX 14.5

Prostitution and the Family

Family problems are common in the prostitute's life. Freudenberger (1973) cited the case of an 11-year-old girl, Maria, who was introduced to prostitution by Dolores, an older girl. A member of a large family, Maria received little love or attention from her parents, but she was expected to be a useful provider for the family. She turned to Dolores, who enjoyed taking care of her. Maria became familiar with the prostitute's life and admired Dolores for it. When Dolores died from an overdose of drugs, Maria's sense of personal isolation and loss drove her to become a prostitute.

- Special services to runaways by youth agencies

- Toll-free phone numbers that are open on a 24-hour basis to counsel runaways

- School programs that explain the causes and problems of running away to teenagers

- Conferences, training sessions, and literature made available to the parents of runaways (see Appendix A).

Prostitution

"It's not so bad, honey," Sherry said. "Flatbackin' ain't the worst thing can happen to ya."

For many years, female runaways have turned to prostitution in order to support themselves. Also of great concern is the finding that the number of teen male prostitutes has been growing rapidly.

Although there are no reliable statistics concerning the number of teenage prostitutes, it is believed that teenage female prostitution has been growing in recent years and that male teenage prostitution has been growing at an even faster rate. There is a definite relationship between the number of runaways and the number of teenagers who turn to prostitution to support themselves. It has been difficult to determine the seriousness of this problem because of the variety of legal definitions of prostitution. Statistics may be distorted by the fact that most police officers are extremely reluctant to charge a female teenager with prostitution but are much less hesitant to do so with a male.

Brown (1979) has studied prostitution among teenage girls. Their common childhood experiences include alienation from family, parental abuse, low level or failure in education, many changes in family and home life, and dismal job prospects. Entrance into prostitution is motivated by desire for financial enterprise and adventure, by delinquent associates, institutionalization, anger and hostility either toward oneself or toward men, sexual promiscuity, and drug abuse. A young girl may also find prostitution a way to gain attention, importance, and the achievement of goals.

Surprisingly, Brown learned that juvenile girls are more seriously punished when arrested for prostitution than are boys (even though boys are more likely to be arrested when caught). As a matter of fact, these girls often receive harsher treatment than do boys who commit more serious crimes. Girls' correctional facilities are generally more rigid than boys' facilities, the fences are higher, and the confinement cells smaller.

Although no extensive survey of the growth in child and adolescent pornography has been conducted by scientists to date, police departments and exposés report a marked increase here, too. Research is badly needed in this area.

Psychologists disagree as to why a teenager enters prostitution. The psychoanalytic school believes that prostitutes have a highly negative self-image, usually because of rejection by the father. Prostitution is a symbolic way to degrade oneself and a way to defend against the need for love. Prostitution also serves as the defense mechanism of compensation (see chap. 2). It can make the teenager feel free of the internal conflicts and anxieties of being unloved. Erikson's theory explains prostitution as a negative identity. It represents a rejection of society's values in general rather than a rejection of self.

Money, drugs, and good times are other attractions of the prostitute's life that seem to be especially appealing to male prostitutes. One male teenage prostitute said that for him, the life offered the appeal of adventure and the risk of danger that is always found in a sexual encounter. He liked the "flashy, fast-paced way you can meet lots of interesting people" (Freudenberger, 1973, p. 11).

The old idea that most prostitutes are nymphomaniacs who simply cannot get enough sex is pretty well discounted by the prostitutes themselves (Kurz, 1977). Kurz interviewed many teenage prostitutes and found that for almost all of them sex is decidedly unpleasant and something that they do because they see it as the only way to survive on their own.

The Juvenile Delinquent

In his eyes is the fixed stare of the blasted spirit.

Poet Ned O'Gorman

Haskell and Yablonsky (1982) point out that the definition of the "delinquent youth" differs from state to state, town to town, and even among neighborhoods within a town. For example, in most areas the law defines a juvenile offender as someone under 18 years old, but this age can be as low as 16 and as high as 21 (Tolan, 1987). The norms for delinquent behaviors frequently depend on the social class of the youth's family (Cohen, Burt, & Bjorck 1987; Griffin, 1987).

When a delinquent act is defined as the violation of legally established codes of conduct, delinquency includes a wide range of illegal behavior from misdemeanors to major crimes against persons and property. Only a small minority of American teenagers have committed major crimes, been arrested, or live a consistently delinquent way of life (Federal Bureau of Investigation, 1988).

A comparison of the number of total crimes committed by age (see Tables 14.5 and 14.6) shows that in every age bracket, the numbers are significantly lower today than in the previous decade (Federal Bureau of Investigation, 1989). This is especially true of three important categories: prostitution, drunkenness, and runaways. (Although complex, these two tables offer a wealth of information. What other conclusions can you come to by studying them?)

It is not easy to explain these findings, but it is possible that the decrease is a result of a movement toward more conservative attitudes, as was found in the 1984 study by the National Association of Secondary School Principals (NASSP, 1984). This study of 1,500 representatively chosen 7th to 12th graders found marked changes in attitude from a similar study conducted by the NASSP in 1974. The students questioned in 1984 were markedly more conservative in their attitudes toward sex, the family, politics, and a number of other topics, including crime. For example, the great majority agreed that:

- the laws concerning the defense of insanity should be much tougher (no doubt reflecting attitudes toward John Hinkley's attempt on President Reagan's life)

Do you know what the statistics of juvenile crime are in your hometown?

BOX 14.6

What's Your Opinion?

It has been suggested that because their crimes are victimless, nonaggressive offenders should not be prosecuted. Some argue that because these youths mainly hurt themselves, they are really the victims of their "crimes." They need help, not punishment by incarceration. In fact, the parents who drive their children from their homes, and the "johns" who solicit the sexual favor of teenagers, are the ones who should be punished by the law.

Parents of runaways or the wives of husbands who catch venereal disease from a prostitute would likely disagree. The parents of the runaway, faced with an "incor-

rigible child," typically feel helpless. They feel that without police involvement, they would have no way to get their child back. Furthermore, it is argued that prostitutes should be treated criminally because they violate the societal rule that the family must be respected. Anyone who tempts people to disregard their marriage vows must be punished for it. (By the way, why is it almost always males, heterosexuals and homosexuals alike, who seek the services of prostitutes?)

You be the judge. Which side is right, or is there a third possible solution?

- the death penalty is appropriate

- violent crime is the third most important problem facing the nation

Learning and Delinquency

Numerous studies have found that "chronic underachievement and a poor school record are . . . predictive of rule breaking and antisocial behavior" (Feldman, Rosenberg, & Peer, 1984). In fact, the evidence indicates that there is a causal link between problems in achieving academic competence and delinquency (Cullinan & Epstein, 1979; Jerse & Fakouri, 1978; Kauffman, 1981; Perlmutter, 1987; Siegel & Senna, 1981; Whelan, 1982).

Perlmutter (1987) looked specifically at the relationship between learning disabilities and delinquency. He found that learning disabled adolescents are

❖ *more likely to develop severe delinquent behaviors than are their non-disabled peers, but unlikely to exhibit a middle ground between delinquent and nondelinquent behavior. It is hypothesized that this difference is due to the ability of most LD children and adolescents to adapt through developing skills that allow them to compensate for their handicapping conditions (p. 89).*

To counteract the link between learning problems and delinquency, (Rosenberg & Anspach, 1973) recommended "educational therapy." This approach includes direct and continuous measurement of student learning activity, individualized instruction, a variety of classroom-wide procedures, and intensive, continuing self-study by administrators and faculty.

Gangs

Gangs often offer youths the fulfillment of basic needs. Some of their functions clearly coincide with those of the larger society. Gangs typically provide protection, recognition of the desire to feel wanted, and rites of passage that mark achievement, status, and acceptance, such as the initiation rite of a potential gang member.

Table 14.5 Total Arrests by Age, 1981 (11,758 Agencies; Estimated Population 204,622,000)

Offense Charged	Total All Ages	Age		
		Under 10	10–12	13–14
Total	9,506,347	74,652	136,754	450,637
Percent distribution	100.0	.8	1.4	4.7
Murder and nonnegligent manslaughter	18,264	14	25	167
Forcible rape	29,164	66	183	832
Robbery	130,753	392	1,837	8,393
Aggravated assault	256,597	898	2,173	7,617
Burglary	468,085	9,366	17,215	55,122
Larceny-theft	1,098,398	23,037	44,947	114,236
Motor vehicle theft	143,654	466	2,164	15,569
Arson	18,387	1,669	1,289	2,275
Violent crime	434,778	1,370	4,218	17,009
Percent distribution	100.0	.3	1.0	3.9
Property crime	1,728,524	34,538	65,615	187,202
Percent distribution	100.0	2.0	3.8	10.8
Crime index total[a]	2,163,302	35,908	69,833	204,211
Percent distribution	100.0	1.7	3.2	9.4
Other assaults	451,475	2,953	6,308	18,847
Forgery and counterfeiting	70,977	71	279	1,357
Fraud	243,461	105	241	1,224
Embezzlement	7,882	6	30	149
Stolen property; buying, receiving, possessing	107,621	583	1,851	7,744
Vandalism	239,246	13,230	16,018	32,712
Weapons: carrying, possessing, etc.	152,731	366	1,031	4,450
Prostitution and commercialized vice	83,088	24	46	303
Sex offenses (except forcible rape and prostitution)	62,633	382	839	2,996
Drug abuse violations	519,377	502	1,585	14,745
Gambling	50,974	15	31	220
Offenses against family and children	53,321	599	158	380
Driving under the influence	1,231,665	162	38	348
Liquor laws	386,957	195	715	9,451
Drunkenness	1,090,233	524	383	3,782
Disorderly conduct	711,730	3,318	6,839	22,023
Vagrancy	34,662	178	203	864
All other offenses (except traffic)	1,595,864	10,728	16,992	59,413
Suspicion	18,135	170	260	1,024
Curfew and loitering law violations	78,147	909	3,183	15,584
Runaways	152,866	3,724	9,891	48,810

[a]Crime index = total of violent and property crimes.
Source: Federal Bureau of Investigation, 1981.

Table 14.5 *Continued*

Offense Charged	Age				
	15	16	17	18	19
Total	407,152	515,979	558,195	595,798	550,079
Percent distribution	4.3	5.4	5.9	6.3	5.8
Murder and nonnegligent manslaughter	283	559	659	884	902
Forcible rape	900	1,213	1,457	1,801	1,701
Robbery	8,327	10,480	11,728	11,559	9,955
Aggravated assault	7,248	9,866	12,058	13,325	13,145
Burglary	46,620	50,508	48,849	41,524	32,041
Larceny-theft	81,749	90,788	89,296	78,170	62,013
Motor vehicle theft	17,213	18,842	16,422	12,241	9,228
Arson	1,440	1,276	1,063	959	754
Violent crime	16,758	22,118	25,902	27,569	25,703
Percent distribution	3.9	5.1	6.0	6.3	5.9
Property crime	147,022	161,414	155,630	132,894	104,036
Percent distribution	8.5	9.3	9.0	7.7	6.0
Crime index total[a]	163,780	183,532	181,532	160,463	129,739
Percent distribution	7.6	8.5	8.4	7.4	6.0
Other assaults	15,621	18,959	21,570	22,487	22,942
Forgery and counterfeiting	1,718	2,663	3,845	4,331	4,362
Fraud	1,417	1,985	3,400	6,551	9,090
Embezzlement	124	268	419	405	467
Stolen property; buying, receiving, possessing	7,333	8,802	9,317	9,082	7,695
Vandalism	21,990	23,173	22,480	16,628	12,870
Weapons: carrying, possessing, etc.	4,623	6,537	7,984	9,546	8,811
Prostitution and commercialized vice	487	781	1,678	4,742	7,468
Sex offenses (except forcible rape and prostitution)	2,250	2,290	2,611	2,719	2,762
Drug abuse violations	21,157	33,690	42,677	48,880	46,253
Gambling	357	618	866	1,106	1,293
Offenses against family and children	412	487	535	2,111	2,102
Driving under the influence	1,077	7,793	20,412	46,310	54,399
Liquor laws	20,009	44,101	64,815	65,282	48,265
Drunkenness	6,721	12,810	21,480	42,440	43,673
Disorderly conduct	22,180	30,508	40,668	51,514	48,425
Vagrancy	942	1,264	1,505	2,230	2,155
All other offenses (except traffic)	53,909	77,577	77,219	97,427	96,016
Suspicion	952	1,137	1,367	1,544	1,292
Curfew and loitering law violations	17,710	23,146	17,615		
Runaways	42,383	33,858	14,200		

Table 14.6   Total Arrests, Distribution by Age, 1987 (10,616 Agencies; 1987 Estimated Population 202,337,000)

Offense Charged	Total All Ages	Age		
		Under 10	10–12	13–14
Total	10,795,869	47,725	135,773	373,780
Percent distribution	100.0	.4	1.3	3.5
Murder and nonnegligent manslaughter	16,714	14	25	164
Forcible rape	31,276	107	362	1,191
Robbery	123,306	299	1,439	5,450
Aggravated assault	301,734	901	2,809	7,574
Burglary	374,963	4,342	12,312	30,947
Larceny-theft	1,256,552	15,418	47,973	98,864
Motor vehicle theft	146,753	238	1,706	12,112
Arson	15,169	1,078	1,152	1,621
Violent crimes	473,030	1,321	4,635	14,379
Percent distribution	100.0	.3	1.0	3.0
Property crime	1,793,437	21,076	63,143	143,544
Percent distribution	100.0	1.2	3.5	8.0
Crime Index total[a]	2,266,467	22,397	67,778	157,923
Percent distribution	100.0	1.0	3.0	7.0
Other assaults	671,938	2,962	9,415	22,736
Forgery and counterfeiting	78,817	37	179	810
Fraud	280,809	212	1,869	5,914
Embezzlement	10,639	10	45	82
Stolen property; buying, receiving, possessing	119,048	333	1,484	6,041
Vandalism	230,088	7,433	14,238	24,182
Weapons: carrying, possessing, etc.	165,650	282	1,243	5,053
Prostitution and commercialized vice	100,950	11	12	165
Sex offenses (except forcible rape and prostitution)	85,627	626	1,752	4,013
Drug abuse violations	811,078	259	870	8,579
Gambling	22,762	2	15	107
Offenses against family and children	48,002	183	158	488
Driving under the influence	1,410,397	100	38	227
Liquor laws	505,021	294	642	8,325
Drunkenness	700,662	109	202	1,920
Disorderly conduct	599,622	2,019	6,028	16,599
Vagrancy	32,518	31	86	422
All other offenses (except traffic)	2,430,913	7,312	16,204	49,762
Suspicion	11,670	83	188	543
Curfew and loitering law violations	77,556	765	3,636	16,426
Runaways	135,635	2,265	9,691	43,463

Source: Federal Bureau of Investigation, 1989.

According to a study commissioned by the New York City Youth Board (*New York Times,* 1989), urban gangs possess the following characteristics:

- Their behavior is normal for urban youths; they have a high degree of cohesion and organization; roles are clearly defined.

- They possess a consistent set of norms and expectations, understood by all members.

- They have clearly defined leaders.

- They have a coherent organization for gang warfare.

Table 14.6 *Continued*

Offense Charged	Age				
	15	16	17	18	19
Total	320,871	422,392	480,699	504,876	500,482
Percent distribution	3.0	3.9	4.5	4.7	4.6
Murder and nonnegligent manslaughter	216	451	722	868	875
Forcible rape	921	1,108	1,220	1,231	1,211
Robbery	5,255	7,201	8,038	7,945	7,345
Aggravated assault	6,840	9,510	11,012	10,786	11,135
Burglary	24,686	29,508	30,367	27,496	22,374
Larceny-theft	67,449	80,347	78,737	70,156	58,682
Motor vehicle theft	13,767	16,167	14,583	11,006	9,057
Arson	882	728	678	572	533
Violent crimes	13,232	18,270	20,992	20,830	20,566
Percent distribution	2.8	3.9	4.4	4.4	4.3
Property crime	106,784	126,750	124,365	109,230	90,646
Percent distribution	6.0	7.1	6.9	6.1	5.1
Crime Index total[a]	120,016	145,020	145,357	130,060	111,212
Percent distribution	5.3	6.4	6.4	5.7	4.9
Other assaults	17,625	21,324	23,818	22,907	24,354
Forgery and counterfeiting	1,011	2,014	3,046	3,825	4,273
Fraud	5,743	1,613	3,038	5,546	8,265
Embezzlement	78	247	446	477	564
Stolen property; buying, receiving, possessing	5,678	7,722	8,592	8,640	7,854
Vandalism	15,176	17,054	16,866	13,094	10,817
Weapons: carrying, possessing, etc.	4,846	6,443	7,786	8,858	8,456
Prostitution and commercialized vice	288	557	1,102	2,751	4,322
Sex offenses (except forcible rape and prostitution)	2,378	2,392	2,383	2,488	2,598
Drug abuse violations	12,700	22,297	31,332	39,816	42,399
Gambling	149	232	335	309	324
Offenses against family and children	538	658	542	1,287	1,279
Driving under the influence	769	5,121	13,462	30,556	39,802
Liquor laws	17,254	40,605	65,339	79,009	68,059
Drunkenness	3,063	5,541	9,519	16,978	19,067
Disorderly conduct	15,064	21,721	27,066	29,690	29,930
Vagrancy	465	668	780	1,367	1,421
All other offenses (except traffic)	45,267	67,616	87,510	106,743	114,972
Suspicion	561	626	558	475	514
Curfew and loitering law violations	16,878	21,750	18,101		
Runaways	35,324	31,171	13,721		

[a]Crime Index = Total of violent and property crimes.

The gang provides many adolescents with a structured life they never had at home. What makes the gang particularly cohesive is its function as a family substitute for adolescents whose strong dependency needs are displaced onto the peer group. The gang becomes a family to its members (Burton, 1978).

Gangs and Social Class

The formation of juvenile gangs typically follows a sudden increase in this country of new ethnic groups due to immigration. The children of new immigrants have a difficult time breaking through cultural barriers such as a new language and racism. Perceiving their prospects of succeeding in the new society as bleak, some of these children form gangs, which provide the structure and security discussed, but also serve as an outlet to attack the society that seemingly will not accept them. In times past these gangs were composed of Jewish, Irish, and Italian Americans. Today's gangs are frequently formed by Hispanic- and Asian-Americans (Vigil, 1988).

Friedman and colleagues (1976) studied the victimization of youth by urban street gangs. He found that

❖   *rituals of street gang warfare and the practices of victimizing both gang members and nonmembers by having them commit serious crimes and violent offenses may serve to maintain the continuity of the group, to give it structure, and to symbolize the gang's power of life and death over others (p. 21).*

The gang becomes a vehicle for tearing its members away from the main social structures and authorities, in particular the family and school.

But today's gangs have some disturbing differences from those of years past. They are much more heavily armed and seemingly much more willing to use their weapons. Movies like *West Side Story* (1961) depict gang members carrying knives, chains, and pipes. Today's urban gangs are often armed with AK-47 assault rifles and UZI submachine guns, grenades, and even cluster bombs.

After a period of decline, urban gangs are again on the rise.

Gang violence has increased dramatically in this decade. Twenty-five percent of all juvenile crimes are committed by urban gangs. Los Angeles, with over 200 gangs and 12,000 members, has perhaps suffered most from this upsurge in violence. That city saw gang-related homicides increase from an already staggering 150 in 1985 to an unfathomable 387 in 1987.

In addition to pride and territory, money and drugs are increasingly motivating the violence. Police in Los Angeles cite the influence of crack, a highly profitable derivative of cocaine, as a major influence in gang violence. Organized urban gangs have now become profit-making enterprises. Drive-by shootings are committed by heavily armed youths in expensive cars protecting their "market."

Gangs are also no longer limited to the large urban areas. Smaller cities and towns in the United States have recently seen an increase in the formation of juvenile gangs (Takata & others, 1987). These gangs are often related to other, well-established gangs from the larger cities. So in effect, a gang such as L.A.'s Crips can set up "franchises" in cities such as Seattle and Shreveport. Suburban gangs have also been on the upswing (Muehlbauer & Dodder, 1983). These suburban gangs usually don't exhibit the same degree of organization or formality. They typically get their "kicks" from the malicious destruction of property.

Characteristics of Gang Joiners

Why do adolescents join gangs? Recent interviews with gang members revealed that companionship, protection, excitement, and peer pressure were the most frequently cited reasons (Hochhaus & Sousa, 1988). Gang members are much more likely to have divorced parents or parents with a criminal history. They are more likely to do poorly in school and score low on IQ tests. Friedman and colleagues (1976) showed that what most differentiates the street gang member from the nonmember is the enjoyment of violence. Female gang members, who also have increased recently, face many of the same societal barriers that cause males to join gangs, with the additional barrier of sexism (Campbell, 1987).

Gang members also have more unrealistic expectations of success than nonmembers, yet perceive less opportunity to be successful (Burton, 1978). Gangs in effect promise a more equal opportunity than does society for members to succeed at something in life. In general, gang members are found to have more drug-abuse problems, more mental disturbance, and are more angry and violent than the average youth. Many are deeply troubled.

Transition

Are adolescents in less or greater trouble than in former years? With the exception of "crack," the abuse of drugs and alcohol has not increased significantly but is still at an intolerably high level. Eating disorders, depression, and suicide attempts are very real new threats to adolescents' happiness. There has been some decrease in individual juvenile crimes, but they still account for a considerably higher percentage of overall crimes than would be expected for their segment of the total population.

These facts certainly are causes for alarm. How can they be explained? What can be done to improve the situation? It seems likely that at least part of the answer lies in finding better ways to help them get ready for the transition to adulthood. The stress of this transition no doubt accounts for a lot of the substance abuse, mental illness, and delinquency problem. An important aspect of this transition is their sexual behavior. This is what we will deal with in the next chapter.

Key Ideas

1. Substance abuse tends to develop through four separate stages.
2. Drugs are alleged to enhance sexuality, but there is little evidence to support this idea.
3. Probably the two most prevalent types of mental disturbance in the teen years are eating disorders and depression.
4. The two major eating disorders are anorexia nervosa and bulimia nervosa.
5. Among the causes of teen depression are the capacity for denial, the tendency to act out feelings, and the desire to avoid dependence and helplessness.
6. Masked depression is a serious complication.
7. Suicide attempts or threats should always be considered serious. They are influenced by age, race, place of residence, and gender.
8. There are three main types of delinquent behavior: the "nonaggressive status offender," the juvenile delinquent, and aggressive gangs.

Key Terms

Aggressive gang
Anorexia nervosa
Bulimia nervosa
Depression
Family status
Hypersensitive youth

Juvenile delinquent
Magical thinking
Nonaggressive status offenders
Parent-child role reversals
Psychopathology
Suggestibility

What Do You Think?

1. Suppose you had a friend with a substance abuse problem. How should you handle it?
2. How would you know if you were developing a serious addiction? What would you do about it?
3. Why do you suppose people develop eating disorders?
4. Think back to the last time you were "down in the mouth" about something. Now suppose it were five times worse than it was. How would you feel? How would you act? How would others treat you?
5. What do you think Hankoff (see "Crisis of Death" section) means when he says "ruminations over suicide and forms of actively promoted death encounters would serve to provide the adolescent with a sense of greater temporal definition in his life"?
6. Try to remember every illegal act you have ever committed (hopefully there won't be too many of them). Can you imagine how any one of those acts could have led you into becoming a juvenile delinquent?

Suggested Readings

Abel, Ernest L. (1981). *Marijuana: The first twelve thousand years.* New York: Plenum. This book chronicles the use of marijuana throughout history. The author is a psychopharmacist who has done a great deal of research on the subject.

Gibson, Margaret. (1980). *The butterfly ward.* New Orleans: Louisiana State University Press. This set of short stories tells what it is like to be between sanity and insanity. It is a sensitive look at the world of the mentally ill both in and out of institutions.

Hinton, S. E. (1967). *The outsiders.* New York: Dell. This remarkable book was written by a 17-year-old girl. It describes gang rituals, class warfare, and coming of age in this truly intense environment. Another popular book by this author is *That Was Then, This Is Now* (1971), a sequel to *The Outsiders.*

Kennedy, William. (1983). *Ironweed.* New York: Penguin Books. Although this book is about adult addicts, it is such an engrossing look at the problem that we have included it here.

Plath, Sylvia. (1971). *The bell jar.* New York: Bantam. This famed book tells the story of Esther Greenwood's painful month in New York City, which leads eventually to her insanity and attempted suicide.

Rebeta-Burditt, Joyce. (1986). *The cracker factory.* New York: Bantam. This novel humorously describes the difficulties of a young woman who takes to drinking because of the pressures in her life and is eventually institutionalized because of an attempted suicide.

Sechehaye, Marguerite. (1970). *Autobiography of a schizophrenic girl.* New York: New American Library. Written by a Swiss psychoanalyst, this book describes the method of therapy as it was applied to a case of schizophrenia. Offers many insights into this malady that often starts during adolescence.

· *Chapter 15* ·

Adolescence: Sexuality and Sex Roles

Sexual Identity and Sex Roles

The problem lay buried, unspoken, for many years in the minds of American women. It was a strange stirring, a sense of dissatisfaction, a yearning that women suffered in the middle of the twentieth century in the United States. Each suburban wife struggled with it alone, as she made the beds, shopped for groceries, matched slipcover material, ate peanut butter sandwiches with her children, chauffeured Cub Scouts and Brownies, lay beside her husband at night—she was afraid to ask even of herself the silent question—"Is this all?"

Betty Friedan, 1963

The beginning of the "feminist revolution" in the 1960s opened an era of changing views toward gender roles. Do you believe that society's views of gender roles are significantly different today from what they were 10 years ago?

This is the opening of the famous book, *The Feminine Mystique,* which began the feminist movement in this country. This was the opening salvo of the revolution that has made such sweeping changes in sex roles in the latter half of this century. Its early effects were mainly on late adolescent and early adult females, but today there is scarcely a woman in the country (or a man, for that matter) whose life has not been affected by this movement.

Contrast it with this statement made over two thousand years ago by the famed Greek philosopher Aristotle: "Woman may be said to be an inferior man." Most of us would disagree with his viewpoint publicly. On the other hand, its underlying attitude is still widespread. People today are far less willing to admit to a belief in female inferiority, but many still act as though it were so. However, the influence of the women's movement, as well as of science and other forms of social change, is profoundly affecting the way we view **sexual identity** and **sex role.**

First, we should make a distinction between the two. Sexual identity results from those *physical characteristics* that are part of our biological inheritance. They are the traits that make us males or females. Genitals and facial hair are examples of sex-linked physical characteristics. Sex role, on the other hand, results largely from the specific traits that are in fashion at any one time and in any one culture. For example, women appear to be able to express their emotions through crying more easily than men, although there is no known physical cause for this difference.

It is possible for people to accept or reject their sexual identity and/or their sexual role. Jan Morris (1974), the British author, spent most of her life as the successful author James Morris. Although born a male she deeply resented the fact that she had a male sexual identity and hated having to perform the male sex role. She always felt that inside she was really a woman.

The cause of these feelings may have been psychological—something that happened in her childhood, perhaps. Or the cause may have been genetic—possibly something to do with hormone balance. Such rejection is rare, and no one knows for sure why it happens. Morris decided to have a **transsexual operation** that changed her from male to female. The change caused many problems in her life, but she says she is infinitely happier to have her body match her feelings about her sex role.

Some people are perfectly happy with their sexual identity, but don't like their sex role. Sex role itself has three aspects:

- **Sex-role orientation.** Individuals differ in how confident they feel about their sex identity. Males often have a weaker sex-role orientation than females. (This will be discussed later in the chapter.)

- **Sex-role preference.** Some individuals feel unhappy about their sex role, as did Jan Morris, and wish either society or their gender could be changed, so that their sex role would be different. The feminist move-

---

BOX 15.1

Sex-Role Stereotype Test

In what ways are males and females really different? There are many stereotypes about sex roles; some are accurate, some are not. Extensive recent research has helped establish the truth about these traits. Check the following statements true or false to learn your "chauvinist" rating (remember, women can be chauvinists, too).

Compared to males, the average female in the United States:

	True	False
1. Is more suggestible.	___	___
2. Is more social.	___	___
3. Has greater verbal ability.	___	___
4. Is smarter.	___	___
5. Is less aggressive.	___	___
6. Is better at rote learning and simple repetitive tasks.	___	___
7. Has less ability to process high-level mental tasks.	___	___
8. Is less analytic, more intuitive.	___	___
9. Has less math ability.	___	___
10. Is more auditory.	___	___
11. Lacks achievement motivation.	___	___
12. Fears success.	___	___

Answers to the Sex-Role Stereotype Test
An F means the statement is false, and a T means it is true.

1. F 2. T 3. T 4. F 5. T 6. F 7. F 8. F 9. T 10. F 11. F 12. T

(a)

(b)

Some people are so unhappy with their sexual identity that they have it changed surgically. Renee Richards (a) before the surgery, and (b), the female tennis star, used to be a man by the name of Richard Raskind.

ment of the last few decades has had a major impact on many of the world's societies in this regard.

- **Sex-role adaptation.** Adaptation is defined by whether other people judge individual behavior as masculine or feminine. If a person is seen as acting "appropriately" according to her or his gender, then adaptation has occurred. People who dislike their sex role, or doubt that they fit it well (e.g., the teenage boy who fights a lot because he secretly doubts he is masculine enough) may be said to be poorly adapted.

Research indicates that while sex *roles* may be modified by differing cultural expectations, sexual *identity* is fixed rather early in a person's development. John Money and his associates at Johns Hopkins University believe there is a critical period for the development of sexual identity, which starts at about age 18 months and ends at about the age of 4. Once sexual identity has been established, it is very difficult to change (Money & Ehrhardt, 1972).

The more traditional view (e.g., Diamond, 1982) holds that sexual identity is the result of interaction between sex chromosome differences at conception and early treatment by the people in the child's environment. However, Baker (1980), in her review of the main body of research on this topic, is unequivocal: she states that gender identity depends on the way the child is reared, "regardless of the chromosomal, gonadal, or prenatal hormonal situation" (p. 95).

Once culture has had the opportunity to influence the child's sexual identity, it is unlikely to change, even when biological changes occur. Even in such extreme cases of **chromosome failure** as gynecomastia (breast growth in the male) and

Table 15.1   Stereotypes of the Differences Between Females and Males

Females differ from males in that females are (by type of finding):

Well-founded	Unfounded	Debatable
Higher in verbal ability	More social	More fearful, timid, and anxious
Lower in visual-spatial ability	More suggestible	Lower in activity level
Weaker in mathematical ability	Higher in self-esteem	Less competitive and more cooperative
Less aggressive	Better in rote learning	Less dominant
More afraid to be successful, especially in mixed competition, but less so for black females than for white females	Better at simple, repetitive tasks	More compliant
	Poorer at higher-level cognitive processing	More nurturant
More easily able to maintain their sex-role identity	Less analytical	More maternal
	More affected by environment motivation	
	More auditory, but less visual	

Most of the findings have been abstracted from a review of the literature, *The Psychology of Sex Differences,* by Maccoby and Jacklin, 1974. Though old, it is still considered the most intensive work on the subject.

hirsutism (abnormal female body hair), sexual identity is not affected. In almost all cases, adolescents desperately want medical treatment so they can keep their sexual identities.

Although sexual identity becomes fixed rather early in life, sex roles usually undergo changes as the individual matures. The relationships between the roles of our two genders also change, and have altered considerably in the past few decades.

Sex Roles of the Two Genders

This section considers two aspects of the social roles of the sexes: **sex-role stereotypes** and the concept of **androgyny.**

Sex-Role Stereotypes

There are a number of stereotypes common in our culture that identify behavior as typically either male or female. Some of them are clearly true, some are clearly false, and some we are not sure about. Test your knowledge of sex-role stereotypes (see following), and then look at Table 15.1. This table lists the most typical stereotypes that differentiate females from males, which the research literature classifies as well-founded, unfounded, or debatable.

It is interesting to note that of the well-founded stereotypical differences between women and men listed in Table 15.1, the only personality trait listed is aggressiveness. There are many other stereotypes about personality differences, but research does not support them. It is also interesting that, although women fear success more than men, it is not because they don't care about achievement.

Erik Erikson's ideas about the biological determinants of male and female sex roles came from his studies of early adolescents (1963). He tossed wooden blocks of various shapes and sizes on a table and asked each child to make something with them. Girls, he found, tend to make low structures like the rooms of a house. Having finished these structures, the girls then use other blocks as furniture, which they move around in the spaces of the rooms. Boys, on the other hand, tend to build towers, which, after completion, they usually destroy.

Erikson likens the roomlike structures of the girls to their possession of a womb, and the towerlike structures of the boys to their possession of a penis. He feels that

Our sex-role stereotypes define what actions are and are not appropriate for each gender. What would most people say if they saw this young woman chopping wood? How about 100 years ago?

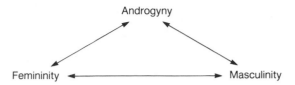

Figure 15.1 *Relationships among the three sex roles.*

these differences account for greater aggressive behavior in males. Penis and tower alike are seen as thrusting symbols of power.

He also suggests that differences in biological function cause the differences we see in male and female mental illness. Males get sick when they are unable to express the anger and hostility resulting from their natural aggressive tendencies. Females, on the other hand, suffer from a lifelong fear of being left empty, or more simply, of being left alone. Women have a natural desire to fill up the womb within them, and if they are unable or unwilling to bear children, they become prone to mental illness.

Although Erikson's ideas have been severely criticized by representatives of the women's movement, he argues that the pervasive anger of many feminists stems from their unconscious fear of being possessed by their own bodies, rather than owning them by choice and using them with deliberation. Although he has frequently espoused complete economic equality between men and women, Erikson continues to insist that genital differences are the cause of many psychological differences. In this he certainly does maintain close ties with the psychoanalytic tradition.

Androgyny

One sex role researcher, Sandra Bem (1975), has argued that typical American roles are actually unhealthy. She says that highly masculine males tend to have better psychological adjustment than other males during adolescence, but as adults they tend to become highly anxious and neurotic, and often experience low self-acceptance. Highly feminine females suffer in similar ways.

Bem believes we would all be much better off if we were to become more androgynous. The word is made up of the Greek words for male, *andro,* and for female, *gyne.* It refers to those persons who have higher than average male *and* female elements in their personalities. More specifically, they are more likely to behave in a way appropriate to a situation, regardless of their gender.

For example, when someone forces his way into a line at the movies, the traditional female role calls for a woman to look disapproving but to say nothing. The androgynous female would tell the offender in no uncertain terms to go to the end of the line. When a baby left unattended starts to cry, the traditional male response is to try to find some woman to take care of its needs. The androgynous male would pick up the infant and attempt to comfort it.

Androgyny is not merely the midpoint between the two poles of masculinity and femininity. Rather, it is a higher level of sex role identification than either of the more traditional roles. Figure 15.1 illustrates this relationship.

Although some aspects of our sex roles appear to be in a state of flux, such as those having to do with the workplace, there has been even more change when it comes to our sexual behavior. We turn now to examine this aspect of social interaction.

The androgynous man is not afraid to be seen being kind to an infant.

Table 15.2	Percentage of Metropolitan-Area Never-Married Women Who Have Experienced Sexual Intercourse				
Age	1971	1976	1979	1983	1989
15	14.4	18.6	22.5	NA	34.2[a]
16	20.9	28.9	37.8	40.2	
17	26.1	42.9	48.5	55.6	43.9

NA = not available
[a]Combines 15 and 16 year olds.
Sources: Dreyer, 1982; Rodman, et al., 1984; Zelnick and Kantner, 1980.

Sexual Behavior

There are few aspects of human behavior that have changed more in this century than sexual behavior. Until the 1970s, the popular belief about sex was, "They're talking more about it now, but they're not doing anything more about it!" This may have been true earlier in this century, but no longer. The situation has changed so much that it is reasonable to call it a **sexual revolution.**

The Sexual Revolution

Seeing their elders founder in a sea of confused values, adolescents have begun to consult one another more often on important matters like sex. Edgar Friedenberg, a far-sighted sociologist, saw the beginning of this change as early as the late 1950s. He described these new attitudes in *The Vanishing Adolescent* (1959). The yearning for love and world peace, perennially scorned by some cynical older adults, began to flourish among late teens and young adults in the 1960s. Many middle-age adults came to the disconcerting realization that they were beginning to admire and even emulate the values of their adolescent children. As the spirit of "love among brothers and sisters" grew, so did its consequence, more open sexuality. And a great many adults were no longer sure this was wrong.

Although most teenagers are not ready for mature love, sexual feelings are unavoidable, and for many they are extremely frightening. Now comes one of the most difficult decisions of life: Shall I say "yes" or "no" to premarital sex? Parents, clergy, teachers, police, and other adults used to be united in their resistance to it. But now, possibly for the first time in history, adult domination of the values of youth has faltered. As Williams (1989) expressed the change:

❖ *Even as adults in America moderate their sexual activity in response to the threat of AIDS and shifting standards of behavior, teen-agers in the last decade have developed a widely held sense that they are entitled to have sex (p. 4).*

Evidence that the forces that traditionally kept the great majority of adolescents from engaging in sex are no longer powerful is presented in Table 15.2. Examine this table. Notice that for the first four years, percentages increase for all age groups. The apparent decline may be due to a growing concern about AIDS and other STDs (Koyle & others, 1989). We can be sure that the rates for males in the 1970s are considerably higher, and that by the end of the teen years, they are quite a bit higher still, for both genders. Results of studies vary, but the most likely percentage of college sophomores who are no longer virgins is about 75% for both males and females (Dacey, 1986).

Stages of Sexuality

Many psychologists believe that human sexuality develops in three steps:

- Love of one's self (**autosexuality**)
- Love of members of one's own sex (**homosexuality**)
- Love of members of the opposite sex (**heterosexuality**).

These stages appear to be natural, although some argue that it is as natural to stay at the second stage as to go on to the third.

In the autosexual stage, the child becomes aware of himself or herself as a source of sexual pleasure, and consciously experiments with masturbation. The autosexual stage begins as early as 3 years of age and continues until the child is about 6 or 7, although in some children it lasts for a considerably longer period of time.

When the child enters kindergarten, the homosexual phase comes to the fore (please note that this does not necessarily refer to sexual touching, but rather to the direction of feelings of love). For most children from the age of 7 to about 13, best friends, the ones with whom he or she dares to be intimate, are people of the same sex. Feelings become especially intense between ages 10 and 12 when young people enter puberty and feel a growing need to confide in others. It is only natural that they are more trusting with members of their own sex who share their experiences. Occasionally these close feelings result in overt sexual behavior (one study found this to be true over one-third of the time). In most cases, however, it appears that such behavior results from curiosity rather than latent homosexuality of the adult variety.

The great majority of teenagers move into the third stage, heterosexuality, at about 13 or 14 years, with girls preceding boys by about a year. These three phases are discussed in the following sections.

Autosexual Behavior

❖   *If a boy in an unguarded moment tries to entice you to masturbatic experiments, he insults you. Strike him at once and beat him as long as you can stand, etc. Forgive him in your mind, but never speak to him again. If he is the best fighter and beats you, take it as in a good cause. If a man scoundrel suggests indecent things, slug him with a stick or a stone or anything else at hand. Give him a scar that all may see; and if you are arrested, tell the judge all, and he will approve your act, even if it is not lawful. If a villain shows you a filthy book or picture, snatch it; and give it to the first policeman you meet, and help him to find the wretch. If a vile woman invites you, and perhaps tells a plausible story of her downfall, you cannot strike her; but think of a glittering, poisonous snake. She is a degenerate and probably diseased, and even a touch may poison you and your children.*

Psychologists have been debating autosexual behavior since the dire warnings of G. S. Hall (see chap. 12). There is still disagreement today in the United States about masturbation, especially among females:

❖   *From the moment we were born we all began making ourselves feel good by touching and playing with our bodies. Some of these experiences were explicitly sexual. From our parents and later, our schools and churches, many of us learned that we were not to continue this pleasurable touching. Some of us heeded their messages and some of us did not. But by the time we were teenagers, whether we masturbated or not, most of us thought it was bad (Boston Women's Health Book Collective, 1976, p. 47).*

Masturbation is probably universal to human sexual experience. Although most people still consider it an embarrassing topic, it has always been a recognized aspect of sexuality, legitimate or not. Kinsey, in his 1948 study of male sexuality, found that 97% of all males masturbated. As for women, approximately two-thirds have masturbated to orgasm by the time they reach 16 (Gagnon & Simon, 1969). Most 4–5 year olds masturbate, are chastised for it, and stop, then start again at an average age of 14 (Masters & Johnson, 1966). If masturbation is so popular, why has it been considered such a problem?

For one reason, it is believed that the Bible forbids it. Dranoff (1974) points out that the Latin word *masturbari* means "to pollute oneself." For generations, people have taken as a prohibition the passage in Genesis 38.8 in which Onan is slain by the Lord because "he spilled his seed upon the ground." Dranoff argues that Onan was not slain by the Lord for masturbating, but because he refused to follow God's directive to mate with his brother's wife. Instead, he practiced coitus interruptus (withdrawal from the vagina before ejaculation).

In addition to the biblical restrictions, for centuries the medical profession believed that masturbation caused disease. In 1760, Tissot asserted that a common consequence of masturbation is "locomotor ataxia and early insanity." There are many myths about masturbation: it causes one to go mad; it causes hair to grow on one's palms; it causes one to reject sex with anyone else. No research evidence shows that there are any intrinsic bad effects of masturbation. In fact, the American Psychiatric Association has stated that it should not be considered the sole cause of any particular psychiatric problem (American Psychiatric Association, 1985).

Although most psychiatrists feel that there is no intrinsic harm in masturbation and believe it to be a normal healthy way for adolescents to discharge their sexual drive, some teens (mainly boys) feel such a sense of shame, guilt, and fear that they develop the "excessive masturbation" syndrome. In this case, masturbation is practiced even though the child feels very bad about it. These feelings are reinforced by solitude and fantasy, which leads to depression and a debilitating sense of self-condemnation.

Most psychiatrists argue that masturbation in childhood is not only normal but helpful in forming a positive sexual attitude. It cannot be obsessive at 4, so it should be ignored at that age. However, it can be obsessive at 14, and if the parent suspects this to be the case, a psychologist should be consulted.

Homosexual Behavior

Historically speaking, homosexuality has been surrounded by a number of myths:

- Male homosexuals are sissies and will never get involved in a fight.

- Boys with frail physiques and girls with muscular physiques have a strong tendency to become homosexuals.

- Homosexuality results from a mental disorder, usually caused by a hormone imbalance.

- Homosexual men have overprotective mothers and rejecting, inept fathers; in lesbians, the reverse is true.

- Homosexuals frequently attempt to seduce young boys. Since they cannot give birth to children themselves, this is the only way they can replenish their ranks.

- You can always tell the homosexual male because he "swishes" like a woman when he walks; looks at his fingernails with his fingers pointing away rather than toward himself; uses his hands in an effeminate way, with "limp wrists"; usually talks with a lisp; and crosses his legs like a woman.

- You can always tell a female homosexual because she has unusually short cropped hair; refuses to wear a dress; hates all men; is unusually aggressive; and crosses her legs like a man.

Although one or more of these beliefs are held by many people, there is no evidence, psychological or otherwise, of their validity. Among the most difficult stereotypes confronting homosexuals is the belief that they are "sick." For 23 years, until 1973, the American Psychiatric Association listed homosexuality among its categories of mental illness. In its decision to exclude homosexuality from that category, the APA Board of Trustees argued that because it cannot be said that homosexuality regularly causes emotional distress or is regularly associated with impairment of social functioning, it does not meet the criteria of a mental illness (American Psychiatric Association, 1985). Shortly after this pronouncement, however, one wing of the APA gained acceptance of a category called "Sexual Orientation Disturbance," established for those people, homosexual or otherwise, who suffer anxiety from the sexual choices they have made.

Clearly, some of the stereotypes about homosexuals are untrue and unfair. What generalizations, if any, do you believe can fairly be made about all homosexuals?

Causes of Homosexuality

There have been a number of suggestions about why people become homosexuals. The majority of Americans no longer assume homosexuality is an innate disease (Gallup, 1977). The two most often cited explanations are the **psychoanalytic theory of homosexuality** and the **learning theory of homosexuality.**

The Psychoanalytic Theory of Homosexuality
Freud's psychoanalytic theory of homosexuality suggested that if the child's first sexual feelings about the parent of the opposite sex are strongly punished, the child may identify with the same-sex parent and develop a permanent homosexual orientation. Because researchers have noted many cases in which the father's suppression of the homosexual's Oedipal feelings was not particularly strong, this theory is not held in much regard today.

The Learning Theory of Homosexuality
The learning theory of homosexuality offers another explanation:

❖   *The reigning theory among sex researchers is that homosexuality, like heterosexuality, is "learned behavior"—the product of subtle interaction of the child and the significant people around home. Only birds and lower mammals are rigidly programmed to mate with the opposite sex. The higher one goes on the mammalian scale, the more the organism is under the sway of learning rather than inherited factors. But that does not really mean anything either. Scientists do not yet know how an individual creates a heterosexual or homosexual value system ("Gays on the March," 1975, p. 37).*

The Onset of Homosexuality

For a long time, psychologists believed that homosexuality does not manifest itself until adulthood. Recent studies of male homosexuals reviewed in the *Journal of the American Medical Association* (Remafedi, 1988), however, indicate that this belief was the result of interviews with teens, most of whom were ashamed or otherwise unwilling to tell about their feelings on the subject. The current studies,

---

BOX 15.2

What's Your Opinion?

We have the behaviorists and the psychoanalysts giving their explanations of homosexuality. We have many homosexuals who believe that their sexual orientation became clear so early in life that it could only have been caused genetically. Each of these positions agrees that being homosexual is not a matter of choice for the homosexual. Thus it is argued that they should be accepted the same as heterosexuals, or at the very least be given sympathy, for their role in today's society is not an easy one.

There are also those who believe that homosexuality is a matter of free choice, and that those who choose it are behaving in an immoral way. Homosexuals don't have to be that way; they want to. Because they are immoral and because they disrupt the "natural order of things," they deserve society's condemnation. What's your opinion?

---

using better methods, are in remarkable agreement that at least one-third of all males have had "a homosexual experience that resulted in an orgasm" at least once during their adolescent years. About 10% "are exclusively homosexual for at least three years between the ages of 16 and 55" (p. 222).

Most adult homosexuals remember feeling that they were "different" at about 13 years old, the age when most boys are beginning to notice girls. One study followed boys who were seen by medical personnel because of **gender-atypical behavior** (dressing in girls' clothes, playing with dolls etc.) between the ages of 3 and 6. The majority developed a homosexual identity during adolescence or adulthood.

Remafedi sums up the situation:

❖   *Professionals may deny the existence of gay or lesbian teenagers for a number of reasons, some benign and others more malignant. It is both reasonable and judicious to avoid applying potentially stigmatizing labels to children and adolescents. It is also understandable. . . . to adopt a 'wait and see' approach to a teenager's homosexuality, while providing appropriate preventative and acute health care. However, the reluctance of some professionals to acknowledge the existence and the needs of homosexual adolescents is primarily related to the emotionalism surrounding the issue (p. 224).*

Two other studies reinforce Remafedi's position: those by Harry (1986) and Sullivan and Schneider (1987).

Whatever one believes about homosexuality being a natural stage of sexual development, it is clear that the great majority of people in the United States today do engage in heterosexual behavior sooner or later—and the evidence indicates that they begin much sooner than they used to.

Heterosexual Behavior

At the beginning of this section we presented some statistics on teen sexuality that may have surprised you. To get a clearer picture of this situation, you will need to look at the data provided by a number of other studies that have researched heterosexual teen behavior.

One societal change that seems to have strongly affected adolescent sexuality is maternal employment. Hansson and colleagues (1981) conducted a study to determine whether maternal employment is associated with teenage sexual attitudes

---

BOX 15.3

How to Talk to Teens About Sex (or Anything Else, for That Matter)

Adolescents are more likely to talk to adults who know how to listen—about sex, alcohol, and other important issues. But there are certain kinds of responses, such as giving too much advice or pretending to have all the answers, that have been shown to block the lines of communication.

Effective listening is more than just "not talking." It takes concentration and practice. Below are six communication skills that are useful to anyone who wants to reach adolescents. By the way, these skills can also enhance communication with other adults.

Rephrase the person's comments to show you understand. This is sometimes called **reflective listening**. Reflective listening serves four purposes:

- It assures the person you hear what she or he is saying.
- It persuades the person that you correctly understand what is being said (it is sometimes a good idea to ask if your rephrasing is correct).
- It allows you a chance to reword the person's statements in ways that are less self-destructive. For example, if a person says "My mother is a stinking drunk!" you can say "You feel your mother drinks too much." This is better, because the daughter of someone who drinks too much usually can have a better self-image than the daughter of a "stinking drunk."
- It allows the person to "rehear" and reconsider what was said.

Watch the person's face and body language. Often a person will assure you that he or she does not feel sad, but a quivering chin or too-bright eyes will tell you otherwise. A person may deny feeling frightened, but if you put your fingers on her or his wrist, as a caring gesture, you may find that the person has a pounding heart. When words and body language say two different things, always believe the body language.

Give nonverbal support. This may include a smile, a hug, a wink, a pat on the shoulder, nodding your head, making eye contact, or holding the person's hand (or wrist).

Use the right tone of voice for what you are saying. Remember that your voice tone communicates as clearly as your words. Make sure your tone does not come across as sarcastic or all-knowing.

Use encouraging phrases to show your interest and to keep the conversation going. Helpful little phrases, spoken appropriately during pauses in the conversation, can communicate how much you care:

"Oh, really?"

"Tell me more about that."

"Then what happened?"

"That must have made you feel bad."

Remember, if you are judgmental or critical, the person may decide that you just don't understand. You cannot be a good influence on someone who won't talk to you.

Source: Adapted from U.S. Department of Health and Human Services Publication [ADM] 88–1417, 1988.

and behaviors and increases the likelihood of pregnancy. They found that those girls whose mothers are employed outside the home have a greater tendency to begin sexual relations before the age of 19.

A number of studies have looked at the relationship between sexual communications among family members and sexual behavior (Chewning, and others, 1986; Daugherty & Burger, 1984; Darling & Hiscks, 1982; Fisher, 1986a, 1986b; Moore, Peterson, & Furstenberg, 1986; Wilks, 1986). All have found that parents can have a powerful effect on the children's behavior, including those who are in their late teens, when the parent-child interaction is good, and talk about sexuality is direct.

Wagner (1980) found that sexuality becomes a part of the adolescent's concept of self, regardless of their personal experience or knowledge. She summarizes what we currently know about certain aspects of adolescent sexuality:

- *Knowledge about sexuality.* There is some evidence that teenagers who receive sex information from their parents or someone important to them behave more conservatively and responsibly. Males and females are about equally informed, but neither group knows as much as they need to. For example, 4 out of 10 teens in one study (Zelnick & Kantner, 1977b) thought that the time when you are most likely to get pregnant is during menstruation. Peers and books are the most common sources of information.

- *Attitudes, values, and standards.* Current research reveals a trend toward change in sexual mores among the young. In general, having sex with one person, for whom "love" is felt, is emerging, at least among older teens, as the most popular standard. Adolescent sexuality appears to be affected as much by social change and historical events as by separation and identity formation.

- *Homosexuality.* Most homosexual contact during adolescence is part of a developmental interlude and will not develop into adult homosexual behavior. It happens more among boys than girls, and usually occurs during early adolescence.

- *Male-female differences.* Differences in heterosexual specific practices are more evident in younger than in older adolescents. There is tremendous variability among adolescents in terms of specific sexual practices. More advanced types of sexual behavior (such as petting and intercourse) are occurring at earlier and earlier ages. While there has been a decline in male promiscuity, there has been an increase in female permissiveness.

Wagner (1980) concludes that each new sexual experience provides the adolescent with opportunities to test autonomous behavior in a conflict situation. She states that societal changes in attitudes, standards, and behavior have all been reflected in sexuality among adolescents.

The Many Nonsexual Motives for Teenage Sex

In recent years, researchers have begun to pay more attention to the notion that teens engage in sex for many reasons other than the satisfaction of their prodigious sexual drives. In one of the most enlightening articles on this subject, two adolescent therapists (Hajcak and Garwood, 1989) concluded that for many adolescents, orgasm becomes a "quick fix" for a wide variety of other problems. Among these alternative motives for sex are the desire to

- *Confirm masculinity/femininity.* For some teens, having sex with one or more partners (sometimes called "scoring") is taken as evidence that their sexual identity is intact. This is particularly relevant to those (especially males) who consciously or unconsciously have their doubts about it.

- *Get affection.* Usually some aspects of sexual behavior include physical indications of affection, such as hugging, cuddling, and kissing. To the youth who gets too little of these, sex is not too high a price to pay to get them.

- *Rebel against parents or other societal authority figures.* There are few more effective ways to "get even" with parents than to have them find out that you are having sex at a young age, especially if it leads to pregnancy.

- *Obtain greater self-esteem.* Many adolescents feel that if someone is willing to have sex with them, then they are held in high regard. Needless to say, this is often an erroneous conclusion.

- *Get revenge on or to degrade someone.* Sex can be used to hurt the feelings of someone else, such as a former boyfriend. In more extreme cases, such as "date-rape," it can be used to show the person's disdain for the partner.

- *Vent anger.* Because sex provides a release of emotions, it is sometimes used to deal with feelings of anger. Some teens regularly use masturbation for this purpose.

- *Alleviate boredom.* Another frequent motive for masturbation is boredom.

- *Ensure fidelity of girlfriend or boyfriend.* Some engage in sex, not because they feel like it, but because they fear their partner will leave them if they don't comply.

Using sex for these reasons often has an insidious result. As Hajcak and Garwood (1989) describe it,

❖   *Adolescents have unlimited opportunities to learn to misuse sex, alone or as a couple. This happens because of the powerful physical and emotional arousal that occurs during sexual activity. Adolescents are very likely to ignore or forget anything that transpired just prior to the sex act. Negative emotions or thoughts subside as attention becomes absorbed in sex. . . . The end result is that adolescents condition themselves to become aroused any time they experience emotional discomfort or ambiguity. . . . sexual needs are only partially satisfied [and] the nonsexual need (for example, affection or to vent anger) is also only partially satisfied, and will remain high. . . . the two needs become paired or fused through conditioning. . . . Indulging in sex inhibits their emotional and sexual development by confusing emotional and sexual needs and, unfortunately, many of these teens will never learn to separate the two (pp. 756–758).*

This is not to say that adolescents don't experience genuine sexual arousal. They definitely do, but this does not, by itself, justify sexual activity. These therapists argue that teens need to be taught to understand their motives, and to find appropriate outlets for them. In fact, this has led some experts to recommend sex education that teaches alternatives to premarital sex.

Sexual Abuse

Sexual harassment and abuse during adolescence has been studied by Herold and colleagues (1979). They surveyed young women in college and found that nearly 85% say they have been victims of some sexual offense. The offenses ranged from obscene phone calls (61%) and sexual molestation (44%) to attempted rape (16%) and rape (1%).

BOX 15.4
Postponing Sexual Involvement

Postponing Sexual Involvement is an approach designed for use with 13- through 15-year-old adolescents. It is aimed at reducing pregnancy by decreasing the number of adolescents who become sexually involved. It was developed in Atlanta, Georgia (Howard, 1983).

This program does not offer factual information about sexual reproduction and it does not discuss family planning. Rather the program concentrates on social and peer pressures that often lead an adolescent into early sexual behavior. Particular emphasis is placed on building social skills to help adolescents communicate better with each other when faced with sexual pressures.

One main difference between this curriculum and most sex education programs is that it starts with a given value—that is, you should not be having sex at such a young age. Everything in the curriculum is designed to support this argument. Traditional sex education programs invariably have the implicit goal of reducing teenage pregnancy, but they usually include information on birth control and reproduction so that if young adolescents choose to have sex, they can behave in a responsible manner. This curriculum avoids the double message implied in such traditional programs.

The series is divided into four sessions, each one and a half hours long. The first three sessions occur fairly close together, while the fourth session is used as a reinforcement some three to six months later. The first session focuses on social pressure, with students given opportunities to explore why they feel adolescents engage in sex at an early age. The reasons they usually give involve various needs, such as to be popular, to hang onto a boyfriend, and so forth. The leaders then help the adolescents to understand that sexual intercourse will not necessarily fulfill these needs.

The second session presents further information about peer pressure, both in group sessions and in one-on-one sessions. Adolescents are provided with opportunities to become familiar with common pressure statements and after responses are modeled for them, they practice responding in their own words. Session three involves information and exercises about problem solving. It encourages an understanding of limiting physical expression of affection and through developing and practicing skits, provides help in handling difficult sexual situations. As indicated earlier, the fourth session occurs a number of months later and is used to reinforce the ideas in the first three sessions by applying them to new situations.

This series on "how to say no" was designed to provide young adolescents with the ability to bridge the gap between their physical development and their cognitive ability to handle the implications for such development. It was not developed to replace the provision of actual factual information about sexuality and family planning.

It should be pointed out that as part of the Postponing Sexual Involvement Series, some adolescents' parents also are participating. The goal of the parental involvement is to determine the acceptance level both by the community (parents) and the young adolescents themselves, as well as to learn which delivery styles are most effective. For instance, some of the series are being delivered by peers several years older than the adolescents, while others have adult leaders.

Adolescents are typically abused by someone they know and trust. It is often just a continuation of abuse that started during childhood. The most common type of serious sexual abuse is incest between father and daughter (Alexander & Kempe, 1984). This type of relationship may last for several years. The daughter is often manipulated into believing it is all her fault, and that if she says anything to anyone, she will be seen as a bad person, one who may even be arrested and jailed. The outcome is usually another adolescent statistic: a runaway or even a prostitute.

Most of these offenses were discussed with friends. Very few were reported to parents, police, social workers, or other authorities. It has also been found that the effects of abuse may influence a youth's future relationships. Directly following the experience there may be such "acting out" behaviors as truancy, running away, sexual promiscuity, and damage to school performance and family relationships.

Gruber and colleagues (1982) interviewed a group of female teenagers ranging in age from 13 to 17 who had been sexually abused. These young women were involved in a residential intervention program. Gruber found that the victims sustained a diminished self-worth and a behavioral change of their interpersonal relationships with males. In addition, VanderMay and Neff (1982), in reviewing research and treatment of adult-child incest, concluded that the long-term effects may result in promiscuity, alcoholism, sexual dysfunction, drug abuse, prostitution, depression, and even suicide.

VanderMay and Neff call for improved education to sensitize people to prevent incest, as well as improved reporting systems, legal definitions, and treatment of victims. These may help us better understand and intervene, so that victims can receive professional attention earlier that may alter the long-term effects of abuse.

It is safe to say that sexuality in the lives of late adolescents and young adults in the last decade of this century is very different from in earlier decades (although perhaps not so different from several centuries ago). What is the relationship between this fact and the problem covered in the next section, sexually transmitted disease? That is a complex question.

Very few cases of sexual molestation are actually reported to the authorities.

Sexually Transmitted Diseases

AIDS

Not long ago, when people thought about **sexually transmitted diseases** (STDs), gonorrhea came to mind. In the 70s, it was herpes. Today, **AIDS (Acquired Immune Deficiency Syndrome)** causes the most concern (Forestein, 1989).

AIDS was first diagnosed at Bellevue-New York University Medical Center in 1979 and has quickly approached epidemic proportions. What is known about AIDS is that a virus attacks certain cells of the body's immune system, leaving the person vulnerable to any number of fatal afflictions such as cancer and pneumonia. In addition, the disease can directly infect the brain and spinal cord, causing acute meningitis.

As of July 1989, 100,000 cases of AIDS had been reported since the first diagnosis. Of these 100,000 reported cases, about 60,000 of the patients have died. AIDS now ranks 15th among the leading causes of morbidity and mortality in children and young adults. The first 50,000 cases of AIDS were reported from 1981 to 1987. The second 50,000 were reported in just the following two years (CDC, 1989b). The CDC estimates over 300,000 cases will be reported by 1992 (CDC, 1989c). Keep in mind that these are only *reported* cases of the full-blown AIDS disease. A combination of underdiagnosis and underreporting makes these estimates conservative at best. The CDC estimates that 1–1.5 million people in the United States are currently infected with the initial virus (Office of the Assistant Secretary for Health, 1988). Studies suggest that about 50% of these people will develop the full-blown AIDS disease within 10 years of infection and that 99% will eventually develop the disease (Lifson, Hessol, & Rutherford, 1989).

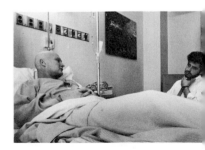

First diagnosed in 1979, AIDS has quickly approached epidemic proportions.

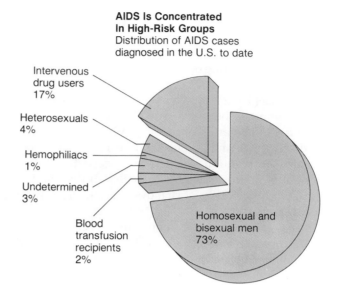

Figure 15.2 *AIDS is concentrated in high-risk groups. The chart shows the distribution of diagnosed AIDS cases to date by group.*
Source: National Center for Health Statistics, 1986.

Trends include increased reporting of AIDS in intravenous drug users, women, children, the elderly, African-Americans, Hispanic-Americans, heterosexuals, small cities, and rural areas (Catania & others, 1989; CDC, 1989a; Kirkland & Ginther, 1988). The only segment of society in which the incidence of AIDS is decreasing are homosexuals with no history of intravenous drug use, although this group still represents the single largest at-risk group (CDC, 1989b).

The AIDS virus is transmitted through the transfer of substantial amounts of intimate bodily fluids such as blood and semen. The virus is most likely to be transferred through sexual contact, the sharing of hypodermic needles and, much less likely, through blood transfusions (a test for AIDS is now available at blood banks and hospitals). In addition, the virus can be transmitted from an infected mother to an infant during pregnancy or birth. Figure 15.2 shows the concentrations of AIDS in each of these groups.

In the initial stages of the spread of the disease in this country, the AIDS virus is most likely to be found in certain segments of the population such as male homosexuals and intravenous drug users, and to a much less degree among hemophiliacs. But that could easily change over time. In some Central African countries, where AIDS is thought to originate, the virus is found equally among men and women throughout the population.

Although there is no cure for AIDS, the disease can be effectively controlled through preventive measures. Use of condoms during sexual intercourse and clean, unused needles during intravenous drug use can drastically reduce the risk of contracting the disease. Figure 15.3 reflects the improvement in protection through use of contraceptives. After a slow start, large scale education efforts by grassroots organizations, as well as by state and federal government agencies, have begun to get these messages out, but the problems remain extremely serious.

First of all, as mentioned, the virus has been highly identified with a few select groups. If you're not gay or a drug user, you might think you don't have to consider preventive measures. However, a person exposed to the AIDS virus may not show any symptoms for between seven and ten years (Curran, 1985). Further, this same person can expose other people to the virus during this incubation phase. Some

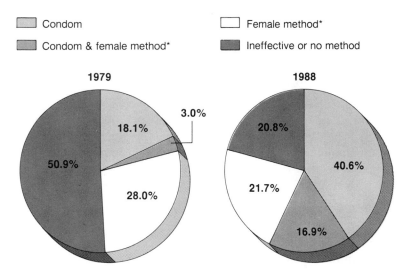

Contraceptive use among US teenage males.

Percent of 17-to-19-year-olds who say they used contraceptives during last sexual intercourse. Source: Knox, 1989.

▢ Condom   ▢ Female method*

▣ Condom & female method*   ▣ Ineffective or no method

1979   **1988**

3.0%
18.1%
50.9%
28.0%

20.8%
40.6%
21.7%
16.9%

*Female methods include pill, IUD, diaphragm, foam, jelly, and sponge

Figure 15.3 *Contraceptive use among United States teenage males. The chart shows the percentage of 17 to 19 year olds who say they used (or didn't use) contraceptives during their last sexual intercourse.*

people have reacted to this by becoming more particular about their sexual partners. Monogamous relationships have been on the rise again during the 1980s after the "liberated" days of the sexual revolution of the 1960s and 1970s. And the educational message seems to be getting through as condom use increases. But many still ignore the dangers and the consequences may be years away.

This may be particularly true among adolescents. Adolescents currently constitute only about one percent of all diagnosed cases of AIDS in the United States (CDC, 1989b). But given the long incubation period and the research findings that suggest that adolescents are not very well informed about AIDS, many researchers think this may be an underestimation. Adolescents are also more prone than the general public to misconceptions and prejudices generated by the frightening new disease. This is particularly true about minority adolescents (Office of the Assistant Secretary for Health, 1988).

For example, there is the misconception that AIDS can be transmitted through casual contact such as kissing or hugging someone with AIDS, or sharing their utensils or bathroom facilities. Such misconceptions unnecessarily increase fear and anxiety in everyone. AIDS prevention efforts aimed at adolescents often have as their main goal the dispelling of such myths (DiClemente, 1987).

Other Sexually Transmitted Diseases

Often lost in the public focus on the burgeoning AIDS problem is a truly epidemic increase in the prevalence of other STDs. Because of its fatal nature, AIDS gets most of the press and the major funding. But STDs such as gonorrhea, syphilis, chlamydia, and herpes are running rampant compared to AIDS, particularly among adolescents. The effects of such venereal diseases range from the mildly annoying to the life threatening. There are more than fifty diseases and syndromes other than AIDS that account for over 13 million cases and 7,000 deaths annually (National Institute of Allergy and Infectious Diseases, 1987).

Some of the more common STDs (other than AIDS) are

- *Chlamydial infection.* **Chlamydia** is now the most common STD, with about 5 to 7 million new cases each year (Subcommittee on Health and the Environment, 1987). There often are no symptoms. It is diagnosed only when complications develop. As with all of these diseases, however, it can be transmitted to another person whether symptoms are present or not.

- *Gonorrhea.* The well-known venereal disease **gonorrhea** accounts for between 1 1/2 and 2 million cases per year. One quarter of those were reported among adolescents (Klassen, Williams, & Levitt, 1989). The most common symptoms are painful urination and a discharge from the penis or the vagina.

- *Pelvic inflammatory disease (PID).* **Pelvic inflammatory disease** (PID) often results from untreated chlamydia or gonorrhea, and frequently causes prolonged problems, including infertility. There are more than one million new cases per year in the United States (Washington, Arno, & Brooks, 1986). Women who are most likely to get it are those who use an intrauterine device for birth control, have multiple sex partners, are teenagers, and/or have had PID before. Symptoms include lower abdominal pain and a fever. PID is so widespread that it causes 2.6 billion dollars in medical costs per year!

- *Genital herpes.* **Genital herpes** is an incurable disease with about 500,000 new cases every year. With no cure, there are now estimated to be about 30 million people in this country who experience recurring pain from this infection.

- *Syphilis.* Although the advent of penicillin has reduced **syphilis** from the killer it used to be, there are 70,000 new cases per year. Its great danger is that in its early stage there are no symptoms. Its first sign is a *chancre* ("shan-ker"), a painless open sore that usually shows up on the tip of the penis and around or in the vagina. After a while this disappears, and if there is not treatment, the disease enters its third stage, which is usually deadly.

Figure 15.4 depicts the relative percentage of new cases of each type of STD in the United States each year.

Studies have shown that the age group at greatest risk for STDs are individuals between 10 and 19 years old (National Institute of Allergy and Infectious Disease, 1987). This is an age group that is particularly difficult to educate in any area concerning sexuality. The obstacles to education include individuals who refuse to take the information seriously, and parents who won't let the information be taught.

The AIDS crisis and the STD epidemic have several features in common. On the negative side, misconceptions contribute to both problems. Many young people believe that only promiscuous people get STDs, and that only homosexuals get AIDS. Having multiple sexual partners does increase the risk of contracting STDs, but most people do not view their sexual behavior, no matter how active, as being promiscuous. Recent research also suggests that *machismo* gets in the way of proper condom use, an effective prevention technique for all STDs. A "real man" doesn't

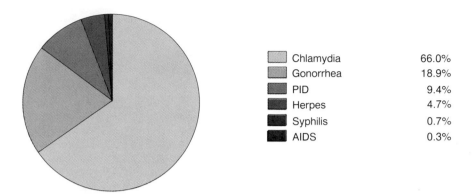

Chlamydia	66.0%
Gonorrhea	18.9%
PID	9.4%
Herpes	4.7%
Syphilis	0.7%
AIDS	0.3%

Figure 15.4 *The relative percentage of new cases of each type of STD in the United States each year.*

use condoms. And finally, when people do contract a disease, strong social stigmas make accurate reporting difficult.

On the positive side, the preventive and educational measures are basically the same for AIDS and other STDs: dispel the myths, increase general awareness and acknowledgment of the problem, and encourage more discriminating sexual practices. Perhaps some of the educational efforts made on behalf of AIDS prevention and treatment will have a helpful effect on the current STD epidemic. Historically, the health focus on STDs has been on treatment, typically with antibiotics, but recently the Public Health Service has shifted its focus for all STDs to prevention. So perhaps comprehensive efforts of this kind that emphasize all STDs will prove fruitful.

In summary, it seems safe to say that major changes in adolescent sexual practices have occurred in recent decades. Many of them must be viewed with considerable alarm, especially when you consider the tragic increases in STDs and pregnancy.

The Teenage Parent

❖   *"You're pregnant," the doctor said, "and you have some decisions to make. I suggest you don't wait too long to decide what you'll do. It's already been seven weeks, and time is running out!"*

"Look, it just can't be true!" I replied. I was trying to convince myself that the clinic doctor was lying. It wasn't supposed to be like this! I was tired of the bitter quarrel I had been having with the doctor. I resented him with every passion. How could I let myself be seen like this?

I had been fearing this answer. I suppose I knew the truth all along, but I really didn't want to face it. I didn't want an abortion, that much I was sure of. Besides, where would I get the money?

For ages now, I had been thinking my period would come any day. Now the truth was in the open! I walked out of the office and headed aimlessly down the street. I looked around and saw only ugliness. I thought about God and how even He had deserted me. It all hurt so much.

"How could this have happened to me?" I thought. "Good girls don't get pregnant!" All of the things my mother had told me were lies. According to her, only the "fast girls got pregnant." The ones who stayed out late and hung around with boys. I wasn't part of that category!

I looked down at my stuffed belly and thought about my family. Would

Table 15.3 Birthrates by Age of Mother (per 1,000 Women) 1960 to 1986												
Age of Mother	**Birthrate**											
	1960	1965	1970	1975	1979	1980	1981	1982	1983	1984	1985	1986
10–14 years	.8	.8	1.2	1.3	1.2	1.2	1.1	1.1	1.1	1.1	1.2	1.2
15–19 years	89.1	70.5	68.3	55.6	51.5	52.3	53.0	52.7	52.9	51.7	50.9	51.3
20–24 years	258.1	195.3	167.8	113.0	109.9	112.8	115.1	111.8	111.3	108.3	107.3	108.9
25–29 years	197.4	161.6	145.1	108.2	108.5	111.4	112.9	112.0	111.0	108.7	108.3	110.5
30–34 years	112.7	94.4	73.3	52.3	57.8	60.3	61.9	61.4	64.2	64.6	66.5	66.5
35–39 years	56.2	46.2	31.7	19.5	19.0	19.5	19.8	20.0	21.1	22.1	22.8	23.9
40–44 years	15.5	12.8	8.1	4.6	3.9	3.9	3.9	3.8	3.9	3.8	3.9	4.0
45–49 years	.9	.8	.5	.3	.2	.2	.2	.2	.2	.2	.2	.2

Source: U.S. National Center for Health Statistics, *Vital Statistics of the United States,* 1989.

> *they be understanding? After all, they had plans for my future. They would be destroyed by the news.*
>
> *"I'm not a tramp," I said to myself. "Then again, I'm only 16 and who would believe that Arthur and I really are in love?"*
>
> *Written by a 17-year-old single parent.*

The feelings of this unmarried girl are all too typical. Children born of these pregnancies have it even harder (Garn & Petzold, 1983). Harvard biological anthropologist Melvin Kohner (1977) sums it up:

❖ *As maternal age drops from age 20, mortality risk for mother and child rise sharply as does the probability of birth defects. Offspring of adolescent mothers, if they survive, are more likely to have impaired intellectual functioning. Poverty, divorce, inept parenting, child neglect, and child abuse are all more frequent in teenage parents (p. 38).*

Trends in Behavior

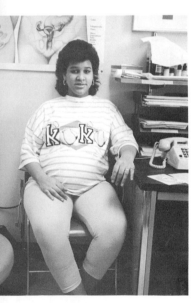

Except for the youngest adolescents, birthrates for adolescents have been dropping in recent years. However, the extent to which young adolescents have been becoming pregnant is certainly a cause for great concern because physically, emotionally, and economically, they are at the greatest risk.

In Table 15.3, it is clear that in the United States the number of live births per 1,000 of married and unmarried females has been dropping steadily and sharply since 1960. The single exception is for 10–14-year-old mothers. This is not to say that pregnancy rates are dropping. In most states, 10%–20% of all females have been pregnant at least once by the time they reach their nineteenth birthday. Clearly this is unfortunate, but the rate for 15–17 year olds, which is about one-third as high, might even be described as catastrophic. And the largest increases in teen pregnancy rates occurred in those under the age of 15 (Westoff, Calot, & Foster, 1983).

Currently over one million teenagers become pregnant in this country every year (Ralph, Lochman, & Thomas, 1984). One in ten girls becomes pregnant before the age of 20 (Foster, 1988). The ramifications of this social problem extend into other social problems. Pregnancy is considered the number one reason for adolescent females dropping out of school (Strobino, 1987). The most likely profile of a pregnant teenager is a girl who is from a minority, grew up in a poor, single-parent home, and has low academic and occupational aspirations (Polit, 1985).

There are many stereotypes about the causes of this epidemic. Some point to earlier menstruation; others talk of the crumbling morals of today's youth. We can say that the images of the fast and easy girl and the sex-obsessed boy are surely false (Elster & Lamb, 1986; Herz & Reis, 1987; Kinard & Reinherz, 1987; Klein & Cordell, 1987; Stiffman and others, 1987). Most of these couples have had a substantial relationship prior to the pregnancy, usually for at least six months. That unmarried

Table 15.4 Birthrate by Race, 1960 to 1986									
Birthrate per 1,000 Women	**118.0**	**96.6**	**87.9**	**66.0**	**65.5**	**67.2**	**67.3**	**65.8**	**65.4**	**66.2**
	1960	1965	1970	1975	1979	1980	1983	1984	1985	1986
White	113.2	91.4	84.1	62.5	61.7	63.4	63.9	62.4	62.2	63.0
Black	153.5	133.2	115.4	87.9	86.7	88.3	84.1	81.7	81.4	82.2

Live-Birth Order	**White**					**Black**				
	1960	**1970**	**1980**	**1984**	**1985**	**1960**	**1970**	**1980**	**1984**	**1985**
Total	113.2	84.1	64.7	62.2	63.0	153.5	115.4	88.1	81.4	82.2
First birth	30.8	32.9	28.4	26.4	26.5	33.6	43.3	35.2	32.2	32.4
Second birth	29.2	23.7	21.0	21.1	21.4	29.3	27.1	25.7	24.1	24.5
Third birth	22.7	13.3	9.5	9.4	9.7	24.0	16.1	14.5	13.7	13.9
Fourth birth	14.1	6.8	3.4	3.2	3.3	18.6	10.0	6.7	6.3	6.3
Fifth birth	7.5	3.4	1.3	1.1	1.1	14.1	6.4	3.0	2.7	2.7
Sixth and seventh	6.1	2.7	.8	.7	.7	18.4	7.0	2.1	1.8	1.8
Eighth and over	2.8	1.2	.3	.2	.2	15.6	5.6	.9	.6	.6

[1]Includes other races not shown separately.
Source: U.S. National Center for Health Statistics, *Vital Statistics of the United States,* 1989.

parents are usually from the lower socioeconomic class and from one-parent families are also untrue generalizations.

Adolescents in the United States have rates of pregnancy that are among the world's highest; this is especially true of inner-city adolescents (Garcia-Coll, Hoffman, & Oh, 1987; Colletta, 1980, 1982; Herz & Reis, 1987; Moore, Jofferth, & Wertheimer, 1979; McKenry, Walters, & Johnson, 1979; Silber, 1980; Stiffman & others, 1987). Six percent of them give birth each year. Of these, one-third give birth out of wedlock, one-third conceive before marriage, and one-third conceive after marriage. In one study, researchers interviewed 1,000 30 year olds and found that 10% of the men and 31% of the women had had a child during adolescence (Russ-Eft, Springer, & Beaver, 1979).

As Lancaster and Hamburg (1986) point out,

❖ *except for the very youngest adolescents, contraception and abortion have lowered the birthrates for adolescents since 1970 to levels that are somewhat lower than those in the 1920s and 1950s. However, the rate of adolescent childbearing outside of marriage has shown steep increases (p. 5).*

What this means is that more and more children are being born without the cultural approval and support that marriage brings.

Racial and Ethnic Differences

Many studies have shown that there are distinct differences among racial and ethnic groups of teenagers in sexual behavior, pregnancy, and the outcomes of such pregnancies (Chilman, 1985; Brooks-Gunn & Furstenberg, 1986). As Table 15.4 shows, African-American teenagers are more likely to give birth, and they have larger families than whites. African-American teenagers also begin sexual experimentation at an earlier age than do white teenagers (Herz & Reis, 1987; Zelnick & Kantner, 1980). The Johns Hopkins University studies determined that African-Americans are more likely to get pregnant than whites during adolescence, but the gap between the two races has been decreasing during the last decade.

One study (Thompson, 1980) compared whites and African-Americans on their beliefs, perceptions, and decisions related to having children. African-American teenagers, both males and females, felt more strongly that having children promotes greater marital success, approval from others, and personal security. They also expressed stronger beliefs that couples should have as many children as they wish. African-American males, more than females, placed a high value on having children, but females felt exposed to stronger social pressures to have children.

A survey by Davis and Harris (1982) of 288 11–18 year olds revealed that females were generally more knowledgeable than males about the facts of maturation and reproduction, pregnancy and contraception. They are also more interested than males in sexual vocabulary.

Urban subjects showed a greater familiarity than rural subjects with several terms, but there were only a few differences between urban and rural teenagers in specific interests. Anglos were generally the most knowledgeable, then Hispanics and Native Americans, and there were a number of differences among ethnic groups in interests. Older subjects knew more facts and were more interested in pregnancy and birth control. The most common source of sexual information was friends; then schools, books/magazines, and parents. Anglos, females, and subjects from rural areas received more information from their parents than male Hispanics, Native Americans, and students from urban areas. Males were more likely to get information from movies than females.

Eberhardt and Schill (1984) compared sexual permissiveness attitudes and the behavior of 53 father-present and 37 father-absent African-American, low socioeconomic status female adolescents (age 14 to 17 years). Within the father-absent group, those subjects whose fathers became absent before they were 5 years old were found to have a significantly higher need for social approval than subjects whose fathers became absent after they were 5 years old. Thus they are more likely to become permissive.

Washington (1983) explored the contraceptive attitudes and practices of 65 13–18-year-old African-American mothers who participated in an inner-city parent education program. The sample was predominantly lower class. A questionnaire was administered to subjects prenatally or shortly postdelivery. Concern over the side effects of contraceptives was the primary reason subjects gave for not using contraception. Motivational factors were secondary, and lack of information about contraception placed last. (It should be noted that the Eberhardt and Washington studies do not look at white attitudes or behaviors.)

A number of studies discovered males are significantly more willing to engage in unprotected intercourse than are females (Clark, Zabin & Hardy, 1984; Cohen & Rose, 1984; Herz & Reis, 1987). Interestingly, however, there were no differences in feelings of responsibility for the pregnancy, should one occur.

Data on 3,568 white, 969 African-American, and 524 Mexican-American women attending a planned parenthood clinic were analyzed by Cummings (1983). Most subjects were age 14 to 24 years, and most sought counseling for an unplanned pregnancy. Analysis showed slight differences among the ethnic groups in terms of sexual and reproductive behavior. There were distinct differences in marital status among the groups, Mexican-Americans being the largest percentage of married clients. African-Americans and Mexican-Americans tended to have given birth to more children than whites and to have experienced their first pregnancy at an earlier age.

Brown (1983) studied 36 African-American adolescent unwed expectant couples (females age 12 to 17 years; males age 16 to 21 years) to assess the quality of their commitment and concerns as couples. It was found that fathers were primarily concerned with financial responsibilities to the child, parenting skills, continued schooling, problems with the girl's parents, and their own future. Results contradict the notion that unwed black fathers exploit their female partners. Regardless of marital status, there is a higher incidence of adolescent parenting among African-Americans than among whites (Russ-Eft & others, 1979).

The Role of Family in Teen Pregnancies

Rosen (1980) examined the extent to which teenagers involve their parents in decision making in resolving unwanted conceptions. Data were obtained from a questionnaire given to 432 unmarried 12–17 year olds with unwanted conceptions. Although few subjects consulted their parents when they first thought they might be pregnant, more than half did involve their mothers in deciding what to do about the pregnancy. The findings indicate that there may be less of a generation gap between parents and teenagers than is often supposed.

However, there is some doubt that communication in and of itself makes much difference. On the basis of their study of 287 African-American and white teens, Furstenberg and colleagues, (1986) concluded that

❖ *most parents do not want to get directly involved and, certainly, most teenagers are reluctant to encourage involvement. . . . [Most parents] are relieved to discover that their teenagers are obtaining contraception. Beyond that, it seems that most are either willing or prefer to respect the adolescent's privacy (p. 241).*

Held (1981) conducted a study of 62 girls, none more than 17 years old, who were in the third trimester of pregnancy. Twenty-two percent were white, 56% African-American, and 16% Mexican-American. Each completed the self-esteem inventory, and rated her perception of the reactions of significant people in her life to the pregnancy.

The person on whom these subjects depended most was the mother; the prospective grandmother was the most disapproving. Social support among the three ethnic groups differed: the African-American woman who was keeping her baby had the highest self-esteem, but she and her mother were least likely to rate the pregnancy as "good" or "OK." White women more often rated the pregnancy highly but had lower self-esteem. The 10 Mexican-Americans reported the least disapproval.

Gabriel and McAnarney (1983) compared the decision about parenthood in two study groups in Rochester, New York: 17 African-American, low-income adolescents (age 15 to 18 years) and 53 white, middle-class adult couples. Their observations showed that the decision to become parents was related to different subcultural values. In contrast to the white adults, the African-American subjects did not see marriage as a prerequisite for motherhood, nor did they view completion of schooling and economic independence as phases of maturation that should precede parenthood.

Instead, these subjects expected that becoming mothers would help them to achieve maturation and acceptance as adults. This may have been due to the fact that the African-American subjects did not see other adult roles as available, whereas middle-class white couples did. At the same time, adolescent pregnancy and out-of-wedlock motherhood were not viewed negatively among the low-income African-American subjects. Health care programs that encourage birth control to avoid "unwanted pregnancies" may be ineffective because they do not address the needs of African-American clients in terms of the values of their own subculture.

In summary, one note of caution: In an extensive review of the literature on adolescent pregnancy, McKenry and colleagues (1979) made an important point about racial difference. They found that while studies of low-income nonwhite girls tended to focus on *social* factors, studies of white, middle-class girls tended to search for *psychological* explanations for the pregnancies and their outcomes. It is important to remember that while racial and social class differences have been reported in the research, some of these differences may have more to do with the researchers than with the teenagers themselves.

Causes of Teenage Pregnancy

Why do so many adolescents get pregnant? According to McKenry and colleagues (1979), many factors combine to create the situation. They divide the causes into four major categories: physiological, psychological, social, and cognitive abilities. A fifth may be added—moral reasoning abilities.

Physiological Causes

It is presently possible for girls to get pregnant at a younger age because of improvements in the general health among Americans. Menarche occurs at an earlier age than in the past. The American Academy of Pediatrics Committee on Adolescence has learned that the fertility rate among girls under 15 years of age has been rising rapidly. Improved nutrition and health care have also contributed to an increase in the potential for young girls to become pregnant (Waltz & Benjamin, 1980).

Psychological Causes

McKenry and colleagues (1979) have stated that sometimes pregnancy is the result of a teenager's conscious or unconscious desire to get pregnant. These researchers found that the psychoanalytic model is preeminent in psychological explanations of adolescent pregnancy. Ego strength and family relationships are the most commonly cited reasons. Low ego strength or a low sense of personal worth is said to lead to sexual acting out or use of sex as an escape. Highly dependent girls with a great need for affection and those experiencing social or psychological stress are more likely to become pregnant. Also, girls who feel they have little control over their lives are more likely to get pregnant.

Social Causes

Poverty influences the pregnancy rate; insufficient economic and social resources may lead to pregnancy (McKenry & others, 1979). Pressure from peers and the influence of the media are also social precursors to pregnancy during adolescence.

Family situations or problems that have been linked to the incidence of adolescent pregnancy include the following: closeness to father, lack of closeness to mother, generally unstable family relationships, father-absence accompanied by resentment of the mother, and feelings of rootlessness.

Cognitive Ability Causes

Another major cause involves young girls' lack of the knowledge and maturity required to prevent unwanted conceptions. One must possess the cognitive ability to foresee the consequences of sexual activity. Epstein (1980) indicated that some teenagers believe they are too young to become pregnant or that their sexual encounters are too infrequent. Many teens do not know it is possible to become pregnant during a single act of intercourse. Others are unable to relate risks of pregnancy to their menstrual cycles or are too menstrually irregular to use such information properly.

Moral Reasoning Ability Causes

Differences in moral reasoning may also contribute, especially in the case of male irresponsibility. Herz and Reis (1987), who studied 251 seventh and eighth grade African-American inner-city teens, summarize the situation:

❖   *Young men may not be able to perceive a cause-and-effect relationship be-*
    tween their interests in sex, their sexual behavior, and the occurrence of preg-
    nancy, retaining instead an egocentric, childlike belief that they will not be
    held accountable for what they do (p. 375).

They are not able to assume mature reasoning in this case. Thus the fact that they feel responsible for the pregnancy is due to their acknowledgment of sexual activity, not to any desire of impregnating their partner. These authors conclude that there is "a clear need for more factual and practical information on the processes of conception and contraception, as well as decision-making and moral-reasoning skill development." (p. 372)

Finally, in their review of the research, Crockett and associates (1986) concluded that we still have much to learn about the causes of teen pregnancy:

❖   *Pubertal change and the development of reproductive potential involve sev-*
    eral interrelated processes. More importantly, we must attend to the meaning
    of these changes to girls. Because in our society we have no puberty rites or
    clear transitional rituals based on maturational status [see the next chapter],
    this change becomes more individually integrated (p. 170).

Thus, because we do not teach them society's expectations (either in school or elsewhere), young teens react to puberty and make sexual decisions on a purely personal basis. There is no one "type" who gets premaritally pregnant in adolescence. All suffer from a lack of knowledge that is probably the major culprit.

Transition

For each of the aspects of social interaction reviewed in this chapter—sexual identity, sex roles, sexual behavior, sexually transmitted diseases, teenage parenthood—there is one consistent trend with which all adolescents must deal: fast-paced change. Some of this change derives from ground swells in today's society, and some results from the nature of adolescence itself.

The advent of feminism has promoted major innovations in our thinking about the appropriate roles males and females should play. The concept of androgyny has been introduced in the past two decades. Yet perhaps nothing has had a more resounding impact on adolescent life than the recent changes in our attitudes toward sexuality. The five areas of greatest change have been in homosexuality, sexually transmitted disease (including AIDS), the earlier and more widespread participation in sex by teenage females, the increase in child pornography and prostitution, and the increase in pregnancy and childbearing among younger teenagers.

Some observers have suggested that the biggest problem facing adolescents today, and one which is intertwined with those just listed, is the difficulty in knowing when childhood and youth have ended and adulthood has begun. When the societal lines between these stages of development are blurred, youth cannot be blamed for not knowing how to behave. A clearer induction into adult life has been advocated. This will be the main topic of the next chapter.

Key Ideas

1.   Sexual identity results from those physical characteristics and behaviors that are part of our biological inheritance.

2.   Sex role, on the other hand, results partly from genetic makeup and partly from the specific traits that are in fashion at any one time and in any one culture.

3.   Many psychologists believe that love feelings develop in three steps: love of one's self (autosexuality); love of members of one's own sex (homosexuality); and love of members of the opposite sex (heterosexuality).

4.   These three stages are also thought to describe the development of human sexuality.

5.   The six major types of sexually transmitted disease are AIDS, chlamydia, gonorrhea, pelvic inflammatory disease, genital herpes, and syphilis.

6.   Although fewer teens are becoming pregnant than in previous years, two disturbing patterns have emerged: the rate among those 15 years old and younger is increasing; and more *unmarried* teenage women are giving birth, with less societal support.

Key Terms

AIDS (Acquired immune deficiency syndrome)
Androgyny
Autosexuality
Chlamydia
Chromosome failure
Gender-atypical behavior
Genital herpes
Gonorrhea
Heterosexuality
Homosexuality
Learning theory of homosexuality
Pelvic inflammatory disease (PID)

Psychoanalytic theory of homosexuality
Reflective listening
Sex role
Sex-role adaptation
Sex-role orientation
Sex-role preference
Sex-role stereotypes
Sexual identity
Sexual revolution
Sexually transmitted diseases
Syphilis
Transsexual operation

What Do You Think?

1.   What aspects of traditional male and female sex roles do you think we should try to keep?

2.   What is your attitude toward androgyny? Would you describe yourself as androgynous? If not, do you wish you were?

3.   Do you agree with the theorists who claim that there are three stages in the development of love and sexuality, and that this development is natural?

4.   Why do you think we are seeing such widespread changes in the sexual aspects of our lives?

5.   If you were the mayor of a medium-size city, what actions would you take to try to reduce the incidence of sexually transmitted diseases?

6.   If you were the mayor of a medium-size city, what actions would you take to try to reduce the incidence of teenage parenthood?

Suggested Readings

Calderone, Mary S., and James Ramsey. (1981). *Talking to your child about sex.* New York: Ballantine. This book offers a creative interpretation of human sexuality in a family setting.

Capote, Truman. [1948] (1988). *Other voices, other rooms.* New York: Signet. Written when Capote was 23 years old, it is considered by many to be his best work. It is the story of a 13-year-old boy who goes to live with his father in Louisiana and meets many eccentric characters. Through this experience he becomes aware of the adult world and his own homosexuality.

Fromm, Erich. (1968). *The art of loving.* New York: Harper & Row. Although most of us think of love as a very personal topic, it would be hard to think of anything that has been the subject of more novels, articles, poems, plays, and psychological treatises. Most of these are not particularly helpful and many are downright corny. Fromm's book is a distinct exception. You will understand what love is and how to give and receive it much better when you have finished reading it.

Tannahill, Reay. (1980). *Sex in history.* New York: Ballantine. This lively book describes the role of sex down through the ages.

Walker, Alice. (1982). *The color purple.* New York: Harcourt Brace Jovanovich. This disturbing story of African-American teenage pregnancy in the South was hailed by all the reviewers for its insight.

PART 7

Early Adulthood

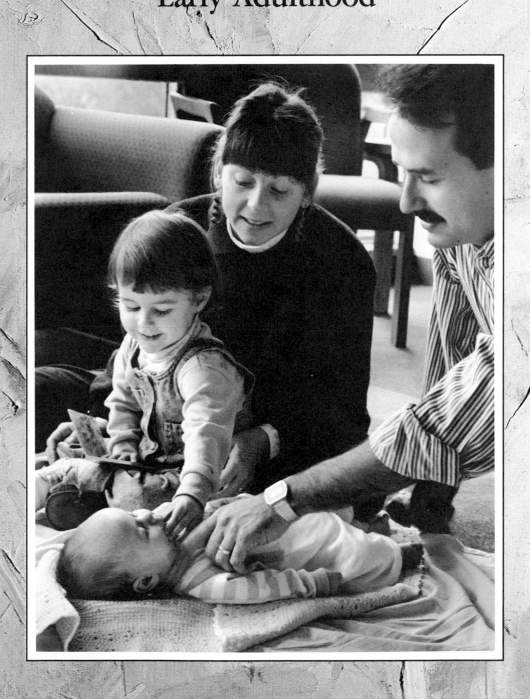

· *Chapter 16* ·

Passages to Maturity

Initiation Rites

❖   *All the young men standing in the living room of the old fraternity house had solemn faces. As the fraternity president began intoning the sacred words that would lead to their induction, Dave and Bill looked at each other out of the corners of their eyes. The two "pledges" were in the front row, waiting along with nine other sheepish-looking freshmen. Each knew the other was remembering the same thing—the long ordeal of their pledge period, which had begun at the start of the semester.*

For weeks they had had to wear ridiculous beanies on their heads and act as virtual slaves to the fraternity brothers. Despite their best efforts to obey the complex rules, each had incurred numerous violations, which the brothers had noted in their pledge books.

Last night, for the initiation opener, they had endured one blow from a thick magazine, rolled up and taped for the purpose, for each of their rules violations. Bent over and holding their ankles, they had managed to get through the bottom-beatings without crying out, but not without becoming very black-and-blue. Then they were taken as a pair and dropped off in the middle of a dark woods with instructions to get back to the frat house by 10 A.M. if they wanted to be initiated.

After numerous scares and mishaps, they made it to the main road and hitched into town. On their return to the house, they thought their initiation was finished, but the ordeal was far from over. Now came a series of lesser trials, including:

- *Being made to lie on their backs while tablespoons of baking soda and then vinegar were poured into their open mouths. They were ordered to close their mouths and keep them that way no matter what. The brothers laughed uproariously when, inevitably, the mixture exploded, shooting a geyser from their tightly-pressed lips high into the air.*

- *Being blindfolded and made to eat warm "dog manure." Actually they had eaten doughnuts soaked in warm water, but the bag of manure held under their noses made them believe it was the real thing.*

- *Having a mixture of Liederkranz cheese and rotten eggs smeared on their upper lips, then being made to run around while inhaling the dreadful odor.*

Now, as the torture was over, and the final ceremony underway, both Dave and Bill had the same thought in their minds: I've done it! I've survived! I'm in!

The horrors of the fraternity initiation have been softened by legal restrictions and by more humane attitudes. For example, Baier and Williams (1983) surveyed 440 active members and 420 alumni members of the fraternity system of a large state university. They compared attitudes of these men toward 22 **hazing practices** (such as those just described) known to be used by the frats. They found the active members were considerably opposed to more of the practices than the alumni.

Nevertheless, most of us have heard of recent cases of maimings and even deaths of young men who have been put through hazing. Such trials are held by people at all socioeconomic levels and racial and ethnic backgrounds. They are organized by sports teams and criminal gangs, and are not limited to males, either.

Nor is the problem limited to the United States. For example, in his study of French juvenile delinquents, Garapon (1983) saw a "symbolic, sacrificial dimension" to their crimes. He notes that often cars and other stolen goods are either dumped in the canals or burned, which he feels parallels the sacrifices of prized goods that preindustrial tribes carry out with fire and water. He points out other links to tribal initiations: most crimes are committed at night, and wind up in courtrooms, where there are symbolic costumes such as the judge's robes. In Germany, Zoja (1984) has suggested similar parallels in the path to drug addiction. He states that "Drug addiction can be an active choice, allowing the user to acquire a solid identity and social role, that of the negative hero, as well as access to an esoteric glimpse of an 'other world' " (p. 125).

Why do some people, and the groups they wish to be associated with, seem to enjoy holding **initiation rites** so much? And why are so many adolescents, many of them otherwise highly intelligent and reasonable, willing and eager to endure such pain? Is it simply because they want to join the group, to feel that they belong? There seems to be more to it than that. Throughout the world, adolescents readily engage in such activities because they seem to want to be tested, to prove to themselves that they have achieved the adult virtues of courage, independence, and self-control. And the adults seem to agree that adolescents should prove they have attained these traits before being admitted to the "club of maturity." Compare the activities that Dave and Bill were put through to those of two members of a "primitive" African tribe, Yudia and Mateya, in Box 16.1.

Analysis of an Initiation Rite

Before discussing the implications of American initiation rites (or the lack of them), we'll provide a more detailed description of the purposes and components of such rites.

The first analysis of initiation ceremonies in preindustrial societies such as the Kaguru was completed by anthropologist Arnold Van Gennep in 1909 (Van Gennep, 1960). His explanation is still highly regarded, as can be seen in more recent studies (e.g., Anderson & Noesjirwan, 1980; Brain & others, 1977; Hill, 1987; Kitahara, 1983; Lidz & Lidz, 1984; Morinis, 1985; Ramsey, 1982). Van Gennep argued that the purpose of the initiation rites, as with all rites of passage (marriage, promotion, retirement, etc.) is to cushion the emotional disruption caused by a change from one status to another. As Brain and associates (1977) put it:

❖ *These rites are seen as a part of general human concern. . . . The particular problem being dealt with is the change from childhood, seen as asexual, to adulthood, seen as sexual. Further, sex is threatening, since it is connected with death and with the unique human knowledge of mortality (p. 191).*

For males, this transition also involves the end of dependence on their mothers and other older women and the beginning of their inclusion in the world of men.

This ceremony is often scheduled to coincide with the peak in adolescent physiological maturation, and therefore has often been called a **puberty rite.** Van Gennep argues that this is inappropriate, since initiation may be held by one tribe when the children are 8 years old, and in another at 16. Children of 8 have not yet started puberty; those of 16 are halfway through it. Also, the age at which puberty starts differs from individual to individual, and now occurs approximately three years earlier than it did one hundred years ago (see chap. 13). Nevertheless, the initiation rite is usually held at one age within each tribe, regardless of the physical maturity of the individual initiates.

Serving as an introduction to sexuality and separation from mother is one purpose of the initiation rite. Several other purposes have been suggested. In his classic text *Totem and Taboo* (1914/1955), Sigmund Freud offered the psychoanalytic

After months of grueling training, teenage members of most pre-industrial tribes, such as these San Carlos Apaches, are inducted into adulthood.

BOX 16.1

Multicultural Focus: Yudia and Mateya Come of Age

Yudia cannot believe how rapidly her feelings keep changing. One moment she is curious and excited, the next, nervous and afraid. Tonight begins her *igubi,* the rite that celebrates her induction into adulthood. Yudia has longed for this day most of her 11 years, but now she wonders if she really wants the responsibilities of a grown-up.

Though it seems much longer, only a week has passed since the excruciating beginning of her initiation. The memory of it is already dimming: the bright fire, her women relatives pinning her down on the table, her grandmother placing a thin sharp stone against her vulva, the searing strips of pain.

The women had held and consoled her, empathizing fully with her feelings. Each had been through the same agony. For them, too, it occurred shortly after their first menstruation. They had explained to her that this was just the beginning of the suffering she must learn to endure as an adult woman. All during the past week, they had been teaching her—about the pain her husband would sometimes cause her, about the difficulties of pregnancy and childbirth, about the many hardships she must bear stoically. For she is Kaguru, and all Kaguru women accept their lot in life without complaint.

It has been a hard week, but tonight the pleasure of the *igubi* will help her forget her wound. There will be singing, dancing, and strong beer to drink. The ceremony, with its movingly symbolic songs, will go on for two days and nights. Only the women of this Tanzanian village will participate, intoning the time-honored phrases that will remind Yudia all her life of her adult duties.

In a large hut less than a mile from the village, Yudia's male cousin Mateya and seven other 13-year-old Kaguru boys huddle close, even though the temperature in the closely thatched enclosure is a stifling 110 degrees. Rivulets of sweat flow from their bodies and flies dot their arms, backs, and legs. They no longer pay attention to the flies, nor to the vivid slashes of white, brown, and black clay adorning all their faces. Their thoughts are dominated by a single fear: will they cry out when the elder's sharpened stone begins to separate the tender foreskin from their penises? Each dreams of impressing his father, who will be watching, by smiling throughout the horrible ordeal.

---

explanation. In his view, such ceremonies are necessitated by the conflict between fathers and sons over who will dominate the women of the tribe. Adolescent males are seen as challenging the father's authority and right to control the women.

In order to make clear their supremacy in the tribe and to ensure the allegiance of the young males, the adults set a series of trials for the youth at which the adults are clearly superior. The ultimate threat held over the young is castration, the loss of sexual power. Most rites include trials of strength, endurance, prowess, and courage. These usually involve forced ingestion of tobacco and other drugs, fumigations, flagellations, beatings with heavy sticks (running the gauntlet), tattooing, cutting of the ears, lips, and gums, and that most Freudian of inflictions, the circumcision of the foreskin of the penis.

The message is clear: "We, the adult males, are in charge. Join us and be loyal, or else!" Psychologist Bruno Bettleheim (1969) agrees with Freud that there is a fear of castration among the males, but argues that the main role of the initiation rite is to ease the stress of becoming an adult, not to exaggerate it.

BOX 16.1

Continued

Three months of instruction and testing have brought the young men to this point. They have learned many things together: how to spear their own food, how to tend their tiny gardens, how to inseminate their future wives, and most important, how to rely on themselves when in danger.

The last three months have been exhausting. They have been through many trials. In some, they had to prove they could work together; in others, their skill in self-preservation was tested. For most of them, being out of contact with their mothers was the hardest part. They have not seen any of the female members of their families since they started their training. Unlike Yudia's initiation, which is designed to draw her closer to the adult women of the tribe, Mateya's initiation is designed to remove him forever from the influence of the females, and to align him with the adult men.

Now it is evening. Mateya is the third to be led out to the circle of firelight. Wide-eyed, he witnesses an eerie scene. His male relatives are dancing in a circle around him, chanting the unchanging songs. The grim-faced elder holds the carved ceremonial knife. Asked if he wishes to go on, the boy nods yes. Abruptly the ritual begins: the hands of the men hold him tight; the cold knife tip touches his penis; a shockingly sharp pain sears his loins; he is surprised to hear a piercing scream; then, filled with shame, he realizes it comes from him.

Thus far, Yudia's and Mateya's initiations have been different. Mateya's has been longer and harder than Yudia's. She is being brought even closer to the women who have raised them both, but Mateya must now align himself with the men. (Freud stated that, unlike females, all males must give up their identification with their mother; this makes adult males subconsciously doubtful of their sexual identity.)

The initiations are similar, though, in that both youths have experienced severe physical pain. In both cases, the operations were meant to sensitize them to the vastly greater role sex will now play in their lives. Furthermore, their mutilations made them recognizable to all as adults of the Kaguru tribe.

At this "coming out" ceremony, males and females also receive new names, usually those of close ancestors. This illustrates the continuity of the society. The beliefs of the tribe are preserved in the continuous flow from infant to child to adult to elder to deceased and to newborn baby again. When all is done, Yudia and Mateya can have no doubt that they have passed from childhood to adulthood.

The Passage to Adulthood in Western Countries

The Transition to Adulthood in the United States

In the industrial past of the United States, it used to be fairly clear when one became an adult. In their late teens, boys and girls usually got married and assumed an adult role. Males were accepted as partners in the family farm or business; females became housewives. This has changed in many ways. What Black (1974) has suggested is still true:

❖ *Today, in modern society, initiation of the boy and girl into adult life is far more complicated. Society is fast, heterogeneous, a network of interdependent groups with many different backgrounds, traditions, and outlooks, the products of religious, racial, national, and class differences. In our age of technology, the young have to learn to deal with cars and trains and planes, machines and other electronic equipment, typewriters, television sets, com-*

BOX 16.2

Multicultural Focus: Initiation Rites in the United States

Do we have initiation rites in United States society? In the spaces below, write down as many initiation rites in which you have participated as you can think of. Did these rites help you become an adult? Were they sufficient? Were they formal or informal? Taken together, do they indicate an American definition of maturity? Some activities that may be considered initiation rites are suggested on this page and page 423.

1.	11.
2.	12.
3.	13.
4.	14.
5.	15.
6.	16.
7.	17.
8.	18.
9.	19.
10.	20.

---

puters, and mass production assembly lines. They face high concentrations of population, high mobility, and relationships on regional, national, and global levels. All this they have to know and understand at a time when customs, laws and institutions are undergoing drastic and rapid change in the midst of a high degree of human differences and human conflict (p. 25).

There are no specific rituals comparable to those in preindustrial societies to help Western youth through this difficult period. For example, religious ceremonies like confirmation and bar mitzvah no longer seem to play the role they had in earlier times. Kilpatrick (1975) argues that

❖ *At some point we grew too sophisticated, at some point the rituals lost their vitality and became mere ornaments. We may still keep their observance, but they are like old family retainers, kept on in vague remembrance of their past service (p. 145).*

In his anthology of adolescent literature, Thomas Gregory (1978) points out that many modern writers find the decline of the initiation rite in the United States a noteworthy theme. He describes their thinking as follows:

❖ *Today's adolescents are faced with not knowing when they have reached maturity. . . . the absence of a formal rite of passage ceremony necessitates a larger and more uncertain transition, with much groping, as adolescents not only try to establish their new adulthood, but also their identity (p. 336).*

Types of Initiation Activities in the United States

This is not to say that Americans have *no* activities that signal the passage to maturity. We have a number of types of activities, which usually happen at various stages and ages of adolescence. Here is a list of the types and some examples of each:

Religious
Bar mitzvah or bat mitzvah
Confirmation
Participating in a ceremony, such as reading from the Bible

Sexual
Menarche (first menstruation)
Nocturnal emmissions (male "wet dreams")
Losing one's virginity

Social
"Sweet Sixteen" debutante party
Going to the senior prom
Joining a gang, fraternity, or sorority
Beginning to shave
Being chosen as a member of a sports team
Moving away from one's family and relatives
Joining the armed forces
Getting married
Becoming a parent
Voting for the first time

Educational
Getting a driver's license
Graduating from high school
Going away to college

Economic
Getting a checking or credit card account
Buying one's first car
Getting one's first job

The tuxedo and party dress might be considered costumes in one of America's initiation rites.

The Adolescent Moratorium

In the late twentieth century, the attitude that youth need a "time out" period to explore possibilities and to continue education has become widespread. This phase of life is known as the **adolescent moratorium** (see chap. 12).

Perhaps it is natural that we have discarded rites of passage into adulthood for the more leisurely moratorium. In preindustrial societies, children must take over the responsibilities of adulthood as quickly as possible. The survival of the tribe depends on getting as much help from all individuals as possible. In industrial societies, and even more so in our "information-processing" society, the abundance of goods makes it less necessary that everyone contribute to the society. There is also a need for more extensive schooling in preparation for technical types of work. The moratorium, then, comes about because of our advanced economic system. For these reasons, the initiation ritual has declined considerably since the nineteenth century. Is our society the better or worse for this change?

Implications of the Lack of an Initiation Ceremony

Today we have doubts that this moratorium is turning out to be effective. In fact, it appears that crime is one of the ways that some youth are *initiating themselves* into adulthood. Males especially seem to need to do something dangerous and difficult. Males raised without fathers or father substitutes are especially vulnerable to the attractions of criminality (Dacey, 1986). When they are leaving adolescence, many of them seem to feel they must prove their adulthood by first proving their manhood in risk-taking behavior.

BOX 16.3

The Components of Maturity

Think of the woman and the man who are the most mature persons you know—people with whom you are personally familiar, or people who are famous. Then ask yourself, "Why do I think these people are so much more mature than others?" In the spaces below, for both the male and the female, create a list of the characteristics that seem to distinguish them in terms of their maturity.

Female
1.
2.
3.
4.
5.
6.
7.
8.
9.
10.

Male
1.
2.
3.
4.
5.
6.
7.
8.
9.
10.

How much do the lists differ? Is male maturity significantly different from female maturity? Which of the two people is older? Which of the two do you admire more? Which of the two are you more likely to want to imitate? Were you able to think of many candidates for this title of "most mature adult," or was it difficult to think of anyone? Are either or both of the people you picked professionals? Are either or both of these persons popular with their own peer group? What is the significance of your answers to you?

For much of their childhood, males in the United States are also highly dependent upon female attention. This is especially true among those whose fathers are absent. Such a youth sometimes compensates by:

❖   *joining tribe-like gangs and undergoing harsh initiation rites, all in the service of proving his manhood. Much of the trouble that these youth get into serves the same function as primitive rituals. To compensate for the dominant role of mother in his childhood, the boy needs a dramatic event or a series of them to establish male identity (Kilpatrick, 1975, p. 155).*

In the 1960s and early 1970s, American youth sought to establish their identities by imitating the very rituals of the preindustrial tribes described earlier in this chapter. Known as "hippies" and "flower children," they attempted a return to a simpler life. Many of them returned to the wilderness, living on farms and communes away from the large cities in which they were brought up. Many totally rejected the cultural values of their parents. The most famous symbol of their counterculture was the Woodstock musical marathon in 1969. With its loud, throbbing music, nudity, and widespread use of drugs, it was similar to many primitive tribal rites. Yet these self-designed initiation rites also seem to be unsuccessful as passages to maturity. Most of the communes and other organizations of the youth movement of the 1960s have since failed. Most American youth have decided "you can't go back again."

Organized sport is another attempt to include initiation rites in American life. The emphasis on athletic ability has much in common with the arduous tasks given to preindustrial youth. In particular, we can see a parallel in the efforts by fathers to get their sons to excel in Little League baseball and Pop Warner football. Fathers

It has been suggested that sports play the same role in life as the arduous tasks performed by youths in centuries past: learning coordination, cooperation, and the other skills necessary in adult work. Can you think of ways that sports might serve as initiation rites?

(and often mothers) are seen exhorting the players to try harder, to fight bravely, and when hurt, to "act like a man" and not cry.

Thus, in delinquency, the counterculture, and sports, we see evidence that members of several age groups today yearn for the establishment of some sort of initiation rite. Adolescents and adults alike seem to realize that something more is needed to provide assistance in this difficult transitional period. But what?

Traditional initiation rites are inappropriate for American youth. In preindustrial societies, individual status is ascribed by the tribe to which the person belongs. Social scientists call this an *ascribed identity*. The successes or failures of each tribe determine the prestige of its members. Family background and individual effort usually make little difference. In earlier times in the United States, the family was the prime source of status. Few children of the poor became merchants, doctors, or lawyers. Today, personal effort and early commitment to a career path play a far greater role in the individual's economic and social success. This is called an *achieved identity*. For this reason (and others), preindustrial customs are not compatible with Western youth today.

A number of prominent thinkers have suggested that human development could be enhanced if the transition from adolescent to adult were clearer. But how to do it? Here are two suggestions that have been studied.

Two Proposals

These following two ideas on an initiation procedure have been lately gaining in popularity. As you read about them, question whether either or both would fulfill the need for some kind of initiation into adulthood.

Outward Bound

The **Outward Bound** program (Outward Bound, 1988) was founded during World War II to help merchant seamen in England survive when their ships were torpedoed. Early in the war, it was learned that many sailors died because they became paralyzed with fear when their ship was hit. Outward Bound was designed to prepare these men to handle their fears in dangerous situations. The program was so successful that after the war it was redesigned for much broader use.

Its basic premise is that when people learn to deal with their fears by participating in a series of increasingly threatening experiences, their sense of self-worth increases and they feel more able to rely on themselves. The program uses such potentially threatening experiences as mountain climbing and rappeling, moving about in high, shaky rope riggings, and living alone on an island for several days. Some of the experiences in the program also involve cooperation of small groups to meet a challenge, such as living in an open rowboat on the ocean for days at a time.

Outward Bound has grown rapidly in recent years, and has installations throughout the country. Each program emphasizes the use of its particular surroundings. For example, the Colorado school emphasizes rock climbing, rappeling, and mountaineering. The Hurricane Island school in Maine uses sailing in open boats on the ocean as its major challenge. The school in Minnesota emphasizes reflection and development of appropriate spiritual needs.

Outward Bound has proven its special worth for teenagers. It originally started with males, but most of its sessions now include equal numbers of males and females. The program operates as a basic rite of passage by offering a chance to prove one's self-worth and to have this feeling validated by others. The philosophy of the program is that participants cannot be told what they are capable of, but must discover it for themselves.

Although they hardly know each other, these boys will find that working together to achieve the goals of this Outward Bound program quickly serves to break down the boundaries society establishes between strangers.

If the Outward Bound experience can effectively reduce **recidivism rates** (the percentage of convicted persons who commit another crime once they are released from prison), it would have widespread implications in treating juvenile delinquents. This program is not punitive as reform schools are, and is considerably less expensive than prison. However, there is reason to believe that the effectiveness of the program decreases significantly after the enrollees have spent some time back in their neighborhoods. Perhaps this just means that they must be brought back for "booster" sessions from time to time.

Although there is a lack of extensive experimental evidence on the effects of Outward Bound, there is no scarcity of testimony from the participants themselves. As one short teenager put it, "Size really doesn't matter up there. What really counts is determination and self-confidence that you can do it!"

Many graduates say that they find life less stressful and feel more confident about their everyday activities as a result of participating in Outward Bound. One of the most positive aspects of the program is its effect on women. Many say that they are surprised to discover how much more self-reliant they have become. Probably the most important result is that most graduates say they feel more responsible and grown-up after having been through the experience.

A number of these types of programs have sprung up over the country. One is the Vision Quest Program in Pine River, Michigan (Wiland, 1986). This approach uses Indian ceremonies to prepare participants for a four-day solo experience designed to "demarcate the questor's entrance into society as a fully responsible and mature adult" (p. 30).

The Walkabout Approach

In the remote regions of Australia, the aborigines have a rite of passage for all 16-year-old males. It is known as the **walkabout.** In the walkabout, the youth, having received training in survival skills throughout most of his life, must leave the village and live for six months on his own. He is expected not only to stay alive, but to sustain himself with patience, confidence, and courage. During this six-month estrangement from home and family, he learns to strengthen his faith in himself. He returns to the tribe with the pride and certainty that he is now accepted as an adult member.

According to educator Maurice Gibbons (1974),

❖   *The young native faces an extreme but appropriate trial, one in which he must demonstrate the knowledge and skills necessary to be a contributor to the tribe rather than a drain on its meager resources. By contrast, the young North-American is faced with written examinations that test skills very far removed from actual experience he will have in real life (p. 597).*

As a result of Gibbons' article, a group was set up by Phi Delta Kappa (PDK), the national education fraternity, to see what could be done about promoting walkabouts for boys and girls in this country. A booklet has been produced that makes specific suggestions. In it, the PDK Task Force suggests that:

❖   *The American walkabout has to focus the activities of secondary school. It does so by demonstrating the relationship between education and action. It infuses the learning process with an intensity that is lacking in contemporary secondary schools. The walkabout provides youth with the opportunity to learn what they can do. It constitutes a profound maturing experience through interaction with both older adults and children. The walkabout enriches the relationship between youth and community (Task Force, 1976, p. 3).*

There is also a monthly magazine that prints stories about the various types of walkabouts that students in participating schools have devised.

The Australian aborigines train their teenaged youth, such as this boy learning to spear a ray, to subsist while on a solo "walkabout," an extended initiation rite. The walkabout has been used as a model to induct American youths into adulthood.

BOX 16.4

What's Your Opinion?

A number of prominent educators believe that schools should concern themselves only with intellectual matters, not with personal and social development. Do you agree? These educators are opposed to ideas like Outward Bound and walkabout.

How do you feel about these two ideas? If you like these ideas, can you use them as a springboard to other methods by which we adults might help youth in their "passage to maturity"?

There are three phases in the process: pre-walkabout, walkabout, and post-walkabout. Each of these phases calls for learning specific skills. In the pre-walkabout, adolescents study personal, consumer, citizenship, career, and lifelong learning skills. In the walkabout itself, the skills to be mastered are logical inquiry, creativity, volunteer service, adventure, practical skills, world of work, and cognitive development. The task force suggests a great number of activities that foster learning in each of these skills. Most involve at least six months of supervised study and activity outside the school, such as working in a halfway house for mental patients.

The post-walkabout is a recognition that the student has engaged in a major rite of passage on his way to adulthood. It is not enough to recognize this experience in a ceremony where members are confirmed en masse, such as the typical graduation. Instead, an individual ceremony involving the graduate's family and friends is held for each walkabout the student undergoes.

❖ *The celebration of transition could take a variety of forms. The ceremonies are varied according to family tastes and imagination, but in each celebration the graduate is the center of the occasion. Parents and guests respond to the graduate's presentation. Teachers drop by to add their comments and congratulations. The graduate talks about his or her achievements, sharing some of the joys and admitting the frustrations (Task Force, 1976, p. 34).*

The Outward Bound and walkabout procedures are becoming popular, and they will almost certainly help to alleviate the need for transitional activities, but they are clearly not sufficient in themselves. The complexity of American adulthood requires a variety of such approaches, if we are to develop in our youth the kind of mature women and men we want.

Before we can specify initiation activities that would be useful in inducting youth into adulthood, perhaps we need a clearer idea of the successful adult. To put this another way: "What is a mature person?" This question has intrigued thinkers throughout recorded history. It has been variously described as a search for peace, for the knowledge of God, for satori, for nirvana, for self-actualization, or for wisdom. We will be exploring the many aspects of maturation in the chapters that follow, but first we want to consider another aspect of "growing up," dealing with the stresses of adult life in a mature way.

Dealing With the Stresses of Adulthood

Table 16.1 contains a list of common life events and the ratings they have been given. To evaluate the amount of stress you are under, check the events that have happened to you in the past year. Total your score; it will be explained later in the chapter.

Table 16.1 Social Readjustment Rating Scale	
Life Events	**Life Crisis Units**
1. Death of spouse	100 _____
2. Divorce	73 _____
3. Marital separation	65 _____
4. Jail term	63 _____
5. Death of close family member	63 _____
6. Personal injury or illness	53 _____
7. Marriage	50 _____
8. Fired at work	47 _____
9. Marital reconciliation	45 _____
10. Retirement	45 _____
11. Change in health of family member	44 _____
12. Pregnancy	40 _____
13. Sex difficulties	39 _____
14. Gain of new family member	39 _____
15. Business readjustment	39 _____
16. Change in financial state	38 _____
17. Death of close friend	37 _____
18. Change to different line of work	36 _____
19. Change in number of arguments with spouse	35 _____
20. Mortgage over $10,000	31 _____
21. Foreclosure of mortgage or loan	30 _____
22. Change in responsibilities at work	29 _____
23. Son or daughter leaving home	29 _____
24. Trouble with in-laws	29 _____
25. Outstanding personal achievement	28 _____
26. Wife begins or stops work	26 _____
27. Begin or end school	26 _____
28. Change in living conditions	25 _____
29. Revision of personal habits	24 _____
30. Trouble with boss	23 _____
31. Change in work hours or conditions	20 _____
32. Change in residence	20 _____
33. Change in schools	20 _____
34. Change in recreation	19 _____
35. Change in church activities	19 _____
36. Change in social activities	18 _____
37. Mortgage or loan less than $10,000	17 _____
38. Change in sleeping habits	16 _____
39. Change in number of family get-togethers	15 _____
40. Change in eating habits	15 _____
41. Vacation	13 _____
42. Christmas	12 _____
43. Minor violations of the law	11 _____
TOTAL	_____

From T. H. Holmes and R. H. Rahe, "A Social Adjustment Scale" in *Journal of Psychosomatic Research,* 11:213–218. Copyright © 1967 Pergamon Press, Inc., Elmsford, NY.

In chapter 12, we cited the oft-repeated warning of parents that adolescence is the last chance to have fun, because becoming an adult means taking on the heavy responsibilities of maintaining a job and a family. Well, this is not to say that infancy, childhood, and the teen years are free of stress—far from it! As adolescent psychologist David Elkind (1989) summarizes the current situation:

❖   *Young teen-agers today are being forced to make decisions that earlier gen-*
      erations didn't have to make until they were older and more mature—and
      today's teen-agers are not getting much support and guidance. This pressure
      for early decision-making is coming from peer groups, parents, advertisers,
      merchandisers and even the legal system (p. 24).

The section that follows applies to these years, too. But we have included this
section in the adult part of our book because the stresses of adulthood are different
in one important way: more and more, adults are expected to deal with stress *en-*
tirely on their own. True, we adults can and should expect help from others, but
there are an increasing number of crises where independent decisions and actions
are called for. For example, many more families today exist in a state of *ongoing,*
unending crisis. In these families, there is often only one parent, who is unable to
work and therefore is below the poverty level, and who has one or more handicapped or highly disruptive children (Smith, 1990).

Sometimes stress may be due to childhood traumas that begin to manifest themselves only during adulthood. This may be due to psychological defense mechanisms such as denial (see chap. 18). Brown and associates (1975) studied depression
in working-class English women. Among those women who suffered with depression, there was a high incidence of separation from or loss of their mothers by death
in early childhood. Many of these women had been born before or during World
War II, and, as a result of the Battle of Britain, were sent as children to the country-
side or to other countries to protect them from the German bombing of the major
British cities. Other research has looked at the delayed effects caused by environmental factors such as noise (Cohen & Spacapan, 1978). Knowing how stress works,
and how to handle it effectively, is a necessary building block in the process of
maturation.

As should be clear by now, there are many sources of stress, regardless of your
age. Mainly, stress is due to change. It is the nature of human development to produce inexorable change in every aspect of our existence. This situation is difficult
enough when we are young, but at least then we have the support of parents, teachers,
and other adults, as well as a more resilient body. There does seem to be more stress
as we get older. As we move from early to late adulthood, we must rely more and
more on knowledge and insight to avoid having a stressful life. What follows is a
detailed description of just what stress is, and how humans try to deal with it.

Change as a Source of Stress

❖   *If the last 50,000 years of man's existence were divided into lifetimes of ap-*
      proximately 62 years each, there have been about 800 such lifetimes. Of these
      800, fully 650 were spent in caves. Only during the last 70 lifetimes has it been
      possible to communicate effectively from one lifetime to another—as writing
      made it possible to do. Only during the last six lifetimes did masses of men
      ever see a printed word. Only during the last four has it been possible to mea-
      sure time with any precision. Only in the last two has anyone anywhere used
      an electric motor. And the overwhelming majority of all the material goods
      we use in daily life today have been developed within the present, the 800th,
      lifetime (Toffler, 1970, p. 148).

With the incredible amount of change in this current "lifetime," it is not surprising
that the twentieth century has been called the most stressful in which humans have
ever lived. So great have been the results of change in terms of stress that sociologist
Alvin Toffler (1970, 1984) has labeled it a new disease: **future shock.** Future shock
is the illness that results from having to deal with too much change in too short a
time. Toffler compares it to culture shock, the feeling we get when arriving in a

foreign country for the first time. We become disoriented and anxious, but in the back of our minds, we know that if this discomfort becomes too great, we have only to get on the plane and go back to our own culture where we can feel safe again. Future shock causes the same kind of stressful feeling, except there is no going home to escape from it.

Why is change so stressful? Toffler suggests that the stress results not so much from the direction or even the kind of changes that we are faced with in this century, but rather from the incredible *rate* of change in our daily lives. He suggests that there are three major aspects of rate of change, each of which is rapidly increasing:

- **Transience.** There is a lack of permanence of things in our lives. Toffler documents in great detail how much more transient (fast-moving) our lives have become in this century.

- **Novelty.** Some changes are more novel than others. New situations in our lives are more dissimilar from old situations than they used to be, and therefore far more stressful.

- **Diversity.** It also matters what percentage of our lives is in a state of change at any one time. People used to maintain stability in most of their lives, allowing only a few aspects to change at any particular point. This stable proportion is now much smaller for most of us.

Although the escalating rate of change in our lives has increased the amount of pressure we are under, research is increasing our understanding of it and so helping us deal with it better.

Stimulus Reduction Versus Optimum Drive Level

Many a gifted person has been done in by a promotion.

(Cassem, 1975)

Practically everything we do or attempt to do involves overcoming some type of obstacle. Therefore to be alive is to be under stress. According to Canadian physiologist Hans Selye (1985), the most successful researcher and theorist in this field, "Crossing a busy intersection, exposure to a draught, or even sheer joy are often enough to activate the body's stress mechanism to some extent." (p. 5).

Freud was the first to espouse the notion that human beings try to avoid stimulation whenever possible. He referred to this tendency as **stimulus reduction.** According to this idea, all our activities are attempts to eliminate stimulation from our lives. Drinking when we are thirsty, sleeping when we are tired, the pursuit of sex—all are efforts to reduce some drive. Thus, Freud believed that the natural state of human beings is **quiescence,** a condition in which we have no needs at all. Some Eastern philosophers have this condition as their main goal of life, a goal they call nirvana.

Most psychologists today believe that Freud's view of stress was wrong. The results of a considerable amount of research (reviewed in Dacey, 1982), indicate that individuals have a level of stimulation that is *optimum* for them. This is referred to as the **optimum drive level** of stimulation. Figure 16.1 compares stimulus reduction theory with optimum drive level theory.

According to the concept of optimum drive, when individuals have too much stimulation, they may seek to reduce the stimulation by satisfying the need causing it. This is Freud's position. But at other times, there may be too little stimulation, as in boredom. Under these circumstances, people *seek* new types of stimulation. Thus the goal is not to reduce stimulation to zero, but to maintain it at some optimum level.

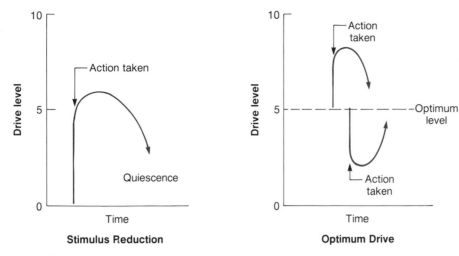

Figure 16.1 *Comparison of stimulus reduction and optimum drive theories.*

What level is optimum differs from individual to individual and from situation to situation. For example, some people enjoy a high level of stimulation in the morning, and become less excitable as the day goes on. Others, who call themselves "night persons," like to be left alone in the morning and only come alive in the evening hours. Some "live wires" demand a great deal of stimulation; others prefer a quieter style of life in general.

Categories of Conflict

Three types of conflict cause stress: approach-avoidance conflict, double-approach conflict, and double-avoidance conflict (Coleman, 1976). There are four kinds of resolutions of conflict: **resolution by choice, resolution by freeze, resolution by oscillation,** and **resolution by leaving the field** (Goldstein, 1979; Jarvik & Russell, 1979).

Approach-Avoidance Conflict
In an **approach-avoidance conflict,** conflict exists because obtaining a pleasurable goal will also result in an unpleasurable one. The more evenly balanced the positive and negative sides of the objective, the greater the conflict. For example, a person who is overweight may want to eat a banana split, but may also anticipate severe guilt feelings if it is eaten.

Double-Approach Conflict
In a **double-approach conflict,** the individual must choose between two pleasant but mutually exclusive choices. An example might be trying to decide whether to buy a television set or a stereo when you desire both but can afford only one.

Double-Avoidance Conflict
In a **double-avoidance conflict,** a choice between two situations must be made, and they are both unpleasant. An example might be deciding whether to let your son go with the Boy Scouts on a hazardous camping trip to the mountains, or putting up with his surliness at being forced to stay home.

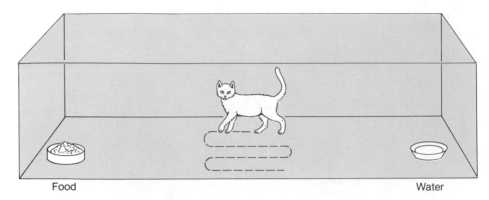

Food   Water

Figure 16.2 An example of oscillation.

Resolutions of Conflict

Choice

In most cases of conflict, people simply choose one option or the other, even if they must do so by arbitrary means, such as by flipping a coin.

Freeze

When the outcomes of two choices are seen to be equal, one possible reaction is to make no choice at all. The chooser is "frozen" in indecision.

Sometimes this may be a positive choice. For example, Jarvik and Russell (1979) found that the elderly are particularly likely to employ the freeze reaction:

❖   *it is proposed that those who have survived into old age have developed strat-*
      egies to successfully deal with stress, that among those strategies is a passive
      stance, termed 'freeze,' and that 'freeze' is a third emergency reaction, one
      which was omitted from the fight-flight paradigm of emergency reactions
      (p. 197).

For many of the elderly in many situations, this may be a wise stance to take. On the other hand, it may also be that the discrimination abilities of older persons, probably limited by age, cause them to perceive more situations as being equal than younger adults do. Finally, since elders have less time left, each decision may seem more important to them, and so they feel they need a longer time to decide what to do.

Oscillation

A variation of the freeze response is known as *oscillation.* Here, rather than being frozen, the individual makes a move toward one goal, then is drawn by an opposite goal and turns toward it. This behavior is repeated over and over, so that the individual seems to be going in circles. Figure 16.2 depicts the situation in a laboratory test of the discrimination abilities of a small animal. Here the animal wants to get to the end of the run to get at some food, but also wants the water at the other end—a double-approach conflict. Unable to choose, it oscillates at the center of the run.

Leaving the Field

The last response to conflict is referred to as *leaving the field.* If the cat in the experiment depicted in Figure 16.2 were to jump over the side of the run rather than freezing or oscillating, it would be leaving the field. The man who departs his country and assumes a new identity, the woman who convinces herself that she does not care about her husband's philandering—each is resolving their conflict by leaving the field. That is, they simply remove themselves, physically or mentally, from the arena of the conflict.

The General Adaptation Syndrome

In 1936, Hans Selye (the father of stress research) was studying a little-known ovarian hormone. This led to the discovery of the **general adaptation syndrome** (Selye, 1956, 1975). In one of the experiments, hormones from cattle ovaries were injected into rats to see what changes would occur. Selye was surprised to find that the rats had a broad range of reactions:

> The cortex became enlarged and hyperactive.
> A number of glands shrank.
> Deep bleeding ulcers occurred in both the stomach and upper intestines.

Further experiments showed that these reactions occurred in response to all toxic substances, regardless of their source. Later experiments also showed them occurring, although to a lesser degree, in response to a wide range of noxious stimuli, such as infections, hemorrhage, and nervous irritation.

Selye calls the entire syndrome an **alarm reaction.** He refers to it as a generalized "call to arms" of the body's defensive forces. Seeking to gain a fuller understanding of the syndrome, he wondered how the reaction would be affected if stress were present for a longer period of time. He found that a rather amazing thing happens. If the organism survives the initial alarm, it enters a **stage of resistance.** In this second stage, an almost complete reversal of the alarm reaction occurs. Swelling and shrinkages are reversed; the adrenal cortex, which lost its secretions during the alarm stage, becomes unusually rich in these secretions; and a number of other shock-resisting forces are marshalled. During this stage, the organism appears to gain strength and to have adapted successfully to the stressor.

However, if the stressor continues, a gradual depletion of the organism's adaptational energy occurs (Selye, 1982). Eventually this leads to a **stage of exhaustion.** Now the physiological responses revert to their condition during the stage of alarm. The ability to handle the stress decreases, the level of resistance is lost, and the organism dies. Figure 16.3 portrays these three stages. And Table 16.2 lists the physical and psychological manifestations of the two. Table 16.3 details these reactions.

As you grow older, your ability to remain in the resistance state decreases. Activity over the years gradually wears out your "machine," and the chances of sustaining life are reduced. As will be discussed in chapter 19, no one dies of old age. Rather, they succumb to some stressor because their ability to resist it has become weakened through aging.

Selye (1975) compares his general adaptation stages to the three major stages of life. Childhood, he says, is characteristic of the alarm state: children respond excessively to any kind of stimulus and have not yet learned the basic ways to resist shock. In early adulthood, a great deal of learning has occurred, and the organism knows better how to handle the difficulties of life. In middle and old age, however, adaptability is gradually lost, and eventually the adaptation syndrome is exhausted, leading ultimately to death.

Selye suggests that all resistance to stress inevitably causes irreversible chemical scars that build up in the system. These scars are signs of aging. Thus, he says, the old adage that you shouldn't "burn the candle at both ends" is supported by the body's biology and chemistry. Selye's work with the general adaptation syndrome has also helped us to discover the relationship between disease and stress.

Table 16.2   Selye's Stress Adaptation Syndrome

Stage	Function	Physical Manifestations	Psychological Manifestations
Stage I: Alarm reaction	Mobilization of the body defensive forces.	Marked loss of body weight. Increase in hormone levels. Enlargement of the adrenal cortex and lymph glands.	Person is alerted to stress. Level of anxiety increases. Task-oriented and defense-oriented behavior. Symptoms of maladjustment, such as anxiety and inefficient behavior, may appear.
Stage II: Stage of resistance	Optimal adaptation to stress.	Weight returns to normal. Lymph glands return to normal size. Reduction in size of adrenal cortex. Constant hormonal levels.	Intensified use of coping mechanisms. Person tends to use habitual defenses rather than problem-solving behavior. Psychosomatic symptoms may appear.
Stage III: Stage of exhaustion	Body resources are depleted and organism loses ability to resist stress.	Weight loss. Enlargement and depletion of adrenal glands. Enlargement of lymph glands and dysfunction of lymphatic system. Increase in hormone levels and subsequent hormonal depletion. If excessive stress continues, person may die.	Personality disorganization and a tendency toward exaggerated and inappropriate use of defense mechanisms. Increased disorganization of thoughts and perceptions. Person may lose contact with reality, and delusions and hallucinations may appear. Further exposure to stress may result in complete psychological disintegration (involving violence or stupor).

From Kneisl, C. R. and Ames, S. W.: *Adult Health Nursing: A Biopsychosocial Approach*, Addison-Wesley Publishing Company, 1986, p. 20.

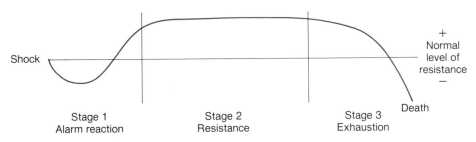

Figure 16.3   The general adaptation syndrome.

Disease as a Result of Stress

A merry heart doeth good like a medicine.

(Proverbs 17:22)

We are all aware of short-term physical upsets such as fainting, rapid heartbeat, and nausea, caused by the strains of living. Table 16.3 lists the various reactions to stress. You can easily see how many of them are impairing. Only recently have we come to understand more about the relationship between long-term emotional stress and illness.

International studies have shown how widespread this relationship is. For example, it is estimated that in Western industrialized countries, up to 70% of all patients being treated by doctors in general practice suffer from conditions whose origins lie in unrelieved stress (Blythe, 1973). The World Health Organization has

Table 16.3   Reactions to Stress

Thoughts	Feelings	Bodily Responses	Actions
Initially: Attentiveness, increased alertness, focus, discrimination, problem-solving, mental coping devices.	Surge of energy, tension, and/or excitement, elation, anxiety, fright, frustration, anger, fulfillment, happiness.	Tachycardia, hypertension, shallow respiration, dry mouth, paleness, perspiring hands, difficulty voiding/defecating, insomnia, fatigue, tremors, diarrhea, nervousness.	Increased activity level: restlessness, irritability, increased sensitivity and responsiveness, cooperation, alternative plans, compromise.
Later: Continued or diminished clarity, focus, discrimination, problem-solving skills, and mental coping devices.	Any emotion is possible: ambivalence, loneliness, sadness, helplessness, or hopelessness.	Hypotension, bradycardia, slow respirations, faintness and dizziness, blurred vision, and incontinence.	Problem solving, work, play, exercise, diversification, withdrawal, overuse of drugs, alcohol, and food, excessive sleeping, regression, daydreaming.
With overwhelming stress: Impaired perception and cognition; disorganized thinking; minimal focus and discrimination; reality distortions.	Panic, detachment.	Fixed, dilated pupils; exhaustion; death.	Disorganization, immobilization.

From S. Jasmin and L. N. Trygstad, *Behavioral Concepts and the Nursing Process.* Copyright © 1979 The C. V. Mosby Company, Inc., St. Louis, MO.

listed a large number of illnesses, such as coronary disease, diabetes mellitus, and bronchial asthma, as being caused almost entirely by stress. Stress can also cause skin disease, ulcers, nervous tension, dizziness, sore throat, impotence, angina, tachycardia, itchiness, and even accident-proneness (Snider, 1975).

What makes one person handle difficult life stress better than another person? One answer is practice. Success with similar situations leaves a person with some experience and confidence to draw on in coping with a new stressful situation. The person is less rattled and able to think more clearly and make more realistic responses to the situation.

Social support has also been found to be an important factor in a person's ability to remain composed and to adapt successfully to stressful situations. According to Bowlby (1973), these social supports are created during infancy when a person learns the essential base of security that will carry him or her throughout life. One study (Nuckolls, Cassel, & Kaplan, 1972) looked at the social supports of a group of pregnant women. These were defined as people with whom the women were close, from whom they could obtain affection, and on whom they could rely. They found that women who had many social supports had significantly fewer pregnancy complications than women who had relatively little support. The lack of social support was even more damaging to those women who had high levels of life change. Close family and friends seem to provide a cushioning effect during the stressful times in our lives.

We now know that being angry a lot of the time (a typical reaction to stress) is highly related to heart attack. There is a growing body of research linking stress with a number of forms of cancer (Cooper, 1984). As a result of the research of Selye and others, we are beginning to get a much better understanding of this interaction.

Measuring the Relationship Between Stress and Physical Illness

Psychologists and psychiatrists have long attempted to measure accurately the relationship between stress and disease. In the early 1900s, Adolph Meyer introduced the concept of *psychobiology,* which emphasized the importance of biographical study in understanding the whole person. He attempted to relate the biology of the person to the likelihood of their getting a variety of diseases. The most successful attempt in this area was by Holmes and Rahe (1967). They developed the *Social Readjustment Rating Scale,* which measures the relationship between events in one's life that require considerable adjustment and the likelihood of getting sick as a result of these crises. The scale is composed of life events that require coping, adaptation, or adjustment. The adult version of this scale was presented at the beginning of this section on stress. Preschool, elementary, and high school versions also exist.

The events in the scale are ranked according to the relative degree of adjustment required by the average individual. A numerical weight, called the life change unit (LCU), is assigned to each of the events. The greater the degree of the life change, the higher the unit number.

Holmes and Rahe designed the original adult scale by developing a list of events that could affect psychological well-being. The list was submitted to a sample of adults who rated each item according to the relative amount of adjustment required. The results of this study were then mathematically interpreted, and a numerical value (LCU) assigned to each event. To find out what your score is, look again at Table 16.1. For each LCU that you checked as having happened to you within the last year, give yourself the number of points indicated. Then total up your score.

Their studies show that a score of 200 or more makes some kind of illness likely. Colligan (1975) reports that 86% of those who experienced over 300 LCUs in a year developed some serious health problem.

Of course this does not mean that every person who has a high number of LCUs in one year will definitely get sick. It only means that the odds of getting sick are considerably increased. One caution is necessary here: there is the danger of a self-fulfilling prophecy. That is, persons who know they have a high number of LCUs in a year may believe they are going to become sick, and therefore they do. Nevertheless, it is clear that people under a high level of stress should take especially good care of their bodies and should be ready to check with their doctors quickly if they do develop symptoms of illness.

Transition

We began this chapter by comparing how youth are inducted into adulthood in preindustrial tribes and in the modern United States. We concluded that our situation is much more complex than that of the tribes; and that although there have been several good suggestions for initiation activities in postindustrial societies, the absence of clear initiation rites still causes problems for us.

We then considered the concept of stress. Three types of conflict cause stress: approach-avoidance conflict; double-approach conflict; and double-avoidance conflict. These may be dealt with through four kinds of resolution: choice, freeze, oscillation, and leaving the field. Hans Selye's "general adaptation syndrome" was also reviewed. It has three stages: alarm reaction, resistance, and exhaustion. Finally, we discussed the major warning that comes out of this research: when one is unable to relieve stress over a prolonged period, disease is likely to result. The mature person is one who learns the many skills that help avoid this dire consequence.

Is there any way to sum up the concept of maturity? We believe that Erikson's term, "integrity," probably comes closest. The mature person is one who has achieved an integrated life. But integration of what? That will be the subject of the rest of this book. In the next chapter, we tackle the development processes of early adulthood.

Key Ideas

1. It is evident that we in modern America lack clear ceremonies for inducting our youth into adulthood, and that this causes a number of problems.

2. Two concepts that have been designed to alleviate the lack of initiation rites are Outward Bound and the walkabout.

3. Three types of conflict cause stress: approach-avoidance conflict; double-approach conflict; and double-avoidance conflict.

4. There are four kinds of resolutions of conflict: choice, freeze, oscillation, and leaving the field.

5. Hans Selye's "general adaptation syndrome" has three stages: alarm reaction, resistance, and exhaustion.

6. When one is unable to relieve stress over a prolonged period, disease is likely to result.

Key Terms

Adolescent moratorium
Alarm reaction
Approach-avoidance conflict
Diversity
Double-approach conflict
Double-avoidance conflict
Future shock
General adaptation syndrome
Hazing practices
Initiation rites
Novelty
Optimum drive level
Outward Bound

Puberty rites
Quiescence
Recidivism rates
Resolution by choice
Resolution by freezing
Resolution by leaving the field
Resolution by oscillation
Stage of exhaustion
Stage of resistance
Stimulus reduction
Transience
Walkabout

What Do You Think?

1. Do you remember any experiences from your own youth that were particularly helpful in your transition to adulthood?

2. The adolescent moratorium seems to be getting longer and longer. Do you think this is a good thing? Why or why not?

3. Can you think of a third plan for initiation along the lines of the walkabout and Outward Bound?

4. How high is your Social Readjustment Rating in total LCUs (life change units)? Do you believe you have anything to worry about? What should you do?

5. Can you name five productive ways of dealing with everyday stress?

Suggested Readings

Benson, Herbert, and William Proctor. (1985). *Beyond the relaxation response.* New York: Berkley. A stress reduction program that has helped millions of people live healthier lives. Includes his concept of the "faith factor."

Bronowski, Jacob. (1973). *The ascent of man.* Boston: Little, Brown. This classic work makes exciting reading when one is beginning to study the psychology of human development.

Erikson, Erik. (Ed.) (1978). *Adulthood.* New York: Norton. A collection of essays on what it means to become an adult. Written by experts from a wide variety of fields.

May, Rollo. (1975). *The courage to create.* New York: Norton. A remarkably insightful psychoanalyst, May brings to this book his many years of experience helping highly creative people deal with their many stresses.

Selye, Hans. (1974). *Stress without distress.* Philadelphia: Lippincott. Offers many suggestions on how to achieve a rewarding life-style.

· *Chapter 17* ·

Early Adulthood: Physical and Cognitive Development

Aging is not something that happens only to old people.

Alexander Spence

Physical Development

The Peak Is Reached

Early adulthood is the period during which physical changes slow down or stop. For example, most females have reached their maximum height by 18; males reach theirs by the time they are 20. There is some increase in muscle and fat tissue into the 20s. From 20 to 35, the average man gains 15 pounds, the average female 14 (U.S. Bureau of the Census, 1986). Women have a higher percentage of body fat than men, relative to total weight, and this gender difference increases with age.

The muscle structure and internal organs attain their greatest physical potential between the ages of 19 and 26. Following this period, the body begins its slowing process:

- Spinal disks settle, which leads to a decrease in height.

- Fatty tissue increases, which leads to weight gain.

- Muscle strength decreases.

- Reaction times level off and stabilize.

There are slight sensory function changes during early adulthood. Women can detect higher pitched sounds than men. Vision changes slightly during early adulthood. The lens of the eye loses some of its flexibility, and it becomes more difficult to focus on close objects. The changes are so slight however, that the individual does not notice any differences in sight. Surprisingly, this process begins as early as 10 and continues until 30. The lens of the eye loses some of its elasticity and strength. Nearsighted persons will become more nearsighted, and farsighted persons will become more farsighted. More persons will require glasses in their 30s. These slight sensory changes are easily adapted to by the adult, who compensates for the changes more easily than a child.

The nervous system has been developing since conception, and will continue to mature until early adulthood. The brain continues to increase in weight and will reach its maximum potential by the adult years. Electroencephalograph (EEG) examinations can be helpful in predicting longevity, especially in those who have suffered some type of brain injury. EEG waves show that mature brain wave activity begins at about age 19 and continues to mature until approximately age 30 (Wang & Busse, 1974).

In sports, young adults are in their prime condition as far as speed and strength are concerned. A healthy individual can continue to partake in less strenuous sports for years. As the aging process continues, however, the individual will realize a loss of the energy and strength felt in adolescence.

Early adulthood is also the time when the efficiency of most body functions begins to decline. For example, cardiac output and vital capacity start to decrease (deVries, 1981). As Table 17.1 clearly shows, these declines are quite steady right through old age. It is important to remember that this chart gives the average changes; there will be considerable differences from individual to individual. (The greatest decline shown is for "male stated frequency of sexual intercourse." Why do you suppose that is?)

Table 17.1 Approximate declines in various human functional capacities with age.			
	Percent of Function Remaining		
	30 Years	60 Years	80 Years
Nerve conduction velocity	100	96	88
Basal metabolic rate	100	96	84
Standard cell water	100	94	81
Cardiac index	100	82	70
Glomerular filtration rate	100	96	61
Vital capacity	100	80	58
Renal plasma flow	100	89	51
Maximal breathing capacity	100	80	42

From Alexander P. Spence, *Biology of Human Aging,* © 1989, p. 8. Adapted by permission of Prentice-Hall, Inc., Englewood Cliffs, New Jersey.

Organ Reserve

Although Table 17.1 makes it look all downhill from what is probably your present age, the actual experience of most people is not that bad. This is because of a human capacity called **organ reserve.** Organ reserve refers to that part of the total capacity of our body's organs that we do not normally need to use. For example, when you walk up the stairs, you probably use something less than half of your total lung capacity. In fact, you could probably get to the top of those stairs in one-third or one-fourth of the time if you ran up them as fast as you could.

This is because your body is designed to do much more than it is usually called upon to do. Much of our total capacity is held in reserve. You may have heard the story of the 60-year-old woman whose son's leg became trapped under her compact car while he was working under it. Although she sometimes had had trouble just opening the hood of the car, in her extreme duress she was actually able to lift the car enough for him to extricate his leg from under its tire. This is a clear example of organ reserve.

As we get older, these reserves grow smaller. The peak performance of which each of our organs (and muscles, bones etc.) is capable declines. A 50-year-old man can fish all day with his 25-year-old son, can usually take a long walk with him without becoming exhausted, but has no chance at all of winning a footrace against him.

This is why people are aware of little decline during the early adult years, and often do not experience a sharp decline in most of their everyday activities even into middle age. Our organ reserves are diminishing, but we are unaware of it because we call on them so seldom.

The Effect of Style of Life on Health

Young adults are healthier than older adults in just about every way. All of the body's systems reach peak functioning at this age. There is less illness, too. For example, there are fewer hospitalizations and visits to the doctor's office than later, and those that do occur are caused mainly by injuries. Even catching a cold happens more rarely at this stage than at any other stage of life (U.S. Bureau of the Census, 1986).

Good health is clearly related to factors such as genetics, age, and the medical treatment that is locally available. But these factors are generally beyond the control of the individual. Increasingly, people are beginning to realize that their style of life plays an enormous role in their own health.

The impact of life-style on health is dramatically illustrated by the observations in the book *The Healing Brain* (Ornstein & Sobel, 1987). These researchers determined that the miraculous technological gains in medicine over the last one hundred years have not had as great an impact on health as one might think. A person who has reached the age of 45 today has a life expectancy of only a couple years more than the person who had reached the age of 45 a hundred years ago, in spite of all the money and effort now spent on medicine after that age.

As a counterexample, Ornstein and Sobel offer the people of Nevada and Utah, two states and populations that are similar in geography, education, income, and availability of medical treatment. Yet Nevada's death rate is 40% higher than Utah's. Utah is largely composed of Mormons who live a relatively quiet and stable life-style, including very low incidences of smoking and drinking. In Nevada, people drink and smoke much more heavily, and it shows. The rate of cirrhosis of the liver and lung cancer are 100% to 600% higher in Nevada than in Utah. A man who reaches the age of 45 in Utah can expect to live 11 years more than the man who reaches age 45 in Nevada. The point is that simple, cost-free choices under the control of the individual are much more effective at improving health than all the expensive, time-consuming medical advances of the last century. Perhaps our priorities are misplaced.

Based on this information one could conclude that a simple difference in style of life can have more of an effect on health than medical advances. Let's look at the influence on health of some specific life-style choices.

Choices of Foods

Nutrition plays an important role throughout human development, from the neonate to the elderly. In middle adulthood, however, increasing evidence demonstrates the influence of nutrition on two major health concerns, heart disease and cancer. Medical science has recently established a link between heart disease and a substance in the blood, **cholesterol.** Cholesterol has been found to leave deposits along the walls of blood vessels, blocking the flow of blood to the heart and resulting in a heart attack. The main culprit in high levels of cholesterol has been found to be diets high in fat. Typically, Americans consume 40% of their total calories as fat. The American Heart Association (1984) recommends changes in diet, such as eating fish and poultry instead of red meat, yogurt and cottage cheese instead of cheese, margarine instead of butter, fewer eggs, and drinking skim milk instead of whole milk, as ways of lowering cholesterol in the body.

A similar link has been found between diet and certain types of cancer, such as cancer of the breast, stomach, intestines, and the esophagus. The American Cancer Society has also come out with a set of recommendations for an improved, healthy diet. They too recommend lowering fat intake, to no more than 30% of the daily caloric total, and a diet that is high in fiber, a substance that helps the digestive process. High fiber foods include leafy vegetables such as cauliflower, broccoli, and brussel sprouts, as well as whole grain cereals and breads. The proliferation of new products that feature lower levels of fat and higher levels of fiber indicate that the American public is taking this new knowledge to heart (no pun intended).

Anyone who is 10% over the normal weight for their height and build is considered overweight. Anyone who is 20% over the normal weight is considered obese. Obesity is now considered a very serious health concern. Over 30 million Americans can be labeled obese (National Institute for Health Statistics, 1986) and the impact on health is significant and widespread. Obesity increases the risk of such diseases as heart disease, diabetes, arthritis, and cancer. In addition, our society places

Young adults today are probably more health-conscious than at any other time in history.

great importance on physical appearance. Overweight persons are likely to suffer from low self-esteem or even depression because of the way they are treated by others.

At the other extreme, there is some disagreement over what is considered to be too thin. Some researchers suggest that it is better to be a little overweight than it is to be underweight. Recent research on animals suggests that a restricted diet that leaves the animal lean and thin might be healthiest (Masoro, 1984; Campbell & Gaddy, 1987). A severely restricted diet leads to some of the complications associated with eating disorders such as anorexia nervosa (see chap. 14). Once again, moderation seems to be the safest course to follow.

Use of Alcohol

The consumption of alcohol is another great health concern to our society. Alcohol abuse is estimated to cost our economy over $100 billion annually (Holden, 1987). This figure includes medical treatment for cirrhosis of the liver, osteoporosis, ulcers, heart disease, nervous system damage, and certain types of cancer such as breast cancer. It includes the insurance and medical costs incurred by automobile accidents resulting from drinking and driving. It includes the drug treatment necessary to help people control their addiction. And it includes the enormous cost of labor that is lost when heavy drinkers are unable to come in to work.

Ingalls (1983) conducted a survey among college students and reported that 82% consumed alcohol and 21% were heavy users. Eight percent admitted to having an alcohol problem. It was found that alcohol consumption was directly related to low grade-point average. White males consume more alcohol than women or African-Americans. Most people consume alcohol to attain the relaxed, uninhibited feeling that alcohol tends to produce. The fact is, alcohol dulls the senses. Specifically, it decreases reaction times in the brain and nervous system. Continued drinking may affect the sex life of males, by making it difficult for them to attain and hold an erection.

Alcohol leads to a variety of problems in the family, with the law, and with one's health. Physical problems associated with alcoholism include cirrhosis of the liver, increased chances of cardiomyopathy, a weakening of the heart muscles, stomach and intestinal ailments, as well as cancer of the mouth, liver, and esophagus (Schemeck, 1983).

Ironically, there is some indication that a daily, moderate intake of alcohol may be beneficial (although not for those over the age of 50—see chap. 19). Such small amounts of alcohol seem to produce a protein in the blood that helps lower cholesterol. Unfortunately, the addictive qualities of alcohol make it impossible for many people to drink in only moderate amounts. This is why treatment programs such as the very successful Alcoholics Anonymous ask their clients to abstain totally from alcohol rather than try to control their drinking.

Use of Tobacco

Tobacco use is also linked to a variety of health problems. The most common way to use tobacco is to smoke cigarettes. Most people are now aware that heavy cigarette smoking greatly increases the risk of lung cancer. They are perhaps less aware of the links between smoking and cancer of the kidney and stomach, along with the links to other diseases such as heart disease and emphysema (Engstrom, 1986).

The main culprit in tobacco is nicotine. Nicotine is a stimulating drug that the Surgeon General of the United States has concluded is as addictive as heroin or cocaine. There are other ways to be affected by nicotine than by smoking cigarettes.

White males consume more alcohol than either white females or African-Americans, according to one study. Can you think of any reasons why this might be so?

Although the dangers of "passive smoke"—smoke inhaled by those in the vicinity of a smoker—are well established, many people still disregard the new no-smoking signs that seem to be springing up everywhere.

Recent attention has focused on the dramatic increase in the use of smokeless chewing tobacco, primarily in young men. This type of tobacco use leads to a higher risk of cancer of the larynx, mouth, esophagus, and stomach. Awareness of this type of health risk is quickly spreading, as people see news photos of teenage boys who have had to have entire portions of their face removed due to cancer.

Smokers are 14 times more likely to die from cancer of the lungs, and twice as likely to die of a heart attack as nonsmokers. Other diseases linked to smoking are bronchitis, emphysema, and increased blood pressure. In 1984, the Federal Office on Smoking and Health reported that 37.9% of American men and 29.8% of American women smoke. They report that 30.5% of men and 15.7% of women have quit smoking.

The Department of Health and Human Services has outlined the personality types of smokers versus nonsmokers (Brody, 1984). Adult smokers tend to be risk-takers, impulsive, defiant, and extroverted. Blue-collar workers tend to be the heaviest smokers among men. For females, white-collar workers are the heaviest smokers, and homemakers tend to smoke more than women who work.

Peer pressure from friends is the major reason that young adults smoke. As in adulthood, young people who smoke tend to be extroverted and more disobedient toward authority than nonsmokers. Some young adults see smoking as a way of appearing older and more mature. Young adults who go on to college smoke less than those who do not continue their education. Among young women, smokers are less athletic, more social, study less, get lower grades, and generally dislike school more than nonsmoking females.

You may also involuntarily be exposed to the dangers of tobacco use. A growing body of research is documenting the deleterious effects of passive smoking. Passive smoking is the breathing in of the smoke around you produced by others. For example, a nonsmoker who is married to a heavy smoker has a 30% greater risk of lung cancer (National Institute for Health Statistics, 1986). There is also evidence that children can be affected by their mothers who smoke (Tager & others, 1984). This mounting evidence has led to a flurry of legislation prohibiting smoking in certain public areas such as elevators, airplanes, and restaurants, and the designation of smoking areas in workplaces.

The message does seem to be reaching the public. Overall, fewer people smoke now than at any time in the last twenty-five years (with the sole exception of teenage females). Numerous stop-smoking programs spring up all the time. These programs run the gamut, from classic behavioral techniques to hypnosis. But perhaps the most telling evidence that smoking is on the decline in the United States is the reaction of the giant tobacco companies. In recent years these companies have increasingly targeted foreign markets (a growing ethical controversy since these markets are typically Third-World countries) while diversifying their domestic market with different and healthier products.

Physical Fitness

One of the most popular trends of recent years has been the so-called fitness craze. The signs are all around us: gyms and spas opening everywhere, exercise classes at home on the TV or videocassette or perhaps even at the workplace, designer clothes and shoes for working out. People in this country are trying to change the old notion of the lazy, fat American.

The health benefits are the obvious reason for this enthusiasm for exercise. Regular, strenuous exercise can increase heart and lung capacity, lower blood pressure, decrease cholesterol in the blood, keep weight at normal levels, enhance cognitive functioning, relieve anxiety and depression, and increase self-esteem (Elsayed, Ismail, & Young, 1980; Lee & others, 1981; McCann & Holmes, 1984).

During a physical workout, oxygen travels more deeply into the lungs, and the heart pumps harder to carry more blood into the muscles. Healthy lungs and heart are vital for a long life. Persons who do not exercise and have inactive jobs are at twice the risk for a heart attack compared to persons who do exercise. Individuals who exercise report other health benefits, including better concentration at work and better sleep patterns (Vander Zanden, 1989).

Johns Hopkins Hospital in Baltimore reported that a family medical history of heart attacks increases a person's chances of having a heart attack (Findlay, 1983). Among individuals under age 50 from at-risk families, 42% have significantly high blood pressure, compared with 20% of the general population. Of the same group, 28% have dangerously high cholesterol levels, compared to 5%–10% of the general population. Nearly 25% show evidence of "silent" coronary artery disease—double the rate of the general population.

Studies at Harvard show that at-risk individuals do not properly metabolize cholesterol, which collects in the arteries and eventually leads to a heart attack (Bishop, 1983). Carey (1983) explains that young adults who gain a large amount of weight after adolescence are more at risk for heart disease. Scientists feel that with greater public awareness of the dangers of cholesterol, and early detection and treatment, they can decrease heart disease among at-risk individuals.

One study (Ossip-Klein & others, 1989) assigned a number of clinically depressed women to one of three groups: a group that did regular running, a group that lifted weights regularly, or a control group that did nothing special. The women in both exercise groups showed increased self-concept over the women in the control group. The types of exercise worked equally well.

Many corporations are now providing the time and facilities so that employees can build regular exercise into their workday. The reasoning is that work time lost in this way is more than made up for by more productive employees who end up losing less time due to illness. In one new trend, some health insurance programs are offering free access to exercise facilities, again looking at the long-term gain of having healthier members.

There was a time when only males did calisthenics. Now exercise classes are becoming very popular with female adolescents.

Marital Status

Another life-style factor that appears to affect health is marital status. Despite comedians' jokes, married people seem to be healthier than single, divorced, or widowed people (Verbrugge, 1979). They tend to have less frequent and shorter stays in hospitals. They tend to have fewer chronic conditions and fewer disabilities. Never married and widowed people are the next healthiest. Divorced and separated people show the most health-related problems. There are a number of possible explanations for this, but clearly one must consider the emotional and economic support that an intact family can provide.

Based on the above information, one could conclude that a healthy life-style consists of a diet with reasonable caloric intake that is low in fat and high in fiber, moderate or no consumption of alcohol, no tobacco use, plenty of regular, strenuous exercise, and a supportive spouse. In fact, this accurately describes the Mormon life-style in Utah, which allows the average resident of Utah to live years longer than the average resident of Nevada. This, of course, is no reason to go out and change your religious preference, but it is reason to examine your current life-style and consider some prudent changes.

As you can see, physical development in young adulthood is a complex affair. The same is true of the mental changes in this period.

Mental Development

As with physical development, there has not been a great deal of research on the mental development of young adults. Possibly this is because mental functioning appears to peak during this period, and so there is less concern over change. A major emphasis of research has been on the relationship between intellectual and ethical growth.

Intellectual/Ethical Development

Perry (1968a, 1968b; 1981) studied the intellectual/ethical development of several hundred Harvard College students, a group of males age 17 to 22. These students responded to several checklists on their educational views and were interviewed extensively on the basis of their responses. The results of these studies led Perry to suggest a sequence of intellectual and ethical development that typically occurs during the transition from late adolescence to early adulthood. This sequence consists of nine positions, which indicate progress from belief in absolute authority to the recognition that one must make commitments and be responsible for one's own beliefs.

Perry's nine stages are divided into three broader categories, as follows:

I. **Dualism** ("Things are either absolutely right or absolutely wrong.")
Position 1: The world is viewed in such polar terms as right versus wrong, we versus they, and good versus bad. If an answer is right, it is absolutely right. We get right answers by going to authorities who have absolute knowledge.
Position 2: The person recognizes that uncertainty exists, but ascribes it to poorly qualified authorities. Sometimes individuals can learn the truth for themselves.
Position 3: Diversity and uncertainty are now acceptable but considered temporary because the authorities do not know what the answers are yet. The person becomes puzzled as to what the standards should be in these cases.

II. **Relativism** ("Anything can be right or wrong depending on the situation; all views are equally right.")
Position 4a: The person realizes that uncertainty and diversity of opinion are often extensive and recognizes that this is a legitimate status. Now he or she believes that "anyone has a right to an opinion." It is now possible for two authorities to disagree with each other without either of them being wrong.
Position 4b: Sometimes the authorities (such as college professors) are not talking about right answers. Rather, they want students to think for themselves, supporting their opinions with data.
Position 5: The person recognizes that all knowledge and values (including even those of an authority) exist in some specific context. It is therefore relative to the context. The person also recognizes that simple right and wrong are relatively rare, and even they exist in a specific context.
Position 6: The person apprehends that because we live in a relativistic world, it is necessary to make some sort of personal commitment to an idea or concept, as opposed to looking for an authority to follow.

III. **Commitment** ("Because of the available evidence and my understanding of my own values, I have come to new beliefs.")

Position 7: The person begins to choose the commitments that she or he will make in specific areas.

Position 8: Having begun to make commitments, the person experiences the implications of those commitments and explores the various issues of responsibility involved.

Position 9: The person's identity is affirmed through the various commitments made. There is a recognition of the necessity for balancing commitments and the understanding that one can have responsibilities that are expressed through a daily life-style. Perry (1981) describes this position:

❖ *This is how life will be. I will be whole-hearted while tentative, fight for my values yet respect others, believe my deepest values right yet be ready to learn. I see that I shall be retracing this whole journey over and over—but, I hope, more wisely (p. 276).*

Life is full of situations in which the difference between right and wrong is far from clear.

Some students move through these stages in a smooth and regular fashion; others, however, are delayed or deflected in one of three ways:

• **Temporizing**: Some people remain in one position for a year or more, exploring its implications, but hesitating to make any further progress.

• **Escape**: Some people use opportunities for detachment, especially those offered in Positions 4 and 5, to refuse responsibility for making any commitments. Since everyone's opinion is "equally right," the person believes that no commitments need be made, and thus escapes from the dilemma.

• **Retreat**: Sometimes, confused by the confrontation and uncertainties of the middle positions, people retreat to earlier positions.

If young adults are able to avoid these traps, they should be able to achieve the commitments that are the hallmark of the mature person.

Although some have criticized Perry's theory (see Kitchener & King, 1981; Brabeck, 1984), it has a certain common sense. At least, his ideas seem to fit well with your authors' many years of experience teaching college students. It should be remembered that the subjects of his research were all males. Now let us turn to research on females that was spurred by Perry's work.

"Women's Ways of Knowing"

In a collaborative study, four female psychologists (Belenky & others, 1986) set out to answer the question, "Do female ways of knowing develop differently from those of males? If so, how do they come to learn and value what they know?" The study was rooted in Perry's work and also the work of Carol Gilligan, whose groundbreaking research on the morality of care and responsibility versus the morality of rights and justice was covered in chapter 9.

Belenky and her associates conducted a series of lengthy and intense interviews with 135 women of diverse socioeconomic background. They found five general categories of ways in which women know and view the world. While some of the women interviewed clearly demonstrated a progression from one perspective to the next, the researchers contend that they are unable to discern a progression of clearcut stages, unlike Perry and Gilligan. The five perspectives are silence, received knowledge, subjective knowledge, procedural knowledge, and constructed knowledge.

1. *Silence.* Females in the **silence** category described themselves as "deaf and dumb." These women feel passive and dependent. Like players in

an authority's game, they feel expected to know rules that don't exist. These women's thinking is characterized by concepts of right and wrong, similar to the men in Perry's first stage. Questions about their growing up revealed family lives filled with violence, abuse, and chaos. The researchers noted that "gaining a voice and developing an awareness of their own minds are the task that these women must accomplish if they are to cease being either a perpetrator or victim of family violence" (p. 38).

2. *Received knowledge.* Women in the **received knowledge** category see words as central to the knowing process. They learn by listening, and assume truths come from authorities. These women are intolerant of ambiguities and paradoxes, always coming back to the notion that there are absolute truths. Received knowers seem similar to the men that Perry described as being in the first stage of dualism, but with a difference. The men interviewed by Perry felt a great affiliation with the knowing authority. The women of this perspective were awed by the authorities, but far less affiliated with them. In contrast to the men of Perry's study, women of received knowledge channel their energies and increased sense of self into the care of others.

3. *Subjective knowledge.* The researchers noted that women in the **subjective knowledge** category often had experienced two phenomena that pushed them toward this perspective: some crisis of male authority that sparked a distrust of outside sources of knowledge, and some experience that confirmed a trust in themselves. Subjectivists value their "gut" or firsthand experience as their best source of knowledge and see themselves as "conduits through which truth emerges" (p. 69). The researchers note that subjectivists are similar to males in Perry's second stage in that they embrace the notion of multiple truths.

4. *Procedural knowledge.* The women in the **procedural knowledge** category have a distrust of both knowledge from authority and their own inner authority or "gut." The perspective of procedural knowledge is characterized by an interest in form over content (how you say something rather than what you say). They also have a heightened sense of control. This category is similar to Perry's relativism subordinate stage, where students learn analytic methods that authorities sanction. But it emerges differently in women because they don't affiliate with authorities.

The researchers describe women as having two kinds of procedural knowledge: separate knowing and connected knowing. The terms are reminiscent of Gilligan's work. Separate knowers are analytical and try to separate out the self, so as to reveal the truth. Connected knowers learn through empathy.

5. *Constructed knowledge.* The hallmark of those in the **constructed knowledge** category is an integration of the subjective and procedural ways of knowing (types 3 and 4). Women of this perspective note that "all knowledge is constructed and the knower is an intimate part of the known" (p. 137). They feel responsible for examining and questioning systems of constructing knowledge. Their thinking is characterized by a high tolerance of ambiguity and internal contradiction. Indeed, the women whose ways of knowing are of this perspective often balance many commitments and relationships, as well as ideas.

The work of Perry and Belenky and her associates (as well as that of Piaget, Kohlberg, and Gilligan, discussed earlier in this book) has greatly advanced our knowledge of intellectual and ethical development in the late adolescent and early adult years. It has also produced much controversy. Many questions remain to be answered. For example, does socioeconomic level make any difference? What about cultural background? We hope that the ongoing research in this area will provide further insights into how we can help youth progress through this period successfully. We could say the same for the next aspect of development we will review, sexuality in young adulthood.

Sexuality

Sexuality has various roles in our lives. Perhaps the broadest definition of these roles is given by the American Medical Association:

❖   *Human sexuality is involved in what we do, but it is also what we are. It is an identification, an activity, a drive, a biological and emotional process, an outlook, and an expression of the self. It is an important factor in every personal relationship, in every human endeavor from business to politics (Roberts & Holt, 1979, p. 2).*

Most people who disregard or repress their sexuality suffer for it. Of course, the sex drive, unlike other instinctual drives such as hunger and thirst, can be thwarted without causing death. There are some people who are able to practice complete celibacy without apparent harm to their personalities. The great majority of us, however, become highly irritable when our sexual needs are not met in some way. There is also reason to believe that our personalities do not develop in healthy directions if we are unable to meet sexual needs in adulthood. Why is it so important to us? Although the answer may seem obvious, there are in fact a number of sexual motivations.

Most people seem to find a strong need to develop a sexual and romantic relationship with another person.

Freud's Theory

For Freud, human sexuality is the underlying basis for all behavior (see chap. 2). He held that genitality (the ability to have a successful adult sex life) is the highest stage of development. He believed that those people who do not have adequate adult sex lives fail to do so because they have become fixated at some earlier and less mature level.

Because sexuality is so important and controlled by such deep-seated genetic forces, those who do not fulfill their sexual needs are likely to suffer from mental illness. Women, he believed, are more vulnerable than men to these problems, and his medical practice seemed to confirm his beliefs.

Many researchers (e.g., Chilman, 1974; Masters & Johnson, 1970, 1979) have disputed this view. For example, it has been found that women who have physiological difficulties with their reproductive systems, such as infertility or menstrual disorders, are no more likely than other women to suffer from neurosis. Most probably Freud's theories were influenced by the attitudes and morals in Victorian Vienna, which were quite different from those in the United States today.

Sexual Scripts—Gagnon and Simon

Psychologists John Gagnon and William Simon (1987) see sexual behavior as "scripted" behavior. They believe that children begin to learn scripts for sexual

Psychologist John Gagnon argues that humans learn to behave sexually according to scripts established by the culture in which they live. For most people, most of this learning takes place during adolescence and young adulthood.

attitudes and behavior from the other people in their society. They view sexuality, therefore, as a cultural phenomenon rather than a spontaneously emerging behavior. They believe that

❖   *In any given society, [children] acquire and assemble meanings, skills, and values from the people around them. Their critical choices are often made by going along and drifting (1987, p. 2).*

Learning sexual scripts occurs in a rather haphazard fashion throughout childhood, but this changes abruptly as children enter adolescence. Here much more specific scripts are learned: in classrooms, from parents, from the media, and most specifically, from slightly older adolescents. This process continues throughout early adulthood, through a process of listening to and imitating older adults whom the individual admires. For these researchers, then, the roles sexuality plays in a society come about largely through transmission of the culture by idealized adults.

Sexual Motivations—Mitchell

In a highly respected article, psychiatrist John Mitchell (1972) has suggested the following six major motives for human sexuality.

The Need for Intimacy   The need for intimacy is one of the deepest that humans experience. It often conflicts with other needs, such as independence and self-protection, but if unmet it can cause intense depression. In the past, sexual interaction usually took place only when two people had achieved a high degree of intimacy.

The Need of Belonging   The vast majority of adults are able to satisfy their sexual needs with one other person. When a person is unable to do so, it tends to strengthen the unpleasant feelings of aloneness and being different.

The Desire for Power   Both sexes have a need to feel they are able to exercise some control over another. Sometimes this is expressed as domination, sometimes as manipulation. Its more mature form is the feeling of personal importance each partner can achieve by giving the other partner satisfaction through love-making.

The Desire for Submission   Submission is the complementary need to the need for power. Just as we sometimes like to be in control, at times we like to be cared for by someone we feel is more powerful than we are.

Curiosity   When their most deep-seated needs are met, most human beings have a desire to explore their environment and their capabilities in dealing with it. It is natural, therefore, for healthy adults to want to find out more about their sexual feelings and to try to increase their competence.

The Desire for Passion and Ecstasy   The Greek word *ekstasis* means "to be outside of oneself." Medical researchers have found that people occasionally need to experience self-transcendence, the feeling of getting outside of and rising above themselves—in other words, a "high." Sebald (1977) suggests that three benefits derive from sexual passion: intense self-awareness, intense awareness of the other person, and a confirmation of the other person as someone who is intensely important to you.

Socially Approved Playfulness   Mitchell does not suggest this seventh category, but there is good evidence for it (Dacey, 1989). Although society tends to equate childlike playfulness with being irresponsible and foolish, most of us who are no longer children like to go back to that relaxed and happy period, at least for brief intervals. In sexual play, we can act silly, use babytalk, and just fool around. This kind of activity can leave us better prepared to return to the heavy burdens of adult responsibility.

The Sociobiological View—Wilson

Whatever we see as our reasons for seeking sex, this complicated behavior has obviously evolved through a number of complex stages over which we have had no control. What genetic purposes has this evolution served? E. O. Wilson (1978) and his fellow sociobiologists have a number of unorthodox suggestions:

Sex is not designed for reproduction. Sociobiologists argue that the primary motivation of all human behavior is the reproduction of the genes of each person. Wilson, however, believes that if reproduction were the primary goal of the human species, many other techniques would have been far more effective:

❖ *Bacteria simply divide in two (in many species, every twenty minutes), fungi shed immense numbers of spores, and hybrids bud offspring directly from their trunks. Each fragment of a shattered sponge grows into an entire new organism. If multiplication were the only purpose of reproductive behavior, our mammalian ancestors could have evolved without sex. Every human being might be asexual and sprout new offspring from the surface cells of a neutered womb (p. 121).*

Sex is not designed for giving and receiving pleasure. Wilson points out that many animal species perform intercourse quite mechanically with virtually no foreplay. Furthermore, lower forms achieve sex without benefit even of a nervous system. Thus, he suggests that pleasure is only one of the means of getting complex creatures to "make the heavy investment of time and energy required for courtship, sexual intercourse and parenting" (p. 122).

Sex is not designed for efficiency. The very complexity of human genital systems makes them subject to a variety of disorders and diseases, such as ectopic pregnancy and venereal disease. The genetic balance brought about by sex is easily disturbed, and if the human being has one sex chromosome too many or too few, abnormalities in behavior and in physiology often result.

Sex is not designed to benefit the individual's drives. If an individual's drive is to reproduce himself or herself, sex is actually an impairment. When sexual reproduction is employed, the organism must accept partnership with an individual whose genes are different. Only with asexual reproduction is multiplication of self totally possible.

Sex does create diversity. Wilson concludes that the only possible reason that evolution brought about the human sexual system is to create a greater diversity of individuals. The purpose of this diversity is to increase the chances of the survival of the species. As conditions have changed throughout history (e.g., during an ice age), some individuals have had a greater chance to survive than others. If there had been only one type of human being with only one set of genes, and that inheritance had not been suited to the changing environment, the species would have become extinct.

Wilson points out that when two different individuals mate, there is the possibility of offspring like individual A, offspring like individual B, and offspring with the characteristics of both. As these individuals mate with others, the possible variations increase exponentially. Diversity, brought about through sex, leads to adaptability of the species, and therefore its greater survival rate.

Why are there not hundreds of sexes instead of just two? Wilson argues that two sexes are enough to create tremendous diversity while keeping the system as simple as possible. Diversity may not only be responsible for variation in the offspring, but contribute to the wide range of values people place on sexuality.

In a recent article, Weinrich (1987) extends the sociobiological theory to explain homosexuality. He suggests that homosexual behavior is the result of a "reproductively altruistic trait." That is, homosexuals give up their right to reproduce their genes. The theory, Weinrich qualifies, is only applicable in societies like ours that do not strictly require marriage and reproductivity.

Practices of Young Adults

Two topics are covered in this section: premarital experiences and marital practices.

Premarital Experiences

We have considerable evidence that sexual experience has increased among college students. For example, in their study of 793 undergraduates, Earle and Perricone (1986) found "significant increases in rates of premarital intercourse, significant decreases in age at first experience, and significant increases in number of partners" (p. 304).

Kinnaird and Gerrard (1986) examined the premarital sexual activity of unmarried female undergraduates. Young women from divorced and reconstituted families reported significantly more sexual behavior than those from intact families. Family conflict, disruption, and father-absence were also related to such behavior.

There have been many studies of the premarital experiences of college students, but few studies of persons who have not gone to college. We know from the classic studies that the noncollege educated are almost always more conservative, that is, less experienced, than those who go to college (Kinsey, Pomeroy, Martin, & Gebhard, 1948, 1953; Masters & Johnson, 1966, 1970), but that they are subject to the same kinds of societal influence. Therefore we can expect that while noncollege populations have a lower experience rate, theirs too is considerably higher than it used to be.

Abernathy and associates (1979) measured sexual attitudes and behavior among adolescents. They compared college students from urban, suburban, and rural areas and found some interesting differences among these groups. A direct relationship appears to exist between sexual values and degree of urbanization. As you might expect, rural teenagers are the most conservative and those from cities are the most liberal.

However, both male and female adolescents from city environments were *less* willing than the others to grant women the same sexual freedom as men. The suburban females were found to have the highest rates of promiscuous behavior, but were not the most permissive in their values. These authors conclude that there is only a moderate relationship between sexual attitude and behavior.

A later study of university students by Story (1982) sought a comparison of various sexual outlets (such as masturbation, premarital intercourse with other than future marriage partner, group sex, sexual experience with person of same sex) over a six-year span. Fifty single males and 50 single females were tested in 1974 and another group of the same size in 1980. Results showed that both males and females appeared to adhere more to society's conservative or traditional sexual behavior in 1980 than the group tested in 1974. This indicates that society's attitude affects and possibly dictates what is acceptable sexual behavior.

What's Your Opinion?

As you might imagine, the whole theory of sociobiology (which is also covered in other sections of this book) is not without its critics. Obviously, genes do affect our behavior, but not nearly as much as they do in the other species of the animal kingdom. Many experts say that sociobiology has made a valuable contribution to the theory of human sexuality, but that it overemphasizes the role of genes.

We find that many of our students reject sociobiology completely. "Wilson treats people as though we are no better than animals," they say. What do you think? Is there a place for sociobiology in your understanding of human sexuality? If so, what is it?

Marital Intercourse

Intercourse between a husband and wife is the only type of sexual activity totally approved by American society. Much is expected of it, and when it is unsatisfactory, it usually generates other problems in the marriage (McCary, 1978). Sexual closeness also tends to lessen significantly with the birth of each child, except in cases where the couple has taken specific steps to maintain the quality of their sexual relationship. Two studies (Whitehead and Mathews, 1986; Whitehead, Mathews, & Ramage, 1987) learned that when young couples who are having sexual difficulties regularly attend therapy sessions, they are usually able to resolve their problems. Interestingly, those couples who received placebos (sugar pills) or small doses of testosterone did better than those who did not.

Physical and Mental Aspects of Love

The words written about love over the course of human history are uncountable. In this book, we will limit ourselves to describing the developmental aspects of this emotion: the seven forms of love suggested by psychologist Robert Sternberg, and the definition of the essence of love offered by psychoanalyst Erich Fromm.

The Seven Forms of Love—Sternberg

Sternberg (1986) argues that love is made up of three different components:

- **Passion**—a strong desire for another person, and the expectation that sex with them will prove physiologically rewarding.

- **Intimacy**—the ability to share one's deepest and most secret feelings and thoughts with another.

- **Commitment**—the strongly held conviction that one will stay with another, regardless of the cost.

Each of these components may or may not be involved in a relationship. The extent to which each is involved defines the type of love that is present in the relationship. Sternberg believes that the various combinations actually found in human relations produce seven forms of love (see Table 17.2).

Table 17.2	Sternberg's Seven Forms of Love
Liking	Intimacy, but no passion or commitment
Infatuation	Passion, but no intimacy or commitment
Empty love	Commitment, but no passion or intimacy
Romantic love	Intimacy and passion, but no commitment
Fatuous love	Commitment and passion, but no intimacy
Companionate love	Commitment and intimacy, but no passion
Consummate love	Commitment, intimacy, and passion

From R. J. Sternberg, "The Triangular Theory of Love" in *Psychological Review,* 93:199–235. Copyright © 1986 American Psychological Association, Arlington, VA.

This is not to say that the more of each, the better. A healthy marriage will usually include all three, but the balance among them is likely to change over the life of the marriage. For example, early in the marriage, passion is likely to be high relative to intimacy. The physical aspects of the partnership are new, and therefore exciting, while there has probably not been enough time for intimacy to develop fully. This is a dangerous time in the marriage, because when intimacy is moderate, there are many situations in which the couple may misunderstand each other, or may make unpleasant discoveries about each other. Such problems are often much more painful than they are later, when deeper intimacy and commitment have developed.

Passion, Sternberg states, is like an addiction. In the beginning, the smallest gesture can produce intense excitement. As the relationship grows older, however, it takes larger and larger "doses" to evoke the same feelings. Inevitably, passion loses some of its power.

Of course, there are wide differences among couples (Traupmann & others, 1981; Hatfield, Traupmann, & Sprecher, 1984). Some never feel much passion, while others maintain at least moderately passionate feelings into old age. Some appear to have strong commitments from the earliest stage of their association (love at first sight?), while others waver for many years.

Sternberg's theory has numerous implications for couples, and for marriage therapists as well. For example, more and more couples are engaging in premarital counseling. In this, they analyze with their counselor the three factors of love, and how each person feels about them. This often helps them to avoid later problems, and to get their relationship off to a good start. For some, it provides information that makes them realize that while their passion is high, their intimacy and commitment may not be, and they wait until these develop, or decide not to get married at all. It is hoped that such counseling will bring about a decrease in our nation's high divorce rate.

For more and more engaged couples, premarital counseling is becoming a part of their plan to marry.

Validation—Fromm

In his highly enlightening book on this subject, *The Art of Loving* (1968), Erich Fromm has given us a respected new understanding of the meaning of love. First, he argues, we must recognize that we are prisoners in our own bodies. Although we assume that we perceive the world around us in much the same way as others, we cannot really be sure. We are the only one who truly knows what our own perceptions are, and we cannot be certain they are the same as other people's. In fact, most of us are aware of times when we have *misperceived* something: we heard a phrase differently from everyone else, had an hallucination when under the influence of a fever, alcohol, or a drug, and so on.

Thus we must constantly check on the reality our senses give us. We do this thousands, maybe millions, of times every day. Let us give you an example. We assume you are sitting or lying down while you are reading this book. Did you make a conscious check of the surface you are sitting or lying on when you got on it? Probably not. Nevertheless your brain did. You know that if it had been cold, sharp, or wet, you would have noticed. That it isn't is something your unconscious mind ascertained without your having to give it a thought.

With some insane people, this is the major problem. Their "reality checker" isn't working right. They cannot tell fact from imagination. They dwell in "castles in the air," out of contact with the real world. We need the feedback from all our senses, doing repeated checks at lightning speeds, in order to keep in contact with reality.

Fromm's point is this: as important as these "reality checks" on our physical environment are, much more important are the checks on our innermost state— our deepest and most important feelings and thoughts! To check on the reality of these, we must get the honest reactions of someone we can trust. Such a person tells us, "No, you're not crazy. At least I feel the same way, too!" Even more important, they *prove* their insight and honesty by sharing with us their own secret thoughts and feelings. In Fromm's words, they give us **validation.**

Validation is essential to our sanity. We are social animals, and we need to know that others approve of us (or, for that matter, when they don't). When someone regularly makes you feel validated, you come to love them. This is the essence of what Erikson calls intimacy, which we will discuss at length in the next chapter. It fulfills what Maslow calls the need for self-esteem.

It is no accident that the first person outside of our family who validates us is almost always a person of the same gender. It usually happens during adolescence, with your "best girlfriend" if you are female, or "best buddy" if you are male. This first intimate relationship is usually with a person of the same gender because the risk of them misunderstanding you is less than in a relationship with the opposite gender.

There is, however, great risk in receiving validation. The person who gives it to you is able to do so only because you have let them in on your deepest secrets. This gives them great power, for good or for ill. Because they know you and your insecurities so well, they have the capability to hurt you horrendously. This is why many divorces are so acrimonious. No one knows how to get you better than a spouse with whom you have shared so many intimacies. This is why it is said that "There is no such thing as an amicable divorce."

Nevertheless, we truly need love and the validation that leads to it. As studies of mental illness make clear, those who try to live without do so at their peril.

Transition

Young adulthood is an exciting period in life, during which many changes are taking place. The peak of physical development is reached, and the decline of certain abilities begins. These are almost never apparent, however, because of organ reserve. Our style of life has a powerful effect on this development, including our diet, use of alcohol, drugs and nicotine, and marital status.

The major change occurring in the area of mental development involves the relationship between intellectual and ethical growth. There are several quite different explanations of why sexuality develops as it does, and a number of important changes in the current sexual practices of young adults. Love, too, may be variously explained. We looked at the theories of Sternberg and Fromm.

Physical and mental development form the basis for our interactions with the world around us. These interactions, which we refer to as psychosocial development, are covered in the next chapter.

Key Ideas

1. During young adulthood, we reach the highest level of most aspects of physical development, and begin the slow decline to old age.

2. Organ reserve, which refers to that part of the total capacity of our body's organs that we do not normally need to use, keeps us from being aware of declines in body functions.

3. The research of William Perry and Mary Belenky and her associates has greatly advanced our understanding of intellectual/ethical development.

4. Several theories have been offered to explain human sexuality: Freud's psychoanalytical theory, Gagnon's sexual scripts, Mitchell's sexual motives, and Wilson's sociobiological theory.

5. There are seven forms of love, according to Sternberg, each of which involves degrees of passion, intimacy, and commitment.

6. Fromm suggests that validation is the essential ingredient in mature love.

Key Terms

Cholesterol
Commitment (Perry's term)
Commitment (Sternberg's term)
Constructed knowledge
Dualism
Escape
Intimacy (Sternberg's term)
Organ reserve
Passion (Sternberg's term)

Procedural knowledge
Received knowledge
Relativism
Retreat
Silence
Subjective knowledge
Temporizing
Validation

What Do You Think?

1. What would life be like if we did not reach the peak of our physical abilities in early adulthood?

2. How would you describe your style of life? According to the research you have read about in this chapter, would you say you are more like or unlike the average American?

3. Make a list of 10 of your best friends. In which of Perry's three stages would you place each of them?

4. Do you agree that there are major differences in the ways males and females view ethical issues? In what ways?

5. Are you clear on your sexual values? Could you state your principles with precision?

6. Do you agree with Wilson's sociobiological theory? Why or why not?

7. How can you tell if you are truly in love?

Suggested Readings

Fromm, Erich. (1968). *The art of loving*. New York: Harper & Row. A highly readable classic in the field. You will never think about love the same way.

Geer, James, Julia Heiman, and Harold Leitenberg. (1984). *Human sexuality*. Englewood Cliffs, NJ: Prentice-Hall. This impressively comprehensive book covers virtually all aspects of sex with a depth of understanding.

Lawrence, D. H. [1920] (1976). *Women in love*. New York: Penguin. This novel probes the relationships between two sisters and their lovers. It offers a timeless examination of the many aspects of adult interactions. Another of his books, *Sons and Lovers,* is also magnificent on this subject.

Peck, Scott M. (1978). *The road less traveled.* New York: Simon & Schuster. "Confronting and solving problems is a painful process, which most of us attempt to avoid. And the very avoidance results in greater pain and the inability to grow both mentally and spiritually." Drawing heavily on his own professional experience, Dr. Peck, a practicing psychiatrist, suggests ways in which confronting and resolving our problems—and suffering through the changes—can enable us to reach a higher level of self-understanding.

Sternberg, Robert J. (1986). The triangular theory of love. *Psychological Review, 93,* 129–135. This, too, offers a penetrating view of this most elusive topic.

· *Chapter 18* ·

Early Adulthood: Psychosocial Development

When Sigmund Freud was asked the purpose of life, he gave his answer in probably the fewest words he ever used: *"Lieben und arbeiten."* This means "To love and to work." Americans apparently agree. Our literature, both popular and scientific, is heavily committed to books and articles on how we grow and change in respect to work and love. In this chapter, these aspects of early adult life are separated into three categories: marriage and the family, work and leisure, and stages of personal development.

Marriage and the Family

When two people are under the influence of the most violent, most divisive and most transient of passions, they are required to swear that they will remain in that excited, abnormal, and exhausting condition continuously until death do them part.

George Bernard Shaw

Changing American Marriages and Families

The modern American family is quite different from those of the last century. Those families were larger and much more likely to live near each other in the same city or town. What are the advantages and disadvantages of this tendency?

It is not difficult to find critics of marriage (e.g., Kathrin Perutz's book, *Marriage Is Hell*). Not many Americans are paying attention, though. Almost 95% of Americans get married at some point in their lives (U.S. National Center for Health Statistics, 1988). To better understand the present situation, let us take a look at the trends in marriage and family relations.

Today, 25% of all people who get married for the first time are likely to marry someone who has been married before (Sweet & Bumpass, 1987). In almost half of all marriages, one of the spouses has been married before, and in 20% both were married previously. Trends in the rates of first marriage, divorce, and remarriage since the early twentieth century reflect patterns of change in economic and social conditions in the United States. These changes can be clearly seen in Table 18.1. One of the most interesting trends has been the change in the average age at first marriage. At the turn of the century, the average age for females was almost 22 years, and for males almost 26 years. With the exception of the late Depression and war years, the trend has been toward earlier and earlier marriages.

This trend led Duvall (1971) to predict that marriages in 1990 would come even earlier, at about age 20 for both males and females. Several other investigators (e.g., Neugarten & Moore, 1968) said the same thing in the late 1960s. But they only demonstrate the difficulty of predicting the behavior of human beings. For reasons that are not entirely clear, the trend has almost completely reversed itself in recent years. For example, as shown in Table 18.1, in 1970 the median age of first marriage for females was 20.6, and for males 22.5. The most recent average for the available data is almost 25 for males and 23 for females. It seems possible that the figures for the year 2000 will be higher than they were in 1900!

We can also see in Table 18.1 that the rates for first marriage were fairly steady from 1970 to 1984. The rate of divorce and, as a result, the rate of remarriage are higher. In their study of the responses of thousands of women, Norton and Moorman (1987) discovered several trends: "currently many young adult women (particularly African-Americans) will never marry, remarriage after divorce is becoming less frequent, and data indicate that divorce is leveling [at almost 50%]" (p. 3). Interracial marriage represents only one-half of one percent of all marriages (Sweet & Bumpass, 1987). However, this number indicates a rapid increase over earlier periods.

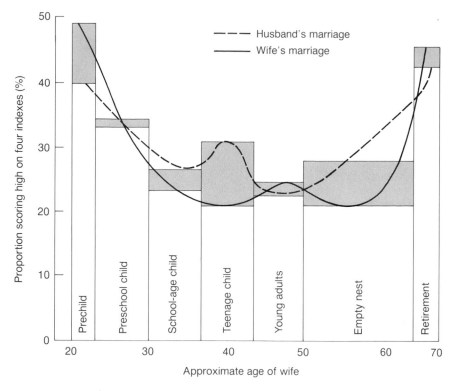

Figure 18.1 *The effect of children on the satisfaction of parents with their marriage.*

The Bureau of the Census suggests that the recent trend is probably caused, at least in part, by four factors:

Liberalization of divorce laws

Growing societal acceptance of divorce, and of remaining single

The reduction in the cost of divorces, largely through no-fault divorce laws

The broadening educational and work experience of women has contributed to increased economic and social independence, a possible factor in marital dissolution

Other factors that affect divorce rates are race, the wife's workforce participation, husband's employment status, and residence status (Buehler & others, 1986; Kalter, 1987; Phillips & Alcebo, 1986; South & Spitze, 1986).

Another of the changing trends has to do with marital satisfaction over the life cycle of the marriage. That is, when are most people the happiest with married life, and when are they the unhappiest, and why? Some older studies (reviewed in Rollins & Feldman, 1970) have reported that marital satisfaction drops when the children arrive (see Figure 18.1). More recent ones have found that such a drop depends on the circumstances. Feldman (1981) found no drop in marital satisfaction at all if the children are planned for and the parents are realistic about the responsibilities involved. Schumm and Bugaighis (1986) found that the drop in marital satisfaction occurs only when the stress of raising new children is combined with other stress such as financial need and overwork.

Table 18.1 Marriages and Divorces: 1970 to 1984					
Marriage and Divorce	**1970**	**1975**	**1977**	**1978**	**1979**
Marriages					
Total (1,000)	2,159	2,153	2,178	2,282	2,331
Rate per 1,000 population	10.6	10.0	9.9	10.3	10.4
Rate per 1,000 unmarried women:					
15–44 years old	140.2	118.5	109.8	109.1	107.9
15 years old and over	76.5	66.9	63.6	64.1	63.6
First marriage of bride (1,000)	1,252	1,191	1,147	1,174	1,214
Rate per 1,000 single women:					
15 years old and over	82.9	68.1	62.7	62.1	62.1
18–19 years old	151.4	115.0	99.6	95.6	91.7
20–24 years old	220.1	143.8	125.6	123.0	121.9
25–44 years old	82.5	81.7	78.6	77.1	76.8
45–64 years old	8.8	9.2	8.6	7.9	7.8
65 years old and over	1.1	1.2	1.0	1.0	.9
Median age at first marriage:					
Male (years)	22.5	22.7	23.0	23.2	23.4
Female (years)	20.6	20.8	21.1	21.4	21.6
Remarriages of bride (1,000)	393	510	532	548	582
Rate per 1,000 widowed and divorced:					
15 years old and over	36.6	40.1	40.0	40.0	40.8
15–24 years old	317.6	319.9	323.5	321.5	312.6
25–44 years old	142.3	144.5	129.0	126.8	127.5
45–64 years old	24.8	23.5	22.1	21.9	21.7
65 years old and over	2.5	2.5	2.4	2.1	3.0
Remarriages of divorced women (1,000)	270	365	391	406	432
Rate per 1,000 divorced women:					
15 years old and over	123.3	117.2	107.3	105.0	104.0
15–24 years old	413.4	319.6	347.3	313.7	309.1
25–44 years old	179.6	158.6	137.3	134.4	135.2
45–64 years old	42.6	40.1	35.6	35.6	35.1
65 years old and over	6.1	9.1	6.4	6.4	7.4
Median age at remarriage:					
Male (years)	37.5	35.5	34.9	35.1	35.3
Female (years)	33.3	32.0	31.4	31.5	31.9
Divorces					
Total (1,000)	708	1,036	1,091	1,130	1,181
Rate per 1,000 population	3.5	4.8	5.0	5.1	5.3
Rate per 1,000 married women, 15 yr. old and over	14.9	20.3	21.1	21.9	22.8
Median duration of marriage (years)	6.7	6.5	6.6	6.6	6.8
Median age at divorce after first marriage:					
Male (years)	30.5	30.2	30.6	30.7	3.10
Female (years)	27.9	28.1	28.4	28.4	26.7
Children involved in divorces (1,000)	870	1,123	1,096	1,147	1,181
Average number of children involved	1.22	1.08	1.00	1.01	1.00

Source: U.S. National Center for Health Statistics, *Vital Statistics of the United States, 1988.*

A recent Gallup poll (1988) asked 1,500 parents "What do you regard as the biggest problem facing you and your family?" Table 18.2 indicates that economic problems are by far the single largest concern of the respondents. Only about one-fifth said they could think of no serious problems.

Although early and middle-age adults are certainly concerned about every aspect of their family lives, the crucial part of family life for most of them is how they manage their relationship with their spouse. Their major concern is: "What kind of marriage will I have, and how can I make it a happy marriage?"

Table 18.1 *Continued*					
Marriage and Divorce	**1980**	**1981**	**1982**	**1983**	**1984**
Marriages					
Total (1,000)	2,390	2,422	2,456	2,446	2,477
Rate per 1,000 population	10.6	10.6	10.6	10.5	10.5
Rate per 1,000 unmarried women:					
15–44 years old	102.6	103.1	101.9	99.3	99.0
15 years old and over	61.4	61.7	61.4	59.9	59.5
First marriage of bride (1,000)	1,221	1,219	1,240	1,218	1,225
Rate per 1,000 single women:					
15 years old and over	66.0	64.9	66.0	63.8	63.5
18–19 years old	87.3	80.7	78.5	72.6	72.1
20–24 years old	119.8	110.0	111.9	106.9	104.4
25–44 years old	74.9	79.3	80.7	79.2	80.5
45–64 years old	7.0	7.9	8.6	8.4	8.3
65 years old and over	.9	.9	.9	.9	.8
Median age at first marriage					
Male (years)	23.6	23.9	24.1	24.4	24.6
Female (years)	21.8	22.0	22.3	22.5	22.8
Remarriages of bride (1,000)	591	616	629	629	635
Rate per 1,000 widowed and divorced					
15 years old and over	38.3	39.9	39.2	38.4	37.6
15–24 years old	231.0	280.0	267.7	268.1	249.2
25–44 years old	117.3	119.7	119.5	117.4	114.4
45–64 years old	19.7	19.9	20.8	20.9	20.5
65 years and over	2.3	2.3	2.2	2.2	2.2
Remarriages of divorced women (1,000)	447	475	487	485	490
Rate per 1,000 divorced women					
15 years old and over	91.3	96.3	94.4	91.6	87.3
15–24 years old	236.4	282.2	263.6	250.1	244.3
25–44 years old	122.8	129.1	129.6	126.0	120.8
45–64 years old	30.3	30.2	31.3	31.2	30.4
65 years and over	5.3	5.7	5.3	4.9	4.8
Median age at remarriage:					
Male (years)	35.2	35.3	35.7	36.2	36.8
Female (years)	32.0	32.1	32.5	32.9	33.3
Divorces					
Total (1,000)	1,189	1,213	1,170	1,158	1,169
Rate per 1,000 population	5.2	5.3	5.0	4.9	5.0
Rate per 1,000 married women, 15 yr. old and over	22.6	22.6	21.7	21.3	21.5
Median duration of marriage (years)	6.8	7.0	7.0	7.0	6.9
Median age at divorce after first marriage					
Male (years)	31.2	31.5	31.9	32.3	32.4
Female (years)	26.9	29.2	29.5	29.8	30.0
Children involved in divorces (1,000)	1,174	1,180	1,108	1,091	1,081
Average number of children involved	96	97	94	94	92

Types of Marriage

Attitudes toward marriage, and therefore types of marriage, vary greatly throughout the world. Despite many variations in the ways humans begin their married lives, there are basically four kinds of marriage throughout the world: monogamy, polygamy, polyandry, and group marriage.

Monogamy is the standard marriage form in the United States and most other nations, in which there is one husband and one wife. In **polygamy,** there is one

Table 18.2   Most Significant Problems Facing Today's Family

What Do You Regard as the Biggest Problem Facing You and Your Family?

Economic problems (total)	56%
Health problems, care	6
Divorce, family well-being	5
Education	3
Dissatisfaction with government	3
Fear of war	3
Old age, Social Security	3
No problems	16
All others	8
No opinion	8
	111%[a]

[a]Total adds to more than 100% due to multiple responses.
Copyright © 1988 The Gallup Poll, Princeton, N.J.

BOX 18.1

Is the Family on the Way Out?

No doubt you have recently heard at least one politician wringing his or her hands over what serious shape the American family is in. In chapter 12, we reported on many of the changes affecting the relationship between parents and children in today's families—for example, the loss of such family functions as job training, values clarification, and economic dependence. Some even worry that the family itself is on the way out. They prophesy that professionals will have ever-increasing roles in raising our children, as more and more American women seek careers.

Are other countries as concerned about this as we are? There are countries in which the family has always been of tremendous importance—Asian countries such as Japan and China, and Western countries such as Italy and Spain, for example. Is this becoming a big problem for them? What about the Soviet Union, where 50% of children 1 to 3 years old, and 90% of children 4 to 5 years old, are in daycare? Do you think they have solved the problem of how to raise children when both parents work full time?

There have been many books and articles written on this subject. For ideas on how you yourself might solve this problem, you may want to look into some of them.

The polygamous family, consisting of one husband and several wives, is almost nonexistent today.

husband but two or more wives. In earlier times in this country, this form of marriage was practiced by the Mormons of Utah. There are still some places in the world where it exists, but the number is dwindling. **Polyandry** is a type of marriage in which there is one wife but two or more husbands. The rarest type of marriage, it is practiced only in situations where there are very few females. **Group marriage** includes two or more of both husband and wives, who all exercise common privileges and responsibilities. In the late 1960s, this form of marriage received considerable attention, but it accounts for a miniscule percentage of the world's population and has lost considerable popularity in recent years.

A different way of looking at marriage is based on the similarity or dissimilarity of the husband and wife in terms of their social, racial, and ethnic backgrounds.

Endogamous marriages are those in which the partners are said to have married into their "own tribe." That is, they have married someone who is similar to them in most ways.

BOX 18.2

Why Marry?

Another way to learn more about types of marriage is to conduct an informal survey of couples from each of three age groups suggested below, asking each person for the major reason he or she decided to marry.

25–35 years	husband _____
	wife _____
	husband _____
	wife _____
35–50 years	husband _____
	wife _____
	husband _____
	wife _____
50 or more years	husband _____
	wife _____
	husband _____
	wife _____

What conclusions can you draw from their answers? Were there important age or gender differences? How many types of marriage did your survey cover?

Exogamous marriages are those in which the spouses are thought to be unlike each other in some important ways. Another term for this is **heterogamous.** An example is an Irish Catholic man marrying a Russian Jewish woman. The customs of the two families would be quite different.

Homogamy is a newer term that describes a marriage in which two people are *extremely* similar in all of their personal characteristics. In previous times, marriages arranged by the parents were usually intended to be homogamous. The closest form of homogamy today is probably the dual-career marriage, in which "couples share equally in the rights and duties of marriage" (Nicola & Hawkes, 1986, p. 47). This type of marriage is seen as contributing to the couple's satisfaction in many cases.

Omnigamy is a term made up by Lionel Tiger (1978) to describe a relatively recent development in American marriage systems. Tiger suggests that because the divorce rate is now two and a half times as great as it was some twenty years ago, and because 80% of people who get divorced eventually remarry, there are many more marriages in our country than there used to be. He says that,

❖ *Many people are married to people who have been married to other people who are now married to still others to whom the first parties may not have been married, but to whom somebody has likely been married. . . . Thus we appear to be moving to a new and imprecise system which you might call omnigamy, in which each will be married to all (p. 14).*

Although there is some variation in the types of marriage and relationships established between spouses, it is slight compared to the variability that exists in adult sexual practices. In the next section, we examine this topic more closely.

Table 18.3 A Brief History of Work	
Approximate Years	**Primary Role of Work**
Early History	Nomadic search for food.
8000 B.C.	Cultivation of cereal grains, domestication of animals.
5000 B.C.	Greater division of labor, surplus production of goods, trade.
500 B.C.	Work seen as degrading and brutalizing by upper classes; done as much as possible by slaves.
A.D. 500	Serfdom (lord of manor system replaces slavery).
A.D. 1350	Black Death makes workers scarce. Move to towns; guilds of craftspersons formed. Cottage industry, capitalism start.
A.D. 1750	Inventions cause "industrial revolution," demise of small business. Factory system takes advantage of cheap labor.
A.D. 1900	Unions, government regulations, electricity and automation, new management policies greatly improve life of workers.
A.D. 1950	Computers, technology create world of highly skilled, white-collar workers.
A.D. 1970	Age of information processing.

Patterns of Work

Waste of time is thus the deadliest of sins. Loss of time through sociability, idle talk, luxury, or more sleep than is necessary for health (six hours) is worthy of absolute moral condemnation. Thus inactive contemplation is also valueless, or even reprehensible if it is at the expense of one's daily work.
Max Weber, The Protestant Ethic and the Spirit of Capitalism.

Weber, a philosopher and economist, was a leading spokesperson on the role of labor at the turn of the century. How differently we view that role today! Table 18.3 displays a brief summary of the history of work in Western society, and indicates how much our attitudes toward work have changed. Changes in the world of work have been coming more rapidly in recent years than ever before. Working in the United States today is complicated. The rest of this section is devoted to explicating the major trends, their causes, and likely results.

Employment Patterns

Most of the total population 16 years old and older who choose to work are working (see Table 18.4). The figure is decidedly lower for the African-American population—around 89%, compared to 95% for whites. Not surprisingly, the highest percentage of unemployment is found among persons 16 to 19 years old. For African-Americans in that age group, the percentage is a disconcerting 40%, as compared to 15% for whites.

Another important aspect of employment patterns has to do with the effects of education. Table 18.5 makes it obvious that the lower the level of education, the more likely a person is to be unemployed. Unfortunately, this is even more true for African-Americans than for whites and Hispanics. Notice, for example, that of those with less than four years of high school, 19.9% of whites and 15.8% of Hispanics are unemployed, compared to 35.9% of African-Americans.

BOX 18.3
Getting a Job
How many jobs have you held so far in your life? Do you remember how you got them? What do the people who hire workers consider when they are hiring? Do blue-collar jobs have significantly different criteria than white-collar jobs?
To find out, you might interview the managers of a bank and a supermarket and ask what they look for in a new employee. Are there differences in behavioral, attitudinal, cognitive, or appearance criteria? Why or why not?

How People Choose Their Careers

On the basis of research still considered to be highly reliable, Holland (1973) developed an interesting theory on how people choose their careers. He suggested that, in our culture, all people can be categorized as one of six personality types: realistic, investigative, artistic, social, enterprising, or conventional. An individual's personality pattern is estimated by figuring out how much a person's attributes resemble each type.

For example, a person might resemble an artistic type most. This type exhibits "a preference for ambiguous, free, unsystematized activities that entail the manipulation of physical, verbal, or human materials to create art forms or products, and an aversion to explicit, systematic, and ordered activities" (p. 120). This kind of person learns to be competent in artistic endeavors such as language, art, music, drama, and writing.

Our hypothetical person may next most resemble the social type. Such an individual is likely to be cooperative, friendly, generous, helpful, idealistic, insightful, responsible, tactful, and understanding. This person is then rated on the remaining four types in descending order. The six-category composite is the person's personality pattern.

The theory also holds that there are six kinds of environments in which people live. These have the same names as the personality types. According to Holland (1973),

❖ *each environment is dominated by a given type of personality, and each environment is typified by physical settings posing special problems and stresses. For example, realistic environments are "dominated" by realistic types of people—that is, the largest percentage of the population in the realistic environment resembles the realistic type. A conventional environment is dominated by conventional types (p. 22).*

The "artistic" type of person, according to Holland, has a preference for ambiguous, free, unsystematized activities.

People tend to search out environments in which they feel comfortable and competent. Artistic types seek out artistic environments, enterprising types seek out enterprising environments, and so forth.

The theory relates to career choice when the assumption is made that a person's behavior is determined by an interaction between their personality and the characteristics of the environment. By knowing someone's personality pattern and the pattern of their environment, predictions can be made about choice of vocation, job changes, vocational achievement, personal competence, and educational and social behavior.

Table 18.4   Employment Status of the Civilian Noninstitutional Population by Age, Sex, and Race

| Age, Sex, and Race | February 1990 Civilian Labor Force | | | | | |
| | Civilian Noninstitutional Population | Total | Percent of Population | Employed | Unemployed | |
					Number	Percent of Labor Force
Black						
16 years and over	21,188	13,292	62.7	11,798	1,494	11.2
16 to 19 years	2,188	744	34.0	532	211	28.4
16 to 17 years	1,097	228	20.8	159	69	30.1
18 to 19 years	1,091	516	47.3	373	143	27.7
20 to 24 years	2,420	1,673	69.1	1,374	299	17.9
25 to 54 years	11,961	9,581	80.1	8,672	909	9.5
25 to 34 years	5,331	4,291	80.5	3,744	547	12.7
25 to 29 years	2,671	2,140	80.1	1,840	300	14.0
30 to 34 years	2,660	2,151	80.9	1,905	246	11.4
35 to 44 years	4,014	3,313	82.5	3,051	261	7.9
35 to 39 years	2,246	1,846	82.2	1,699	147	7.9
40 to 44 years	1,769	1,467	82.9	1,352	115	7.8
45 to 54 years	2,616	1,977	75.6	1,876	101	5.1
45 to 49 years	1,387	1,101	79.3	1,040	61	5.5
50 to 54 years	1,229	877	71.3	836	41	4.6
55 to 64 years	2,132	1,045	49.0	979	66	6.3
55 to 59 years	1,113	641	57.6	598	43	6.7
60 to 64 years	1,020	404	39.6	381	23	5.7
65 years and over	2,485	249	10.0	241	8	3.4
65 to 69 years	915	143	15.6	136	7	4.9
70 to 74 years	647	74	11.5	73	2	(1)
75 years and over	923	32	3.5	33	—	(1)
White						
16 years and over	160,007	106,113	66.3	100,689	5,425	5.1
16 to 19 years	11,265	6,046	53.7	5,184	862	14.3
16 to 17 years	5,333	2,290	42.9	1,897	393	17.2
18 to 19 years	5,932	3,756	63.3	3,287	469	12.5
20 to 24 years	14,714	11,487	78.1	10,578	909	7.9
25 to 54 years	88,931	74,997	84.3	71,833	3,164	4.2
25 to 34 years	35,875	30,407	84.8	28,851	1,556	5.1
25 to 29 years	17,506	14,845	84.8	14,000	845	5.7
30 to 34 years	18,369	15,562	84.7	14,852	711	4.6
35 to 44 years	31,439	27,119	86.3	26,124	995	3.7
35 to 39 years	16,667	14,330	86.0	13,817	514	3.6
40 to 44 years	14,772	12,788	86.6	12,307	482	3.8
45 to 54 years	21,617	17,471	80.8	16,858	613	3.5
45 to 49 years	11,812	9,880	83.6	9,505	375	3.8
50 to 54 years	9,805	7,591	77.4	7,353	238	3.1
55 to 64 years	18,612	10,439	56.1	10,062	377	3.6
55 to 59 years	9,192	6,227	67.7	5,978	248	4.0
60 to 64 years	9,421	4,212	44.7	4,084	128	3.0
65 years and over	26,484	3,145	11.9	3,032	113	3.6
65 to 69 years	8,964	1,922	21.4	1,851	70	3.7
70 to 74 years	7,085	790	11.2	762	28	3.6
75 years and over	10,436	433	4.2	419	14	3.3

Source: U.S. National Center for Health Statistics, 1990.

This theory represents a departure from earlier vocational measures that looked at vocational choice in terms of interest patterns. In these, vocational interests and preferences were considered independent of personality. But Holland draws on a body of research to support his claim that vocational interests are just a further expression of personality.

Table 18.4 *Continued*

Age, Sex and Race	February 1990 Not in Labor Force				
	Total	Keeping House	Going to School	Unable to Work	Other Reasons
Black					
16 years and over	7,895	2,787	1,737	792	2,580
16 to 19 years	1,445	75	1,252	1	117
16 to 17 years	869	8	826	—	35
18 to 19 years	576	67	426	1	82
20 to 24 years	747	261	306	26	154
25 to 54 years	2,380	1,286	171	356	567
25 to 34 years	1,040	601	118	75	246
25 to 29 years	531	296	77	36	123
30 to 34 years	509	305	41	40	124
35 to 44 years	701	356	34	133	178
35 to 39 years	400	197	27	59	117
40 to 44 years	302	159	7	74	61
45 to 54 years	639	329	20	148	142
45 to 49 years	286	149	17	62	57
50 to 54 years	352	179	2	85	85
55 to 64 years	1,088	442	4	192	449
55 to 59 years	472	230	4	94	145
60 to 64 years	615	212	1	98	304
65 years and over	2,235	722	3	217	1,293
65 to 69 years	773	259	4	60	450
70 to 74 years	573	197	—	35	341
75 years and over	890	266	—	122	502
White					
16 years and over	53,894	22,990	7,128	2,515	21,260
16 to 19 years	5,219	328	4,512	29	350
16 to 17 years	3,043	74	2,824	5	140
18 to 19 years	2,177	254	1,688	24	211
20 to 24 years	3,228	1,140	1,649	74	365
25 to 54 years	13,934	9,623	932	992	2,388
25 to 34 years	5,468	3,799	618	233	818
25 to 29 years	2,661	1,761	416	109	375
30 to 34 years	2,807	2,038	202	124	443
35 to 44 years	4,320	3,088	234	324	674
35 to 39 years	2,336	1,710	128	154	343
40 to 44 years	1,984	1,377	106	170	331
45 to 54 years	4,146	2,736	80	434	896
45 to 49 years	1,932	1,292	55	200	385
50 to 54 years	2,215	1,444	24	234	512
55 to 64 years	8,173	3,849	26	556	3,742
55 to 59 years	2,965	1,647	12	272	1,034
60 to 64 years	5,208	2,202	14	284	2,708
65 years and over	23,339	8,052	10	864	14,414
65 to 69 years	7,042	2,455	4	215	4,368
70 to 74 years	6,295	2,184	2	183	3,926
75 years and over	10,003	3,412	4	467	6,120

Note: Numbers in thousands

The development of a vocational choice theory based on personality is useful in many ways. It can be used to help explain social science problems. It can be used to help people whose careers seem to have gotten off track. And it can be used in the obvious area of vocational guidance. Holland developed the Self-Directed Search (1970) for this purpose. It essentially helps people determine their resemblance

Table 18.5 Employment Status of the Civilian Noninstitutional Population, 16 to 24 Years of Age by School Enrollment, Years of School Completed, Sex, Race, and Hispanic Origin

Employment Status, Years of School Completed, Race, and Hispanic Origin	February 1990 Civilian Labor Force					
	Civilian Noninstitutional Population	Total	Percent of Population	Employed		
				Total	Full Time	Part Time
Total Not Enrolled						
Total, 16 to 24 years	16,029	13,025	81.3	11,514	9,923	1,591
16 to 19 years	3,320	2,418	72.8	1,938	1,499	440
20 to 24 years	12,709	10,607	83.5	9,576	8,424	1,151
Less than 4 years of high school	4,052	2,582	63.7	2,014	1,628	385
4 years of high school	8,075	6,830	84.6	6,091	5,238	853
1 to 3 years of college	2,469	2,221	90.0	2,066	1,812	254
4 years of college or more	1,433	1,392	97.1	1,344	1,245	99
Men, 16 to 24 years	7,712	6,975	90.4	6,079	5,466	613
16 to 19 years	1,632	1,336	81.9	1,038	851	186
20 to 24 years	6,080	5,640	92.8	5,041	4,615	426
Less than 4 years of high school	2,124	1,727	81.3	1,340	1,141	198
4 years of high school	3,955	3,674	92.9	3,255	2,955	300
1 to 3 years of college	1,063	1,015	95.5	945	864	81
4 years of college or more	570	559	98.0	540	506	34
Women, 16 to 24 years	8,317	6,050	72.7	5,435	4,457	978
16 to 19 years	1,688	1,082	64.1	901	647	253
20 to 24 years	6,629	4,967	74.9	4,535	3,810	725
Less than 4 years of high school	1,929	855	44.3	674	487	187
4 years of high school	4,120	3,156	76.6	2,836	2,283	553
1 to 3 years of college	1,405	1,206	85.8	1,121	947	174
4 years of college or more	863	833	96.5	804	739	65
White						
Total, 16 to 24 years	13,197	10,949	83.0	9,849	8,546	1,304
16 to 19 years	2,718	2,039	75.0	1,673	1,311	363
20 to 24 years	10,479	8,910	85.0	8,176	7,235	941
Men	6,391	5,898	92.3	5,227	4,742	485
Women	6,806	5,052	74.2	4,622	3,804	819
Less than 4 years of high school	3,255	2,165	66.5	1,733	1,430	303
4 years of high school	6,578	5,668	86.2	5,136	4,423	713
1 to 3 years of college	2,049	1,836	89.6	1,741	1,541	200
4 years of college or more	1,316	1,280	97.3	1,239	1,151	87
Black						
Total, 16 to 24 years	2,360	1,721	72.9	1,343	1,112	231
16 to 19 years	509	317	62.2	214	151	63
20 to 24 years	1,850	1,404	75.9	1,130	962	168
Men	1,088	880	80.9	675	578	98
Women	1,272	841	66.1	668	535	133
Less than 4 years of high school	660	335	50.8	215	153	62
4 years of high school	1,310	1,017	77.6	820	706	114
1 to 3 years of college	323	303	93.7	249	202	46
4 years of college or more	67	66	—	59	51	8
Hispanic Origin						
Total, 16 to 24 years	2,174	1,569	72.2	1,375	1,198	177
16 to 19 years	547	353	64.5	275	231	44
20 to 24 years	1,627	1,216	74.7	1,100	967	133
Men	1,143	1,012	88.5	896	810	86
Women	1,031	557	54.0	479	388	91
Less than 4 years of high school	1,112	726	65.2	611	539	71
4 years of high school	783	608	77.7	551	467	84
1 to 3 years of college	238	199	83.6	181	164	17
4 years of college or more	41	36	—	31	27	5

Source: U.S. National Center for Health Statistics, 1990.

Table 18.5 *Continued*

Employment Status, Years of School Completed, Race, and Hispanic Origin	February 1990 Civilian Labor Force			
	Total	Unemployed		
		Looking for Full-Time Work	Looking for Part-Time Work	Percent of Labor Force
Total Not Enrolled				
Total, 16 to 24 years	1,511	1,381	130	11.6
16 to 19 years	480	415	65	19.8
20 to 24 years	1,031	966	65	9.7
Less than 4 years of high school	568	506	63	22.0
4 years of high school	739	695	44	10.8
1 to 3 years of college	155	134	21	7.0
4 years of college or more	48	46	2	3.5
Men, 16 to 24 years	896	859	37	12.9
16 to 19 years	298	270	28	22.3
20 to 24 years	599	589	10	10.6
Less than 4 years of high school	388	371	17	22.4
4 years of high school	419	406	14	11.4
1 to 3 years of college	70	65	5	6.9
4 years of college or more	19	17	1	3.4
Women, 16 to 24 years	614	522	93	10.2
16 to 19 years	182	145	37	16.8
20 to 24 years	433	377	55	8.7
Less than 4 years of high school	181	135	46	21.2
4 years of high school	320	289	30	10.1
1 to 3 years of college	85	69	16	7.0
4 years of college or more	29	29	—	3.5
White				
Total, 16 to 24 years	1,100	1,007	93	10.0
16 to 19 years	366	314	52	18.0
20 to 24 years	734	693	41	8.2
Men	670	641	29	11.4
Women	430	366	64	8.5
Less than 4 years of high school	432	390	41	19.9
4 years of high school	532	496	36	9.4
1 to 3 years of college	95	82	13	5.2
4 years of college or more	41	39	2	3.2
Black				
Total, 16 to 24 years	377	342	36	21.9
16 to 19 years	103	92	12	32.6
20 to 24 years	274	250	24	19.5
Men	205	197	8	23.3
Women	173	145	28	20.5
Less than 4 years of high school	120	100	20	35.9
4 years of high school	197	190	7	19.3
1 to 3 years of college	54	46	8	17.9
4 years of college or more	7	7	—	—
Hispanic Origin				
Total, 16 to 24 years	194	175	20	12.4
16 to 19 years	78	62	16	22.0
20 to 24 years	117	113	4	9.6
Men	116	109	7	11.5
Women	78	66	12	14.0
Less than 4 years of high school	115	103	12	15.8
4 years of high school	57	50	7	9.3
1 to 3 years of college	18	17	—	8.9
4 years of college or more	5	5	—	—

Note: Numbers in thousands.

to each of the six personality types. They can then search through occupations that correspond to their personality pattern.

The Phenomenon of the Dual-Career Family

The old family pattern of the husband who goes off to work to provide for his family and the wife who stays home and manages that family is almost extinct. Economic realities and feminist social upheaval have combined to change all that. Now most women do some sort of paid work and contribute 30% of the family income. This phenomenon of the **dual-career family** has manifested itself in some unusual ways.

First, women are still considered responsible for the maintenance of the family (Gerson, 1985; Szinovacz, 1984). Therefore, women are often considered unreliable by employers for the more important, higher paying jobs. Women in general have better access to low-pay jobs with little opportunity for advancement. In addition, women don't yet seem to need paid work to define themselves in the way men do (Rubin, 1979). Women often choose jobs that fit in well with the needs of their family. Women tend to work shorter hours and change the nature of their work more often than men do (Berk, 1985; Moen, 1985).

Second, men have had to adjust psychologically to the increased role of their wives as providers for the family. Men have historically derived much of their self-image and personal satisfaction from their work and their ability to "provide" for their family. Women now contribute much more of the family income than in previous times, and in a small but increasing number of cases, women are the primary breadwinners.

The assumption was that the more conservative blue-collar worker would have more trouble dealing with this new division of labor than the better educated and more "enlightened" upper-class and middle-class husbands. Recent research suggests just the opposite. Upper-middle-class men seem to have the most problem sharing their roles as family providers, unless they make considerably more than their wives (Fendrich, 1984; Hood, 1983). Other research suggests that these men feel cheated because they have no wife at home full time to support them, as their fathers perhaps had.

Working-class men have adapted better to this change, perhaps because the financial reality gave them little choice. The more dependent a family is on the contributions of a wife's income, the more accepting the husband is of the new role of his spouse (Rosen, 1987). All classes of men and women, however, try to continue to portray the husband as the primary provider and the wife as providing secondary support. Many women still seem to believe that much of a man's pride and identity is wrapped up in his work and will try to preserve that position.

While women are entering the workforce in increasing numbers, men are in general not participating more in the family work. While some research suggests that men are doing more housework than ever before (Pleck, 1985), others conclude that men do about the same amount of housework as they did in the nineteenth century (Cowan, 1987).

Most wives do about two to three times as much family work as the husbands (Berk, 1985). Women tend to do all the everyday work, including most of the childcare, washing of clothes, cooking, and general cleaning. They tend to work alone, during the week and on the weekends, and during all parts of the day.

Men tend to do the less frequent, irregular work, such as household repairs, taking out the trash, mowing the lawn, and so on. They tend to do family work in the company of others, on the weekend, or perhaps during the evening. In the evening, this work may involve childcare while the wife does the after-dinner chores.

On the average, the wife in a family does two to three times as much of the family's work as does the husband.

The tasks that men are most willing to share are the very tasks that women find most enjoyable: cooking and childcare. During the inevitable argument over who does what around the house, the husband may point out that he helped out in these areas, not recognizing that he left the more onerous jobs for his wife.

We mentioned that men seem to derive their self-image and identity from their work, and that this is increasingly threatened by the entrance of women into the workplace. One obvious way men could derive more satisfaction is by taking on a greater role in the care of their children. This change, however, does not appear to be occurring at the same pace as women entering the workforce. It is estimated that mothers are actively involved with their children three to five times as much as fathers (Lamb, 1987). Mothers do all the routine chores such as feeding, bathing, and dressing. Fathers primarily play with their children. Fathers tend to spend their time with the children when the mothers are around, while mothers spend much more time alone with the children.

This participation is true, regardless of whether the mother is employed or not. However, as economic necessity forces women to spend more time at a paid job, they are demanding that men help out more equitably. Recent research suggests that men who are forced to participate more in childcare may form better relationships with their children. At the same time, this results in significantly more marital distress (Crouter & others, 1987). One of the challenges of the family in the 1990s will be to get husbands to take on voluntarily more of the responsibility of childcare.

Stages of Personal Development

Transformations—Gould

To better understand how adults try to gain maturity, psychoanalyst Roger Gould and his colleagues at the University of California at Los Angeles combined their findings on a large number of outpatients. They discussed the primary concerns of patients at various age levels. Also at that time, Gould administered a questionnaire on this same topic to 524 persons who were not outpatients. Based on the results of these two investigations, Gould generated a theory of adult growth that is reported in his book *Transformations* (1978).

Transformations is not a scientific report of the data, statistics, and research conclusions derived from these studies. Rather, it is a theoretical discussion illustrated by selected case studies, in the manner of Freud. Gould contends that there are four developmental periods in adult life up through middle age (he does not go into later adulthood). At each of these stages, there is a **major false assumption** remaining from childhood, which must now be reexamined and readjusted by each individual if he or she is to progress in maturity. A summary of the stages, typical ages, and major false assumptions at each stage is presented in Table 18.6. In this chapter, we will look only at the first three stages, the transition from late adolescence up to the midlife decade.

As Gould (1978) defines adult development, "Growing and reformulating our self-definition becomes a dangerous act. It is the act of transformation" (p. 25). Reexamining one's childhood angers and hatred (he refers to them as demons) is often a painful and difficult task. Many adults avoid it or soon give up on the struggle after they have entered it. This prevents them from reaching true maturity.

Gould recommends seven steps, called an **inner dialogue,** which he believes can help in mastering the demons of one's childhood experiences. These steps are

---

BOX 18.4

Multicultural Focus: A Letter to Mama

What follows is a letter written by a 36-year-old woman to her 64-year-old mother. She did this as part of her effort to follow Gould's recommendations for "mastering the demons of her childhood experiences." Do any of the issues she raises with her mother seem relevant to you? Do you know anyone else for whom these issues are relevant?

Dear Mama,

This is a very difficult letter to write. There are some things you won't want to hear, but I think I should say, because you and I will bear the brunt of them, stated or not.

I am ANGRY. I'm angry with me, but a lot of that anger stems from feelings I have about unfair treatment from my childhood. I know you have always said "Don't blame your parents for your failings as an adult." That philosophy certainly helps an adult to consider changing, but to say your parents have not contributed in some basic ways—good and bad—to the adult you have become, is ignoring what seems to me a very basic truth. Some people have to work harder to become happy, productive adults, and I feel I am one of those people.

For years I have not been at peace with myself. As I write this, I am experiencing one of the most painful times in my life, because I am unable to be nice to myself on any level. If a stranger treated me as badly as I do, I would simply walk away. The sad part is that I must live in constant disapproval of myself. The last seven years have been spent trying to understand my own lack of acceptance. I have recently had several revelations, and I wish you to know about them.

First, I have not always realized the depth and breadth of my self-hatred. Just recently its full intensity has become clear to me. The catalyst was that I thought I was beginning to go through menopause, and even though I am only in my mid-thirties, I immediately thought "Gee, I deserve that!" At that moment, I realized that I have been speaking this way to me for years and didn't realize the extent to which I denigrate myself.

This is where you come in. How did I learn to have so little value for my self? I learned it from the things grownups said to me, and YOU had the strongest influence. For many years I have known that you were not the first in our family to send negative messages to their children on a regular basis. I recall not liking Grandma very much after about the age of twelve. It must be just about that time that I figured out she had been unkind to you in many ways. I'm sure her childhood experiences were quite similar, too. However, the fact that upbringings can make generations of unhappy people does not nullify my anger that it also happened to ME.

I have had my doubts about telling you exactly how I feel, because, after all, we can't go back and do it again and change the outcome. However, expressing anger is half the battle in leaving it behind and getting on with life.

---

1. Recognize your tension and confusion.

2. Understand that people are faced with contradictory realities.

3. Give full intensity to the childhood reality; that is, accept the fact that it is real.

4. Realize that contradictory realities still exist (between childhood and adulthood).

5. Test reality. Pick a risk that discriminates one view from another.

6. Fight off the strong urge to retreat when just on the verge of discovery.

BOX 18.4

Continued

There are times when I would like to point out ludicrousies that still continue, but I don't know if you could even spot them if they were identified. The other day you looked at my living room, knowing that I (and you) had spent an ungodly amount of time laboring over it. It thrilled me to hear you say it was beautiful. (I still care what you think about things.) I was also dumbfounded and sad that you were capable of seeing fingerprints on the highboy, and angry that you should spoil my pleasure in the room by saying they detracted from it. This probably seems like a nothing to you, but I pick the incident because I could easily replace the room with myself.

It is not a supportive and loving parent who praises her child, and then quickly lets her know that there are still faults—so not to think too highly of one's self. There is some level of performance which is *adequate,* and even more than adequate, which is not perfect. (You hope, I realize, that perfect is a personal standard, and therefore no one can be perfect in another's eyes.) This constant reminder that "better" was still to be had, has left me an angry adult, incapable of taking pleasure in my accomplishments.

There is another issue associated with taking realistic inventory of my worth, which also stems from my childhood. When I have done a good job, the credit is owed to someone else—a good mother (and, as an adult, any number of other powerful people). When something bad happens, it is because I have it coming to me because I am so worthless. This is a terrible supposition which allows me no way of taking pleasure in my accomplishments, and no realization that many of the bad things that happen to me are factors beyond my control. I CANNOT control all aspects of life's incidents, and certainly no one else is totally to blame or praise for them either. The best I can do is try, and then accept the rest as outside my jurisdiction. "Trying" is more than good enough, and therefore worthy of my self-respect, no matter what the outcome.

All of this cannot be undone, but it can certainly be discontinued, now that its cost is apparent. I intend to set more realistic standards for myself in the future and I wish you would bear this in mind as I continue to share my life with you.

Be sure that you know I am angry about the above. I'm not infallible, and no amount of criticism could ever achieve that. I am angry with YOU because I wanted you to care more about how my behavior affected ME, than what other people thought of me. Other people don't have to live with me and they shouldn't have been more important to you than I was. I am not telling you that I don't love you, only that I am very angry. In fact, if I did not love you, this letter would not be worth the effort—I would just write you out of my life. The exercise has been worthwhile, and I would heartily recommend that you might benefit from the process as well.

I love you always,

---

7. Reach an integrated, trustworthy view of reality, unencumbered by the demonic past.

At every stage, in addition to major false assumptions, there are several component false assumptions. These steps are aimed at helping us recognize false assumptions and eventually reject them in favor of a more realistic view of the world.

Stage One—Age 17 to 22—"Leaving Our Parents' World"
At Stage One, youth begin to recognize the difficulties in accepting their *major false assumption*: "I'll always belong to my parents and believe in their world." As a result of this misunderstanding, there are five other false assumptions, which derive from the first:

Table 18.6   Gould's Four Stages of Adult Development
Stage One—Age 17 to 22—Leaving Our Parents' World
Major False Assumption: "I'll always belong to my parents and believe in their world."
Stage Two—Age 22 to 28—I'm Nobody's Baby Now
Major False Assumption: "Doing things my parents' way, with willpower and perseverance, will bring results. But if I become too frustrated, or tired, or am simply unable to cope, they will step in and show me the right way."
Stage Three—Age 28 to 34—Opening Up to What's Inside
Major False Assumption: "Life is simple and controllable. There are no significant coexisting contradictory forces within me."
Stage Four—Age 35 to 45—Midlife Decade
Major False Assumption: "There is no evil or death in the world. The sinister has been destroyed."

Source: Data from R. Gould, *Transformations.* Copyright © 1978 Simon & Schuster, New York, NY.

- "If I get any more independent, it will be a disaster."

- "I can see the world only through my parents' assumptions."

- "Only my parents can guarantee my safety."

- "My parents must be my only family."

- "I don't own my own body."

Stage Two—Age 22 to 28—"I'm Nobody's Baby Now"
The major *false* assumption here: "Doing things my parents' way, with will power and perseverance, will bring results. But if I become too frustrated, confused, or tired, or am simply unable to cope, they will step in and show me the way." Thus even though the direct dependence on parents is, or should have been, mastered at the previous stage, the strong influence of parents must be dealt with now. The following *false* assumptions need to be recognized and exorcised:

- "Rewards will come automatically if we do what we're supposed to."

- "There is only one right way to do things."

- "My loved ones can do for me what I haven't been able to do for myself."

- "Rationality, commitment, and effort will always prevail over all other forces."

Now one's adult sex role begins to take decisive form. Young adults decide on their careers, their relationships with other persons, and whether or not to become parents. Their dreams for the rest of their lives now take clear form.

Over nine-tenths of all Americans eventually marry, and the great majority of them marry during this stage. Gould believes that, in part, the motivation for those marriages and the choice of the specific partner result from our inability to deal adequately with our relationship with our parents. As he puts it:

❖ *Each and every one of us pick partners that, in subtle ways at least, recreate a parent-child relationship that has not yet been mastered. Our separateness from our parents in our twenties is really just a fiction (1978, p. 145).*

For most young adults, society's sex roles determine their careers and the type of relationships they have.

BOX 18.5

Responsibility for Self

One of the clearest indices of maturity is the ability to be responsible for one's own life and behavior. This exercise asks a number of questions involving responsibility for one's own behavior.

1. Name two major purchases you have made in the past year by yourself without a strong influence by anyone else.

   _____

   _____

2. Wherever it is that you live, are you supported by your parents, or do you pay for your own housing?

   _____

   _____

3. Are you completely in charge of what time you come home at night, or do you have to answer to someone else?

   _____

   _____

4. Are you the sole person who decides what clothing you wear?

   _____

   _____

5. To what extent have your parents influenced your career, that is, whether you have chosen to go to college or work, the acceptability of your grades or pay, and so on?

   _____

   _____

6. Are you able to make independent decisions about your sex life? Do you let your parents know what you have decided?

   _____

   _____

   You might compare your answers with those of some of your friends to get a relative idea of how responsible for your life you are.

Stage Three—Age 28 to 34—''Opening Up to What's Inside''

At Stage Three, the major erroneous belief of most individuals is that "Life is simple and controllable. There are no significant contradictory forces within me." People at this stage begin to realize that life is really quite relativistic, and that there are very few "eternal verities." The dream of the crack salesman or the fulfilled mother now comes to be questioned. Both men and women seem to need to reevaluate their entire lives as they enter the fourth decade of their existence.

According to Gould, this reevaluation forces an examination of four *false* assumptions. They are

"What I know intellectually, I know emotionally."

"I am not like my parents in ways that I don't want to be."

"I can see the reality quite clearly of those close to me."

"Threats to my security aren't real."

The major cause of conflict at this stage of life is parenthood. In explaining to children what their values ought to be, we are often forced to see how unsure we are of our own values. Divorce increases at this time, too, as spouses attempt to adjust to each other's developing values.

There is a good side to all of this conflict, however. Gould cites Bertrand Russell's statement that this stage was "intellectually the highest point of my life." Gould believes that the age-30 crisis often forces us to come to know ourselves finally for what we really are. "Our confidence in the world increases as we accept the limitations of our powers and the complexity of reality. . . .in short, we come to see that life is not fair" (1978, p. 61).

The Adult Life Cycle—Levinson

Working with his colleagues, Yale psychologist Daniel Levinson has derived a theory of adult development based on intensive interviews with 40 men and 40 women. Rather than depend on questionnaire data from a large number of individuals, Levinson decided that intensive interviewing and psychological testing with a small number of representative cases would more likely provide him with the information for a theory of adult development. Because of the number of hours necessary in this study (almost 20 hours were spent on interviews with each subject), Levinson decided to limit the number of cases so that he could get more detailed information.

Key to Levinson's theory of adult development is the notion of **life course** (1986). "Life" refers to all aspects of living—everything that has significance in a life. "Course" refers to the flow or unfolding of an individual's life. Life course, therefore, looks at the complexity of life as it evolves over time.

Equally important to Levinson's theory is the notion of **life cycle.** Building on the findings of his research, Levinson proposes that there is "an underlying order in the human life course; although each individual life is unique, everyone goes through the same basic sequence" (1986, p. 4). The life cycle is a *general* pattern of adult development, while the life course is the unique embodiment of the life cycle by an *individual.*

Through his studies, Levinson further defines parts of the life cycle. He defines the life cycle as a sequence of eras. Each era is **biopsychosocial** in character: it is composed of the interaction of the individual, complete with his or her own biological and psychological makeup, with the social environment. Each era is important in itself and in its contribution to the whole of the life cycle. A new era begins as the previous era approaches its end. That in-between time is characterized as a **transition.**

The intricacies of Levinson's theory of adult life course and life cycle are further elaborated by his concept of the adult **life structure.** Life structure is the underlying pattern or design of a person's life *at a given time.* Levinson notes that "a theory of life structure is a way of conceptualizing answers to a different question: 'What is my life like *now?*'" (1986, p. 6) The primary components of a life structure are the relationships that an individual has with significant others. It is through relationships that we "live out" various aspects of ourselves. Levinson regards relationships as actively and mutually shaped. Life structure may have many components, but generally only one or two components are central in the structure at a given time. The central component(s) is the one that most strongly influences the life structure of the individual.

The evolutionary sequence of the life structure includes an alternating series of **structure-building** and **structure-changing** transitions. During the structure-*building* periods, individuals face the task of building a stable structure around choices they have made. They seek to enhance the life within that structure. This period of relative stability usually lasts five to seven years. During that time, the stability of the life structure affords individuals the freedom to question their choices and to consider modifying their life.

This process of reappraising the existing life structure and exploring new life structures characterizes the structure-*changing* period. This period usually lasts around five years. Its end is marked by the making of critical life choices around which the individual will build a new life structure. Levinson notes that the individual decides at this point, "This I will settle for" (1986, p. 7).

In considering the periods of stability and change in the adult life cycle, Levinson notes, "We remain novices in every era until we have had a chance to try out an entry life structure and then to question and modify it in the mid-era transition" (1986, p. 7). Individuals enter into new stages of adult development as they become focused on certain developmental tasks. You will understand these tasks better when we describe each stage below.

Levinson gives equal weight to periods of stability and transition. This captures the evolution of the focus of an individual and the flowing quality of adult development. Unlike most theories of child development where development takes the form of positive growth, Levinson's study of adult development recognizes a coexistence of growth and decline.

Seasons of a Man's Life—Levinson

Levinson has made two separate studies, one of men (1978) and one of women (in progress—to be described in chapter 20). In his first study, which was solely of men, 40 male subjects ranging in age from 35 to 45 were selected, representing four categories (10 each): blue-collar workers paid on an hourly basis, middle-level executives, academic biologists, and novelists.

The hourly workers and the executives were employees of an industrial firearms manufacturer or an electronics plant (about half from each). The biologists were employed at two highly rated universities located between Boston and New York. Of the writers, some were highly gifted novelists whose work had already been accepted by critics; others were less well known, but were regarded as promising and worthy of serious consideration. Of course, this sample cannot be considered to represent the average male in the United States, but the diversity of the people selected in terms of social class origins, racial, ethnic, and religious backgrounds, education, and marital status does make it typical of a great deal of American society today.

The study concentrates on the choices made by each man during his life and how he has dealt with the consequences of his choices, especially as they affect the main components of living: occupation, marriage, and family. After studying these components, Levinson suggested that there are four main seasons of life: (1) childhood and adolescence—birth to 22 years; (2) early adulthood—17 to 45 years; (3) middle adulthood—40 to 65 years; and (4) older adulthood—60 years and older.

Obviously, there is considerable overlap between each of his stages. Between these major stages are substages that help to bring about the transitions necessary for development. Figure 18.2 gives a description of various stages and substages. Levinson himself concentrates on the early and middle adult periods, leaving further consideration of the childhood and late adult periods to others.

He believes that "even the most disparate lives are governed by the same underlying order—a sequence of eras and developmental periods" (1978, p. 64). The

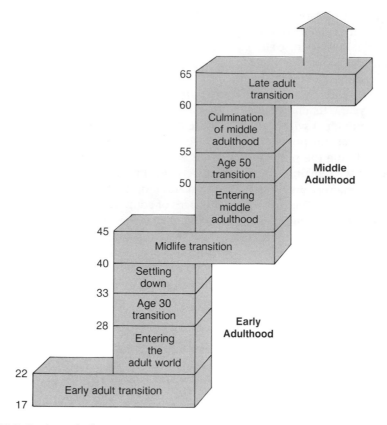

Figure 18.2 Levinson's theory.

purpose of these developmental transitions is to cause greater **individuation.** Individuation refers to our becoming more individual; we develop a separate and special personality, derived less and less from our parents and teachers and more from our own behavior.

Although he hypothesizes more than 10 substages in the course of life, Levinson chooses to concentrate on three phases in male development. These are the **novice phase,** the settling-down phase, and the midlife transition (the latter two will be discussed in the next chapter).

The Novice Phase

The **novice phase** of human development extends from age 17 to 33, and includes the early adult transition, entering the adult world, and the age 30 transition (see Figure 18.2). In this phase of life, four major tasks are to be accomplished. The individual in the novice phase should form

- The dream: "a vision, an imagined possibility that generates excitement and vitality" (p. 91).

- Mentor relationships: Each man should find someone who is older, more experienced, and willing to make suggestions at each of the choice points in his early adult life.

- An occupational decision: A man should begin to build on his strengths and to choose a vocation that values those strengths.

Love relationships: Each man should make decisions on a marriage partner, the number of children, and the type of relationship that he wants to have with wife and children.

The Mentor

The concept of **mentoring** has received considerable attention in recent years (e.g., Frey & Noller, 1983; Moyers & Bly, 1990; Noller, 1983; and Rivchun, 1980). Of particular interest are Robert Bly's notions on the subject (which, by the way, he calls "male mothering").

Bly suggests that two events have wreaked havoc with the modern American male's sense of himself. The first, which began in the first half of the nineteenth century, was the Industrial Revolution. As a result of this, fathers were forced to leave home, where they traditionally worked by the side of their sons, and seek employment in factories. The second, which began in the 1960s with "no-fault" divorce, led to the proliferation of single-parent families, about 90% of which are headed by females.

With each of these events, much of the teaching and appreciation that boys used to get from their ever-present fathers was lost. Mothers have tried to make up for this loss, but because of deep-seated gender differences, only another male can induct a boy into adulthood successfully. Bly believes that only those young men who achieve a mentor relationship with some other older man are likely to attain a mature personality. This man may be an uncle, one of the father's friends, or some older man at work. Without such a person, the young man will not be brave enough to confront himself, and he will sink into a defensive, self-deluding life-style. Bly also suggests that because the typical conflicts that exist between son and fathers are absent in the mentor relationship, the mentor actually can be more helpful to the young man.

Levinson found that after each man selects a dream, mentor relationship, occupation, and love relationship, there is a time at around age 30 (plus or minus two years) when he comes to reexamine his feelings about the four major tasks. Important decisions are made at this time, such as an alteration of the dream, a change in mentor, a change in occupation, and sometimes a change in marital status. For some, this transitional period proves to be very smooth. In most cases, however, it challenges the very foundations of life itself. Although he often keeps it to himself, the typical male at this stage undergoes a seriously disturbing period of self-doubt. Fortunately, most emerge from these doubts with a clearer understanding of their strengths and weaknesses, and a clearer view of what they wish to make of themselves.

Thus, for both Gould and Levinson, the transition from late adolescence to early adulthood (and also for the years to come) tends to proceed in stages as orderly as those we have seen in the earlier stages of life. There is more variation as we grow older, because we are controlled less and less by our genetic inheritance and more and more by the environment in which we find ourselves, and by our own individual decisions. This growing independence from our genes and our early experiences is reflected clearly in these two theories. Even if we have had a hard childhood, with alcoholic parents and traumatic accidents, we should be developing the ability to be in charge of our lives. As we grow older, we have the opportunity, and indeed the responsibility, to re-invent ourselves. The next personality theorist we will cover, Erikson, would certainly agree.

A solid relationship with an older mentor is crucial to the career success of a young adult, according to Levinson. Why is it, do you think, that older males are more likely to take a mentoring attitude toward their younger colleagues than are older females toward their younger colleagues?

Intimacy Versus Isolation—Erikson

We last talked about Erikson's theory in chapter 12, where we discussed his fifth stage (adolescence), Identity and Repudiation versus Identity Confusion. Now we will consider his sixth stage, Intimacy and Solidarity versus Isolation. This stage applies to what he defines as young adulthood, ages 18 to 25.

In his definition of **intimacy,** Erikson states that it should include:

1. Mutuality of orgasm

2. with a loved partner

3. of the other sex

4. with whom one is able and willing to share a mutual trust

5. and with whom one is able and willing to regulate the cycles of
    a. work
    b. procreation
    c. recreation

6. so as to secure to the offspring, too, all the stages of a satisfactory development (1963, p. 266).

He points out, however, that it should not be assumed that sexual intercourse is the most important aspect of intimacy between individuals. He is speaking here of far more than sexual intimacy. He is talking about the ability to relate one's deepest hopes and fears to another person and to accept another's need for intimacy in turn.

Those who have achieved the stage of intimacy are able to commit themselves to concrete affiliations and partnerships with others, and have developed the "ethical strength to abide by such commitments, even though they may call for significant sacrifices and compromises" (1963, p. 262). This leads to **solidarity** between partners.

Erikson is fond of quoting Freud's response when asked what he thought a normal person should be able to do well (mentioned as this chapter began): *"Lieben und arbeiten,"*—"to love and to work." To Freud, then, sharing responsibility for mutual achievements and the loving feelings that result from them are the essence of adulthood. Erikson fully agrees with this. Thus when Freud uses the term "genitality" to describe this same period, he does not merely mean sexual intercourse; he is referring rather to the ability to share one's deeply held values, needs, and secrets with another through the generosity that is so important in intimacy.

It must be admitted, nevertheless, that Freud was far more concerned with the physical aspects of sex than Erikson, who deserves major credit for moving the school of psychoanalysis away from its fascination with genitalia and toward a greater concern for adult intimacy in general.

The counterpart of intimacy is **distantiation.** This is the readiness all of us have to distance ourselves from others when we feel threatened by their behavior. Distantiation is the cause of most prejudices and discrimination. Propaganda efforts mounted by countries at war are examples of attempts to increase distantiation. It is what leads to **isolation.**

Most young adults vacillate between their desires for intimacy and their need for distantiation. They need social distance because they are not sure of their identities. They are always vulnerable to criticism, and since they can't be sure whether the criticisms are true or not, they protect themselves by a "lone wolf" stance.

Although intimacy may be difficult for some males today, Erikson believes that it used to be even more difficult for females. "All this is a little more complicated with women, because women, at least in yesterday's cultures, had to keep their identities incomplete until they knew their man'' (1978, p. 49). Now that there is less emphasis in the female sex role on getting married and pleasing one's husband, and more emphasis on being true to one's own identity, Erikson believes that both sexes have a better chance of achieving real intimacy.

A growing number of theorists, however, many of them feminist psychologists, argue that females *still* have a harder time "re-inventing" themselves, because of the way our society educates them. In the next section, we present their position.

Male Versus Female Individuation

Identity precedes intimacy for men. . . . For women, intimacy goes with identity, as the female comes to know herself as she is known, through her relationships with others.

Sigmund Freud would have concurred with this statement by Gilligan (1982, p. 12), but for reasons with which many modern women disagree. According to feminist Betty Friedan, he believed "that women need to accept their own nature, and find fulfillment the only way they can, through 'sexual passivity, male domination, and nurturing maternal love' " (Friedan, 1983, p. 43).

The view of the feminists is that because females are trained to believe in the necessity of their maintaining relationships within the family, and because this role often involves self-sacrifice, women find it harder to **individuate**—that is, to develop a healthy adult personality of their own. They argue that for the young adult male, identity formation "involves separating himself from dependency on his family and taking his place in the adult world as an autonomous, independent being, competent, with a clear sense of career and confidence in his ability to succeed" (Wolfson, 1989, p. 11).

For the young adult female, career and self-assurance are not so emphasized. Winning the attention and then the commitment of a man are more important aspects of her identity, and intimacy is the major goal. This is seen as unhealthy. As Wolfson (1989) puts it, "It is difficult to have a sense of yourself that is internally consistent and congruent if your identity is dependent on the identity of someone else. 'I am who you are' is very different from 'I am who I am' " (p. 12).

This new point of view arose in the 1960s, primarily with the publication of Betty Friedan's book *The Feminine Mystique* (1963). The affluent 1950s had "created a generation of teenagers who could forego work to stay in school. Inhabiting a gilded limbo between childhood and adult responsibility, these kids had money, leisure, and unprecedented opportunity to test taboos" (Matusow, 1984, p. 306). At this time many youth, particularly those of the newly affluent middle class, "wanted to live out the commitments to justice, peace, equality and personal freedom which their parents professed" (Gitlin, 1987, p. 12) but, the young people felt, failed to live up to. Groups such as the Students for a Democratic Society sprang up. There developed programs such as Rennie Davis' Economic Research and Action Project, whose goal was to "change life for the grassroots poor" (Matusow, 1984, p. 315). This movement worked for justice and equality not only for the poor and racial minorities, but also for women.

The movement fostered a new commitment to women's issues, and to studies of women themselves. For example, as a result of her research on the female perspective (see chap. 9), Harvard psychologist Carol Gilligan has come to believe that

The 1960s were a time when many grass roots action groups, such as Students for a Democratic Society, came into being. They were anxious to promote "justice, peace, equality and personal freedom."

BOX 18.6

How's Your Individuation Index?

A number of theorists have stressed that maturity involves becoming more and more of an individual as one goes through life's stages. That is, one becomes less dependent on the opinions of one's parents, other relatives, teachers, and friends. The person is better able to determine her or his own personality, using these other influences only as guides. Thus one index of maturity level is the extent to which one is "individuating." Fill in the blanks below to get an idea of your own individuation.

1. Can you think of any occasion within the last month when your friends asked you to do something with them and you refused?

   _____

   _____

2. Can you think of three important decisions you have made within the past year that were definitely not influenced by your parents?

   _____

   _____

3. Can you name at least two things about yourself that you used to hate, but that you now feel are not all that bad?

   _____

   _____

4. Can you name at least two people who used to have a big influence on your life, but who are no longer able to influence you very much?

   _____

   _____

❖ *for girls and women, issues of femininity or feminine identity do not depend on the achievement of separation from the mother or on the progress of individuation. Since masculinity is defined through separation while femininity is defined through attachment, male gender identity is threatened by intimacy while female gender is threatened by separation (1982, p. 9).*

Research has also pointed to two other concerns. One has been the tendency of society to "objectify" women, which means seeing them as a particular type of creature or object rather than as individuals. Psychoanalyst Erich Fromm (1955) suggested that "To be considered an object can lead to a deep inner sense that there must be something wrong and bad about oneself" (p. 323).

The second concern involves the ability to admit vulnerability. "Men are taught to avoid, at all costs, showing any signs of vulnerability, weakness, or helplessness, while women are taught to cultivate these qualities" (Wolfson, 1989, p. 44). Psychologist Jean Baker Miller writes that a "necessary part of all experience is a recognition of one's weakness and limitations. The process of growth involves admitting feelings, and experiencing them so one can develop new strengths" (1976, p. 31).

BOX 18.6
Continued

5. Can you name two things that you now like to do by yourself that you previously didn't like to do?

_____

_____

6. Can you name two beliefs or values you hold with which your friends would disagree?

_____

_____

7. Can you name three things you do of which your parents would disapprove? Three things of which they would approve?

_____

_____

8. Do you think you organize your time differently from most of your friends? Name three ways in which you do things differently from them.

_____

_____

9. Are you an "individual"? Suggest five ways in which you are different from everybody else.

_____

_____

The answers to these questions do not prove or disprove that you are fully mature. To a large extent, however, individuation does consist of the behaviors suggested in this exercise.

Miller sums up the feminist indictment of Erikson's position. His theory is flawed, she argues, because of his belief that

❖   *women's reality is rooted in the encouragement to 'form' themselves into the person who will be of benefit to others. . . . This selfhood is supposed to hinge ultimately on the other person's perceptions and evaluations, rather than one's own (1976, p. 72).*

Obviously, more work is needed to resolve this conflict about the role of gender in the development of the adult personality. Erikson (1963) himself appears to have endorsed this point of view, by stating that

❖   *There will be many difficulties in a new joint adjustment of the sexes to changing conditions, but they do not justify prejudices which keep half of mankind from participating in planning and decision-making, especially at a time when the other half [men], by its competitive escalation and acceleration of technological progress, has brought us and our children to the gigantic brink on which we live, with all our affluence (p. 293).*

Transition

By now you can see that the study of human development is mainly the study of change. Few chapters in this book, however, have described a more changing scene than this one.

Americans are getting married later and for a larger variety of reasons. They are staying married for shorter periods, having fewer children, and are more reluctant to remarry if they become divorced or widowed. As we discussed in chapter 12, the functions of the family itself have changed tremendously in this century, and some have even predicted the family's demise.

The nation's workers experience a very different environment than their predecessors of fifty years ago, as we leave the industrial age and enter the age of "information processing." There are still many problems to solve— including the treatment of minorities and women— but progress can be seen.

Perhaps the liveliest area in developmental study in recent years has been the field of personality research. More and more, we are realizing that, just as in childhood and adolescence, there are predictable stages in adulthood. There appear to be distinct life cycles, the goals of which are individuation and maturity. And differences between male and female development, some desirable and some not so desirable, are becoming apparent.

In the next chapter, we return to the topics of physical and mental development, because they are worth understanding for their own sake, and so that you can see the foundations of psychosocial development in the middle adult years.

Key Ideas

1. Marriage is still enormously important in the United States, but so is divorce.
2. There are four basic types of marriage: monogamy, polygamy, polyandry, and group marriage.
3. There are five categories of marriage based on similarity of spouses: endogamous, exogamous, homogamous, heterogamous, and omnigamous.
4. People tend to choose their jobs on the basis of personal traits, and the interaction of the traits with a set of environmental conditions.
5. A relatively new phenomenon, the dual-career family, has resulted in a number of new problems.
6. Gould's main concept is "major false assumptions."
7. Levinson's central theme has to do with individuation during the novice phase.
8. Erikson sees early adulthood as a crisis between intimacy and isolation.
9. These theories are in accord on several points:
   In many ways, people improve with age.
   Change is manifested in a series of observable stages, just as it is in childhood and adolescence.
   As with earlier age periods, these developmental stages may be seen as obstacles to be overcome, or as crises to be resolved.
   Adult stages are less rigid, and as yet, we know less about them.

Key Terms

Biopsychosocial	Life cycle
Distantiation	Life structure
Dual-career family	Major false assumptions
Endogamous	Mentoring
Exogamous	Monogamy
Group marriage	Novice phase

Heterogamous
Homogamous
Individuation
Inner dialogue
Intimacy
Isolation
Life course

Omnigamous
Polyandry
Polygamy
Solidarity
Structure-building
Structure-changing
Transition

What Do You Think?

1. Which of the four types of marriage described in this chapter do your parents have? Your grandparents?

2. Which of the five categories of marital similarity best describes the marriage your parents have? Your grandparents?

3. What is the best way of resolving the dilemma of the dual-career family?

4. How well do Gould's major false assumptions fit the early and middle adult periods?

5. Gould suggests seven steps in what he calls an "inner dialogue." What is your opinion of this approach?

6. Levinson believes that forming a mentor relationship is an essential part of the novice phase. Have you formed such a relationship? What are its characteristics?

7. To be intimate, you must know your own identity. But to achieve an identity, you need the feedback you get from being intimate with at least one other person. How can this catch-22 be resolved?

8. Which gender has the most difficulty with individualization? Why?

Suggested Readings

Fowles, John. (1977). *The magus (rev. ed.)*. Boston: Little, Brown. This is surely one of the best psychological mystery stories ever written. It concerns a young man who is unable to keep commitments. A secret society decides to try and help him to become more mature.

Friedland, Ronnie, and Carol Kort. (Eds.) (1981). *The mother's book: Shared experiences*. Boston: Houghton-Mifflin. A moving and realistic collection of essays by mothers about motherhood.

Gordon, Mary. (1978). *Final payments*. New York: Random House. The heroine of this marvelously revealing novel struggles with numerous obstacles, from within and without, to gain her independence as a responsible adult.

Kilpatrick, William K. (1975). *Identity and intimacy*. New York: Delacorte. This highly readable examination of Erikson's fifth and sixth stages is brilliant. We guarantee you will see yourself in a new light after reading this book.

Miller, Jean Baker. (1976). *Toward a new psychology of women*. Boston: Beacon. A classic in the field of feminist psychology.

Roth, Philip. (1969). *Portnoy's complaint*. New York: Random House. A wildly comic look at the relationship between a mother and her son, from the standpoint of the son.

Updike, John. (1960). *Rabbit, run*. New York: Knopf. This is the first of four books that chronicles the development of an ordinary man whose nickname is "Rabbit." (He got that name because of his speed as a high school basketball player.) In the book, we follow his efforts to leave behind his exciting life as a sports star and become a responsible family man. It is not an easy trip.

PART 8

Middle Adulthood

· *Chapter 19* ·

Middle Adulthood:
Physical and Cognitive Development

Physical Development

"You're not getting older, you're getting better!"

You may hear middle-age people saying this to each other. They hope that the changes they are experiencing are minor and not too negative, but let's face it, physical systems do decline with age. Table 19.1 traces this decline from age 30 to 80. As can be seen in the table, the slightest decline is in the function most related to thinking, nerve conduction velocity. This involves the speed with which electrical impulses move along the nervous pathways. Unfortunately, the greatest decline is in the cardiac index, which reflects the heart's blood-pumping ability, an ability vital to many other functions of the body. Now let us take a closer look at some of these functions.

Health

Weight and Metabolism

As one moves into middle adulthood, weight gain becomes a matter of concern. For example, about one-half of the United States adult population weighs over the upper limit of the "normal" weight range. For some, this is the result of genetic inheritance—about 40% of the people with one obese parent become obese, as compared to only 10% of those whose parents are not obese (U.S. National Center for Health Statistics, 1986). Others become overweight simply because they do not compensate for their lowering **basal metabolism rate (BMR).**

BMR is the minimum amount of energy an individual tends to use when in a resting state. As you can see from Figure 19.1, this rate varies with age and sex. Females have a slightly higher rate than males. The rate drops most quickly during adolescence, and then more slowly during adulthood. This is caused by a drop in the ratio of lean body mass to fat, "results in a lower BMR, since the metabolic needs of fat tissue are less than those of lean. Even for those who exercise regularly, fewer calories need to be consumed" (Kart, Metress, & Metress, 1988, p. 171).

Thus if you continue to eat at the same rate throughout your life, you will definitely gain weight. If you add to this a decreased rate of exercise, the weight gain (sometimes called "middle-age spread," referring to wider hips, thicker thighs, a "spare tire" around the waist, and a "beer belly") will be even greater. If you expect this to happen, it probably will (another **self-fulfilling prophecy).**

On the other hand, the warnings against "crash diets" should be heeded, especially by middle-aged people. Probably the most popular diet these days includes the use of dietary supplements, and the most popular ingredient in them is an amino acid known as **L-tryptophan.** This acid has been linked to a blood disorder in which white blood cells increase to abnormally high numbers (American Association of Retired Persons, 1990a). This can result in swelling of extremities, severe pain in muscles and joints, fever, and skin rash. To date there have been almost 300 cases in 37 states, and one known death.

Use of Alcohol

Anyone over the age of fifty should go on the wagon and stay there, according to Teri Manolio of the National Heart, Lung and Blood Institute (cited in AARP, 1990b, p. 7). Even one or two drinks each day can be dangerous, because they can cause enlargement of the left ventricle of the heart. Such enlargement causes the heart to work harder, and often can cause irregular heartbeats. If a person's heart is already enlarged, the danger is even greater. This data comes from the Framingham (Massachusetts) Heart Study, which has also furnished the following findings:

- The older the person and the larger the number of drinks per day, the greater the risk.

Table 19.1 Approximate Declines in Various Human Functional Capacities With Age.			
	Percent of Function Remaining		
	30 Years	**60 Years**	**80 Years**
Nerve conduction velocity	100	96	88
Basal metabolic rate	100	96	84
Standard cell water	100	94	81
Cardiac index	100	82	70
Glomerular filtration rate[a]	100	96	61
Vital capacity	100	80	58
Renal plasma flow[a]	100	89	51
Maximal breathing capacity	100	80	42

[a]Glomerular filtration rate and renal plasma flow refer to the ability of the kidneys to do their work.

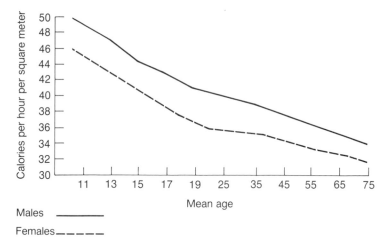

Males ———
Females — — — —

Figure 19.1 The decline of basal metabolism rate through the life cycle. BMR varies with age and sex. Rates are usually higher for males and decline proportionally with age for both sexes.

- The risk is smaller for women.

- Men who are obese or have high blood pressure are at the greatest risk.

Muscular Ability

Muscle growth is complete in the average person by age 17, but improvement in speed, strength, and skill can occur throughout the early adult years. In fact, most people reach their peak around age 25—females somewhat earlier than that and males somewhat later. Variations in peak muscular ability depend very much on the type of activity. Consider, for example, the 20-year-old female Olympic gymnast who is thought of as an "old lady" because peak ability in this area tends to come at around age 16.

Between the ages of 30 and 60, there is a gradual loss of strength—about 10% on the average (Gimby & Saltin, 1983; Spence, 1989). Most of this loss occurs in the back and leg muscles, with considerably less in the arm muscles. Muscle tone and flexibility also slowly decrease during this time. Injuries take longer to heal. Muscle is gradually replaced by fat. A 175-pound man has 70 pounds of muscle at age 30, but typically loses 10 pounds of that muscle to fat by the time he reaches old age (Schulz & Ewen, 1988). However, the current popularity of jogging, swimming, and other exercise techniques may be reversing this trend (Buskirk, 1985).

Many men in their 30s find it hard to accept that their muscular ability is slowly declining. Unfortunately, this sometimes causes them to overexert themselves, leading to such dire results as serious injury and heart attack.

Jogging, in particular, appears to help maintain general health because it demands that the heart pump a great deal of blood to the large muscles of the legs.

In the middle period of adulthood (35 to 64) there is a common but unnecessary decline in muscular ability. Unfortunately, the majority of people in this stage of life do not get much exercise. Both males and females also undergo a marked change in life-style. Growing success in one's chosen field often leads to greater leisure and indulgence in the so-called finer things of life.

Sensory Abilities

The five senses—vision, hearing, smell, taste, and touch—are responsible for gathering information about the world around us. Although the stereotyped image of an elderly person losing her hearing or vision is sometimes good for a laugh, the gradual loss of function of one of the senses is a serious concern for all of us. We often take everyday experiences such as reading a good book, watching television, driving a car to the grocery store, tasting or even smelling a good meal, or just holding a child in our arms for granted. Yet all these experiences depend on one or more of the five senses. What changes in sensory ability can we expect as we pass from early to late adulthood? The following trends are only general and vary widely from one individual to another.

Vision

Vision is the sense that we most depend on for information about what's going on around us. The eye begins to change physically at about age 40. The lens becomes less elastic and more yellow. The cornea begins to loose its luster. By age 50 the cornea is increasing in curvature and thickness. At 50, the iris begins to respond less well to light (Eifrig & Simons, 1983; Schulz & Ewen, 1988).

What do these physical changes mean for our vision? In general, our eyes don't adapt to sudden intense light or darkness as effectively as they once did. The ability to focus on nearby objects decreases, leading to a diagnosis of farsightedness and possibly a prescription for bifocals. The ability to detect certain colors can also be hampered by age-related changes in the eye. As the lens yellows, shades of blue and green become more difficult to discern. The ability to detect moving objects may also decrease as we grow older (Leigh, 1982; Warabi, Kase, & Kato, 1984). For most people, these changes in visual ability are more discomforting than disabling.

Eye disease is a more serious matter. Increasing age often brings a heightened risk for such diseases. **Glaucoma** results from a buildup of pressure inside the eye due to excessive fluid. The resulting damage can destroy one's vision. Glaucoma is increasingly common after the age of 40, and is the leading cause of blindness by age 70. About 60,000 people in the United States are blind because of it (Johnson & Goldfinger, 1981). Routine eye examinations, however, now usually include a glaucoma test and blindness is often prevented.

Cataracts are the result of cloudy formations on the lens of the eye. They form very gradually and inhibit the passage of light through the eye. Cataracts are most common after the age of 60. If they become large enough, they can be surgically removed.

Less well-known but more dangerous is **senile macular degeneration.** This disease of the retina is a leading cause of blindness. It begins as blurred vision and a dark spot in the center of the field of vision. Advances in laser surgery have shown promise in treating diseases of the retina such as this.

Because of changes in the eye that occur when we reach our 40s, glasses are often necessary.

Hearing

Hearing also seems to be susceptible to decline at about age 40. This is when we begin to lose the ability to detect certain tones. As you progress from middle to old age, certain frequencies, the higher ones in particular, may need to be much louder for you to hear them (Schulz & Ewen, 1988). Our ability to understand human speech also appears to decrease as we grow older. The most likely result is an inability to hear certain consonants, especially *f, g, s, t, z, th,* and *sh* (Marshall, 1981). Cognitive capacity may play a role in the fact that the ability to listen to speech in a crowded environment (e.g., a party) declines faster than the ability to listen to someone alone with no background noise (Bergman & others, 1976; Bergman, 1980).

Our visual system is a more reliable sense than our auditory system. In fact, in contrast to the success that medical science has made in fighting blindness, it appears that deafness in the United States is increasing. In 1940 you could expect to find deafness in 200 out of every 10,000 people in this country. By 1980, you could expect to find 300 (Hunt & Hertzog, 1981). Bear in mind, however, that these effects are partly a result of choice. Cross-cultural studies have shown that our relatively loud, high-tech culture contributes to our society's general loss of hearing (Bergman, 1980).

One curious aspect of the age-related decline in hearing is that, of the five senses, hearing is easily the most stigmatized loss. People who wouldn't think twice about getting prescription eyeglasses will refuse to get a hearing aid or even admit they are suffering a hearing loss.

Smell

Although not as important a sense as vision or hearing, the **olfactory sense** does a little more than just tell us when dinner is about ready. First, the olfactory sense works closely with our taste buds to produce what we think of as the "taste" of a given food. In fact, it is difficult in studies to separate which sense—taste or smell— is actually contributing to the decline in performance on a certain task. Besides bringing us pleasurable smells, this sense warns us against spoiled foods, smoke or fire, and leaking gas (Stevens & Cain, 1987).

Various studies suggest that our sense of smell decreases as we grow older (Schiffman & Pasternak, 1979; Murphy, 1983; Stevens & Cain, 1987). The decline seems to begin slowly around age 50 and increases rapidly after age 70.

Taste

As mentioned above, our sense of taste is closely tied to our sense of smell, which makes studying age-related effects on taste very difficult. One estimate is that 95% of taste derives from the olfactory nerves. Not coincidentally, taste seems to begin to decline around the age of 50 (Cooper, Bilash, & Zubek, 1959; Schiffman, 1977).

Recent studies have suggested that older adults may experience a decline in the ability to detect weak tastes, but retain their ability to discriminate among those tastes that they can sense (Spence, 1989). The decline in the ability to taste (and smell) may account in part for the decrease in weight that many elderly persons experience.

Touch

The tactile sense also declines somewhat after the age of 65 (Turner & Helms, 1989), but the evidence for this comes strictly from the reports of the elderly. Until scientific studies are performed, this finding must be accepted with caution.

In summary, we can say that while our senses do decline throughout middle age, we are finding more and more ways to compensate for the losses. Another physical concern in our middle years is the climacteric.

The Climacteric

At this critical time of life the female sex are often visited with various diseases of the chronic kind. . . . Some are subject to pain and giddiness of the head, hysteric disorders, colic pains, and a female weakness. . . . intolerable itching at the neck of the bladder and contiguous parts are often very troublesome to others. . . . Women are sometimes affected by low spirits and melancholy.

John Leake, 1777

The word **climacteric** refers to a relatively abrupt change in the body, brought about by changes in hormonal balances. In women, this change is called **menopause.** It normally occurs over a four-year period at some time during a woman's 40s or early 50s (Masters & Johnson, 1966). The climacteric also refers to the **male change of life,** whereas the word *menopause* refers only to the cessation of menstruation, most often between the ages of 48 and 52. The term **climacterium** refers to the loss of reproductive ability. This occurs at menopause for women, but men tend to be quite old when they are no longer able to produce fertile sperm.

The main physical change in menopause is that the ovaries cease to produce the hormones estrogen and progesterone, although some estrogen continues to be produced by the adrenal glands (Santrock, 1989). Does this decline in hormonal output always cause significant changes in female behavior? The question is difficult to answer. In the first place, women seem to react to menopause in many different ways. As Neugarten (1968) discovered in her extensive study of white mothers, there is not much agreement as to what menopause means or how it feels. Only 4% of the women interviewed thought that menopause was the worst thing about middle age, and many found it much less difficult than they had expected. On the other hand, half the women thought that menopause caused a negative change in their appearance, and a third experienced negative changes in their physical and emotional health. The great majority thought that menopause had no effect on their sexual relationships. Many other things are happening in a woman's life at the same time as her menopause, so it is difficult to sort out what is causing what. Undoubtedly a lack of understanding of menopause, coupled with normal fears of growing old, accounts for at least some of the negative feelings about menopause.

Even for those women who experience serious problems with menopause, **estrogen replacement therapy** (ERT) can offer considerable relief. When it was first instituted, ERT was found to increase the risk of cancer. Today, however, it is given in quite low levels and is combined with progesterone, which greatly reduces the risk. In addition, a recent study (Myers & Morokoff, 1986) found that postmenopausal women who are receiving ERT demonstrate a higher level of arousal when watching an erotic movie than those who are not receiving ERT.

At one time, it was thought that the male hormone balance parallels that of the female. According to a well-designed study conducted by the National Institute on Aging (1979), however, the level of testosterone declines only very gradually with age. Dr. Mitchell Hermann, who conducted the study on men from age 25 to 89, says that his findings contradict earlier results because most of those previous studies were of men in hospitals and in nursing homes who were afflicted with obesity, alcoholism, or chronic illness. All of his subjects were healthy, vigorous men.

Hermann suggests that the decrease in sexual potency that men experience in later years is probably not the result of hormone changes, but rather slowing down in the central nervous system, together with a self-fulfilling prophecy (men expect to become impotent, so they do). The effects of hormonal changes on the appearance and emotional state of men are unclear at present.

It seems likely that as we better understand precisely how hormone balances change and how the different changes interact with each other, the impairments that have been attributed to these changes will decrease (Rowland & others, 1987).

The experts pretty well agree on the nature of physical alterations that occur through the middle years of adulthood. There is, however, much less agreement on the course of mental development in these years.

Mental Development

The Development of Intelligence

> *It was a very curious thing. When I was about 13, my father's intelligence started to drop. His mental ability continued to decline until I reached 21, when these abilities miraculously began to improve.*
> *Mark Twain,* **Pudd'nhead Wilson,** *1884*

Of course, Twain's statement is a sarcastic commentary of the misperceptions youth often have of their parents. Nevertheless, the question of declining intelligence across adulthood has long concerned humans.

Indeed, no aspect of adult functioning has received more research than intelligence (e.g., Botwinick, 1978; Cooney, Schaie, & Willis, 1988; Nesselroade & others, 1988). Despite this considerable research, investigators still do not agree as to whether or not we lose intellectual ability as we grow old. In fact, there are three basic positions: yes, it does decline; no, it does not decline; and yes, it does in some ways, but no, it doesn't in others. The evidence for these positions will now be considered.

Yes, intelligence does decline with age. Undoubtedly the strongest proponent of the decline hypothesis is psychologist David Wechsler. He stated his position as follows:

> ❖ *Beginning with the investigation by Galton in 1883 . . . nearly all studies dealing with the age factor in adult performance have shown that most human abilities . . . decline progressively, after reaching a peak somewhere between ages 18 and 25 (1958, p. 135).*

The most widely used test of adult intelligence is the one designed by Wechsler himself (1955).

No, intelligence does not decline. The Terman study (1925) is an excellent longitudinal study that found an *increase* in intelligence with age. That study was started in 1924 and used the *Stanford-Binet Intelligence Test* for children. The subjects were tested 10 years later, in 1941, and then retested in 1956 with the Wechsler Adult Intelligence Scale (WAIS), which is highly correlated with the Stanford-Binet. At the end of the second, 15-year interval, when the subjects were in their 20s, there was an average increase of scores (Bradway, Thompson, & Cravens, 1958).

The subjects were retested in 1969 by Kangas and Bradway (1971). The subjects were now approximately 40 years old; their scores were found to have increased to an average of nearly 130! Another study supporting the no-decline hypothesis is reported by Owens (1953). In 1919, 363 students entering Ohio State College had their intelligence tested. Thirty years later, Owens retested 127 of them, and all but one of the subjects showed an increase over the 30 years. In 1966, when the individuals were approximately 61 years old, 97 of the subjects were retested and none of the scores had changed significantly.

Lewis Terman began his study of the development of intelligence in the 1920s.

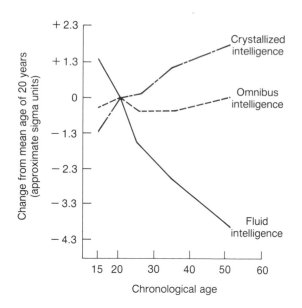

Figure 19.2 *Horn's three types of intelligence.*

From J. L. Horn, "Remodeling Old Models of Intelligence" in B. B. Wolman (ed.), *Handbook of Intelligence: Theories, Measurements, and Applications.* Copyright © 1975 John Wiley & Sons, Inc., New York, NY.

Canestrari (1963) found that adults in middle age do more poorly on speed tests than do younger subjects. However, when they were given more time, for example, to memorize digits, they did as well as the younger subjects.

Yes, intelligence does decline in some ways, but no, in other ways it does not. The picture is probably more complicated than either of the first two positions reveals. There is evidence that

- One type of intelligence declines, while another does not.

- Some individuals decline while others do not.

- Although decline does eventually occur, it happens only late in life.

The main researcher offering support for this position is J. L. Horn, who has described two dimensions of intelligence, fluid and crystallized (see Box 19.1).

Horn (1975, 1978) hypothesized that whereas crystallized intelligence does not decline and may even increase, fluid intelligence probably does deteriorate, at least to some extent (see Figure 19.2). Horn and his colleagues (1981) have found that this decline in fluid intelligence averages three to seven IQ points per decade for the three decades spanning the period from 30 to 60 years of age.

Some research suggests that some types of achievement may rely more on one type of intelligence than on the other (Lehman, 1964). For example, in fields such as mathematics, music, chemistry, and poetry, the best work is usually produced at a relatively young age and therefore may rely most on fluid intelligence. Other major achievements, such as in history, astronomy, philosophy, writing, and psychology, usually occur later in life, which may indicate greater reliance on crystallized intelligence (more on this later).

Earlier work on mental abilities was flawed because the studies were cross sectional rather than longitudinal. A cross-sectional study looks at different groups of people at different ages and then makes inferences about age-related changes (see chap. 2). The problem is that people of different ages, having grown up at different periods, have necessarily had different life experiences. Therefore the results may be more due to this "cohort" effect than to aging.

BOX 19.1

Horn's Description of Two Major Dimensions of Intelligence

To further investigate the decline hypothesis, Horn and Cattell (1967) administered 30 tests of what they called "primary mental abilities." Then, using a complex statistical procedure known as factor analysis, they examined the result of these measurements to see which mental abilities seemed to be associated with one another. They found two distinct types of mental ability, **fluid intelligence** and **crystallized intelligence**. Horn and his colleagues (Horn, 1975; Horn, Donaldson, & Engstrom, 1981) have described these abilities in some detail.

Fluid intelligence involves perceiving relationships, educing correlates, maintaining span of immediate awareness in reasoning, abstracting, concept formation, and problem solving, as measured in unspeeded as well as speeded tasks involving figural, symbolic, or semantic content. These are tasks in which there is little advantage from education. Examples are

- Letter grouping: Find the rule that relates three of four sets of letters and mark the one set that does not fit.
- Dominoes: Insert a domino into a pattern of dominoes in accordance with the rules of the game and in such a way as to extend the pattern.
- Recall paired associates. Recall a number that had been paired with a picture.

Crystallized intelligence involves perceiving relationships, educing correlates, reasoning, abstracting, concept of attainment, and problem solving, as measured primarily in unspeeded tasks involving various kinds of content (semantic, figural, symbolic). The content clearly represents relatively advanced education and acculturation either in the fundamentals of the problems or in the operations that must be performed on the fundamentals. Examples are

- Synonyms vocabulary: Select the best synonym for a word among five choices.
- Inference: Select the most justifiable conclusion to be drawn from a set of statements.
- Arithmetical reasoning: Solve word problems of a kind similar to those presented in elementary algebra courses.
- Tools: Indicate use intended for a wide range of tools.

A longitudinal study avoids this weakness because it looks at the same group of people over an interval of time. Schaie and Hertzog (1983) conducted a longitudinal study on mental abilities and found evidence that they decline as one ages. The evidence for a decline after the age of 60 was strong. They also found evidence that this process starts slowly after the age of 50, although it is probably not observable in everyday life. Making the situation even more complex, Hertzog's latest research suggests that a decline in speed of performance makes declines in intelligence look worse than they are. "It may be the case that a substantial proportion of the age changes actually observed by Schaie in his longitudinal studies is not loss of thinking capacity per se but, rather, slowing in rate of intelligent thought" (Hertzog, 1989, p. 650). Perhaps you simply need more time to think and respond when you get older.

The Definition of Intelligence

Part of the debate is a matter of definition. What, exactly, is intelligence? How is it measured? It is certainly composed of several different mental abilities such as memory, language, reasoning, and the ability to manipulate numbers. Each of these mental processes can, in turn, be divided into various subprocesses.

Different definitions of intelligence lead to different measures of it. Each measure emphasizes different mental abilities. For example, if you define intelligence as rank in class or school achievement, then mental abilities such as verbal comprehension and general information may be much more important than rote memory and perceptual tasks (for a review see Horn & Donaldson, 1980). In fact, most of the commonly used IQ tests measure only a few of the mental abilities that could be measured. Under these circumstances, the question of whether or not intelligence declines with age becomes unanswerable. Clearly, more specific questions must be asked.

Increasingly, general intelligence is being abandoned as a scientific concept and subject of study. More and more, researchers are proposing several quite distinct cognitive abilities. Horn has now added supporting abilities to the concepts of fluid and crystallized intelligence. These include short-term memory, long-term memory, visual processing, and auditory processing (Horn, 1985; Horn & Donaldson, 1980). Howard Gardner (1983) contends there are seven different mental abilities. His list includes linguistic, musical, logical-mathematical, spatial, bodily-kinesthetic, self-understanding, and social understanding abilities. Other lists have been generated by other researchers.

Memory

Certainly intelligence cannot be separated from memory. Your mind can process information like lightning, but if you cannot recall the proper information, processing abilities are useless. Does memory decline with age? There is the stereotype of the doddering old person who can't quite seem to remember the names of his grandchildren. But the research does not always confirm the existence of a decline.

We mentioned above that memory itself can be separated into different types of memory. Horn and his colleagues make a distinction between short-term acquisition and retrieval factors, SAR, and the tertiary storage and retrieval dimension, TSR. Simply put, SAR refers to short-term memory and TSR refers to long-term memory. Short-term memory allows the individual to keep the details of a reasoning problem in awareness so that it can be processed. Long-term memory allows the individual to recall information from the relatively distant past and use it to solve the current problem. They found that SAR declined with age in much the same way as fluid intelligence, and TSR either did not decline or improved, just as crystallized intelligence did (Horn & Donaldson, 1980).

Baltes and his associates (Baltes, Reese, & Nesselroade, 1977; Baltes & Schaie, 1976) have suggested a resolution to the question of how intelligence develops with age. They have proposed a **dual-process model** of intelligence. There is likely to be a decline in the *mechanics* of intelligence, such as classification skills and logical reasoning, but the *pragmatics* are likely to increase. Pragmatics include social wisdom, which is defined as "good judgment about important but uncertain matters of life" (Baltes, Reese, & Nesselroade, 1977, p. 66).

This seems the most reasonable position. There are just too many famous people whose thinking obviously got better as they got older. To name a few: George Burns, Coco Chanel, Benjamin Franklin, Albert Einstein, Mahatma Gandhi, Helen Hayes, Michelangelo, Grandma Moses, Georgia O'Keefe, Pope John XXIII, Eleanor Roosevelt, Bertrand Russell, George Bernard Shaw, Sophocles, Frank Lloyd Wright, and so on and so on. It is no coincidence that these people also maintained their *creative* abilities well into old age.

The Development of Creativity

As the world changes more and more rapidly, the role of creativity becomes more crucial. In this section, we explore the development of creative ability in the adult years. But first, here is a description of creative individuals.

BOX 19.2

What's Your Opinion?

Think of five people over 35 whom you know and most admire. Write their names here:

_____   _____

_____   _____

_____

   Now, ask yourself, how many of these people are among the most creative people you know? If most are, do you think there is something about growing old that contributes to creativity? If your answer is no, what do you think does contribute? Would you say that, on the average, most people get more creative as they grow older?

Traits of the Highly Creative Adult

A number of studies (reviewed in Dacey, 1989) have compared highly creative and average adults in terms of a number of important traits. In general, highly creative adults

- Like to do their own planning, make their own decisions, and need the least training and experience in self-guidance.

- Do not like to work with others, and prefer their own judgment of their work to the judgment of others. They therefore seldom ask others for opinions.

- Take a hopeful outlook when presented with complex difficult tasks.

- Have the most ideas when a chance to express individual opinion is presented. These ideas frequently invoke the ridicule of others.

- Are most likely to stand their ground in the face of criticism.

- Are the most resourceful when unusual circumstances arise.

- Can tolerate uncertainty and ambiguity better than others.

- Are not necessarily the ''smartest'' or ''best'' in competitions.

In their compositions, creative adults typically

- Show an imaginative use of many different words.

- Are more flexible; for example, in a narrative they use more situations, characters, and settings. Rather than taking one clearly defined train of thought and pursuing it to its logical conclusion, creative adults tend to switch the main focus quickly and easily and often go off on tangents.

- Tend to elaborate on the topic assigned, taking a much broader connotation of it to begin with, and then proceeding to embellish even that.

- Are more original. (This is the *most important* characteristic. The others need not be evidenced, but this one must be.) Their ideas are qualitatively different from the average person's. Employers frequently react to the creative person's work in this way: ''I know what most of my people will do in a particular situation, but I never know what to expect from this one!''

The ''grande dame'' of modern dance, Martha Graham's contributions to choreography make her one of the most creative adults in the 20th century.

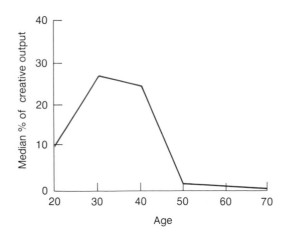

Figure 19.3 *Graph of Lehman's findings.*
Source: Data from Lehman, 1953.

Now let us turn to the research on the development of creativity.

Psychohistorical Studies of Creative Achievement
Lehman (1953) examined biographical accounts of the work of several thousand individuals born since 1774. He studied the ages at which these persons made their creative contributions. He compared the contributions of deceased persons with those still living. On the basis of his study, he concluded:

❖   *On the whole it seems clear that both past and present generation scientists have produced more than their proportionate share of high-quality research not later than at ages 30 to 39, and it is useless to bemoan this fact or to deny it (p. 26).*

Figure 19.3 portrays Lehman's general results.

In his report of his own research on this subject, Dennis (1966) criticized Lehman's work, stating that it included many individuals who died before they reached old age. Dennis points out that this biased the study statistically, because we cannot know what proportion of creative contributions these deceased people would have made had they lived longer.

Dennis himself studied the biographies of 738 creative persons, all of whom *lived to age 79 or beyond* and whose contributions were considered valuable enough to have been reported in biographical histories. He did this because, "It is our view that no valid statements can be made concerning age and productivity except from longitudinal data involving no dropouts due to death" (1966, p. 8).

He looked at the percentage of works done by these persons in each of the decades between the ages of 20 and 80. When creative productivity is evaluated in this way, the results are quite different. He found that scholars and scientists (with the exception of mathematicians and chemists) usually have little creative output in their 20s. For most of them, the peak period is between their 40s and 60s, and most produce almost as much in their 70s as they did in their earlier years. The peak period for artists tended to be their 40s, but they were almost as productive in their 60s and 70s as they were in their 20s. Figure 19.4 depicts these relationships.

Dennis offers an interesting hypothesis to explain the difference in creative productivity between the three groups. The output curve of the arts rises earlier and declines earlier and more severely because productivity in the arts is primarily a matter of *individual* creativity. Scholars and scientists require a greater period of training and a greater accumulation of data than do others. The use of accumulated

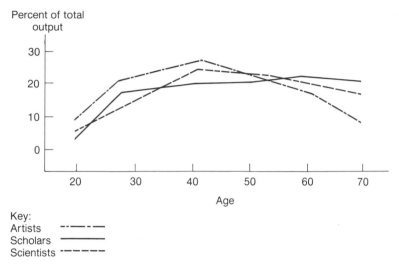

Figure 19.4 *Graph of Dennis's findings.*
Source: Data from Dennis, 1966.

data and the possibility of receiving assistance from others causes the scholars and scientists to make more contributions in later years than do people in art, music, and literature.

Most of the productive persons in Dennis' study were males. It would be interesting to investigate the patterns of productivity among a comparable all-female group.

More recent studies by Simonton (1975, 1976, 1977a, 1977b) have attempted to resolve the differences between the Lehman and Dennis research. In general, he found evidence that quantity declines with age, which favors Lehman, but that quality does not, which favors Dennis. Unfortunately, because of differences in design and criteria (e.g., differing data sources, differing criteria for inclusion in the studies), it cannot be said that this issue is fully resolved at this time.

We started this section on intellectual development by looking at the measurement of changes in intelligence over the adult years. Next we reviewed what we know about creative development. Now we will consider a third aspect, one that attempts to pull together a variety of intellectual factors.

Information Processing

The information-processing approach to the study of intelligence involves looking at different processing capabilities in areas such as attention, perception, memory, and problem solving (e.g., Craik & Simon, 1980; Kintsch, 1970; Sternberg & Detterman, 1979). This view looks at the flow of information from the moment it is attended to, perceived, placed in memory, organized with previous memory, and then considered and acted upon. We will now turn to some of the findings of the information-processing research.

The flow of information through the brain begins at the sensory receptors. At this initial point, the evidence suggests that age-related declines do occur. This part of the process, perhaps more than any other, is affected by the readily observed physical changes brought on by increasing age. For example, the vast majority of sensory information comes through the eyes. It is commonly accepted that as one increases in age, the diameter of the eye decreases and the lens thickens and yellows. These structural changes cannot help but limit the amount of sensory information that can be received at any one time (Fozard & others, 1977).

BOX 19.3

Obstacles and Aids to Creativity

We may agree that creativity is a valuable trait and should be fostered, but how? A number of theorists have offered excellent suggestions (e.g., Adams, 1986; Treffinger, Isaksen, & Firestien, 1983), but educator Ralph Hallman's suggestions (1967) on the obstacles and aids to creativity are still classic. According to him, there are several persistent obstacles to creativity:

- *Pressures to conform.* The pressure on the individual to follow standardized routines and inflexible rules is probably the major inhibitor. Authoritarian parents, teachers, and managers who demand order are responsible for destroying a great deal of creative talent.
- *Ridicule of unusual ideas.* This destroys one's feelings of worth and makes one defensive and compulsive.
- *An excessive quest for success and the rewards it brings.* An overconcern with material success is often the result of trying to meet the standards and demands of others in order to obtain the rewards they have to give. In the long run, this distorts one's view of reality and robs one of the strength of character to be creative (Amabile, Hennessey, & Grossman, 1986).
- *Intolerance of a playful attitude.* Innovation calls for playing around with ideas, a willingness to fantasize and make believe, and a healthy disrespect for accepted concepts. Often creative persons are seen as childlike and silly and their activity wasteful, but these are only appearances. As Hallman remarks, ''Creativity is profound fun.''

In addition to recommending that we avoid these obstacles, Hallman urges that we promote the following aids in ourselves and others:

- *Engage in self-initiated learning.* Most people who are in charge of others (managers, teachers, parents) find it hard to encourage others to initiate and direct their own learning. After all, this is certainly not the way most people were taught. They fear that if their subordinates are given greater freedom to explore

Once the information is made available to the senses, the question becomes whether one can or will attend to it. First, a distinction has been made between effortful and automatic attention (Hasher & Zacks, 1979). **Effortful attention** refers to processing novel tasks, such as trying to learn a new phone number or a new surgical technique. **Automatic attention** refers to common tasks that require little of a person's limited capacity for attention. Anyone who has worked for many years at a job that initially requires a great deal of attention, such as a pilot or a surgeon, usually finds that they use less and less of their total attention capacity to accomplish their tasks. Effortful attention capacity seems to decline with age, while automatic attention does not (Hoyer & Pludes, 1980). So as one gets older, attending to new tasks may get more difficult but performance on familiar tasks should stay the same.

Once the information is attended to, is it properly stored in memory? Can previous information be recalled in order to help reorganize and process new information? The answer to whether memory declines with age depends on what kind of memory is being considered. Fozard (1980) summarized the findings according to five types of memory: sensory, primary, secondary, working, and tertiary. Table 19.2 provides some examples of these five types of memories.

In general, the findings suggest that secondary and working memory decline with age (Botwinick, 1977; Belbin & Belbin, 1968), while primary and tertiary memory do not (Craik, 1977; Botwinick, 1977).

BOX 19.3

Continued

reality on their own, they will learn wrong things, and/or will not learn the right things in the proper sequence. We must put less emphasis on learning "the right facts," and more on learning how to learn. Even if we do temporarily mislearn a few things, in the long run the practice in experimentation and imagination will be greatly to our benefit.

- *Become deeply knowledgeable about your subject.* Only when people make themselves fully familiar with a particular situation can they detach themselves enough to get an original view of it.

- *Defer judgment.* It is important to make wild guesses, to juggle improbable relationships, to take intellectual risks, to take a chance on appearing ridiculous. Refrain from making judgments too early.

- *Be flexible.* Shift your point-of-view; to dream up new ideas for things, imagine as many possible solutions to a particular problem as possible.

- *Be self-evaluative.* When a person comes up with a creative idea, he or she is always a minority of one. History is replete with examples of ideas that were rejected for years before people began to realize their worth. Therefore, the creative person must be one who knows his or her own mind and is relatively independent of the judgment of others. To become a good judge of their own thinking, people must practice making many judgments.

- *Ask yourself lots of open-ended questions.* One extensive study showed that 90% of the time the average teacher asks questions to which there can be only one right answer, which the teacher already knows. Questions that pique curiosity and allow many possible right answers were asked only 10% of the time. Realize that you were probably taught that way, and take steps to rectify the tendency.

- *Learn to cope with frustration and failure.* Thomas Edison tried more than 2,000 combinations of metal before he found just the right kind for the electric element in his first light bulb.

Table 19.2	**Examples of Remembering with Different Types of Memory**
Sensory	Shortest time required to identify the letters in the name of someone you have just met.
Primary	Ability to recall the name of someone you have just met immediately after meeting the person.
Secondary	Ability to recall the name of someone you have met after meeting 10 other people.
Working	Ability to recall a rule, such as using only the first names of the 11 people you just met.
Tertiary	Ability to recall information learned long ago, such as vocabulary (what Horn calls *crystallized intelligence*).

From James L. Fozard, "The Time for Remembering" in L. W. Poon (ed.), *Aging in the 1980's: Psychological Issues.* Copyright © 1980 by the American Psychological Association, Arlington, VA.

We also need to consider how the speed of memory processing is affected by age. Fozard's (1980) review found that the time required to recognize a task and prepare a response seems to increase with age with all types of memory. He also found that the time it takes to search memory for a correct response—the time for decision making—increases for most memory types except tertiary.

One of the implications of this research on memory is that since tertiary or long-term memory does not seem to decline with age, generally the older we get, the larger the knowledge base from which we draw information. An older person, by virtue of a greater number of retained experiences, remembers more things than a younger person.

Of course, all of these processes are interrelated. They can be studied separately but actually they work together. Declines in one process, such as memory, can affect the performance of another, such as problem solving. By the way, the evidence of decline in problem-solving skills is conflicting and far from clear. Research in this area is relatively recent compared to memory or perception research.

So some mental processes seem to decline with age and some do not. This leads us to one final question. When all the pieces are put together, how well can adults learn new things as they get older?

Learning Ability

Is there a serious drop in ability to learn from early to late adulthood? Despite some excellent studies (e.g., Eisdorfer & Wilkie, 1973; Hulicka, 1967; Knowles, 1984; Taub, 1975), there is still considerable disagreement over this matter.

For example, many studies have shown a marked decline in paired associate learning (the ability to remember associations between two lists of words) (Kimmel, 1974). Obviously, memorizing pairs of words is itself of no great importance, but much essential learning is based on this skill. In most of these studies, however, the measure of how well the associations have been learned is speed of response. Do older persons perform poorly because they are slower to *learn,* or only because they take longer to *show what they have learned?* As Botwinick (1978) reports:

❖ *The research strategy has been to vary both the amount of time the stimulus is available for study and the amount of time that is available for response. A general finding is that elderly people need more time for responding than typically is provided; they are at a disadvantage when this time is not available. When sufficient time for response is available, the performance of elderly people is only slightly inferior, or not inferior at all, to that of young people (p. 278).*

Another factor in learning ability that has been studied is motivation to learn (Botwinick, 1978). It has been suggested that persons in middle and late adulthood are less motivated to learn than younger people. Further, it appears that often they are aroused and anxious when placed in a laboratory situation for testing their learning ability. To the extent that this is true, their ability to learn is underestimated.

It has also been found in laboratory experiences that older adults are more likely than younger adults to make the "omission error." That is, when they suspect they may be wrong, they are more likely to refrain from responding at all, and therefore are scored as having not learned the task. But when asked what they think the answer is, they are often right.

Also, the meaningfulness of the task affects motivation. It is clear that the motivation for middle-age and elderly adults is different from that of younger adults, and many experiments have not taken this into consideration in studying learning ability.

For example, some highly abstract tasks that may be meaningful to younger adults are not nearly so meaningful to older people. When the meaningfulness of the learning task allows older persons to organize the incoming information in ways that are familiar to them, they suffer much less detriment.

BOX 19.4

The Lifelong Learning Resource System

Malcolm Knowles (1984) has proposed what he calls a **learning community**. In such a community, many resources (social agencies, school systems, businesses and industries, churches, government etc.) would form an alliance to promote learning in many forms. Such learning opportunities would be open to people of all ages. His concept is based on the following principles of human learning:

1. Learning in a world of accelerating change must be a lifelong process.
2. Learning is a process of active inquiry with the initiative residing in the learner.
3. The purpose of education is to facilitate the development of the competencies required for performance in life situations.
4. Learners are highly diverse in their experiential backgrounds, pace of learning, readiness to learn, and styles of learning; therefore, learning programs need to be highly individualized.
5. Resources for learning abound in every environment; a primary task of a learning system is to identify these resources and link learners with them effectively.
6. People who have been taught in traditional schools have on the whole been conditioned to perceive the proper role of learners as being dependent on teachers to make decisions for them as to what should be learned, how it should be learned, when it should be learned, and if it has been learned; they therefore need to be helped to make the transition to becoming self-directed learners.
7. Learning (even self-directed learning) is enhanced by interaction with other learners.
8. Learning is more efficient if guided by a process structure (e.g., learning plan) than by a content structure (e.g., course outline).

Knowles makes a marked distinction between teaching aimed at children and youth (**pedagogy**) and the teaching of adults (**androgogy**). Adults differ from younger persons in the following ways:

1. *The need to know.* Adults need to know why they need to learn something before undertaking to learn it.
2. *The learners' self-concept.* Adults have a self-concept of being responsible for their own decisions, for their own lives.
3. *The role of the learners' experience.* Adults come into an educational activity with both a greater volume and a different quality of experience than youths.
4. *Readiness to learn.* Adults become ready to learn those things they need to know and be able to do in order to cope effectively with their real-life situations.
5. *Orientation to learning.* In contrast to children's and youths' subject-centered orientation to learning (at least in school), adults are life-centered (or task-centered or problem-centered) in their orientation to learning.
6. *Motivation.* While adults are responsive to some external motivators (better jobs, promotions, higher salaries, and the like), the most potent motivators are internal pressures (the desire for increased job satisfaction, self-esteem, quality of life, and the like).

New Opportunities to Learn

Decline in mental ability due to aging can often be offset through motivation and new learning experiences. This is shown by the growing number of adults who return to formal education in middle age.

Does the apparent drop in learning ability from early to late adulthood occur strictly because of ability or because of factors such as motivation and dexterity?

Why are more and more adults going back to school? In the past, children could be educated to deal with a society and workplace that would remain essentially unchanged for their entire lives. Today the rate of change and innovation is too rapid. Fifty-year-old men and women who were born before the computer was being invented, and certainly didn't learn about computers in school as children, are now routinely asked to use them at work. It is now commonplace for people to return to school in order to advance or even maintain their present career. Also, sometimes an adult will return to school in order to learn a new skill or hobby that will be enjoyable during retirement.

Women in particular are going back to school in large numbers. Middle-age women of today were not encouraged to pursue higher education when they were young. Some women are trying to catch up in order to be competitive with their male counterparts. Other women may return to school, not to study accounting or computer science, but to study literature or history, just to broaden their knowledge and for their own personal enjoyment.

The education system is having to adapt to this change. Most adults cannot afford to quit their current jobs to go back to school. More schools are now offering evening and part-time programs. Many schools offer courses that can be taken at home, in some cases taking advantage of technology such as TV or computers.

Not all new learning by middle-age adults takes place in a formal school setting. Employees in many different types of work settings are asked to keep abreast of new innovations. Other social experiences, such as practicing a religion, going to a library, watching television, and serving as a volunteer, involve new learning. Learning is now more than ever a lifelong task.

Sex in Middle Age

Practices of Middle-Age Adults

While the sexual lives of college students and the elderly have been studied in detail in recent years, there is little information about the practices of middle-age adults. What we know of the situation indicates a slowly declining incidence of sexual intercourse over the course of the couple's relationship. Pearlman (1972) found that married men between the ages of 30 and 39 have intercourse on the average of from one to three times per week. Men in the 40 to 49 age bracket make love about once a week. About one-third have sex one time or less per month. In the 60 to 69 group, well over half have sex once a month or less, and a third no longer engage in intercourse.

It is important to note that Pearlman's data are made up of averages. That is to say, about one-half of people make love more often than his figures show, and one half less. Ethnic background (see Box 19.5) and years of having been married (see Figure 19.5) also play an important role.

One explanation for a decline in sexual activity in middle age is physiological changes. Evidence for such changes is clearer for men than for women. As men age, they generally need more direct stimulation to achieve an erection. The amount of stimulation needed for orgasm increases. The orgasm is generally less intense, and there is a longer recovery time before a man can have another orgasm (Katcha-dourian, 1987).

The picture of women's sexual response in middle age is less clear, since women's orgasms are harder to measure. One change is that after menopause, a woman's sexual lubrication seems to decrease. Most research findings, however, seem to sug-

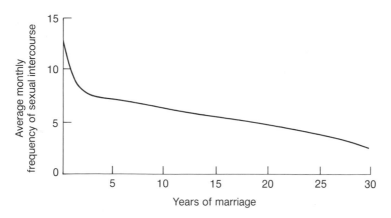

Figure 19.5 *Average monthly frequency of sexual intercourse by duration of marriage.*

BOX 19.5

Multicultural Focus: Sexual Repression in Inis Beag

John Messenger, an anthropologist, spent nineteen months between the years 1958 and 1966 studying the community and culture of a small island off the coast of Ireland. In his study he named the island, fictitiously, Inis Beag. The major livelihood for the 350 people residing in this community was agriculture. At the time of this study, there was no electricity or running water and no motorized vehicles on the island. A small steamer delivered supplies and mail once a week, and Messenger observed that the inhabitants seldom visited the mainland. The following quotes from Messenger provide a flavor of the attitude toward sex that existed in this small community.

A considerable amount of evidence indicates . . . that foreplay is limited to kissing and rough fondling of the lower body, especially the buttocks. Sexual activity invariably is initiated by the husband. Only the male superior position is employed; intercourse takes place with underclothes not removed; the orgasm, for the man, is achieved quickly, almost immediately after which he falls asleep.

Women have been taught . . . that sexual relations with their husbands are a duty which must be rendered, for to refuse coitus is a mortal sin. A frequently encountered assertion affixes the guilt for male sexual strivings on the enormous intake of potatoes of the Inis Beag male. Asked to compare the sexual proclivities of Inis Beag men and women, one mother of nine said, "Men can wait a long time before wanting it, but we can wait a lot longer." There is much evidence that the female orgasm is unknown—or at least doubted or considered a deviant response.

Source: Geer, Heiman, & Leitenberg, 1984, p. 231.

Many couples find that when they reach middle age, their relationship becomes more romantic.

gest that sex has at least the potential of getting better as a woman passes through her middle years (Masters & Johnson, 1966; Rubin, 1979). There are certainly fewer distractions and concerns. After menopause a woman no longer has to worry about getting pregnant, and there are no children around to interrupt lovemaking.

Of course, this potential is only realized if a husband complies. Some research points out that men, influenced by the current standard of youthful beauty, lose interest in their wives in middle age because of the natural physical changes that are brought about by aging. Women in their middle and later years are considered less attractive by many.

Even in today's society, and especially for the current middle-age generation, men still are responsible for taking the initiative in sex (Blumstein & Schwartz, 1983). So if the man does not take the initiative, sex may not occur. Women are particularly reluctant to take the initiative when their husbands are feeling troubled, vulnerable, and insecure, emotions that are not uncommon in middle age.

Although Santrock's data (Figure 19.5) indicate a continuing drop in sexual intercourse over the years, this does not mean that satisfaction in marriage also drops. Satisfaction in marriage depends much more on the stage of childbearing the parents are at than on anything else. There is a definite drop in satisfaction in the earlier years, but if the marriage lasts, the level of happiness, on the average, rises to its earliest level.

Another aspect of middle-age sex is the effect of both spouses working full time. It was suggested that this would have a negative effect on the couple's sex life, but Avery-Clark (1986) found just the opposite. Men married to working women were, in fact, less likely to suffer from sexual problems than were single-earner males.

Furthermore, intercourse apparently does not account for as much of the sex of middle-age people as you might think. Making several calculations on available data, McCary (1978) came to the following interesting conclusion:

❖ *Only 60 percent of the American male population are married at any one time, yet between adolescence and old age each 100 men average 231 orgasms a week. Correcting for the increased incidence of coition and total sexual outlet in marriage, we conclude that only 106 orgasms per 100 men are from marital coitus (45.9 percent of their total sexual outlet). If five percent of the total outlet is accounted for in nocturnal emissions, then approximately 50 percent of men's total sexual outlet is obtained through other sources, which are or have been socially disapproved (e.g., oral sex) or illegal (e.g., homosexuality and nonmarital sex) (p. 281).*

Let us comment on McCary's statement. First, please note that his data mean that the average *individual* male has 2.31 orgasms per week. Also note that this includes men of all ages; younger men no doubt have a higher average. Finally, although he does not mention it, probably a significant part of the 50% of sexual outlet not attributable to sex with a partner is due to masturbation, which does not necessarily end when one marries.

As you can see, by the time people reach middle adulthood, sexual preferences are clearly a very individual matter. Some couples engage in sexuality a lot right into their old age, and some have a fine marriage without making love very much at all.

Transition

What is true of personality and social development appears to be especially true of physical and mental development: *What you expect is what you get*. If you expect

> Your weight to go up,
> Your muscles to grow flabby and weak,
> Your senses to dull,
> Your climacteric to be disruptive,
> Your intelligence to drop,
> Your creativity to plummet,
> Your sexual interest and ability to decline, they probably will.

This is called the self-fulfilling prophecy. People who take a positive outlook, who enthusiastically try to maintain their bodies and minds, have a much better chance at success. They also will be better able to deal with the stresses that life naturally imposes on us all.

This is not to say that we can completely overcome the effects of aging. It means that through our attitudes, we can learn to deal with them more effectively. In the next chapter, we look at the psychosocial features of middle age, which depend so much, as we have said before, on physical and mental development.

Key Ideas

1. Four aspects of our physical system are of special interest when we consider early and middle adulthood: weight and its relationship to metabolism, muscular ability, sensory abilities, and the climacteric.

2. There are three views on whether intelligence drops during adulthood: it does; it does not; and in some ways it does and in others it does not.

3. The last position holds that fluid intelligence does deteriorate to some extent, but crystallized intelligence continues to increase somewhat.

4. Studies indicate that many types of creativity peak in early or middle adulthood, but that those types that can employ the assistance of others peak quite late in life.

5. The "lifelong learning system" is an approach that advocates using learning centers to facilitate continued learning by adults.

6. Males in middle age often experience a decline in sexual interest, usually for nonphysical reasons, whereas females often experience an increase.

Key Terms

Androgogy
Automatic attention
Basal metabolism rate (BMR)
Cataracts
Climacteric
Climacterium
Crystallized intelligence
Dual-process model
Effortful attention
Estrogen replacement therapy

Fluid intelligence
Glaucoma
Learning community
L-tryptophan
Male change of life
Menopause
Olfactory sense
Pedagogy
Self-fulfilling prophecy
Senile macular degeneration

What Do You Think?

1. When you look at the physical shape your parents and grandparents are in, and their attitudes toward the subject, do you see evidence of the self-fulfilling prophecy?

2. If you are a female and have not yet gone through menopause, what do you anticipate your feelings will be about it?

3. If you are a male, can you imagine what women facing menopause must be feeling?

4. What are some ways in which our society might try to foster the intellectual abilities of its adult citizens?

5. What are some ways in which our society might try to foster the creative abilities of its adult citizens?

6. What are some ways in which our society might try to foster the learning of its adult citizens?

7. What is your attitude toward your parents' sexuality?

Suggested Readings

Gardner, Howard. (1983). *Frames of mind: The theory of multiple intelligences.* New York: Basic Books. Offers a comprehensive view of the numerous faces of intelligence.

The Journal of Creative Behavior. Pick up any volume of this fascinating journal at your library and browse through it. A wide variety of interesting topics are covered, and more often than not the articles are written creatively.

Nilsson, Lennart, and Jan Lindberg. (1974). *Behold man: A photographic journey of discovery inside the body.* New York: Delacorte. A book of photographs, many of them pictures enlarged thousands of times. This is a magnificent description of the human body.

Wolfe, Tom. (1987). *The bonfire of the vanities.* New York: Farrar, Straus & Giroux. With his customary verve, Wolfe looks inside the heads of five men and two women, all New Yorkers in early middle age, and shows us how they think.

· *Chapter 20* ·

Middle Adulthood: Psychosocial Development

Marriage must continually vanquish the monster that devours everything: the monster of habit.

Honoré de Balzac

Marriage and Family Relations

In this section, we consider four important aspects of middle-age life today: relationships in marriage; relationships with aging parents; relationships with brothers and sisters; and divorce.

Marriage at Middle Age

Middle age is often a time when husbands and wives reappraise their marriage. The midlife transition often causes a person to simultaneously evaluate past relationships and consider changes for the future. Often, whatever tension that exists in a marriage is suppressed while the children still live at home. As they leave to go off to college or to start families of their own, these tensions are openly expressed.

Sometimes couples learn to "withstand" each other rather than live with each other. The only activities and interests that they shared were ones that revolved around the children. When the children leave, they are forced to recognize how far apart they have drifted. In effect, they engage in **emotional divorce** (Fitzpatrick, 1984).

The period in a marriage after there is no longer a need to care for children is often a time for pursuing dreams that were previously impractical.

But most couples whose marriages have lasted this long have built the type of relationship that can withstand reappraisal and continue for the rest of their lives. Census data suggest that the highest rates for separation and divorce occur about five years after the beginning of the marriage (Sweet & Bumpass, 1987).

In fact, some studies suggest that this period after the children leave home is like a second honeymoon (Campbell, 1975; Rhyne, 1981). After the initial period of negative emotions that follow this disruption of the family, often called the **empty nest syndrome,** married couples can evaluate the job they have done with their children. They can pat themselves on the back for a job well done and then relax now that a major life goal has been accomplished. They then realize that they have more freedom and privacies and fewer worries. They usually have more money to spend on themselves. And this period after the children leave home is now much longer than it used to be. Husbands and wives now can look forward to spending twenty or thirty years together as a couple rather than as a large family.

The Happy Marriage

What does research have to say about the components of a happy, or at least a lasting, marriage? Gottman and Krokoff (1989) conducted a longitudinal study looking at the types of interactions between husband and wife and the effect on marital satisfaction. Earlier research suggested that there was always more negative interaction in unhappy marriages than in happy marriages.

Gottman and Krokoff decided to look at the effect of different types of negative interactions rather than one global category. They found that certain types of conflict may in fact be positive factors in a happy, lasting marriage. They also found that certain types of conflict, particularly defensiveness, stubbornness, and withdrawal on the part of the husband, indicated that a marriage was in trouble.

Gottman and Krokoff assign to the wife the role of manager of marital disagreements, and suggest she get her husband to "confront areas of disagreement and to openly vent disagreement and anger" (p. 50). Most husbands tend to try to avoid relational confrontations (Moyers & Bly, 1990). Therefore, overcoming this reluctance can have extremely beneficial long-term effects on the marriage.

The Unmarried

About 1 in 20 people in middle age have never been married (Sweet & Bumpass, 1987). In general, a person who has never married by middle age will not get married. Such people tend either to have very low or very high education levels. At the low extreme, of those who have less than five years of school, 1 person in 7 has never married. The factors that kept these people from completing school, such as mental illness or other handicaps, are probably the same ones that make them less likely to get married. At the other extreme, 13% of middle-age women with 17 or more years of education have never been married.

There are a number of possible explanations for this. These women may choose higher education and a career over marriage. They may believe marriage will hold them back. A cultural factor may be at work, since some men feel threatened by women with more education than them. Perhaps women who delay marriage to pursue an education end up having a smaller pool of available men to choose from.

Relationships With Aging Parents

Middle age is also a time when most people develop improved relationships with their parents. Middle-age children gain a new perspective on parenthood, most of them being parents themselves, and so reevaluate the actions taken by their own parents (Farrell & Rosenberg, 1981). Also, grandchildren can strengthen bonds that may have weakened when people left their parents' home during early adulthood.

In many cases, however, the relationship begins to reverse itself: as elderly parents grow older and weaker, they often become as dependent on the middle-age children as those children once were on them. Most people fail to anticipate the costs and emotional strains that the aging of their parents can precipitate. This can lead ultimately to new sources of tension and rancor in the relationship.

There are two other features of family life in middle adulthood that we will deal with here: relationships with siblings, and the problem of divorce.

Relationships With Siblings

Developmental psychology has, for some time now, recognized the importance of sibling relationships for a child's cognitive and social growth. But do these special relationships stop contributing to a person's development after adolescence? Does the relationship slowly decline in importance as one ages? Are the characteristics of the relationship the same in middle adulthood as they were in childhood? Psychological research has recently begun to focus on some of these questions.

The fact is, sibling relationships have the potential to be the most enduring that a person can have. You don't usually meet your spouse until young adulthood or at least adolescence. Your parents usually pass away before you do. You usually pass away before your children do. But most siblings are born within a few years of each other, and such a relationship can last 60, 80, or even 100 years!

Nevertheless, sibling relationships do change. As Cicirelli (1980), a prominent researcher on adult sibling relationships, notes:

❖ *At the beginning it is one of intimate daily contact and sharing of most experiences, including the socializing influence of the same parents. Throughout the school years, siblings may have different teachers and different friends and peer groups, but they still have their home experiences in common. Later, when they leave their parents' home to pursue a career or to marry and establish families of their own, they tend to separate from each other as well. They may live in different cities or even different countries. Contact becomes voluntary except on certain ritual occasions, and most life experiences are no longer shared. Still later, they may share the obligations of caring for their parents*

Relationships and roles among the generations are always changing.

*during their declining years. With the death of the parents, sibling contact re-
turns to a more voluntary level until the end of life (p. 455).*

What then are some of the characteristics and effects of such a long and evolving relationship?

Although the research on adulthood sibling relationships is considerably less than that on childhood and adolescent sibling relationships, there are some partial answers to this question. Some researchers have measured change of the relationship with age by looking at how close siblings live to one another and how often they see one another (Rosenberg & Anspach, 1973). They reason that such contact is necessary for a relationship to exist. This research indicates that sibling relationships do decline with age. However, other researchers (Allan, 1977; Cicirelli, 1979) suggest that measures of feelings of closeness and affection are better indicators of a relationship than proximity and frequency of contact. This research supports the notion of strong sibling relationships even in old age. One consistent finding is that the relationship between sisters tends to be stronger than the relationship between brothers.

What is the nature of adult sibling relationships? As in childhood, there is often rivalry, in addition to closeness. Some researchers have found this rivalry to be very common, especially among adult brothers (Adams, 1968). Other researchers suggest that childhood rivalry dissipates in adulthood (Allan, 1977), largely because the siblings have less contact with each other as they grow older.

One would hope that a growing maturity would also lessen rivalry. Certainly adult siblings are faced with more serious and important tasks than are childhood siblings. For example, most middle-age siblings must make mutual decisions concerning the care of their elderly parents and eventually deal with the aftermath of their death.

Another consideration is the effect of changing family patterns on sibling relationships. Couples now are having fewer or even no children. Children will therefore be less available to parents for companionship and psychological support. On the other hand, parents and their siblings will be living longer, more active lives. The obvious conclusion is that sibling relationships will become more and more important in the future.

The Gray Divorcee

With the rapid increase in divorce rates over the last several decades, much has been studied and written about the effects of divorce on the children. Recently, more attention has been given to the effects of divorce on adults. Although most divorces happen within the first five years of marriage, as Figure 20.1 illustrates, most of the people who get divorced are in their middle years of adulthood.

In general, new divorce laws were considered to have a liberating effect on women. Until the liberalization of divorce laws and attitudes, women usually had no choice but to endure a difficult and sometimes even abusive marriage. Cultural norms allowed men much more moral latitude: the so-called double standard. Women basically just had to put up with it.

Before liberalization, it was necessary to establish "reasonable grounds" for divorce, such as adultery or physical abuse. Women who were granted divorces were almost always given relatively generous alimony settlements in order to make up for the loss of income. This was necessary because women lagged far behind men in their earning potential, and often women stayed at home to raise the children and run the household while the husband advanced a career. A woman could not survive a divorce if it left her and her family destitute.

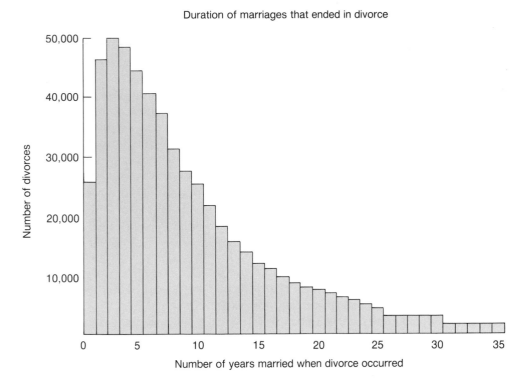

Duration of marriages that ended in divorce

Figure 20.1 *The chart of divorces in the United States shows that most divorces occur within the first five years of marriage, with the peak at three years. Interestingly, the same pattern is found in most other societies, ranging from contemporary Sweden to the hunting and gathering groups of southwest Africa.*

In 1970, the divorce laws were liberalized in California, a change soon followed across the country. This was the introduction of **no-fault divorce.** Suddenly, people could get divorced without proving some atrocious act on the part of one of the spouses. This new law recognized that people could, in the course of their lives, simply grow apart from each other to the point that they no longer made good marriage partners. In legal language, this is known as an irretrievable breakdown of a marriage. It eliminated much of the expensive, time-consuming, and often painful courtroom procedures of the past. Every state except South Dakota now has some form of no-fault divorce.

The intent of these changes in divorce law was to lessen the negative psychological impact of divorce, while making it quicker and less of a burden on the legal system. A less acrimonious divorce was supposed to make parenting after the divorce easier and more successful. But the new laws have had some far-reaching economic consequences that have only recently been explored. An excellent analysis of this impact is contained in Lenore Weitzman's book *The Divorce Revolution* (1985).

It is Weitzman's contention that the new divorce laws have impoverished divorced women and their children. A major facet of the new laws is supposed to be their gender neutrality. Men and women are to be treated equally under the divorce law, and this includes the division of property and alimony.

But perhaps these laws were premature. Men and women did not in 1970, and still do not today, live in an economically equitable system. Men still possess a competitive advantage in terms of earning potential, and women are still held responsible by the culture for raising the children and running the household. When a divorce judge divides up the property equally, grants little or no alimony, and provides inadequate child support, it is the woman and children who suffer.

This is particularly true of middle-age homemakers. The courts seldom give much recognition to the years spent running the household while the husband invested time in advancing a career. Such a woman cannot reasonably be expected to compete with others who have been gaining experience in the marketplace while she stayed at home.

In the year following a divorce, a woman and her children can expect a 73% decline in their standard of living, according to Weitzman's research. The former husband can expect a 42% increase. After five years, the woman's standard of living will likely be 30% of what it was during the marriage, while the husband's will be 14% more.

Another effect is that no-fault divorce laws mandate an even division of property. This often means that the family house must be sold. Before these laws, the house was almost always given to the woman and her children. Besides being an economic burden, the loss of the house has psychological consequences for the development of the children. The dislocation often requires that the children leave their school, neighborhood, and friends. And this usually comes just after the divorce, a period of tremendous stress for any child.

There are some indications that reform is on the way. In California, the rules for division of property and spousal support are being revised. More things are now being considered family assets, to be divided equally, such as the major wage earner's salary, pension, medical insurance, and future earning power. In addition, some states have now become aggressive at pursuing husbands who are delinquent on child support payments. Their names are being published and a part of their wages is being withheld and given to the ex-wife.

Divorce will probably never be the "civilized" process that the early proponents of no-fault divorce laws hoped it would become. At best, we can expect the suffering of spouses to become more equal, and the suffering of the children to be reduced.

Marriage and family life are but two of the factors that have a marked effect on personality development, to which we now turn.

Personality Development—Continuous or Changing?

Continuity Versus Change

All of us have heard someone say, "Oh, he's been like that ever since he was a baby!" Such a comment doesn't sound like a philosophical statement, but think about what it implies. It implies that a person can remain basically the same throughout his or her life span. This is the fundamental question addressed by the issue of *change versus continuity of development*. Do human beings ever really change or do we all stay pretty much the same? It is the focus of great debate by child-development and lifespan psychologists alike because of its implications.

If we assume that people remain the same regardless of what happens to them as their life continues, then the period of early childhood takes on great meaning (Brim & Kagan, 1980; Kagan, 1984; Rubin, 1981). Several of the developmental theorists we have discussed (e.g., Freud and Piaget) have focused much energy on the early years of childhood because they believe that what happens to a person during childhood determines much of what will happen to him or her in the future.

Conversely, others (e.g., Erickson and other adult development theorists) believe that people are constantly changing and developing, and so all life experiences must be considered important. In that case, early childhood becomes a somewhat less significant period in the whole of development, and adolescence and adulthood come more into focus. It also implies that getting children "off on the right foot" is not enough to assure positive development. These are just some of the implications of the debate about personality continuity versus change.

In the study of adulthood, the issue of continuity versus change gets even more complex. In general, there are two distinct theoretical positions in the study of adult personality. There are those who feel that adults remain basically the same—that the adult personality is stable. This is *continuity* in adult development. There are other theorists who view the adult as constantly in a process of change and evolution. That is what the position of *change* refers to.

The study of continuity versus change in adulthood is complicated by the many ways that the issue is studied. Some researchers look at pieces of the personality (personality traits), as measured by detailed questionnaires. They think that the answers to such questionnaires assess adult personality. They are known as **trait theorists.**

Others note that such questionnaires measure only parts of the personality. They argue that adult personality is much more complicated than any list of personality traits. What is interesting to them is how those traits fit with the whole of the person. Beyond that they are also interested in how an adult's personality interacts with the world around him or her. They believe that research based on personality traits is too narrow in focus, and that we must also look at the stages of change each person goes through. They are known as **stage theorists.** The old saying "you can't see the forest for the trees" sums up their position—the parts prevent you from seeing the whole.

The differences in how to go about measuring adult personality complicates the study of continuity and change in adulthood. Researchers use extremely different methods of measuring adult personality and then relate their findings to support either the position of continuity or change. In general, trait theorists have found that the adult personality remains the same: their work supports *continuity* (McCrae & Costa, 1984). McCrae and Costa summed up their research in the title of an article: "Still stable after all these years." Researchers looking at the whole of the adult personality through extensive interviews have found support for the notion of *change* in adulthood (Erikson, 1963, 1975; Gould, 1978; Levinson, 1978, 1986, in progress; Vaillant, 1977).

The study of continuity versus change in adult psychology has important implications, just as it does in childhood psychology. The findings of personality studies add to our knowledge of what "normal" adult development means. Yet as we have seen, the studies vary in their definition of what adult personality is and how it should be measured. Not surprisingly, they also differ in what their studies tell us about normal adult development. They have different answers to the question: "If nothing very unusual happens (like a catastrophe), how will the adult personality develop?"

Trait theorists like McCrae and Costa might say, "If nothing unusual happens, then the adult personality will stay relatively the same. Normal adult personality development is really the *maintenance* of personality." Gould, Levinson, Vaillant, and Erickson, looking at the whole of the adult, would respond differently. They might say, "The adult personality naturally and normally develops through change. Normal adult personality development is a continual process of growth and change."

Who is right? We suggest you read our summary of the studies that each camp provides, and try to make up your own mind. We begin with Roger Gould's theory, as it applies to middle age.

Transformations—Gould

The part of Roger Gould's theory of personality development that deals with middle adulthood is labeled Stage IV. Let us remind you that the basis of his theory is the concept that all of us unconsciously learn assumptions about the nature of life. Healthy personality development depends on rejecting these "major false assumptions."

Stage IV: Age 35 to 45— "The Midlife Decade"

The midlife decade is a time in life when parents, other relatives, and some close friends often go through serious illness and death. Also, this is the time when our self-deceptions and the lies of others can have repercussions far more serious than ever before, because of the greater power that middle-age persons usually have. Therefore, the major false assumption that tends to be rejected at this time of life is "There is no evil or death in the world. Everything sinister has been destroyed."

Five false assumptions accompany this erroneous belief, all of which should now be abandoned:

"The illusions of safety can last forever."

"Death can't happen to me or to my loved ones."

"It is impossible to live without a protector" (this assumption is especially common among women).

"There is no life beyond this family."

"I am innocent."

Even if one's parents are still living and well at this time, most adults experience a role reversal with them. Parents who are in their 60s and 70s often become dependent on their middle-age children, thus bringing the cycle full circle. There is a growing sense of vulnerability, of the passage of time, and a realization of what is truly important. Men at this time say that they no longer fear their bosses or idealize their mentors. Women begin to realize that male protectors really are not all that necessary. Those who come to this realization, both male and female, have a feeling of freedom never before experienced.

Gould realizes, of course, that there are developments in life after the midlife transition, but his research ends at this period.

Seasons of a Man's Life—Levinson

This section continues a discussion of Levinson's (1978) theory that was begun in the previous chapter. Figure 20.2 reproduces that part of his theory that applies to middle adulthood.

Settling Down

The settling-down phase usually extends from age 33 to 40. At this time, most men have pretty well decided what occupation they choose to pursue, and they wish to go from the bottom rung to a place much higher than that. During this period, most men attempt to achieve two tasks: (1) establish a niche in society, and (2) advance up the ladder of the occupational group. During this phase, the male attempts to overcome his dependency on his mentor, and slowly is able to "become his own man." This is a step in the direction of greater individuation, in that the man thinks less and less as others want him to, and more and more as he feels he should. He is now ready to go into the third phase of his adulthood, the midlife transition.

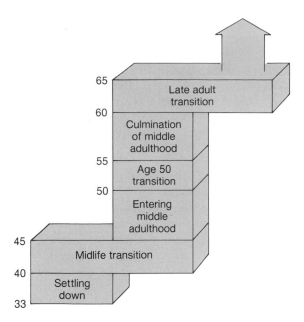

Figure 20.2 Levinson's theory—middle age.

The Midlife Transition

The **midlife transition,** which usually lasts for five years, generally extends from age 40 to 45. It involves three major developmental tasks:

1. The review, reappraisal, and termination of the early adult period.

2. Decisions as to how the period of middle adulthood should be conducted.

3. Dealing with the polarities that are the source of deep division in the man's life at this stage. These polarities, which represent the continual struggle toward greater individuation, are (1) young/old, (2) destruction/creation, (3) masculinity/femininity, and (4) attachment/separation.

Young/Old Young/old is the major polarity to be dealt with during the midlife transition. Levinson refers to Freud's disciple Carl Jung. Jung (1966) suggested that the experience of thousands of generations of human beings has gradually produced deep-seated ideas with which each of us must learn to deal. The major one is that although we begin to grow old even at birth, we are also terribly interested in maintaining our youth, if only to avoid the ultimate consequence of our mortality: death.

In tribal symbolism, the word "young" represents fertility, growth, energy, potential, birth, and spring. "Old," on the other hand, encompasses termination, death, completion, ending, fruition, and winter. Until the age of 40, the man has been able to maintain his youthful self-image. Through producing and raising children, and in many cases through a creative product such as a book, invention, or painting, he has been able to see himself as part of a new and youthful recycling of life. Subconsciously, at least, he has been able to maintain the myth of immortality.

At about the time of his 40th birthday, he is confronted with evidence of his own declining powers. He is no longer able to run, play tennis, or shoot basketballs as effectively as he could in his 20s. He sometimes forgets things, and his eyesight may not be as good. Even more damaging to his hope for immortality is the illness of his friends. There are more frequent heart attacks, strokes, and other serious illnesses among people of his age. In many cases, his parents suffer serious illnesses,

The so-called "midlife crisis"—do you think most middle-aged men go through one?

or even die. These events lead to one inevitable realization: he is going to die, and perhaps in the not-too-distant future. Even the 32 years left him (on the average) do not seem like much, because over half of life is now already past.

Now there is a sense of wanting to leave a legacy. Most individuals want to feel that their life has made some difference, and they want to leave something behind them that can be remembered. Therefore, it is typical at this time that the individual becomes more creative and often works harder than he has in the past to make a contribution considered worthwhile by those who follow him.

Destruction/Creation   The male going through a midlife transition realizes not only the potential of the world to destroy, but also his own capacity to be destructive. He recognizes the evil within himself and his own power to hurt, damage, and injure himself and others. He knows, if he is honest with himself, that he has not only hurt others inadvertently, but sometimes with clear purpose. He sees himself as both victim and villain in the "continuing tale of man's inhumanity to man" (Levinson, 1978, p. 224).

The more honest he is with himself, the more he realizes how tremendous is his capacity to destroy. There is a bonus to this honesty, however: in recognizing his power to be destructive, he begins to realize how truly powerful he can be in creating new and useful forms of life. As with the young/old polarity, he now attempts to strike a new balance between his destructive and creative sides.

Masculinity/Femininity   Levinson again borrows from Jung, using his concept that all persons have a masculine and feminine side, and that they emphasize one over the other because of the demands of society. This emphasis often costs us greatly. A rich adulthood can be achieved only by compensating for that part of us that was denied during our childhood. In most males, the feminine side has typically been undernourished, and now must come to the fore if we are to be all we are capable of being.

According to Levinson, in early adulthood, femininity has a number of undesirable connotations for the male. To the young man, masculinity connotes bodily prowess and toughness, achievement and ambition, power, and intellectuality. To him, the feminine role represents physical ineptness, incompetence and lack of ambition, personal weakness, and emotionality. Now is the time when the polarity between these self-concepts must be reconciled.

The male who is to achieve greater individuation now recognizes that these dichotomies are false, and that he does indeed have a feminine side that must also be nourished. The mature male is able to allow himself to indulge in what he before has disparaged as feminine aspects of his personality. Such a male feels secure enough in his masculinity to enjoy his ability to feel, to nurture, to be dependent. Levinson suggests such men are now freer to assume more independent relationships with their mothers, to develop more intimate love relationships with peer women, and to become mentors to younger men and women alike.

Attachment/Separation   By the attachment/separation dichotomy, Levinson means that each of us needs to be attached to our fellow members of society, but also to be separate from them. As the human being develops, there is a fascinating vacillation between each of these needs. In childhood, there is a clear-cut attachment to mother and later to family. Children need support because of their incompetence in dealing with the complexity of the world around them.

During adolescence, this need switches toward an emphasis on separateness from family, as the individual proceeds through the identity moratorium. During this time, most adolescents need to separate themselves not only from their parents, but from the entire society around them in order to try out new ways of being. This need vacillates back toward attachment during early adulthood.

Throughout their 20s and 30s, most men are involved in entering the world of work and in family and have a strong attachment to others who can help them be successful in these goals. Now, in the midlife transition, a new separateness, perhaps a second adolescence, takes place. The man, especially the successful man, begins to look inside and to gain greater awareness of his sensual and aesthetic feelings. He becomes more in touch with himself by being temporarily less in touch with the others around him.

Because the men interviewed so extensively by Levinson and his colleagues were between the ages of 35 and 45, their study of adult development ends at the midlife transition. Levinson recognizes, however, that there is still a great deal to be learned about development after this stage. He ends his book by encouraging those who are attempting to develop theory and research on the periods following this stage of life.

Farrell and Rosenberg's Findings

Contrary to Levinson's position, some researchers feel that although midlife crises do occur in some individuals, they are not a universal part of adult development (Costa & McCrae, 1980). Further, they believe that because middle-age adults have such a strong tendency to deny the experience of crises of any kind, it is difficult to confirm or deny the existence of a middle-age crisis by simply taking adults' responses at face value. When interviewed or when completing questionnaires, adults may consciously or unconsciously give the socially desirable responses. To get a true understanding of adult development, it may be necessary to look beyond the answers and narratives given by adults.

The work of Farrell and Rosenberg (1981) is a good example. They interviewed and gave a battery of personality tests to two groups of men: those between the ages of 25 and 30 and those between the ages of 38 and 48. Included in that battery was a Midlife Crisis Scale developed for the purpose (see Table 20.1). They asked the participants about tasks central to midlife development, such as:

- Assuming the role of "patron" of the family

- Becoming a source of financial/emotional stability for younger and older generations

- Learning to live with changing physical abilities and accepting unfulfilled dreams of youth

These tasks probably sound familiar, as they are similar to some in Levinson's theory.

Farrell and Rosenberg analyzed the responses of the men in their study in a manner radically different from Levinson. They listened to the responses and then assessed the responses on two dimensions: ability to confront stress, and amount of life satisfaction. Figure 20.3 is a summary of the four personality types that result from their findings.

The researchers confirmed the idea that many middle-age men work hard at denying feelings of weakness or distress. Glaring differences across socioeconomic lines were also found: those who typically confronted their stressful feelings (Types I and II) were much more likely to be affluent than those who had not (Types III and IV).

Men who deny stress showed manifestations of coping with it in different ways. Those whose responses were grouped in the category of Pseudo-Developed (III)

	Denial of Stress	Open Confrontation with Stress
Dissatisfied	**IV Punitive-Disenchanted** 1. Highest in authoritarianism 2. Dissatisfaction associated with environmental factors 3. Conflict with children	**I Anti-Hero** 1. High alienation 2. Active identity struggle 3. Ego-oriented 4. Uninvolved interpersonally 5. Low authoritarianism
Satisfied	**III Pseudo-Developed** 1. Overtly satisfied 2. Attitudinally rigid 3. Denies feelings 4. High authoritarianism 5. High on covert depression and anxiety 6. High in symptom formation	**II Transcendent-Generative** 1. Assesses past and present with conscious sense of satisfaction 2. Few symptoms of distress 3. Open to feelings 4. Accepts out-groups 5. Feels in control of fate

Figure 20.3 Typology of responses to middle-age stress.

represented themselves as being similar to the Transcendent-Generative, with "cheery self-confidence," when really they were not. Responses of this type were interpreted to be "masks" of true feelings. "We call the men's reports of their experiences 'masks' to emphasize our suspicion that the subjective experience of the men and their presentations of self are not necessarily congruent with each other" (Farrell & Rosenberg, 1981, p. 31). The researchers hypothesize that these men create a highly structured life, one that leaves little room for self-exploration or expression.

The fourth type of response, termed Punitive-Disenchanted (IV), was also one that avoided confronting the stress of midlife. Responses of this type reflect a faulty interpretation of feelings. Men in this category interpreted personal feelings of dissatisfaction to be feelings of dissatisfaction with others and the world around them. This transformation of feelings is called projection (see chap. 2).

In distinction to the findings of other theorists, Farrell and Rosenberg's findings do not suggest the existence of a universal midlife crisis, per se. They suggest, instead, that there are universal *stresses* at midlife, and thus each man must create a buffer from or resolution of those stressors. "For most men, then, the movement toward midlife is a process of self-insulation" (Farrell & Rosenberg, 1981, p. 212).

Either most men experience a distinct crisis during their early 40s that alters their self-perceptions and behavior (as Levinson says), or most react to middle age by attempting to "insulate" themselves from reality (as Farrell and Rosenberg argue). It cannot be both ways. What do you think?

Seasons of a Woman's Life—Levinson

In recent years, Levinson (in progress) has turned his attention to female progress toward maturity. For his research, he has selected three groups of women who are between the ages of 35 and 45. One-third are homemakers whose lives have followed the traditional family-centered pattern, one-third are teachers at the college level, and one-third are business women. He sees these women as representing a continuum from the domestic orientation to the public orientation, with the college teachers being somewhere in between. Each of the 45 women has been seen 8 to 10 times by the research staff (half of whom are female) for a total of 15 to 20 hours of interviewing.

Of greatest importance is the finding that females go through a sequence of stages very similar to the stages experienced by the males who were studied. Each

Table 20.1   Midlife Crisis Scale

Unless noted otherwise, all questions are answered with this six-point scale:

| 1. Strongly Agree | 2. Agree | 3. Slightly Agree |
| 4. Slightly Disagree | 5. Disagree | 6. Strongly Disagree |

1. Marriage is as rewarding and enjoyable after 15 or 20 years as it is in the earlier years.
2. Many men I know are undergoing what you would call a change of life or middle-age identity crisis.
3. Almost any job or occupation becomes routine and dull if you keep at it for many years.
4. I am still finding new challenges and interest in my work.
5. In some ways, I wish my children were young again.
6. When your child grows up, he is almost bound to disappoint you.
7. Many people claim that middle age is one of the most difficult times of life. Has it been (or do you think it will be) that way for you? (1. Very Much So; 2. Somewhat; 3. Perhaps; 4. I Doubt It; 5. Not at All)
8. I wish I had the opportunity to start afresh and do things over, knowing what I do now.
9. Many of the things you seek when you are young don't bring true happiness.
10. I find myself thinking about what kind of person I am and what I really want out of life.
11. A person must remain loyal to his commitments if they do not turn out the way he expected.
12. How would you characterize your relationship to your wife now? (1. Very Close; 2. Close; 3. Neither Close Nor Distant; 4. Distant; 5. Far Apart)

Physical Health Questions

1. Do you have any particular physical or health trouble?
   If yes, what is it? _____

   _____

2. Have you ever had the following diseases:
   Asthma
   If yes, when was that? _____

   _____

3. Hay fever
   If yes, when was that? _____

   _____

4. Skin trouble
   If yes, when was that? _____

   _____

5. Stomach ulcer
   If yes, when was that? _____

   _____

6. Do you feel you are bothered by all sorts of pains and ailments in different parts of your body?

   _____

7. Have you ever felt you were going to have a nervous breakdown? _____

From M. P. Farrell and S. D. Rosenberg, *Men at Midlife.* Copyright © 1981 Auburn House, Dover, MA.

gender may be seen as going through an alternating series of structure-building and structure-changing stages. Levinson found, for example, that men in their late 30s want to "become their own man." He also found that at just this time women desire to "become their own woman"; that is, they want greater affirmation both from the people in their world and from themselves.

Although male and female growth toward maturity may be similar in terms of stages, Levinson and his associates also believe that there are major differences between the genders within these similar stages. There are important sociohistorical differences. For women, the central themes are **gender splitting**, the **traditional marriage enterprise,** and the emerging **gender revolution.**

Gender Splitting

All societies support the idea that there should be a clear difference between what is considered appropriate for males and for females: gender splitting appears to be universal. Women's lives have traditionally been devoted to the domestic sphere, men's to the public sphere. Human societies have seen a need for females to stay at home to protect the small number of offspring (compared to other species), while the male goes about being the "provisioner" (getting the resources the family needs outside of the home).

The Traditional Marriage Enterprise

In the final analysis, everyone gets married because they believe they can have a better life by doing so. There may be exceptions, but they are probably rare. At any rate, the main goal is to form and maintain a family. Gender splitting is seen as contributing to this goal. Being supportive of the husband's "public" role—that is, getting resources for the family—is seen by the woman as a significant part of her role. When she goes to work, this goal is not largely different. Levinson reports that it is still a source of conflict when a female does get to be the boss. Women pay a heavy price for the security this role affords. Many find it dangerous to develop a strong sense of self.

The Gender Revolution

But the meanings of gender are changing, and becoming more similar. This is because there is so much more work to be done by young and middle-age adults. The increase in life expectancy has created a large group, the elderly, who consume more than they produce. This, together with the decrease in birthrate, has brought many more women out of the home and into the workplace. Two other factors have also been at work: the divorce rate, which has reached 50%, and the increase in the educational levels of women.

In his study of women, Levinson found support for the existence of the same stages and a similar midlife crisis as for men (Levinson, 1986). A major study of women's development (Reinke & others, 1985) used a methodology similar to Levinson's and found there to be important transitions in the lives of women, but not exclusively clustered around the midlife (40–45-year-old) period. Instead, women described important transitions in their lives at age 30, 40, and 60.

Interestingly, Reinke found a universal turning point for women to occur between the ages of 27 and 30. Among women in their 20s and 30s, 80% of those with preschool children experienced a major transition, and of these, 50% were between the ages of 27 and 30. Women who manifested the transition were more likely to have been employed outside their home in their mid-20s (63%) than women who did not manifest the transition. The 27–30-year-old transition period was characterized by personal disruption, reassessment, and reorientation. The transition lasted an average of 2.7 years, and generally ended in increased life satisfaction. Many women in their early 40s also manifested a transition that included decreases in marital satisfaction and increases in assertiveness. This transition was not as widespread as the transition occurring at age 30 and seemed to be tied to children growing up.

Their data led the researchers to conclude that transitions in a woman's life may be integrally tied to family life cycle. "My research on women suggests that the course of relationships exerts a greater press on women's development than does chronological age" (Reinke, 1985, p. 275). The cycle of female adult development is not a process of increasing individuation from the family but rather of interrelated growth.

For women, it appears that there is an important transition at about 30 years of age. The transition involves a period of self-evaluation that usually leads to greater satisfaction with life.

We are, in Levinson's opinion, at a cultural crossroads. The old division of female homemakers and male providers is breaking down, but no clear new direction has yet appeared. Researchers will be watching this dramatic change closely.

Both Gould and Levinson are psychologists. The next theory is that of a psychiatrist, most of whom are trained in the Freudian tradition. As we shall see, that makes for a rather different view of adult personality development.

Adaptations to Life—Vaillant

The subtitle of George Vaillant's book *Adaptation to Life* (1977) is "How the Best and the Brightest Came of Age." Vaillant's claim that the subjects of his study were among the smartest young men of their time seems to be justified. He has investigated mountains of data collected on a carefully selected group of students from Harvard University's classes of 1939 through 1944. The investigation included 260 white males.

The young men were selected because of the superiority of their bodies, minds, and personalities. A major consideration was that each subject be highly success oriented. Although their intelligence was not greatly higher than that of other students at Harvard, almost two-thirds of them graduated with honors (as compared to one-fourth of their classmates), and three-fourths went on to graduate school.

Almost all had solid, muscular builds and were in excellent health. Their average height was 70 inches, and their average weight was 160 pounds. Interestingly, 98% were right-handed. If the current theory is correct (Dacey, 1989), persons dominated by the left side of the brain (which is indicated by right-handedness) tend to be intelligent but not very imaginative. Left-handed people are thought to be more creative. It would be interesting to know how creatively productive this group of men has been, but because he was interested only in their mental health, Vaillant has not addressed this question.

Almost 20 hours of physical, mental, and psychological tests were administered to the men. Their brain waves were recorded, and anthropologists measured each man to determine his body type, although these last two measurements had little bearing on the results of the study. Finally, the family history of each of the subjects was carefully recorded. Using this voluminous data, Vaillant set out to describe the personal development of these special people.

As in the theories of Sigmund Freud and Erik Erikson, defense mechanisms are important in Vaillant's explanation of the mental health of these subjects. He believes that everyone uses defense mechanisms regularly. Thus defense mechanisms can range all the way from serious psychopathology to perfectly reasonable "adaptations to life." As he puts it:

❖ *These intrapsychic styles of adaptation have been given individual names by psychiatrists (projection, repression, and sublimation are some well-known examples.)... In this book, the so-called mechanisms of psychoanalytic theory will often be referred to as coping or adaptive mechanisms. This is to underscore the fact that defenses are healthy more often than they are psychopathological (1977, p. 7).*

On the basis of his data, Vaillant concluded that adaptive mechanisms, as he calls them, are as important to the quality of life as any other factor. Nevertheless, he does not challenge Freud's definition: these mechanisms are subconscious defenses of the ego (see chap. 2). Vaillant makes a number of generalizations about these mechanisms on the basis of his observations. He believes that they

Are not inherited
Do not run in families

Are not related to mental illness in the family
Cannot be taught
Are discrete from one another
Are dynamic and reversible

He believes that four other generalizations also emerge from the data:

- Life is shaped more by good relationships than by isolated traumatic occurrences during childhood.

- The constantly changing nature of human life may qualify a behavior as mentally ill at one time and adaptive at another.

- In order to understand the healthiness or psychopathology of the individual, it is necessary to understand what part these adaptive mechanisms play in the healing process. Furthermore, there is a natural tendency in most people to progress to higher level mechanisms as they grow toward maturity.

- Since human development continues into adulthood, it is necessary to have a longitudinal study such as this to understand that development.

Generativity Versus Stagnation—Erikson

Let us turn now to a theory that is considered a classic. In this final section, we will put forth Erikson's explanation of personality development in middle adulthood: generativity versus stagnation.

Generativity means the ability to be useful to ourselves and to society. As in the industry stage (see chap. 2), the goal here is to be productive and creative. However, productivity in the industry stage is a means of obtaining recognition and material reward. In the generativity stage, which takes place during middle adulthood, one's productivity is aimed at being helpful to others. The act of being productive is itself rewarding, regardless of recognition or reward. Erikson adds that generativity is

❖ *that middle period of the life cycle when existence permits you and demands you to consider death as peripheral and to balance its certainty with the only happiness that is lasting: to increase, by whatever is yours to give, the good will and the higher order in your sector of the world (1978, p. 124).*

Generativity, Erikson's term for the major goal of the middle years of adulthood, includes coming to understand those who are different from you and desiring to make a lasting contribution to their welfare.

Although Erikson certainly approves of the procreation of children as an important part of generativity for many people, he does not believe that everyone needs to become a parent in order to be generative. There are, of course, people who from misfortune or because of special and genuine gifts in other directions cannot apply this drive to offspring of their own, and instead apply it to other forms of altruistic concern and creativity (1968, p. 138).

It is at this stage of adulthood that some people become bored, self-indulgent, and unable to contribute to society's welfare; they fall prey to stagnation. Such adults act as though they were their own only child. People who have given birth to children may fail to be generative in their parenthood, and come to resent the neediness of their offspring.

Although generativity can provide great satisfaction to those who reach it, several theorists (e.g., Roazen, 1976) have suggested that the majority of adults never do. Many males appear to become fixed in the industry stage, doing their work merely to obtain the social symbols of success—a big car, a fancy house, a color television. Many women, they suggest, may become fixed in the identity stage, confused and

---

Box 20.1

What's Your Opinion?

As you can see, there is a clear conflict between the trait researchers and the positions of the four stage theorists. It appears that they cannot both be correct, although the truth may lie somewhere in between. We have devoted much more space to the stage theories. In part this is because they have received so much attention in the popular press as well as by scholars. It is

also because we are biased toward them. (It is certainly obvious throughout this book that we have a great deal of admiration for the ideas of Erikson.)

Whatever the case may be, the important thing is that, through discussion, further reading, and observation, you try to come to your own opinion. What do you think?

---

conflicted about their proper role in life. They rarely achieve intimacy and therefore rarely reach the stage of generativity.

Becoming generative is not easy. It depends on the successful resolution of the six previous Eriksonian crises we have described in this book. Although you, the reader, are probably not yet at the middle stage of adulthood, you can see that it is by no means too soon to start preparing for it. Getting a clear understanding of Erikson's ideas and the ideas of other theorists covered in this chapter would make a good start. Those people who are able to achieve generativity have a chance to reach the highest level of personhood in Erikson's hierarchy: integrity. This will be examined in chapter 22.

As you can see, all of the theories described thus far hold that as we age, we go through many important changes. Let us turn now to the other side of the coin: the position that the adult personality is made up of traits that remain continuously stable, in most cases, throughout adulthood.

Continuous Traits Theory

In their extensive study of men at midlife, McCrae and Costa (1984) found no evidence for personality change over the adult years, nor any evidence for the existence of any midlife crisis. The research measured the stability of several different personality traits over a period of six years (longitudinal study) and also looked at those same personality traits in a cross-age population (cross-sectional analysis).

At the first testing, McCrae and Costa administered several personality inventories to men ranging in age from 17 to 97. When they combined the data they gathered from the inventories, they defined three major personality traits that they feel govern the adult personality: neuroticism, openness to experience, and extroversion. Each of those three traits is supported by six subtraits or 'facets' (see Figure 20.4). The three major traits together are termed the **NEO model of personality.** The researchers found relative stability of those traits throughout male adulthood.

Neuroticism is described as an index of instability or a predisposition for some kind of breakdown under stress. Behaviors associated with this trait include:

• A tendency to have more physical and psychiatric problems (without medical problems).

• Greater tendencies to smoke and drink.

• More general unhappiness and dissatisfaction with life.

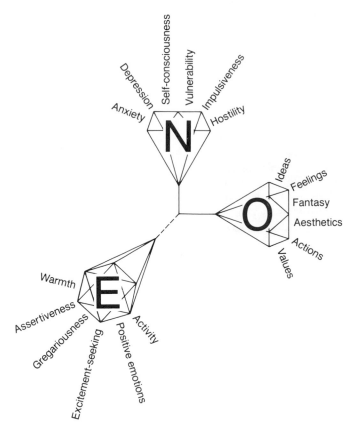

Figure 20.4 *Schematic representation of the three-dimensional, 18-facet NEO (Neuroticism, Extroversion, Openness) model.*

Openness to experience, the second general trait, is exactly that: an openness to new ideas, fantasies, actions, feelings, and values. Overall, a lack of rigidity in regard to the unfamiliar characterizes openness to experience.

Extroversion, the tendency to be outgoing and social, is the third global trait found by McCrae and Costa. Extroversion seems to spill over almost all aspects of the personality, since it implies an overriding interest in people and social connections.

The researchers note that while habits, life events, opinions, and relationships may change over the life span, the basic personality of an individual does not (McCrae & Costa, 1984). They feel that people who experience a midlife crisis probably have the personality makeup that biases them toward that behavior. The Costa and McCrae research, however, lacks consideration of the reciprocal nature of influence of a person with his or her environment. Even so, the rigor of McCrae and Costa's work warrants careful consideration from those interested in personality development across the life span.

Another recent study that has looked at stability of traits across adult periods has been conducted by Dorothy Eichorn and her associates at Berkeley (1981; see also Sears & Sears, 1982). These researchers examined stability by looking at the relationship between traits in adolescence and in middle age. They found that middle-age blood pressure, goodness-of-health, IQ, IQ gain, political ideology, and drinking problems can be predicted fairly well in adolescence. Other traits, however, such as the status of marriage and psychological health are less stable.

Patterns of Work

As the "baby boom" generation enters middle age, many changes are beginning to occur in the workplace. There will be fewer and fewer new young workers available to enter the workforce. Employers will find themselves with a larger number of older workers. This shrinking labor pool is leading many employers to pay more attention than ever to the welfare of their employees. Some of the new issues of the 1990s are childcare, elderly care, home-based work, nontraditional work schedules, and the spiraling cost of health care benefits.

Employers are also attempting more creative approaches to development and training. In the past, employers have tended to spend the majority of their training and development resources on younger employees. Perhaps this is just a matter of employers being unaware of the problems and concerns of their older employees. Or perhaps money and time invested in younger employees were considered better spent than that on older employees.

But recent years have seen a trend among employers to recognize some of the concerns of middle-age employees. Among them are

- Awareness of advancing age and awareness of death

- Awareness of body changes related to aging

- Knowing how many career goals have been or will be attained

- Search for new life goals

- Marked change in family relationships

- Change in work relationships

- Sense of work obsolescence

- Feeling of decreased job mobility and increased concern for job security

Businesses have responded to these issues with continuing education, seminars, workshops, degree programs, and other forms of retraining (Super & Hall, 1978). As the labor pool shrinks, the welfare of the older, established workforce becomes more valuable.

Special Problems of the Working Woman

It is probably not news to you that the problems facing women in the workplace are different from those of men. But what actual differences does being a woman make? Some recent research has been unable to establish clear differences (Northcott & Lowe, 1987), but many more reveal important differences. The difficulties working women face have been studied intensively in recent years (Amato, 1987; Galambos & Lerner, 1987; Smart & Ethington, 1987). A review of this literature reveals the following five major problem areas.

Sexual Harassment on the Job
Sexual harassment can take many forms (Garvey, 1986) such as verbal sexual suggestions or jokes, leering, "accidentally" brushing against your body, a "friendly" pat, squeeze, or pinch, or arm around you, catching you alone for a quick kiss, explicit propositions backed by the threat of losing your job, and forced sexual relations (Faier, 1979).

Equal Pay

The Equal Pay Act was passed in 1963, and states that men and women in substantially similar jobs in the same company should get the same pay. Under this act, the complainant may remain anonymous while the complaint is being investigated. This law has been administered since July, 1979.

In spite of these new legal protections, women make less money on the average than men. Why? In addition to male prejudice, women may be absent more from work due to illness of children, women seem to have greater anxiety about using computers, and females take much less math in school than males.

Career and/or Family

There can be little doubt that the family woman has more difficulty in maintaining a full-time job, especially a professional job, than the family man. Although dual-career families have become commonplace, the responsibility and recognition for family provision still falls to men (Szinovacz, 1984), and women continue to be responsible for the work of the family (Gerson, 1985). Of course there is considerably less acknowledgment of family work since it is private and unpaid. This responsibility for the family work has in turn resulted in fewer job opportunities for women (Haggstrom, Kanouse, & Morrison, 1976). Employers often see women as unreliable because of their commitment to families. The economic reality of a shrinking labor pool is forcing a change in this pattern, but the change has been slow in coming.

"Fiscal Fitness"

Financial advisor Froma Joselow (1979) has suggested that many women lack **fiscal fitness**; that is, they are not experienced in managing money. The lack of financial knowledge has definitely impeded the progress of many women up the ladder to success in business.

Travel Safety

Working women are exposed to a considerable number of hazards to which the average housewife and mother is not subjected. Crimes against women are no longer limited to the inner city, now occurring in suburban and even rural areas with a high frequency.

These five problems are gradually being recognized in the workplace, and there is hope that they will be alleviated. Another type of problem, which is more likely to affect men than women, is the midcareer crisis.

The Midcareer Crisis

Considerable attention is now being given to the crisis many people undergo in the middle of their careers. For some it is a problem of increasing anxiety, which is troublesome but no serious problem. For others the difficulty is truly threatening.

A number of changes in the middle years are not caused by work: the awareness of advancing age, the death of parents and other relatives, striking changes in family relationships, and a decrease in physical ability. Other changes are entirely work related.

Coming to Terms With Attainable Career Goals

By the time a person reaches the age of 40 in a professional or managerial career, it is pretty clear whether she or he will make it to the top of the field. If they haven't reached their goals by this time, many people adjust their level of aspirations and start over in a new career. Many, however, are unable to recognize that they have unrealistic aspirations, and suffer from considerable stress.

Even people whose career patterns are stable, such as Catholic priests, often have a midcareer letdown. Nor is this crisis restricted to white-collar workers. Many blue-collar workers, realizing that they have gone about as far as they are going to go on their jobs, suffer from depression.

This is also the time when family expenses, such as college education for teenage children, become great. If family income does not rise, this obviously creates a conflict, especially if the husband is the sole provider for the family. If the wife goes back to work, other types of stress often occur.

The Change in Work Relationships

Relationships with fellow employees obviously change when one has come to the top of one's career. Some middle-age adults take a mentoring attitude toward younger employees, but others feel resentful toward the young because they still have a chance to progress. When people reach their 40s and 50s they often try to establish new relationships with fellow workers, and this contributes to the sense of conflict.

A Growing Sense of Obsolescence

Kaufman's definition of *obsolescence* (1974) still stands: it is the

❖   *degree to which organizations and professions lack the up-to-date knowledge or skills necessary to maintain effective performance in either their current or future work (p. 23).*

Often employers are unwilling to spend money on the training of older workers.

In many cases, an individual has to work so hard just to stay in a job that it is impossible to keep up to date. Sometimes a younger person, fresh from an extensive education, will join the firm and will know more about modern techniques than the middle-age person does. These circumstances usually cause feelings of anxiety and resentment in the older employee because he or she is afraid of being considered incompetent.

Inability to Change Jobs

Mayer (1978) finds that age discrimination in employment starts as early as 35 in some industries, and becomes pronounced by age 45. A federal law against age discrimination in employment was passed in 1968 to ease the burden on the older worker, but to date the law has been poorly enforced on both the federal and state levels. Many employees get around the law by simply telling older applicants that they are "overqualified" for the available position.

The Generativity Crisis

Erikson suggests that people in the middle years ought to be in the generativity stage (discussed earlier in this chapter). This is a time when they should be producing something of lasting value, making a gift to future generations. In fact, this is definitely a concern for middle-age workers. The realization that the time left to make such a contribution is limited can come with shocking force.

The generativity crisis is similar to the identity crisis of late adolescence in many ways. Both often produce psychosomatic symptoms such as indigestion and extreme tiredness. Middle-age persons often get chest pains at this time. These symptoms are rarely caused by organic diseases in people younger than 50, and usually are due to a depressed state associated with career problems (Levinson, 1978, in progress).

The resolution of this crisis, and of other types of crises that occur during early and middle adulthood, depends on how the person's personality has developed during this period. In the following section, we continue our examination of this topic, which began in the previous chapter.

Some Suggestions for Dealing With the Midlife Crisis

One of the major ways of dealing with the midlife crisis is for the middle-age worker to help younger employees make significant contributions. Furthermore, companies should take a greater responsibility for fostering continuing education of their employees.

We should continue the type of job transfer programs for middle-age people that we now have for newer employees. Although sometimes the changes can be threatening, the move to a new type of job and the requisite new learning experiences can bring back a zest for work.

Perhaps the federal government should consider starting midcareer clinics. Such clinics could help workers reexamine their goals, consider job changes, and provide information and guidance. Another solution might be the establishment of "portable pension plans" that would move with workers from one company to another so they would not lose all they have built up when they change jobs.

Can you imagine any other remedies?

Transition

Dealing with change is as serious a challenge in midlife as at any other time. Learning new ways to get along with one's spouse, parents, siblings, and children is necessary at this time of life. There is considerable debate over whether personality changes much during this period. Some think it goes through a series of predictable changes; others view it as continuous with earlier life. Workers often experience a "midlife crisis" at this time, and women workers have an additional set of burdens to handle.

Yet with any luck, we make it safely through middle age and move on to late adulthood. In the next two chapters, we investigate the pluses and minuses of this development.

Key Ideas

1. Marriage is still enormously important in the United States, but divorce rates have increased rapidly over the past few decades.
2. Our relationships with our parents, siblings, spouses, and children undergo significant changes in middle adulthood.
3. The debate over continuity versus change in personality still rages among developmental scientists.
4. Four theorists have made major contributions to personality stage theory: Roger Gould, Daniel Levinson, George Vaillant, and Erik Erikson.
5. Most people experience a crisis in the middle of their careers. Women experience a number of additional problems.

Key Terms

Emotional divorce	Midlife transition
Empty nest syndrome	NEO model of personality
Fiscal fitness	No-fault divorce
Gender revolution	Stage theorists
Gender splitting	Traditional marriage enterprise
Generativity	Trait theorists

What Do You Think?

1. What is the best way for middle-age people to take care of their ailing elderly parents?
2. What changes would you make in our divorce laws?
3. Would you agree that almost everyone has a midlife crisis, but they just deny it?
4. What are the main differences between male and female personality development?
5. Who's right, the stage theorists or the trait theorists?
6. What laws would you make to improve the workplace for women?

Suggested Readings

Breslin, Jimmy. (1986). *Table money*. New York: Ticknor & Fields. An empathetic tale of matrimony, alcoholism, and the struggle to attain maturity, focusing on a poor Irish-American couple.

Guest, Judith. (1976). *Ordinary people*. New York: Ballantine. The evocative story of the relationships among a middle-age couple, their teenage son, and his psychiatrist.

Hansberry, Lorraine. (1959). *A raisin in the sun*. A moving drama portraying the inner lives of an African-American family.

Updike, John. (1981). *Rabbit is rich*. New York: Knopf. The third in Updike's series about an ordinary American male. In this volume Rabbit reaches middle age.

PART 9

Late Adulthood

· *Chapter 21* ·

Late Adulthood: Physical and Cognitive Development

❖   *Mary Pickford gazes around the magnificent living room of the mansion she and Douglas Fairbanks purchased over a half century earlier. Dwarfed by the baronial chair in which she sits, she looks small and vulnerable. As she admires her collection of antique furniture and artwork, she is aware of how few more times she will be seeing it. The thought of her impending death is not an unhappy one.*

     "America's Sweetheart" she was called in the years during and after World War I. The country had adored her for her superb acting in numerous roles in the silent movies of those times. Her bright smile and cheerful disposition always charmed the throngs that attended her public appearances. It was her eyes for which she was famous. They used to say she could express more with her eyes than most actors could with their mouths. Now, at eighty-six, those wonderfully expressive eyes are covered with a hazy film, the result, no doubt, of the quart of gin she sips her way through every day.

· · · · · · ·

❖   *After hearing many compliments paid to him at a dinner given by his friends on his eightieth birthday, author Somerset Maugham rose and said, "There are many advantages to growing old!" He paused and looked down at the table. Many seconds went by. The audience became tense, worrying whether his health was failing him. Finally, he lifted his head, looked back out at his audience, and said, "I'm just trying . . . to think . . . of some."*

· · · · · · ·

❖   *A special session of the British House of Lords was being held to honor Winston Churchill on his ninetieth birthday. As he descended the stairs of the amphi-theater, one member turned to another and said, "They say he's really getting senile." Churchill stopped, and leaning toward them, said in a stage whisper loud enough for many to hear, "They also say he's deaf!"*

· · · · · · ·

Even when he was very old and ill, Winston Churchill's fabled sense of humor never left him. In addition, it was only in his later years that he found time to sharpen his artistic skills, which brought him world renown in that realm. He was an excellent example of how fruitful the last third of life can be.

These vignettes portray old age rather negatively. Must growing old mean decline? Must the teeth and hair fall out, the eyes grow dim, the skin wrinkle and sag? Must intelligence, memory, and creativity falter? Must old age be so awful?

Or is there actually only a relatively slight decline in capacity, a decline greatly exaggerated by our values and presumptions? Many elderly people seem to be having the time of their lives! Could it be that aging is largely a matter of self-fulfilling prophecy (people expect to deteriorate, so they stop trying to be fit, and then they *do* deteriorate)? Could most of us in our later years be as capable as those famous few who seem to have overcome age today?

These questions concern most of the 23 million men and women over 65 who constitute 10% of our population today. In 1900, the over-65 population was 3 million, only 3% of the total. By the year 2040, it will have reached 20% (see Figure 21.1). Such questions should also concern those of us who hope to join their ranks some day. The next section looks at the answers to these questions, as revealed by considerable new research.

Must We Age and Die?

"Nothing is inevitable except death and taxes," the old saying goes. But is death inevitable? True, no one so far has attained immortality; the oldest known person in the United States, as certified by the Social Security Administration, is 114 years old. And, of course, the vast majority of those people who have ever lived are dead.

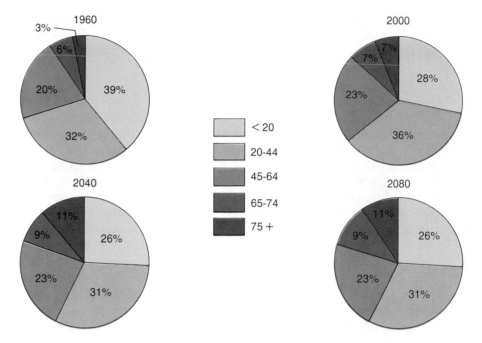

Figure 21.1 *Age distribution of United States population, selected years.*
Source: Social Security Administration

But not all organisms die. There are trees alive today that are known to be over 2,500 years old; they have aged, but show no sign of dying. Bacteria apparently are able to live indefinitely, as long as they have the requirements for their existence. The fact is, we are not sure why we age, and until we are, we cannot be certain that aging and death are absolutely inevitable. Let us look now at the three types of explanations that have been offered (Spence, 1989): physiological, genetic, and environmental aspects of aging.

Physiological Aspects of Aging

It is apparent that organisms inherit a tendency to live for a certain length of time. An animal's durability depends on the species to which it belongs. The average human life span of approximately seventy years is the longest of any mammal. Elephants, horses, hippopotamuses, and asses are known to live as long as fifty years, but most mammals die much sooner. Sacher (1959) has suggested that the ratio of the weight of the brain to the body is the best predictor of longevity in mammals; there may be some causative factor involved here, but it has not yet been identified.

Some doctors are fond of stating that "no one ever died of old age." This is true. People die of some physiological failure that is more likely to occur the older one gets. One likely explanation of aging, then, is that the various life-support systems gradually weaken. Illness and death come about as a cumulative result of these various weaknesses. Seven different physiological factors have been suggested as accounting for this process.

These olive trees found in Greece are over 2,500 years old. Do you think it's possible that they might live forever?

Wear and Tear Theory
The **wear and tear theory** seems the most obvious explanation for aging, but there is actually little evidence for it. To date, no research has clearly linked early deterioration of organs with either hard work or increased stress alone.

A complex interaction, however, may be involved. It is known that lower rates of metabolism are linked to longer life, and that certain conditions, such as absence of rich foods, cause a lower metabolism. Therefore, the lack of the "good life" may prolong life. On the other hand, it is also known that poor people who seldom get to eat rich foods tend to die at an earlier age than middle-class or wealthy people. Therefore, the evidence on this theory is at best conflicting.

Aging by Program

According to this theory, we age because it is programmed into us. It is hard to understand what evolutionary processes govern longevity (if any). For example, the vast majority of animals die at or before the end of their reproductive period, but human females live twenty to thirty years beyond the end of their reproductive cycles. This may be related to the capacities of the human brain. Mead (1972) argued that this extra period beyond the reproductive years has had the evolutionary value of helping to keep the children and grandchildren alive. For example, in times when food is scarce, older people may remember where it was obtained during the last period of scarcity. On the other hand, it may be that we humans have outwitted the evolutionary process, and due to our medical achievements are able to live on past our reproductive usefulness.

Another enduring hypothesis, proposed by Birren (1960), is known as the "counterpart" theory. According to this concept, factors in human existence that are useful in the earlier years become counterproductive in later years. An example is the nonreplaceability of most cells in the nervous system. The fact that brain cells are not constantly changing enhances memory and learning abilities in the earlier years, but it also allows the nervous system to weaken as dead cells are not replaced.

Spence (1989) suggests that the hypothalamus may well be an "aging chronometer" (p. 17) that keeps track of the age of cells and determines how long they should keep reproducing. Although research on **aging by program** is in its infancy, some findings indicate that older cells may act differently from younger cells. Although cells in the nervous system and muscles do not reproduce themselves, all the other cells in the body do reproduce, at least to some extent. But these cells are able to reproduce only a limited number of times, and they are more likely to reproduce imperfectly as they get older. There is also reason to believe that reproduced older cells do not pass on information accurately through the DNA. This weakens the ability of older cells to continue high level functioning.

Homeostatic Imbalance

Comfort (1964) has suggested that it may be a failure in the systems that regulate the proper interaction of the organs, rather than wear of the organs themselves, that causes aging and ultimately death. He states that aging results from "an increase in homeostatic faults" (p. 178). These homeostatic (feedback) systems are responsible, for example, for the regulation of the sugar and adrenalin levels in the blood. Apparently there is not a great deal of difference in the systems of the young and the old when they are in a quiet state. It is when stress is put on the systems (death of a spouse, loss of a job, a frightening experience) that we see the effects of the elderly **homeostatic imbalance.** The older body simply isn't as effective, qualitatively or quantitatively, in reacting to these stresses. Figure 21.2 shows graphically the relationship between problems with the homeostatic systems and the competence of the organism to react effectively to dangers in the environment.

Cross-Linkage Theory

The proteins that make up a large part of cells are themselves composed of peptides. When cross-links are formed between peptides (a natural process of the body), the proteins are altered, often for the worse. For example, **collagen** is the major connective tissue in the body; it provides, for instance, the elasticity in our skin and

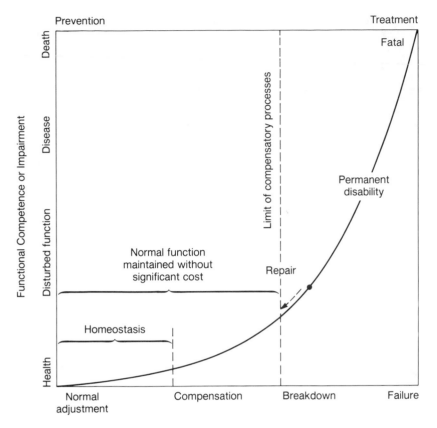

Figure 21.2 *Homeostasis and health. Progressive stages of homeostasis from adjustment (health) to failure (death). In the healthy adult, homeostatic processes ensure adequate adjustment in response to stress, and even for a period beyond this stage compensatory processes are capable of maintaining overall function without serious disability. When stress is exerted beyond compensatory capacities of the organism, disability ensues in rapidly increasing increments to severe illness, permanent disability, and death. When this model is viewed in terms of homeostatic responses to stress imposed on the aged and to aging itself, a period when the body can be regarded as at the point of "limit of compensatory processes," it is evident that even minor stresses are not tolerable, and the individual moves rapidly into stages of breakdown and failure.*

blood vessels. When its proteins are altered, skin and vessels are adversely affected. This is known as the **cross-linkage theory.**

Accumulation of Metabolic Waste
Although the connection has not been clearly established as yet, Curtis (1966) argued that waste products resulting from metabolism build up in various parts of the body, contributing greatly to the decrease in competence of those parts. Examples of this effect of the **accumulation of metabolic waste** are cataracts on the eye, calcification in the arteries, and brittleness of bones.

Autoimmunity
With increasing age, there is increasing **autoimmunity,** the process by which the immune system in the body rejects the body's own tissue. Examples of this are rheumatoid arthritis, diabetes, vascular diseases, and hypertension. It may be that, with age, the body's tissues become more and more self-rejecting.

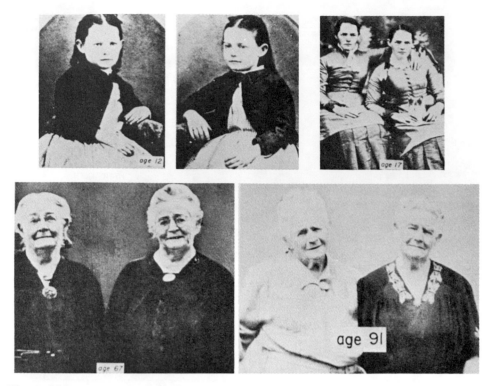

Figure 21.3 *One-egg twins before and after long separations (between the ages of 18 and 65).*

This may be the result of the production of new **antigens,** the substances in the blood that fight to kill foreign bodies. These new antigens may come about for one of two reasons:

* Mutations that cause the formation of altered RNA or DNA.

* Some cells may be "hidden" in the body during the early part of life. When these cells appear later, the body does not recognize them as its own, and forms new antigens to kill them. This in turn may cause organ malfunction.

Accumulation of Errors
As cells die, they must synthesize new proteins to make new cells. As this is done, occasionally an error occurs. Over time, these errors mount up. This **accumulation of errors** may finally grow serious enough to cause organ failure.

Genetic Aspects of Aging

Gene theory also suggests that aging is programmed, but says that the program exists in certain harmful genes. As Spence (1989) explains it,

❖   *perhaps there are genes which direct many cellular activities during the early years of life that become altered in later years, thus altering their function. In their altered state, the genes may be responsible for the functional decline and structural changes associated with aging (p. 19).*

Whatever the reason, there is little doubt that genes affect how long we live. Kallman and Jarvik's (1959) research into identical twins still offers strong evidence

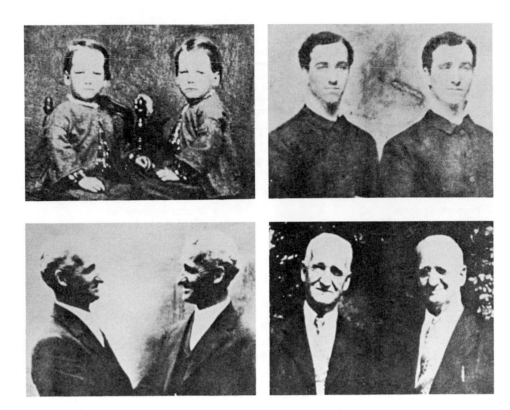

Figure 21.4   One-egg twins at the ages of 5, 20, 55, and 86 years.

of this. They found that monozygotic twins (those born from the same egg) have more similar lengths of life than do dizygotic twins (those born from two eggs). This effect is illustrated in Figures 21.3 and 21.4.

Environmental Aspects of Aging

Our genes and the physiology of our organs greatly affect the length of our lives. This may be seen in the extreme accuracy with which insurance companies are able to predict the average number of deaths at a particular age. A mathematical formula to predict the number of deaths within a population was produced as early as 1825 by Gomertz. The formula is still quite accurate except for the early years.

Today there are many fewer deaths in early childhood, since vaccines have eliminated much of the danger of diseases at this age. This shows that the environment is also an important factor in the mortality rate. Many of today's elderly would have died in childhood had they been born in the early part of the nineteenth century.

Considering mortality rates for specific cultures rather than world population shows the effects of the environment more specifically. Starvation in Africa and earthquakes in Guatemala obviously had a tragic effect on the mortality rates of those two countries. A number of authors have reported on the effects of radiation (Curtis, 1966; Demoise & Conrad, 1972; Spence, 1989). There is reason to believe that the nuclear testing in the Pacific in the 1950s is affecting the aging process of some of the residents there. There is little or no evidence, however, that the radiation to which all of us are exposed every day is having any impact on aging. It remains to be seen if events such as the nuclear accident at Three Mile Island will have adverse effects.

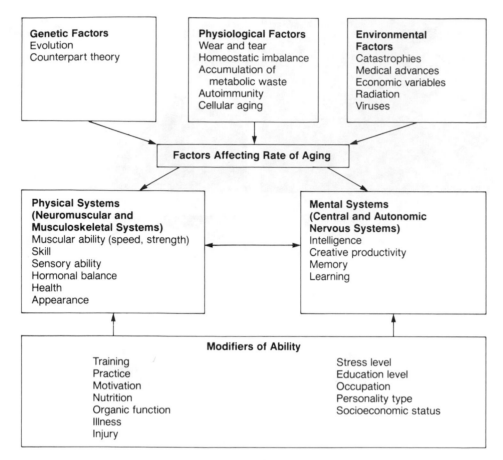

Figure 21.5 *Influences on adult mental and physical systems.*

Researchers (Hotcin & Sikora, 1970) have suggested that several illnesses thought to be largely genetic, such as cancer and cardiovascular disease, may in fact be caused by viruses. Discovery and elimination of these viruses, therefore, would have an effect on the mortality rate of humankind. But even if cardiovascular and kidney diseases were totally curable, it would add only about seven years to the average life span. Even more surprising, the elimination of cancer would add only one and one-half years to the average life span (Myers & Pitts, 1972).

Other Modifiers of Ability

In addition to genetic, physiological, and environmental factors that indirectly affect the individual's rate of aging, there are factors that can modify a person's level of ability more directly. Many of these modifiers interact with one another in complex ways. Some of the major modifiers are training, practice, motivation, nutrition, organic malfunction, illness, injury, stress level, educational level, occupation, personality type, and socioeconomic status.

Figure 21.5 summarizes the relationships between the hypothesized factors that affect aging of physical and mental systems. These include two genetic, five physiological, and five environmental factors, as well as twelve other modifiers of human abilities. Now we will take a closer look at the effects of aging on specific aspects of the elderly: reaction time, sensory abilities, other body systems, hormonal balance, health, and appearance.

Before reading the next section, try your hand at the true-false test on the topic of aging in Box 21.1.

BOX 21.1
The Facts on Aging Quiz

Mark the items *T* for true or *F* for false.

1. A person's height tends to decline in old age.
2. More older persons (over 65) have chronic illnesses that limit their activity than younger persons.
3. Older persons have more acute (short-term) illnesses than persons under 65.
4. Older persons have more injuries in the home than persons under 65.
5. Older workers have less absenteeism than younger workers.
6. The life expectancy of African-Americans at age 65 is about the same as whites'.
7. The life expectancy of men at age 65 is about the same as women's.
8. Medicare pays over half of the medical expenses for the aged.
9. Social Security benefits automatically increase with inflation.
10. Supplemental Security Income guarantees a minimum income for needy aged.
11. The aged do not get their proportionate share (about 11%) of the nation's income.
12. The aged have higher rates of criminal victimization than persons under 65.
13. The aged are more fearful of crime than are persons under 65.
14. The aged are the most law abiding of all adult groups according to official statistics.
15. There are two widows for each widower among the aged.
16. More of the aged vote than any other age group.
17. There are proportionately more older persons in public office than in the total population.
18. The proportion of African-Americans among the aged is growing.
19. Participation in voluntary organizations (churches and clubs) tends to decline among the healthy aged.
20. The majority of the aged live alone.
21. About 3% less of the aged have incomes below the official poverty level than the rest of the population.
22. The rate of poverty among aged African-Americans is about 3 times as high as among aged whites.
23. Older persons who reduce their activity tend to be happier than those who remain active.
24. When the last child leaves home, the majority of parents have serious problems adjusting to their "empty nest."
25. The proportion widowed is decreasing among the aged.

The key to the correct answers is simple: alternating pairs of items are true or false (i.e., 1 and 2 are true, 3 and 4 are false, 5 and 6 are true etc., and 25 is true).

Seniors usually find that their coordination declines with the years, and so they often quit playing sports. Now there is a strong movement to reverse this trend.

Physical Development

Reaction Time

It is obvious that physical skills decline as people grow older. This appears to be especially true of manual dexterity (Ringel & Simon, 1983). As one psychologist (Troll, 1975) puts it, "After about 33, hand and finger movements are progressively more clumsy" (p. 20). Although older people are able to perform short coordinated manual tasks, a long series of tasks, such as playing a stringed instrument, becomes

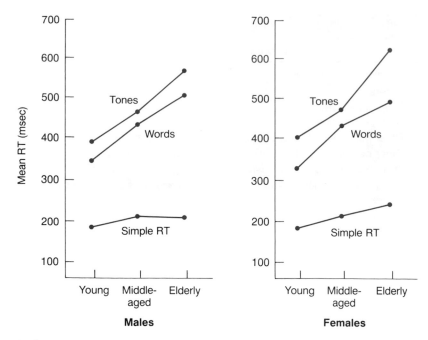

Figure 21.6   Research on reaction time. Mean RT for a simple RT task, subjects were asked to respond to a tone as quickly as possible. In the matching RT task, subjects were asked to identify a pair of stimuli (nonverbal or verbal) as "same" or "different" as quickly as possible.

increasingly difficult for them. Famed Spanish guitarist Andrés Segovia and pianist Vladimir Horowitz are notable exceptions.

Is this because the human nervous system is deteriorating through aging? To answer this question, psychologists have completed numerous studies of "reaction time," the time between the onset of a stimulus and the actual muscle activity that indicates a reaction to it. Studying reaction time is a scientific way of separating the effects of the central nervous system from the ability of the rest of the body to perform manual tasks.

In their excellent review of this research, Elias and associates (1977) present a much more positive picture. They report that in simple discrimination tasks, where the subject is asked to respond to a sensory cue, there is essentially no decrease in reaction time with age. Even when tasks are made more complicated, such as when a series of responses are called for or a number of stimuli must be matched, increases in reaction time with age are not great.

An example of this research can be seen in the study by Elias and Elias (1976). As Figure 21.6 indicates, there is a greater increase in reaction time scores between simple and complicated tasks than between the young and the elderly. This finding holds for both males and females. If the ability of older people to respond quickly does not decline greatly, why does it appear that their actual performance is slower and less capable? Elias and associates (1977) point to a number of variables that cause this decline. Among the most important are the following:

- *Motivation.* Because they have had many experiences, older adults are often less likely than younger people to believe that doing well on tests in general is important. Therefore they probably do not try as hard to do well.

- *Depression.* The elderly are frequently seen as having lost mental abilities, when in fact they are slow to respond because they care less about everything—a standard effect of being depressed.

- *Anxiety.* Some seniors find being tested an unusual experience, which makes them afraid.

- *Response strategies.* Over the years, we have made progress in teaching our children how to respond to problems. The older adult probably was not taught these strategies.

- *Response style.* The older we get, the more we tend to use a single trusted response to all problems. But the best problem solvers are those who have at their command a number of styles for dealing with problems (Rowe and Troen, 1980).

We may conclude that variables other than sheer neural or motor activities account for most change in physical skills over time. Older adults can improve their ability in any of these areas if they desire.

Sensory Abilities

Vision

A number of problems may affect the eye as the adult ages (Eifrig & Simons, 1983). The lenses may become less transparent, thicker, and less elastic. This tends to result in farsightedness (Corso, 1971; McFarland, 1968). The illumination required to perceive a stimulus also increases with age (McFarland, 1968). Timiras (1972) stated that retina changes almost never occur before the age of 60, but Elias and associates (1977) argued that conditions that affect the retina, such as glaucoma, are often not detected, so problems may occur without causing noticeable changes in the eye. At any rate, with the improvements in recent years in ophthalmology and optical surgery (Kornzweig, 1980), the declining ability of the human eye need not greatly affect vision in older age.

Hearing

Decline in hearing ability may be a more serious problem than decline in vision. However, we seem to be much less willing to wear hearing aids than we are to wear glasses, perhaps because we rely on vision more.

Most people hear fairly well until older, but men seem to lose some of their acuity for higher pitches during their middle years (Marshall, 1981). This difference may occur mostly in men who are exposed to greater amounts of noise in their occupations and in traveling to and from their jobs.

One of the few instances in which the elderly perform better than young adults involves verbal transformations. These have been studied by a number of researchers (Lass & Golden, 1971; Warren & Warren, 1971). A verbal transformation occurs when a person inadvertently reproduces a sound in an order different from the way it was first said: for example, saying the word "does" after the word "suds" is given. Children and the elderly rarely make such transformations. One explanation is that both children and the elderly are more careful in their listening habits—children because they are just learning, and the elderly because they may be suffering from diminished hearing ability (Mader, 1984).

Smell

Some atrophy of olfactory fibers in the nose occurs with age. When artificial amplifiers are added, however, the ability of the older people to recognize foods by smell is greatly improved.

Taste

It is difficult to study the effects of aging on the sense of taste because taste itself is so dependent on smell. About 95% of taste derives from the olfactory nerves. It is clear, however, that there is decline in tasting ability among the elderly (Grzegorczyk, Jones, & Mistretta, 1979).

Rogers (1979) reported that whereas young adults have an average of 250 taste buds, 70 year olds have an average of no more than 100. The decrease begins between the ages of 50 and 60 in men and 40 to 55 in women. Although the ability to distinguish between sweetness, sourness, saltiness, and bitterness remains fairly constant with age, sweetness is the first to be affected when the decline begins.

Many factors affect taste besides the aging process (Moscowitz & others, 1975). Among these are culture, state of hunger, dietary history, expectations, gender, and genotype. Nevertheless, it appears that the decline in the ability to taste may account in part for the decrease in weight that many elderly persons experience.

Touch

The tactile sense also declines somewhat after the age of 65 (Turner & Helms, 1989), but the evidence for this comes strictly from the reports of the elderly. Until scientific studies are performed, and apparently at present none have been, this finding must be accepted with caution.

Other Body Systems

Skeletal System

Although the skeleton is fully formed by age 24, changes in stature can occur because of the shrinking of the discs between spinal vertebrae (Mazess, 1982). As was mentioned earlier, collagen changes. Frequently this causes bone tissue to shrink (Hall, 1976; Twomey, Taylor, & Furiss, 1983). Thus the bones become more brittle. Because the entire skeletal system becomes tighter and stiffer, there is frequently a small loss of height in the aged. Diseases of the bone system such as arthritis are probably the result of changes in the collagen in the system with age (Aloia, 1978).

Skin

There are a number of factors that can cause the body to become shorter and stiffer with age.

Collagen is also a major factor in changes in the skin. Because continuous stretching of collagen causes it to lengthen, the skin begins to lose its elasticity with age. Other changes are a greater dryness and the appearance of spots due to changes in pigmentation (Dotz & German, 1983; Robinson, 1983; Walther & Harber, 1984). The skin becomes coarser and darker, and wrinkles begin to appear. Darkness forms under the eyes, more because of a growing paleness of the skin in the rest of the face than because of any change in the under-eye pigmentation. Years of exposure to the sun also contribute to these effects.

Another important cause of the change in skin texture has to do with the typical weight loss among the elderly. There is a tendency to lose fat cells, which decreases the pressure against the skin itself. This tends to cause sagging, folds, and wrinkles in the skin. Older persons not only need less nourishment, but they also lose the social motivation of eating at meetings and parties that younger persons have (Carnevali & Patrick, 1986). As the elderly eat less, their skin becomes less tight and wrinkles appear.

Teeth

The loss of teeth is certainly one physical aspect that makes a person look older (Pizer, 1983). Even when corrective measures are taken, the surgery involved and the adjustment to dentures have a major impact on the person's self-image. In most cases, the loss of teeth is more the result of gum disease than decay of the teeth themselves. It appears likely that education, the use of fluorides, the use of new brushing techniques, and daily flossing will make this aspect of aging far less of a problem in the future.

Hair

Probably the most significant signature of old age is change of the hair. Thinness, baldness, grayness, stiffness, and a growing amount of facial hair in women are all indications of growing old. Hormonal changes are undoubtedly the main culprit here. Improvements in hair coloring techniques and hair implants may make it possible to avoid having "old-looking" hair.

Hormonal Balance

The relationship between hormone balance and physical ability is an extremely difficult one to determine. Not only do hormones affect behavior, but behavior affects the level of hormone balance. Furthermore, while it is clear that hormones are vital to the ability of the individual to deal with environmental stress, it is not clear that age is a major factor in this relationship (Spence, 1989).

Early research on the relationship between hormones and physical ability is reminiscent of Ponce de León's search for the Fountain of Youth. In early studies, researchers hoped to discover the right combination of hormones to prolong life, perhaps indefinitely. One early endocrinologist went so far as to inject himself with a solution made from dog testicles. Elias and associates (1977) have described the extent to which others have gone:

❖ *The medieval Indian kings of Chandell are said to have pursued longevity through ritual coition with well-trained maids, and in the 1700s a Dutch physician named Boerhave (1668–1738) advised an elderly patient to renew his strength by lying between two young girls. Apparently he was not too concerned about the effects of this treatment on the young girls, and we do not know whether he was motivated to give elderly women similar advice with regard to young men. Perhaps we will never know, but we do know that it has not been established that such a treatment will lengthen life. Perhaps it only seems longer (p. 200).*

Even today some wealthy persons will travel to Switzerland to receive secret injections of hormones that are said to promote sexual vitality and physical ability in general. Actually, however, the endocrine system is incredibly complicated, and it is extremely unlikely that an injection of any single hormone will have an effect on longevity (Green, 1981; Korenman, 1982; Vernandakis, 1982). Even though there is a slowing down of hormone production over this period, a detriment in one area is almost always compensated for by some other gland. The single exception to this rule has been the human sexual system.

Health

It is well known that health declines when one reaches the older years. This decline, however, usually does not occur until quite late in life (Kart, 1988). Table 21.1 shows years of life expectancy at various elderly ages.

Table 21.1	Years of Life Expectancy at Various Elderly Ages, 1900–1902 and 1980			
	White		Black	
Year and Age	Male	Female	Male	Female
1900–1902				
65	11.5	12.2	10.4	11.4
70	9.0	9.6	8.3	9.6
75	6.8	7.3	6.6	7.9
80	5.1	5.5	5.1	6.5
85	3.8	4.1	4.0	5.1
1980				
65	14.2	18.5	13.5	17.3
70	11.3	14.8	11.1	14.2
75	8.8	11.5	8.9	11.4
80	6.7	8.6	6.9	9.0
85	5.0	6.3	5.3	7.0

From C. S. Kart, et al., *Aging, Health and Society.* Copyright © 1988 Jones and Bartlett Publishing Company, Boston, MA.

Illness is not a major cause of death until one reaches the 30s, and only then among African-American females. This is probably because they receive fewer preventive health services, and because medical treatment is frequently delayed until the later stages of disease. Not until adults reach the age of 40 does ill health, as opposed to accidents, homicide, and suicide, become the major cause of death. Arteriosclerotic heart disease is the major killer after the age of 40 in all age, sex, and race groups.

Table 21.2 summarizes the diseases and other conditions from the teen years through older adulthood according to type of condition, age, sex, and family income. The most striking finding reported in this table is that at every age level you are more likely to have one of these problems if you are poor than if you are in the middle or upper class. Whether males or females are more likely to have one of the conditions depends on age level.

Alzheimer's Disease

Probably the single greatest scourge of the elderly, and in many ways the most debilitating, is Alzheimer's disease. Alzheimer's was discovered by the German neurologist Alois Alzheimer in 1906, but it did not gain much attention until the 1970s. Researchers are not much closer to unraveling the cause of this mysterious disease, nor in finding a cure for it. Alzheimer's is difficult to diagnose and even more difficult to treat. Relatively few of its symptoms respond to any type of treatment, and then only in the earliest stages. The single exception is that the depression that normally accompanies the disease can be treated effectively (Gierz, Haris, & Lohr, 1989). Alzheimer's disease usually follows a 6- to 20-year course.

The normal brain consists of billions of nerve cells (neurons), which convey messages to one another chemically by way of branchlike structures called dendrites and axons. Neuron groups generate specific chemical transmitters that travel between cells at the synapses. While Alzheimer's victims look normal externally, their brains are undergoing severe changes. One particular trait of Alzheimer's is the breakdown of the system in the brain that produces the chemical transmitter acetylcholine. A decrease in the enzyme that tells the system to produce acetylcholine is directly related to insanity. Brain autopsies unmask severe damage, abnormalities, and even death of neurons. There is often as little as 10% of the normal

---

BOX 21.2

Facts About Alzheimer's

- Approximately 10% of the 65-and-over population may have Alzheimer's. Forty-seven percent over 85 already have the disease.
- The National Institute of Health allocated $5.1 million for Alzheimer's research in 1978, and $123.4 million for research in 1989. Though the dollar amount allocated for research has increased each year, more money is needed.
- Heredity is the cause in 10%–30% of all Alzheimer's cases.
- There are always at least two victims of Alzheimer's: the afflicted person and the primary caregiver. The stress of caring for Alzheimer's patients makes the primary caregiver much more vulnerable to infectious disease, as well as vulnerable to all the problems that go with dealing with high levels of stress.

---

amount of acetylcholine, and the degree of its loss corresponds closely to the severity of the disease. Box 21.2 contains some pertinent facts about Alzheimer's (Gelman, 1989).

There are several theories as to the causes of Alzheimer's. Some feel that a virus causes the disease, while others feel that environmental factors are involved. A popular theory is that the disease is caused by an overabundance of metal accumulation in the neurons, mainly aluminum. Some dispute this theory, since although we all ingest aluminum, our body rejects it by refusing to digest it.

Some think that Alzheimer's may be transmitted genetically, since we know that a sibling of an Alzheimer's patient has a 50% chance of contracting the disorder. Almost all persons with Down syndrome, a genetic disorder, will develop Alzheimer's disease if they live long enough. The President of the Alzheimer's Association reports that the cost of caring for an Alzheimer's patient in the home is $18,000–$20,000 per year, while nursing home care may reach as high as $36,000 per year (Cowley, 1989; Kantrowitz, 1989). The financial burden is usually placed on the patient's family, since Medicare does not cover the cost and Medicaid will cover only families who are in poverty. Sadly, a family must exhaust all its resources before becoming eligible for Medicaid.

Another alternative to chronic care is the daycare facility. These programs provide help with daily tasks such as feeding, washing, toileting, and exercising. The average cost of daycare centers is $27 per day, including meals. One drawback to many of the daycare facilities is that the staff often does not include medical personnel.

At this time the outlook is bleak for patients and families suffering with Alzheimer's. If you desire further information on what is known about the disease, write to the Alzheimer's Association, 70 East Lake Street, Suite 600, Chicago, Illinois, 60601.

The Relationship Between Physical and Mental Health

In their study of the general health of 1,139 elderly persons living in an urban community, Gerson and associates (1987) had a number of interesting findings:

- There is a strong relationship between physical and mental health.

- Married men have better health than unmarried men (this is not so for women). This may be because their wives take care of them, or because they feel responsible to their families to maintain their health.

Table 21.2   Chronic Conditions Among Persons 17 Years of Age and Over, United States

Age, Sex, and Family Income	Type of Chronic Condition and Year: Prevalence per 1,000 Population				
	Arthritis, 1969	Asthma, 1970	Chronic Bronchitis, 1970	Diabetes, 1973	Heart Conditions, 1972
17–44 Years					
Total	40.3	26.2	23.2	8.9	24.6
Sex					
Male	28.0	24.6	16.7	6.9	19.5
Female	51.3	27.6	29.1	10.8	29.3
Family Income					
Less than $5,000	46.9	34.1	28.4	11.4	32.5
$5,000–$9,999	40.5	23.6	22.3	9.1	23.3
$10,000–$14,999	38.7	24.4	21.8	8.4	22.5
$15,000 or more	35.9	26.8	23.7	8.0	24.3
45–64 Years					
Total	204.2	33.1	35.4	42.6	88.8
Sex					
Male	148.0	29.3	28.5	40.6	97.4
Female	255.3	36.7	41.6	44.4	81.0
Family Income					
Less than $5,000	297.8	53.5	44.2	74.1	139.3
$5,000–$9,999	200.3	33.5	38.7	43.8	92.5
$10,000–$14,999	163.7	23.7	29.0	37.8	74.3
$15,000 or more	159.8	22.7	30.3	30.5	66.6
65 Years and Over					
Total	380.3	35.8	41.2	78.5	198.7
Sex					
Male	287.0	42.3	47.3	60.3	199.3
Female	450.1	31.1	36.6	91.3	198.3
Family Income					
Less than $5,000	411.7	41.4	45.4	82.0	219.0
$5,000–$9,999	353.3	32.6	37.2	76.1	190.0
$10,000–$14,999	310.9	•	27.4	81.1	158.9
$15,000 or more	300.8	•	40.7	62.7	174.8

From C. S. Kart, et al., *Aging, Health and Society.* Copyright © 1988 Jones and Bartlett Publishing Company, Boston, MA.

- Social resources are strongly associated with mental health for women, but less so for men. Probably women are more likely than men to *use* their social resources to help them maintain their mental health. Many men hate to admit to their friends that they are having a mental disturbance, because it is not considered "manly."

- Economic resources are clearly related to mental health. As was pointed out, this is especially true for African-American women.

A study by Lohr and associates (1988) supports some of these findings.

Another aspect of mental health, the desire for and belief in the ability to have self-control, was studied by Pointer-Smith and associates (1988). They looked at this variable in nearly 600 adults, about half of whom were about to undergo barium enemas, chemotherapy, or surgery. There was a clear decline in the perception of self-control with age.

Table 21.2 *Continued*

Age, Sex, and Family Income	Type of Chronic Condition and Year: Prevalence per 1,000 Population			
	Hypertensive Disease, 1972	Impairments of Back or Spine (Except Paralysis), 1971	Hearing Impairments, 1971	Vision Impairments, 1971
17–44 Years				
Total	37.8	49.0	42.4	31.9
Sex				
Male	36.4	51.9	51.4	44.7
Female	39.1	46.4	34.2	20.3
Family Income				
Less than $5,000	48.9	59.4	55.4	43.2
$5,000–$9,999	40.8	50.5	44.0	31.7
$10,000–$14,999	35.9	47.4	39.3	28.7
$15,000 or more	29.8	42.4	35.8	30.9
45–64 Years				
Total	126.7	68.2	114.1	63.0
Sex				
Male	101.3	68.2	140.2	73.6
Female	149.6	68.2	90.5	53.4
Family Income				
Less than $5,000	172.7	102.8	158.9	114.1
$5,000–$9,999	125.4	67.2	118.1	57.4
$10,000–$14,999	121.3	62.3	107.3	45.9
$15,000 or more	105.3	52.2	85.9	48.9
65 Years and Over				
Total	199.4	67.1	294.3	204.6
Sex				
Male	141.2	54.6	338.2	183.1
Female	240.9	76.3	262.1	220.4
Family Income				
Less than $5,000	216.1	78.7	232.0	232.0
$5,000–$9,999	179.5	57.3	271.6	163.2
$10,000–$14,999	192.6	39.3	247.3	181.3
$15,000 or more	161.4	48.5	259.2	169.2

Health and Retirement

Muller and Boaz (1988) state: "Many studies of the retirement decision have found that poor health increases the probability of retirement. Yet doubts have been expressed whether self-reported deterioration of health is a genuine cause of retirement, rather than a socially acceptable excuse" (p. 52). They studied the actual health status of retirees, and found support for the idea that the majority of those who say they are retiring for health reasons are telling the truth.

There is no question that health affects the physical abilities of adults across the age range. Yet it is also clear that social circumstances are the main factor in health in the older years. Thus, the healthiness of adults appears to be more a result of the cultural conditions in which they find themselves than of their age.

BOX 21.3

A Comparison of Physical Abilities

One of the best ways of comprehending adult development is to do a miniseries of experiments of your own. In this activity, you can compare the physical development of friends and relatives with just a few simple pieces of equipment. Pick at least three people in at least two age groups. The results might surprise you.

You may find that you need to alter the instructions of the following experiments to make it more convenient for you to do the study. This is perfectly all right, as long as you make sure that each test is the same for every person who takes it. The greater the variety of the adults you enlist in the study, in factors such as age, sex, and religion, the more interesting your results will be.

A. *Muscular strength.* Several of the following tests require a heavy table. Simply have each subject grasp a leg of the table with one hand and raise the leg off the ground three inches. Subjects who can hold it up for three inches for 30 seconds have succeeded in Step 1. Now have them try to hold it up another three inches, and if they succeed they get credit for Step 2 (each step must be done for 30 seconds). In Step 3 they must hold it at a height of one foot, in Step 4 they must hold it at a height of one and a half feet, and in Step 5 at a height of two feet. Record one point for each step successfully completed.

B. *Vision.* The subject should be seated at the table with chin resting on forearms and forearms resting on the table. Set a magazine at a distance of 2 feet and ask the subject to read two lines. Next 3 feet, then 4 feet, then 5 feet, and finally at 6 feet. One point is given for each step.

C. *Hearing.* The subject is seated with his or her back to the table. You will need some instrument that makes the same level of noise for the same period of time. For example, a portable radio might be turned on a brief moment and turned back off, each time at the same volume. A clicker might be used. Whatever you use, make the standard noise at 2 feet behind the subject, and have him or her raise a hand when the sound is heard. Then make the sound at 4 feet, 6 feet, 10 feet, and 20 feet. You may need to vary these distances, depending upon the volume of the instrument you are using. Be sure to vary the intervals between the noises that you make, so that you can be sure the subject is really hearing

Appearance

All of the physical factors treated earlier have an effect on the person's self-concept, but none has a stronger impact than physical appearance. Appearance is of great importance in the United States. A youthful appearance matters a great deal, and to women more than to men. Because women are affected by the "double standard" of aging, they are more likely to use diet, exercise, clothing, and cosmetics to maintain their youthful appearance. Nevertheless, there are significant changes in physical appearance with age that cannot be avoided.

As you can see from the data presented in this chapter, there is a certain amount of physical decline in later life, but it does not occur until most people are quite advanced in age. And with the new medical technologies and marked trend toward adopting more healthy living styles, you can expect to see a much more capable elderly population. Will this happy news also be true for mental development?

Sales of products that promote youth and beauty are booming.

BOX 21.3

Continued

the noise when you make it. Give points for each appropriate response.

D. *Smell,* E. *Taste,* and F. *Touch.* For these three tests, you will need five cups of equal size. The cups should hold milk, cola, soft ice cream, yogurt, and applesauce. Each food should be chilled to approximately the same temperature. Blindfold subjects and ask them to tell you what the five substances are.

G. *Reaction Time—I.* For this test you will need three squares, three circles, three triangles; one of each is one inch high, two inches high, and three inches high. Make them of cardboard, plastic, or wood. Arrange the nine figures in random order in front of the subject. Tell the subject that when you call out the name of one of the figures (e.g., a large square), he or she is to put a finger on it as quickly as possible. Call out the name of one of the figures, and time the response. Repeat this test five times, calling out a different figure each time, and compute the total time required for the five trials.

H. *Reaction Time—II.* Again arrange the nine pieces randomly in front of the subject. You will call out either the shape ("circle") or a size ("middle-size"). The subject puts the three circles or the three middle-size pieces in a pile as quickly as possible. Repeat this experiment five times, using a different designator each time, and compute the total time the task requires.

I. *Health—I.* Ask subjects to carefully count the number of times they have been in the hospital. Give them one point if they have been hospitalized 10 times or more, two points for 5 through 9 times, three points for 3 times, four points for no more than one time, five points if they have never been hospitalized for any reason (pregnancy should not be counted).

J. *Health—II.* Ask subjects to carefully remember how many times they have visited a doctor within the past year. Give one point for four or more times, two points for three times, three points for two times, four points for one time, five points for no visits at all.

Compare the scores for each test for persons within the age groups you have chosen. Do you see any patterns? Are the results of aging evident? What other conclusions can you draw?

Mental Development

In chapter 19, we examined the research on the developmental trends for intelligence, creativity, and learning ability. In this chapter, we concentrate more specifically on research implications for the elderly.

Intelligence

One of the most interesting developments in the research on changes in adult intelligence has been that of **terminal drop.** Birren (1964) defines terminal drop as the period preceding the person's death, from a few weeks up to two years prior. According to Birren,

❖ *The individual himself may or may not be aware in himself of diffuse changes in mood, in mental functioning, or in the way his body responds. Terminal [drop] may be paced by a disease initially remote from the nervous system, such as a cancer of the stomach. Thereafter, over a series of months, a rapid sequence of changes might be observed in overt behavior or in measured psychological characteristics of the individual. It is as though at this point the physiology of the individual had started on a new phase, that the organism is unable to stop (p. 280).*

This research looks at the relationship, not between IQ and age (which is the number of years from birth till the time of testing), but between IQ and survivorship (which is the number of years from the time of testing till death). The hypothesis is that the decline in intelligence in the later years may be caused by the person's perception, consciously or unconsciously, of impending death. This perception causes the person to begin withdrawing from the world. Consequently, performance on an IQ test drops markedly.

There is considerable support for the terminal drop hypothesis. Siegler (1975) reviewed eight studies of the phenomenon and discovered a strong positive relationship between the length of survivorship and high level of intellectual ability. That is, the higher the IQ, the longer the person is likely to live after the time of testing. However, this is not the only aspect of aging that affects change in intelligence.

Researchers have come to several different conclusions concerning the effect of age on intelligence level.

Other Factors in the Relationship Between IQ and Aging

Nonintellectual Factors

A number of factors could cause older people to appear less intelligent than younger people, even when they are not. For example, older people tend to be less healthy and this may impair their performance on tests.

There also may be personality differences in the aged that affect taking tests. Certainly many older people are less motivated to try hard on tests. Younger adults, most of whom have only recently left school, have been strongly conditioned to do their best on any test. Older adults may be much less interested in impressing others and therefore do not try as hard.

Obviously education, occupation, and socioeconomic status also influence a person's intellectual abilities, apart from genetic inheritance. Finally, it may be that the experience, judgment, and wisdom of the elderly compensate for some decline in IQ, such that they function better even with less intelligence.

Location of the Problem

Even if we were able to define the course of intellectual development throughout adulthood, it still would remain a problem to define the causes of change in intellectual functioning. Elias and associates (1977) point to three sources of problems in intellectual functioning. These are

- Input (The individual may have difficulty understanding or even being aware of relevant information.)

- Throughput (There may be difficulty in processing information in the cortex of the brain.)

- Output (The individual might have difficulty expressing conclusions or solutions, even when the problem was fully understood and expertly processed.)

We need to know considerably more about the contributions of each of these three aspects of mental functioning to fully understand the development of the adult mental system.

Table 21.3	Means for Divergent Thinking and Self-Esteem Scores			
Age Group	Fluency	Flexibility	Originality	Self-Esteem
	Mean	Mean	Mean	Mean
10–12	20	13	14	30
13–17	29	18	18	33
18–25	31	19	19	34
26–39	30	18	19	37
40–60	36	21	20	38
61–84	22	15	15	32

From G. Jaquish and R. E. Ripple, "Cognitive Creative Abilities Across the Adult Life Span" in *Human Development*. Copyright © 1980 Educational Center for Human Development, Cambridge, MA.

One final warning: although virtually all studies described here use IQ tests to measure intelligence, the two are not identical. IQ involves school-related abilities, whereas intelligence is made up of these and many other abilities (e. g., spatial ability and "street smarts"). It is not possible at present to discern how much this discrepancy affects the research. Another mental trait that is hard to study, but is even more vital to understand and cultivate, is creativity.

Creativity

In chapter 19, we concluded that quantity of creative production probably drops in old age but that quality of production may not. This is based on studies of actual productivity. But what about *potential* for production? Might it be that the elderly are capable of great creativity but that, as with IQ, factors like motivation and opportunity prevent them from fulfilling this ability? That is the question addressed by the next set of studies we'll discuss.

Cross-Sectional Studies of Creative Productivity

The first large-scale study to look at the creative productivity of *typical* people at various ages *who are still alive* was completed by Alpaugh and associates (1976; also Alpaugh & Birren, 1977). They administered two batteries of creativity tests to 111 schoolteachers age 20 to 83. Their findings support the idea that creativity does decline with age. One major criticism of their research is that the tests they used are probably not equally valid for all age groups. The younger subjects are more likely to have had practice with these types of materials than the older ones.

Jaquish and Ripple attempted to evaluate the effects of aging while avoiding the problem of using age-related materials (1980). These researchers gathered data on six age groups across the life span: 10–12 years (61 people); 13–17 years (71 people); 18–25 years (70 people); 26–40 years (58 people); 40–60 years (51 people); and 60–81 years (39 people). There were a total of 350 subjects in the study.

The definition of creativity in this study was restricted to the concepts of fluency, flexibility, and originality; these are collectively known as divergent thinking abilities. These three traits were measured through the use of an auditory exercise, which was recorded on cassette. Known as the Sounds and Images Test, it elicits responses to the "weird" sounds presented on the tape. Responses are then scored according to the three traits of divergent thinking. The researchers believe that this test is so unusual that no age group is likely to have had more experience with it than any other.

A number of interesting findings have resulted from this study, as may be seen from Table 21.3. On all three measures of divergent thinking, the scores generally

Table 21.4 Peak Periods of Life During Which Creativity May Most Readily Be Cultivated	
For Males	**For Females**
1. 0–5 years old	0–5 years old
2. 11–14 years old	10–13 years old
3. 18–20 years old	18–20 years old
4. 29–31 years old	29–31 years old
5. 40–45 years old	40 (37?)–45 years old
6. 60–65 years old	60–65 years old

From J. S. Dacey, *Fundamentals of Creative Thinking.* Copyright © 1989 D. C. Heath/Lexington Books, Lexington, MA.

increased slightly across the first five age groups. Scores for the 40–60-year-old group increased significantly, while scores for the 61–84-year-old group decreased significantly below the scores of any of the younger age groups. Furthermore, when decline in divergent thinking did occur, it was more pronounced in quantity than in quality. That is, there were greater age differences in fluency (a measure of quantity) than in originality (a measure of quality). Finally, it is not known to what extent the oldest subjects were affected by hearing loss, particularly of high and low tones. Obviously, this could be an alternative explanation of the findings for this oldest group.

Probably the most important finding of the study had to do with the relationship between divergent thinking and self-esteem, which was measured by the Coopersmith Self-Esteem Inventory. Table 21.3 indicates that self-esteem follows a pattern quite similar to the other three traits.

Of special interest is the relationship between self-esteem and divergent thinking for the oldest group: the correlations were moderately high in every case. This indicates that self-esteem may have a positive effect on creative abilities over the years, or that creativity may enhance self-esteem, or both. Jaquish and Ripple (1980) conclude that

❖   *There is much more plasticity in adult development than has been traditionally assumed. Such an interpretation should find a hospitable audience among those people concerned with educational intervention. If the creative abilities of older adults were to be realized in productivity, it would be difficult to overestimate the importance of the formation of new attitudes of society, teachers in continuing adult education programs, and in the older adults themselves (p. 152).*

The Stages of Life During Which Creativity May Best Be Cultivated
In this final section we present Dacey's theory (1989) that there are certain critical periods in life during which creative ability can be cultivated most effectively. Its relevance to the study of late adulthood will be obvious. Table 21.4 presents a list of these periods for males and females.

The basic premise of this theory is that a person's inherent creativity can blossom best during a period of crisis and change. The six periods chosen in the table above are ages at which most people experience stress due to life changes.

The chart above presents a new theory, and thus it must be considered speculative. Nevertheless there is some direct evidence from research to support it. There is also some excellent research from the fields of personality and cognitive development to indicate that these periods are more volatile than any others.

Included in the theory is the concept that major gains in creative performance are less likely with each succeeding period. That is, what happens to the person in the early years is far more influential than what happens in the later years. The older people become, the less likely they are to have a sudden burst of high creative production.

The Sixth Peak Period

Evidence for the first five peak periods has been presented earlier in this book. The rationale for the sixth period, from 60 to 65, is reviewed here.

For most men and for a growing number of women, this is the period in which retirement occurs. Even if a woman has not been in the labor force, she has many adjustments to make because of her husband's retirement. Thus most adults are faced with a major adjustment of self-concept at this time in their lives.

Although some do not adjust well and begin withdrawing from society, others take advantage of the change to pursue creative goals that had previously been impossible for them. Obviously a majority of the "young old" (the new term for those who are 60 to 70) do not suddenly become creative, but a substantial number do. Of the several thousand highly productive people he studied, Lehman (1953, 1962) found over 100, or almost 5%, whose major productivity began in the years after 60.

Research indicates that the time right after retirement can be a period of creative growth, as the individual turns from the demands of a work schedule to the opportunities offered by an artistic endeavor.

In addition to highly visible contributions, many of the elderly become creative in less newsworthy ways. Gerontologist Jack Botwinick, who presents an excellent analysis of this topic in his book *We Are Aging* (1981), suggests that many elderly persons exercise a newfound creativity by mentoring younger people. Though largely unheralded, such guidance and encouragement of younger creators unquestionably has invaluable benefits for society.

This is not to say that maintaining or increasing creative performance in one's later years is easy. There are inherent problems that are not readily overcome. Psychologist B. F. Skinner (1983), who had a 60-year-long career of high creative achievement, states that productivity is difficult for the elderly because they tend to lose interest in work, find it hard to start working, and work more slowly:

❖   *It is easy to attribute this change to them, but we should not overlook a change in their world. For motivation, read reinforcement. In old age, behavior is not so strongly reinforced. Biological aging weakens reinforcing consequences. Behavior is more and more likely to be followed by aches and pains and quick fatigue. Things tend to become 'not worth doing' in the sense that the aversive consequences exact too high a price. Positive reinforcers become less common and less powerful. Poor vision closes off the world of art, faulty hearing the enjoyment of highly fidelitous music. Foods do not taste as good, and erogenous tissues grow less sensitive. Social reinforcers are attenuated. Interests and tastes are shared with a smaller number of people (p. 28).*

It is increasingly clear that creativity may blossom at any age. This theory of "the peak periods of creative growth" is not meant to disparage that fact. There is solid evidence, however, that the best opportunities lie in the six periods identified by the theory. Are there also periods in the development of sex roles in later life that have special importance? of sexuality? of family relations? of work and retirement? We'll examine these questions in the next chapter.

Transition

At the beginning of this chapter we asked, "Must growing old mean decline?" The answer is that some decline is inevitable, but the picture is much less gloomy than we have been led to believe. The loss of mental and physical abilities is, on the average, relatively slight; some individuals experience only moderate physical loss and no mental loss at all. For many older adults, compensatory skills and abilities may replace lost capacities. The same is true for personal and social development.

Here once again we run into the bugaboo of all human development: the self-fulfilling prophecy. Because American society has been changing rapidly for many decades, older adults are frequently viewed as incompetent—their experience appears to have little relevance in "modern times." Yet carefully controlled laboratory measurements of their abilities make clear that their losses may be relatively slight.

Perhaps as we learn to understand the aging process, and as the process is better understood by the public in general, the majority of adults will not assume that their abilities must undergo severe decline. In such a situation, the quality of life of the elderly will surely improve greatly! As you shall see in the next chapter, such improvements are already taking place in the social and personal lives of the elderly.

Key Ideas

1.   There are three aspects of aging: physiological, genetic, and environmental.

2.   Seven different *physiological* factors have been suggested to account for the process of aging: wear and tear; aging by program; homeostatic imbalance; cross-linkage theory; accumulation of metabolic wastes; autoimmunity; and accumulation of errors.

3.   Other major modifiers that affect the aging process are training, practice, motivation, nutrition, organic malfunction, illness, injury, stress level, educational level, occupation, personality type, and socioeconomic status.

4.   Six aspects of the decline of physical systems were discussed in this chapter: reaction time, sensory abilities, other body systems, hormonal balance, health, and appearance.

5.   It is hypothesized that terminal drop brings about a significant decline in intelligence. It occurs about two years before the person's death.

6.   Although actual creative achievement usually peaks earlier in adulthood, there is evidence that creative *ability* remains high well into old age.

Key Terms

Accumulation of errors
Accumulation of metabolic waste
Aging by program
Antigens
Autoimmunity
Collagen

Cross-linkage theory
Gene theory
Homeostatic imbalance
Terminal drop
Wear and tear theory

What Do You Think?

1.   Must we grow old and die?

2.   Which factors do you believe most strongly affect aging: physiological, genetic, environmental, or some others?

3.   Regarding the decline of physical systems, which has the greatest impact on the person's life: reaction time, sensory abilities, other body systems, hormonal balance, health, or appearance? Why?

4.   Regarding the decline of mental systems, which has the greatest impact on the person's life: intelligence, creativity, memory, or learning? Why?

Suggested Readings

Cunningham, Walter, and John Brookbank. (1988). *Gerontology*. New York: Harper & Row. An up-to-date general reference on the psychological, biological, and sociological factors in aging.

Olsen, Tillie. (1961). *Tell me a riddle*. New York: Dell. The superb title story details the difficulties of old age and terminal illness as they occurred to a working-class woman during the Great Depression.

Sarton, May. (1973). *As we are now*. New York: Norton. A novel in the form of the diary of a retired schoolteacher, this is a powerful portrayal of her experiences when she is put in a nursing home by her relatives.

Skinner, B. F., and M. E. Vaughan. (1983). *Enjoy old age: A program of self-management*. New York: Norton. In this book, the grandfather of behaviorism explains how to use behavior modification to better handle the problems of aging. A good read, whether you are elderly or plan to help someone who is.

Spence, Alexander. (1989). *Biology of human aging*. Englewood Cliffs, NJ: Prentice-Hall. A highly detailed look at the systems of the body and how they are affected by aging.

· *Chapter 22* ·

Late Adulthood: Psychosocial Development

Social Development

Sex Roles

When people enter their sixties, they enter a new and final stage in the life cycle. At this point they confront the loss of many highly valued roles, the need to establish a new life structure for the remaining years, and the undeniable fact of life's termination. Widowhood and retirement are the central role transitions likely to occur at this time, but the death of friends and relatives also diminishes one's social network. Although people are aware of the inevitability of these role losses as they enter old age, their often abrupt reality may result in severe role discontinuity (Sales, 1978, p. 185).

In this section, you will learn about several aspects of growing old: sex roles, sexuality, family life, and work and retirement. Each of them often involves abrupt and disruptive change. This is known as **role discontinuity.** See Box 22.1 for several questions you should keep in mind as you read the theories and research summaries on each of these aspects.

A number of gerontologists have noted that people in late adulthood experience a **cross-over** in sex roles. Older men become more like women, and older women become more like men. They do not actually cross over—they just become more like each other. This is what Neugarten (1968) found in her studies of aging men and women. She states that "women, as they age, seem to become more tolerant of their own aggressive, egocentric impulses; whereas men, as they age, [become more tolerant] of their own nurturative and affiliative impulses" (p. 71). In Gutman's terms (1973), men pass from "active to passive mastery," and women do just the opposite.

The differences between men and women, so many of which seem to be based on sexuality, are no longer as important. With the barriers breaking down, older men and women seem to have more in common with each other, and thus may be more of a solace to each other as they deal with the disruptive changes of growing old. This is not to say that men and women reverse sex roles. Rather, they move toward androgyny (see chap. 15), accepting whatever role, male and female, is appropriate in the situation.

On the basis of data obtained by University of California at Berkeley, Norma Haan (1976, 1981) concludes that the sex role changes that result from aging generally lead toward greater candor with others and comfort with one's self. For the most part, she says, "people change, but slowly, while maintaining some continuity" (1985, p. 25).

Sexuality

Until the 1980s, most reports on sex among the elderly agreed that sexual practices drop off sharply in old age. For example, Pearlman (1972) reported that only 20% of elderly males have sex two times or more per month. There are serious doubts, however, about the reliability of these reports. Society disapproves of the idea of sex among the elderly, so it may be that many do not report what actually goes on.

A study at Duke University centered primarily on the social and emotional aspects of sexuality in later adulthood, but included the physical component as well (Williamson, Munley, & Evans, 1980). Since 1960, when the study began, researchers at Duke University have interviewed and medically evaluated 270 people over age 60. Their main goal was to define interest in sex and amount of sexual activity as people age. The study's main conclusions are the following:

- At age 68, about 70% of males engage in intercourse, and 1 out of 5 are sexually active in their 80s.

The "cross-over effect" concerns the tendency of men to do more things that are considered feminine, such as caring for flowers, and for women to do more things that are considered male, such as taking charge of repairs to the home.

BOX 22.1

What's Your Opinion?

Role discontinuity occurs when people experience an abrupt change in their style of life and their role in it. Is this a natural part of growing old? Should we expect our world to shrink and our power to erode? Or is this just a stereotype of old age?

Is role discontinuity a problem only for the poor, who have less control over their lives than the wealthy? Does high intelligence make a difference? How about gender? What's your opinion?

- For women, activity does not decrease with age as it does for men.

- Older men are more sexually active and more interested in sex than older women.

- Interest decreases for both sexes but not as much as activity does.

- Sexual interest is positively linked to health for males. Healthier individuals are more interested in sex.

- For women, interest is dependent upon the enjoyment and quality of sex in the past.

Widowhood

Gender differences in attitudes and interest in sex are accounted for by a number of factors. For example, women outlive men by approximately seven years. Most married women will become widows because they marry men nearly four years older than themselves. In contrast, most men in society will not become widowers unless they reach age 85. There are five widows for every one widower (Metropolitan Life, 1977). Due to this imbalance of elderly males and females, it is more difficult for women to find sexual partners in their aging years.

Whether or not a woman is sexually active depends mainly on her marital status. In contrast, single men in the Duke study were just as sexually active as their married counterparts. Men have generally had more opportunity for extramarital sexual relations than women, due to the **differential opportunity structure** (Glenn, 1978). This means that due to social disapproval and more rigid rules enforced by parents, peers, and the legal system, women have not had the same access to sex as men.

For females, masturbation increases after widowhood. Throughout the life span, however, only 58% of women masturbate compared with 88% of the men (Kinsey, 1953). Thus, women are more sexually restrained, even when no partner is involved.

Impotency

One of the biggest fears in males of increasing age is **impotency.** Physical changes, nonsupportive partners and peers, and internal fears may be enough to inhibit or terminate sexual activity in males. It may become a self-fulfilling prophecy.

Sleep laboratory experiments have shown that many men in their 60s to 80s who have labeled themselves as impotent regularly experience erections in their sleep (Rubin, 1979). In many cases a man is capable of having intercourse, but a physical condition such as diabetes impedes it.

One pervading myth is that surgery of the prostate gland inevitably leads to impotency. Many elderly men experience pain and swelling of this small gland, and

Table 22.1   Findings of the Starr-Weiner Study of Sexual Activity in Later Life

Frequency of intercourse is 1.4 times per week. (Kinsey had reported a frequency of once every two weeks for 60 year olds.)

- The ideal or fantasized lover for most, particularly women, is close to their own age.
- Most see their sex lives remaining pretty much the same as they grow even older.
- Most have a strong continuing interest in sex.
- The belief that sex is important for physical and mental well-being.
- The perception of most of the respondents that sex is as good as when they were younger.
- For a large number, both male and female, sex is *better* in the later years.
- Orgasm is considered an essential part of the sexual experience.
- Most of the women are orgasmic and always have been.
- The orgasm for many is stronger now than when they were younger.
- Masturbation is an acceptable outlet for sexual needs.
- For a majority, living together without marriage is acceptable.
- An overwhelming number of respondents, including widows, widowers, divorcees, and singles, are sexually active.
- Most are satisfied with their sex lives.
- Many vary their sexual practices to achieve satisfaction.
- For a surprising number of older people, oral sex is considered the most exciting sexual experience.
- Respondents typically show little embarrassment or anxiety about sex.
- Most enjoy nudity with their partners.

Source: Data from B. Starr and M. Weiner, *The Starr-Weiner Report on Sex and Sexuality in the Mature Years,* 1981, p. 241.

a **prostatectomy** (removal of all or a part of this gland) is necessary. Most impotency that results from the removal of this gland is psychological rather than physical.

Most sexual problems experienced by women are due to hormonal changes. The vaginal walls begin to thin, and intercourse may become painful, with itching and burning sensations. Estrogen pills and hormone creams relieve many of these symptoms (Butler & Lewis, 1977). Further, if women *believe* that sexual activity ceases with menopause and/or aging, it probably will. Although women have fewer concerns about sex, they are often worried about losing their attractiveness, which can also have a negative effect on their sex lives (McCary, 1978).

More recently, Starr and Weiner (1981) surveyed 800 adults between the ages of 60 and 91, drawn from all parts of the country and representing all ethnic and racial groups. Half were married, a third were widowed, 11% were divorced, and 4% had never married. They asked them to answer 50 open-ended questions about their sexual lives and then mail back the questionnaire anonymously. Table 22.1 presents their surprising findings.

Sex in Nursing Homes

In their study of the sexual behavior of 63 residents in nursing homes, Wasow and Loeb (1979) reported the following findings:

The question of whether or not to allow residents of nursing homes to engage in sex has been a growing problem, as elders' attitudes toward sexual mores change with the rest of us.

❖ *The aged interviewees believed that sexual activity was appropriate for other elderly people in the homes; they personally were not involved, chiefly because of lack of opportunity. Most of them admitted having sexual thoughts and feelings. Medical and behavioral personnel showed great reluctance to discuss the subject. It would seem that, if the quality of life in old age is to be improved, there should be some provision in nursing homes for those who desire appropriate sexual activity (p. 73).*

Sex and the "Old-Old"

In a fascinating study only of those 80 to 102 years old by Bretschneider and McCoy (1988), we get a look at the sexual activities of those elderly who used to be thought totally inactive. Table 22.2 gives us some surprises! In their past lives, the men claim to have engaged in intercourse more than the women, but there was no difference in enjoyment. In their present lives, 62% of the men and 30% of the women say they have intercourse at least sometimes, and 76% of the men and 39% of the women say they enjoy it at least mildly. Another interesting finding of this study is that the men reported having their first intercourse at an average age of 22, and women at age 25. What a difference from today's figures (see chap. 15)!

Nevertheless, it is quite likely that there is a real decline in sexual activity among the elderly. Men are often concerned about their ability to consummate intercourse. They also worry about their loss of masculinity, in terms of looks and strength. Nevertheless, the literature on sex among the elderly shows a new attitude emerging. Datan and Rodeheaver (1983) describe very well a difference between **generative love** and **existential love.**

❖ *We believe that existential love, the capacity to cherish the present moment, is one of the greatest gifts of maturity. Perhaps we first learn this love when we first confront the certainty of our own personal death, most often in middle adulthood. Generative love is most characteristic of parenthood, a time during which sacrifices are gladly made for the sake of the children. However, it is existential love, we feel, that creates the unique patience and tenderness so often seen in grandparents, who know how brief the period of childhood is, since they have seen their own children leave childhood behind them.*

We have not yet awakened to the potential for existential love between old women and old men, just as we are not yet prepared to recognize the pleasures of sexuality as natural to the life span, particularly to the postparental period.

Those old people who have had the misfortune of spending their last days in nursing homes may learn that love can be lethal. We have been told of an old woman and an old man who fell in love. The old man's children thought this late flowering was 'cute'; however, the old woman's children thought it was disgraceful, and over her protests, they removed her from the nursing home. One month later she registered her final protest: she died (p. 287).

Out of all the hundreds and hundreds of studies of monkeys, there is only one finding that applies to every type: from the largest gorilla to the tiniest spider monkey, they all spend about four hours a day in "grooming." Grooming refers to their different ways of touching—stroking, removing bugs, hugging, sex. It is obviously genetic. It seems likely that we humans have something in common with them. We all need to be touched, too.

The elderly get less touching than the rest of us, perhaps because they are not seen as being attractive. But they need physical contact just as much as everyone else. It is hoped that a new attitude will spread and make their lives that much happier.

White (1981) has reviewed the literature on sexuality and offers the following summary.

1. Males are more active than females, except for very old age groups (those 85 or older) in which males and females do not significantly differ.

2. When sexual interest or activity ceases or declines in the aging female, it is usually due to declining interest or illness in her male partner.

| Table 22.2 | Reported Frequency and Enjoyment of Sexual Intercourse by 80–102-Year-Old Men and Women in the Past (Younger Years) and in the Present | | | | | | | | | |

| | Entire Sample | | Frequency | | | | | | | |
| | | | Never (1) | | Sometimes (2–3) | | Often (4–5) | | Very Often (6–7) | | |
	N	%	n	%	n	%	n	%	n	%	x²
Past											
Men	92	92	3	3	3	3	60	65	26	28	
Women	90	88	2	2	10	11	70	78	8	9	14.2
Present											
Men	80	80	30	38	27	34	21	26	2	3	
Women	80	78	56	70	16	20	8	10	0	0	18.5

From J. G. Bretschneider and N. L. McCoy, "Sexual Interest and Behavior in Healthy 80 to 102 Year Olds" in *Archives of Sexual Behavior,* 17(2):109–129. Copyright © 1988 Plenum Press, New York, NY.

3. Males do show a gradual decline in sexual activity with advancing age, though this decline may be a cohort difference, because some males actually show an increased interest in sex with age. In the absence of longitudinal data, a cohort explanation cannot be ruled out.

4. Physiological changes in the sexual organs in advanced age cause some difficulties for some individuals but do not adequately explain decreased or nonexistent sexual activity in either sex.

5. It is difficult to find research on aging and sexuality that does not suffer from sample bias and methodological problems.

The Elderly and Their Families

The familial relationship undergoes changes in membership, organization, and role during the aging process. Due to improved health care, individuals can expect to live longer, which means that married couples will have more years together after their children leave home. Though there are exceptions (those who are divorced, childless, or who never married), most middle-age and aged couples go through similar stages in the life cycle (Williamson & others, 1980). There are four basic phases:

> The child-launching phase
> The childless preretirement period
> The retirement phase
> Widowhood

The duration of each stage in the life cycle, and the ages of the family members for each stage, vary from family to family. Childbearing patterns have a lot to do with life in the late stages of life. Couples who complete their families in their early years will have a different life-style when their last child leaves home than couples with "change of life" babies, who may have a dependent child at home when they are ready to retire. This can pose serious economic problems for those retirees on fixed incomes, trying to meet the staggering costs of education. In addition, with children in the home, it is difficult to save for retirement.

The period after the last offspring leaves home is frequently referred to as the *empty nest syndrome.* Some women experience depression, a sense of loss and

Table 22.2 *Continued*

	Entire Sample		Enjoyment							
			None (1)		Mild (2–3)		Moderate (4–5)		Great (6–7)	
	N	%	n	%	n	%	n	%	n	%
Past										
Men	91	91	3	3	5	6	23	25	60	66
Women	92	90	5	5	9	10	34	37	44	48
Present										
Men	79	79	19	24	11	14	21	27	28	35
Women	82	80	50	61	10	12	13	16	9	11

purposelessness, when the active role of motherhood ends. Aging and menopause contribute to this syndrome. On rare occasions, a father becomes depressed, too, although the majority of couples do not suffer from the syndrome (Treas, 1975).

Retirement may bring about changes for both spouses, but it may be particularly stressful for wives who have not properly prepared themselves emotionally and financially for retirement. Retirement generally signifies a decrease in income and a lowering of the standard of living, but it may take a while before some of these problems are noticed. Household duties may change, with the husband generally helping more.

Widowhood
Widowhood is the final phase in the life cycle. With women outliving men by large margins, the wife is most often the survivor. Only half of women over 65 are living with a partner. Helena Lopata's (1973) study of Chicago area widows sought to find what changes occur with the death of a spouse. She found that "widowhood means the loss, reorganization, and acquisition of social roles" (p. 6). A widow forfeits the role of her partner's "nurse, confidant, sex partner and housekeeper."

Many widows have to take on additional duties, including managing household finances and janitorial tasks, and some will have to seek employment. Widowhood affects social relationships with family and friends. Often a widow is the "fifth wheel" in social settings, and former relationships may dissipate. Fortunately, new social activities and friends emerge and replace the old ones. Many of Lopata's widows came to realize some compensations in widowhood, including increased independence and a decline in their work load.

Children may play an integral part in their mother's adjustment to widowhood in three ways: (1) by taking over some of the father's responsibilities; (2) by supplanting the father as the mother's center of attention; and (3) by being supportive and maintaining relationships (Lopata, 1973).

Remarriage is an alternative to the loneliness that most widows and widowers feel after losing their spouse. However, remarriage rates for senior citizens are low and it is not an option for most. The reasons for not remarrying include the following:

• Many of the elderly view it as improper.

• Children may oppose remarriage.

Older women, who are more likely to be widowed than men because the men die earlier, often turn to activities with other widows for enjoyment.

BOX 22.2

Decisions Most Older Couples Must Make

Most older couples need to make a number of decisions that will be vital to their family lives (Cox, 1988), including whether or not to

- Remain in their current home with its history and memories, or move to a new home or apartment
- Remain in the same community or move to a different one, or perhaps move to a retirement community
- Remain active in current organizations, join new ones, or simply not be bothered with organizational affiliations
- Try to locate near children and close friends or move to a different section of the country
- Seek activities satisfying to both husband and wife, or participate independently

Obviously the decisions they make can have a major impact on their families and themselves. Each of these decisions has the capacity to cause considerable stress for all the family's members.

- Social Security laws penalize widows who remarry.
- There are three single women for every unmarried man over age 65.

Seniors who choose to remarry, however, enjoy much success if the ingredients of love, companionship, financial security, and offspring consent are present.

An important aspect of happiness in the elderly person's family life is whether he or she is living with a spouse, with children, or with another relative. The former has been more common in recent years (Turner & Helms, 1989), probably as a result of better health among the elderly, and better support systems for them. In most cases, living with one's spouse is preferred, so this is probably contributing to an increase in happiness in our senior citizens.

The Older Worker

Only a small percentage of all older adults are in the labor force—about 11%. Much of this is due to forced retirement (Sommerstein, 1986). However, even with the extension of the mandatory age of retirement from 65 to 70 by Congress in 1978, not many people want to continue working past 65. For example, a large steel corporation that has never had mandatory retirement finds that less than one percent of their 40,000 workers stay on past 65. The average age of retirement at this company is below 62.

Interest in Work

Older people clearly care less about working than younger people. For example, Cohn (1979) reports that "Toward the end of the period of labor force participation, the satisfactions men derive from work are transferred from the actual experience of work to its consequences" (p. 264). It seems likely that these percentages are even lower today. That is, no more than half of older workers may be willing to work for its own sake. Of course, many younger workers do it only for the pay, too. The social value of the work itself is probably the most significant differential.

Lack of interest in work for its own sake as one grows older may be natural, but it also has a severe impact on the income of older persons when it leads to retirement. For example, Paul Nathanson, Executive Director of the National Senior Citizens Law Center, states that almost 22% of all older people live in households below the poverty level. Furthermore, more than 50% of all single women above the age of 60 live at or below the poverty level. He says that "older women in America today constitute the single poorest group in our society." If these older women are also minority persons, they have an even more difficult time existing.

Discrimination

Discrimination against the older worker can be subtle and hard to detect (Findley, 1979). For example, one 61-year-old female designer was told by the company she worked for that they were going out of business and that she would not be able to collect her company pension. Also losing their jobs were two other persons who had the same job as her, ages 32 and 29. After the company folded, the older woman learned that the owners had formed a new company and had reemployed the two younger designers. She complained to the United States government, who took the case to court and won $125,000 in benefits for her.

Performance

As this society ages through greater longevity, the aging of the baby boom generation, and decreased birthrates, some of the stereotypes about aging are coming under closer scrutiny. One stereotype is that work performance necessarily declines with age (Rhodes, 1983). This stereotype is getting more research attention because the number of workers in the last two decades of their careers will *grow* 41% while the number of workers 16 to 35 years old will *decline* slightly (Johnston, 1987).

The stereotype is bolstered by research on aging that demonstrates a decline in abilities such as dexterity, speed of response, agility, hearing, and vision. If all these abilities decline, then surely job performance must decline with age. However, McEvoy and Cascio (1989) recently conducted an extensive meta-analysis (a study that compiles the results of many other studies) of 96 studies and found no relationship between age and job performance. It made no difference whether the performance measure was ratings or productivity measures or whether the type of job was professional or nonprofessional.

What explanation is there for these results? How can a worker deal with declining physical abilities? Experience is one answer. There is said to be no substitute for it and it is certainly valued by employers. Other reasons cited are that older workers have lower absenteeism, turnover, illness, and accident rates (Kacmar & Ferris, 1989; Martocchio, 1989) . They also tend to have higher job satisfaction and more positive work values than younger workers (Rhodes, 1983). These qualifications seem to offset any decreases in physical ability caused by increasing age.

We are making strides in understanding the special problems of the older worker, especially in measuring their individual needs. The key seems to lie in improvements in career counseling. A number of new programs are being set up for this purpose (Brady & Gray, 1988). When older workers are adequately advised, they can remain a useful and satisfied part of the workforce (Bove, 1987; Bornstein, 1986; Cahill & Salomone, 1987).

Retirement

"I just don't want to retire," said Charlie, a 65-year-old shipping clerk. "But you've worked hard, and you should get the fruits of your labor," said his boss. "Fruits of my labor, my backside! I know lots of guys, as soon as they retire, they get sick or something and then they die. I know if I retire I'm gonna die. I'm gonna die!" Despite his protestations, Charlie was retired. Three months later he was dead.

BOX 22.3
The Effects of Retirement

- Mandatory retirement has deleterious effects on society by excluding talented individuals from the workplace, by decreasing public funding sources, by encumbering the pension system, and by insulting the dignity of some elderly persons.
- Many retirees prefer to combine the positive aspects of both work and retirement.
- New assessment techniques, geared specifically toward measuring the job performance of older individuals, need to be devised.
- The midlife years are critical to adjustment in retirement. Gerontologists urge a midlife assessment of one's abilities and desires relating to work and retirement.
- Minority workers often feel that retirement is a meaningless concept, since many have not been employed in meaningful work positions that would lead to retirement benefits.
- Alternative employment programs should be available for older workers, including (1) changes in time spent on the job, such as phased retirement, job sharing, and part-time work; (2) allowing older employees to work at a decreased pace; and (3) allowing for lateral promotions and transfers.
- Industrialized nations will have to find additional methods for dealing with an increasing population of unemployed individuals, if current trends of early retirement, decreasing birthrates, increasing longevity, abnormal inflation, and low productivity continue.
- States that abolish mandatory retirement are responsible for older employees through affirmative action and civil rights, retirement planning, and retraining programs.

For many people, retirement is a welcome relief from a frustrating and boring job. For others, it is just as difficult as being unemployed. Retirement requires changing the habits of an adult lifetime. This probably explains why over 11% of those 65 and over are employed.

Nevertheless, the great majority of the elderly do not choose to work. Money is probably not the major factor in that decision (Hayward, 1986). The decision is a complicated one, but most people now feel they have enough financial security so that they need not work. Health may be the biggest factor. Crowley (1986) found that the well-being of 1,200 retirees was highly dependent on the state of their health at the time of retirement.

Retirement seems to be harder on males than females. Many feel that they have nothing to do, while their wives still have a job. The home still must be taken care of, the meals cooked, the clothes cleaned. Most older wives have already adjusted to a reduction in their roles because their children have left home. For men, the change usually comes all at once.

Women's attitudes toward retirement are clearly different from those of men (Campione, 1987). For example, Barfield and Morgan (1978) found that even in families where the husband is planning to retire early, the wife often is not. Campbell (1979) has suggested that because women make up a larger percentage of the older population, extending the retirement age to 70 will benefit them more. It may also alleviate some of the strain on programs such as Social Security. Gerontologists agree on a number of things about retirement and its effects on the retiree (Gonda, 1981). These are listed in Box 22.3.

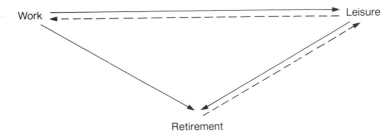

Figure 22.1 *The interrelatedness of work, leisure, and retirement.
Solid lines denote the direct influence of (1) work on leisure, and
(2) work and leisure upon retirement. Broken lines suggest a possible feedback
influence whereby preferences for uses of leisure time may affect choice of jobs, and the
availability of more time in retirement may affect content of leisure activities.*

Retirement and Leisure

How one views retirement is contingent upon the work and leisure experiences one
has had up to the point of retirement. The leisure activities one has pursued
throughout life play a crucial role in one's social adjustment later on. The relationships among work, retirement, and leisure can be seen in Figure 22.1.

The type of work one does directly affects how one spends leisure time in two
ways. The scheduling of work affects when leisure time is available. A person who
works second or third shift might be unable to take part in activities that are often
thought of as evening activities, such as dining and dancing. Secondly, the content
of work may influence how much time will be left over for leisure activities. Persons
with physically draining positions may be too tired to do anything but nap after
work. On the other hand, a person with a desk job may choose physically challenging activities during leisure hours.

When leisure is no more than an extension of work experiences and attitudes,
it performs what leisure theorists call a *spillover function.* For example, some people
try to relax by performing some of their easier tasks at home—the "stuffed briefcase" syndrome. Conversely, when leisure time is engaged in to make up for disappointment and stress at work, it is described as a *compensatory function.* An
example would be excessive partying at the end of the work day or week. An
overabundance of compensatory leisure will leave one as unprepared to face retirement as an overabundance of work-related activities.

Sociologists and economists contend that education prepares workers for the
independence they will need when they retire. Those with low levels of education
often have jobs that require little creativity or a particular skill, and consist largely
of following directions. Workers with higher levels of education are usually found
in occupations that require more initiative and responsibility, and ones that they
have been specifically prepared for (Bowles & Gintis, 1976). Those in "deadend"
jobs may seek relief in early retirement but then find that their pensions are insufficient. Therefore their independence is lessened in retirement.

*The "stuffed briefcase"
syndrome refers to people
who feel they must work
even when they are
pursuing such relaxing
activities as watching
television.*

The Seven Phases of Retirement

Williamson and associates (1980) have suggested that there are phases through
which most retirees pass. These are illustrated in Figure 22.2, and explained in Table
22.3.

The seven phases of retirement have no specific timing because people retire
at different ages and retire under different circumstances. Some individuals adapt

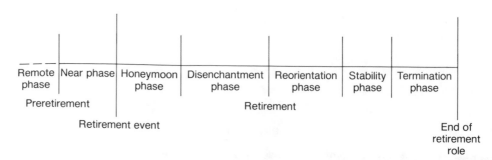

Figure 22.2 *The seven phases of retirement.*
Source: Data from Williamson and Associates, 1980.

rather quickly and leap from the honeymoon stage to the stable phase. Obviously, the person's progress through the seven phases depends on his or her attitude toward departure from the workforce.

Making Retirement More Enjoyable

There is a growing belief that retired persons are an important resource to the community. Numerous efforts have been made in recent years to tap this powerful resource. There are a number of national programs that now make an effort to involve retired persons in volunteer and paid work of service to society.

Recent surveys seem to indicate that the "golden years" are not so golden for many retired persons. But with improving health conditions (see chap. 18), improved understanding of the nature of life after 65, and a considerable increase in government involvement, the lives of retirees have a far better chance of being fruitful.

Contrary to the stereotype, getting old need not, and usually does not, mean being lonely. In fact, the elderly, most of whom have a good deal of free time, often use it to develop their social lives. We now move to a consideration of their personal development.

Personal Development

Personal Development—Committee on Human Development

What are the effects of aging on personal development? The Committee on Human Development has addressed this question for many years. Gerontologist Bernice L. Neugarten and her associates at the University of Chicago have been responsible for the highly respected research of this committee (e.g., Havighurst, Neugarten, & Tobin, 1968; Neugarten, 1968).

Adults between the ages of 54 and 94 who were residents of Kansas City were asked to participate in a study of change across the adult life span. The sample is somewhat biased in that it represents only white persons who were living on their own (i.e., not institutionalized) at the time of the study. They were somewhat better educated and of a higher socioeconomic group than is typical for this age group. Nevertheless, the sample is reasonably well balanced, and because of the thoroughness with which these persons were studied, this research has become a classic in the field of adult psychology. Neugarten summarizes the findings:

- In the middle years (especially the 50s), there is a change in the perception of time and death and the relationship of the self to them. Introspection, contemplation, reflection, and self-evaluation become important aspects of life. People at this age become more interested in their "inner selves."

Table 22.3   The Seven Phases of Retirement

1. *Remote Phase.* A stage of denial where the person does little to prepare himself or herself for the transition into retirement.
2. *Near Phase.* Some workers partake in preretirement programs that are offered by the employer. Preretirement programs help the worker to understand pension and benefit plans along with the legal, health, and leisure aspects of retirement.
3. *Honeymoon Phase.* A time of euphoria in which individuals try to overcompensate for all the things they never had time for. Persons who were involuntarily forced to retire do not go through the honeymoon phase. This euphoria eventually leads to disenchantment.
4. *Disenchantment Phase.* A sense of loss or disappointment as the pace of life lessens, due to unrealistic expectations of what retirement should be like.
5. *Reorientation Phase.* The retiree tries to rebuild a satisfying, stable, and realistic life-style.
6. *Stability Phase.* The individual learns to adjust to change because his life becomes balanced and routine.
7. *Termination Phase.* The retirement role is cancelled if the retiree accepts a job or becomes disabled.

- Perception of how well one can control the environment undergoes a marked change:

  ❖ *Forty-year-olds, for example, seem to see the environment as one that rewards boldness and risk-taking, and to see themselves as possessing energy congruent with the opportunities perceived in the outer world. Sixty-year-olds, however, perceive the world as complex and dangerous, no longer to be reformed in line with one's wishes, and the individual as conforming and accommodating to outer-world demands (1968, p. 140).*

- **Psychic energy** declines with age. Tests showed that intensity of emotion and amount of psychic energy invested in tasks undergo a definite decline in the later years.

- **Sex-role reversals** also occur with age. Older men see themselves and other males as becoming submissive and less authoritative with advancing years. Conversely, older women see themselves and other women as becoming more dominant and self-assured as they grow older.

- **Age-status** becomes more rigid with development. Age-status refers to society's expectations about what is normal at various ages. These expectations change not only with advancing years but according to the particular society and to the historical context. For example, in 1940 a woman who was not married by age 22 was not considered unusual, but if she had not married by the time she was 27, people began to worry. In the late 1980s, the expected age of marriage is much less rigid. This holds only for the United States; in Samoa, for example, there is concern if a person is not married by age 15.

A more recent study that has also looked at the stability of traits across adult periods has been conducted by Dorothy Eichorn and her associates at Berkeley (1981; see also Sears & Sears, 1982). These researchers examined stability by looking at the relationship between traits in adolescence and in middle age. They found that middle-age blood pressure, goodness-of-health, IQ, IQ gain, political ideology, and drinking problems can be predicted fairly well in adolescence. Other traits such as the status of marriage and psychological health are less stable (see chap. 20 for more on this topic).

BOX 22.4

National Retirement Programs

- *The Foster Grandparents Program.* People over 60 are eligible for part-time work in infant homes, schools for the retarded, and convalescent homes. They do not replace regular staff, but establish a one-to-one relationship with the people they serve.
- *The Retired Executives' Service Corps.* In this program, retired executives offer consultation on a part-time basis, usually to new or struggling companies.
- *Senior Worker Action Program.* Offered under the Office of Economic Opportunity, this program offers senior citizens work as school aides, babysitters, companions, handymen, homemakers, and seamstresses. It also supplies training to obtain new skills or brush up on old ones such as typing.
- *The National Council of Senior Citizens.* This large organization has 21 projects throughout the country that offer various kinds of employment to senior citizens.
- *Mature Temps.* This is the free employment service that is offered by the American Association of Retired Persons. It has offices in at least thirteen major cities, and helps to place older people in temporary paid jobs.
- *Senior citizen's centers.* There are over 1,200 senior citizen centers in the United States, which offer a wide variety of services to retirees.
- *Other employment services.* On a more local basis, retirees can get employment help from Senior Placement Bureaus, Senior Home Craftsmen, Good Neighbor Family Aides, Red Cross Centers, the Grey Panthers, and the home economic departments of many state universities.

Activity Versus Disengagement

What is the optimum pattern of aging in terms of our relationships with other people? This question has also been investigated by the Committee on Human Development. For many years, there have been two different positions on this question, known as the **activity theory** and the **disengagement theory.**

According to the activity theory, human beings flourish through interaction with other people and through keeping physically active. They are unhappy when, as they reach the older years, their contacts with others shrink as a result of death, illness, and societal limitations. Those who are able to keep up the social activity of their middle years are considered to be the most successful.

Disengagement theory contradicts this idea. According to this position, the belief that activity is better than passivity is a bias of the Western world. This was not always so; the Greeks, for example, valued their warriors and athletes but reserved the highest distinction for such contemplative philosophers as Sophocles, Plato, and Aristotle (Bellah, 1978). Many people in the countries of the Eastern hemisphere also hold this view. According to disengagement theory, the *most mature* adults are likely to gradually disengage themselves from their fellow human beings in preparation for death. They become less interested in their interactions with others, and more concerned with internal concerns. They accept the decreasing attention of a society that views them as losing power.

In a second aspect of the study by the Committee (Havighurst & others, 1968), a distinction is made between social and psychological disengagement. Social disengagement refers to restricting interactions with other human beings; psychological disengagement has to do more with concentrating one's attention within oneself. In a sense, they are opposite sides of the same coin. The results were quite clear: both social and psychological disengagement increase with age. The investigators found that psychological disengagement is more prevalent in a person's 50s, apparently as a precursor to social disengagement, which becomes more apparent in 60 and 70 year olds.

Does this mean that the tendency toward disengagement is more normal than the tendency toward activity? Not necessarily. Researchers found that as disengagement increases, the individual's feelings of happiness also usually decrease. This seems to indicate that activity is more desired by the elderly, but they simply cannot achieve it. On the other hand, the unhappiness that results from disengagement is really quite moderate, which may support the disengagement theory.

In a third part of the Committee's study, reported by Havighurst (1963), it was concluded that there are eight patterns of successful aging. Havighurst explains how each of these eight types view their lives:

1. *Reorganizers*: life satisfaction means preserving a high level of activity and replacing old roles with new ones.

2. *Focused*: life satisfaction means an average amount of role activity and concentration on a few favorite roles and activities.

3. *Disengaged*: involves taking a "back seat" approach in which they have voluntarily withdrawn from role involvement.

4. *Holding on*: only middle-age activities can be enjoyed; if they cannot be enjoyed, then disengagement occurs. Such people are very defensive and reject dependence.

5. *Constricted personality*: life satisfaction is gained by reducing role activity. Such individuals have a less integrated personality.

6. *Succorance-seeking*: life satisfaction is maintained by dependent relationships with others.

7. *Apathetic*: derives little life satisfaction due to limited interests and role activity.

8. *Disorganized*: life satisfaction is minimal because thought processes have deteriorated.

Havighurst and associates (1968) found that, in terms of "successful aging," a person who stays at home and pursues a hobby can be just as happy and adjusted as one who joins many postretirement activities and work. The different personality types have their unique ways of adjusting to life stresses and changing life occurrences.

In summary, neither the activity theory nor the disengagement theory of optimal aging is totally supported by the Committee. The authors conclude that some older persons

❖ *accept this drop in activity as an inevitable accompaniment of growing old; and they succeed in maintaining a sense of self-worth and a sense of satisfaction with past and present life as a whole. Other older persons are less successful in resolving these conflicting elements (Havighurst & others, 1968, p. 171).*

Neugarten (1968) concludes that most elderly persons are conflicted. They wish to remain active in order to maintain their sense of self-worth, but they also wish to withdraw from social commitments in order to protect themselves from the pain of loss, caused by the deaths of people they care about and by thoughts of their own death. She suggests that this conflict is resolved in different ways by people of different personality types; therefore, neither the activity theory nor the disengagement theory can completely explain the process of aging.

Clearly the group on the top is enjoying itself more than the woman on the bottom, but does that mean that the disengagement theory is wrong? Isn't it only natural for people to slowly disengage from society as they approach death?

BOX 22.5

What Kind of Old Person Will You Be?

We expect that most of the readers of this text are college students. If you are of college age, thinking about what it will be like to be old is probably not foremost in your mind. But if you hope to be the kind of person who ends his or her life with a sense of integrity, the time to begin is really now. You don't get to be a happy elderly person unless you plan and work for it. There are many ways to do this, but we have some suggestions to pass along to you.

Whenever you are about to make an important decision, follow these four steps:

1. Come to some tentative conclusion about what you should do.

2. Close your eyes and picture yourself as a 75-year-old woman or man.

3. Imagine yourself explaining your decision to that old person, and try to picture her or him telling you what she or he thinks of what you have decided.

4. If you don't like what you hear, rethink the decision and go through this process again.

Use this technique to get a better perspective on your thinking, and we think you will be surprised by how much wisdom you already have.

Nevertheless, it is unfortunate that some administrators of retirement programs and nursing homes have used the disengagement theory to justify restricting the activities of some elderly. Cath (1975) believes that because some of these individuals have "unconscious gerontophobic [fear of the elderly] attitudes . . ., they interpreted [disengagement] according to their personal motivation and limitation—often colored by financial considerations" (p. 212).

Personal Development—Erikson

For Erikson, resolution of each of the first seven crises in his theory should lead us to achieve a sense of personal **integrity.** Older adults who have a sense of integrity feel their lives have been well spent. The decisions and actions they have taken seem to them to fit together—their lives are *integrated.* They are saddened by the sense that time is running out and that they will not get many more chances to make an impact, but they feel reasonably well satisfied with their achievements. They usually have a sense of having helped to achieve a more dignified life for humankind.

The acceptance of human progress, including one's own, is essential for this final sense of integrity. This is the path to wisdom, which Erikson defines as "the detached and yet active concern with life itself in the face of death itself" (1978, p. 26).

When people look back over their lives and feel that they have made many wrong decisions, or more commonly, that they have frequently not made any decisions at all, they tend to see life as lacking integrity. They feel **despair,** which is the second half of this last stage of crisis. They are angry that there can never be another chance to make their lives make sense. They often hide their fear of death by appearing contemptuous of humanity in general, and those of other religions and races in particular. As Erikson puts it, "Such despair is often hidden behind a show of disgust" (1968, p. 140).

Erikson (1978) has provided a panoramic view of his life cycle theory in an analysis of Swedish film director Ingmar Bergman's famous film *Wild Strawberries.* In this picture, an elderly Swedish doctor goes from his hometown to a large city where he is to be honored for fifty years of service to the medical profession. On the way, he stops by his childhood home and, resting in an old strawberry patch, begins an imaginary journey through his entire life, starting with his earliest memories. In the ruminations of this old man, Erikson sees clear and specific reflections of the eight stages he proposes.

Erikson demonstrates through Bergman's words that, like his other seven stages, this last stage involves a life crisis. Poignantly, the old doctor struggles to make sense out of the events of his life. He is ultimately successful in achieving a sense of integrity. The film is well worth seeing, and Erikson's analysis makes it an even more meaningful experience.

Erikson believes that the character of the old Swedish doctor in Ingmar Bergman's famous film Wild Strawberries, *excellently reflects the eight stages he proposes.*

Transition

Many changes happen during later adulthood. There is a "cross-over" effect in sex roles, sexual activity declines (but not nearly as much as was commonly believed), and the nature of family relationships undergoes several alterations.

As we leave the industrial age and enter the age of "information processing," the nation's older workers experience an incredibly different environment from that of their predecessors of fifty years ago. Even retirement is a much-changed adventure. As in each of the preceding chapters, life appears as never-ending change, but change with discernible patterns. There is, perhaps, more stress in old age than before, but there are also more effective techniques for dealing with it.

In the next, final chapter, we examine the final experience of life, one that is itself often a very significant stressor—dying. We will also review research on the principal method of dealing with both stress and death, and a vital part of life for most Americans: spirituality.

Key Ideas

1. Social change among older adults involves sex roles, sexual practices, family relationships, work roles, and retirement.

2. In later life, males and females return to being more like each other, just as they were as infants.

3. As more is learned about elderly sexuality, the elderly themselves feel less restricted about engaging in it.

4. Family life in later adulthood is a matter of adapting to changes in life-style, including, for many women, living in widowhood.

5. Work and retirement for the elderly have changed greatly in recent years, partly because of new legislation, and partly because of research that has led to a new understanding of the needs of the older worker.

6. In a classic set of studies, the Committee on Human Development investigated the disengagement and the activity theories of aging.

7. Erikson believes that the key crisis for the elderly pits a sense of integrity against a sense of despair.

Key Terms

Activity theory
Age-status
Cross-over
Despair
Differential opportunity structure
Disengagement theory
Existential love

Generative love
Impotency
Integrity
Prostatectomy
Psychic energy
Role discontinuity
Sex-role reversals

What Do You Think?

1. Which would you rather be, an old man or an old woman? Why?

2. What is your position on sex in old age institutions? Should there be any restrictions at all?

3. Which aspect of your family life do you most fear change in as you get old?

4. Which is most right, the activity theory or the disengagement theory?

5. Some have said that whereas Erikson's first seven stages describe crises in which action should be taken, the last stage, integrity versus despair, is merely reactive. All he has the elderly *doing* is sitting in a rocking chair and looking back over their lives. Do you believe that this criticism is valid?

Suggested Readings

Beauvoir, Simone de. (1971) *Coming of age*. This magnificent psychological study gives one an intense look at what it means rather than how it feels to become old.

Cowley, Malcolm. (1980). *The view from 80*. New York: Penguin. Critic Donald Hall describes this book as "Eloquent on the felt disparity between an unchanged self and the costume of altered flesh." Cowley wrote this intensely personal book when he himself was 82.

Publications of the American Association of Retired Persons (AARP). With about 30 million members, the powerful AARP is a rich source of information on the elderly. Write to them in Washington, D.C.

Roff, Lucinda, and Charles Atherton. (1989). *Promoting successful aging*. Chicago: Nelson-Hall. This readable book is half about theory and research and half about the specific strategies for dealing with the needs of the elderly. A bible for those who want to work with older adults.

· *Chapter 23* ·

Dying and Spirituality

The Role of Death in Life

When the time did come, though, Margaret Mead was ready. When she learned that she had a generally fatal form of cancer, she refused to let it slow her down. Instead, the scientist who had spent a lifetime observing others turned her still keen powers of observation on herself, and continued to keep her thorough records on her own process of aging. Her attention was appropriate. Of all the people she studied, few were as interesting as Mead herself (Jones, 1978).

Americans, who have long been accused of abhorring the subject of death, are now giving it considerable attention. From the ways we teach the young about death (Duncan, 1979; Gutierrez, 1978; Lown, 1978; Pack, 1978; Williams, 1979) to the ways in which we bury our dead (Cassell, 1979; Fulton & Markusen, 1979; Pine, 1979; Schneider, 1984; Swanson & Bennett, 1983), we seem to have switched to an eager confrontation of the problem.

In this section, we review research and theory from the social and physical sciences to examine three major concerns: What is death? How do we deal with the death of others? How do we deal with our own death?

What Is Death?

The matter of my friend rests heavy upon me.
How can I be salved?
How can I be stilled?
My friend, who I loved, has turned to clay.
Must I, too, lie me down
Not to rise again for ever and ever?

Gilgamesh, c. 2,000 B.C.

In the movies, death is almost invariably portrayed in the same sequence: dying people make a final statement, close their eyes, fall back on the pillow or into the arms of a loved one, and are pronounced dead. In fact, death rarely occurs that way (Veatch, 1981, 1984). In most cases, the person dies gradually. "Death is a process, not a moment" (Schulz, 1978, p. 90).

Ascertaining when people are truly and finally dead has been a medical problem for centuries. For example, in the early 1900s, Franz Hartmann claimed to have collected approximately 700 cases of premature burial or "close calls" (Hardt, 1979). In 1896 the "Society for the Prevention of Premature Burial" was founded. Fear of premature burial was so strong that in 1897 in Berlin a patent was granted for a life signal device that sent up a warning flag and turned on a light if there was movement inside the coffin.

We no longer have any serious problem in determining whether or not a person is dead. But determining exactly *when* death occurred has come to be of even greater importance because of organ donations. All the body's systems do not cease simultaneously, so there are disagreements over which system is most significant in judging whether a person is dead.

Since the first historian, Homer, began recording the lives of the Greeks, the meaning of death has been a central issue.

Four Types of Death

Today, four types of death are recognized: clinical death, brain death, biological or cellular death, and social death.

Clinical Death

In one sense, the individual is dead when his or her respiration and heartbeat have stopped. This is the aspect of dying that is referred to in the movies when the doctor turns and sadly announces "I'm sorry, but he's gone." Actually, **clinical death** is the least useful to the medical profession and to society at large because it is unreliable.

Since the advent of **cardiopulmonary resuscitation** (CPR), many individuals whose lungs and heart had ceased to function were saved. In other cases, spontaneous restarting of the heart and lungs has occurred after failure.

Brain Death

Death of the brain occurs when it fails to receive a sufficient supply of oxygen for a short period of time (usually 8 to 10 minutes). The cessation of brain function occurs in three stages: first, the cortex stops, then the midbrain fails, and finally the brain stem ceases to function. When the cortex and midbrain stop operating, **brain death** has occurred and the person enters an irreversible coma. The body can remain alive in this condition for a long time, because the autonomic processes are governed by the brain stem. Consciousness and alertness, however, will never be regained.

Biological Death

The cells and the organs of the body can remain in a functioning condition long after the failure of the heart and lungs. **Biological death** occurs when it is no longer possible to discern an electrical charge in the tissues of the heart and lungs.

Social Death

Sudnow (1967) has suggested the concept of **social death,** which "within the hospital setting, is marked at that point in which a patient is treated essentially as a corpse although perhaps still 'clinically' or 'biologically' alive" (p. 74). He cites cases in which body preparations (e.g., closing the eyes, binding the feet) were started while the patient was still alive, in order to make things easier for the staff. Also, in some cases, autopsy permissions have been signed by the family members while the patient was still alive.

So when is a person really dead? If a person has suffered brain death, but the heart is still beating, should the heart be removed and used for a transplant operation? Schulz (1978) cites a case in Texas in which the heart of a man killed in a fight was removed for a transplant. The autopsy that is usually required in such cases was not performed. Later, the doctor who did the transplant was brought to a court. He was accused by the defense attorney of the man's killer of being the one actually responsible for the man's death, because he may have acted too soon. Since the doctor had received prior permission to remove the heart, he was not found at fault. The case illustrates the complexity and extreme importance of defining the moment of legal death.

Another complex case (Goldsmith, 1988) involved the Loma Linda University Medical Center, famous for its work in the area of organ transplants. They attempted to initiate a program that would provide scarce organs for transplants. In this program, healthy hearts and other organs would be taken from babies born with anencephaly, a condition where part or all of the brain is missing at birth. Ninety-five percent of these babies die within one week. When the anencephalic infants were born, they were flown to Loma Linda and given traditional "comfort care" (warmth, nutrition, and hydration). In addition, they were put on artificial breathing support for a maximum of seven days. The hospital maintained that they were put on respirators until a technical definition of brain death could be ascertained. But critics contended that this was done because the organs needed the time to mature for a successful transplant to occur. A storm of controversy ended the program before any donations could be made. Critics accused the hospital of "organ farming." The

It is possible to ensure that all or part of your body be donated for use after your death, usually by a designation on your driver's license. Have you done this? If not, why do you think you have refrained from doing so?

hospital argued that it was not only trying to increase the number of organ donors for infants but giving the families of anencephalic babies an opportunity to "turn their tragedy into something good." With the advent of more advanced technology, the distinction between life and death becomes blurred and the ethical considerations grow increasingly complex.

The Legal Definition of Death

In 1968 the "Harvard Ad Hoc Committee to Examine the Criteria of Brain Death" suggested the following criteria for **legal death:** "Unreceptivity and unresponsivity, no movements or breathing, no reflexes, and a flat **electroencephalogram** (EEG) reading that remains flat for 24 hours" (Schulz, 1978, p. 98).

Such criteria preclude the donation of organs in most cases, because the organs would probably suffer irreparable damage in the 24 hours needed to check the EEG. Others have suggested that the time at which the cerebral cortex has been irreparably damaged should be accepted as the time when organs can be removed from the body.

Organ donation is not the only difficulty involved. An increasing number of cases illustrate the ethical problem created by maintaining the life of the comatose individuals with the support of technical equipment. A number of medical personnel, philosophers, and theorists have suggested that maintaining life under these conditions is wrong. What do you think?

Although scientists may disagree on the exact nature of death itself, we have been learning a great deal about how people deal, and how they *should* deal, with the death of their loved ones. We turn to that subject now.

Dealing Successfully With the Death of Others

> *Representative Bryan had the true passion of a runner. It's a shame he's gone, but I can't help feeling that he might not have regretted the manner of his death. Outdoors on a brisk autumn afternoon, in the company of a friend, with a feeling of life in all of the nerve ends that a long life excites (McCarthy, 1979, p. 120).*

In modern Western societies, death comes mostly to the old. For example, 55% of all males are 65 or over when they die, and almost a third are past 75. The mortality rate has declined in our country from 17 per 1,000 population in 1900 to slightly less than 9 per 1,000 today. For the first time in history a family may expect to live twenty years (on the average) without one of its members dying.

The causes of this lower mortality are clear: virtual elimination of infant and child mortality, and increasing control over the diseases of youth and middle age. For this reason, the subject of death became more and more taboo in the first half of this century. Probably as a result, social scientists spent little time studying our reactions to it or trying to find better ways to help us deal with it. Fortunately, in recent decades, this has changed.

Grief Work

> *No one ever told me that grief felt so like fear. I am not afraid, but the sensation is like being afraid. The same fluttering in the stomach, the same restlessness, the yawning. I keep on swallowing (Lewis, 1963, p. 7).*

In fact, grief has a great deal in common with fear, and most grieving people really are afraid, at least unconsciously. They are frightened by the strength of their feelings, and they often fear that they are losing their sanity. They feel that they cannot go on, that their loss is so great that their own lives are in danger.

In fact, in some cases they are. Seligman (1975) notes documented cases in which persons have died as a direct cause of grief. Most people who have experienced a loss of a loved one have felt that they never want to love that deeply again. Fortunately, when the grieving is over at last, most people find a renewed capacity and desire to love, together with a deepened capacity to do so. As Kübler-Ross (1975) puts it, "If we choose to love, we must also have the courage to grieve" (p. 96).

Grief not only *follows* death; when there is advanced warning, it frequently precedes it. Fulton (1977) finds that there are four phases in anticipatory grief: depression, a heightened concern for the ill person, rehearsal of death, and finally an attempt to adjust to the consequences that are likely to occur after the death.

The topic of anticipatory grief has received increasing attention lately. There have been major debates about its exact nature. For example, Hill and associates (1988) found that those widows who had anticipated their husband's death reported a higher level of mental health than those who had not. Most researchers agree that a forewarning of the impending death of a loved one can have therapeutic consequences (Parke & Weiss, 1983):

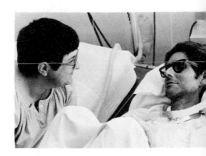

Anticipatory grief, which precedes the sick person's death, is usually very difficult. It often provides a number of benefits to the grieving, however.

- Avoiding the shock and fear that often accompanies sudden death

- Being able to make plans for the future that won't be regarded as betrayals

- Expressing thoughts and feelings to the dying loved ones, thereby avoiding a sense of lost opportunity

- A time to prepare for the changes ahead

But researchers disagree over whether an actual grief process is experienced before the death. Some say that true grief and an actual confrontation of the realities of the death of a loved one can come only after the death has occurred (Silverman, 1974; Parke & Weiss, 1983). Other scientists contend that there is some type of grieving process at work when a person is forewarned of an impending death. One need only look at the anguish of a parent or spouse to recognize it. This process should not be expected to take the same form as post-death grieving and surely won't fully reconcile those who grieve to the realities ahead (Rando, 1986).

Rando (1986) and others have begun to devise therapeutic intervention techniques to facilitate the unique aspects of anticipatory grief. As medical technology increasingly makes it possible to at least stall death, such work will continue to grow in importance.

Stages of Grief After an Unexpected Death

In his study of persons dealing with the unexpected death of a loved one (most notably the relatives of victims of the Coconut Grove fire in Boston), Lindemann (1944) posited three stages of grief:

- An initial period of shock followed by intense emotionality

- An intermediate phase in which the individual has to break emotional ties with the deceased

- A recovery period in which the individual forms new relationships

Other studies, reviewed by Schulz (1978), support Lindemann's findings. Lindemann refers to the process of grieving as *grief work* and argues that it is essential to go through each of the stages.

1. *Initial shock and emotionality.* The numbness and disbelief that characterize most people's reaction to death allow time for the person to

summon strength to deal with the situation. Disbelief or denial provide a cushion, almost a sense of hope, while the person is trying to grasp the enormity of the pronouncement. Typical of the emotionality that follows the shock are five basic symptoms: physical distress; preoccupation with the image of the deceased; intense guilt feelings; hostile reactions and anger; and distortion of normal patterns of conduct. Physical distress includes feelings of choking and tightness in the throat, a need to sigh, a feeling of emptiness in the abdomen, weakness, and headaches.

2. *Intermediate distress.* During the phase of intermediate distress, the person is preoccupied with thoughts about the deceased, and relives and recounts the events leading up to the death. Guilt is usually manifested, together with thoughts about what should have been done differently to prevent the death.

In his ground-breaking book *Mourning and Melancholia* (1915, 1957), Freud expressed the belief that this process is essential in the gradual breaking of emotional ties to the deceased. Attachment is achieved through calling to mind each memory of interaction with the deceased, and realizing that it is a memory, rather than anticipation of the future.

Hostility and anger are frequently expressed, quite inappropriately, toward anyone who had anything to do with the death, such as medical personnel and clergy. Fury at God is also common at this time. These strong emotions frequently cause distorted patterns of conduct, the result of thought disorganization. For example, the grieving individual frequently is incapable of making decisions, and is willing to allow others to decide important questions.

This stage often lasts as long as a year, while the individual learns to live in an environment where the deceased was once an integral part. The reality of death is gradually understood and accepted emotionally as well as intellectually. Schulz (1978) believes that three behavior patterns are common in this stage: an "obsessional review" of all the memories related to the deceased; a "search for an understanding of death"; and a "search for the presence of the deceased" (p. 141).

3. *The recovery phase.* Generally, after living through a year of important dates and occasions, including the first anniversary of the death, the bereaved person progresses to the third state. New relationships begin to be formed and a new sense of purpose develops. Gradually, memories of the deceased bring warm feelings rather than the intense pain of the loss.

Pathological Grieving

The stages described, painful as they are, are experienced by most individuals. In some cases, however, morbid grief reactions occur that prevent the successful conclusion of the life crisis. There are three types: delayed reaction; distorted reaction; and pathological mourning.

Delayed Reaction

In some cases, the intense reaction of the first stage is postponed for days, months, and in some cases years. In these cases, it is common for some seemingly unrelated incident to bring to the surface an intense grieving, which the individual does not even recognize.

Lindemann (1944) gives the example of a 42-year-old man who underwent therapy to deal with an unaccountable depression. It was soon discovered that when

---

BOX 23.1

A Personal Experience of One of the Authors

I would like to step out of my role as "objective observer" and relate an experience of mine that is relevant to this discussion of the function of grief. In April 1957, I joined the United States Navy and sailed to the Mediterranean for a six-month tour of duty on an oil supply ship. In early November I returned home to a joyful reunion with my family. After this wonderful weekend at home, I returned to my ship. Two days later I received a telegram informing me of a tragedy: my mother, two younger brothers, and two younger sisters had been killed in a fire that had destroyed our house. My father and three younger brothers and a sister had escaped with serious burns.

On the long train ride home from the naval port, I recall thinking that, as the oldest, I should be especially helpful to my father in the terrible time ahead. I was also aware of a curious absence of dismay in myself.

In our medium-sized upstate New York town, the catastrophe was unprecedented, and expressions of grief and condolences were myriad. People kept saying to me, "Don't try to be so brave. It's good for you to let yourself cry." And I tried to, but tears just wouldn't come.

At the funeral, the caskets were closed, and I can remember thinking that maybe, just maybe, this was all just a horrible dream. I distinctly remember one fantasy about my brother Mike. He was born on my first birthday and in the several years before the fire, I had become especially close to him. I imagined that he had actually hit his head trying to escape and had wandered off to Chicago with a case of amnesia, and that no one was willing to admit that they didn't know where he was. I knew this wasn't true, but yet I secretly clung to the possibility. After a very difficult period of time, our family gradually began a new life. Many people generously helped us, and eventually the memories faded.

Several times in the years that followed, I went to doctors because of a stomach ache, a painful stiff neck, or some other malady that couldn't be diagnosed physically. One doctor suggested that I might be suffering from an unresolved subconscious problem, but I doubted it.

Then one night in 1972, fifteen years after the fire, I was watching "The Walton's Christmas," a television show in which the father of a close family is lost and feared dead. Although dissimilar from my own experience, this tragedy triggered an incredible response in me. Suddenly and finally it occurred to me: "My God, half my family is really gone forever!" I began sobbing and could not stop for over three hours. When I finally stopped, I felt weak and empty, relieved of an awful burden. In the days that followed I believe I went through a clear-cut "delayed grief" reaction.

Therefore, the answer to the question, at least in my experience, is clear: grief work really is essential, and we avoid it only at the cost of even greater pain. My father died some years ago, and my grief was immediate and intense. I cannot help but feel that my emotional response this time was considerably more appropriate and healthy.

---

he was 22, his 42-year-old mother committed suicide. Apparently, the occurrence of his own forty-second birthday brought to the surface all the feelings that he had managed to repress since that time.

Distorted Reactions

In most cases distorted reactions are normal symptoms carried to an extreme degree. They include adopting the behavior traits of the deceased, such as aspects of the deceased's fatal illness and other types of psychosomatic ailments, particularly colitis, arthritis, and asthma.

An example we know of is a young man whose mother died of lymphomic cancer. At her death, she had large boils on her neck. Some weeks after she died, her son discovered lumps on his neck that quickly developed into boils. On examination, it was found that they were benign. In fact, it was determined that they were entirely psychosomatic. That is, the doctors decided that the only explanation of their existence was the great stress in the young man's mind over the loss of his mother.

Pathological Mourning

In pathological mourning, the stages are not skipped but they are prolonged and intensified to an abnormal degree. Frequently, the person suffering from pathological mourning tries to preserve every object of the deceased in perpetual memory.

An example of this illness is the man who worked hard with his wife to renovate an old cottage they had bought in order to live by a lake not far from their home. A few days before they were going to move in, she died of a heart attack. Some months later, friends noticed that he would disappear for several days at a time. One friend followed him to the cottage, and found that he had created a shrine to her memory in it. Her clothes and other possessions were laid out in all the rooms, and her picture was on all the walls. Only after extensive therapy was he able to give up the shrine.

The Role of Grief

Most psychologists who have examined the role of grief have concluded that it is an essential aspect of a healthy encounter with the crisis of death. They believe that open confrontation with the loss of a loved one is essential to accepting the reality of a world in which the deceased is no longer present. Attempts to repress or avoid thoughts about the loss are only going to push them into the subconscious, where they will continue to cause problems until they are dragged out and accepted fully.

And yet, dealing with grief is also costly. For example, Fulton (1977) found that the mortality rate among grieving persons is seven times higher than a matched sample of nongrieving persons. The first five items on Holmes and Rahe's *Social Readjustment Rating Scale* (see chap. 18) all involve separation and loss from loved ones. These five most stressful events, in descending order, are death of a spouse, divorce, marital separation, going to jail, and death of a close family member. These events and the grief attached to them are most likely to cause illness.

On the other hand, anthropologist Norman Klein (1978) has suggested that psychologists may be too insistent that our grief be public and deep:

❖ *In our own society, faddish therapies stress the idea that expressing sorrow, anger, or pain is a good thing, and the only means for "dealing with one's feelings" honestly . . . yet it is surely conceivable that some Americans can work through grief internally and privately, without psychological cost. It is even more conceivable that whole cultural subgroups may have different ways of conceding and responding to such experience (p. 122).*

Klein goes on to cite the Japanese, who are most reticent about public grief and yet seem to suffer no ill effects from this reticence. The Balinese frequently laugh at the time of death, because, they say, they are trying to avoid crying; yet they seem to be psychologically healthy. Some cultures employ "keeners" who wail loudly so that the bereaved will not have to do so themselves.

Is the expression of grief essential? At this time, the studies of social and medical scientists do not offer us a conclusive answer.

The Role of the Funeral

One of the hardest aspects of dealing with the death of a loved one is deciding how the funeral (if there is to be one) is to be conducted. Funerals have always been an important part of American life, as demonstrated by the elaborate burial rituals practiced by Native Americans. Some research indicates that the rituals surrounding funerals have a therapeutic benefit that facilitates the grieving process (Bolton & Camp, 1989; Kraeer, 1981; Rando, 1983).

Once the intimate responsibility of each family, care for the dead in the United States has been transferred to a paid service industry. The need for this new service was brought about by changes in society during the first part of this century. The more mobile, urbanized workforce had less family support and less time to devote to the task of caring for the dead. In a relatively short time, funeral homes and funeral directors became the accepted form of care for one's dead relatives (Fulton & Owen, 1988).

In your opinion, what are the appropriate arrangements for a funeral? Are you in favor of formal religious services or not? Why or why not?

This commercialization of care for the dead has had mixed results. During the 1950s and 1960s, funeral homes came under stinging criticism for their expense and their lack of sensitivity to the needs of the surviving family members (Bowman, 1959; Mitford, 1963). The bereaved often felt that the funeral directors were more interested in dramatic and expensive presentations of the body rather than what might be best for the family members.

A more current survey has revealed that only about 42% of funeral directors have had any formal education in the physical and psychological effects of the death of a loved one, and most of those who had some education felt it was inadequate (Weeks, 1989). Recent trends such as cremations and memorial services without the body (often because some body parts have been donated for transplants or science research) have relieved people of the more unpleasant and expensive aspects of funeral services.

In Box 23.2, a view of the various ways of burying the dead over the centuries is presented.

Dealing Successfully With One's Own Death

> *Having nearly died, I've found death like that sweet feeling that people have that let themselves slide into sleep. I believe that this is the same feeling that people find themselves in whom we see fainting in the agony of death, and I maintain that we pity them without cause. If you know not how to die, never trouble yourself. Nature will in a moment fully and sufficiently instruct you; she will exactly do that business for you; take you no care for it. (Michel de Montaigne, "Of Physiognomy" 1585–88).*

Why is the acceptance of death so painful to so many of us? Why does it come up in every developmental stage, only to be partially resolved and partially denied?

Many people find dying a much harder experience than Montaigne would have us believe it is. Many dying patients feel seriously depressed before their deaths, and a large number have suicidal feelings. Among the reasons for these depressions are the following:

- Medication-induced mood alterations

- Awareness of how little time is left

BOX 23.2

Multicultural Focus: The Funeral Throughout History

Looking at the funeral practices of former cultures shows us not only how they buried their dead but something about their values.

Ancient Egypt

Upon the death of the head of the house in ancient Egypt, women would rush frantically through the streets, beating their breasts from time to time and clutching their hair. The body of the deceased was removed as soon as possible to the embalming chambers, where a priest, a surgeon, and a team of assistants proceeded with the embalming operation. (The Egyptians believed in the life beyond; embalming was intended to protect the body for this journey.) While the body was being embalmed, arrangements for the final entombment began. When the mummified corpse was ready for the funeral procession and installation in its final resting place, it was placed on a sledge drawn by oxen or men and accompanied by wailing servants, professional mourners simulating anguished grief, and relatives. It was believed that when the body was placed in an elaborate tomb (family wealth and prestige exerted an obvious influence on tomb size), its spirits would depart and later return through a series of ritualistic actions.

Ancient Greece

Reverence for the dead permeated burial customs during all phases of ancient Greek civilization. Within a day after death the body was washed, anointed, dressed in white, and laid out in state for one to seven days, depending on the social prestige of the deceased. Family and friends could view the corpse during this time. For the funeral procession, the body was placed on a bier carried by friends and relatives and followed by female mourners, fraternity members, and hired dirge singers. Inside the tomb were artistic ornaments, jewels, vases and articles of play and war. Like the Egyptians, the ancient Greeks prepared their tombs and arranged for subsequent care while they were still alive. About 1000 B.C. the Greeks began to cremate their dead. While earth burial was never entirely superseded, the belief in the power of the flame to free the soul acted as a strong impetus to the practice of cremation. A choice of inhumation (burial) or cremation was available during all late Greek periods.

The Roman Empire

Generally speaking, the Romans envisioned some type of afterlife and, like the Greeks, practiced both cremation and earth burial. When a wealthy person died, the body was dressed in a white toga and placed on a funeral couch, feet to the door, to lie in state for several days. For reasons of sanitation, burial within the walls of Rome was prohibited;

Source: Turner & Helms, 1989, pp. 492–493.

- Feelings of isolation from relatives and friends who are withdrawing
- Feelings of grief for the losses that are close at hand
- Feelings of disillusion and resentment over injustice

The increased feeling of depression was the greatest difference between a group of terminal and nonterminal cancer patients (Schulz, 1978). This depression is sometimes described as cognitive withdrawal, because many patients have a decreasing ability and/or motivation to process stimuli as death nears (see *terminal drop,* chap. 21). Also common is a strong sense of fear and a deep sense of sorrow (Feifel, 1977).

Must dying, then, always be such an unhappy experience? It is really more complicated than that, according to the European psychiatrist Elisabeth Kübler-Ross.

BOX 23.2

Continued

---

consequently, great roads outside the city were lined with elaborate tombs erected for the well-to-do. For the poor, there was no such magnificence; for slaves and aliens, there was a common burial pit outside the city walls.

Anglo-Saxon England

In Anglo-Saxon England (approximately the time when invading Low German tribes conquered the country in the fifth century), the body of the deceased was placed on a bier or in a hearse. On the corpse was laid the book of the Gospels as a symbol of faith and the cross as a symbol of hope. For the journey to the grave, a pall of silk or linen was placed over the corpse. The funeral procession included priests bearing lighted candles and chanting psalms, friends who had been summoned, relatives, and strangers who deemed it their duty as a corporal work of mercy to join the party. Mass was then sung for the dead, the body was solemnly laid in the grave (generally without a coffin), the mortuary fee was paid from the estate of the deceased, and liberal alms were given to the poor.

Colonial New England

Burials and funeral practices were models of simplicity and quiet dignity in eighteenth-century New England. Upon death, neighbors (or possibly a nurse if the family was well-to-do) would wash and lay out the body. The local carpenter or cabinetmaker would build the coffin, selecting a quality of wood to fit the social position of the deceased. In special cases, metal decorations imported from England were used on the coffin. In church, funeral services consisted of prayers and sermons said over the pall-covered bier. Funeral sermons often were printed (with skull and crossbones prominently displayed) and circulated among the public. The funeral service at the grave was simple, primarily a brief prayer followed by the ritual commitment of the body to the earth. The filling of the grave, with neighbors frequently supplying the necessary labor because there were no professional gravediggers, marked the formal end of the early-colonial funeral ceremony.

Let's hope it won't happen, but what would you do if you were called upon to organize a funeral tomorrow? Would you know whom to notify? How would you arrange for the preparation and disposition of the body? What kind of ceremony, religious or otherwise, would you ask for? What would you do about a funeral home, a cemetery plot, and the will and death benefits of the deceased?

Perhaps you could discuss this with some of your friends or classmates, to see how they would feel. Take note of how you feel about your differences of opinions with them.

Kübler-Ross—The Stages of Dying

Dr. Kübler-Ross is the most famous student of the process of death. Her three books on the subject have all been best sellers: *On Death and Dying* (1969), *Death—The Final Stage of Growth* (1975), and *To Live Until We Say Goodbye* (1978).

Kübler-Ross discovered that, far from wanting to avoid the topic of death, many dying patients have a strong urge to discuss it. She interviewed hundreds of terminally ill persons. On the basis of these interviews, she developed a five-stage theory, describing the emotions that underlie the process of dying. The stages in her theory are flexible, in that people can move through them quickly, slowly, or not at all. There is some fluctuation between the stages, but by and large people tend to move through them in sequential order. The recognition of these stages has had a great impact on professionals and others, so the stages are described in some detail here. They are portrayed in Figure 23.1.

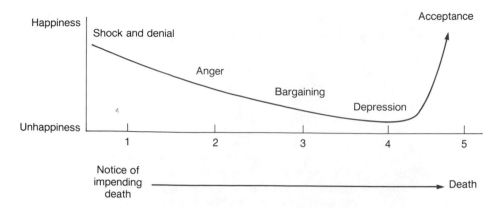

Figure 23.1 *Kübler-Ross' stages of dying.*

Source: E. Kübler-Ross, *On Death and Dying.* Copyright © 1969 Macmillan Publishing Company, New York, NY.

1. <u>*Shock and denial.*</u> The defense mechanism of denial is a very basic one. It protects the individual by filtering out information that threatens the person's equilibrium. As with the first stage of grief, denial allows time for the person to gather strength and to marshall other defenses. Dr. Laurens Weisman (cited in Feifel, 1977) suggests that

❖ *Most of us have come to view denial as a bad thing, and to see those persons who use denial as making some sort of error. A long series of patients, who have taught me so much else, have also convinced me that denial is not necessarily a mistake, particularly in patients who have to face certain realities (p. 100).*

Apparently, denial helps prevent many persons from being overwhelmed by initial shock. Typically, such persons go from doctor to doctor hoping to receive a different diagnosis. They hope desperately that a phone call will come, explaining that the test results were mixed up, and that the correct diagnosis will show only a minor illness.

Dying persons also often use the defense mechanism of *compartmentalization.* That is, they simultaneously hold contradictory beliefs. For example, a patient may admit that she is going to die soon, but still discuss her long-term plans for the future. Another patient may say that he believes that death is imminent, but also really doubts it.

2. <u>*Anger.*</u> The most common feeling at this stage is, "Why me?" Strong feelings of resentment toward others, and especially envy of healthy individuals, prevail. Kübler-Ross suggests that this is usually the most difficult stage for everyone involved, because "this anger is misplaced in almost all directions and projected onto the environment at times almost at random" (1969, p. 50). It is not unusual for patients to suffer full-blown paranoia at this time, suspecting that someone is "trying to get them." Nevertheless, the anger stage is essential and usually passes into Stage Three rather rapidly.

3. <u>*Bargaining.*</u> Now the individual tries to think of ways to postpone death. Most of these bargains are made with God. The person makes some kind of deal in which, if spared, he or she will undertake some unusual sacrifice to help others. This kind of thinking is similar to the so-called

magical thinking often seen in young children, where they feel responsible for causing events over which they could not possibly have control. When the individual realizes that there is no hope in this direction, a period of depression almost always sets in.

4. *Depression.* As was stated earlier in this section, depression is common in dying persons, and serious depression has been found in approximately half the cases. Kübler-Ross refers to this as *preparatory depression,* because it usually functions as an attempt to anticipate the future loss of one's life. In this, it is similar to anticipatory grief. It is also a clear instance of disengagement (see chap. 21).

Family members and others often work at cross purposes to the patient at this time. The patient is trying to get ready to leave, and the family keeps encouraging him or her to hang on a little longer. The patient is often confused by a jumble of feelings. For some, especially those in pain, there is guilt at wanting to die.

There is considerable evidence that people have at least minimal control of the exact time when they die. For example, some patients, even those in considerable pain, manage to linger on, waiting for a birthday, holiday, or some significant person to arrive before letting go of life.

Kavanaugh (1972) suggests that there are two prerequisites at this stage for peaceful, dignified dying:

❖ *First, the dying person needs to receive permission to pass away from every important person he will leave behind. Only then can he go on to the other problem, the need to let go of every person whose possession he holds dear (p. 75).*

A friend of ours who is a surgeon tells us that even those poor souls who have no one close to them at the time of their dying seem to need permission to go. In such cases, he says, he finds he is the only one who can say it is all right, and so he does.

5. *Acceptance.* In the final stage of dying, a peaceful time almost devoid of feeling sets in. The patient withdraws from others and from worldly concerns, and more calmly awaits death. Kübler-Ross describes this acceptance as being neither happy nor resigned but as a quiet time of contemplation. There is a certain degree of quiet expectation.

Erikson (1963) believes that dying persons can be categorized into one of two groups. He says that some are characterized by a sense of *despair,* which is exemplified by their strong fear of death. They act as though they cannot accept the life they have lived:

❖ *The lack of this accrued ego integration is signified by fear of death: the one and only life cycle is not accepted as the ultimate of life. Despair expresses the feeling that time is now too short, too short to start another life and to try out alternate roads to integrity (pp. 268–269).*

Others feel that their lives have been well lived. They are suffused with a sense of *integrity,* and they can view their impending death with equanimity.

No matter how well prepared we are, death is always sad and stressful. Most of the time, though, we know that there is nothing we can do about it, and so we must accept the inevitable. How different it is when the death was not inevitable, but was chosen by the person because life had become no longer worth living.

Suicide—The Saddest Death

The Overall Picture

Suicide and attempted suicide among adolescents are a growing national problem (Holinger & others, 1987) and an increasingly common response to stress and depression among young persons (Kienhorst & others, 1987). Suicide now ranks as the second leading cause of death among persons age 15 to 19, and many experts believe that if no suicides were "covered up," it would be the leading cause. Teenagers have not only become more suicidal but apparently more reckless and self-destructive in general. As the suicide rate has risen steadily over the past twenty years, so too has the rate for motor vehicle accidents (the leading cause of death), accidents of other types, and homicides (Bem, 1987; Vital Statistics of the U.S., 1982).

Although suicide rates for teenagers have risen 72% since 1986, the rate for most other age groups has decreased. It would be safe to say that while the United States as a whole has become slightly less suicidal, teenagers and young people in general (age 30 and under) have become dramatically more suicidal. The increase has risen most steadily and most consistently among teenagers.

There are two groups that are much more prone to suicide, however: the so-called middle-old and old-old groups. While the suicide rate for 15–24 years olds is high—12.5 per 100,000—the rate for those 75 and older is almost double that, with males accounting for almost all the difference (U.S. National Center for Health Statistics, 1986). In fact, the older single white male is by far the person most likely to die of suicide. Woodruff-Pak (1988) states that adolescent suicides are paid more attention to because they are usually in good health. For the elderly, poor health is often both a cause of suicide and a way of covering it up. Loneliness is a second major factor.

Woodruff-Pak relates the story of an elderly retiree from the police force who had made an excellent adjustment to leaving the force. When he discovered that he had a large brain tumor, however, he became very depressed at the thought of leaving his wife, children, and nine grandchildren, to all of whom he was deeply attached. One day, after asking his wife to go to the store for his favorite candy, he shot himself. His wife discovered him and threw away his pistol. She told the paramedics she saw a man fleeing from her house. The "case" remained unsolved, and she was able to bury her husband in a Catholic cemetery.

It is in the area of attempted suicide that adolescents are truly a distinctive population (Rotherham, 1987; Spirito & others, 1987). Weisman (1974) attributed 50% of all attempted suicides to those under the age of 30, and points out that the modal age is dropping. It is believed that there are 200 to 300 suicide attempts for every committed suicide in the 15–19-year-old age group; estimates range from 220 to 1 (McIntire, 1980) to 312 to 1 (Curran, 1984). There are no official estimates of suicide attempts since data of this type is very difficult to gather and assess on a national scale.

It is estimated that the actual rate of adolescent suicide is as much as 50% greater than the official figure (Burvill, 1982; Frederick, 1971; Malla, 1983; Weiner, 1970). Holinger (1979) and Phillips (1979) have suggested that a significant number of fatal single-car accidents are in fact undetected suicides. It is a commonly stated suicide fantasy among teenagers to die in a car crash.

The Influence of Race and Place of Residence on Suicide

Suicidal behavior remains, as it has consistently for decades, a behavior in which whites (Vital Statistics of the U.S., 1982) and the middle class (Jacobziner, 1965;

Table 23.1 Suicide Rates per 100,000 by Gender—1985			
White Males **White Females** **Black Males** **Black Females**			
All Ages* 19.9 5.3 11.3 2.1			
Age Group	Females		Males
15–24	4.4		21.4
25–34	5.9		24.5
35–44	7.1		22.3
45–54	8.3		25.5
55–64	7.7		26.8
65–74	6.9		33.9
75–84	6.8		53.1
85+	4.6		55.4

***Total Males** 17.4 **Females** 4.9
Source: *Statistical Abstracts of the United States, 1988.*

Tishler, 1981; Weisman, 1974) are overrepresented. A comparative chart for white versus African-American suicide rates is presented in Table 23.1.

In regard to place of residence, since the late 1960s persons from rural areas have had a higher rate of suicide than those from urban areas (Wilkinson & Isreal, 1984).

The Influence of Gender on Suicide

Table 23.1 also presents the suicide rates by gender. As is obvious from looking at this table, major gender differences exist. The rate for males is much higher because of the type of suicidal behavior engaged in, the methods used, the lethality of the attempt, and the degree of psychiatric disturbance present. Males and females are two very different suicidal types.

Universally, males are 3.6 times more likely to die of suicide than females. For adolescents in the United States, a ratio of more than 4 to 1 is being reported (Vital Statistics of U.S., 1982). This difference is even greater between white male (14.6) and female (3.4) teenagers.

Attempt rates show even more dramatic gender differences, but in the opposite direction. *Failed* attempts at suicide among females are much higher than for males (Woodruff-Pak, 1988). The literature consistently has cited female-to-male ratios of at least 3 to 1. Jacobziner (1965), Weiner (1970), and White (1974) reported ratios of four to one. More recent studies show a far greater number of females among teenage suicide attempters: 5 to 1 (Curran, 1984), 9 to 1 (Hawton 1982b, 1982c; McIntire, 1980), 9.5 to 1 (Birtchnell & Alarcon, 1971), and 10 to 1 (Toolan, 1975).

A major reason for the high survival rate among females is the method used. While males often resort to such violent and effective means as firearms and hanging, females tend to choose less violent and less deadly means, such as pills. Male suicidals are considered to be significantly more disturbed than female (Hawton, 1982a, 1982b, 1982c; Otto, 1972; Teicher, 1973). Males are usually more committed to dying and therefore succeed far more often.

Sad and stressful though all dying is, some ways of doing it seem better than others. And it does matter. Whether you believe in Heaven and Hell in an afterlife, reincarnation back on earth, or some variation of the two, how one dies must have an effect on these results. And even if you believe death leads to an eternity of nothingness, how you die can greatly influence the lives of those you leave behind. In this next section, we look at several proposals for "successful dying."

Males are three to four times more likely to die of suicide attempts than are females.

BOX 23.3

My Attempts at Suicide (Anonymous)

My first psychiatrist told my parents that my psychological tests indicated that I was potentially suicidal. I was 14 then. At 22, I had made five suicide attempts and had been in six mental institutions, which add up to 29 months as a mental patient and five years of intensive therapy. My diagnosis was borderline schizophrenia, chronic depression, and sadomasochism. Why? How had I become so obsessed with suicide?

When I flash back on my adolescent days, I remember feeling ugly, socially awkward, stuck away in an all-girls' boarding school reading Camus and Hesse, unpopular, and stupid! In fact, I was not quite as dreadful as all that, but in my mind I was. I felt different. I once wrote, "I'm at the bottom of an upside-down garbage can and it's so ugly." The world was horrible, but I was the worst part of it.

Suicide was my escape. Unsuccessful suicide attempts put me in the care of others who delicately forced me to confront my feelings of sadness and anger. I had to learn to share with others and sometimes that was what I secretly wanted. Two of my attempts, however, were calculated, purposeful acts. Despite what shrinks may say, I wanted to be dead, not taken care of.

What did death mean to me? One of my earliest memories is sitting on moss-covered ground in a grove of pines, reading *The Prayer for the Dead* with my basset hound curled up beside me. Suicide meant escape from hell on earth. No other purgatory could be worse than this one. Even if I were reincarnated, I would end up being some "lowly animal" with the kind of mind that could not plague me with frightening, lonely, depressing thoughts. I clung to my friends and family, but it only increased my anger and self-contempt. I treated those people as my keepers who temporarily saved me from being left alone with my tormenting mind.

The final blow hit in Boston. I gradually withdrew from the few friends I had as well as my family. Death had grown so close that I no longer felt that I had much time. It was impossible to commit myself to anyone or anything. I was reserved, yet few people could sense how obsessed I was with death. Signs of affection terrified me because I knew I could not let anyone count on me. I needed death if life became too unbearable.

It finally did. I had become so passive that I no longer made contact with people. They had to call me. So much time had elapsed since I had felt close to someone that it seemed my "disappearance" would not really upset anyone. In addition to this, I was convinced that I was too stupid to handle academics or even a menial job (even though I had two jobs at the time). On a day when I knew no one would try and reach me, I took three times the lethal dosage of Seconal.

I was found 24 hours later and came out of a coma after 48 more. My arm was paralyzed. This time, I was placed in a long-term hospital. Another try at life began. With the help of an excellent therapist and the patient love of those whom I had thus far rejected, I have started once more. It has been two years since I took the pills. I think I know why people bother to live now.

"Successful" Dying

Thus far, this chapter has been pretty depressing, we know. Death and dying, by whatever means, are not our favorite topics, but they do have an important place in our study of life. In the next section of this chapter, however, we will be talking about two of the ways we humans have to deal with death in a mature and satisfying way.

BOX 23.4

What's Your Opinion?

Many things spread in popularity even if they are not always good for people. Although the "death with dignity" concept does appear to grant greater control over life to the person whose life it is, it has been argued that many individuals will invoke the law only when they believe they are dying. It won't occur to most people to think about it before then.

When people know they are likely to die, they are frequently in a depressed state. They may feel that now they are becoming worthless, and so should not be a burden on those around them. They may feel that they "just want to get it over with." Opponents of the law say that this is no time for a person to be making judgments about what should happen if death appears imminent. Their judgment is impaired by the depression. As Attorney Thomas Marzen has remarked, "People who are not dying are being denied treatment. The family doesn't object, the doctor doesn't object, and no one seems to care" (Gest, 1989, p. 36). What do you think?

The "Death With Dignity" Law

On September 30, 1976, Governor Edmund Brown, Jr. of California signed the "Natural Death Act," the first death with dignity law in the nation. The statute states the right of an adult to sign a written directive instructing her or his physician to withhold or withdraw life-sustaining procedures in the event of a terminal condition. The law contains specific definitions for "terminal condition," "life-sustaining procedure," and "qualified patient." The directive must be drawn up in the form set forth by the statute. It must be signed and dated by an adult of sound mind and witnessed by two persons not related by blood or entitled to the estate of the declarant.

Since then, all but 10 states have established such procedures. In June, 1990, the Supreme Court ruled that because the desires of a Missouri woman who has been lying in a coma since 1983 had not been made explicit (through a signed document), she could not be allowed to die despite her parents' wishes. However, the Court has ruled that when procedures established within each state are followed, the "right to die" would be constitutional.

Almost 80% of Americans die in hospitals, and 70% of those deaths involve some aspect of medical technology such as breathing, feeding, and elimination equipment. Hence it is essential that those who do not want to be maintained on life support systems if they are terminal put their wishes in writing according to their state's laws.

A Better Way of Dying

The "death ward" in most hospitals is not a nice place to be. The atmosphere is one of hushed whispers and fake smiles. No children below the age of 12 are allowed. Medications to control the pain are usually given on a schedule rather than as needed. Machines are used to continue life at all costs, though the patient may desire death. Viewing a typical American death ward made British historian Toynbee conclude that "Death is un-American."

The modern hospice is organized to afford a more "natural death" to the dying. Although this woman knows she does not have long to live, she is able to maintain a positive attitude with the help of the hospice staff.

In reaction to this, some have reached back to the Middle Ages, when religious orders set up havens where dying pilgrims could come to spend their last days (Stoddard, 1977). The modern **hospice** was established to provide for a more "natural" death for those who are terminally ill. The first United States hospice opened in New Haven, Connecticut, in 1971. Since then the National Hospice Organization has been formed to help promulgate this movement. A 1981 survey by the Joint Commission on Accreditation of Hospitals identified over 800 hospice programs in various stages of development (Falknor & Kugler, 1981). By 1984, this number had risen to 1,429 (Joint Commission on the Accreditation of Hospitals, 1984).

The hospice is more than a facility; it is a new philosophy of patient care in the United States (although not new in Europe). "What people need most when they are dying is relief from the distressing symptoms of their disease, security of a caring environment, sustained expert care, and the assurance that they and their families won't be abandoned" (Craven & Wald, 1975, p. 1816).

Hospices do pioneering work in such neglected areas as the easing of pain and psychological counseling of patients and their families. Even before patients begin to suffer pain, which in diseases such as cancer can be excruciating, they are given a mixture of morphine, cocaine, alcohol, and syrup so that they come to realize that pain can be controlled. Known as "Brompton's Mixture," this concoction is used only when the patient's need is severe; it is very effective in alleviating both pain and the fear accompanying it. A major goal of the hospice is to keep the person's mind as clear as possible at all times.

Whenever advisable, the hospice allows the patient to remain at home, and provides daily visits by staff nurses and volunteers. Jane Murdock, a California schoolteacher,

❖   *recalls how her dying mother at first refused to see her grandchildren after she was brought home from the hospital. But when the visiting hospice team began reducing her pain and reassuring her and her family in other ways, a new tranquility set in. Finally the woman even let the youngsters give her medication, and assist her about the house. Says Murdock: "I felt when she died that it was a victory for all of us. None of us had any guilt" ("A Better Way of Dying," Alban, 1978, p. 66).*

The hospice program movement has now grown to the point that it supports its own journal. Articles in the *Hospice Journal* often provide supplementary information about special issues concerning the terminally ill. For example, one recent article on hospice care for patients with AIDS (Schofferman, 1987) delved into additional issues of concern: irrational fear of contagion, homophobia (fear of homosexuals) by friends and relatives, and special difficulties in caring for substance abusers.

One of the major questions now being considered is whether the hospice should continue as a separate facility run solely for that purpose or become a standard part of all major hospitals. Currently, hospice programs in the United States are primarily home-based care, with the sponsorship of such programs being evenly divided between hospitals and community agencies (Torrens, 1985).

Whatever the case, it seems clear that this movement will continue to grow considerably. This is because hospices have already proved that they are better places to die. As Cronin and Wald (1975) put it, they are places "where we can finally come to terms with the self—knowing it, loving it reasonably well, and being ready to giving it up" (p. 53); in short, they are places where we have an opportunity for successful dying.

For most of us, though, dying is frightening and, ultimately, very hard to understand. To come to terms with it, we almost always rely on our spirituality rather than our cognitive powers.

Spirituality

There is but one true philosophical problem, and this is suicide: Judging whether life is or is not worth living amounts to answering the fundamental question of philosophy.

Albert Camus, The Plague, *1948*

Spirituality is concerned not only with whether life is worth living but why it is worth living. It may involve the attempt to better understand the reasons for living, through striving to know the intentions of a Supreme Being. An example is reading inspired books such as the Bible. Another is trying to discern the purposes and goals of some universal life force by, for example, examining historical trends in biological changes of species. In any case, spirituality includes all of our efforts to gain insight into the underlying, overriding forces of life. For many, it is the only justification for morality.

How important a role does spirituality play in the lives of typical American adults? One way this question has been investigated is through looking at religious participation and at religious attitudes. These factors are sometimes misleading, but together they offer one fairly reliable answer to the question.

Religious Participation

Americans have always been highly religious. This statement is supported by numerous Gallup polls (Gallup, 1988). A majority of the elderly consider religious practice to be of major importance in their lives. According to surveys, 96% of those over 65 believe in God and 82% report that religion plays a significant role in their lives (Koenig, Kvale, & Ferrell, 1988).

Religious life is of great importance to many of the elderly.

Furthermore, the influence of religion appears to be highly related to a sense of well-being. Studies of the relationship, however, may be criticized. It is known that those who attend services regularly are healthier than those who do not, but perhaps it is good health rather than religion that is causing the good feelings (George & Landerman, 1984; Lawton, 1984; Levin & Markides, 1986).

In their study of 836 elderly persons, Koenig and associates (1988) attempted to clear this up. They looked at nonorganizational practices (prayer, Bible reading, etc.) and subjective religious feelings, as well as organized religious practices. They found moderately strong correlations between morale and all three religious measures. The relationships were especially strong for women and for those over 75.

In recent decades, participation in religious activities has been growing among almost all adult age groups. Berkowitz (1979) offers a number of reasons for this:

- Disenchantment with the belief that mental health professionals can solve problems.

- Willingness to recognize guilty feelings, and the conclusion that church is a place where guilt can be absolved.

- Desire to do things together with the whole family.

- Recognition that church activity can relieve feelings of loneliness. College students, "engulfed by a huge university, or men and women starting careers in strange cities" are among those who are going back to church in large numbers.

- Realization that church is a good place to meet people of similar interests.

- A new awareness of heritage and the value of tradition among many young people.

- Popularity of study groups interested in the history, psychology, and sociology of religion.

- Desire for discipline and responsibility in life.

- In an era of growing anxiety, the hope that sacraments may be of some help.

- Decrease in role playing and an increase in individuality among the clergy.

- An increase in conservative attitudes toward sexuality and other aspects of life, and a desire to feel "clean and good."

- Decrease in pressure from parents and society. Because many feel that they do not have to go to church, they are more willing to do so.

Spirituality does appear to develop with age. There have been a number of theories offered as to how and why this is so. Among them, four views have come to receive highest regard: those of Viennese psychoanalysts Viktor Frankl and Carl Jung, sociobiologist E. O. Wilson, and theologian James Fowler.

Frankl's Theory of Spirituality

Dr. Victor Frankl, survivor of six years in a Nazi concentration camp, has made many contributions to the field of psychology and spirituality.

Frankl (1967) describes human life as developing in three interdependent stages according to the predominant dimension of each stage.

1. *The somatic (physical) dimension.* According to the **somatic dimension,** all persons are motivated by the struggle to keep themselves alive and to help the species survive. This intention is motivated entirely by instincts. It exists at birth and continues throughout life.

2. *The psychological dimension.* Personality begins to form at birth and develops as a result of instincts, drives, capacities, and interactions with the environment. The **psychological dimension** and the somatic dimension are highly developed by the time the individual reaches early adulthood.

3. *The noetic dimension.* The **noetic dimension** has roots in childhood but primarily develops in late adolescence. It is spiritual not only in the religious sense but in the totality of the search for the meaningfulness of life. This aspect distinguishes humans from all other species. The freedom to make choices is the basis of responsibility. Reason exists in the noetic realm. Conscience, which greatly affects the meaningfulness that one discovers in life, resides in the noetic.

Frankl believes that development in the physical and personality dimensions results from the total sum of the influences bearing upon an individual. The noetic, on the other hand, is *greater than the sum of its parts.* This means that we as adults are responsible for inventing (or re-inventing) ourselves! Whatever weaknesses our parents may have given us, we can and should try to overcome them. They need not govern our lives.

It is in the noetic dimension that the person is able to transcend training and to aspire to the higher levels of spiritual thought and behavior. For example, Teilhard de Chardin (1959) urges that if a person uses this noetic capacity to perceive the "Omega" or final point toward which human life is moving, frailties and foolishness can be overcome, and a high level of morality becomes natural.

Jung's Theory of Spirituality

Jung (1933, 1971), a student of Freud's, agreed to a large extent with his mentor's description of development in the first half of the human life. But he felt that Freud's ideas were inadequate to describe development during adulthood. Jung saw spiritual development as occurring in two stages.

The First Half of Life In each of the Jungian functions of thinking, feeling, sensing, and intuiting, the personality develops toward differentiation. Most individuals are well differentiated by the middle of life, at approximately age 35. That is, we are most different from each other at this age.

The Second Half of Life The goal of human development in the second half of life is just the opposite. Here a movement toward wholeness or unity of personality is the goal. Somewhere around midlife, the individual should begin to assess the various systems of his or her personality and come to acknowledge the disorganized state of these systems. There should be a turning inward or self-inspection that marks the beginning of true adult spirituality. The goals of this introspection are:

Dr. Carl Jung, a student of Freud's, introduced many concepts into psychology, including the anima *and* animus.

- Discovering a meaning and purpose in life

- Gaining a perspective on others, determining values and activities in which one is willing to invest energy and creativity

- Preparing for the final stage of life—death

Spirituality in the second half of life develops as a complement to the first half of life. By nourishing one's undeveloped side of life, one comes to a recognition of the spiritual and supernatural aspects of existence. For men, this means developing the **anima,** and for females the **animus.**

In contrast to the self-determination of spirituality seen in Frankl's and Jung's psychological points of view, sociobiology sees spirituality as determined almost entirely by instinct, that is, as a function of the genes.

Wilson's Theory of Spirituality

❖ *The predisposition to religious belief is the most complex and powerful force in the human mind and in all probability an ineradicable part of human nature (Wilson, 1978, p. 169).*

Harvard sociobiologist Edward O. Wilson, the leading spokesperson for the socio-biological point of view (see chap. 15 and 17), argues that religion and spirituality are inseparable. Together they grant essential benefits to believers. He argues that all societies, from hunter-gatherer bands to socialist republics, have religious practices with roots that go back at least as far as the Neanderthal period.

For example, he argues that even modern Soviet Union society, with its May Day rallies, its worship at the tomb of Lenin, and its insistence on belief in socialism, is as much a religious society as any other. Wilson (1978) cites one of Lenin's closest disciples, Grefori Pyatakov, who describes what it is to be "a real Communist"—one who

❖ *will readily cast out from his mind fears in which he has believed for years. A true Bolshevik has submerged his personality in the collectivity, the 'Party,' to such an extent that he can make the necessary effort to break away from his opinions and convictions and can honestly agree with the 'Party'—that is the test of a true Bolshevik (p. 184).*

Wilson says that in this statement we see the essence of religious spirituality. Humans, he argues, have a need to develop simple rules for handling complex problems. We also have a strong need for an unconscious sense of order in our daily lives. We strongly resist attempts to disrupt this order, which religion almost always protects.

Religion is one of the few uniquely human behaviors. Rituals and beliefs that make up religious life are not seen among any other animals. Some scientists, notably Lorenz and Tinbergen (Hinde, 1970), argue that animal displays, dances, and rituals are similar to human religious ceremonies. Wilson believes this comparison is wrong; animal displays are for the purpose of communicating (sexual desire, etc.), but religious ceremonies intend far more than mere communication.

Their goal is to "reaffirm and rejuvenate the moral values of the community" (Wilson, 1978, p. 179). Furthermore, religious learning is almost entirely unconscious. Most religious tenets are taught and deeply internalized early in life. Early teaching is a necessity if children are to learn to subvert their natural self-interests to the interest of society.

The sociobiological explanation of spirituality, then, is that through religious practice, the survival of practitioners is enhanced. Those who practice religion are more likely to stay alive (or at least they were in the past) than those who do not.

Wilson believes that even a person's willingness to be controlled may be genetic. Although all societies need some rebels, they also require that the vast majority of people be controllable, typically through religious and political beliefs. Therefore, Wilson believes that over the long run genes that favor willingness to be controlled have been favored by natural selection.

The potential for self-sacrifice can be strengthened in this manner, because the willingness of individuals to relinquish rewards or even surrender their own lives will favor group survival. The Jonestown mass suicide, for example, appears to have occurred because of the group's hope to remain united in afterlife. This concept of self-sacrifice is also the basis for Weinrich's (1987) assertion that homosexuality is an altruistic behavior (see chap. 17).

Wilson (1978) says that the United States is the second most religious country in the world, preceded only by India. He notes that only the form of religion has changed in the United States:

❖   *The self-fulfilling cults of the present day, including Esalen, EST, Arica, and scientology, are the vulgar replacements of the traditional forms. Their leaders receive a degree of obedience from otherwise intelligent Americans that would win smiles of admiration from the most fanatic Sufi shaykh. In the Erhard Training Centers (EST), novitiates are pounded from the lectern with simplistic truths from the behavior sciences and Eastern philosophy, while being simultaneously bullied and soothed by attendants. They are not allowed to leave their seats to eat or go to the bathroom or even to stand and stretch. The reward . . . is the masochistic relief that results from placing oneself into the hands of a master to whom omnipotence has been granted (p. 185).*

Religions usually favor survival of their believers. This is not always true, though, and is true to differing degrees. It has been estimated that there have been over 100,000 different religious faiths since humankind began. Obviously most have failed. Some are even contrary to the survival needs of their believers.

The Shaker religion, which disallows sexual intercourse to any of its participants, is an example. Shakerism lasted in this country for no more than two centuries. It flourished in the nineteenth century, but there are only a very few believers today. With no new recruits, it seems doomed to extinction. This, Wilson argues, is always the case for those religions that do not somehow enhance the vitality and hardiness of the groups that support them. The constant pursuit of a better chance for survival is why new ones are started.

The Birth of a Religion

Religions, according to the sociobiological point of view, develop through three steps:

1. **Objectification.** First, a perception of reality is described—abstractions become **objective.** This includes images and definitions that are easy to understand. Examples are good versus evil, heaven versus hell, and the control of the forces of nature by a god or gods.

2. **Commitment.** People devote their lives to these objectified ideas. Out of this **commitment,** they are willing under any circumstances to help those who have done the same.

3. **Mythification.** In **mythification,** stories are developed that tell why the members of the religion have a special place in the world. These stories are rational and enhance the person's understanding of the physical as well as spiritual world. The stories include explanations of how and why the world, as well as the religion, came to be. In earlier, less sophisticated religions, the faith is said to have been founded at the same time as the beginning of the race. These rarely include all-powerful or all-knowing gods. In less than one-third of the known religions is there a highly placed god, and in even fewer is there a notion of a moral god who has created the world. In the later religions, God is always seen as male, and almost always as the shepherd of a flock.

Not surprisingly, Wilson sees science as taking the place of theology today, because science has explained natural forces more effectively than theology. In fact, he asserts that science has explained theology itself. Although he sees theology as being phased out, he argues that the demise of religion is not at all likely. As long as religions make people more likely to survive and propagate themselves, Wilson suggests, they will enjoy worldwide popularity.

Wilson's theory attempts to explain spiritual development within societies. Theologian James Fowler has offered a description of the development of faith throughout the life cycle of individuals, without regard to the culture in which faith forms.

Fowler's Theory of Spirituality

James Fowler (1974, 1975a, 1975b) offers a theoretical framework built on the ideas of Piaget, Erikson, and Kohlberg. He believes strongly that cognitive and emotional needs are inseparable in the development of spirituality. Spirituality cannot develop faster than intellectual ability, and also depends on the development of personality. Thus Fowler's theory of faith development integrates the role of the unconscious, of needs, of personal strivings, and of cognitive growth.

Fowler sees faith developing in six steps. He says that the stages in faith development can be delayed indefinitely, but the person must have reached at least a certain *minimal age* at each stage in order to move on to a succeeding stage. His six stages are as follows.

1. **Intuitive-projective faith.** For **intuitive-projective faith,** minimal age is 4 years. In this stage, the individual focuses on surface

qualities, as portrayed by adult models. This stage depends to a great extent on fantasy. Conceptions of God or a supreme being reflect a belief in magic.

2. **Mythical-literal faith.** For **mythical-literal faith,** minimal age is 5 to 6 years. Fantasy ceases to be a primary source of knowledge at this stage, and verification of facts becomes necessary. Verification of truth comes not from actual experience but from such authorities as teachers, parents, books, and traditions. Faith in this stage is mainly concrete, and depends heavily on stories told by highly credible storytellers. For example, the traditional story of Adam and Eve is taken quite literally.

3. **Poetic-conventional faith.** For **poetic-conventional faith,** minimal age is 12 to 13 years. The child is entering Piaget's codification stage. Faith is still conventional and depends on a consensus of opinion of other, more authoritative persons. Now the person moves away from family influence and into new relationships. Faith begins to provide a coherent and meaningful synthesis of these relationships.

There is an awareness of symbolism and a realization that there is more than one way of knowing truth. Learned facts are still taken as the main source of information, but individuals in Stage Three begin to trust their own judgment and the quality of selected authorities. Nevertheless, they do not yet place full confidence in their own judgment.

4. **Individuating-reflective faith.** For **individuating-reflective faith,** minimal age is 18 to 19 years. Youth in Stage Three are unable to synthesize new areas of experience because depending on others in the community does not always solve problems. Individuals in Stage Four begin to assume responsibility for their own beliefs, attitudes, commitments, and life-style. The faith learned in earlier stages is now disregarded, and greater attention is paid to one's own experience. In those individuals who still need authority figures, there is a tendency to join and become completely devoted to clubs and cults.

5. **Paradoxical-consolidation faith.** For **paradoxical-consolidation faith,** minimal age is 30. In this stage such elements of faith as symbols, rituals, and beliefs start to become understood and consolidated. The person begins to realize that other approaches to dealing with such complex questions as the supernatural and supreme being can be valid as her or his own. The individual at this stage considers all people to belong to the same universal community and has a true regard for the kinship of all people.

6. **Universalizing faith.** For **universalizing faith,** minimal age is 40 years. As with Kohlberg's final stage, very few people ever reach this level. Here the individual lives in the real world but is not of it. Such persons do not merely recognize the mutuality of existence; they act on the basis of it. People at this stage appear to be truly genuine and lack the need to "save face" that exists at the lower stages.

Stage Six, as described by Fowler, compares closely to a hypothetical Stage Seven of morality proposed by Kohlberg (1973). Although he never found anyone at a Stage Seven level of morality, Kohlberg believed that theoretically there should be a stage for those few persons who rise above the purely cognitive and achieve a place where they transcend logic. These individuals, who are rare indeed, come to understand why one should be just and ethical in a world that is unjust. A burning love of universal humankind presses them always to act in truly moral ways.

The development of spirituality and morality appears to be parallel all along the sequence, especially in the Kohlberg and Fowler models. At the early levels, the orientation is basically selfish; ethical thinking and behavior are virtually nonexistent. The child is "good" only in order to please more powerful persons.

At the second two levels, concern for the opinion of the community in general takes over. "What will people think!" is uppermost in religion as well as in moral decisions. Only if and when the highest levels are reached do true spirituality and morality emerge. And for a few individuals at the highest level, the distinction between the moral and the spiritual no longer exists.

Transition

"The distinction between the moral and the spiritual no longer exists." What a wonderful goal to choose as a means of living the good life. It is probably also the best way to ensure a successful death. We sincerely hope that reading this book will contribute in some small way to your achievement of those two preeminent goals.

Key Ideas

1. There are four types of death: clinical death, brain death, biological or cellular death, and social death.

2. The legal definition of death is "Unreceptivity and unresponsivity, no movements or breathing, no reflexes, and a flat electroencephalogram (EEG) reading that remains flat for 24 hours."

3. There are three stages of grief: initial shock and emotionality, intermediate distress, and the recovery phase.

4. Sometimes grief does not follow its normal path. Abnormal grief patterns include delayed mourning, distorted reactions, delayed reactions, and pathological mourning.

5. Elisabeth Kübler-Ross suggests five stages in the process of dying: shock and denial; anger; bargaining; depression; and acceptance.

6. Suicide attempts are influenced by race, place of residence, and gender.

7. Two efforts to make dying a more dignified experience are the "death with dignity" law, which allows persons to state the terms of their treatment while they are still coherent, and the hospice movement.

8. According to surveys, 96% of those over 65 believe in God and 82% report that religion plays a significant role in their lives.

9. This chapter reports on four theoretical explanations of spirituality: those of Viktor Frankl, Carl Jung, E. O. Wilson, and James Fowler.

Key Terms

Anima
Animus
Biological death
Brain death
Cardiopulmonary resuscitation
Clinical death
Commitment
Electroencephalogram
Hospice
Individuating-reflective faith
Intuitive-projective faith

Legal death
Mythical-literal faith
Mythification
Noetic dimension
Objectification
Paradoxical-consolidation faith
Poetic-conventional faith
Psychological dimension
Social death
Somatic dimension
Universalizing faith

What Do You Think?

1. What do you think is the best way to define death?

2. Most of us think of grief as something that happens to us. Do you think it makes sense to describe it as "work"?

3. How do you feel about the idea of "successful death"?

4. Are there some old people—those who have lost their spouse and all their friends, or those who are undeniably terminal—who should be allowed to take their own lives? Should these people be helped to have a "ceremony of death"?

5. This chapter has suggested two ways of making death more dignified. Can you think of any others?

6. Are you satisfied with your own level of religious participation? What do you think you should do differently?

7. How would you define your own spirituality?

Suggested Readings

Agee, James. [1957] (1971). *A death in the family.* New York: Bantam. This Pulitzer Prize winning novel focuses on the effect of a man's death on his young son.

Becker, Ernest. (1973). *The denial of death.* New York: Free Press. This is a brilliant analysis of the human failure to acknowledge death. Looks into the theories of Freud, Rank, Jung, Fromm, and others. Becker was awarded the Pulitzer Prize for this work.

Caine, Lynn. (1987). *Widow.* New York: Bantam. Describes the feelings of a woman about her husband's death and the ways she finds to deal with her grief.

Freud, Sigmund. (1950). *Totem and taboo.* New York: Norton. One of Freud's most famous works, it explains how psychoanalysis looks at death and dying.

Kübler-Ross, Elisabeth. (1969). *On death and dying.* New York: Macmillan. Briefly described in this chapter, this is a classic in the field.

Tolstoy, Leo. [1886] (1981). *The death of Ivan Illich.* New York: Bantam. Upon learning that he has terminal cancer, a man starts a lonely journey into understanding of the meaning of life and the ability to accept his own death.

Glossary

❖

a

Accommodation: When we modify our schemata to meet the demands of the environment; that is, we make our minds fit reality (ch. 2).

Accumulation-of-Errors Theory: As cells die, they must synthesize new proteins to make new cells. As this is done, occasionally an error occurs. Over time, these errors mount up and may finally grow serious enough to cause organ failure (ch. 21).

Accumulation of Metabolic Waste: Waste products resulting from metabolism build up in various parts of the body, contributing greatly to the decreasing competence of those parts. Some examples of this effect are cataracts on the eye, calcification in the arteries, and brittleness of bones (ch. 21).

Acrosome: Tip of the sperm (ch. 3).

Activity Theory: Human beings flourish through interaction with other people. They are unhappy when, as they reach the older years, their contacts with others shrink as a result of death, illness, and societal limitations. Those who are able to keep up the social activity of their middle years are considered to be the most successful (ch. 22).

Adaptation: Piaget states that a tendency in all human beings is to adapt to the environment. Adaptation consists of two complementary processes: **assimilation** and **accommodation** (ch. 2). Also refers to how an individual, child or adult, adjusts to his or her environment (ch. 9).

Adhesion: The prepared surface of the uterus and the outer surface of the fertilized egg, now called the trophoblast, touch and actually "stick together" (ch. 4).

Adolescent Egocentrism: The reversion to the self-centered thinking patterns of childhood that sometimes occurs in the teen years (ch. 13).

Adolescent Moratorium: A "time-out" period during which the adolescent experiments with a variety of identities, without having to assume the responsibility for the consequences of any particular one (ch. 16).

Afterbirth: The period following birth in which the placenta and other membranes are discharged (ch. 4).

Age Cohorts: Groups of people born at about the same time (ch. 1).

Age-Status: Refers to society's expectations about what is normal at various ages. These expectations change not only with advancing years, but according to the particular society and to the historical context (ch. 22).

Aggressive Gang: An organized group of juvenile delinquents who engage in a variety of illegal activities (ch. 14).

Aging by Program: The vast majority of animals die at or before the end of their reproductive period, but human females live twenty to thirty years beyond the end of their reproductive cycles. Nevertheless, all animals seem to die when their "program" dictates (ch. 21).

AID: An acronym for "Artificial Insemination by Donor" (ch. 3).

AIDS (Acquired Immune Deficiency Syndrome): A condition caused by a virus that invades the body's immune system, making it vulnerable to infections and life-threatening illnesses (ch. 4, 15).

Alarm Reaction: Selye's term for a generalized "call to arms" of the body's defensive forces (ch. 16).

Allele: Alternate forms of a specific gene; there are genes for both blue and brown eyes (ch. 3).

Amenorrhea: The suppression of menstruation, often seen in anorexics and bulimics (ch. 13).

Amniocentesis: Entails inserting a needle through the mother's abdomen, piercing the amniotic sac, and withdrawing a sample of the amniotic fluid (ch. 4).

Amniotic Sac: The sac that is filled with amniotic fluid and in which the embryo and fetus develop (ch. 4).

Anal Stage: Freud's stage of psychosexual development during which the anus is the main pleasure center. The function here is successful toilet training (ch. 2).

Androgyny: Refers to those persons who have higher than average male *and* female elements in their personalities. Such persons are more likely to behave in a manner appropriate to a situation, regardless of their gender (ch. 15).

Anima: The female side of the personality. Males tend to repress it until later in life (ch. 23).

Animism: Children consider a large number of objects as alive and conscious that adults consider inert (ch. 7).

Animus: The male side of the personality. Females tend to repress it until later in life (ch. 23).

Anorexia Nervosa: A syndrome of self-starvation that mainly affects adolescent and young adult females. It is characterized by an "intense fear of becoming obese, disturbance of body image, significant weight loss, refusal to maintain a minimal normal body weight, and amenorrhea. The disturbance cannot be accounted for by a known physical disorder" (ch. 14).

Anoxia (lack of oxygen): If something during the birth process should cut the flow of oxygen to the fetus, there is the possibility of brain damage or death (ch. 4).

Anticipatory Images: Piaget's term for images (which include movements and transformation) that enable the child to anticipate change (ch. 6).

Antigens: The substances in the blood that fight to kill foreign bodies (ch. 21).

Anxiety: An unpleasant feeling of apprehension and uneasiness (ch. 11).

Apgar: A scale to evaluate a newborn's basic life signs; administered one minute after birth and repeated at three-, five-, and ten-minute intervals; it uses five life signs: heart rate, respiratory effort, muscle tone, reflex irritability, and skin color (ch. 5).

Apposition: The fertilized egg, now called a blastocyst, comes to rest against the uterine wall (ch. 4).

Approach-Avoidance Conflict: Conflict exists because obtaining a pleasurable goal will also result in an unpleasurable one. The more evenly balanced the positive and negative sides of the objective, the greater the conflict (ch. 16).

Artificialism: Consists in attributing everything to human creation (ch. 7).

Assimilation: When we perceive the environment in a way that fits our existing schemata; that is, we make reality fit our minds (ch. 2).

Attachment: Behavior intended to keep a child (or adult) in close proximity to a significant other (ch. 6).

Attention Deficit: A short attention span; associated with hyperactivity (ch. 11).

Authoritarian Parenting Style: The parents strive for complete control over their children's behavior by establishing complex sets of rules. They enforce the rules through the use of rewards and, more often, strong discipline (ch. 12).

Authoritarian Parents: Baumrind's term for parents who are demanding and want instant obedience as the most desirable child trait (ch. 8).

Authoritative Parenting Style: In this, the most common style, parents are sometimes authoritarian and sometimes permissive, depending to some extent on the mood they happen to be in. They believe that both parents and children have rights, but that parental authority must predominate (ch. 12).

Authoritative Parents: Baumrind's term for parents who respond to their children's needs and wishes; believing in parental control, they attempt to explain the reasons for it to their children (ch. 8).

Autism: A severe and rare disorder that appears before 30 months of age; its characteristics include withdrawal from contact with other people, severe language problems, obsessive preservation of the status quo (insists on sameness, exhibits repetitive behavior), skill in fine motor movements, and inability to deal with people (ch. 11).

Autoimmunity: The process by which the immune system in the body rejects the body's own tissue. Examples are rheumatoid arthritis, diabetes, vascular diseases, and hypertension (ch. 21).

Automatic Attention: Refers to common tasks that require little of a person's capacity for attention (ch. 19).

Autonomy: Erikson's term for a child's growing sense of independence (ch. 7).

Autosexuality: The love of oneself; the stage at which the child becomes aware of himself or herself as a source of sexual pleasure, and consciously experiments with masturbation (ch. 15).

b

Babbling: The sounds that children make that sound like speech (ch. 5).

Basal Metabolism Rate (BMR): The minimum amount of energy an individual tends to use when in a resting state (ch. 19).

Behavior Disorders: Fighting, temper tantrums, defiance, destructiveness, and other similar behaviors (ch. 11).

Behavioral Theory: The theory of human learning that says that all learning is ultimately determined by forces outside the control of the organism. What we learn and how we learn it is determined completely by genetic inheritance and by the influences of our environment, past and present (ch. 2).

Behavioristic Model: This model sees subcultures starting out as a result of a series of trial-and-error behaviors, which are reinforced if they work. Peer group members behave the way they do because they have no other choice (ch. 12).

Bilingual Education Act: Schools must make provisions for students who find instruction incomprehensible because they do not understand English (ch. 10).

Binocular Coordination: Three-dimensional vision; appears around age 4 months (ch. 5).

Biological Death: Death occurs when it is no longer possible to discern an electrical charge in the tissues of the heart and lungs (ch. 23).

Biopsychosocial: A term for the idea that development proceeds by the interaction of biological, psychological, and social forces (ch. 1, 18).

Birth Order: The position that a child occupies in the family (first born, second born, etc.); also called *ordinal position* (ch. 10).

Blastocyst: Name of the fertilized egg after initial divisions (ch. 3).

Bodily-Kinesthetic Intelligence: The control of bodily motions and ability to handle objects skillfully; one of Gardner's multiple intelligences (ch. 9).

Brain Death: Death of the brain occurs when it fails to receive a sufficient supply of oxygen for a short period of time (usually eight to ten minutes). The cessation of brain function occurs in three stages: first the cortex stops, then the midbrain fails, and finally the brain stem ceases to function (ch. 23).

Breech Birth: About four out of every hundred babies are born feet first, or buttocks first, while one out of a hundred are in a cross-wise position (transverse presentation) (ch. 4).

Bulimia Nervosa: This disorder is characterized by "episodic binge-eating accompanied by an awareness that the eating pattern is abnormal, fear of not being able to stop eating voluntarily, and depressed mood and self-deprecating thoughts following the eating binges. The bulimic episodes are not due to anorexia nervosa or any known physical disorder" (ch. 14).

C

Capacitation: A process by which the layer surrounding the sperm is removed; may be done externally or naturally in the woman's genital tract (ch. 3).

Cardiopulmonary Resuscitation: A technique for reviving an individual's lungs and/or heart that have ceased to function (ch. 23).

Cataracts: The result of cloudy formations on the lens of the eye. They form very gradually and inhibit the passage of light through the eye. Cataracts are most common after the age of 60. If they become large enough, they can be surgically removed (ch. 19).

Centration: A feature of preoperational thought—the centering of attention on one aspect of an object and the neglecting of any other features (ch. 7).

Cerebral Hemispheres: The two halves of the brain; the left side of the brain controls the right side of the body, the right side of the brain controls the left side of the body (ch. 7).

Cesarean Section: Surgery to deliver the baby through the abdomen when a vaginal delivery is impossible (ch. 4).

Child Abuse: The physical or mental injury, sexual abuse, negligent treatment, or maltreatment of a child under the age of 18 by a person who is responsible for the child's welfare, under circumstances that indicate that the child's health or welfare is harmed or threatened (ch. 11).

Childhood Schizophrenia: This severe disorder is characterized by a combination of extreme isolation, noncommunicative use of speech, repetitive body movements, self-injurious behavior, abnormal responses to light or sound, problems in eating and sleeping, abnormal fears or lack of fears, and delusional behavior (ch. 11).

Children at Risk: Children who show early signs of physical or psychological difficulties; unless helped by appropriate intervention, they may continue to experience problems, perhaps with increasing intensity, throughout the life span (ch. 11).

Chlamydia: This is now the most common STD, with about 5 to 7 million new cases each year. There often are no symptoms; it is diagnosed only when complications develop (ch. 15).

Cholesterol: A substance in the blood that comes to adhere to the walls of the blood vessels, restricting the flow of blood and causing strokes and heart attacks (ch. 17).

Chorionic Villi Sampling (CVS): A catheter (small tube) is inserted through the vagina to the villi and a small section is suctioned into the tube (ch. 4).

Chromosomal Sex: The biological sexual program initially carried by either the X or Y sex chromosome (ch. 8).

Chromosome Failure: A genetic abnormality such as gynecomastia (breast growth in the male) or hirsutism (abnormal female body hair) (ch. 15).

Chromosomes: Stringlike bodies that carry the genes (ch. 3).

Classification: Concrete operational children can group objects with some similarities within a larger category (e.g., brown wooden beads and white wooden beads are all beads) (ch. 9).

Climacteric: Refers to a relatively abrupt change in the body, brought about by changes in hormonal balances (ch. 19).

Climacterium: Refers to the loss of reproductive ability (ch. 19).

Clinical Death: The individual is dead when his or her respiration and heartbeat have stopped (ch. 23).

Closed Adoption: Biological parents are removed from the lives of their adopted child (ch. 3).

Cofigurative Culture: A culture in which the young pattern their behavior on that of their peers, rather than on older models (ch. 12).

Cognitive Development: The growth of those mental processes by which we gain knowledge, such as perception, memory, representation (ch. 8).

Cognitive Structuralist Theory: The theory that a child's intelligence develops through the gradual addition of specific quantitative and qualitative mental abilities (ch. 2).

Collagen: The major connective tissue in the body; it provides the elasticity in our skin and blood vessels (ch. 21).

Color Blindness: A condition affecting the ability to detect some colors; caused by a defective gene on the X chromosome (ch. 3).

Commitment (Fowler's term): For Fowler, the third step in the birth of a religion, in which people devote their lives to objectified ideas. They are willing under any circumstances to help those who have done the same (ch. 23).

Commitment (Perry's term): The third phase in Perry's theory. The individual realizes that certainty is impossible, but that commitment to a certain position is necessary, even without certainty (ch. 17).

Commitment (Sternberg's term): One of Sternberg's three aspects of love; the strongly held conviction that one will stay with another, regardless of the cost (ch. 17).

Communication Disorders: Language behaviors that differ from what might be expected from a child of a particular age (ch. 11).

Compensation: The cognitive ability to recognize an inequality of quantity and then add to the lesser amount to create an equality (ch. 13).

Competition: Efforts to excel by achieving a particular goal; may come at the expense of others (ch. 9).

Concrete Operational Stage: Piaget's stage of mental development in which children become concerned with *why* things happen. The intuitive thinking style of the preoperational stage is replaced by elementary logic, as operations begin to develop that enable children to form more complex mental actions on concrete elements of their world (ch. 2).

Conditioned Reflexes: Reflexes that are not innate, but come about through learning (ch. 2).

Confluence Model: The premise that the intellectual growth of each family member depends on the intellectual level of all the other family members (ch. 10).

Conservation: Concrete operational children gradually master the idea that something may remain the same even though its surface features change (ch. 7).

Consolidation: A quantitative cognitive change from childhood to adulthood whereby improved problem-solving techniques are employed in a wider variety of situations and with greater skill (ch. 13).

Constructed Knowledge: Belenky's fifth phase of women's thinking; characterized by an integration of the subjective and procedural ways of knowing (types 3 and 4) (ch. 17).

Content Theory of Intelligence: Perkins' term, which means that intelligence is a rich knowledge base; mastery of factual material is at the heart of thinking and problem solving (ch. 9).

Continuity: The lasting quality of experiences; development proceeds steadily and sequentially (ch. 1).

Controlled Scribbling: Drawing in which children carefully watch what they are doing, whereas before they looked away; they have better control of the crayon and hold it now like an adult (ch. 7).

Conventional Level of Morality: Kohlberg's stage of moral development during which children desire approval from individuals and society (ch. 9).

Coordination of Secondary Schemes: Infants combine secondary schemes to obtain a goal (ch. 5).

Crawling: Locomotion in which the infant's abdomen touches the floor and the weight of the head and shoulders rests on the elbows (ch. 5).

Creative Parenting Style: A parenting style in which parents are devotedly interested in their children's behavior but seldom make rules to govern it. Instead, by modeling and family discussions, they espouse a well-defined set of values and expect their children to make personal decisions based on these values (ch. 12).

Creeping: Movement is on hands and knees and the trunk does not touch the ground; creeping appears after age 9 months in most youngsters (ch. 5).

Cross-Linkage Theory: A theory of aging that states that the proteins that make up a large part of cells are themselves composed of peptides. When cross-links are formed between peptides (a natural process of the body), the proteins are altered, often for the worse (ch. 21).

Cross-Over: Older men become more like women, and older women become more like men. They do not actually cross over—they just become more like each other (ch. 22).

Cross-Sectional Studies: This method compares groups of individuals of various ages at the same time in order to investigate the effects of aging (ch. 1).

Crystallized Intelligence: Involves perceiving relationships, educing correlates, reasoning, abstracting, concept of attainment, and problem solving, as measured primarily in unspeeded tasks involving various kinds of content (semantic, figural, symbolic) (ch. 19).

Culture Transmission Model: A new subculture arises as an imitation of the subculture of the previous generation. This takes place through a learning process by which younger teenagers model themselves after those in their 20s (ch. 12).

Cystic Fibrosis: A chromosomal disorder that produces a malfunction of the exocrine glands (ch. 3).

Cytomegalovirus (CMV): A virus that can cause damage such as mental retardation, blindness, deafness, and even death. One of the major difficulties in combating this disease is that it remains unrecognized in pregnant women (ch. 4).

d

Daycare: A child spends part of the day outside of his or her own home in the care of others (ch. 8).

Decentering: Concrete operational children can concentrate on more than one aspect of a situation (ch. 9).

Decoding: The technique by which we recognize words (ch. 9).

Defense Mechanisms: Freud's concept of unconscious mental mechanisms that protect our conscious minds from becoming aware of truths we would rather not know (ch. 2).

Deferred Imitation: Imitation that continues after the disappearance of the model to be imitated (ch. 7).

Delayed Puberty: The stages of pubertal change do not begin until a significant time after the normal onset (ch. 13).

Depression: A condition marked by a sorrowful state, fatigue, and a general lack of enthusiasm about life; children are now thought to be subject to this problem (ch. 11); Depression is not a specific syndrome or illness in itself. It is a basic affective state that, like anxiety, can be of long or short duration and of low or high intensity, and can occur in a wide variety of conditions at any stage of development (ch. 14).

DES (Diethylstilbestrol): In the late 1940s and 1950s, DES (a synthetic hormone) was administered to pregnant women supposedly to prevent miscarriage. It was later found that the daughters of the women who had received this treatment were more susceptible to vaginal and cervical cancer (ch. 4).

Descriptive Studies: Information is gathered on subjects without manipulating them in any way (ch. 1).

Despair: The counterpart to integrity in the last stage of Erikson's theory. When people look back over their lives and feel that they have made many wrong decisions, or more commonly, that they have frequently not made any decisions at all, they tend to see life as lacking integrity. They are angry that there can never be another chance to make their lives make sense (ch. 22).

Developmentally Delayed: A condition in which a child's growth rate slows; it need not cause any permanent retardation if corrected. Its causes may be either physical or psychological (ch. 7).

Developmental Risk: A term used to describe those children whose well-being is in jeopardy due to a range of biological and environmental conditions (ch. 4).

Developmental Tasks: Havighurst suggests these specific tasks at each stage of life, which lie midway between the needs of the individual and the ends of society. These tasks, such as skills, knowledge, functions, and attitudes, are needed by an individual in order to succeed in life (ch. 1, 12).

Differential Opportunity Structure: Due to social disapproval and more rigid rules enforced by parents, peers, and the legal system, women have not had the same access to sex that men have had (ch. 22).

Difficult Children: Children whose temperament causes conflicts with those around them (ch. 6).

Discontinuity: Behaviors that are apparently unrelated to earlier aspects of development (ch. 1).

Disengagement Theory: According to this position, the belief that activity is better than passivity is a bias of the Western world. In disengagement theory, the *most mature* adults are likely to gradually disengage themselves from their fellow human beings in preparation for death. They become less interested in their interactions with others, and more concerned with internal concerns (ch. 22).

Distantiation: The readiness of all of us to distance ourselves from others when we feel threatened by their behavior. Distantiation is the cause of most prejudices and discrimination (ch. 18).

Diversity: According to Toffler, stress is increased by what percentage of our lives is in a state of change at any one time (ch. 16).

DNA: Deoxyribonucleic acid; often referred to as the structure of life (ch. 3).

Dominant: The gene that tends to be expressed in a trait (ch. 3).

Double-Approach Conflict: In this case, the individual must choose between two pleasant, but mutually exclusive choices. An example might be trying to decide whether to buy a television set or a stereo when both are desired but only one can be afforded (ch. 16).

Double-Avoidance Conflict: Under these circumstances, a choice between two situations must be made, and they are both unpleasant. An example might be deciding whether to let your son go with the Boy Scouts on a hazardous camping trip to the mountains, or putting up with his surliness at being forced to stay home (ch. 16).

Down Syndrome: Genetic abnormality caused by a deviation on the 21st pair of chromosomes (ch. 3).

Drawing: The ability to form lines into objects that reflect the world; a physical activity that often reveals cognitive and emotional development (ch. 7).

DSM-III—R: Diagnostic and Statistical Manual III—Revised. This classification scheme was devised by the American Psychiatric Association to aid in defining atypical behavior (ch. 11).

Dual-Career Family: A family in which the wife does some sort of paid work and also manages the family's functions (ch. 18).

Dual-Process Model: A model of intelligence that says there may be a decline in the *mechanics* of intelligence, such as classification skills and logical reasoning, but that the *pragmatics* are likely to increase (ch. 19).

Dualism: Perry's initial phase of ethical development where "Things are either absolutely right or absolutely wrong" (ch. 17).

e

Easy Children: Those children whose temperament enables them to adjust well and to get along with others (ch. 6).

Ectoderm: The outer layer of the embryo that will give rise to the nervous system, among other developmental features (ch. 4).

Ectopic Pregnancy: The fertilized egg attempts to develop in one of the fallopian tubes; sometimes referred to as a **tubal pregnancy** (ch. 4).

Effortful Attention: Refers to processing novel tasks, such as trying to learn a new phone number or a new surgical technique (ch. 19).

Ego: One of the three structures of the psyche, according to Freud; it is in contact with reality, and mediates between the id and superego (ch. 2).

Egocentrism: Refers to children's belief that everything centers on them; *sensorimotor egocentrism* refers to the inability to distinguish oneself from the world (ch. 5, 7).

Electroencephalogram: A graphic record of the electrical activity of the brain (ch. 23).

Embryonic Period: Third through the eighth week following fertilization (ch. 4).

Emotional Divorce: Sometimes a couple learns to "withstand" each other, rather than live with each other. The only activities and interests that they shared were ones that revolved around the children. When the children leave, they are forced to recognize how far apart they have drifted; in effect, they are emotionally divorced (ch. 20).

Empirico-Inductive Method: A method of problem solving used by young children in which they look at available facts and try to induce some generalization from them (ch. 13).

Empty Nest Syndrome: Refers to the feelings parents may have as a result of their last child leaving home (ch. 20).

Encoding: Translating objects and events into language (ch. 9).

Endoderm: The inner layer of the embryo that will give rise to the lungs and liver, among other developmental features (ch. 4).

Endogamous: Marriages in which the partners are said to have married into their "own tribe"; that is, they have married someone who is similar to them in most ways (ch. 18).

Escape: Perry's term for refusing responsibility for making any commitments. Since everyone's opinion is "equally right," the person believes that no commitments need be made, and so escapes from the dilemma (ch. 17).

Estrogen Replacement Therapy: A process in which estrogen is given in low levels to a woman experiencing severe problems with menopause (ch. 19).

Existential Love: The capacity to cherish the present moment, perhaps first learned when we confront the certainty of our own personal death (ch. 22).

Exogamous: Marriages in which the spouses are thought to be unlike each other in some important ways (ch. 18).

Exosystem: An environment in which you are not present, but which nevertheless affects you (e.g., your father's job) (ch. 1).

Expressive Language: Children move from purely receptive speech to expressing their own ideas and needs through language (ch. 7).

External Fertilization: Fertilization that occurs outside of the woman's body (ch. 3).

Extinction: According to behavioral theory, refraining from reinforcing behavior is the best way to extinguish it; extinction differs from punishment in that no action is taken (ch. 2).

Extragenetic: Sources of information other than genetic (ch. 3).

Extrasomatic: Sources of information outside of the body (e.g., computers, books) (ch. 3).

f

Failure-to-Thrive (FTT): The weight and height of FTT infants consistently remain far below normal (the bottom 3% of height and weight measures); there are two types of FTT cases: **organic** and **nonorganic** (ch. 5).

Fallopian Tubes: Passageway for the egg once it is discharged from the ovary's surface (ch. 3).

Family Status: An indication of how close and strong family ties are. A strong family status is associated with a lower incidence of adolescent suicide (ch. 14).

Fear: An emotional condition that, unlike anxiety, is caused by something specific; a child will usually try to avoid or escape from the situation that causes this reaction (ch. 11).

Fertilization: Union of sperm and egg (ch. 3).

Fetal Alcohol Syndrome (FAS): Refers to babies affected when their mothers drink alcohol during pregnancy; they manifest four clusters of symptoms: physiological functioning, growth factors, physical features, and structural effects (ch. 4).

Fetal Hydrocephalus: Surgery to cure a condition in which the brain regions fill with fluid and expand (ch. 4).

Fetal Period: The period extending from the beginning of the third month to birth (ch. 4).

Fetoscopy: A tiny instrument called a fetoscope is inserted into the amniotic cavity, making it possible to see the fetus (ch. 4).

Fiscal Fitness: The idea that many women lack experience in managing money, and need to become "fiscally fit" (ch. 20).

Fixation: Freud's term for when the personality fails to progress beyond one of its first four stages (ch. 2).

Fluid Intelligence: Involves perceiving relationships, educing correlates, maintaining span of immediate awareness in reasoning, abstracting, concept formation, and problem solving, as measured in unspeeded as well as speeded tasks involving figural, symbolic, or semantic content (ch. 19).

Forceps Delivery: Occasionally, for safety, the physician will withdraw the baby with forceps during the first phase of birth (ch. 4).

Formal Operational Stage: Piaget's fourth stage of mental development, in which children are able to perform abstract operations entirely in their minds (ch. 2).

Fraternal Twins: Nonidentical twins (ch. 3).

Free Will: The concept that some of our decisions are entirely controlled by us, without the influence of outside forces (ch. 2).

Future Shock: The illness that results from having to deal with too much change in too short a time (ch. 16).

g

Gender Constancy: Refers to children understanding the unchanging nature of gender (ch. 8).

Gender Identity: Refers to children cognitively realizing that they are males or females (ch. 8).

Gender Revolution: Levinson's term; the meanings of gender are changing and becoming more similar (ch. 20).

Gender Splitting: Levinson's term; all societies support the idea that there should be a clear difference between what is considered appropriate for males and for females: gender splitting appears to be universal (ch. 20).

Gender Stability: Refers to children understanding that gender typically remains the same throughout life (ch. 8).

Gene Theory: The theory that aging is due to certain harmful genes (ch. 21).

General Adaptation Syndrome: Selye's theory about the three stages of reaction to stress (ch. 16).

Generative Love: Most characteristic of parenthood, a time during which sacrifices are gladly made for the sake of the children (ch. 22).

Generativity: Erikson's term for the ability to be useful to ourselves and to society. As in the industry stage, the goal is to be productive and creative, but in the generativity stage, which

takes place during middle adulthood, one's productivity is aimed at being helpful to others (ch. 20).

Genetic: Refers especially to the information genes contain (ch. 3).

Genital Herpes: This is an incurable sexually transmitted disease, with about 500,000 new cases every year. With no cure, there are now estimated to be about 30 million people in this country who experience the recurring pain of this infection (ch. 15).

Genital Sex: Sex is determined not only by chromosomes and hormones but by external sex organs (ch. 8).

Genital Stage: During this, the fifth of Freud's stages, the personality reaches the fulfillment of psychic development, in which sexuality becomes mature (ch. 2).

Genotype: An individual's genetic composition (ch. 3).

German Measles (Rubella): A typically mild childhood disease caused by a virus; pregnant women who contract this disease may give birth to a baby with a defect: congenital heart disorder, cataracts, deafness, mental retardation. The risk is especially high if the disease appears early in the pregnancy (ch. 4).

Germinal Choice: Refers to attempts to match the sperm and egg of selected individuals (ch. 3).

Germinal Period: The first two weeks following fertilization (ch. 4).

Gifted and Talented: Those who possess abilities that have evidence of high performance capabilities in areas such as intellectual, creative, specific academic or leadership ability, or in the performing and visual arts (ch. 11).

Glaucoma: Results from a buildup of pressure inside the eye due to excessive fluid. The resulting damage can destroy one's vision (ch. 19).

Gonadal Sex: The XX or XY combination pass on the sexual program to the undifferentiated gonads if the program is XY; the gonads will then

differentiate into testes. If the program is XX, the gonads differentiate into the ovaries, starting at about the 12th week (ch. 8).

Gonorrhea: This well-known venereal disease accounts for between one and a half and two million cases per year. One quarter of those were reported among adolescents. The most common symptoms are painful urination and a discharge from the penis or the vagina (ch. 15).

Goodness of Fit: Compatibility between parental and child behavior; how well parents and their children get along (ch. 6).

Group Marriage: A marriage that includes two or more of both husbands and wives, who all exercise common privileges and responsibilities (ch. 18).

Gynecomastia: Inappropriate physical development marked by male breast growth (ch. 13).

h

Hazing Practices: The often dangerous practices used by some fraternities to initiate new members (ch. 16).

Hearing Impairment: A hearing loss that ranges in severity from mild to profound (ch. 11).

Hemophilia: A genetic condition causing incorrect blood clotting; called the "bleeder's disease" (ch. 3).

Herpes Simplex: An infection that usually occurs during birth; a child can develop the symptoms during the first week following the birth. The eyes and nervous system are most susceptible to this disease (ch. 4).

Heterogamous: Marriages in which the spouses are thought to be unlike each other in some important ways (ch. 18).

Heterosexuality: Love of members of the opposite sex (ch. 15).

Hirsutism: Inappropriate physical development in females marked by the development of facial and chest hair (ch. 13).

Holophrase: Children's first words; they usually carry multiple meanings (ch. 5).

Holophrastic Speech: One word to communicate many meanings and ideas (ch. 5).

Homeostatic Imbalance: The theory that aging is due to a failure in the systems that regulate the proper interaction of the organs (ch. 21).

Homogamy: A marriage in which two people are *extremely* similar in all of their personal characteristics (ch. 18).

Homosexuality: Love of members of one's own sex (ch. 15).

Hormonal Balance: One of the triggering mechanisms of puberty that may be used to indicate the onset of adolescence (ch. 13).

Hormonal Sex: Once the testes or ovaries are differentiated, they begin to produce chemical agents called sex hormones (ch. 8).

Hospice: A facility and/or program dedicated to assisting those who have accepted the fact that they are dying and desire a "death with dignity." Provides pain control and counseling, but does not attempt to cure anyone (ch. 23).

Hyperactivity: Hyperactive children are never still, can't remain seated, and are constantly on the move; hyperactivity is characterized by its severity, its early onset, its persistence, and its association with disorders of attention and concentration; it usually appears at about age 3 or 4 years when parents begin to notice that their children have a short attention span and are easily distracted. The problem seems to lie in an attention-deficit whose underlying cause may be a brain problem; only occasionally can hyperactivity be traced to temperament. These youngsters typically experience educational difficulties and developmental delays (ch. 11).

Hypersensitive Youth: The hypersensitive youth will have an extreme reaction to situations that would only mildly disturb most people. The disruptions caused by seemingly trivial events may come together in a suicide attempt (ch. 14).

Hypothetico-Inductive Method: A method of problem solving used by adolescents in which they hypothesize about the situation and then deduce from it what the facts should be if the hypothesis is true (ch. 13).

i

Id: One of the three structures of the psyche, according to Freud. Present at birth, it is the source of our instinctive desires (ch. 2).

Identity Achievement: Marcia's final status, where numerous crises have been experienced and resolved, and relatively permanent commitments have been made (ch. 12).

Identity Confusion: Marcia's initial status, where no crisis has been experienced and no commitments have been made (ch. 12).

Identity Crisis: Erikson's term for the situation, usually in adolescence, that causes us to make major decisions about our identity (ch. 2, 12).

Identity Foreclosure: One of Marcia's statuses, where no crisis has been experienced, but commitments have been made, usually forced on the person by the parent (ch. 12).

Identity Moratorium: One of Marcia's statuses of adolescence, where considerable crisis is being experienced but no commitments are yet made (ch. 12).

Identity Status: Refers to Marcia's four types of identity formation (ch. 12).

Implantation: When a fertilized egg becomes embedded in the uterine wall (ch. 3, 4).

Impotency: The inability to engage in the sexual act (ch. 22).

Inconsistent Conditioning: A situation in which children are sometimes expected to behave in a certain way, but at other times are not (ch. 12).

In Vitro Fertilization: Fertilization that occurs "in the tube" or "in the glass"; an external fertilization technique (ch. 3).

Individuating-Reflective Faith: The fourth developmental step of Fowler's theory of faith. Individuals in stage four begin to assume responsibility for their own beliefs, attitudes, commitments, and life-style. The faith learned in earlier stages is now disregarded, and greater attention is paid to one's own experience (ch. 23).

Individuation: Refers to our becoming more individual; we develop a separate and special personality, derived less and less from our parents and teachers and more from our own behavior (ch. 8 and 18).

Information Processing: The study of how children (and adults) perceive, comprehend, and retain information (ch. 7).

Information-Processing Strategy: A cognitive problem-solving plan (ch. 13).

Initiation Rites: A cultural and sometimes ceremonial task that signals the entrance to some new developmental stage. Such rites can indicate the passage from adolescence to adulthood (ch. 16).

Initiative: Erikson's term for children's ability and willingness to explore the environment and test their world (ch. 7).

Inner Dialogue: Gould's seven steps, which he believes can help in mastering the demons of one's childhood experiences (ch. 18).

Integrity: The resolution of each of the first seven crises in Erikson's theory should lead us to achieve a sense of personal integrity. Older adults who have a sense of integrity feel their lives have been well spent. The decisions and actions they have taken seem to them to fit together (ch. 22).

Inter-Propositional Thinking: The ability to think of the ramifications of *combinations* of propositions (ch. 13).

Interaction: Behaviors involving two or more people (ch. 6).

Intergenerational Continuity: The connection between childhood experiences and adult behavior (ch. 6).

Internal Fertilization: A natural process in which fertilization occurs within the woman (ch. 3).

Interpersonal and Intrapersonal Intelligences: Gardner's personal intelligences; interpersonal intelligence builds on an ability to recognize what is distinctive in others, while intrapersonal intelligence enables us to understand our own feelings (ch. 9).

Intimacy: Erikson's stage that represents the ability to relate one's deepest hopes and fears to another person and to accept another's need for intimacy in turn (ch. 18).

Intra-Propositional Thinking: The ability to think of a number of possible outcomes that would result from a *single* choice (ch. 13).

Intuitive-Projective Faith: The first developmental step of Fowler's theory of faith. In this stage, the individual focuses on surface qualities, as portrayed by adult models. This stage depends to a great extent on fantasy. Conceptions of God or a supreme being reflect a belief in magic (ch. 23).

Invasion: During invasion the trophoblast "digs in" and begins to bury itself in the uterine lining (ch. 4).

Inversion: The cognitive ability to recognize an inequality of quantity and then subtract from the greater amount to create an equality (ch. 13).

Invulnerable Children: Those children who sustain some type of physical or psychological trauma yet remain on a normal developmental path (ch. 10).

Irreversibility: A child's inability to reverse thinking; a cognitive act is reversible if it can utilize stages of reasoning to solve a problem and then proceed in reverse, tracing its steps back to the original question or premise (ch. 7).

Irritable Infants: Infants who are generally more negative in their behavior and more irregular in their biological functioning than typical children (ch. 6).

Isolation: This is the readiness all of us have to isolate ourselves from others when we feel threatened by their behavior (ch. 18).

j

Juvenile Delinquent: A minor who commits illegal acts (ch. 14).

k

Knowledge-Acquisition Components: Sternberg's term for those components that help us to learn how to solve problems in the first place (ch. 9).

l

L-tryptophan: This amino acid has been linked to a blood disorder in which white blood cells increase to abnormally high numbers (ch. 19).

Language Disorders: Refers to the difficulty some children have in learning their native language with respect to content, form, and usage; and possibly to those children with delayed language development (ch. 11).

Laparoscope: A thin, tubular lens used to identify mature egg(s) (ch. 3).

Latency Stage: During this, the fourth of Freud's stages, sexual desire becomes latent. This is especially true for males, through the defense mechanism of introjection (ch. 2).

Lateralization: There is a preferred side of the brain for a particular activity (if you are right-handed in writing, you are left-lateralized for writing) (ch. 7).

Learning Community: In such a community, many resources (social agencies, school systems, businesses and industries, churches, government, etc.) would form an alliance to promote learning in many forms. Such learning opportunities would be open to people of all ages (ch. 19).

Learning Disability: A general term that refers to multiple disorders leading to difficulties in listening, speaking, reading, writing, reasoning, or mathematical abilities (ch. 11).

Learning Theory of Homosexuality: Homosexuality is the result of learned experiences from significant others (ch. 15).

Least Restrictive Environment: *See* mainstreaming (ch. 11).

Legal Death: Defined as "unreceptivity and unresponsivity, no movements or breathing, no reflexes, and a flat **electroencephalogram** (EEG) reading that remains flat for 24 hours" (ch. 23).

Life Course: Levinson's term. "Life" refers to all aspects of living—everything that has significance in a life; "course" refers to the flow or unfolding of an individual's life (ch. 18).

Life Cycle: Levinson's term. The life cycle is a *general* pattern of adult development, while the life course is the unique embodiment of the life cycle by an *individual* (ch. 18).

Life Structure: Levinson's term. The underlying pattern or design of a person's life *at a given time* (ch. 18).

Lifespan Psychology: A study of development as a life-long process beginning at conception and ending in death (ch. 1).

Linguistic Intelligence: One of Gardner's multiple intelligences (ch. 9).

Logical-Mathematical Intelligence: One of Gardner's multiple intelligences (ch. 9).

Longitudinal Studies: The experimenter makes several observations of the same individuals at two or more times in their lives. Examples are determining the long-term effects of learning on behavior; the stability of habits and intelligence; and the factors involved in memory (ch. 1).

m

Macrosystem: A term indicating society at large (ch. 1).

Magical Thinking: Many adolescents have an unrealistic view of death's finality and use suicide as a means to radically transform the world and solve their problems or to join a loved one who has already died. These feelings are often aided and abetted by the glorification of suicide that sometimes occurs in the media (ch. 14).

Mainstreaming: Mainstreaming legislation requires communities to provide an appropriate education for children with special needs; this law is expressly designed to accommodate such youngsters by requiring that they be placed in the least restrictive environment in which they can achieve success (ch. 11).

Major False Assumptions: Remaining from childhood, these must be reexamined and readjusted by each individual if he or she is to progress in maturity (ch. 18).

Male Change of Life: Change in hormonal balance and sexual potency (ch. 19).

Manipulative Experiments: The experimenter attempts to keep all variables (all the factors that can affect a particular outcome) constant except one, which is carefully manipulated (ch. 1).

Maturation: The process of physical and mental development due to physiology (ch. 13).

Maximum Growth Spurt: The period of adolescence when physical growth is at its fastest (ch. 13).

Meiosis: Division of the germ cells, resulting in 23 chromosomes; also called *reduction division* (ch. 3).

Menarche: The onset of menstruation (ch. 13).

Menopause: The cessation of menstruation (ch. 19).

Menstrual Cycle: The interaction between the pituitary and the ovaries that occurs in four-week phases (ch. 3).

Mental Imagery: Mental processing involving visual depiction of people, events, and objects (ch. 7).

Mental Retardation: Refers to significantly subaverage general intellectual functioning resulting in or associated with concurrent impairments in adaptive behavior and manifested during the development period (ch. 11).

Mental Structures: The blueprints in our minds that equip us to have an effect on our environment. They are the tools of adaptation (ch. 2).

Mentoring: The act of assisting another, usually younger, person with his work or life tasks (ch. 18).

Mesoderm: The middle layer of the embryo that gives rise to muscles, the skeleton, and the circulatory and excretory systems (ch. 4).

Mesosystem: The relationship among microsystems (ch. 1).

Metacomponents: Sternberg's term for those components that help us to plan, monitor, and evaluate our problem-solving strategies (ch. 9).

Metalinguistics Awareness: A capacity to think about and talk about language (ch. 9).

Microsystem: The immediate setting that influences development, such as the family (ch. 1).

Midlife Transition: Levinson's term for the phase that usually lasts for five years and generally extends from age 40 to 45. It involves three major developmental tasks (ch. 20).

Miscarriage: When a pregnancy ends spontaneously before the 20th week (ch. 4).

Miseducation: David Elkind's term for excessive academic pressure placed on young children (ch. 8).

Mitosis: Cell division in which each chromosome is duplicated, maintaining the number at 46 (ch. 3).

Monogamy: The standard marriage form in the United States and most other nations, in which there is one husband and one wife (ch. 18).

Monozygotic Twins: Identical twins (ch. 3).

Moral Dilemma: A modified clinical technique used by Kohlberg to discover the structures of moral reasoning and the stages of moral development; a conflict leads subjects to justify the morality of their choices (ch. 9).

Moratorium of Youth: A "time-out" period during which the adolescent experiments with a variety of identities, without having to assume the responsibility for the consequences of any particular one (ch. 12).

Musical Intelligences: One of Gardner's multiple intelligences (ch. 9).

Mutation: A change in the structure of a gene (ch. 3).

Mythical-Literal Faith: The second developmental step of Fowler's theory of faith. Fantasy ceases to be a primary source of knowledge at this stage, and verification of facts becomes necessary. Verification comes not from actual experience, but from such authorities as teachers, parents, books, and traditions (ch. 23).

Mythification: Stories are developed that tell why members of a religion have a special place in the world. These stories are rational and enhance the person's understanding of the physical as well as the spiritual world (ch. 23).

n

Naturalistic Experiments: In these experiments, the researcher acts solely as an observer and does as little as possible to disturb the environment. "Nature" performs the experiment, and the researcher acts as a recorder of the results (ch. 1).

Negative Identity: Persons with a negative identity adopt one pattern of behavior because they are rebelling against demands that they do the opposite (ch. 12).

Negative Reinforcement: Any event which, when it *ceases to occur* after a response, makes that response more likely to happen in the future (ch. 2).

NEO Model of Personality: McCrae and Costa's theory that there are three major personality traits, which they feel govern the adult personality. Each of those three traits is supported by six subtraits or "facets" (ch. 20).

Neonate: Term for an infant in the days immediately following birth (ch. 5).

Neurological Assessment: Identifies any neurological problem, suggests means of monitoring the problem, and offers a prognosis about the problem (ch. 5).

New York Longitudinal Study: Long-term study by Chess and Thomas of the personality characteristics of children (ch. 6).

No-Fault Divorce: The law that lets people get divorced without proving some atrocious act by one of the spouses. This new law recognized that people could, in the course of their lives, simply grow apart from each other to the point that they no longer made good marriage partners. In legal language, this is known as an irretrievable breakdown of a marriage (ch. 20).

Noetic Dimension: Frankl's third stage of human development has roots in childhood, but primarily develops in late adolescence. It is spiritual, not only in the religious sense but in the totality of the search for the meaningfulness of life. This aspect makes humans specifically different from all other species (ch. 23).

Nonaggressive Status Offenders: Anyone who commits a crime in which there is no aggressive intent. Usually refers to prostitutes and runaways (ch. 14).

Normal Range of Development: The stages of pubertal change occur at times that are within the normal range of occurrence (ch. 13).

Novelty: Toffler's term for the dissimilarity of new situations in our lives (ch. 16).

Novice Phase: Levinson's initial phase of human development extends from ages 17 to 33, and includes the early adult transition, entering the adult world, and the age-30 transition (ch. 18).

Nucleotides: The small blocks of the DNA ladder (ch. 3).

Numeration: Concrete operational children grasp the meaning of number, the oneness of one (ch. 9).

O

Object Permanence: Refers to children gradually realizing that there are permanent objects around them, even when these objects are out of sight (ch. 5).

Objectification: Fowler's term for the first step in the birth of a religion, where a perception of reality is described. This includes images and definitions that are easy to understand. Examples are good versus evil, heaven versus hell, and the control by a god or gods of the forces of nature (ch. 23).

Observational Learning: A term associated with Bandura, meaning that we learn from watching others (ch. 10).

Oedipal Conflict: According to Freud, the unconscious sexual desire for the parent of the opposite sex, which occurs in children between the ages of 4 and 5. In females it is called the *Electra conflict* (ch. 2).

Olfactory Sense: The sense of smell, which uses the olfactory nerves in the nose and tongue (ch. 19).

Omnigamy: A situation coined by Lionel Tiger to describe the situation in this country where increasing numbers of divorces and subsequent remarriages imply that "each will be married to all." (ch. 18).

One-Time, One-Group Studies: Studies that are carried out only once on only one group of subjects (ch. 1).

Open Adoption: Biological parents may remain in contact with their adopted child (ch. 3).

Operant Conditioning: The theory that when operants (actions that people or animals take of their own accord) are reinforced, they become conditioned (more likely to be repeated in the future) (ch. 2).

Operations: Mental events that take the place of actual behavior (ch. 2).

Optimum Drive Level: The level of optimum stimulation for an individual (ch. 16).

Oral Stage: During this, the fourth of Freud's stages, the oral cavity (mouth, lips, tongue, gums) is the pleasure center. Its function is to obtain an appropriate amount of sucking, eating, biting, and talking (ch. 2).

Organ Reserve: Refers to that part of the total capacity of our body's organs that we do not normally need to use. For example, when you walk up the stairs, you probably use less than half of your total lung capacity (ch. 17).

Organization: Our innate tendency to organize causes us to combine our schemata more efficiently. The schemata of the infant are continuously reorganized to produce a co-ordinated system of higher-order structures (ch. 2).

Organogenesis: The formation of organs during the embryonic period (ch. 4).

Outward Bound: A program where people learn to deal with their fears by participating in a series of increasingly threatening experiences. As a result, their sense of self-worth increases and they feel more able to rely on themselves. The program uses such potentially threatening experiences as mountain climbing and rappeling, moving about in high, shaky rope riggings, and living alone on an island for several days (ch. 16).

Overregularities: At a certain point in their language development, children inappropriately use the language rules they have learned—for example, "I comed home" (ch. 7).

Ovulation: That time when the egg is released from the ovary's surface (ch. 3).

Ovum: Another term for the egg (ch. 3).

P

Paradoxical-Consolidation Faith: The fifth developmental step of Fowler's theory of faith. In this stage, such elements of faith as symbols, rituals, and beliefs start to become understood and consolidated. The person begins to realize that others' approaches to dealing with such complex questions as the supernatural and supreme being can be as valid as her or his own (ch. 23).

Parent-Child Role Reversals: Parents and children sometimes exchange traditional role behaviors. In the parent-child interaction, the child adopts some parent-type behavior (e.g., caretaking, supporting, nurturing, advising), and the parent acts more as a child is expected to act (ch. 14).

Passion: Sternberg's term for a strong sense of desire for another person, and the expectation that sex with them will prove physiologically rewarding (ch. 17).

Pedagogy: The science of teaching children (ch. 19).

Peer: Refers to a youngster who is similar in age to another child, usually within 12 months (ch. 10).

Pelvic Inflammatory Disease (PID): This disease often results from chlamydia or gonorrhea, and frequently causes prolonged problems, including infertility. Symptoms include lower abdominal pain and a fever (ch. 15).

Performance Components: Sternberg's term for those components that help us to execute the instructions of the metacomponents (ch. 9).

Permissive Parenting Style: The parents have little or no control over their children, and refrain from disciplinary measures (ch. 12).

Permissive Parents: Baumrind's term for parents who take a tolerant, accepting view of their children's behavior, including both aggressive and sexual urges; they rarely use punishment or make demands of their children (ch. 8).

Permutations: The act of altering a given set of objects in a group in a systematic way. One of the abilities described by Flavell (ch. 13).

Phallic Stage: During this, the third of Freud's stages, the glans of the penis and the clitoris are the pleasure centers (ch. 2).

Phenotype: The observable expression of gene action (ch. 3).

Phenylketonuria: Chromosomal disorder resulting in failure to break down the amino acid phenylalanine (ch. 3).

Phobia: When fears and anxieties become so overwhelming that they dominate a child's feelings and behavior for lengthy periods (ch. 11).

Phonology: Describes how to put sounds together to form words (ch. 7).

Placenta: The placenta supplies the embryo with all its needs, carries off all its wastes, and protects it from danger (ch. 4).

Plasticity: Resiliency; the ability to recover from either physiological or psychological trauma and return to a normal developmental path (ch. 1, 10).

Poetic-Conventional Faith: The third developmental step of Fowler's theory of faith. Faith is still conventional and depends on a consensus of opinions of other, more authoritative persons. Now the person moves away from family influence and into new relationships. Faith begins to provide a coherent and meaningful synthesis of these relationships (ch. 23).

Polyandry: A type of marriage in which there is one wife but two or more husbands (ch. 18).

Polygamy: A marriage in which there is one husband but two or more wives (ch. 18).

Positive Reinforcement: Any event which, when it *occurs after* a response, makes that response more likely to happen in the future (ch. 2).

Postconventional Level of Morality: Kohlberg's stage of moral development during which individuals make moral decisions according to an enlightened conscience (ch. 9).

Postnatal Depression: Many women feel "down" a few days after giving birth; this is fairly common and is now thought to be a normal part of pregnancy and birth for some women (ch. 4).

Power Theory of Intelligence: Perkins' term; the view that intelligence is solely dependent on the neurological efficiency of the brain; a genetic interpretation (ch. 9).

Pragmatics: The rules of pragmatics describe how to take part in a conversation (ch. 7).

Precociousness: The ability to do what others are able to do, but at a younger age (ch. 13).

Preconventional Level of Morality: Kohlberg's stage of moral development during which children respond mainly to cultural control to avoid punishment and attain satisfaction (ch. 9).

Premature Foreclosure: A situation in which a teenager chooses an identity too early, usually because of external pressure (ch. 12).

Prematurity: About 7 out of every 100 births are premature, occurring less than 37 weeks after conception; prematurity is defined by low birth weight and immaturity (ch. 4).

Preoperational Stage: Piaget's second stage, during which the ability to represent objects symbolically in the mind begins (ch. 2, 17).

Prepared Childbirth: A combination of relaxation techniques and information about the birth process; sometimes called the *Lamaze method,* after its founder (ch. 4).

Pretend Play: A characteristic of the early childhood youngster; these children show an increasing ability to let one thing represent another, a feature that carries over to their play (ch. 8).

Primary Circular Reactions: Infants repeat some act involving their bodies (ch. 5).

Procedural Knowledge: Belenky's fourth phase of women's thinking; characterized by a distrust of both knowledge from authority and the female thinker's own inner authority or "gut" (ch. 17).

Prodigiousness: The ability to do *qualitatively* better than the rest of us are able to do; such a person is referred to as a prodigy (ch. 13).

Prosocial Behavior: Refers to behaviors such as friendliness, self-control, and being helpful (ch. 10).

Prostatectomy: The removal of all or part of the male prostate gland (ch. 22).

Psychic Energy: As compared to physical energy, Freud's term for mental/sexual energy (ch. 22).

Psychoanalysis: Sigmund Freud's explanation of the psychic development of humans. Also his method of psychological therapy (ch. 2).

Psychoanalytic Theory: Freud's theory of the development of the personality (ch. 2).

Psychoanalytic Theory of Homosexuality: Freud's theory suggests that if the child's first sexual feelings about the parent of the opposite sex are strongly punished, the child may identify with the same-sex parent and develop a permanent homosexual orientation (ch. 15).

Psychogenic Model: Teenagers form a subculture because they are avoiding or escaping from reality (ch. 12).

Psycholinguistic: That language theory that attempts to identify the psychological mechanisms by which individuals learn their native language (ch. 5).

Psychological Dimension: The second stage of Frankl's theory of human development, in which personality begins to form at birth and develops as a result of instincts, drives, capacities, and interactions with the environment. This and the somatic dimension are highly developed by the time the individual reaches early adulthood (ch. 23).

Psychopathology: Mental illness, relatively rare during adolescence (ch. 14).

Psychosocial Dwarfism: Where puberty is so delayed that the teenager looks like a child. This condition is the result of an extremely negative environment (ch. 13).

Psychosocial Theory: Erikson's theory of the development of the personality (ch. 2).

Puberty: A relatively abrupt and qualitatively different set of physical changes that normally occur at the beginning of the teen years (ch. 13).

Puberty Rites: An initiation ceremony often scheduled to coincide with the peak in adolescent physiological maturation (ch. 16).

Punishment: In behavioral theory, any action that makes a behavior less likely to happen. Differs from extinction in that an action is taken (ch. 2).

q

Quiescence: A condition in which an individual has no needs at all (ch. 16).

r

Random Scribbling: Drawing in which children use dots and lines with simple arm movements (ch. 7).

Reading Comprehension: Understanding the concepts and relationships that words represent (ch. 9).

Real Versus the Possible: The growing ability of the adolescent to imagine possible and even impossible situations (ch. 13).

Realism: Children distinguish and accept the real world surrounding them, meaning that they now have identified an external as well as internal world (ch. 7).

Received Knowledge: Belenky's second phase of women's thinking; characterized by being awed by the authorities, but far less affiliated with them (ch. 17).

Recessive: A gene whose trait is not expressed unless paired with another recessive gene; for example, both parents contribute genes for blue eyes (ch. 3).

Recidivism Rates: The percentage of convicted persons who commit another crime once they are released from prison (ch. 16).

Reciprocal Interactions: We respond to those around us and they change; their responses to us thus change and we in turn change (ch. 1); similar to transactional model; recognizes the child's active role in its development; "I do something to the child, the child changes; as a result of the changes in the child, I change" (ch. 5).

Reconciliation Fantasies: When children wish their parents could get together again following divorce (ch. 8).

Reflective Listening: A method of talking to adolescents; you rephrase the person's comments to show you understand (ch. 15).

Reflex: When a stimulus repeatedly elicits the same response (ch. 5).

Reinforcement: Increasing the probability that a response will recur under similar conditions (ch. 8).

Relationship: A pattern of intermittent interactions between two individuals over a period of time (ch. 6).

Relativism: The second phase in Perry's theory. An attitude or philosophy that says anything can be right or wrong depending on the situation; all views are equally right (ch. 17).

Representation: Recording or expressing information in a manner different from the original; the word *auto* represents the actual car (ch. 7).

Reproductive Image: Mental images that are faithful to the original object or event being represented; Piaget's term for images that are restricted to those sights previously perceived (ch. 7).

Repudiation: Choosing an identity involves rejecting other alternatives (ch. 12).

Resiliency: *See* plasticity (ch. 10).

Resolution by Choice: One of the resolutions of conflict, in which people simply choose one option or the other, even if they must do so by arbitrary means such as flipping a coin (ch. 16).

Resolution by Freezing: When the outcomes of two choices are seen to be equal, one possible reaction is to make no choice at all. The chooser is "frozen" in indecision (ch. 16).

Resolution by Leaving the Field: Resolution of conflict in which individuals simply remove themselves, physically or mentally, from the arena of the conflict (ch. 16).

Resolution by Oscillation: A variation of the freeze response. Here, rather than being frozen, the individual makes a move toward one goal, then is drawn by an opposite goal and turns toward it. This behavior is repeated over and over, so that the individual seems to be going in circles (ch. 16).

Respiratory Distress Syndrome (RDS): This problem is most common with prematures, but it may strike full-term infants whose lungs are particularly immature; RDS is caused by the lack of a substance called *surfactant,* which keeps the air sacs in the lungs open (ch. 5).

Retreat: According to Perry's theory of ethical development, when someone retreats to an earlier ethical position (ch. 17).

Rh Factor: Rh incompatibility is an incompatibility between the blood types of mother and child; if the mother is Rh-negative and the child Rh-positive, miscarriage or even infant death can result (ch. 4).

Ritalin: A drug, actually a stimulant, used to calm hyperactive children; it helps them to concentrate and maintain attention for a longer time (ch. 11).

Role Discontinuity: Abrupt and disruptive change caused by conflicts among one's various roles in life (ch. 22).

S

Schemata: Patterns of behavior that we use to interact with the environment (ch. 2).

Secondary Circular Reactions: Infants direct their activities toward objects and events outside themselves (ch. 5).

Secular Trend: The phenomenon of adolescents entering puberty sooner and growing taller and heavier in recent centuries (ch. 13).

Self-fulfilling Prophecy: Making an idea come true simply by believing it will (ch. 19).

Semantics: The rules of semantics describe how to interpret the meaning of words (ch. 7).

Senile Macular Degeneration: This disease of the retina is a leading cause of blindness, beginning as blurred vision and a dark spot in the center of the field of vision. Advances in laser surgery have shown promise in treating diseases of the retina such as this (ch. 19).

Sensitive Periods: Certain times in the life span when a particular experience has a greater and more lasting impact than at another time (ch. 1).

Sensitive Responsiveness: Refers to the ability to recognize the meaning of a child's behavior (ch. 6).

Sensorimotor Stage: Piaget's first stage, during which mental operations are not yet possible (ch. 2).

Sequential (Longitudinal/Cross-Sectional) Studies: A cross-sectional study done at several times with the same groups of individuals (ch. 1).

Seriation: Concrete operational children can arrange objects by increasing or decreasing size (ch. 9).

Sex Cleavage: The custom that youngsters of the same sex tend to play together (ch. 8).

Sex Identity: A conviction that one belongs to the sex of birth (ch. 8).

Sex Role: A pattern of behavior that results partly from genetic makeup and partly from the specific traits that are in fashion at any one time and in any one culture. For example, women are able to express their emotions through crying more easily than men, although there is no known physical cause for this difference (ch. 8, 15).

Sex Stereotypes: Reflects beliefs about the characteristics associated with male or female (ch. 8).

Sex-linked Inheritance: Sex-linked inheritance is explained by the fact that the female carries more genes on the 23rd chromosome (ch. 3).

Sex-Role Adaptation: Defined by whether the individual's behavior may be seen as in accordance with her or his gender (ch. 15).

Sex-Role Orientation: Individuals differ in how *confident* they feel about their sexual identity. Those with low confidence have a weak orientation toward their gender role (ch. 15).

Sex-Role Preference: Some individuals feel unhappy about their sex role, and wish either society or their gender could be changed, so that their sex role would be different (ch. 15).

Sex-Role Reversals: Older men see themselves and other males as becoming submissive and less authoritative with advancing years. Conversely, older women see themselves and other women as becoming more dominant and self-assured as they grow older (ch. 22).

Sex-Role Stereotypes: Behavior common in our culture that can be identified as typically either male or female. Some stereotypes are more or less true, some are clearly false, and some we are not sure about (ch. 15).

Sexual Abuse: Refers to any sexual activity between a child and an adult whether by consent or force (ch. 11).

Sexual Identity: Sexual identity results from those *physical characteristics* and *behaviors* that are part of our biological inheritance. They are the traits that make us males or females. Examples of sex-linked physical characteristics are the penis and testes of the male. A corresponding behavior is the erection of the penis when stimulated (ch. 15).

Sexual Revolution: The extraordinary change in human sexual behavior that occurred in the 1960s and 1970s (ch. 15).

Sexually Transmitted Diseases: A class of diseases transmitted through sexual behavior, such as AIDS, gonnorhea, herpes, and chlamydia (ch. 15).

Sibling: A brother or sister (ch. 10).

Sickle-Cell Anemia: A chromosomal disorder resulting in abnormal hemoglobin (ch. 3).

Silence: Belenky's first phase of women's thinking, characterized by concepts of right and wrong; similar to the men in Perry's first stage (ch. 17).

Skeletal Growth: The development of the bone structure in the body (ch. 13).

Sleeping Disorders: Problems with a child's sleeping pattern, such as an inability to sleep or sleepwalking (ch. 5).

Slow-to-Warm-Up Children: Children whose reactions are initially mildly negative but then show slow adaptation (ch. 6).

Social Death: That point in which a patient is treated essentially as a corpse, although perhaps still "clinically" or "biologically alive" (ch. 23).

Social Learning: Another name for observational learning; children (and all of us) learn from watching others. The term is associated with Albert Bandura (ch. 8).

Social Perspective-Taking: Children's views on how to relate to others emerge from their personal theories about the traits of others (ch. 10).

Socialization: The need to establish and maintain relations with others and to regulate behavior according to society's demands (ch. 8).

Solidarity: Erikson's term for the personality style of persons who are able to commit themselves in concrete affiliations and partnerships with others, and have developed the "ethical strength to abide by such commitments, even though they may call for significant sacrifices and compromises" (ch. 18).

Solidification: Cognitive growth in which the thinker is more certain and confident in the use of newly gained mental skills and is more likely to use them in new situations (ch. 13).

Somatic Dimension: The first stage of Frankl's theory of human development, in which all persons are motivated by the struggle to keep themselves alive and to help the species survive. This intention is motivated entirely by instincts. It exists at birth and continues throughout life (ch. 23).

Spatial Intelligence: One of Gardner's multiple intelligences (ch. 9).

Speech Disorders: Refers to difficulties children have with how they speak (ch. 11).

Sperm: The germ cell that carries the male's 23 chromosomes (ch. 3).

Spina Bifida: A genetic disorder resulting in the failure of the neural tube to close (ch. 3).

Stage of Exhaustion: The third stage in Selye's theory of stress, caused by a gradual depletion of the organism's adaptational energy. The physiological responses revert to this condition during the stage of alarm. The ability to handle the stress decreases, the level of resistance is lost, and the organism dies (ch. 16).

Stage of Resistance: The second stage in Selye's theory of stress. If the organism survives the initial alarm, an almost complete reversal of the alarm reaction occurs. Swelling and shrinkages are reversed, the adrenal cortex that lost its secretions during the alarm stage becomes unusually rich in these secretions, and a number of other shock-resisting forces are marshalled. During this stage, the organism appears to gain strength and to have adapted successfully to the stressor (ch. 16).

Stage Theorists: Researchers who believe that research based on personality traits is too narrow in focus, and that we must also look at the stages of change each person goes through (ch. 20).

Stanford-Binet Intelligence Test: Usually refers to the intelligence test originally designed by Alfred Binet, then brought to America and revised on subjects near Stanford University (ch. 9).

State of Identity: According to Erikson, the main goal of adolescence (ch. 12).

Stillbirth: After the 20th week, the spontaneous end of a pregnancy is called a *stillbirth* if the baby is born dead (ch. 4).

Stimulus Reduction: Freud's notion that human beings try to avoid stimulation whenever possible. According to this idea, all our activities are attempts to eliminate stimulation from our lives (ch. 16).

Storm and Stress: Hall's description of the rebirth that takes place during adolescence (ch. 12).

Stress: Anything that upsets our equilibrium—both psychological and physiological (ch. 10).

Structure-Building: Levinson's term. During structure-building periods, individuals face the task of building a stable structure around choices they have made. They seek to enhance the life within that structure. This period of relative stability usually lasts five to seven years (ch. 18).

Structure-Changing: Levinson's term. A process of reappraising the existing life structure and exploring the possibilities for new life structures characterizes the *structure-changing* period. This period usually lasts for around five years. Its end is marked by the making of critical life choices around which the individual will build a new life structure (ch. 18).

Subjective Knowledge: Belenky's third phase of women's thinking; characterized by some crisis of male authority that sparked a distrust of outside sources of knowledge, and some experience that confirmed a trust in women thinkers themselves (ch. 17).

Sudden Infant Death Syndrome (SIDS): Estimates are that 10,000 2–4-month-old infants die each year from this syndrome; thought to be brain-related (ch. 5).

Symbolic Play: The game of pretending; one of five preoperational behavior patterns (ch. 7).

Suggestibility: Adolescent behavior resulting from the perceived wishes of others. Some adolescents may attempt suicide out of the perception, true or not, that their parents wish them dead (ch. 14).

Superego: One of the three structures of the psyche, according to Freud (ch. 2).

Syntax: The rules of syntax describe how to put words together to form sentences (ch. 7).

Syphilis: A sexually transmitted disease, which presents a great danger in that in its early stage there are no symptoms. Its first sign is a chancre ("shan-ker"), a painless open sore that usually shows up on the tip of the penis and around or in the vagina. After a while, this disappears, and if there is not treatment, the disease enters its third stage, which is usually deadly (ch. 15).

t

Tactical Theory of Intelligence: Perkins' term; the view that those who think better do so because they know more tactics about how to use their minds (ch. 9).

Tay-Sachs Disease: A fatal disease in which a gene fails to produce proper enzyme action (ch. 3).

Telegraphic Speech: Initial multiple word utterances, usually two or three words (ch. 5).

Temperament: A child's basic personality, which is now thought to be discernible soon after birth (ch. 6).

Temporizing: An aspect of Perry's theory of ethical development, in which some people remain in one position for a year or more, exploring its implications but hesitating to make any further progress (ch. 17).

Teratogens: Any agents that can cause abnormalities, including drugs, chemicals, infections, pollutants, and the mother's physical state (ch. 4).

Terminal Drop: The period of from a few weeks up to two years prior to the person's death, during which his or her intelligence is presumed to decline rapidly (ch. 21).

Tertiary Circular Reaction: Repetition with variation; the infant is exploring the world's possibilities (ch. 5).

Thalidomide: During the early 1960s, thalidomide was a drug popular in West Germany as a sleeping pill and an anti-nausea measure that produced no adverse reactions in women. In 1962, physicians noticed a sizeable increase in children born with either partial or no limbs. Feet and hands were directly attached to the body. Other outcomes were deafness, blindness, and occasionally mental retardation. Investigators discovered that the mothers of these children had taken thalidomide early in their pregnancy (ch. 4).

Thinking Frames: Representations intended to guide the process of thought; a guide to organizing and supporting thought processes (ch. 9).

Total Range: The behaviorists' explanation of attachment that focuses on all the reinforcements provided by the environment (ch. 6).

Traditional Marriage Enterprise: Levinson's term. The main goal of this type of marriage is to form and maintain a family (ch. 20).

Trait Theorists: Researchers who look at pieces of the personality (personality traits), as measured by detailed questionnaires (ch. 20).

Transactional Model of Development: Similar to reciprocal interactions; recognizes the child's active role in its development; "I do something to the child, the child changes; as a result of the changes in the child, I change" (ch. 1 and 6).

Transience: Toffler's term for the lack of permanence of things in our lives that leads to increased stress (ch. 16).

Transition: Levinson's concept that each new era begins as an old era is approaching its end. That "in-between" time is a transition (ch. 18).

Transsexual Operation: An operation that changes the physical characteristics of an individual to those of the opposite sex (ch. 15).

Triarchic Model: A three-tier explanation of intelligence proposed by Robert Sternberg (ch. 9).

Trophoblast: The outer surface of the fertilized egg (ch. 4).

Type T Personalities: (T for Thrills)—Adolescents who seem to have inherited a proneness to taking risks (ch. 1).

u

Ultrasound: The use of sound waves to produce an image that enables a physician to detect structural abnormalities (ch. 4).

Umbilical Cord: Contains blood vessels that go to and from the mother through the arteries and veins and supply the placenta (ch. 4).

Universalizing Faith: The final developmental step of Fowler's theory of faith. Here the individual lives in the real world, but is not of it. Such persons do not merely recognize the mutuality of existence; they act on the basis of it (ch. 23).

Use of Metaphor: The ability to think of a word or phrase that by comparison or analogy can be used to stand for another word or phrase (ch. 13).

V

Validation: Fromm's term for the main ingredient of love (ch. 17).

Variable Accommodation: Focusing on objects at various distances; appears at about 2 months (ch. 5).

Verbal Evocation: Using language to indicate somebody or something not present or occurring at that time (ch. 7).

Verbal Processing: Mental processing involving language (ch. 7).

Virilism: The development of several masculine traits in the girl, including *hirsutism* (facial and chest hair) and voice deepening (ch. 13).

Visual Impairment: Any reduction in vision (ch. 11).

Vocables: Consistent sound patterns to refer to objects and events (ch. 5).

Vocabulary: Knowing the meaning of words, not just how to pronounce them (ch. 9).

W

WAIS: The Wechsler Adult Intelligence Scale, an intelligence test devised by David Wechsler (ch. 9).

Walkabout: Originally an Aborigine initiation rite, the American version attempts to focus the activities of secondary school by demonstrating to the student the relationship between education and action (ch. 16).

Wear and Tear Theory: The theory that aging is due to the cumulative effects of hard work and lifelong stress (ch. 21).

WISC-R: The Wechsler Intelligence Scale for Children (revised), a children's intelligence test devised by David Wechsler (ch. 9).

WPPSI-R: The Wechsler Preschool and Primary Scale of Intelligence (revised), an intelligence scale for children age 4 to 6 1/2 years, devised by David Wechsler (ch. 9).

Z

Zygote: The fertilized egg (ch. 3).

References

Aban, D. F. (1978, June 5). A better way of dying. *Time, 66*.

Abernathy, T., Robinson, I., Balswick, J., & King, K. (1979). A comparison of the sexual attitudes and behavior of rural, suburban, and urban adolescents. *Adolescence, 14*(54), 289–95.

Ackerman, J. W. (1958). *The psychodynamics of family life*. New York: Basic Books.

Adalbjarnardottir, S. & Selman, R. (1989). How children propose to deal with the criticisms of their teachers and classmates: Developmental and stylistic variations. *Child Development, 60,* 539–50.

Adams, B. N. (1968). *Kinship in an urban setting*. Chicago: Markham.

Adams, J. (1986). *Conceptual blockbusting* (3rd ed.). Reading, MA: Addison-Wesley.

Ainsworth, M. D. S. (1973). The development of infant-mother attachment. In B. Caldwell & H. Ricciuti (Eds.), *Review of child development research*. Chicago: University of Chicago Press.

Ainsworth, M. D. S. (1979). Infant-mother attachment. *American Psychologist, 34,* 932–37.

Alexander, A. & Kempe, R. S. (1982). The role of the lay therapist in long-term treatment. *Child Abuse and Neglect, 6*(30), 329–34.

Allan, G. (1977). Sibling solidarity. *Journal of Marriage and the Family, 39,* 177–84.

Alpaugh, P. & Birren, J. (1977). Variables affecting creative contributions across the adult life span. *Human Development, 20,* 240–48.

Alpaugh, P., Renner, V., & Birren, J. (1976). Age and creativity. *Educational Gerontology. E.G., 1,* 17–40.

Amato, P. R. (1987). Maternal employment: Effects on children's family relationships and development. *Australian Journal of Sex, Marriage and Family, 8*(1), 5–16.

American Association of Retired Persons. (1990a, January). FDA warns against dietary supplement. *A. A. R. P., 31*(1), 7.

American Association of Retired Persons. (1990b, January). Study links alcohol to heart damage. *A. A. R. P., 31*(1), 7.

American Heart Association. (1984). *Eating for a healthy heart: Dietary treatment of hyperlipidemia*. Dallas: American Heart Association.

American Psychiatric Association. (1980). *Diagnostic and statistical manual of mental disorders* (3rd ed.). Washington, DC: Author.

Anderson, A. M. & Noesjirwan, J. A. (1980). Agricultural college initiations and the affirmation of rural ideology. *Mankind, 12*(4), 341–47.

Angle, C. (1983). Adolescent self-poisoning: A nine-year follow-up. *Developmental and Behavior Pediatrics, 4*(2), 83–87.

Anselmo, S. (1987). *Early childhood development*. Columbus, OH: Merrill.

Apgar, V. (1953). A proposal for a new method of evaluation of the newborn infant. *Anesthesia and Analgesia, 32,* 260–67.

Aries, P. (1962). *Centuries of childhood*. New York: Knopf.

Arieti, S. & Bemporad, J. (1978). *Severe and mild depression*. New York: Basic Books.

Armsden, G. C. & Greenberg, M. T. (1987). The inventory of parent and peer attachment: Individual differences and their relationship to psychological well-being in adolescence. *Journal of Youth and Adolescence, 16*(5), 427–54.

Ashton, J. & Donnan, S. (1981). Suicide by burning as an epidemic phenomenon: An analysis of 82 deaths and inquests in England and Wales in 1978–9. *Psychological Medicine, 11*(4), 735–39.

Asian-American Drug Abuse Program. (1978). *Pacific Asians and alcohol*. Los Angeles: Author.

Aslin, R. (1987). Visual and auditory development in infancy. In J. Osofsky (Ed.), *Handbook of infant development*. New York: Wiley.

Avery, M. E. & Litwack, G. (1983). *Born early*. New York: Little, Brown.

Avery-Clark, C. (1986). Sexual dysfunction and disorder patterns of husbands of working and nonworking women. *Journal of Sex and Marital Therapy, 12*(4), 282–96.

Bachman, J. G., O'Malley, P. M., & Johnston, P. (1978). *Adolescence to adulthood: Change and stability in the lives of young men*. Ann Arbor, MI: Institute for Social Research.

Baier, J. L. & Williams, P. S. (1983, July). Fraternity hazing revisited: Current alumni and active member attitudes toward hazing. *Journal of College Student Personnel, 24*(4), 300–5.

Baker, S. & Henry, R. (1987). *Parents' guide to nutrition*. Reading, MA: Addison-Wesley.

Baker, S. W. (1980, Autumn). Biological influence on human sex and gender. *Signs, 17,* 80–96

Baltes, P. B., Reese, H. W., & Nesselroade, J. R. (1977). *Life-span developmental psychology: Introduction to research methods*. Monterey, CA: Brooks/Cole.

Baltes, P. B. & Schaie, K. W. (1976). On the plasticity of intelligence in adulthood and old age—Where Horn and Donaldson fail. *American Psychologist, 31,* 720–25.

Bancroft, L. (1979). The reasons people give for taking overdoses: A further inquiry. *British Journal of Medical Psychology, 52,* 353–65.

Bandura, A. (1972). The stormy decade: Fact or fiction? In D. Rogers (Ed.), *Issues in adolescent psychology*. New York: Appleton-Century-Crofts.

Bandura, A. (1986). *Social foundations of thought and action*. Englewood Cliffs, NJ: Prentice-Hall.

Bandura, A., Ross, D., & Ross, S. (1963). Imitation of film-mediated aggressive models. *Journal of Abnormal and Social Psychology, 66,* 3–11.

Banks, S. & Kahn, M. (1982). *The sibling bond*. New York: Basic Books.

Barfield, R. & Morgan, J. (1978). Trends in planned early retirement. *Gerontologist, 18,* 13–18.

Baumrind, D. (1967). Child-care practices anteceding three patterns of preschool behavior. *Genetic Psychology Monographs, 75,* 43–88.

Baumrind, D. (1971). Current patterns of parental authority. *Developmental Psychology Monographs, 4,* 1–103.

Baumrind, D. (1983). Are androgynous individuals more effective persons and parents? *Child Psychology, 53*, 44–75.

Baumrind, D. (1986). *Familial antecedents of social competence in middle childhood.* Unpublished manuscript.

Beaconsfield, P., Birdwood, G., & Beaconsfield, R. (1983). The placenta. *Scientific American, 34*, 94–102.

Beck, A. T. (1967). *Depression: Clinical, experimental, theoretical aspects.* New York: Hoeber Medical Division, Harper & Row.

Beidelman, T. (1971) *The Kaguru: A matrilineal people of East Africa.* New York: Holt, Rinehart & Winston.

Belbin, E. & Belbin, R. M. (1968). New careers in middle age. In B. L. Neugarten (Ed.), *Middle age and aging.* Chicago: University of Chicago Press.

Belenky, M., Clinchy, B., Goldberger, N., & Tarule, J. (1986). *Women's ways of knowing.* New York: Basic Books.

Bellah, R. (1978). To kill and survive or to die and become. In E. Erikson (Ed.), *Adulthood* (pp. 61–80). New York: W. W. Norton.

Belsky, J. & Rovine, M. (1988). Nonmaternal care in the first year of life and the security of infant-parent attachment. *Child Development, 59*, 157–67.

Bem, A. (1987). Youth suicide. *Adolescence, 22*(86), 271–90.

Bem, S. L. (1975). Androgyny vs. the light little lives of fluffy women and chesty men. *Psychology Today, 9*(4), 58–59, 61–62.

Berdine, W. & Blackhurst, A. E. (1985). *An introduction to special education.* Boston: Little, Brown.

Bergman, M. (1980). *Aging and the perception of speech.* Baltimore, MD: University of Baltimore Press.

Bergman, M., Blumenfield, V. G., Cascardo, D., Dash, B., Levitt, H., & Margulios, M. K. (1976). Age-related decrements in hearing for speech: Sampling and longitudinal studies. *Journal of Gerontology, 31*, 533–38.

Berk, L. (1989). *Child development.* Boston: Allyn & Bacon.

Berk, S. F. (1985). *The gender factory: The apportionment of work in American households.* New York: Plenum Press.

Berkowitz, G. (1979, August). Religion: Does it have the answers you want? *Glamour*, 252.

Berman, M. (1975, March 30). [Review of *Life history and the historical movement* by E. Erikson.] *New York Times Magazine*, 2.

Bettelheim, B. (1969). *The children of the dream.* New York: Macmillan.

Bettelheim, B. (1976). *The uses of enchantment.* New York: Knopf.

Bettelheim, B. (1987, March). The importance of play. *The Atlantic*, 35–46.

Binet, A. & Simon, T. R. (1905). The development of intelligence. *L'Annee Psycholique*, 163–91.

Birren, J. (1960). Behavioral theories of aging. In N. Shock (Ed.), *Aging.* Washington, DC: American Association for the Advancement of Science.

Birren, J. (1964). *The psychology of aging.* Englewood Cliffs, NJ: Prentice-Hall.

Birren, J., Cunningham, W., & Yamamoto, K. (1983). Psychology of adult development and aging. In M. Rosenzweig & L. Porter (Eds.), *Annual review of psychology.* Palo Alto, CA: Annual Reviews.

Birren, P., Renner, V., & Birren, J. (1976). Age and creativity. *Educational Gerontology, 1*, 17–40.

Birtchnell, J. & Alarcon, J. (1971). The motivation and emotional state of 91 cases of attempted suicide. *British Journal of Medical Psychology, 44*, 45–52.

Bishop, J. E. (1983, December 23). New gene probes may permit early predictions of disease. *Wall Street Journal*, 11.

Black, A. (1974). *Without burnt offerings.* New York: Viking.

Blake, J. (1989). *Family size and achievement.* Berkeley, CA: University of California Press.

Block, J. (1983). Differential premises arising from differential socialization of the sexes: Some conjectures. *Child Development, 54*, 1335–54.

Block, J., Block, J., & Gjerde, P. (1986). The personality of children prior to divorce: A prospective study. *Child Development, 57*, 822–40.

Block, R. & Langman, L. (1974). Youth and work: The diffusion of counter-cultural values. *Youth and Society, 5*(4), 411–32.

Bloom, B. (Ed.). (1956). *Taxonomy of educational objectives.* New York: McKay.

Bloom, B. (1964). *Stability and change in human characteristics.* New York: Wiley.

Bloom, B. (1985). *Developing talent in young people.* New York: McGraw-Hill.

Bloom, L. & Lahey, M. (1979). *Language development and language disorders.* New York: Wiley.

Blume, J. (1970). *Are you there, God? It's me, Margaret.* New York: Bradbury.

Blume, J. (1972). *Otherwise known as Shelia the great.* New York: E. P. Dutton.

Blumenthal, S. J. & Kupfer, D. J. (1988). Overview of early detection and treatment strategies for suicidal behavior in young people. *Journal of Youth and Adolescence, 17*(1), 1–24.

Blumstein, P. & Schwartz, P. (1983). *American couples: Money, work, sex.* New York: William Morrow.

Blythe, P. (1973). *Stress and disease.* London: Barker.

Boas, F. (1911). Growth. In H. Kiddle (Ed.), *A cyclopedia of education.* New York: Steiger.

Boivin, M. & Begin, G. (1989). Peer status and self-perception among early elementary school children: The case of the rejected children. *Child Development, 60*, 591–96.

Bollen, K. & Phillips, D. (1982). Imitative suicides: A national study of the effects of television news stories. *American Sociological Review, 47*, 802–9.

Bolton, C. & Camp, D. J. (1989). The post-funeral ritual in bereavement counseling and grief work. *Journal of Gerontological Social Work, 13*, 49–59.

Bornstein, J. M. (1986). Retraining the older worker: Michigan's experience with senior employment services. Special issue: Career counseling of older adults. *Journal of Career Development, 13*(2), 14–22.

Bos, C. & Vaughn, S. (1988). *Strategies for teaching students with learning and behavior problems.* Boston: Allyn & Bacon.

Boston Women's Health Book Collective. (1976). *Our bodies, ourselves* (2nd ed.). New York: Simon & Schuster.

Botwinick, J. (1977). Intellectual abilities. In J. E. Birren & K. W. Schaie (Eds.), *Handbook of the psychology of aging.* New York: Van Nostrand Reinhold.

Botwinick, J. (1981). *Aging and behavior* (2nd ed.). New York: Springer.

Bourne, R. (1913). *Youth and life.* Boston: Little, Brown.

Bove, R. (1987). Retraining the older worker. *Training and Development Journal, 41*(3), 77–78.

Bower, R. G. (1977). *A primer of infant development.* San Francisco: W. H. Freeman.

Bowlby, J. (1969). *Attachment.* New York: Basic Books.

Bowlby, J. (1973). *Separation: Anxiety and anger.* New York: Basic Books.

Bowlby, J. (1982). Attachment and loss: Retrospect and prospect. *American Journal of Orthopsychiatry, 52,* 664–78.

Bowles, S. & Gintis, H. (1976). *Schooling in capitalist America.* New York: Basic Books.

Bowman, L. (1959). *The American funeral: A study in guilt, extravagance, and sublimity.* Washington: Public Affairs Press.

Brabeck, M. (1983). Moral judgment: Theory and research on differences between males and females. *Developmental Review, 3,* 274–91.

Brabeck, M. (1984). Longitudinal studies of intellectual development during adulthood. *Journal of Research and Development in Education, 17*(3), 12–25.

Bradway, K., Thompson, C., & Cravens, R. (1958). Preschool IQs after 25 years. *Journal of Educational Psychology, 49,* 278–81.

Brady, B. A. & Gray, D. D. (1988). Employment services for older job seekers. *The Gerontologist, 27,* 565–68.

Brain, J. L., Blake, C. F., Bluebond-Langner, M., Chilungu, S. W., Coelho, V. P., Domotor, T., Gorer, G., LaFontaine, J. S., Levy, S. B., Loukotos, D., Natarajan, N., Raphael, D., Schlegel, A., Stein, H. G., & Wilder, W. D. (1977). Sex, incest, and death: Initiation rites reconsidered. *Current Anthropology, 18*(2), 191–98.

Bransford, J. & Stein, B. (1984). *The IDEAL problem solver.* New York: W. H. Freeman.

Brazelton, T. B. (1981). *On becoming a family: The growth of attachment.* New York: Delacorte.

Brazelton, T. B. (1984). *Neonatal behavioral assessment scale.* London: Heinemann.

Brazelton, T. B. (1987). *Working and caring.* Reading, MA: Addison-Wesley.

Brazelton, T. B. & Als, H. (1979). Four early stages in the development of mother-infant interaction. *The Psychoanalytic Study of the Child, 34,* 349–69.

Brenner, A. (1984). *Helping children cope with stress.* San Diego, CA: Lexington Books.

Bretherton, I. & Waters, E. (Eds.). (1985). Growing points of attachment theory and research. *Monographs of the Society for Research in Child Development, 50* (Serial No. 209).

Bretschneider, J. G. & McCoy, N. L. (1988). Sexual interest and behavior in healthy 80 to 102 year olds. *Archives of Sexual Behavior, 17*(2), 109–29.

Bridges, K. (1930). A genetic theory of the emotions. *Journal of Genetic Psychology, 37,* 514–27.

Brim, O. G. & Kagan, J. (Eds.) (1980). *Constancy and change in human development.* Cambridge, MA: Harvard University Press.

Brim, O. S. (1958). Family structure and sex role learning by children: A further analysis of Kler Koch's data. *Sociometry, 21,* 1–16.

Brittain, W. L. (1979). *Creativity, art, and the young child.* New York: Macmillan.

Brody, J. E. (1984, January 15). The growing militance of the nation's nonsmokers. *New York Times,* 31.

Bronfenbrenner, U. (1977). Nobody home: The erosion of the American family. *Psychology Today, 10*(12), 40.

Bronfenbrenner, U. (1978). *The ecology of human development.* Cambridge, MA: Harvard University Press.

Bronowski, J. (1973). *The ascent of man.* Boston: Little, Brown.

Brooks, J. & Lewis, M. (1976). Midget, adult and child: Infants' responses to strangers. *Child Development, 47,* 323–32.

Brooks-Gunn, J. & Furstenberg, F. (1986). The children of adolescent mothers: Physical, academic, and psychological outcomes. *Developmental Review, 6*(3), 224–51.

Brown, G. W., Bhrolchain, M. N., & Harris, R. (1975). Social class and psychiatric disturbance among women in an urban population. *Sociology, 9,* 225–54.

Brown, M. (1979). Teenage prostitution. *Adolescence, 14*(56), 665–80.

Brown, S. V. (1983). The commitment and concerns of black adolescent parents. *Social Work Research and Abstracts, 19*(4), 27–34.

Browne, A. & Finkelhor, D. (1986). Impact of child sexual abuse: A review of the research. *Psychological Bulletin, 99,* 66–77.

Bruch, H. (1981). *Eating disorders.* Canada: Basic Books.

Bruner, J., Jolly, A., & Sylva, K. (1978). *Play: Its role in development and evolution.* New York: Basic Books.

Buehler, C. A., Hogan, M. J., Robinson, B. E., & Levy, R. J. (1985–86). The parental divorce transition: Divorce-related stressors and well-being. *Journal of Divorce, 9*(2), 61–81.

Buffum, J. (1988). Substance abuse and high-risk sexual behavior: Drugs and sex—the dark side. *Journal of Psychoactive Drugs, 20*(2), 165–68.

Buffum, J. & Moser, C. (1986). MDMA and human sexual function. *Journal of Psychoactive Drugs, 18*(4), 355–59.

Burnham, W. (1911). Hygiene and adolescence. In H. Kiddle (Ed.), *A cyclopedia of education.* New York: Steiger.

Burton, C. A. (1978). *Juvenile street gangs: Predators and children.* Unpublished manuscript, Boston College.

Burvill, P. & Johnson, C. (1982). The relationship between suicide, undetermined deaths, and accidental deaths in the Australian born and immigrants in Australia. *Australian and New Zealand Journal of Psychiatry, 16*(3), 179–84.

Buskirk, E. R. (1985). Health maintenance and longevity: Exercise. In C. E. Finch & E. L. Schneider (Eds.), *Handbook of the biology of aging* (2nd ed.). New York: Van Nostrand Reinhold.

Butler, R. N. & Lewis, M. I. (1977). *Aging and mental health* (2nd ed.). St. Louis: Mosby.

Cahill, M. & Salomone, P. R. (1987). Career counseling for work life extension: Integrating the older worker into the labor force. *Career Development Quarterly, 35*(3), 188–96.

Campbell, A. (1975). The American way of mating: Marriage si; children only maybe. *Psychology Today, 8,* 37–43.

Campbell, A. (1987). Self definition by rejection: The case of gang girls. *Social Problems, 34,* 451–66.

Campbell, B. & Gaddy, J. (1987). Rates of aging and dietary restrictions: Sensory and motor function in the Fischer 344 rat. *Journal of Gerontology, 42*(2), 154–59.

Campbell, S. (1979). Delayed mandatory retirement and the working woman. *The Gerontologist, 19,* 257–63.

Campione, W. A. (1987). The married woman's retirement decision: A methodological comparison. *Journal of Gerontology, 42*(4), 381–86.

Camus, A. (1948). *The plague.* New York: The Modern Library.

Canestrari, J. (1963). Paces and self-paced learning in young and elderly adults. *Journal of Gerontology, 18,* 165–68.

Cangemi, J. & Kowalski, C. (1987). Developmental tasks and student behavior: Some comments. *College Student Journal, 21,* 321–29.

Cantwell, D. P. & Carlson, G. A. (1983). *Affective disorders in childhood and adolescence.* New York: Spectrum.

Caplan, T. & Caplan, F. (1983). *The early childhood years.* New York: Bantam Books, Inc.

Carey, J. (1983, December 16). Weight gained later in life is more risky for the heart. *USA Today,* 3.

Carey, W. (1981). The importance of temperament-environment interaction. In M. Lewis & L. Rosenblum (Eds.), *The uncommon child.* New York: Plenum.

Carlson, G. A. (1983). Depression and suicidal behavior in children and adolescents. In D. P. Cantwell & G. A. Carlson (Eds.), *Affective disorders in childhood and adolescence* (pp. 335–51). New York: Spectrum.

Carnevali, D. L. & Patrick, M. (Eds.). (1986). *Nursing management for the elderly* (2nd ed.). Philadelphia: J.B. Lippincott.

Cassell, E. (1979, February 18). Medical technology raises moral issues. *Boston Globe,* A12.

Cassem, N. (1975). Bereavement as a relative experience. In B. Schoenberg & others, (Eds.), *Bereavement* (pp. 3–9). New York: Columbia University Press.

Catania, J. A., Turner, H., Kegeles, S. M., Stall, R., Pollack, L., & Coates, T. J. (1989). Older Americans and AIDS: Transmission risks and primary prevention research needs. *The Gerontologist, 29,* 373–81.

Cath, S. H. (1975). The orchestration of disengagement. *International Journal of Aging and Human Development, 6,* 199–213.

Celotta, B., Jacobs, G., & Keys, S. G. (1987). Searching for suicidal precursors in the elementary school child. Special issue: Identifying children and adolescents in need of mental health services. *American Mental Health Counselors Association Journal, 9*(1), 38–50.

Center for Disease Control. (1989a). AIDS and human immunodeficiency virus infection in the United States: 1988 update. *Morbidity and Mortality Weekly Report, 38,* 1–35.

Center for Disease Control. (1989b). First 100,000 cases of Acquired Immunodeficiency Syndrome—United States. *Morbidity and Mortality Weekly Report, 38,* 561–62.

Center for Disease Control. (1989c). Update: Heterosexual transmission of Acquired Immunodeficiency Syndrome and Human Immunodeficiency virus infection—United States. *Morbidity and Mortality Weekly Report, 38,* 36–40.

Chall, J. S. (1983). *Stages of reading development.* New York: McGraw-Hill.

Chebator, P. (1984). *The bar exam.* Boston, MA: Boston College.

Chess, S. & Hassibi, M. (1978). *Principles and practices in child psychiatry.* New York: Plenum.

Chewning, B., Lohr, S., Van Koningsveld, R., Hawkins, R., Bosworth, K., Gustafson, D., & Day, T. (1986, April). *Family communication patterns and adolescent sexual behavior.* Paper presented at the Society for Research on Adolescence, Madison, WI.

Chilman, C. (1974). *Adolescent sexuality in a changing American society.* Washington, DC: ERIC document.

Chilman, C. (1985). Feminist issues in teenage parenting. Special issue: Toward a feminist approach to child welfare. *Child Welfare, 64*(3), 225–34.

Chomsky, N. (1957). *Syntactic structures.* The Hague: Mouton.

Christiansen, B. A., Roehling, P. V., Smith, G. T., & Goldman, M. S. (1989). Using alcohol expectancies to predict adolescent drinking behavior after one year. *Journal of Consulting and Clinical Psychology, 57*(1), 93–99.

Cicirelli, V. G. (1979). *Social services for elderly in relation to the kin network.* Report to the NRTA-AARP Andrus Foundation, Washington, DC.

Cicirelli, V. G. (1980). Sibling relationships in adulthood: A lifespan perspective. In L. W. Poon (Ed.), *Aging in the 1980s: Psychological issues* (pp. 455–62). Washington, DC: American Psychological Association.

Clark, S. D., Zabin, L. S., & Hardy, J. B. (1984). Sex, contraception and parenthood: Experience and attitudes among urban black young men. *Family Planning Perspective, 16*(2), 77–82.

Clarke, A. & Clarke, A. D. (1976). *Early experience: Myth and evidence.* New York: The Free Press.

Clarke-Stewart, A. (1978). And daddy makes three: The father's impact on mother and young child. *Child Development, 49,* 466–78.

Clarke-Stewart, A. (1982). *Daycare.* Cambridge, MA: Harvard University Press.

Clemens, S. (1907–1919). Pudd'nhead Wilson and those extraordinary twins. In *The Writings of Mark Twain* (Vol. 14). New York: Harper.

Cohen, L. H., Burt, C. E., & Bjorck, J. P. (1987). Life stress and adjustment: Effects of life events experienced by young adolescents and their parents. *Developmental Psychology, 23*(4), 583–92.

Cohen, S. & Spacapan, S. (1978). The aftereffects of stress: An attentional interpretation. *Environmental Psychology and Nonverbal Behavior, 3,* 43–57.

Cohn, R. (1979). Age and the satisfactions from work. *Journal of Gerontology, 34,* 264–72.

Colby, A., Kohlberg, L., Gibbs, J., & Lieberman, M. (1983). A longitudinal study of moral judgment. *Monographs of the Society for Research in Child Development, 48* (Serial No. 200).

Cole, C. (1986). Developmental tasks affecting the marital relationship in later life. *American Behavioral Scientist, 29,* 389–403.

Coleman, J. (1976). *Abnormal psychology and modern life.* Glenview, IL: Scott, Foresman.

Coleman, J. S. (1961). *The adolescent society.* Glencoe, IL: Free Press.

Coleman, J. S. (1974). Comments on responses to youth: Transition to adulthood. *School Review, 83*(1), 139–44.

Colletta, N. (1982). How adolescents cope with problems of early motherhood. *Adolescence, 16*(63), 499–512.

Colligan, J. (1975). Achievement and personality characteristics as predictors of observed tutor behavior. *Dissertation Abstracts International, 35,* 4293–94.

Comfort, A. (1964). *Aging: The biology of senescence.* New York: Holt, Rinehart & Winston.

Conrad, R. (1964). Acoustic confusion in immediate memory. *British Journal of Psychology, 55,* 75–84.

Cooney, T. M., Schaie, K. W., & Willis, S. L. (1988). The relationship between prior functioning on cognitive and personality dimensions and subject attrition in longitudinal research. *Journal of Gerontology: Psychological Sciences, 43*(1), 12–17.

Cooper, C. L. (Ed.). (1984). *Psychosocial stress and cancer.* New York: Wiley & Sons.

Cooper, C. R. & Grotevant, H. D. (1987). Gender issues in the interface of family experience and adolescents' friendship and dating identity. *Journal of Youth and Adolescence, 16*(3), 247–65.

Cooper, R. M., Bilash, I., & Zubek, J. P. (1959). The effect of age on taste sensitivity. *Journal of Gerontology, 14,* 56–58.

Corder, B. G., Shorr, W., & Corder, R. E. (1974). A study of social and psychological characteristics of adolescent suicide attempts in an urban, disadvantaged area. *Adolescence, 9* (33), 1–6.

Corso, J. (1971). Sensory processes and age effects in normal adults. *Journal of Gerontology, 26,* 90.

Costa, P. T., Jr. & McCrae, R. (1980). Still stable after all these years: Personality as a key to some issues in adulthood and old age. In P. B. Baltes (Ed.), *Life-span development and behavior* (Vol. 3, pp. 65–102). New York: Academic Press.

Cote, J. E. & Levine, C. (1988). The relationship between ego identity status and Erikson's notions of institutionalized moratoria, value orientation stage, and ego dominance. *Journal of Youth and Adolescence, 17*(1), 81–100.

Cowan, R. S. (1987). Women's work, housework, and history: The historical roots of inequality in work-force participation. In N. Gerstel & H. E. Gross (Eds.), *Families and work* (pp. 164–77). Philadelphia: Temple University Press.

Cowley, G. (1989, December 18). Medical mystery tour. *Newsweek,* 59.

Cox, H. (1988). *Later life.* Englewood Cliffs, NJ: Prentice-Hall.

Craig-Bray, L., Adams, G. R., & Dobson, W. R. (1988). Identity formation and social relations during late adolescence. *Journal of Youth and Adolescence, 17*(2), 173–88.

Craik, F. I. M. (1977). Age differences in human memory. In J. E. Birren & K. W. Schaie (Eds.), *Handbook of the psychology of aging.* New York: Van Nostrand Reinhold.

Craik, F. I. M. & Simon, E. (1980). Age differences in memory: The roles of attention and depth of processing. In L. W. Poon, J. L. Fozard, L. S. Cermak, D. Arenberg, & L. W. Thompson (Eds.), *New directions in memory and aging: Proceedings of the George Talland Memorial Conference.* Hillsdale, NJ: Lawrence Erlbaum.

Cratty, B. (1979). *Perceptual and motor development in infants and children.* Englewood Cliffs, NJ: Prentice-Hall.

Craven, J. & Wald, F. (1975, October). Hospice care for dying patients. *American Journal of Nursing,* 1816–22.

Cristante, F. & Lucca, A. (1987). Cognitive functioning as measured by various developmental tasks and social competence in late childhood. *Archivio-di-Psycologia, 48,* 62–74.

Crockenberg, S. (1981). Irritability, mother responsiveness, and social support influences on the security of infant-mother attachment. *Child Development, 52,* 857–65.

Crockett, L., Losaff, M., & Petersen, A. (1986). Perceptions of the peer group and friendship in early adolescence. *Journal of Early Adolescence, 4*(2), 155–81.

Cronin, K. & Wald, K. (1979). *Successful dying.* Unpublished manuscript, Boston College, Chestnut Hill, MA.

Crouter, A. C., Perry-Jenkins, M., Huston, T. L., & McHale, S. M. (1987). Processes underlying father involvement in dual-earner and single-earner families. *Developmental Psychology, 23,* 431–40.

Crowley, J. E. (1986). Longitudinal effects of retirement on men's well-being & health. *Journal of Business and Psychology, 1*(2), 95–113.

Crumley, F. (1982). The adolescent suicide attempt: A cardinal symptom of a serious psychiatric disorder. *American Journal of Psychotherapy, 36*(2), 158–65.

Cullinan, D. & Epstein, M. H. (1979). *Special education for adolescents: Issues and perspectives.* Columbus, OH: Merrill.

Curran, D. (1984). Peer attitudes toward attempted suicide in mid-adolescents. *Dissertation Abstracts International, 44*(12), 3927B.

Curtis, H. (1966). *Biological mechanisms of aging.* Springfield, IL: Ch. Thomas.

Curtiss, S. (1977). *Genie: A psycholinguistic study of a modern-day "wild child."* New York: Academic Press.

Cutler, S. J. & Grams, A. E. (1988). Correlates of self-reported everyday memory problems. *Journal of Gerontology: Social Sciences, 43*(3), 82–90.

Dacey, J. (1976). *New ways to learn.* Stamford, CT: Greylock.

Dacey, J. S. (1981). *Where the world is.* Glenview, IL: Goodyear.

Dacey, J. S. (1982). *Adult development.* Glenview, IL: Scott, Foresman.

Dacey, J. S. (1986). *Adolescents today* (3rd ed.). Glenview, IL: Scott, Foresman.

Dacey, J. S. (1989). *Fundamentals of creative thinking.* Lexington, MA: D.C. Heath/Lexington Books.

Dacey, J. S. (1989a). Peak periods of creative growth across the life span. *The Journal of Creative Behavior, 24*(4), 224–47.

Dacey, J. S. (1989b). Discriminating characteristics of the families of highly creative adolescents. *The Journal of Creative Behavior, 24*(4), 263–71.

Dacey, J. S. (in progress). *The psychology of self-control.*

Dacey, J. S. & Gordon, M. (1971, February). *Implications of post-natal cortical development for creativity research.* Paper presented at the American Education Research Association Convention, New York City.

Dacey, J. S. & Leona, M. (in press). Recent attitude changes among adolescents as observed by adults who work with them. *Adolescence.*

Dacey, J., Madaus, G., & Crellin, D. (1968, November). *Can creativity be facilitated? The critical period hypothesis.* Paper presented at Ninth Annual Convention of the Educational Research Association of New York State, Kiamesho Lake.

Dacey, J. S. & Ripple, R. E. (1967). The facilitation of problem solving and verbal creativity by exposure to programmed instruction. *Psychology in the School, 4*(3), 240–45.

Dacey, J. S. & Williams, F. (in press). Some proposals for the improvement of adolescent life. *Adolescence.*

Damon, W. (1983). *Social and personality development.* New York: Norton.

Darling, C. A. & Hicks, M. W. (1982). Parental influence on adolescent sexuality: Implications for parents as educators. *Journal of Youth and Adolescence, 11,* 231–45.

Daugherty, L. R. & Burger, J. M. (1984). The influence of parents, church, and peers on the sexual attitudes and behaviors of college students. *Archives of Sexual Behavior, 13,* 351–59.

Davis, G. A. (1971). Teaching for creativity: Some guiding lights. *Journal of Research and Development in Education, 4*(3), 29–34.

Davis, S. M. & Harris, J. (1982). Sexual knowledge, sexual interests, and sources of sexual information of rural and urban adolescents from three cultures. *Adolescence, 17*(66), 471–92.

De Casper, A. & Fifer, W. (1980). Studying learning in the womb. *Science, 208,* 1174.

De Chardin, T. (1959). *The phenomenon of man* (B. Wall, Trans.). New York: Harper & Row.

Dellas, M. & Jernigan, L. P. (1987). Occupational identity status development, gender comparisons, and internal-external locus of control in first-year Air Force cadets. *Journal of Youth and Adolescence, 16*(6), 587–600.

Dembo, R. (1981). Examining a causal model of early drug involvement among inner-city junior high school youths. *Human Relations, 34*(3), 169–93.

Demoise, C. & Conrad, R. (1972). Effects of age and radiation exposure on chromosomes in a Marshall Island population. *Journal of Gerontology, 27*(2), 197–201.

Dennis, W. (1966). Creative productivity between 20 and 80 years. *Journal of Gerontology, 21,* 1–8.

Detting, E. R. & Beauvais, F. (1987). Peer cluster theory, socialization characteristics, and adolescent drug use: A path analysis. *Journal of Counseling Psychology, 34*(2), 205–13.

Devilliers, J. & Devilliers, P. (1978). *Language acquisition.* Cambridge, MA: Harvard University Press.

DeVries, H. A. (1981). Physiology of exercise and aging. In D. F. Woodruff & J. E. Birren (Eds.), *Aging: Scientific perspectives and social issues* (pp. 464–65). New York: Van Nostrand Reinhold.

Dewey, J. (1933). *How we think.* Boston: Heath.

Diamond, M. (1982). Sexual identity, monozygotic twins reared in discordant sex roles, and a BBC follow-up. *Archives of Sexual Behavior, 11,* 181–85.

Doman, G. (1983). *How to teach your baby to read.* New York: Doubleday.

Dotz, W. & German, B. (1983). The facts about treatment of dry skin. *Geriatrics, 38,* 93.

Douvan, E. & Adelson, J. (1985). *The adolescent experience.* New York: Wiley.

Dranoff, S. M. (1974). Masturbation and the male adolescent. *Adolescence, 9*(34), 16–176.

Duncan, C. (1979). *A death curriculum.* Unpublished doctoral dissertation, Boston College, Chestnut Hill, MA.

Dunn, J. (1983). Sibling relationships in early childhood. *Child Development, 54,* 787–811.

Dunn, J. (1985). *Sisters and brothers.* Cambridge, MA: Harvard University Press.

Dunn, J. (1988). Sibling influences on childhood development. *Journal of Child Psychology and Child Psychiatry, 29,* 119–29.

Duvall, E. (1971). *Family development.* Philadelphia: Lippincott.

Earle, J. R. & Perricone, P. J. (1986). Premarital sexuality: A ten-year study of attitudes and behavior on a small university campus. *Journal of Sex Research, 22*(3), 304–10.

Eberhardt, C. A. & Schill, T. (1984). Differences in sexual attitudes and likeliness of sexual behaviors of black lower-socioeconomic father-present vs. father-absent female adolescents. *Adolescence, 19*(73), 99–105.

Eichorn, D. (1979). Physical development: Current face of research. In J. Osofsky (Ed.), *Handbook of infant development.* New York: Wiley.

Eichorn, D. H., Clausen, J. A., Haan, N., Honzik, M. P., & Mussen, P. H. (Eds.). (1981). *Past and present in middle life.* New York: Academic Press.

Eifrig, D. E. & Simons, K. B. (1983). An overview of common geriatric ophthalmologic disorders. *Geriatrics, 38,* 55.

Eisdorfer, C. & Wilkie, F. (1973). Intellectual changes and advancing age. In L. Jarvik (Ed.), *Intellectual functioning in adults.* New York: Springer.

Elias, M. & Elias, J. (1976). Matching of successive auditory stimuli as a function of age and year of presentation. *Journal of Gerontology, 31,* 164.

Elias, M., Elias, P., & Elias, J. (1977). *Basic processes in adult developmental psychology.* St. Louis: Mosby.

Elkin, F. & Handel, G. (1989). *The child and society.* New York: Random House.

Elkind, D. (1971). *A sympathetic understanding of the child six to sixteen.* Boston: Allyn & Bacon.

Elkind, D. (1978). *The child's reality: Three developmental themes.* Hillsdale, NJ: Erlbaum.

Elkind, D. (1981). *The hurried child.* Reading, MA: Addison-Wesley.

Elkind, D. (1987). *Miseducation: Preschoolers at risk.* New York: Knopf.

Elkind, D. (1989, June 30). Under pressure. *The Boston Globe Magazine,* 24 ff.

Elkind, D. & Bowen, R. (1979). Imaginary audience behavior in children and adolescents. *Developmental Psychology, 15,* 38–44.

Elsayed, M., Ismail, A. H., & Young, J. R. (1980). Intellectual differences of adult men related to age and physical fitness before and after an exercise program. *Journal of Gerontology, 35,* 383–87.

Engstrom, P. F. (1986). Cancer control objectives for the year 2000. In L. E. Mortenseon, P. F. Engstrom, & P. N. Anderson (Eds.), *Advances in cancer control.* New York: Alan R. Liss.

Ennis, R. (1987). A taxonomy of critical thinking dispositions and abilities. In J. Baron & R. Sternberg (Eds.), *Teaching thinking skills.* New York: W. H. Freeman.

Enright, R. D., Levy, V. M., Harris, D., & Lapsley, D. K. (1987). Do economic conditions influence how theorists view adolescents? *Journal of Youth and Adolescence, 16*(6), 541–60.

Epstein, J. L. (1980). *A longitudinal study of school and family effects on student development.* Baltimore, MD: The Johns Hopkins University Press.

Erikson, E. H. (1958). *Young man Luther: A study in psychoanalysis and history.* New York: W. W. Norton.

Erikson, E. H. (1959). Identity and the life cycle. *Psychological Issues, 1,* 18–164.

Erikson, E. H. (1963). *Childhood and society* (2nd ed.). New York: W. W. Norton.

Erikson, E. H. (1968). *Identity: Youth and crisis.* New York: W. W. Norton.

Erikson, E. H. (1969). *Gandhi's truth: On the origins of militant nonviolence.* New York: W. W. Norton.

Erikson, E. H. (1975). *Life, history and the historical moment.* New York: W. W. Norton.

Erikson, E. H. (1978). *Adulthood.* New York: W. W. Norton.

Erickson, M. (1982). *Child psychopathology.* Englewood Cliffs, NJ: Prentice-Hall.

Estrada, A., Rabow, J., & Watts, R. K. (1982). Alcohol use among Hispanic adolescents: A preliminary report. *Hispanic Journal of Behavioral Sciences, 4*(3), 339–51.

Fagot, B. (1985). Changes in thinking about early sex role development. *Developmental Review, 5,* 83–98.

Faier, J. (1979, August). Sexual harassment on the job. *Harper's Bazaar,* 90–91.

Falco, M. (1988). *Preventing abuse of drugs, alcohol, and tobacco by adolescents.* Washington, DC: Carnegie Council on Adolescent Development.

Falknor, H. P. & Kugler, D. (1981). *JCAH hospice project, interim report: Phase I*. Chicago: Joint Commission on Accreditation of Hospitals.

Fantz, R. (1961). The origin of form perception. *Scientific American, 204,* 66–72.

Farber, E. & Egeland, B. (1987). *The invulnerable child*. New York: Guilford.

Farber, S. (1981). *Identical twins reared apart: A reanalysis*. New York: Basic Books.

Farley, F. (1986). The big T in personality. *Psychology Today, 70,* 44–52.

Farrell, M. P. & Rosenberg, S. D. (1981). *Men at midlife*. Boston: Auburn House.

Federal Bureau of Investigation. (1981). *Uniform crime reports for the U.S.* Washington, DC: U.S. Government Printing Office.

Federal Bureau of Investigation. (1989). *Uniform crime reports for the U.S.* Washington, DC: U.S. Government Printing Office.

Feifel, H. (1977). *New meanings of death*. New York: McGraw-Hill.

Feingold, M. & Pashayan, H. (1983). *Genetic and birth defects in clinical practice*. Boston: Little, Brown.

Feldman, D. (1979). The mysterious case of extreme giftedness. In A. H. Passow (Ed.), *The gifted and the talented: Their education and development*. Chicago: University of Chicago Press (NSSE).

Feldman, D., Rosenberg, M. S., & Peer, G. G. (1984). Educational therapy: A behavior change strategy for predelinquent and delinquent youth. *Journal of Child and Adolescent Psychotherapy, 1*(1), 34–37.

Feldman, H. (1981). A comparison of intentional parents and intentionally childless couples. *Journal of Marriage and the Family, 43,* 593–600.

Fendrich, M. (1984). Wives' employment and husbands' distress: A meta-analysis and a replication. *Journal of Marriage and the Family, 46,* 871–79.

Ferber, R. (1985). *Solve your child's sleep problems*. New York: Simon & Schuster.

Ferreira, A. J. (1960). The pregnant mother's emotional attitude and its reflection upon the newborn. *American Journal of Orthopsychiatry, 30,* 553–61.

Findlay, S. (1983, December 6). Study finds family link to heart ills. *USA Today,* 1.

Findley, P. (1979, December 13). This law is for you. *Parade,* 5–6.

First, J. (1988). Immigrant students in U.S. public schools: Challenges with solutions. *Phi Delta Kappan, 70,* 205–10.

Fischer, K. & Silvern, L. (1985). Stages and individual differences in cognitive development. In M. Rosenzweig & L. Porter (Eds.), *Annual review of psychology*. Palo Alto, CA: Annual Reviews.

Fischer, M., Rolf, J., Hasazi, J., & Cummings, L. (1984). Follow-up of a preschool epidemiological sample: Cross-age continuities and predictions of later adjustment with internalizing and externalizing dimensions of behavior. *Child Development, 55,* 137–50.

Fisher, T. D. (1986a). An exploratory study of communication about sex and similarity in sexual attitudes in early, middle, and late adolescents and their parents. *Journal of Genetic Psychology, 147,* 543–57.

Fisher, T. D. (1986b). Parent-child communication and adolescents' sexual knowledge and attitudes. *Adolescence, 21,* 517–27.

Fitzpatrick, M. A. (1984). A typological approach to marital interaction: Recent theory and research. In L. Berkowitz (Ed.), *Advances in experimental social psychology* (Vol. 18). New York: Academic Press.

Flavell, J. H. (1963). *The developmental psychology of Jean Piaget*. New York: Van Nostrand.

Flavell, J. H. (1977). *Cognitive development*. Englewood Cliffs, NJ: Prentice-Hall.

Florian, V. & Zernicky-Shurka, E. (1986). Vocational instructor burnout in two national rehabilitation systems in Israel. *Journal of Applied Rehabilitation Counseling, 17*(1), 41–44.

Forstein, M. (1989, April 7–9). *Sexuality and AIDS*. Paper presented at the Conference on the Psychiatric Treatment of Adolescents and Young Adults, Harvard Medical School, Boston, MA.

Foster, S. (1988). *The one girl in ten: A self portrait of the teenage mother*. Washington, DC: The Child Welfare League of America.

Fowler, J. (1974). Toward a developmental perspective on faith. *Religious Education, 69,* 207–19.

Fowler, J. (1975a). *Stages in faith: The structural developmental approach*. Harvard Divinity School Research Project on Faith and Moral Development.

Fowler, J. (1975b, October). *Faith development theory and the aims of religious socialization*. Paper presented at annual meeting of the Religious Research Association, Milwaukee, WI.

Fox, L. H. & Washington, J. (1985). Programs for the gifted and talented: Past, present, and future. In F. D. Horowitz & M. O'Brien (Eds.), *The gifted and talented*. Washington, DC: American Psychological Association.

Fozard, J. L. (1980). The time for remembering. In L. W. Poon (Ed.), *Aging in the 1980s: Psychological issues* (pp. 273–87). Washington, DC: American Psychological Association.

Fozard, J. L., Wolf, E., Bell, B., McFarland, R. A., & Podolsky, S. (1977). Visual perception and communication. In J. E. Birren & K. W. Schaie (Eds.), *Handbook of the psychology of aging*. New York: Van Nostrand Reinhold.

Fraiberg, S. (1959). *The magic years*. New York: Scribner.

Frankl, V. (1967). *Psychotherapy and existentialism*. New York: Simon & Schuster.

Frederick, C. (1971). The present suicide taboo in the United States. *Mental Hygiene, 55*(2), 178–83.

Freeman, E. W. (1982). Self-reports of emotional distress in a sample of urban black high school students. *Psychological Medicine, 12*(4), 809–17.

Freud, A. (1968). Adolescence. In A. E. Winder & D. L. Angus (Eds.), *Adolescence: Contemporary studies*. New York: American Book.

Freud, S. (1955). Totem and taboo. In J. Strachey (Ed. and Trans.), *The standard edition of the complete psychological works of Sigmund Freud* (Vol. 13). London: Hogarth Press. (Original work published 1914)

Freud, S. (1957). *Mourning and melancholia*. In J. Strachey (Ed. and Trans.), *The standard edition of the complete psychological works of Sigmund Freud* (Vol. 14, 239–58). London: Hogarth Press. (Original work published 1915)

Freudenberger, H. (1973). A patient in need of mothering. *Psychoanalytic Review, 60*(1), 7–10.

Frey, B. A. & Noller, R. B. (1983). Mentoring: A legacy of success. *Journal of creative behavior, 17*(1), 60–64.

Friedan, B. (1963). *The feminine mystique*. New York: W. W. Norton.

Friedenberg, E. (1959). *The vanishing adolescent*. Boston: Beacon Press.

Friedenberg, E. (1967). *Society's children*. New York: Random House.

Friedman, C. J., Mann, F., & Friedman, A. (1976). Juvenile street gangs: The victimization of youth. *Adolescence, 11,* 527.

Frisch, R. (1978). Menarche and fatness. *Science, 200,* 1509–13.

Fromm, E. (1955). *The sane society.* New York: Holt, Rinehart & Winston.

Fromm, E. (1968). *The art of loving.* New York: Harper & Row.

Fulton, R. (1977). General aspects. In N. Linzer (Ed.), *Understanding bereavement and grief.* New York: Yeshiva University Press.

Fulton, R. & Owen, G. (1988). Death and society in twentieth century America. *Omega, 18,* 379–95.

Gabriel, A. & McAnarney, E. R. (1983). Parenthood in two subcultures: White, middle-class couples and black, low-income adolescents in Rochester, New York. *Adolescence, 18*(71), 595–608.

Gagnon, J. H. & Simon, W. (1969). They're going to learn on the street anyway. *Psychology Today, 3*(2), 46 ff.

Gagnon, J. H. & Simon, W. (1987). The sexual scripting of oral genital contacts. *Archives of Sexual Behavior, 16*(1), 1–25.

Galambos, N. L. & Lerner, J. V. (1987). Child characteristics and the employment of mothers with young children: A longitudinal study. *Journal of Child Psychology and Psychiatry and Allied Disciplines, 28*(1), 87–98.

Gallup, G. (1988). *The Gallup poll.* New York: Random House.

Gallup, G. E. (1977). Ninth Annual Gallup poll of the public's attitudes. *Phi Delta Kappan, 59*(1), 34–48.

Galton, F. (1870). *Hereditary genius.* New York: Appleton.

Galton, F. (1879). Psychometric experiments. *Brain, 2,* 148–62.

Garapon, A. (1983, August/September). Place de l'initiation dans la délinquance juvénile. (Initiation role in juvenile delinquency.) *Neuropsychiatrie de l'Enfance et de l'adolescence, 31*(8–9), 390–403.

Garcia-Coll, C., Hoffman, J., & Oh, W. (1987). The social ecology and early parenting of Caucasian adolescent mothers. *Child Development, 58*(4), 955–63.

Gardner, H. (1980). *Artful scribbles.* New York: Basic Books.

Gardner, H. (1982). *Art, mind, and brain: A cognitive approach to creativity.* New York: Basic Books.

Gardner, H. (1982). *Developmental psychology.* Boston: Little, Brown.

Gardner, H. (1983). *Frames of mind: The theory of multiple intelligences.* New York: Basic Books.

Gardner, H. (1985). *The mind's new science: A history of the cognitive revolution.* New York: Basic Books.

Gardner, H. & Winner, E. (1982). Children's conceptions (and misconceptions) of the arts. In H. Gardner, *Art, mind, and brain.* New York: Basic Books.

Garmezy, N. (1987). Stress, competence, and development: The search for stress-resistant children. *American Journal of Orthopsychiatry, 57,* 159–74.

Garmezy, N. & Rutter, M. (Eds.). (1988). *Stress, coping, and development in children.* Baltimore: The Johns Hopkins University Press.

Garn, S. M. & Petzold, A. (1983). Characteristics of the mother and child in teenage pregnancy. *American Journal of Diseases of Children, 137*(4), 365–68.

Garner, H. G. (1975). An adolescent suicide, the mass media and the educator. *Adolescence, 17*(2), 23–27.

Garvey, M. S. (1986). The high cost of sexual harassment suits. *Personnel Journal, 65*(1), 75–78, 80.

Gay, P. (1988). *Freud: A life for our time.* New York: W. W. Norton.

Gays on the March. (1975, September 8). *Time,* 32–43.

Geer, J., Heiman, J., & Leitenberg, H. (1984). *Human sexuality.* Englewood Cliffs, NJ: Prentice-Hall.

Gelman, D. (1989, December 18). The brain killer. *Newsweek,* 54–83.

Gelman, R. (1969). Conservation acquisition: A problem of learning to attend to relevant attributes. *Journal of Experimental Child Psychology, 7,* 167–87.

Gelman, R. & Baillargeon, R. (1983). A review of some Piagetian concepts. In P. Mussen (Ed.), *Handbook of child psychology.* New York: Wiley.

George, L. K. & Landerman, R. (1984). Health and subjective well-being. *International Journal of Aging and Human Development, 19,* 133–56.

Gerson, J. M. (1985). *Hard choices: How women decide about work, career, and motherhood.* Berkeley, CA: University of California Press.

Gerson, L. W., Jarjoura, D., & McCord, G. (1987). Factors related to impaired mental health in urban elderly. *Research on Aging, 9*(3), 356–71.

Gesel, A. (1940). *The first five years of life.* New York: Harper.

Gest, T. (1989, December 1). Is there a right to die? *Time,* 35–37.

Gibbons, M. (1974). Walkabout: Searching for the right passage from childhood and school. *Phi Delta Kappan, 55*(9), 596–602.

Gibson, E. & Wolk, R. (1960). The visual cliff. *Scientific American, 202,* 64–71.

Gierz, M., Haris, J., & Lohr, J. B (1989). Recognition and treatment of depression in Alzheimer's disease. *Geriatrics, 36,* 901–11.

Gilligan, C. (1977). In a different voice: Women's conception of self and morality. *Harvard Educational Review, 47,* 481–517.

Gilligan, C. (1982). *In a different voice: Psychological theory and women's development.* Cambridge, MA: Harvard University Press.

Gimby, G. & Saltin, B. (1983). The aging muscle. *Clinical Physiology, 3,* 209–18.

Gitlin, T. (1987). *Years of hope, days of rage.* New York: Bantam Books, Inc.

Glaser, K. (1965). Attempted suicide in children and adolescents. *American Journal of Psychotherapy, 19*(2), 220–27.

Glaser, K. (1978). The treatment of depressed and suicidal adolescents. *American Journal of Psychotherapy, 32*(2), 252–69.

Glass, A., Holyoak, K., & Santa, J. (1987). *Cognition.* Reading, MA: Addison-Wesley.

Glenn, E. N. (1978). *Behavior in the human male.* Philadelphia: Saunders.

Gloecker, T. & Simpson, C. (1988). *Exceptional students in regular classrooms.* Mountain View, CA: Mayfield.

Goertzel, V. & Goertzel, M. (1962). *Cradles of eminence.* Boston: Little, Brown.

Goethals, G. & Klos, D. (1976). *Experiencing youth.* Boston: Little, Brown.

Goetting, A. (1986). The developmental tasks of siblingship over the life cycle. *Journal of Marriage and the Family, 48,* 703–14.

Gold, M. & Douvan, E. (1969). *Adolescent development: Readings in research and theory.* Boston: Allyn & Bacon.

Goldberg, S. (1983). Parent-infant bonding: Another look. *Child Development, 54,* 1355–82.

Goldberg, S. & DiVitto, B. (1983). *Born too soon.* San Francisco: Freeman, Cooper.

Goldman-Rakic, P., Isseroff, A., Schwartz, M., & Bugbee, N. (1983). The neurobiology of cognitive development. In P. Mussen (Ed.), *Handbook of child psychology.* New York: Wiley.

Goldsmith, H. H. (1983). Genetic influences on personality from infancy to adulthood. *Child Development, 54,* 331–55.

Goldsmith, M. F., (1988). Anencephalic organ donor program suspended; Loma Linda report expected to detail findings. *Journal of the American Medical Association, 260,* 1671–72.

Goldstein, S. (1979). Depression in the elderly. *Journal of the American Geriatrics Society, 27,* 38–42.

Goleman, D. (1987, October 13). Thriving despite hardship: Key childhood traits identified. *New York Times, 82,* 104.

Gonda, J. (1981). Convocation on work, aging and retirement: A review. *Human Development, 24,* 286–92.

Goode, E. (1972). Drug use and sexual activity on a college campus. *American Journal of Psychiatry, 128*(10), 1272–76.

Gottman, J. M. & Krokoff, L. J. (1989). Marital interaction and satisfaction: A longitudinal view. *Journal of Consulting and Clinical Psychology, 57,* 47–52.

Gould, R. (1978). *Transformations.* New York: Simon & Schuster.

Gray, R. E. (1987). Adolescent response to the death of a parent. *Journal of Youth and Adolescence, 16*(6), 511–26.

Green, A. (1978). Self-destructive behavior in battered children. *American Journal of Psychiatry, 135*(5), 579–83.

Green, A. W. (1968). *Sociology.* New York: McGraw-Hill.

Green, M. (Ed.) (1981). *Clinics in endocrinology and metabolism: Endocrinology and aging.* London: Saunders.

Greenspan, S. & Greenspan, N. T. (1985). *First feelings.* New York: Viking.

Gregory, T. (1978). *Adolescence in literature.* New York: Longman.

Griffin, G. W. (1987). Childhood predictive characteristics of aggressive adolescents. *Exceptional Children, 54*(3), 246–52.

Grobstein, C. (1981). *From chance to purpose.* Reading, MA: Addison-Wesley.

Grobstein, C. (1988). *Science and the unborn.* New York: Basic Books.

Grossman, H. J. (1983). *Classification in mental retardation.* Washington, DC: American Association on Mental Deficiency.

Grotevant, H. D., Thorbeck, W., & Meyer, M. L. (1982). An extension of Marcia's identity status interview into the interpersonal domain. *Journal of Youth and Adolescence, 11*(1), 33–47.

Gruber, K., Jones, R. J., & Freeman, M. H. (1982). Youth reactions to sexual assault. *Adolescence, 17*(67), 541–51.

Grzegorczyk, P. B., Jones, S. W., & Mistretta, C. M. (1979). Age-related differences in salt taste acuity. *Journal of Gerontology, 34,* 834–40.

Guilford, J. P. (1975). Creativity: A quarter century of progress. In I. A. Taylor & J. W. Getzels (Eds.), *Perspectives in creativity.* Chicago: Aldine.

Gutierrez, I. (1978). Death for credit? *Massachusetts Teacher, 58,* 19–20.

Gutman, D. (1973, December). Men, women and the parental imperative. *Commentary,* 59–64.

Guttmacher, A. & Kaiser, I. (1986). *Pregnancy, birth and family planning.* New York: Signet.

Haan, N. (1976). ". . . change and sameness . . ." reconsidered. *International Journal of Aging and Human Development, 7,* 59–65.

Haan, N. (1981). Common dimensions of personality development. In D. M. Eichorn (Ed.), *Present and past in middle life.* New York: Academic Press.

Haggstrom, G. W., Kanouse, D. E., & Morrison, P. A. (1976). Accounting for the educational shortfalls of mothers. *Journal of Marriage and the Family, 48,* 175–86.

Hajcak, F. & Garwood, P. (1988). Quick-fix sex: Pseudosexuality in adolescents. *Adolescence, 23*(92), 75–76.

Hakim-Larson, J. & Hobart, C. J. (1987). Maternal regulation and adolescent autonomy: Mother-daughter resolution of story conflicts. *Journal of Youth and Adolescence, 16*(2), 153–66.

Hall, D. A. (1976). *Aging of connective tissue.* London: Academic Press.

Hall, G. S. (1904). *Adolescence.* (2 vols.) New York: Appleton-Century-Crofts.

Hall, G. S. (1905). *Adolescence.* New York: Appleton-Century-Crofts.

Hallahan, D. & Kauffman, J. (1988). *Exceptional children: Introduction to special education.* Englewood Cliffs, NJ: Prentice-Hall.

Hallman, R. (1967). Techniques for creative teaching. *Journal of Creative Behavior, 1*(3), 325–30.

Hankoff, L. D. (1975). Adolescence and the crisis of dying. *Adolescence, 10*(39), 373–90.

Hansson, R., O'Connor, M., Jones, W., & Blocker, T. (1981). Maternal employment and adolescent sexual behavior. *Journal of Youth and Adolescence, 10*(1), 55–60.

Hardt, D. (1979). *Death: The final frontier.* Englewood Cliffs, NJ: Prentice-Hall.

Haring, N. & McCormick, L. (1986). *Exceptional children and youth.* Columbus, OH: Merrill.

Harre, R. & Lamb, R. (1983). *The encyclopedic dictionary of psychology.* Cambridge, MA: The MIT Press.

Harrison, H. & Kositsky, A. (1983). *The premature baby book.* New York: St. Martin's Press.

Harry, J. (1986). Sampling gay men. *Journal of Sex Research, 22,* 21–34.

Harter, S. (1983). Developmental perspectives on the self-system. In P. Mussen (Ed.), *Handbook of child psychology.* New York: Wiley.

Hartup, W. (1983). Peer relations. In P. Mussen (Ed.), *Handbook of child psychology.* New York: Wiley.

Hasher, L. & Zacks, R. T. (1979). Automatic and effortful processes in memory. *Journal of Experimental Psychology: General, 108,* 356–88.

Haskell, M. R. & Yablonsky, L. (1974). *Juvenile delinquency.* Chicago: Rand-McNally.

Hatfield, E., Traupmann, J., & Sprecher, S. (1984). Older women's perceptions of their intimate relationships. *Journal of Social and Clinical Psychology, 2*(2), 108–24.

Hauser, S., Book, B., Houlihan, J., & Powers, S. (1987). Sex differences within the family: Studies of adolescent and parent family interactions. Special issue: Sex differences in family relations at adolescence. *Journal of Youth and Adolescence, 16*(3), 199–220.

Havighurst, R. (1972). *Developmental tasks and education.* New York: McKay.

Havighurst, R. J. (1951). *Developmental tasks and education.* New York: Longmans, Green.

Havighurst, R. J. (1963). Perceived life space: Patterns of consistency and change. *Contributions to Human Development, 3,* 93–112.

Havighurst, R., Neugarten, B., & Tobin, S. (1968). Disengagement and patterns of aging. In B. Neugarten (Ed.), *Middle age and aging.* Chicago: University of Chicago Press.

Hawton, K., (1982a). Motivational aspects of deliberate self-poisoning in adolescents. *British Journal of Psychiatry, 141,* 286–90.

Hawton, K., (1982b). Adolescents who take overdoses: Their characteristics, problems and contacts with helping agencies. *British Journal of Psychiatry, 140,* 118–23.

Hawton, K., (1982c). Classification of adolescents who take overdoses. *British Journal of Psychiatry, 140,* 124–31.

Hay, D. (1986). Infancy. In M. Rosenzweig & L. Porter (Eds.), *Annual review of psychology.* Palo Alto, CA: Annual Reviews.

Hayes, J. (1981). *The complete problem solver.* Philadelphia: The Franklin Institute Press.

Hayward, M. D. (1986). The influence of occupational characteristics on men's early retirement. *Social Forces, 64*(4), 1032–45.

Held, L. (1981). Self-esteem and social network of the young pregnant teenager. *Adolescence, 16*(64), 905–12.

Herold, E., Mantle, D., & Zemitis, O. (1979). A study of sexual offenses against females. *Adolescence, 14*(53), 65–72.

Hertzog, C. (1989). Influences of cognitive slowing on age differences in intelligence. *Developmental Psychology, 25,* 636–51.

Herz, E. & Reis, J. (1987). Family life education for young inner city teens: Identifying needs. *Journal of Youth and Adolescence, 16*(4), 361–77.

Hetherington, E. M. (1972). Effects of father absence on personality development in adolescent daughters. *Developmental Psychology, 7,* 313–26.

Hetherington, E. M. (1973). Girls without fathers. *Psychology Today, 6*(9), 47–52.

Hetherington, E. M., Cox, M., & Cox, R. (1985). Long-term effects of divorce and remarriage on the adjustment of children. *Journal of the American Academy of Child Psychiatry, 5,* 518–30.

Hetherington, E. M. & Parke, R. (1986). *Child psychology.* New York: McGraw-Hill.

Higgins, S. T. & Stitzer, M. L. (1986). Acute marijuana effects on social conversation. *Psychopharmacology, 89*(2), 234–38.

Hill, C. D., Thompson, L. W., & Gallagher, D. (1988). The role of anticipatory bereavement in older women's adjustment to widowhood. *The Gerontologist, 28*(6), 7–12.

Hill, J. P. & Holmbeck, G. N. (1987). Disagreements about rules in families with seventh-grade girls and boys. *Journal of Youth and Adolescence, 16*(3), 221–46.

Hill, P., Jr. (1987, July). *Passage to manhood: Rearing the male African-American child.* Paper presented at the annual conference of the National Black Child Development Institute, Detroit, MI.

Hill, R. & Aldous, J., Jr. (1969). Socialization for marriage and parenthood. In D. Goslin (Ed.), *Handbook of socialization theory and research.* Chicago: Rand-McNally.

Hinde, R. (1970). *Animal behavior* (2nd. ed.). New York: McGraw-Hill.

Hinde, R. (1979). *Towards understanding relationships.* New York: Academic Press.

Hinde, R. (1987). *Individuals, relationships and culture.* New York: Cambridge University Press.

Hochhaus, C. & Sousa, F. (1988). Why children belong to gangs: A comparison of expectations and reality. *High School Journal, 71,* 74–77.

Holden, C. (1987). Alcoholism and the medical cost crunch. *Science, 235,* 1132–33.

Holden, C. (1987). Genes and behavior. *Psychology Today, 21,* 18–19.

Holinger, P. (1979). Violent death among the young: Recent trends in suicide, homicide and accidents. *American Journal of Psychiatry, 139*(9), 1144–47.

Holinger, P. C., Offer, D., & Ostrov, E. (1987). Suicide and homicide in the United States: An epidemiologic study of violent death, population changes, and the potential for prediction. *American Journal of Psychiatry, 144*(2), 215–19.

Holland, J. L. (1970). *The self-directed search.* Palo Alto, CA: Consulting Psychologists Press.

Holland, J. L. (1973). *Making vocational choices: A theory of careers.* Englewood Cliffs, NJ: Prentice-Hall.

Holmes, J. & Rahe, S. (1967). A social adjustment scale. *Journal of Psychosomatic Research, 11,* 213–18.

Honig, A. (1986, May). Stress and coping in children. Part 1. *Young Children,* 50–63.

Hood, J. C. (1983). *Becoming a two-job family.* New York: Praeger.

Horn, J. L. (1975). *Psychometric studies of aging and intelligence.* New York: Raven Press.

Horn, J. L. (1978). Human ability systems. In P. B. Baltes (Ed.), *Life-span development and behavior* (Vol. 1). New York: Academic Press.

Horn, J. L. (1985). Remodeling old models of intelligence. In B. B. Wolman (Ed.), *Handbook of intelligence: Theories, measurements, and applications.* New York: Wiley.

Horn, J. L. & Cattell, R. (1967). Age differences in fluid and crystallized intelligence. *Acta Psychologica, 26,* 107.

Horn, J. L. & Donaldson, G. (1980). Cognitive development in adulthood. In O. G. Brim, Jr. & J. Kagan (Eds.), *Constancy and change in human development* (pp. 445–529). Cambridge, MA: Harvard University Press.

Horn, J. L., Donaldson, G., & Engstrom, R. (1981). Apprehension, memory, and fluid intelligence decline in adulthood. *Research on Aging, 3,* 33–84.

Horwitz, A. V. & White, H. R. (1987). Gender role orientations and styles of pathology among adolescents. *Journal of Health and Social Behavior, 28*(2), 158–70.

Hotcin, J. & Sikona, E. (1970). Long-term effects of virus infection on behavior and aging in mice. *Proceedings of the Society for Experimental Biology and Medicine, 134*(1), 204.

Howard, M. (1983, March). Postponing sexual involvement: A new approach. *Siecus Report, 5–6,* 8.

Hoyer, W. J. & Pludes, D. J. (1980, March). *Aging and the attentional components of visual information processing.* Paper presented at the symposium on Aging and Human Visual Function, National Academy of Sciences, Washington, DC.

Huba, G., Wingard, J., & Bentler, P. (1979). Beginning adolescents' drug use and peer and adult interaction patterns. *Journal of Consulting Clinical Psychology, 47,* 830–41.

Huba, G., Wingard, J., & Bentler, P. (1980a). A longitudinal analysis of the role of peer support, adult models, and peer subcultures in beginning adolescent substance use. *Multivariate Behavior Research, 15,* 259–80.

Huba, G., Wingard, J., & Bentler, P. (1980b). Framework for an interactive theory of drug use. In D. Lettieri, M. Sayers, & H. Pearson (Eds.), *Theories on drug abuse.* Rockville, MD: National Institute on Drug Abuse.

Huba, G., Wingard, J., & Bentler, P. (1980c). Applications of a theory of drug use prevention. *Journal of Drug Education, 10,* 25–38.

Hudgens, R. (1975). Suicide communications and attempts. In *Psychiatric disorders in adolescents* (chap. 5). Baltimore, MD: William & Wilkins.

Hulicka, I. (1967). Short-term learning and memory. *Journal of the American Geriatrics Society, 15,* 285–94.

Huston, A. (1983). Sex-typing. In P. Mussen (Ed.), *Handbook of child psychology.* New York: Wiley.

Ingalls, Z. (1983, January 19). Although drinking is widespread, student abuse of alcohol is not rising, new study finds. *The Chronicle of Higher Education, 9.*

Izard, C. E. (1978). On the ontogenesis of emotions and emotion-cognition relationships in infancy. In M. Lewis & L. Rosenblum (Eds.), *The development of affect.* New York: Plenum.

Izard, I. & Malatesta, C. (1987). Perspectives on emotional development I: Differential emotions theory of early emotional development. In J. Osofsky (Ed.), *Handbook of infant development.* New York: Wiley.

Jacobs, J. (1971). *Adolescent suicide.* New York: Wiley.

Jacobziner, H. (1965). Attempted suicide in adolescence. *Journal of the American Medical Association, 10,* 22–36.

Jaquish, G. A., Block, J., & Block, J. H. (1984). *The comprehension and production of metaphor in early adolescence: A longitudinal study of cognitive childhood antecedents.* Unpublished manuscript.

Jaquish, G. & Ripple, R. E. (1980). Cognitive creative abilities across the adult life span. *Human Development, 34,* 143–52.

Jarvik, L. & Russell, D. (1979). Anxiety, aging, and the third emergency reaction. *Journal of Gerontology, 34,* 197–200.

Jasmin, S. & Trygstad, L. (1979). *Behavioral concepts and the nursing process.* St. Louis: Mosby.

Jerse, F. W. & Fakouri, M. E. (1978). Juvenile delinquency and academic deficiency. *Contemporary Education, 49,* 108–9.

Jersild, A. & Holmes, F. B. (1935). Children's fears. *Child Development Monographs, 6*(20). New York: Teachers College Press.

Johnson, T. G. & Goldfinger, S. E. (1981). *The Harvard Medical School health letter book.* Cambridge, MA: Harvard University Press.

Johnston, L. D., O'Malley, P. M., & Bachman, J. G. (1987). *National trends in drug use and related factors among American high school students and young adults, 1975–1986.* Rockville, MD: National Institute on Drug Abuse.

Johnston, W. B. (1987). *Workforce 2000: Work and workers for the 21st century.* Indianapolis, IN: Hudson Institute.

Joint Commission on Accreditation of Hospitals. (1984). *JCAH hospice provider profile.* Chicago: Author.

Jones, R. (1978, November 2). Margaret Mead. *Time,* 21–22.

Joselow, F. (1979, August). Fiscal fitness: How to manage money. *Harper's Bazaar,* 91.

Jung, C. G. (1933). *Modern man in search of a soul.* New York: Harcourt, Brace & World.

Jung, C. G. (1966). *The spirit in men, art and literature.* New York: Bollingen Foundations.

Jung, C. G. (1971). *The portable Jung.* (Joseph Campbell, Ed.). New York: Viking Press.

Jurich, A. P., Schumm, W. R., & Bollman, S. R. (1987). The degree of family orientation perceived by mothers, fathers, and adolescents. *Adolescence, 22*(85), 119–28.

Kacmar, K. M. & Ferris, G. R. (1989). Theoretical and methodological considerations in the age-job satisfaction relationship. *Journal of Applied Psychology, 74,* 201–7.

Kagan, J. (1984). *The nature of the child.* New York: Basic Books.

Kagan, J., Kearsley, R., & Zelazo, P. (1978). *Infancy: Its place in human development.* Cambridge, MA: Harvard University Press.

Kagan, J. & Moss, H. (1962). *Birth to maturity: A study in psychological development.* New York: Wiley.

Kail, R. (1990). *The development of memory in children.* New York: W. H. Freeman.

Kallman, F. & Jarvik, L. (1959). Individual differences in constitution and genetic background. In J. Birren (Ed.), *Handbook of aging and the individual.* Chicago: University of Chicago Press.

Kalter, N. (1987). Long-term effects of divorce on children: A developmental vulnerability model. *American Journal of Orthopsychiatry, 57*(4), 587–600.

Kangas, J. & Bradway, K. (1971). Intelligence at midlife: A 38-year follow-up. *Developmental Psychology, 5,* 333–37.

Kanner, L. (1944). Early infantile autism. *Journal of Pediatrics, 25,* 211–17.

Kantner, J. F. (1982). Sex and pregnancy among American adolescents. *Educational Horizons, 61*(4), 189–94.

Kantrowicz, B. (1989, December 18). Trapped inside her own world. *Newsweek,* 56–58.

Kart, C. S., Metress, E. K., & Metress, S. P. (1988). *Aging, health and society.* Boston: Jones & Bartlett Publishers, Inc.

Kastenbaum, R. (1959). Time and death in adolescence. In H. Feifel (Ed.), *The meaning of death.* New York: McGraw-Hill.

Katchadourian, H. A. (1987). *Fifty: Midlife in perspective.* New York: W. H. Freeman.

Kauffman, J. M. (1981). *Characteristics of children's behavior disorders* (2nd ed.). Columbus, OH: Charles E. Merrill.

Kaufman, H. (1974). *Obsolescence and professional career development.* New York: AMACOM.

Kavanaugh, R. (1972). *Facing death.* New York: Penguin Books.

Kelley, S. (1986). Learned helplessness in the sexually abused child. *Pediatric Nursing, 9,* 193–207.

Kelley-Buchanan, C. (1988). *Peace of mind during pregnancy.* New York: Dell.

Kellog, J. (1988). Forces of change. *Phi Delta Kappan, 70,* 199–204.

Kempe, R. & Kempe, H. (1978). *Child abuse.* Cambridge, MA: Harvard University Press.

Kessler, J. (1988). *Psychopathology of childhood.* Englewood Cliffs, NJ: Prentice-Hall.

Kienhorst, C. W., Wolters, W. H., Diekstra, R. F., & Otto, E. (1987). A study of the frequency of suicidal behavior in children aged 5 to 14. *Journal of Child Psychology and Psychiatry and Allied Disciplines, 28*(1), 153–65.

Kilpatrick, W. (1975). *Identity, and intimacy.* New York: Delacorte.

Kilpatrick, W. (1976). Boy, girl, or person? In J. Travers (Ed.), *The new children: The first six years.* Stamford, CT: Greylock.

Kimmel, D. (1974). *Adulthood and aging.* New York: Wiley.

Kimmel, D. C. & Weiner, I. B. (1985). *Adolescence: A developmental transition.* Hillsdale, NJ: Erlbaum.

Kinard, E. & Reinherz, H. (1987). School aptitude and achievement in children of adolescent mothers. *Journal of Youth and Adolescence, 16*(1), 69–87.

King, I. (1914). *The high school age.* Indianapolis: Bobbs-Merrill.

Kinnaird, K. & Gerrard, M. (1986). Premarital sexual behavior and attitudes toward marriage and divorce among young women as a function of their mothers' marital status. *Journal of Marriage and the Family, 48*(4), 757–65.

Kinsey, A., Pomeroy, W., Martin, C., & Gebhard, P. (1948). *Sexual behavior in the human male.* Philadelphia: Saunders.

Kinsey, A., Pomeroy, W., Martin, C., & Gebhard, P. (1953). *Sexual behavior in the human female.* Philadelphia: Saunders.

Kintsch, W. (1970). *Learning, memory, and conceptual processes.* New York: Wiley.

Kirkland, M. & Ginther, D. (1988). Acquired Immune Deficiency Syndrome in children: Medical, legal, and school related issues. *School Psychology Review, 17,* 304–5.

Kitahara, M. (1983). Female puberty rites: Reconsideration and speculation. *Adolescents, 18*(72), 957–64.

Kitchener, K. & King, P. (1981). Reflective judgment: Concepts of justification and their relationship to age and education. *Journal of Applied Developmental Psychology, 2,* 89–116.

Klassen, A. D., Williams, C. J., & Levitt, E. E. (1989). *Sex and morality in the U.S.: An empirical enquiry under the auspices of the Kinsey Institute.* Middletown, CT: Wesleyan University Press.

Klaus, M. & Kennell, J. (1976). *Maternal-infant bonding.* St. Louis: Mosby.

Klaus, M. & Kennell, J. (1983). *Bonding.* New York: Mosby.

Klein, H. & Cordell, A. (1987). The adolescent as mother: Early risk identification. *Journal of Youth and Adolescence, 16*(1), 47–58.

Klein, N. (1978, October). Is there a right way to die? *Psychology Today, 12,* 122.

Knobloch, H. & Pasamanick, B. (1974). *Gesell and Amatruda's developmental diagnosis.* New York: Harper & Row.

Knowles, M. (1984). *The adult learner: A neglected species.* Houston: Gulf.

Koch, H. (1960). The relation of certain formal attributes of siblings to attributes held toward each other and toward their parents. *Monographs of the Society for Research in Child Development, 25* (no. 4), 1–124.

Koenig, H. G., Kvale, J. N., & Ferrell, C. (1988). Religion and well-being in later life. *The Gerontologist, 28*(1), 18–20.

Koff, E., Rierdan, J., & Sheingold, K. (1980, April). *Memories of menarche: Age and preparedness as determinants of subjective experience.* Paper presented at the annual meeting of the Eastern Psychological Association, Hartford, CT.

Kogan, N. (1973). Creativity and cognitive style: A life-span perspective. In P. B. Baltes & K. W. Schaie (Eds.), *Lifespan developmental psychology.* New York: Academic Press.

Kogan, N. (1983). Stylistic variation in childhood and adolescence: Creativity, metaphor, cognitive styles. In P. H. Mussen (Ed.), *Handbook of child psychology* (Vol. 3). New York: Wiley.

Kohlberg, L. (1966). A cognitive-developmental analysis of children's sex-role concepts and attitudes. In E. Maccoby (Ed.), *The development of sex differences.* Stanford, CA: Stanford University Press.

Kohlberg, L. (1973). The claim to moral adequacy of a highest stage of moral judgment. *Journal of Philosophy, 60,* 630–46.

Kohlberg, L. (1975). The cognitive-developmental approach to moral education. *Phi Delta Kappan, 56,* 670–77.

Kohlberg, L. (1981). *The philosophy of moral development.* New York: Harper & Row.

Kohner, M. (1977, October 11). Adolescent pregnancy. *The New York Times,* 38.

Kopp, C. (1987). Developmental risk: Historical reflections. In J. Osofsky (Ed.), *Handbook of infant development.* New York: Wiley.

Korenman, S. G. (Ed.). (1982). *Endocrine aspects of aging.* New York: Elsevier Biomedical.

Kornzweig, A. L. (1980). New ideas for old eyes. *Journal of the American Geriatrics Society, 28,* 145.

Kosslyn, S. (1980). *Images and mind.* Cambridge, MA: Harvard University Press.

Koyle, P. R., Jensen, L. C., Olsen, J., & Cundick, B. (1989). Comparison of sexual behaviors among adolescents. *Youth and Society, 20*(4), 461–76.

Kraeer, R. J. (1981). The therapeutic value of the funeral in post-funeral counseling. In O. S. Margolis & others (Eds.), *Acute grief.* New York: Columbia University Press.

Kreider, D. G. & Motto, J. A. (1974). Parent-child role reversal and suicidal states in adolescence. *Adolescence, 10*(35), 365–70.

Kroger, J. & Haslett, S. J. (1988). Separation-individuation and ego identity status in late adolescence. *Journal of Youth and Adolescence, 17*(1), 59–80.

Krouse, H. (1986). Use of decision frames by elementary school children. *Perceptual and Motor Skills, 63,* 1107–12.

Kübler-Ross, E. (1969). *On death and dying.* New York: Macmillan.

Kübler-Ross, E. (1975). *Death: The final stage of growth.* Englewood Cliffs, NJ: Prentice-Hall.

Kübler-Ross, E. & Warshaw, W. (1978). *To live until we say goodbye* Englewood Cliffs, NJ: Prentice-Hall.

Kurz, S. (1977, November 23). Teenage prostitutes. *Equal Times,* 6.

Lamb, M. & Campos, J. (1982). *Development in infancy.* New York: Random House.

Lamb, M. E. (1987). *The father's role: Cross-cultural perspectives.* Hillsdale, NJ: Erlbaum.

Lamb, M., Elster, A., & Tavare, J. (1986). Behavioral profiles of adolescent mothers and partners with varying intra-couple age differences. *Journal of Adolescent Research, 1*(4), 399–408.

Lancaster, J. B. & Hamburg, B. A. (1986). *School-age pregnancy and parenthood.* New York: Aldine de Gruyter.

Langlois, J. & Downs, A. C. (1979). Peer relations as a function of physical attractiveness: The eye of the beholder or behavioral reality. *Child Development, 50,* 409–18.

Langlois, J. H. & Downs, A. C. (1980). Mothers, fathers and peers as socialization agents of sex-typed play behaviors in young children. *Child Development, 51,* 1237–47.

Larson, L. G. (1972). The influence of parents and peers during adolescence: The situation hypothesis revisited. *Journal of Marriage and the Family, 34*(1), 67–74.

Larson, R. & Johnson, C. (1981). Anorexia nervosa in the context of daily experience. *Journal of Youth and Adolescence, 10*(6), 455–71.

Lass, N. & Golden, S. (1971). The use of isolated vowels as auditory stimuli in eliciting the verbal transformation effect. *Canadian Journal of Psychology, 25,* 349.

Lawton, M. P. (1984). Health and subjective well-being. *International Journal of Aging and Human Development, 19,* 157–66.

Lazar, I. & Darlington, R. (1982). Lasting effects of early education: A report from the consortium for longitudinal studies. *Monographs of the Society for Research in Child Development, 47* (No. 195).

Leake, J. (1777). *Medical disorders.* London: Benchley.

Leboyer, F. (1975). *Birth without violence.* New York: Knopf.

Lee, P. R., Franks, P., Thomas, G. S., & Paffenberger, R. S. (1981). *Exercise and health: The evidence and its implications.* Cambridge, MA: Oelgeschlager, Gunn, & Hain.

Lehman, H. C. (1953). *Age and achievement.* Princeton, NJ: Princeton University Press.

Lehman, H. C. (1962). The creative production rates of present versus past generations of scientists. *Journal of Gerontology, 17,* 409–17.

Lehman, H. C. (1964). The relationship between chronological age and high level research output in physics and chemistry. *Journal of Gerontology, 19,* 157–64.

Leigh, R. J. (1982). The impoverishment of ocular motility in the elderly. In R. Sekuler, D. Kline, & K. Dismukes (Eds.), *Aging and human visual function* (pp. 173–80). New York: Alan R. Liss.

Lenneberg, E. (1967). *Biological foundations of language.* New York: Wiley.

Leventhal, H. & Tomarken, A. (1986). Emotions: Today's problems. In M. Rosenzweig & L. Porter (Eds.), *Annual review of psychology.* Palo Alto, CA: Annual Reviews.

Levin, J. S. & Markides, K. S. (1986). Religious attendance and subjective health. *Journal for the Scientific Study of Religion. 25,* 31–38.

Levine, R. (1977). Childrearing as cultural adaptation. In P. Leiderman, S. Tulkin, & A. Rosenfeld (Eds.), *Culture and infancy.* New York: Academic Press.

Levinson, D. (1978). *The seasons of a man's life.* New York: Knopf.

Levinson, D. (1986). A conception of adult development. *American Psychologist, 41*(1), 3–13.

Levinson, D. (in progress). *Seasons of a woman's life.* New Haven, CT: Yale University Press.

Lewis, C. (1963). *A grief observed.* New York: Seabury Press.

Lewis, D. & Greene, J. (1982). *Thinking better.* New York: Rawson, Wade.

Lewis, M. & Brooks-Gunn, J. (1979). *Social cognition and the acquisition of self.* New York: Plenum.

Lickona, T. (1983). *Raising good children.* New York: Bantam Books, Inc.

Lidz, T. & Lidz, R. W. (1984). Oedipus in the Stone Age. *Journal of the American Psychoanalytic Association, 32*(3), 507–27.

Liebert, R. M., Sprafkin, J. N., & Davidson, E. (1982). *The early window.* Elmsford, New York: Pergamon.

Lifson, A., Hessol, N., & Rutherford, G. W. (1989, June). *The natural history of HIV infection in a cohort of homosexual and bisexual men: Clinical manifestations, 1978–1989.* Paper presented at the Fifth International Conference on AIDS, Montreal.

Lindemann, E. (1944). Symptomology and management of acute grief. *American Journal of Psychiatry, 101,* 141–48.

Lips, H. (1988). *Sex and gender.* Mountain View, CA: Mayfield.

Lisina, M. I. (1983). The development of interaction in the first seven years. In W. Hartup (Ed.), *Review of child development research.* Chicago: University of Chicago Press.

Lohr, M. J., Essex, M. J., & Klein, M. H. (1988). The relationships of coping responses to physical health status and life satisfaction among older women. *Journal of Gerontology: Psychological Sciences, 43*(2), 54–60.

Lopata, H. Z. (1973). *Widowhood in an American city.* Cambridge, MA: Schenkman.

Lorand, S. & Schneer, H. I. (Eds.). (1961). *Adolescence: Psychoanalytic approaches to problems and theory.* New York: Hoeber.

Lott, B. (1989). *Women's lives.* Monterey, CA: Brooks/Cole.

Lowenkopf, E. (1982, May/June). Anorexia nervosa: Some nosological considerations. *Comprehensive Psychiatry, 23*(3), 233–39.

Lown, F. (1978). There really is no old age. *Massachusetts Teacher, 58,* 12–15.

Lynn, S. (1985, October). A twinkle in the teacher's eye. *Instructor,* 74–76.

Maccoby, E. (1988). Social emotional development and response to stressors. In N. Garmezy & M. Rutter (Eds.), *Stress, coping and development in children.* Baltimore: The Johns Hopkins University Press.

Maccoby, E. & Jacklin, C. (1974). What we know and don't know about sex differences. *Psychology Today, 8*(7), 109–12.

Macfarlane, A. (1977). *The psychology of childbirth.* Cambridge, MA: Harvard University Press.

Mader, S. (1984). Hearing impairment in elderly persons. *Journal of the American Geriatrics Society, 32,* 548.

Maher, E. L. (1983). Burnout and commitment: A theoretical alternative. *Personnel and Guidance Journal, 61*(7), 390–93.

Malla, A. (1983). Differences in suicide rates: An examination of underreporting. *Canadian Journal of Psychiatry, 28*(4), 291–93.

Manaster, G. (1977). *Adolescent development and the life tasks.* Boston: Allyn & Bacon.

Manaster, G. (1989). *Adolescent development.* Itasca, IL: Peacock.

Manchester, W. (1983). *The last lion: Winston Spencer Churchill.* Boston: Little, Brown.

Marcia, J. E. (1966). Development and validation of ego identity status. *Journal of Personality and Social Psychology, 3,* 551–58.

Marcia, J. E. (1967). Ego identity status: Relationship to change in self-esteem, general maladjustment and authoritarianism. *Journal of Personality, 35,* 118–33.

Marcia, J. E. (1968). The case history of a construct: Ego identity status. In E. Vinacke (Ed.), *Readings in general psychology.* New York: Van Nostrand Reinhold.

Marcia, J. E. (1980). Identity in adolescence. In J. Adelson (Ed.), *Handbook of adolescent psychology.* New York: Wiley.

Marcia, J. E. (1983). Some directions for the investigation of ego development in early adolescence. *Journal of Early Adolescence, 3*(3), 215–23.

Marshall, L. (1981). Auditory processing in aging listeners. *Journal of Speech and Hearing Disorders, 46,* 226–40.

Martocchio, J. J. (1989). Age-related differences in employee absenteeism: A meta-analysis. *Psychology and Aging, 4,* 409–14.

Masoro, E. J. (1984). Nutrition as a modulator of the aging process. *Physiologist, 27*(2), 98–101.

Masters, W. & Johnson, V. (1966). *Human sexual response.* Boston: Little, Brown.

Masters, W. & Johnson, V. (1970). *Human sexual inadequacy.* Boston: Little, Brown.

Matheny, A. P. (1980). Bayley's infant behavior record: Behavioral components and twin analyses. *Child Development, 51,* 466–75.

Matusow, A. J. (1984). *The unraveling of America.* New York: Harper & Row.

Maurer, D. & Maurer, C. (1988). *The world of the newborn.* New York: Basic Books.

Mayer, M. (1978). *The male mid-life crisis—Fresh start after 40.* New York: Doubleday.

Mazess, R. B. (1982). On aging bone loss. *Clinical Orthopaedics and Related Research, 165,* 239–52.

McAnarney, E. (1979). Adolescent and young adult suicide in the U.S.—A reflection of social unrest? *Adolescence, 14*(56), 765–74.

McCall, R. (1979). *Infants.* Cambridge, MA: Harvard University Press.

McCann, I. L. & Holmes, D. S. (1984). Influence of aerobic exercise on depression. *Journal of Personality and Social Psychology, 46*(5), 1142–47.

McCarthy, J. (1979, May 5). Jogging. *Time,* 46.

McCary, J. (1978). *McCary's human sexuality.* New York: Van Nostrand Reinhold.

McCrae, R. & Costa, P. T., Jr. (1984). *Emerging lives, enduring dispositions: Personality in adulthood.* Boston: Little, Brown.

McEvoy, G. M. & Cascio, W. F. (1989). Cumulative evidence of the relationship between employee age and job performance. *Journal of Applied Psychology, 74,* 11–17.

McFarland, R. (1968). The sensory and perceptual processes in aging. In K. Schaie (Ed.), *Theory and methods of research on aging.* Morgantown, WV: West Virginia University Press.

McGhee, P. (1979). *Humor: Its origin and development.* San Francisco: W. H. Freeman.

McIntire, J. (1980). Suicide and self-poisoning in pediatrics. *Resident and Staff Physician, 21,* 72–85.

McKenry, D., Tishler, C., & Kelley, C. (1982). Adolescent suicide: A comparison of attempters and non-attempters in an emergency room population. *Clinical Pediatrics, 21*(5), 911–16.

McKenry, P., Walters, L., & Johnson, C. (1979). Adolescent pregnancy: A review of the literature. *Family Coordinator, 33,* 17–29.

Mead, M. (1970). *Culture and commitment: A study of the generation gap.* New York: Doubleday.

Mead, M. (1972, April). *Long living in cross-sectional perspective.* Paper presented to the Gerontological Society, San Juan, Puerto Rico.

Meilman, P. (1979). Cross-sectional age changes in ego identity status during adolescence. *Developmental Psychology, 15*(2), 230–31.

Meltz, B. F. (1988, November 26). Saving the magic moments. *Boston Globe,* 56.

Menyuk, P. (1982). Language development. In C. Kopp & J. Krakow (Eds.), *The child.* Reading, MA: Addison-Wesley.

Metropolitan Life Insurance Company. (1977). *Widows in the United States.* Boston, MA: Statistical Bulletin, 8–10.

Miller. J. B. (1976). *Toward a new psychology of women.* Boston: Beacon Press, Inc.

Mintz, B. I. & Betz, N. E. (1988). Prevalence and correlates of eating disordered behaviors among undergraduate women. *Journal of Counseling Psychology, 35,* 463–71.

Minuchin, P. & Shapiro, E. (1983). The school as a context for social development. In P. Mussen (Ed.), *Handbook of child psychology.* New York: Wiley.

Mitchell, J. (1972). Some psychological dimensions of adolescent sexuality. *Adolescence, 7,* 447–58.

Mitford, J. (1963). *The American way of death.* New York: Simon & Schuster.

Moen, P. (1985). Continuities and discontinuities in women's labor force activity. In G. H. Elder (Ed.), *Life course dynamics: Trajectories and transitions, 1968–1980* (pp. 113–55). Ithaca, NY: Cornell University Press.

Money, J. (1980). *Love and love sickness.* Baltimore: The Johns Hopkins University Press.

Money, J. & Ehrhardt, A. (1972). *Man and woman/boy and girl.* New York: New American Library.

Money, J. & Wolfe, G. (1974). Late puberty, retarded growth, and reversible hyposomatotropism. *Adolescence, 9*(33), 121–34.

Montemayor, R. & Brownlee, J. R. (1987). Fathers, mothers, and adolescents: Gender-based differences in parental roles during adolescence. *Journal of Youth and Adolescence, 16*(3), 281–91.

Moore, B. N. & Parker, R. (1986). *Critical thinking.* Mountain View, CA: Mayfield Publishing Co.

Moore, E. W., McCann, H., & McCann, J. (1985). *Creative and critical thinking.* Boston, MA: Houghton Mifflin.

Moore, K., Jofferth, S., & Wertheimer, I. (1979). Teenage motherhood. *Children Today, 6,* 12–16.

Moore, K. A., Peterson, J. L., & Furstenberg, F. F. (1986). Parental attitudes and the occurrence of early sexual activity. *Journal of Marriage and Family, 48,* 777–82.

Morinis, A. (1985). The ritual experience: Pain and the transformation of consciousness in ordeals of initiation. *Ethos, 13*(2), 150–74.

Morris, J. (1974, July). Conundrum. *Ms. Magazine,* 57–64.

Morsink, C. V. (1983). *Teaching special needs students in regular classrooms.* Boston: Little, Brown.

Moscowitz, H., Kumaraith, U., Sharma, K., Jacobs, H., & Sharma, S. (1975). Cross-cultural differences in simple taste preferences. *Science, 190,* 1217.

Moskowitz, B. (1979). The acquisition of language. *Scientific American, 239,* 92–108.

Moyers, W. & Bly, R. (1989). *A gathering of men.* New York: N.E.T.

Muehlbauer, G. & Dodder L. (1983). *The losers: Gang delinquency in an American suburb.* New York: Praeger Pubs.

Muller, C. F. & Boaz, R. F. (1988). Health as a reason or a rationalization for being retired? *Research on Aging, 10*(1), 37–55.

Murphy, C. (1983). Age-related effects on the threshold, psychophysical function, and pleasantness of menthol. *Journal of Gerontology, 38,* 217–22.

Mussen, P. & Eisenberg-Berg, N. (1982). *Roots of caring, sharing, and helping: The development of prosocial behavior in children.* San Francisco: W. H. Freeman.

Muuss, R. (1982). *Theories of adolescence* (4th ed.). New York: Random House.

Myers, G. & Pitts, A. (1972, April). Paper presented at the meeting of the Gerontological Society, San Juan, Puerto Rico.

Myers, L. S. & Morokoff, P. J. (1986). Physiological and subjective sexual arousal in pre- and postmenopausal women and postmenopausal women taking replacement therapy. *Psychophysiology, 23*(3), 283–92.

Nagy, P. (1982). Limitations of recent research relating Piaget's theory to adolescent thought. *Review of Educational Research, 52*(4), 513–56.

National Association of Secondary School Principals. (1984). *The mood of American youth.* Reston, VA: Author.

National Institute of Allergy and Infectious Diseases. (1987). *STDA.* Atlanta: Center for Disease Control.

National Institute on Aging. (1979). *Is male menopause a myth?* Washington, DC: U.S. Government Printing Office.

National Research Council. (1986). *Environmental tobacco smoke: Measuring exposures and assessing health effects.* Washington, DC: National Academy Press.

Nelson, D. A. (1980). *Frequently seen stages in adolescent chemical use.* CompCare Publications, 2415 Annapolis La., Suite 140, Minneapolis, MN 55441.

Nesselroade, J. R., Pedersen, N. L., McClearn, G. E., Plomin, R., & Bergeman, C. S. (1988). Factorial and criterion validities of telephone-assessed cognitive ability measures: Age and gender comparisons in adult twins. *Research on Aging, 10*(2), 220–34.

Neugarten, B. (Ed.). (1968). *Middle age and aging.* Chicago: University of Chicago Press.

Neugarten, B. & Moore, J. (1968). The changing age-status system. In B. Neugarten (Ed.), *Middle age and aging.* Chicago: University of Chicago Press.

New York Times. (1989, August 18). Study outlines traits of urban gangs. 23.

Newman, P. R. & Newman, B. M. (1976). Early adolescence and its conflict: Group identity versus alienation. *Adolescence, 11*(42), 261–73.

Nicola, J. S. & Hawkes, G. R. (1986). Marital satisfaction of dual-career couples: Does sharing increase happiness? *Journal of Social Behavior and Personality, 1*(1), 47–60.

Nightingale, E. O. & Wolverton, L. (1988). *Adolescent rolelessness in modern society.* Washington, DC: Carnegie Council on Adolescent Development.

Nilsson, L., Furuhjelm, M., Ingleman-Sundberg, A., & Wirsen, C. (1987). *A child is born.* New York: Delacorte.

Noller, R. B. (1983). *Mentoring: An annotated bibliography.* Buffalo, NY: Bearly Limited.

Northcott, H. C. & Lowe, G. S. (1987). Job and gender influences in the subjective experience of work. *Canadian Review of Sociology and Anthropology, 24*(1), 117–31.

Norton, A. J. & Moorman, J. E. (1987). Current trends in marriage and divorce among American women. *Journal of Marriage and the Family, 49*(1), 3–14.

Nuckolls, K. B., Cassell, J., & Kaplan, B. H. (1972). Psychosocial assets, life crisis, and the prognosis of pregnancy. *American Journal of Epidemiology, 95,* 431–41.

Nuttall, R. & Nuttall, E. (1979). *The impact of disaster on coping behaviors of families.* Unpublished manuscript, Boston College, Chestnut Hill, MA.

Office of the Assistant Secretary for Health. (1988). Report of the second Public Health Service AIDS Prevention and Control Conference. *Public Health Report, 3,* 103.

Olds, S. (1983). *The working parents survival guide.* New York: Bantam Books, Inc.

Olson, G. & Sherman, T. (1983). Attention, learning and memory in infants. In P. Mussen (Ed.), *Handbook of child psychology.* New York: Wiley.

Ornstein, R. & Sobel, D. (1987). *The healing brain.* New York: Simon & Schuster.

Osofsky, J. (1976). Neonatal characteristics and mother-infant interaction in two observational situations. *Child Development, 47,* 1138–47.

Ossip-Klein, D. J., Doyne, E. J., Bowman, E. D., Osborn, K. M., McDougall-Wilson, I. B., & Neimeyer, R. A. (1989). Effects of running or weight lifting on self-concept in clinically depressed women. *Journal of Consulting and Clinical Psychology, 57,* 158–61.

Otto, V. (1972). Suicidal attempts in childhood and adolescents—today and after ten years: A follow-up study. In A. L. Annell (Ed.), *Depressive states in childhood and adolescence.* New York: Halstead Press.

Outward Bound, U.S.A. (1988). *Outward bound.* Greenwich, CT: Outward Bound National Office.

Owens, W. (1953). Aging and mental abilities. *Genetic Psychology Monographs, 48,* 3–54.

Pack, B. (1978). Death: A classroom perspective. *Massachusetts Teacher, 58,* 16–18.

Packer, L. & Rosenblatt, R. (1979). Unpublished manuscript. Issues in the study of social behavior in the first week of life. In D. Shaffer and J. Dunn (Eds.). *The First Year of Life.* New York: Wiley.

Palmore, E. B. (1981). The facts on aging quiz: Part two. *The Gerontologist, 21*(4), 431–37.

Parke, C. M. & Weiss, R. S. (1983). *Recovery from bereavement.* New York: Basic Books.

Parke, R. (1981). *Fathers.* Cambridge, MA: Harvard University Press.

Parke, R. & Slaby, R. (1983). The development of aggression. In P. Mussen (Ed.), *Handbook of child psychology.* New York: Wiley.

Parten, M. (1932). Social participation among preschool children. *Journal of Abnormal and Social Psychology, 27,* 243–69.

Paul, R. W. (1987). Dialogical thinking. In J. B. Baron & R. J. Sternberg (Eds.), *Teaching thinking skills.* New York: W. H. Freeman.

Pearlman, C. (1972, November). Frequency of intercourse in males at different ages. *Medical Aspects of Human Sexuality,* 92–113.

Perkins, D. N. (1987). Thinking frames: An integrative perspective on teaching cognitive skills. In J. Baron & R. Sternberg (Eds.), *Teaching thinking skills: Theory and practice.* San Francisco: W. H. Freeman.

Perlmutter, B. F. (1987). Delinquency and learning disabilities: Evidence for compensatory behaviors and adaptation. *Journal of Youth and Adolescence, 16*(2), 89–96.

Perry, W. (1968a). *Forms of intellectual and ethical development in the college years.* New York: Holt, Rinehart & Winston.

Perry, W. (1968b, April). *Patterns of development in thought and values of students in a liberal arts college: A validation of a scheme.* Washington, DC: U.S. Department of Health, Education, and Welfare, Office of Education, Bureau of Research. Final report.

Perry, W. (1981). Cognitive and ethical growth. In A. Chickering (Ed.), *The modern American college.* San Francisco: Jossey-Bass.

Petersen, A. (1988). Adolescent development. In M. Rosenzweig & L. Porter (Eds.), *Annual review of psychology.* Palo Alto, CA: Annual Reviews.

Petzel, S. V. & Cline, D. (1978). Adolescent suicide: Epidemiological and biological aspects. *Adolescent Psychiatry, 6,* 249–66.

Phillips, D. (1979). Suicide, motor vehicle fatalities, and the mass media: Evidence toward a theory of suggestion. *American Journal of Sociology, 84*(5), 1150–74.

Phillips, R. T. & Alcebo, A. M. (1986). The effects of divorce on black children and adolescents. *American Journal of Social Psychiatry, 6*(1), 69–73.

Piaget, J. (1929). *The child's conception of the world*. New York: Harcourt, Brace & World.

Piaget, J. (1932). *The moral judgment of the child*. New York: Macmillan.

Piaget, J. (1952). *The origins of intelligence in children*. New York: International Universities Press.

Piaget, J. (1953). *The origins of intelligence in the child*. New York: Harcourt, Brace, Jovanovich.

Piaget, J. (1966). *Psychology of intelligence*. Totowa, NJ: Littlefield, Adams & Co.

Piaget, J. (1967). *Six psychological studies*. New York: Random House.

Piaget, J. (1973). *The child and reality*. New York: Viking Press.

Piaget, J. & Inhelder, B. (1969). *The psychology of the child*. New York: Basic Books.

Pine, V. (1979, March 25). Funerals criticized. *Boston Globe*, C17.

Pines, M. (1985). Aggression: The violence within. *Science Digest, 88,* 36–39.

Pinon, M., Huston, A., & Wright, J. (1989). Family ecology and child characteristics that predict young children's educational television viewing. *Child Development, 60,* 846–56.

Pizer, H. (Ed.). (1983). *Over fifty-five, healthy and alive*. New York: Van Nostrand Reinhold.

Pleck, J. H. (1985). *Working wives/Working husbands*. Beverly Hills, CA: Sage.

Plomin, R. (1983). Developmental behavioral genetics. *Child Development, 54,* 255–59.

Polit, D. (1985). *A review of the antecedents of adolescent sexuality, contraception, and pregnancy outcomes*. Jefferson City, MO: Humanalysis.

Poole, W. (1987). The first 9 months of school. *Hippocrates, 1,* 68–73.

Postman, N. (1982). *The disappearance of childhood*. New York: Dell Publishing Co., Inc.

Powledge, T. (1983, July). The importance of being twins. *Psychology Today, 17,* 20–27.

Prechtl, H. (1977). *The neurological examination of the full-term newborn infant*. London: Heinemann.

Ralph, N., Lochman, J., & Thomas, T. (1984). Psychosocial characteristics of pregnant and multiparous adolescents. *Adolescence, 19,* 283–94.

Ramsey, P. (1987). *Teaching and learning in a diverse world*. New York: Teachers College, Columbia University.

Ramsey, P. W. (1982). Do you know where your children are? *Journal of Psychology and Christianity, 1*(4), 7–15.

Rando, T. A. (1986). Creation of rituals in psychotherapy. *Forum Newsletter, 6,* 8–9.

Raphael, D., Feinberg, R., & Bachor, D. (1987). Student teachers' perceptions of the identity formation process. *Journal of Youth and Adolescence, 16*(4), 331–44.

Reinke, B., Ellicott, A., Harris, R., & Hancock, E. (1985). Timing of psychosocial change in women's lives. *Human Development, 28,* 259–80.

Remafedi, G. (1988). Homosexual youth. *Journal of the American Medical Association, 258*(2), 222–25.

Resener, M. (1979, August). Burnout: The new stress disease. *Harper's Bazaar,* 92–93.

Rest, J. (1983). Morality. In P. Mussen (Ed.), *Handbook of child psychology*. New York: Wiley.

Rhodes, S. (1983). Age-related differences in work attitudes and behavior: A review and conceptual analysis. *Psychological Bulletin, 93,* 328–67.

Rhyne, D. (1981). Basis of marital satisfaction among men and women. *Journal of Marriage and the Family, 43,* 941–55.

Ricks, M. (1985). The social transmission of parental behavior: Attachment across generations. In I. Bretherton & E. Waters (Eds.), *Growing points of attachment: Theory and research*. Monographs of the Society for Research in Child Development. Chicago: University of Chicago Press.

Ringel, S. P. & Simon, D. B. (1983). Practical management of neuromuscular diseases in the elderly. *Geriatrics, 38,* 86.

Ritter, J. & Langlois, J. (1988). The role of physical attractiveness in the observation of adult-child interactions: Eye of the beholder or behavioral reality? *Developmental Psychology. 24,* 254–63.

Rivchun, S. B. (1980, August). Be a mentor and leave a lasting legacy. *Association Management, 32*(8), 71–74.

Roazen, P. (1976). *Erik H. Erikson: The power and limits of a vision*. New York: Free Press.

Roberts, E. & Holt, S. (1979). *Sexuality and social policy: Project on human sexual development*. Harvard University: Population Education.

Robinson, J. K. (1983). Skin problems of aging. *Geriatrics, 38,* 57–65.

Rodman, H. (1989). Controlling adolescent fertility. *Society, 23*(1), 35–37.

Rogers, D. (1977). *The psychology of adolescence* (3rd ed.). Englewood Cliffs, NJ: Prentice-Hall.

Rogers, D. (1979). *Adult psychology*. Englewood Cliffs, NJ: Prentice-Hall.

Rogoff, B. & Morell, G. (1989). Perspectives and children's development from cultural psychology. *American Psychologist, 44*(2), 343–48.

Rogow, A. M., Marcia, J. E., & Slugoski, B. R. (1983). The relative importance of identity status interview components. *Journal of Youth and Adolescence, 12*(5), 387–400.

Rohn, R., (1977). Adolescents who attempt suicide. *The Journal of Pediatrics, 90,* 636–38.

Roll, S. & Miller, L. (1978, Spring). Adolescent males' feelings of being understood by their fathers as revealed through clinical interviews. *Adolescence,* 83–94.

Rollins, B. & Feldman, H. (1970). Marital satisfaction over the family life cycle. *Journal of Marriage and the Family, 32,* 20–28.

Roper Organization. (1987). *The American Chicle youth poll*. Storrs, CT: University of Connecticut (Roper).

Rosen, B. M., Bahn, A. K., Shellow, R., & Bower, E. M. (1965). Adolescent patients served in outpatient clinics. *American Journal of Public Health, 55,* 1563–77.

Rosen, E. I. (1987). *Bitter choices: Blue-collar women in and out of work*. Chicago: University of Chicago Press.

Rosen, J. C., Gross, J., & Vara, L. (1987). Psychological adjustment of adolescents attempting to lose or gain weight. Special issue: Eating disorders. *Journal of Consulting and Clinical Psychology, 55*(5), 742–47.

Rosen, R. (1980). Adolescent pregnancy decision-making: Are parents important? *Adolescence, 15*(57), 43–54.

Rosenberg, G. S. & Anspach, D. F. (1973). Sibling solidarity in the working class. *Journal of Marriage and the Family, 35,* 108–13.

Rosenthal, D. A., Gurney, R. M., & Moore, S. M. (1981). From trust to intimacy: A new inventory for examining Erikson's stages of psychosocial development. *Journal of Youth and Adolescence, 10*(6), 525–37.

Rotheram, M. J. (1987, May). *Evaluation of imminent danger for suicide among youth*. Paper presented at the annual meeting of the American Orthopsychiatric Association, Chicago, Illinois.

Rotter, J. (1971, June). External control and internal control. *Psychology Today, 5,* 37ff.

Rourke, B., Bakker, D., Fisk, J., & Strang, J. (1983). *Child neuropsychology.* New York: Guilford Pr.

Rovee-Collier, C. (1987). Learning and memory in infancy. In J. Osofsky (Ed.), *Handbook of infant development.* New York: Wiley.

Rowe, I. & Marcia, J. E. (1980). Ego identity status, formal operations, and moral development. *Journal of Youth and Adolescence, 9*(2), 87–99.

Rowland, D. L., Heiman, J. R., Gladue, B. A., & Hatch, J. P. (1987). Endocrine, psychological and genital response to sexual arousal in men. *Psychoneuroendocrinology, 12*(2), 149–58.

Rubin, K., Fein, G., & Vandenberg, B. (1983). Play. In P. Mussen (Ed.), *Handbook of child psychology.* New York: Wiley.

Rubin, L. B. (1979). *Women of a certain age: The midlife search for self.* New York: Harper & Row.

Rubin, R. H. (1981). Attitudes about male-female relations among black adolescents. *Adolescence, 16*(61), 159–74.

Rubin, Z. (1980). *Children's friendships.* Cambridge, MA: Harvard University Press.

Russ-Eft, D., Springer, M., & Beever, A. (1979). Antecedents of adolescent parenthood and consequences at age 30. *Family Coordinator, 16,* 173–78.

Rutter, M. (1975). *Helping troubled children.* New York: Plenum.

Rutter, M. (1979). *Fifteen thousand hours.* Cambridge, MA: Harvard University Press.

Rutter, M. (1981). *Maternal deprivation reassessed.* New York: Penguin Bks., Inc.

Rutter, M. (1983). Behavioral studies: Questions and feelings on the concept of a distinctive syndrome. In M. Rutter (Ed.), *Developmental neuropsychology.* New York: Guilford Pr.

Rutter, M. (1987, July). Psychosocial resilience and protective mechanisms. *American Journal of Orthopsychiatry,* 316–31.

Rutter, M. (1987). Continuities and discontinuities from infancy. In J. Osofsky (Ed.), *Handbook of infant development.* New York: Wiley.

Rutter, M. (1988). Stress, coping, and development: Some issues and some questions. In N. Garmezy & M. Rutter (Eds.), *Stress, coping and development in children.* Baltimore: The Johns Hopkins University Press.

Rutter, M. & Garmezy, N. (1983). Developmental psychopathology. In P. Mussen (Ed.), *Handbook of child psychology.* New York: Wiley.

Sabbath, J. (1969). The suicidal adolescent: The expendable child. *Journal of the American Academy of Child Psychiatry, 8*(2), 272–85.

Sacher, G. (1959). Relation of life span to brain weight. In E. Wolstenholme & M. O'Connor (Eds.), *Ciba symposium on the life span of animals.* London: Churchill.

Sadler, T. W. (1985). *Langman's medical embryology.* Baltimore: Williams & Wilkins.

Sagan, C. (1977). *The dragons of Eden.* New York: Random House.

Sales, E. (1978). Women's adult development. In I. Fieze (Ed.), *Women and sex roles.* New York: W. W. Norton.

Sameroff, A. (1975). Early influence on development: Fact or fancy. *Merrill-Palmer Quarterly of Behavior and Development, 21*(4), 23–34.

Sameroff, A. (1986). Environmental context of child development. *Journal of Pediatrics, 109,* 192–200.

Santana, G., (1979, September). *Social and familial influences on substance use among youth.* Paper presented to the American Psychological Association, New York.

Santrock, J. W. (1987). The effects of divorce on adolescents: Needed research perspectives. *Family Therapy, 14*(2), 147–59.

Santrock, J. W. (1989). *Life-span development.* Dubuque, IA: Wm. C. Brown Publishers.

Scarr, S. & Kidd, K. (1983). Developmental behavior genetics. In P. Mussen (Ed.), *Handbook of child psychology.* New York: Wiley.

Scarr, S., Weinberg, R., & Levine, A. (1986). *Understanding development.* New York: Harcourt, Brace, Jovanovich.

Schachter, S. (1959). *The psychology of affiliation.* Stanford, CA: Stanford University Press.

Schaie, K. W. & Hertzog, C. (1983). Fourteen-year cohort-sequential analyses of adult intellectual development. *Developmental Psychology, 19,* 531–43.

Schemeck, H. M. (1983, September 2). Alcoholism tests back disease idea. *New York Times,* A10.

Schibuk, M. (1989). Treating the sibling subsystem: An adjunct of divorce therapy. *American Journal of Orthopsychiatry, 59,* 226–37.

Schiedel, D. S. & Marcia, J. E. (1985). Ego identity, intimacy, sex role orientation, and gender. *Developmental Psychology, 21*(1), 149–60.

Schiffman, S. (1977). Food recognition of the elderly. *Journal of Gerontology, 32,* 586–92.

Schiffman, S. & Pasternak, M. (1979). Decreased discrimination of food odors in the elderly. *Journal of Gerontology, 34,* 73–79.

Schneider, J. (1984). *Stress, loss and grief.* Rockville, MD: Aspen Pubs., Inc.

Schofferman, J. (1987). Hospice care of the patient with AIDS. *The Hospice Journal, 3,* 51–84.

Schowalter, J. E. (1978). Parent death and child bereavement. In A. Weiner, I. Gerber, A. Kutscher, & B. Schoenberg (Eds.), *Bereavement.* New York: Columbia University Press.

Schulz, R. (1978). *The psychology of death, dying, and bereavement.* Reading, MA: Addison-Wesley.

Schulz, R. & Ewen, R. B. (1988). *Adult development and aging: Myths and emerging realities.* New York: Macmillan.

Schumm, W. R. & Bugaighis, M. A. (1986). Marital quality over the marital career. *Journal of Marriage and the Family, 48,* 165–68.

Schwartz, M. & Baden, M. A. (1973). Female adolescent self-concept: An examination of the relative influence of peers and adults. *Youth and Society, 5*(1), 115–28.

Scott, D. (Ed.). (1988). *Anorexia and bulimia.* New York: New York University Press.

Sears, R. (1975). Your ancients revisited: A history of child development research. In E. M. Hetherington (Ed.), *Review of child development research.* Chicago: University of Chicago Press.

Sears, R. R. & Sears, P. S. (1982). Lives in Berkeley. *Contemporary Psychology, 27*(12), 925–27.

Sebald, H. (1977). *Adolescence: A social psychological analysis* (2nd ed.). Englewood Cliffs, NJ: Prentice-Hall.

Seginer, R. & Flum, H. (1987). Israeli adolescents' self-image profile. *Journal of Youth and Adolescence, 16*(5), 455–72.

Seiden, R. H. & Freitas, R. P. (1980). Shifting patterns of deadly violence. *Suicide and Life Threatening Behavior, 10,* 195–209.

Select Committee on Children, Youth and Families. (1985). *Emerging trends in mental health care for adolescents.* Washington, DC: U.S. Government Printing Office.

Seligman, M. (1975). *Helplessness.* San Francisco: W. H. Freeman.

Selman, R. (1980). *The growth of interpersonal understanding.* New York: Academic Press.

Selye, H. (1956). *The stress of life.* New York: McGraw-Hill.

Selye, H. (1975, October). Implications of stress concept. *New York State Journal of Medicine,* 2139–45.

Selye, H. (1982). History and present status of the stress concept. In L. Goldberger & S. Breznitz (Eds.), *Handbook of stress: Theoretical and clinical aspects.* New York: Free Press.

Senn, M. (1975). Insights on the child development movement in the United States. *Monographs of the Society for Research in Child Development, 40,* (Serial No. 161).

Shaffer, D. & Fisher, P. (1981). The epidemiology of suicide in children and young adolescents. *Journal of the American Academy of Child Psychiatry, 20,* 545–65.

Shirk, S. R. (1987). Self-doubt in late childhood and early adolescence. *Journal of Youth and Adolescence, 16*(1), 59–68.

Siegal, L. J. & Senna, J. J. (1981). *Juvenile delinquency: Theory, practice, and law.* New York: West.

Siegler, I. (1975). The terminal drop hypothesis: Fact or artifact? *Experimental Aging Research, 1,* 169.

Silber, T. (1980). Values relating to abortion as expressed by the inner city adolescent girl—Report of a physician's experience. *Adolescence, 15*(57), 183–89.

Silverberg, S. B. & Steinberg, L. (1987). Influences on marital satisfaction during the middle stages of the family life cycle. *Journal of Marriage and the Family, 49*(4), 751–60.

Silverman, P. (1974). Anticipatory grief from the perspective of widowhood. In B. Schoenberg, A. Carr, A. Kutscher, D. Peretz, & I. Goldberg (Eds.), *Anticipatory grief* (pp. 320–30). New York: Columbia University Press.

Simonton, D. K. (1975). Age and literary creativity. *Journal of Cross-cultural Creativity, 6,* 259–77.

Simonton, D. K. (1976). Biographical determinants of achieved eminence. *Journal of Personality and Social Psychology, 33,* 218–76.

Simonton, D. K. (1977a). Creativity, age and stress. *Journal of Personality and Social Psychology, 35,* 791–804.

Simonton, D. K. (1977b). Eminence, creativity and geographical marginality. *Journal of Personality and Social Psychology, 35,* 805–16.

Singer, S. (1985). *Heredity.* San Francisco: W. H. Freeman.

Skinner, B. F. (1938). *The behavior of organisms.* New York: Appleton-Century-Crofts.

Skinner, B. F. (1948). *Walden two.* New York: Macmillan.

Skinner, B. F. (1953). *Science and human behavior.* New York: Macmillan.

Skinner, B. F. (1957). *Verbal behavior.* New York: Appleton-Century-Crofts.

Skinner, B. F. (1971). *Beyond freedom and dignity.* New York: Knopf.

Skinner, B. F. (1983, September). Origins of a behaviorist. *Psychology Today, 17*(2), 22–33.

Slugoski, B. R., Marcia, J. E., & Koopman, R. F. (1984). Cognitive and social interactional characteristics of ego identity statuses in college males. *Journal of Personality and Social Psychology, 47*(3), 646–61.

Smart, J. C. & Ethington, C. A. (1987). Occupational sex segregation and job satisfaction of women. *Research in Higher Education, 26*(2), 202–11.

Smart, M. S. & Smart, R. C. (1973). *Adolescents: Development and relationships.* New York: Macmillan.

Smith, R. (1990). *A theoretical framework for explaining the abuse of hyperactive children.* Unpublished doctoral dissertation, Boston College, Chestnut Hill, MA.

Smith-Pointer, R. A., Woodward, N. J., Wallston, B. S., Wallston, K. A., Rye, P., & Zylstral, M. (1988). Health care implications of desire and expectancy for control in elderly adults. *Journal of Gerontology: Psychological Sciences, 43*(1), 1–7.

Snider, A. & Adatto, I. J. (1984). *A doctor discusses learning to live with nervous tension.* Chicago: Budlong Pr. Co.

Solow, R. A. & Solow, B. K. (1986). Mind-altering drugs: Effects on adolescent sexual functioning. *Medical Aspects of Human Sexuality, 20*(1), 64–74.

Sommerstein, J. C. (1986). Assessing the older worker: The career counselor's dilemma. Special issue: Career counseling of older adults. *Journal of Career Development, 13*(2), 52–56.

South, S. J. & Spitze, G. (1986). Determinants of divorce over the marital life course. *American Sociological Review, 51*(4), 583–90.

Spence, A. (1989). *Biology of humanaging.* Englewood Cliffs, NJ: Prentice-Hall.

Spirito, A., Stark, L., Fristad, M., & Hart, K., (1987). Adolescent suicide attempters hospitalized in a pediatric unit. *Journal of Pediatric Psychology, 12*(2), 171–89.

Sprafkin, J. N., Liebert, R. M., & Poulos, R. W. (1975). Effects of a prosocial televised example on children's helping. *Journal of Experimental Child Psychology, 20,* 119–26.

Spreen, O., Tuppet, D., Risser, A., Tuokko, H., & Edgell, D. (1984). *Human developmental neuropsychology.* New York: Oxford University Press.

Sroufe, L. A. (1979). Socioemotional development. In J. Osofsky (Ed.), *Handbook of infant development.* New York: Wiley.

Sroufe, L. A. & Cooper, R. (1988). *Child development.* New York: Knopf.

Starr, B. & Weiner, M. (1981). *The Starr-Weiner report on sex and sexuality in the mature years.* New York: Stein & Day.

Statistical Abstracts of the U.S. (1988). Washington, DC: The Bureau of the Census.

Stein, K. B., Soskin, W. F., & Korchin, S. J. (1974). Interpersonal trust and disaffected high school youth. *Journal of Youth and Adolescence, 3*(4), 281–92.

Steinberg, L. (1987). Single parents, step-parents, and the susceptibility of adolescents to antisocial peer pressure. *Child Development, 58*(1), 269–75.

Stern, D. (1977). *First relationships.* Cambridge, MA: Harvard University Press.

Sternberg, R. (Ed.). (1982). *Handbook of human intelligence.* New York: Cambridge University Press.

Sternberg, R. (1986). *Intelligence applied.* New York: Harcourt, Brace, Jovanovich.

Sternberg, R. (1988). *The triarchic mind: A new theory of human intelligence.* New York: Viking Press.

Sternberg, R. J. (1986). The triangular theory of love. *Psychological Review, 93,* 129–35.

Sternberg, R. J. & Detterman, D. K. (Eds.). (1979). *Human intelligence: Perspectives on its theory and measurement.* Norwood, NJ: Ablex.

Stevens, J. C. & Cain, W. S. (1987). Old-age deficits in the sense of smell as gauged by thresholds, magnitude matching, and odor identification. *Psychology and Aging, 2,* 36–42.

Stiffman, A., Earls, F., Robins, L., & Jung, K. (1987). Adolescent sexual activity and pregnancy: Socioenvironmental problems, physical health, and mental health. *Journal of Youth and Adolescence, 16*(5), 497–569.

Stoddard, S. (1977). *The hospice movement: A better way of caring for the dying.* New York: Stein & Day.

Stoneman, Z., Brody, G. L., & MacKinnon, C. E. (1986). Same-sex and cross-sex siblings: Activity choices, roles, behavior and gender stereotypes. *Sex Roles, 15,* 495–512.

Story, M. D. (1982). A comparison of university student experience with various sexual outlets in 1974 and 1980. *Adolescence, 17*(68), 737–47.

Strobino, D. (1987). Health and medical consequences. In C. Hayes & S. Hofferth (Eds.), *Risking the future: Adolescent sexuality, pregnancy, and childbearing* (pp. 107–23). Washington, DC: National Academy Press.

Subcommittee on Health and the Environment. (1987). *Incidence and control of chlamydia.* Washington, DC: U.S. Government Printing Office.

Sudnow, D. (1967). *Passing on.* Englewood Cliffs, NJ: Prentice-Hall.

Sullivan, T. & Schneider, M. (1987). Development and identity issues in adolescent homosexuality. *Child and Adolescent Social Work Journal, 4*(1), 13–24.

Suomi, S. J., Harlow, H., & Novak, M. A. (1974). Reversal of social deficits produced by isolation rearing in monkeys. *Journal of Human Evolution, 3,* 527–34.

Super, D. E. & Hall, D. T. (1978). Career development: Exploration and planning. *Annual Review of Psychology, 29,* 333–72.

Surgeon General. (1982). *Television and behavior: Ten years of scientific progress and implications for the eighties.* Washington, DC: U.S. Department of Health and Human Services.

Sutton-Smith, B. (1988). *Toys as culture.* New York: Gardner Press.

Swanson, E. A. & Bennett, T. F. (1983). Degree of closeness: Does it affect the bereaved's attitudes toward selected funeral practices? *Omega, 13,* 43–50.

Sweet, J. A. & Bumpass, L. L. (1987). *American families and households.* New York: Sage.

Szinovacz, M. E. (1984). Changing family roles and interactions. In B. B. Hess & M. B. Sussman (Eds.), *Women and the family: Two decades of change* (pp. 164–201). New York: Haworth Press.

Tager, I. B., Weiss, S. T., Munoz, A., Rosner, B., & Speizer, F. E. (1984). Longitudinal study of the effects of maternal smoking on pulmonary function in children. *New England Journal of Medicine, 309,* 699–703.

Takata, S. R., Zevitz, R. G., Berger, R. J., Salem, R. G., Gruberg, M., & Moore, J. (1987). Youth gangs in Racine: An examination of community perceptions. *Wisconsin-Sociologist, 24,* 132–41.

Tanner, J. M. (1978). *Foetus into man.* Cambridge, MA: Harvard University Press.

Task Force. (1976). *The walkabout.* Bloomington, IN: Phi Delta Kappa.

Taub, H. (1975). Effects of coding cues upon short-term memory. *Developmental Psychology, 11,* 254.

Tauber, M. A. (1979). Parental socialization techniques and sex differences in children's play. *Child Development, 50,* 225–34.

Teicher, J. (1973). A solution to the chronic problem of living: Adolescent-attempted suicide. In J. C. Schoolar (Ed.), *Current issues in adolescent psychiatry.* New York: Brunner/Mazel.

Teicher, J. & Jacobs, J. (1966). The physician and the adolescent suicide attempter. *Journal of School Health, 36,* 406.

Terman, L. M. (1925). *Genetic studies of genius.* Stanford, CA: Stanford University Press.

Terman, L. M. & Oden, M. H. (1959). The gifted group in mid-life. In L. M. Terman (Ed.), *Genetic studies of genius* (Vol. 5). Stanford, CA: Stanford University Press.

Tessler, D. J. (1980). *Drugs, kids, and schools.* Santa Monica, CA: Goodyear.

Thomas, A. (1981). Current trends in developmental theory. *American Journal of Orthopsychiatry, 51,* 580–609.

Thomas, A. & Chess, S. (1977). *Temperament.* New York: Brunner/Mazel.

Thomas, A., Chess, S., & Birch, H. (1970). The origin of personality. *Scientific American, 223,* 102–9.

Thomas, L. (1983). *Late night thoughts on listening to Mahler's ninth symphony.* New York: Viking Press.

Thomas, L. E. (1971). Family correlates of student political activism. *Development Psychology, 4,* 206–14.

Thompson, K. (1980). A comparison of black and white adolescents' beliefs about having children. *Journal of Marriage and the Family, 8*(2), 133–39.

Tiger, L. (1978, July). Omnigamy: The new kinship system. *Psychology Today,* 14–17.

Timiras, R. S. (1972). *Developmental physiology and aging.* New York: Macmillan.

Tishler, C. (1981). Adolescent suicide attempts: Some significant factors. *Suicide and Life Threatening Behavior, 11*(2), 86–92.

Tishler, C. & McKenry, P. (1983). Intrapsychic symptom dimension of adolescent attempted suicide. *The Journal of Family Practice, 16*(4), 731–34.

Toffler, A. (1970). *Future shock.* New York: Bantam Books, Inc.

Toffler, A. (1984). *The third wave.* New York: Bantam Books, Inc.

Tolan, P. H. (1987). Implications of age of onset for delinquency risk. *Journal of Abnormal Child Psychology, 15*(1), 47–65.

Toman, W. (1976). *Family constellation.* New York: Springer.

Toolan, J. (1975). Depression in adolescents. In J. Howell (Ed.), *Modern perspectives in adolescent psychiatry.* New York: Brunner/Mazel.

Topol, P. & Rezinkoff, M. (1984). Locus of control as factors in adolescent suicide attempts. *Suicide and Life Threatening Behavior, 12*(3), 141–50.

Torgersen, A. M. (1982). Genetic factors in temperamental individuality: A longitudinal study of same-sexed twins from two months to six years of age. *Journal of the American Academy of Child Psychiatry, 20,* 702–11.

Torrens, P. R. (1985). Current status of hospice programs. In P. R. Torrens (Ed.), *Hospice programs and public policy* (pp. 35–59). Chicago, IL: American Hospital Publishing.

Traupmann, J., Peterson, R., Utne, M., & Hatfield, E. (1981). Measuring equity in intimate relations. *Applied Psychological Measurement, 5*(4), 467–80.

Travers, J. (1982). *The growing child*. Glenview, IL: Scott, Foresman.

Treas, J. (1975). Aging and the family. In D. S. Woodruff & J. Birren (Eds.), *Aging: Scientific perspectives and social issues*. New York: Van Nostrand Reinhold.

Treffinger, D. J., Isaksen, S. G., & Firestien, R. (1983). Theoretical perspectives on creative learning and its facilitation: An overview. *Journal of Creative Behavior, 17*(1), 9–17.

Troll, L. E. (1975). *Early and middle adulthood*. Monterey, CA: Brooks/Cole.

Trotter, R. J. (1987, December). Project day-care. *Psychology Today*, 32–38.

Tudor, C., Petersen, D., & Elifson, K. (1980). An examination of the relationship between peer and parental influences in adolescent drug use. *Adolescence, 60*, 783–98.

Turner, J. S. & Helms, D. B. (1989). *Contemporary adulthood*. New York: Holt, Rinehart & Winston.

Tversky, A. & Kahneman, D. (1981). The framing of decisions and the psychology of choice. *Science, 211*, 453–58.

Twomey, L., Taylor, J., & Furiss, B. (1983). Age changes in the bone density and structure of the lumbar vertebral column. *Journal of Anatomy, 136*, 15–25.

U.S. Bureau of the Census. (1986). *Statistical abstract of the United States, 1986*. Washington, DC: U.S. Government Printing Office.

U.S. Department of Commerce. (1988). *Household and family characteristics: March, 1987*. Washington, DC: Bureau of the Census, 3.

U.S. Department of Health and Human Services. (1988). *10 Steps to help your child say "NO."* Rockville, MD: Office for Substance Abuse Prevention.

U.S. Department of Transportation. (1976). *How to talk to your teenager about drinking and driving*. Washington, DC: National Highway Traffic Safety Administration (GPO 1976, 0–625–636).

U.S. National Center for Health Statistics. (1986). *Advance data from vital and health statistics*, No. 125. DHHS Pub. No. (PHS) 86–1250. Hyattsville, MD: Public Health Service.

U.S. National Center for Health Statistics. (1988). *Vital statistics of the United States, 1968-1987. Death rates by age, race, sex—5 and 10 year age groupings*. Washington, DC: U.S. Government Printing Office.

U.S. National Center for Health Statistics. (1989). *Vital statistics of the United States*. Washington, DC: U.S. Government Printing Office.

U.S. National Center for Health Statistics. (1990). *Vital statistics of the United States*. Washington, DC: U.S. Government Printing Office.

Vaillant, G. (1977). *Adaptation to life*. Boston: Little, Brown.

VanderMay, B. J. & Neff, R. L. (1982). Adult child incest: A review of research and treatment. *Adolescence, 17*(68), 717–35.

VanderZanden, J. (1989). *Human development* (4th ed.). New York: Knopf.

Van Gannep, A. [1909] (1960). *The rites of passage*. (M. Vizedom & G. Caffee, Trans.) Chicago: The University of Chicago Press.

Veatch, R. M. (1981). *A theory of medical ethics*. New York: Basic Books.

Veatch, R. M. (1984). Brain death. In J. Schneidman (Ed.), *Death: Current perspectives* (3rd. ed.). Mountain View, CA: Mayfield.

Verbrugge, L. M. (1979). Marital status and health. *Journal of Marriage and the Family, 41*, 267–85.

Vernandakis, A. (Ed.). (1982). *Hormones in development and aging*. New York: Spectrum.

Vigil, J. D. (1988). *Barrio gangs: Street life and identity in southern California*. Austin: Texas Press.

Vorhees, C. & Mollnow, E. (1987). Behavioral teratogenesis. In J. Osofsky (Ed.), *Handbook of infant development*. New York: Wiley.

Wade, N. L. (1987). Suicide as a resolution of separation-individuation among adolescent girls. *Adolescence, 22*(85), 169–77.

Wagner, C. (1980). Sexuality of American adolescents. *Adolescence, 15*(59), 567–80.

Walch, S. (1976). Adolescent attempted suicide: Analysis of the differences in male and female behavior. *Dissertation Abstracts International, 38*, 2892B.

Walker, L. S. & Greene, J. W. (1987). Negative life events, psychosocial resources, and psychophysiological symptoms in adolescents. *Journal of Clinical Child Psychology, 16*(1), 29–36.

Wallach, M. A. & Kogan, N. (1965). *Modes of thinking in young children*. New York: Holt, Rinehart & Winston.

Wallerstein, J. (1984). Children of divorce: Preliminary report of a ten-year follow-up of young children. *American Journal of Orthopsychiatry, 54*, 444–58.

Wallerstein, J. & Blakeslee, S. (1989). *Second chances: Men, women and children. Decade after divorce*. New York: Ticknor & Fields.

Walther, R. R. & Harber, L. C. (1984). Expected skin complaints of the geriatric patient. *Geriatrics, 39*, 67.

Waltz, G. & Benjamin, L. (1980). *Adolescent pregnancy and parenthood*. ERIC document 184528.

Wang, J. S. & Busse, E. W. (1974). EEG of healthy persons. In E. Palmore (Ed.), *Normal aging II*. Durham, NC: Duke University Press.

Warabi, T., Kase, M., & Kato, T. (1984). Effect of aging on the accuracy of visually guided saccadic eye movement. *Annals of Neurology, 16*, 449–54.

Warren, R. M. & Warren, R. P. (1971). Some age differences in auditory perception. *Bulletin of the New York Academy of Medicine, 47*, 1365–77.

Washington, A. C., Rossier, P. L., & Cox, E. P. (1983). Contraceptive practices of teenage mothers. *Journal of the National Medical Association, 75*(11), 1059–63.

Washington, A. E., Arno, P. S., & Brooks, M. A. (1986). The economic cost of pelvic inflammatory disease. *Journal of the American Medical Association, 225*(13), 1021–33.

Wasow, M. & Loeb, M. B. Sexuality in nursing homes. *Journal of the American Geriatric Society, 28*(2), 73–79.

Watson, J. (1968). *The double helix*. New York: Atheneum Press.

Webb, L., DiClemente, C., Johnstone, E., Sanders, J., & Perley, R. (Eds.). (1981). *DSM—III Training Guide*. New York: Brunner/Mazel.

Weber, M. (1904). *The protestant ethic and the spirit of capitalism*. New York: Charles Scribner's Sons.

Wechsler, D. (1955). *Manual for the Wechsler adult intelligence test*. New York: Psychological Corp.

Wechlser, D. (1958). *The measurement and appraisal of adult intelligence*. Baltimore: Williams & Wilkins.

Weeks, D. (1989). Death education for aspiring physicians, teachers, and funeral directors. *Death Studies, 13*, 17–24.

Weiner, I. B. (1970). *Psychological disturbances in adolescence*. New York: Wiley Interscience.

Weinrich, J. D. (1987). A new sociobiological theory of homosexuality applicable to societies with universal marriage. *Ethology and Sociobiology, 8*(1), 37–47.

Weisman, A. (1974). *On dying and denying*. New York: Behavioral Publications.

Weisman, M. (1974). The epidemiology of suicide attempts, 1960–1971. *Archives of General Psychiatry, 30,* 737–46.

Weiss, G. (1983). Long-term outcome: Findings, concepts, and practical implications. In M. Rutter (Ed.), *Developmental neuropsychology.* New York: Guilford Press.

Weitzman, L. J. (1985). *The divorce revolution: The unexpected social and economic consequences for women and children in America.* New York: Macmillan.

Welch, C. (1989). *In the matter of Claire C. Conroy: Pulling the plug on precedent.* Unpublished manuscript, Boston, MA.

Wenz, F. (1979). Economic status, family anomie, and adolescent suicide potential. *Journal of Psychology, 98*(1), 45–47.

Wertheimer, M. (1962). Psychomotor coordination of auditory-visual space at birth. *Science, 134.*

Westoff, C. F., Calot, G., & Foster, A. D. (1983). Teenage fertility in developed nations. *Family Planning Perspectives, 15,* 105.

Whelan, R. (1982). Presidential message. *Society for Learning Disabilities and Remedial Education Newsletter, 2,* 1–3.

White, C. B. (1981, September). *Sexual interests, attitudes and knowledge and sexual history.* Paper presented at the Annual Meeting of the American Psychological Association, Los Angeles, CA.

White, H. C. (1974). Self-poisoning in adolescents. *British Journal of Psychiatry, 124,* 24–35.

Whitehead, A. & Mathews, A. (1986). Factors related to successful outcome in the treatment of sexually unresponsive women. *Psychological Medicine, 16*(2), 373–78.

Wiland, L. J. (1986). Vision quest: Rites of adolescent passage. *Camping Magazine, 58*(7), 30–33.

Wilkinson, K. & Isreal, G. (1984). Suicide and rurality in urban society. *Suicide and Life Threatening Behavior, 14*(3), 187–200.

Wilks, J. (1986). The relative importance of parents and friends in adolescent decision making. *Journal of Youth and Adolescence, 15,* 323–34.

Will, J., Self, P., & Datan, N. (1976). Maternal behavior and perceived sex of infant. *American Journal of Orthopsychiatry, 46,* 135–39.

Williams, G. (1979, March 11). How to explain death to a child. *Boston Globe,* A12.

Williams, L. (1989, July 21). Teens feel having sex is their own right. *The New York Times,* 13.

Williams, R. M., Jr. (1960). *American society: A sociological interpretation.* New York: Knopf.

Williamson, J. B., Munley, A., & Evans L. (1980). *Aging and society: An introduction to social gerontology.* New York: Holt, Rinehart & Winston.

Wilson, E. O. (1978). *Sociobiology.* Cambridge, MA: Harvard University Press.

Wilson, H. S. & Kneisl, C. (1979). *Psychiatric nursing.* Menlo Park, CA: Addison-Wesley.

Wilson, P. (1987). Psychoanalytic therapy and the young adolescent. *Bulletin of the Anna Freud Centre, 10*(1), 51–79.

Winn, M. (1983). *Children without childhood.* New York: Pantheon Books.

Wittrock, M. (1986). Students' thought processes. In M. Wittrock (Ed.), *Handbook of research on teaching.* New York: Macmillan.

Wolf, M. & Dickinson, D. (1985). From oral to written language: Transitions in the school years. In J. B. Gleason (Ed.), *The development of language.* Columbus, OH: Merrill.

Wolfson, M. (1989). *A review of the literature on feminist psychology.* Unpublished manuscript, Boston College, Chestnut Hill, MA.

Woodruff-Pak, D. (1988). *Psychology and aging.* Englewood Cliffs, NJ: Prentice-Hall.

Wynne, E. (1978). Beyond the discipline problem: Youth suicide as a measure of alienation. *Phi Delta Kappan, 59*(5), 307–15.

Wyshak, G. & Frisch, R. (1982). Evidence for a secular trend in age of menarche. *New England Journal of Medicine, 306,* 1033–35.

Yao, E. L. (1988, November). Working effectively with Asian immigrant parents. *Phi Delta Kappan,* 223–25.

Yogman, M. (1982). Development of the father-infant relationship. In H. Fitzgerald, B. Lester, & M. Yogman (Eds.), *Theory and research in behavioral pediatrics.* New York: Plenum.

Young, T. J. (1987). PCP use among adolescents. *Child Study Journal, 17*(1), 55–86.

Youniss, J. & Smollar, J. (1985). Parent-adolescent relations in adolescents whose parents are divorced. *Journal of Early Adolescence, 5*(1), 129–44.

Zajonc, R. & Marcus, G. B. (1975). Birth order and intellectual development. *Psychological review, 82,* 74–80.

Zelnick, M. & Kantner, J. F. (1977). Sexual and contraceptive experience of young unmarried women in the U.S., 1976 and 1971. *Family Planning Perspectives, 9*(2), 101–11.

Zigler, E. & Finn-Stevenson, M. (1987). *Children: Development and social issues.* Lexington, MA: D.C. Heath.

Zigler, E. & Gordon, E. (1982). *Daycare: Scientific and social policy issues.* Boston: Auburn House.

Zoja, L. (1984, June). Sucht als unbewusster Versuch zur initiation, Teil I./ Addiction as an unconscious attempt toward initiation: I. *Analyische Psychologie, 15*(2), 110–25.

Credits

❖

Text Art and Tables

Chapter 1

Figure 1.1 From John F. Travers, *The Growing Child.* Copyright © 1982 Scott, Foresman and Company, Glenview, IL. Reprinted by permission of the author; **Figure 1.3** From John F. Travers, *The Growing Child.* Copyright © 1982 Scott, Foresman and Company, Glenview, IL. Reprinted by permission of the author; **Table 1.5** From John Dacey, *Adolescents Today,* 3d ed. Copyright © 1986 Scott, Foresman and Company, Glenview, IL. Reprinted by permission of the author.

Chapter 3

Table 3.1 From John F. Travers, *The Growing Child.* Copyright © 1982 Scott, Foresman and Company, Glenview, IL. Reprinted by permission of the author; **Figure 3.1** From John F. Travers, *The Growing Child.* Copyright © 1982 Scott, Foresman and Company, Glenview, IL. Reprinted by permission of the author; **Figure 3.2** From John F. Travers, *The Growing Child.* Copyright © 1982 Scott, Foresman and Company, Glenview, IL. Reprinted by permission of the author; **Figure 3.3** From John F. Travers, *The Growing Child.* Copyright © 1982 Scott, Foresman and Company, Glenview, IL. Reprinted by permission of the author; **Figure 3.5** From John F. Travers, *The Growing Child.* Copyright © 1982 Scott, Foresman and Company, Glenview, IL. Reprinted by permission of the author; **Figure 3.8** From John F. Travers, *The Growing Child.* Copyright © 1982 Scott, Foresman and Company, Glenview, IL. Reprinted by permission of the author; **Table 3.3** From John F. Travers, *The Growing Child.* Copyright © 1982 Scott, Foresman and Company, Glenview, IL. Reprinted by permission of the author; **Table 3.4** From John F. Travers, *The Growing Child.* Copyright © 1982 Scott, Foresman and Company, Glenview, IL. Reprinted by permission of the author.

Chapter 4

Figure 4.2 From Stuart Ira Fox, *Human Physiology,* 3d ed. Copyright © 1990 Wm. C. Brown Publishers, Dubuque, Iowa. All Rights Reserved. Reprinted by permission; **Figure 4.5** From K. L. Moore, *The Developing Human: Clinically Oriented Embryology,* 4th ed. Copyright © 1988 W. B. Saunders Company, Philadelphia, PA. Reprinted by permission.

Chapter 5

Table 5.1 From John F. Travers, *The Growing Child.* Copyright © 1982 Scott, Foresman and Company, Glenview, IL. Reprinted by permission of the author; **Figure 5.1** From *The Conscious Brain* by Steven Rose. Copyright © 1973 by Steven Rose. Reprinted by permission of Alfred A. Knopf, Inc.; **Table 5.3** From John F. Travers, *The Growing Child.* Copyright © 1982 Scott, Foresman and Company, Glenview, IL. Reprinted by permission of the author; **Figure 5.2** From Richard Ferber, *Solve Your Child's Sleep Problems.* Copyright © 1985 by Richard Ferber, M.D. Reprinted by permission of Simon & Schuster, Inc.; **Table 5.4** From John F. Travers, *The Growing Child.* Copyright © 1982 Scott, Foresman and Company, Glenview, IL. Reprinted by permission of the author.

Chapter 7

Figure 7.1 From John F. Travers, *The Growing Child.* Copyright © 1982 Scott, Foresman and Company, Glenview, IL. Reprinted by permission of the author; **Table 7.1** From John F. Travers, *The Growing Child.* Copyright © 1982 Scott, Foresman and Company, Glenview, IL. Reprinted by permission of the author; **Figure 7.4** From John W. Santrock and Steve R. Yussen, *Child Development: An Introduction,* 4th ed. Copyright © 1989 Wm. C. Brown Publishers, Dubuque, Iowa. All Rights Reserved. Reprinted by permission; **Figure 7.3** From John F. Travers, *The Growing Child.* Copyright © 1982 Scott, Foresman and Company, Glenview, IL. Reprinted by permission of the author.

Chapter 9

Table 9.1 From John F. Travers, *The Growing Child.* Copyright © 1982 Scott, Foresman and Company, Glenview, IL. Reprinted by permission of the author; **Figure 9.1** From John F. Travers, *The Growing Child.* Copyright © 1982 Scott, Foresman and Company, Glenview, IL. Reprinted by permission of the author; **Figure 9.2** From John F. Travers, *The Growing Child.* Copyright © 1982 Scott, Foresman and Company, Glenview, IL. Reprinted by permission of the author; **Table 9.3** From John F. Travers, *The Growing Child.* Copyright © 1982 Scott, Foresman and Company, Glenview, IL. Reprinted by permission of the author.

Chapter 11

Figure 11.1 From John F. Travers, *The Growing Child.* Copyright © 1982 Scott, Foresman and Company, Glenview, IL. Reprinted by permission of the author.

Chapter 14

Figure 14.1 From The Roper Organization, *American Chicle Youth Poll.* Copyright © 1987 University of Connecticut, Storrs, CT.; **Figure 14.2** From The Roper Organization, *American Chicle Youth Poll.* Copyright © 1987 University of Connecticut, Storrs, CT.

Chapter 15

Figure 15.3 Reprinted courtesy of The Boston Globe.

Chapter 18

Figure 18.1 From Boyd C. Rollins and Harold Feldman, "Marital Satisfaction Over the Family Life Cycle" in *Journal of Marriage and the Family,* 32:20-28. Copyright © National Council on Family Relations, St. Paul, MN. Reprinted by permission; **Table 18.3** From John Dacey, *Adult Development.* Copyright © 1982 Scott, Foresman and Company, Glenview, IL. Reprinted by permission of the author.

Chapter 19

Figure 19.1 From L. L. Langley, *Physiology of Man.* Copyright © 1971 Van Nostrand Reinhold Company, New York, NY; **Figure 19.5** From *From Now to Zero: Fertility, Contraception and Abortion in America.* Copyright © 1968, 1971 by Charles F. Westoff and Leslie Aldridge Westoff. Little, Brown and Company, Boston, MA.

Chapter 20

Figure 20.1 From John W. Santrock. Copyright © 1989 Wm. C. Brown Publishers, Dubuque, Iowa. All Rights Reserved. Reprinted by permission; **Figure 20.2** From *The Seasons of a Man's Life* by Daniel J. Levinson, et al. Copyright © 1978 by Daniel J. Levinson. Reprinted by permission of Alfred A. Knopf, Inc; **Figure 20.4** From R. McCrae and P. Costa, Jr., *Emerging Lives, Enduring Disposition: Personality in Adulthood.* Copyright © 1984 Little, Brown and Company, Boston, MA.

Chapter 21

Figure 21.2 *Developmental Physiology and Aging* by Paola S. Timiras. Copyright © 1972 P. S. Timiras. Reprinted with permission of Macmillan Publishing Company, a Division of Macmillan, Inc.; **Figure 21.6** From J. W. Elias and M. F. Elias, *Journal of Gerontology,* 31:164. Copyright © 1976 Gerontological Society of America, Washington, DC. Reprinted by permission.

Illustrations

Majority of art provided by Rolin Graphics.

Photo Credits
Photo Research done by Toni Michaels

Part Openers
1: © John R. Jurras; **2:** © Ed Lettau/Photo Researchers, Inc.; **3:** © Robert Kalman/The Image Works; **4:** © Ulrike Welsch; **5:** © James Carroll; **6:** © Ulrike Welsch/Photo Researchers, Inc.; **7:** © Ulrike Welsch; **8:** © Alan Carey/The Image Works; **9:** © Toni Michaels

Chapter 1
Page 5 a: © John R. Jurras; **b,c:** AP/Wide World Photos; **d:** UPI/Bettmann Newsphotos; **e:** AP/Wide World Photos; **p. 7 top left:** © Sarah Putnam/The Picture Cube; **top right:** © Dan Chidester/The Image Works; **bottom left:** © Stan Levy/Photo Researchers, Inc.; **bottom right:** © Bob Daemmrich/The Image Works; **p. 11:** © Omikron/Photo Researchers, Inc.; **p. 13:** © David Hurn/Magnum Photos; **p. 14:** © W. Marc Bernsau/The Image Works; **p. 17:** © Alan Carey/The Image Works

Chapter 2
Page 34: The Bettmann Archive; **p. 36:** © Elizabeth Crews/The Image Works; **p. 38:** Courtesy of Dr. Andrew Schwebel; **p. 41:** © Harriet Gans/The Image Works; **p. 43 top:** The Bettmann Archive; **bottom:** Courtesy of Prof. Benjamin Harris, Univ. of Wisconsin-Parkside; **p. 44:** © Christopher Johnson/Stock Boston; **p. 47:** UPI/Bettmann Newsphotos; **p. 51:** © Ulrike Welsch

Chapter 3
Page 61: © Spencer Grant/The Picture Cube; **p. 63 top:** © Walter Dawn/Photo Researchers, Inc.; **bottom:** © SIU/Photo Researchers, Inc.; **Fig. 3.4:** From L. P. Wisniewski and K. Kirshhorn, *A Guide to Human Chromosome Defects,* 2d ed., White Plains, NY: The March of Dimes Birth Defects Foundation, BD:OAS, 16(6) 1980, with permission of the copyright holder; **p. 76:** The Granger Collection; **p. 77:** © Alan Carey/The Image Works

Chapter 4
Page 86 top: © D.W. Fawcett/D. Phillips/Photo Researchers, Inc.; © Omikron/Photo Researchers, Inc.; **p. 87 top:** © Dr. C. Reather/Photo Researchers, Inc.; **p. 87 bottom and Fig. 4.4:** © Petit Format/Nestle/Science Source/Photo Researchers, Inc.; **p. 92 top:** © Michael J. Okoniewski/The Image Works; **bottom:** © John Griffin/The Image Works; **p. 93:** A.P. Streissguth, S.K. Clarren, and K. L. Jones (1985, July). "Natural History of the Fetal Alcohol Syndrome: A Ten-Year Follow-Up of Eleven Patients. *Lancet, 2,* 85–92; **p. 96:** © Nancy Dureell McKenna/Photo Researchers, Inc.; **p. 98:** © Robert Goldstein/Photo Researchers, Inc.; **p. 105:** © Eric Roth/The Picture Cube

Chapter 5
Page 113: Figure 2 from "Discrimination and Imitation of Facial Expressions by Neonates," I. Field et al., *Science,* Vol. 218, 4568, pp. 179–181, October 8, 1982. Copyright 1982 by the AAAS.; **p. 117, 118:** Dr. John Travers; **p. 119:** © Alan Carey/The Image Works; **Fig. 5.3:** © William Vandivert and *Scientific American,* April 1960; **p. 124:** Dr. John Travers; **p. 128:** © Julie O'Neil/The Picture Cube

Chapter 6
Page 140: © Ulrike Welsch; **p. 144:** © Elizabeth Crews/The Image Works; **p. 146:** © Janice Fullman/The Picture Cube; **p. 148:**

© Sandra Johnson/The Picture Cube; **p. 151:** © Majorie Nichols/The Picture Cube; **p. 157:** © Alan Carey/The Image Works

Chapter 7
Page 165: © Elizabeth Crews/The Image Works; **p. 168:** © Annie Hunter; **p. 171:** © Henry Horenstein/The Picture Cube; **p. 174:** © Sharon L. Fox/The Picture Cube; **p. 176:** © Carol Palmer/The Picture Cube; **p. 184:** © Lynn McLaren/Photo Researchers, Inc.

Chapter 8
Page 191: © Carol Palmer/The Picture Cube; **p. 193:** © Steve Takatsuno/The Picture Cube; **p. 194:** © Erika Stone/Photo Researchers, Inc.; **p. 197 left:** © Nancy Lutz/The Picture Cube; **right:** © Carol Palmer/ The Picture Cube; **p. 201:** © Ulrike Welsh/Photo Researchers, Inc.; **p. 205 top:** © Elizabeth Crews/The Image Works; **bottom:** © Linda Benedict-Jones/The Picture Cube; **p. 210:** © Alan Carey/The Image Works

Chapter 9
Page 221: © Alan Carey/The Image Works; **p. 222:** © Mimi Forsyth/Monkmeyer Press; **p. 225:** © Elizabeth Crews/The Image Works; **p. 229:** © James Carroll

Chapter 10
Page 247: © Alan Carey/The Image Works; **p. 249:** © Ulrike Welsch; **p. 251:** © Meri Houtchens-Kitchens/The Picture Cube; **p. 254:** © Elizabeth Crews/The Image Works; **p. 257:** © Jack Spratt/The Image Works; **p. 265:** © Bob Kalman/The Image Works

Chapter 11
Page 277: © David Grossman/Photo Researchers, Inc.; **p. 280:** © Rick Friedman/The Picture Cube; **p. 281 left:** Photo Researchers, Inc.; **middle and right:** © Topham/The Image Works; **p. 285:** © James Carroll; **p. 289:** © Eric Roth/The Picture Cube; **p. 291:** © John Griffin/The Image Works

Chapter 12
Page 304: © Elizabeth Crews/The Image Works; **p. 306:** Giraudon/Art Resource; **p. 307:** Archives of the History of American Psychology, University of Akron, Akron, OH; **p. 312:** University of Chicago; **p. 315 top:** © Archive/Photo Researchers, Inc.; **bottom:** © Antman Archives/The Image Works; **p. 320:** © Ulrike Welsch; **p. 321:** © Thelma Shumsky/The Image Works; **p. 322:** © Margaret Thompson/The Picture Cube; **p. 325:** © Barbara Rios/Photo Researchers, Inc.

Chapter 13
Page 336: © Annie Hunter; **p. 337:** Walt Disney Productions, photo courtesy of Museum of Modern Art/Film Stills Archive; **p. 341:** © James Carroll; **p. 345:** © Spencer Grant/Photo Researchers, Inc.; **p. 347:** © Alan Carey/The Image Works; **p. 349:** The Granger Collection

Chapter 14
Page 354: © Michael Weisbrot/Stock Boston; **p. 357:** © Frank Siteman/The Picture Cube; **p. 361:** © Toni Michaels; **p. 364:** © Steve Takatsuno/The Picture Cube; **p. 365:** © Susan Rosenberg/Photo Researchers, Inc.; **p. 369:** © Ulrike Welsch; **p. 371:** © David Strickland/The Image Works; **p. 374:** © Jim Shaffer; **p. 377:** © **John Maher/The Picture Cube; p. 378:** © Alan Carey/The Image Works; **p. 384:** UPI/Bettmann Newsphotos

Chapter 15
Page 388: © Bob Daemmrich/The Image Works; **p. 389 top:** AP/Wide World Photos; **bottom:** © Jaye R. Phillips/The Picture Cube; **p. 390, 391:** © Alan Carey/The Image Works; **p. 395:** © Robert V. Eckert, Jr./The Picture Cube; **p. 401 top:** © Rohn Engh/The Image Works; **bottom:** © John Griffin/The Image Works; **p. 406:** © Susan Kuklin/Photo Researchers, Inc.

Chapter 16
Page 420: Anthro Photo; **p. 423, 424:** © Ellis Herwig/The Picture Cube; **p. 425:** © Mark Antman/The Image Works; **p. 426:** © Irven DeVore/Anthro Photo

Chapter 17
Page 442: © Annie Hunter; **p. 443 top:** © Eric Breitenbach/The Picture Cube; **bottom:** © Thelma Shumsky/The Image Works; **p. 445:** © Therese Frare/The Picture Cube; **p. 447:** © Lorraine Rorke/The Image Works; **p. 449:** © Bob Kalman/The Image Works; **p. 450:** © Alan Carey/The Image Works; **p. 454:** © Annie Hunter

Chapter 18
Page 460: © Bobbi Carrey/The Picture Cube; **p. 464:** AP/Wide World Photos; **p. 467:** © Dion Ogust/The Image Works; **p. 472:** © Toni Michaels; **p. 476:** © Ulrike Welsch; **p. 481:** © Annie Hunter; **p. 483:** © Charles Gatewood/The Image Works

Chapter 19
Page 493: © Ellis Herwig/The Picture Cube; **p. 494:** © Annie Hunter; **p. 497:** Archives of the History of American Psychology, University of Akron, Akron, OH; **p. 501:** UPI/Bettmann Newsphotos; **p. 508:** © Ellis Herwig/The Picture Cube; **p. 509:** © Mikki Ansin/The Picture Cube

Chapter 20
Page 514: © Ulrike Welsch; **p. 515:** © Elizabeth Crews/The Image Works; **p. 521:** © Toni Michaels; **p. 526:** © Annie Hunter/The Image Works; **p. 528:** © Nita Winter/The Image Works; **p. 533:** © Mark Antman/The Image Works

Chapter 21
Page 540: © Topham/The Image Works; **p. 541:** © F. B. Grunzweig/Photo Researchers, Inc.; **p. 544, 545:** The University of Chicago Press; **p. 547:** © Toni Michaels; **p. 550:** © Alan Carey/The Image Works; **p. 556:** © Toni Michaels; **p. 558:** © Annie Hunter; **p. 561:** © Toni Michaels

Chapter 22
Page 566: © Annie Hunter; **p. 568:** © Frank Siteman/The Picture Cube; **p. 571:** © Toni Michaels; **p. 575:** © Annie Hunter; **p. 579 top:** © Frank Siteman/The Picture Cube; **bottom:** © Toni Michaels; **p. 581:** The Museum of Modern Art/Film Stills Archives

Chapter 23
Page 584: The Granger Collection; **p. 585:** © Annie Hunter; **p. 587:** © William Thompson/The Picture Cube; **p. 591:** © Michael J. Okoniewski/The Image Works; **p. 597:** © Alan Carey/The Image Works; **p. 599:** © Annie Hunter/The Image Works; **p. 601:** © Alan Carey/The Image Works; **p. 602:** © Topham/The Image Works; **p. 603:** © Keystone/The Image Works

Name Index

❖

Subject Index

❖